Auditing and Security

Auditing and Security

AS/400, NT, UNIX, Networks, and Disaster Recovery Plans

Yusufali F. Musaji

John Wiley & Sons, Inc.
New York • Chichester • Weinheim • Brisbane • Singapore • Toronto

This book is printed on acid-free paper. ♾

Published simultaneously in Canada.

Library of Congress Cataloging-in-Publication Data:

Musaji, Yusufali F.
Auditing and security: AS/400, NT, UNIX, networks, and disaster recovery plans/
Yusufali F. Musaji.
p. cm.
ISBN 0-471-38371-6 (cloth: alk. paper)
1. Electronic data processing—Auditing. 2. Computer security. I. Title.

QA76.9.A93 M87 2001
005.8—dc21 00-064922

10 9 8 7 6 5 4 3 2

DEDICATION

This book is dedicated to my grandmother, Mrs. Kulsumbai Nurbhai, who taught me to sacrifice so I could grow.

To my mother, Mrs. Fatima Musaji, who sacrificed her material well-being so I could pay my school fees.

To my son, Ali Musaji, who taught me perseverance, patience, and the marvels of life.

To my wife, Naomi Musaji, for her love, tolerance, and faith.

PREFACE

Because information technology is a combination of science and arts, auditing information systems requires knowledge of many disciplines. Management science, computer science, information security, accounting, finance, business, and human resources are just a few of the physical, intellectual, and emotional energies one would need to effectively undertake the job.

Before one begins to study the aspects of auditing information technology, one needs an understanding of the most advanced platforms with an idea of their scope. The management of information technology, including the motivation and mobilization of the necessary human resources, is the cornerstone for any information technology audit. Once we begin to grasp the hardware and operating system connections and the management of information systems, we can concentrate on the networks that enable the interconnection of all these platforms and the applications for the logistics and deployment of information technology. Finally, a review of the disaster recovery plan is needed since without it there is the imminent danger that the utility of information technology may never reach its full potential.

Chapter 1 introduces the auditor to the overall structure of the management of Information Security (IS) and to the considerations that apply to the dynamic company's need for IS manager/leaders. These IS manager/leaders are change agents committed to the transformation to a dynamic culture and who inspire that commitment in others. IS manager/leaders need to understand the big picture, see their roles within it, continuously improve their skills, and coach and mentor others' learning. They need to know how and when to lead, manage, and do. Consequently, they become role models for a dynamic company's core values.

Chapter 2 discusses the Physical Safeguarding or Physical Security of information technology resources and reiterates the age old adage: Security Is a Management Issue . . . Not a Technological One!

In the heyday of the mainframe, physical and logical security were synonymous in that they were both viewed as significant. This was because the mainframe was huge and there was no question of where the information was processed. As computers evolved (paradoxically computers became more powerful as they became smaller in size), and with the emergence of networking capabilities, logical security became more significant and physical security became more obscure. In part, because logical security required technical expertise and computer resources could be accessed remotely, computer owners concentrated on logical security to protect their resources. However, in trying to protect computer resources from hackers and computer thieves, corporations neglected the physical security aspects and as a result suffered financial loss from lack of physical security controls, thus becoming easy game for crooks. In spite of this, physical security continued to be regarded as being limited to the perimeter controls and bodyguards at the front doors.

Theft or damage to information processing resources, unauthorized disclosure or erasure of proprietary information, and interruption of support for proprietary business processes are all risks that managers who own or are responsible for information resources must evaluate. Since physical access to information processing resources exposes a company to all of these risks, management must institute physical access controls that are commensurate with the risk and potential loss to the company.

The objective of the physical security audit is to determine if management processes have been implemented, are effective, and are in compliance with established instructions and standards as formulated in the company security policy. Do they ensure that the company's information resources are protected from unauthorized access or loss?

Chapters 3, 4, 5, and 6 discuss auditing the most advanced platforms: AS/400, Microsoft NT, and Unix.

Why are system concepts and architecture important to understand? Business leaders do not start by choosing a computer platform. They start by choosing an application that fits their business needs. Because of this, the computer system is very often considered first.

Why should the computer architecture matter? The accelerating rate of change of both hardware and software technologies necessitates that the system selected has been designed with the future in mind. Do the platforms accommodate inevitable, rapid, and dramatic technology changes with minimum relative effort? Are the systems future-oriented? Paradoxically, the characteristic of the most advanced design and technology is subtle. It accommodates the rapidly changing hardware and software components—permitting one to fully exploit the latest technologies.

Is the operating system conceived as a single entity? Are the facilities such as relational database, communications and networking capabilities, online help, and so on fully integrated into the operating system and the machine?

Successful audits of computer platforms are intended to provide an analysis of the computing and network hardware components with potential risks and recommendations. If the computing platform is not secure, neither is the company's data.

Chapter 7 continues the discussion of auditing networks. Corporations deploy networks to lower the total cost of network ownership, maximize their return on investment, provide seamless, enterprise-wide services, enable applications, enhance their performance, control network resources, speed up project implementation, and minimize risk and complexity.

Driven by the rush to e-commerce, security has rapidly become a mission-critical component of the corporate IT infrastructure. By protecting these mission-critical networks from corruption and intrusion, network security has enabled new business applications by reducing risk and providing a foundation for expanding business with intranet, extranet, and electronic commerce applications.

Therefore, network security should be a continuous cycle, consisting of establishing a security policy that defines the security goals of the enterprise, implementing security in a comprehensive and layered approach, and auditing the network on a recurring basis to ensure that good network security is easier and more cost-effective. Also, network security should ensure that no irregularities have developed as the network evolves, and the results of the audits should be used to modify the security policy and the technology implementation as needed.

Chapter 8 discusses auditing the disaster recovery plan. Large pools of shared databases, time-sharing, vast teleprocessing networks, telecommunications connections to noncompany facilities, multiple distributed printers and systems, and thousands of users characterize the state-of-the-art computer centers in corporations. Disruption of service or the intentional or inadvertent destruction of data could potentially bring business processes to a halt.

Across this entire computer infrastructure, the Information Security (IS) processes must be implemented to ensure the confidentiality, integrity, and availability of the company's information assets. The responsibility for the implementation of an effective IS program is assigned according to the company's goals and objectives. Generally, this responsibility is delegated to the information system because of its traditional role as Provider of Service. However, IS is often not the Provider of Service for smaller systems that exist at a location. Regardless of the organizational roles and responsibilities, the corporate information officer (CIO) is responsible for the overall implementation.

With the emergence of disaster recovery planning, physical security is regarded as the cornerstone to developing a viable disaster recovery plan. The pundits have suddenly proclaimed "Eureka," and the dawn of physical security as the foundation on which the disaster recovery plan can be built has begun to take hold. Protecting assets from disasters is now one edge of a double-edged sword with the other edge preventing losses from theft and human errors, which in fact pays partly if not wholly for the costs of disaster recovery planning. The auditor must ensure that the computing environments supporting vital business processes are recoverable in the event of a disaster.

Auditing and Security has been developed for IT managers, IT operations management, and practitioners and students of IT audit. The intent of this book is to highlight the primary areas of computer controls and to present them to the reader in a practical and pragmatic manner. Each chapter contains usable audit programs and control methods that can be readily applied to information technology audits. As an added value, two presentations are available on the World Wide Web. The first presentation is a proposal for investing in a disaster recovery plan and the second is a firewall selection guide. Please visit www.wiley.com/musaji. The user password is: auditing. These documents are in Powerpoint format.

AUTHOR BIOGRAPHY

Yusufali F. Musaji is the Founder, Director and President of Ali's Y. Consulting Inc., an IT and Financial Consulting firm specializing in computer consulting. Yusufali has a strong computer science and financial background. He embraces the full spectrum of financial, operational, and IT disciplines required of a state-of-the-art organization. His functional and technical areas of expertise include system development and implementation, project management, computer security and financial systems.

Yusufali F. Musaji is widely published in IT, financial, and security journals regarding IT/User Relationships, and has also developed numerous business continuity plans.

He holds a Bachelor of Computer Science from York University, Toronto, Canada, and is a C.G.A., CISA and CISSP.

CONTENTS

CHAPTER 1

SECURITY MANAGEMENT

INFORMATION SECURITY THROUGH DYNAMIC CULTURE

What drives revenue and profit in today's economy is undoubtedly the mix of hardware, software, and services. Often the differentiator for this mix is the highly skilled, motivated, leading-edged employee who determines the company's competitiveness and its growth in the marketplace. Growth is linked to satisfied customers whose loyalty is the foundation for success. Thus, the factor that determines a company's growth and its customer satisfaction is the quality of its employees.

Employees are committed and highly motivated when their work environments enable them to go the extra mile for their customers, their company, and their colleagues. This is what builds a network of dynamic employees who strive to be the best at providing value to their customers. Similarly, what mobilizes the employees to understand the elements of the security culture and to see its relevance to the company's business success as well as their own personal success are the dedicated Information Security (IS) manager–leaders. It takes dedicated IS manager–leaders to guide the transformation to a dynamic security-conscious culture.

Employees continue to be a company's greatest asset, perhaps more so now than ever before. That's why IS manager–leaders must not allow the urgency of their daily workload to take precedence over the important time needed for the employee aspects of their roles. Following are five factors that contribute to customer satisfaction:

1. Image
2. Value
3. Price
4. Quality
5. Technology-Leadership

Of these, image is considered to be four times more important than any of the other factors. Image is a composite of four employee-related issues:

1. Highly skilled employees who are committed to excellence.
2. Employees who are responsive and helpful and who take charge.
3. A company that is customer oriented and easy to do business with.
4. A company you can trust.

Fulfilling customer satisfaction on these four issues, especially the first two, is very dependent on IS manager–leaders being the best at leading employees and managing employee processes. Without highly skilled and motivated employees, the company's image regarding security conscientiousness will be low. IS managers need to ensure that employee management processes are world class. It is not the managers who are more important than nonmanagers, rather it is the employee management process that is more important than ever before. It is important to differentiate the processes from employees, some of whom are managers and some professionals, who share responsibility for their collective success.

INFORMATION SECURITY MANAGER–LEADER ROLES

To define IS manager–leader roles, the following questions need to be addressed:

- What is the mission of IS manager–leaders currently and in the future?
- How does their mission relate to a company's Information Security culture, and what would a security-conscious culture/company look like?
- What roles should IS manager–leaders use to accomplish their mission?
- How do the new realities of team-based and process-managed matrix organizations impact the roles of IS manager–leaders?
- What skills are required for IS manager–leaders to accomplish their roles?
- Is the employee aspect of IS management/leadership as important as it used to be?

Answers to these questions lead us into the realm of dynamic culture, the creation of which requires the redefinition of manager–leader roles. Redefinition requires understanding the following terms:

- Information security manager versus information security leader
- Information dynamic culture
- Roles versus jobs and titles
- Past versus current and future expectations

Also, the title of this section refers to "roles" versus "the role" of the information security manager–leader. The plural form suggests that the information security manager–leader job is composed of multiple roles, and that it is the mix of these roles that is changing.

Next, we will redefine the mission and roles of information security manager–leaders, as well as position the "Information Security Manager-Basic" skills template against the expected Information Security manager–leader roles in a dynamic culture.

DYNAMIC CULTURE IS A PREREQUISITE FOR GROWTH

Any successful business strategy is geared toward being the leader in creating value for customers. This is also a competitive imperative. Highly satisfied customers whose loyalty is contagious drive a company's ongoing growth of revenue, profit, and market share. Therefore, it is the loyal customers who drive a company's long-term growth.

Loyal and very satisfied customers are created when they experience world-class technology, integrated solutions, services, and support and above all else, a sense of security and privacy about their personal business. Only dynamic companies that thrive on challenge and change can sustain these customer loyalties. A dynamic company is synonymous with a dynamic culture, symbolized in the starburst of energy in Exhibit 1.1.

Culture is defined as the climate of behaviors, norms and values, and assumptions in which we are immersed and on which we depend. Culture surrounds and permeates our jobs and roles and is embodied in our systems, structures, and processes.

Transformation to a dynamic culture is a "must do" not a "nice to do," driven by the realities of the external environment (competition, regulations, marketplace demands), as Exhibit 1.1 shows. The desire for growth of market share, revenue, and profit provides the "pull" for the dynamic culture. The external environment and the fear of business efforts failing provide the "push." The collective reengineering work, which is the most massive reengineering effort in corporate history, is geared toward business success. The required supporting cultural context is discussed in Exhibit 1.2. The failure rate of reengineering

Exhibit 1.1 Dynamic Culture Company

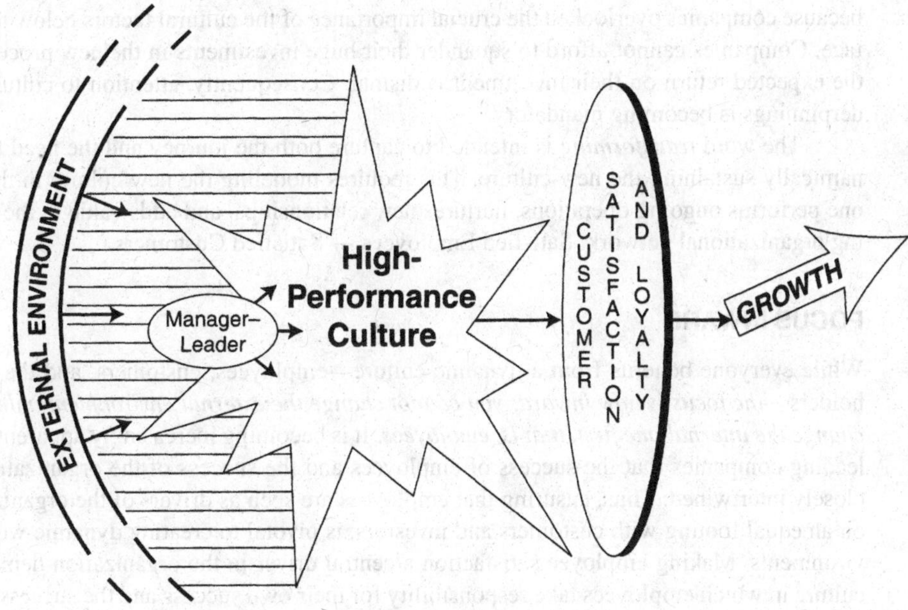

Exhibit 1.2 Process Improvement

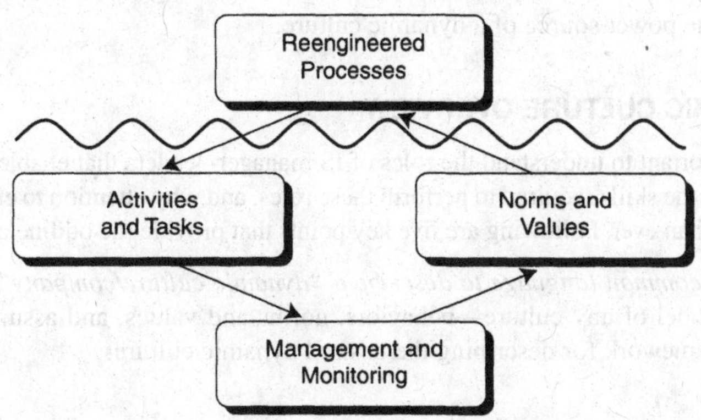

efforts in corporations—attributed to failure to transform cultures in conjunction with reengineering efforts—has been high.

SUSTAINING CULTURE FOR PROCESS IMPROVEMENT

The diamond-shaped chart in Exhibit 1.2 shows the four factors that must be present for reengineered processes to be effectively implemented. It is not enough to only have reengineered processes. The new processes will fail without the accompanying changes in job activities, the management and monitoring methods, and norms and values embedded in the organizational culture—the intangible cultural factors below the surface depicted by the wavy line in Exhibit 1.2.

Think of the reengineered processes as the visible tip of the iceberg above the surface. Just dropping new methods and ideas on employees will not work, especially if the processes have been truly reengineered. More than half the reengineered efforts have failed because companies overlooked the crucial importance of the cultural factors below the surface. Companies cannot afford to squander their huge investments in the new processes if the expected return on their investment is dismal. Consequently, attention to cultural underpinnings is becoming mandatory.

The word *transforming* is intended to capture both the journey and the need for dynamically sustaining the new culture. This requires modeling the new culture in the way one performs ongoing operations, nurtures new relationships, and adds value in the evolving organizational network: Satisfied Employees → Satisfied Customers.

FOCUS INWARD

While everyone benefits from a dynamic culture—employees, customers, and the shareholders—*the focus is now inward; you cannot change the external environment unless you change the internal one first, that is, employees.* It is becoming increasingly apparent to the leading companies that the success of employees and the success of the organization are closely intertwined. Thus, ensuring that employees are seen as drivers of the organization, on an equal footing with customers and investors, is pivotal to creating dynamic work environments. Making employee satisfaction a central driver in the organization demands a culture in which employees take responsibility for their own success and the success of the organization. Customer relations mirror employee relations: "Do unto your employees as you would have them do unto your customers."

Employees must be motivated to *invest their discretionary effort in goals that both maximize their satisfaction and maximize the company's success.* It is this "volunteerism" that is the power source of a dynamic culture.

DYNAMIC CULTURE OVERVIEW

It is important to understand the roles of IS manager–leaders that enable the transformational mission, the skills required to perform these roles, and why attention to employees is more important than ever. Following are five key points that provide the outline of a dynamic culture:

1. *A common language to describe a "dynamic culture/company":* The three-layered model of any culture—behaviors, norms and values, and assumptions—provides a framework for describing the desired dynamic culture.

- *Twenty behaviors:* A twenty-behavior "starter set" and a self-assessment of these behaviors in a dynamic culture/company is provided.
- *Three norms and four values:* The three essential commitments of win, execute, and team are presented as the categories for the "norms." The four "values" are respect, integrity, teamwork, and excellence.
- *Assumptions:* These include the eight key principles and fundamental mind sets about human nature.

2. *Transformation requires IS managers to lead and IS leaders to manage:* That's why the term *IS manager–leader* is used. Terminology such as "IS manager," "IS leader," and "IS manager–leader" will be defined.
3. *IS manager–leaders lead, manage, and do:* IS manager–leaders accelerate the transformation to the new behaviors of a dynamic culture/company as they perform five roles that blend leading employees, managing processes, and doing tasks:
   - *Leading:* "Leading the Organization/Setting Direction" and "Leading by Example/Leading Day to Day"
   - *Managing:* "Managing Business Processes" and "Managing HR/Employees Processes"
   - *Doing:* "Doing Specific Business Tasks"
4. *The IS manager–leaders' skills template is aligned with their roles:* The "IS Manager-Basic" skills template in the Skills tool has fifty skills—fifteen of which are key skills—that map to the IS manager–leader roles.
5. *Employees are the most important asset:* A dynamic company/culture requires highly skilled and motivated employees, and IS manager–leaders must maintain top priority on creating an environment that attracts and retains dynamic employees.

LEADERSHIP NEEDED FROM IS MANAGER–LEADERS

Ideally, IS manager–leaders have to be impatient with themselves and with the obstacles that inhibit the pace of the transformation. They need to have a sense of urgency, driven by the realization that business results depend on the success of these changes.

First, as implied by the transformation mission, IS manager–leaders need to be change sponsors, change agents, change advocates, and change adopters. They need to embrace these change roles and to be "change shock absorbers" who reduce pain, confusion, and frustration as they "unfreeze" the contemporary culture/company. Second, they need to collaborate cross-functionally and model teamwork in their network of relationships. Third, IS manager–leaders need to be coaches and facilitators as they engage others in a long-term commitment to the journey. Commitment is not compliance. Commitment requires that the energy and creativity of employees' hearts, minds, and hands be engaged—compliance just requires employees' hands. Commitment requires clarity, relevance, involvement, and meaning, as shown in Exhibit 1.3.

Commitment Model

Compliance requires clarity and involvement in executing someone else's idea. IS manager–leaders need to understand the profound difference between commitment and com-

Exhibit 1.3 The Four-Factor Commitment Model

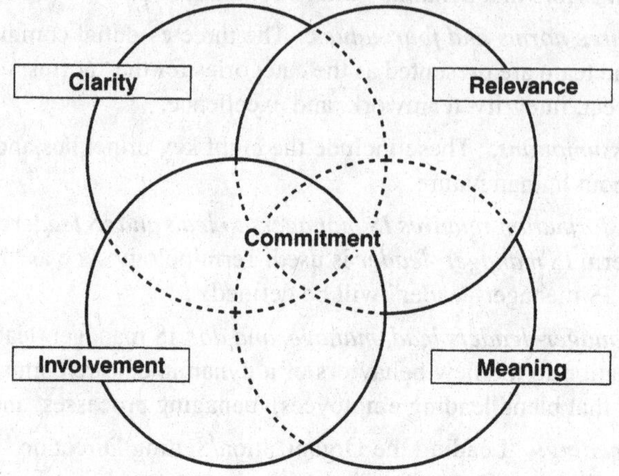

pliance. A dynamic culture/company unleashes the potential of employees who are committed to clear, relevant, and meaningful purposes that they have helped shape.

Employees will commit to the new dynamic culture when four factors are in place:

1. *Clarity:* Staff members understand what the new dynamic culture is—the characteristics of the culture are clear to them and they can articulate them to others.
2. *Relevance:* Staff members see the relevance of the new dynamic culture to the company's business success—they see how it will be good for the company's customers and help the company grow.
3. *Meaning:* Staff members see the personal meaning of the new dynamic culture—what it means to them personally, and they can get excited about it.
4. *Involvement:* Staff members want to be, and are, involved in the shaping and deployment of the new dynamic culture—without involvement, no commitment. When it is impractical to involve everyone in shaping a large-scale change, their chosen representatives may be involved. Giving employees the *choice* to be involved is the key point, even if they choose not to be.

The need should be for everyone, especially IS manager–leaders, to help sustain the journey and not slip back—to be comfortable reinforcing, evolving, and nurturing the dynamic culture/company. In summary, IS manager–leaders enable the dynamic culture that generates a dynamic company, producing highly satisfied and loyal customers that fuel company growth.

The Change Model

Transformation is about change. There are many models that describe stages of personal change and organizational change. The Change Model in Exhibit 1.4 outlines five phases that are a helpful context for cultural change. This book supports the early phases of cultural change as follows:

- *Phase 1: Identify needs.* This phase is supported by the pull of growth and by the push of the external environment. There is also the push to avoid squandering the company's huge investment in reengineering, as explained in Exhibit 1.2.

Exhibit 1.4 The Change Model

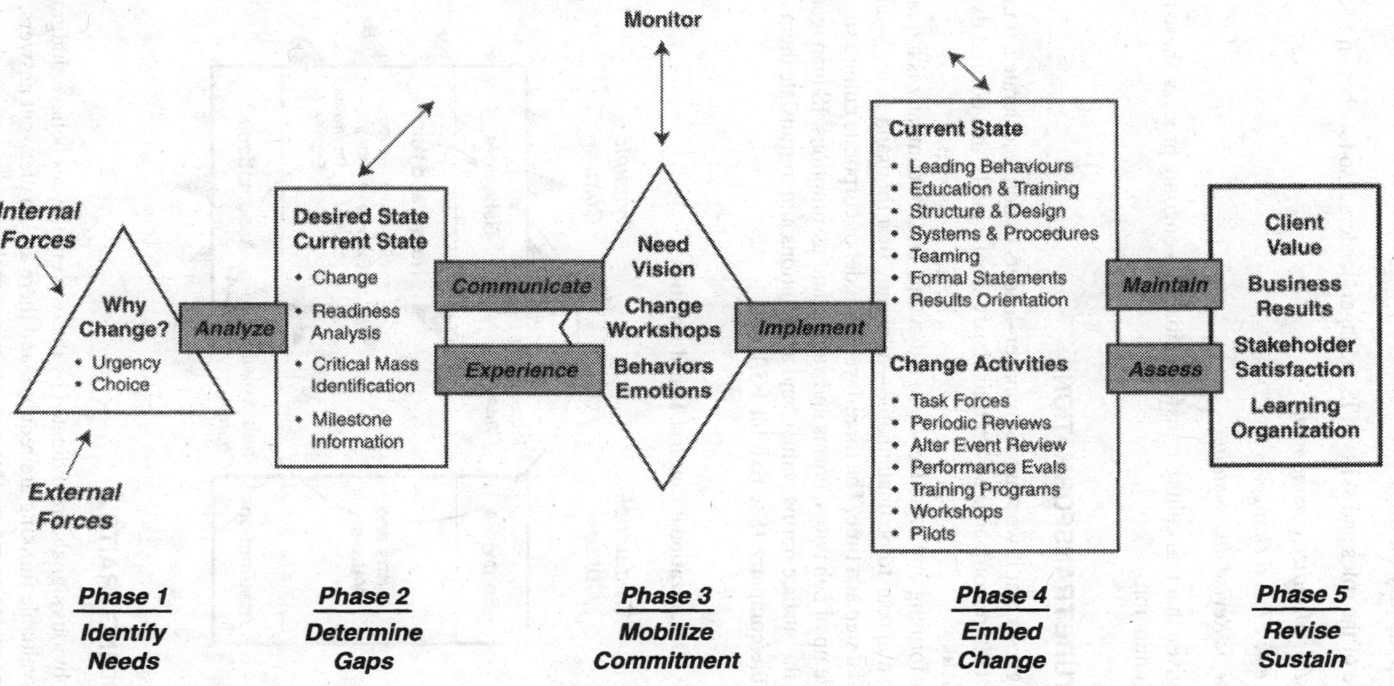

Monitor
Internal Forces
External Forces
Why Change?
• Urgency
• Choice
Analyze
Desired State
Current State
• Change
• Readiness Analysis
• Critical Mass Identification
• Milestone Information
Communicate
Experience
Need
Vision
Change
Workshops
Behaviors
Emotions
Implement
Current State
• Leading Behaviours
• Education & Training
• Structure & Design
• Systems & Procedures
• Teaming
• Formal Statements
• Results Orientation
Change Activities
• Task Forces
• Periodic Reviews
• Alter Event Review
• Performance Evals
• Training Programs
• Workshops
• Pilots
Maintain
Assess
Client Value
Business Results
Stakeholder Satisfaction
Learning Organization
Phase 1
Identify Needs
Phase 2
Determine Gaps
Phase 3
Mobilize Commitment
Phase 4
Embed Change
Phase 5
Revise Sustain

- *Phase 2: Determine gaps.* The "desired state" will be described in the following section "Dynamic Culture Transformation," which includes an assessment questionnaire to help identify the gaps.

Our outline of the roles and skills of IS manager–leaders also touches on the following:

- *Phase 3: Mobilize commitment.*
- *Phase 4: Embed change.*
- *Phase 5: Revise and sustain.*

However, given that real culture transformation is an ongoing process, these phases will require much iteration.

DYNAMIC CULTURE TRANSFORMATION

Phase 2 suggests that if we want IS manager–leaders to help accelerate a transformation to a dynamic culture/company, we need to clarify what exactly this desired dynamic culture would look like.

Transforming any organization to a dynamic culture/company is a quantum change. Progress can appear to be unattainable—a journey of a thousand miles—yet it can be accomplished a step at a time. The three-layered model of corporate culture suggests that culture is made up of behaviors, norms and values, and assumptions. IS manager–leaders help to bring to the surface norms, values, and assumptions and to translate them into a new dynamic culture/company. (See Exhibit 1.5.)

Exhibit 1.5 Organizational Cultural Transformation

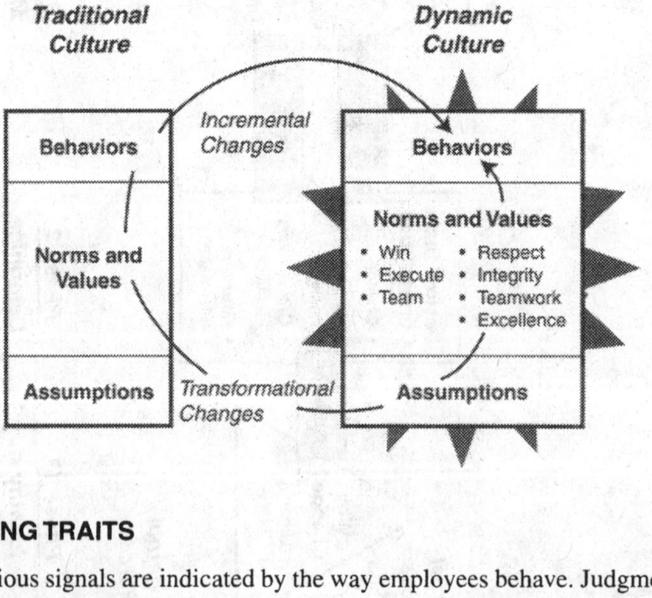

RECOGNIZING TRAITS

The most obvious signals are indicated by the way employees behave. Judgment and experience and valuable thinking are required and there are no clear-cut answers.

From articles on management, executive speeches, and numerous discussions, twenty behaviors in the dynamic security culture were identified. They are a starter set intended to be a catalyst to more specific behaviors agreed to in dialogues throughout dynamic organ-

Exhibit 1.6 What it Means to Be a Dynamic Company

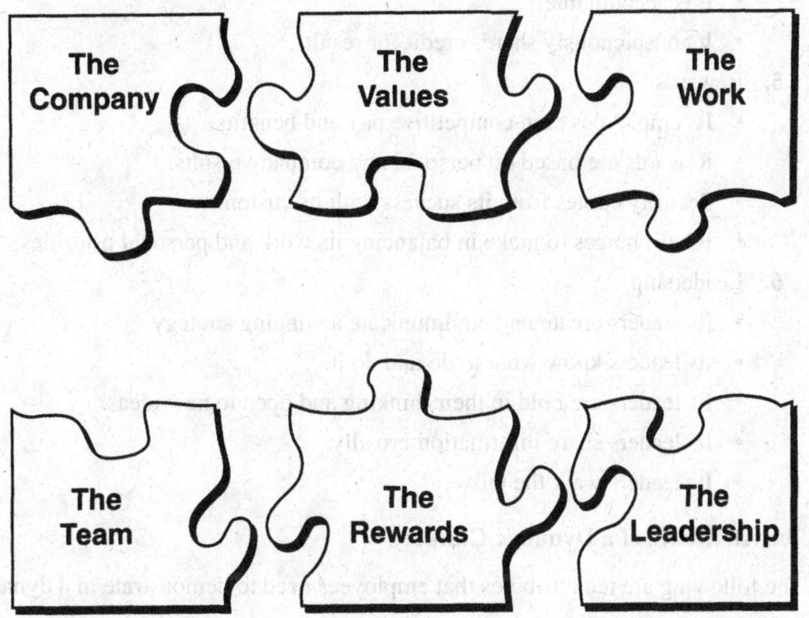

izations. To help understand these behaviors in the context of an existing framework, they are organized around the three foundational organizational commitments of win, execute, and team.

A dynamic company has six core elements as shown in Exhibit 1.6. The pieces of the dynamic culture/company puzzle are as follows:

1. Company
   - Its employees are an energetic global team.
   - It leads in creating value for customers.
   - It wins through technology, integrated solutions, and services.
   - It builds shareholder value.
   - It is involved with our communities.
2. Values
   - It expects teamwork, integrity, respect, and excellence from each employee.
3. Work
   - It works on the right things.
   - It is invigorated by work that helps it win and learn.
   - It works by principles—not rules.
   - It is proud of its products and services.
   - It uses what it sells.
4. Team
   - Its employees are diverse.
   - It shares and leverages knowledge.

- It pays never-ending attention to improving its skills.
- It is accountable.
- It conspicuously shares credit for results.

5. Rewards
   - Its employees earn competitive pay and benefits.
   - Rewards are based on personal and company results.
   - Security comes from its success with its customers.
   - It has choices to make in balancing its work and personal priorities.
6. Leadership
   - Its leaders create and communicate a winning strategy.
   - Its leaders know what to do and do it.
   - Its leaders are bold in their thinking and open to new ideas.
   - Its leaders share information broadly.
   - Its leaders walk the talk.

Ten Attributes of a Dynamic Culture

The following are ten attributes that employees need to demonstrate in a dynamic culture.

1. Focus on winning
2. Insistence on results
3. Disgust with bureaucracy
4. Desire to set aggressive targets
5. Belief in accountability and commitment; concern for the truth even when it's unpleasant
6. Keen recognition of diverse, dynamic co-workers
7. Concern for quality and productivity
8. Fierce loyalty to the company's products
9. Outstanding communication with customers and co-workers; ability to capitalize on change
10. Unburdened by boundaries of place or thought

Fifteen-Point Dynamic Checklist

1. Is there a focus on winning?
2. An insistence on results?
3. A disgust with bureaucracy?
4. A desire to set aggressive targets?
5. A belief in accountability and commitment?
6. A concern for the truth even when it's unpleasant?
7. A keen recognition of diverse, high-performance co-workers?
8. A concern for quality and productivity?
9. A fierce loyalty to the company's products?

10. Outstanding communications with customers and co-workers?
11. An ability to capitalize on change?
12. A sense of being unburdened by boundaries of place or thought?
13. Do you share and leverage knowledge?
14. Do you work continuously to improve your skills?
15. Do you expect teamwork, integrity, respect, and excellence from your colleagues?

DESIRED BEHAVIORS: WIN, EXECUTE, TEAM

From the ten attributes and fifteen positive answers to the checklist, the following steps for organizational commitments of win, execute, and team are defined. (Also see Exhibit 1.7.)

Win

1. Focusing on winning/creating the best customer value
2. Putting the customer first/the company second/the unit third
3. Setting aggressive targets
4. Insisting on results
5. Holding employees accountable for their commitments

Execute

6. Showing concern for quality and productivity
7. Using and being loyal to the company's products
8. Communicating/listening effectively
9. Welcoming the truth
10. Capitalizing on change
11. Showing disgust with bureaucracy
12. Putting never-ending attention to skills improvement
13. Committing to being a process-managed business
14. Modeling a work/life balance

Team

15. Walking the talk on respect, integrity, teamwork, and excellence
16. Valuing diversity
17. Sharing and leveraging knowledge
18. Acting unburdened by boundaries
19. Empowering individuals and teams
20. Energetically building cross-functional/global teamwork

DYNAMIC CULTURE SELF-ASSESSMENT

On a scale of 1 to 5, with 1 being "low-performance" and 5 being "dynamic," assess the environment on each of the following aspects of a dynamic culture/company.

Exhibit 1.7 Initiatives Supporting the Dynamic Culture Behaviors

Desired Behaviors	Initiatives to Support a Dynamic Company/Culture
Win	• Established objectives • Examples • Targets • Results • Accountability
1. Focusing on winning/creating best customer value	
2. Putting customer first/company second/unit third	
3. Setting aggressive targets	
4. Insisting on results	
5. Holding employees accountable for their commitments	
Execute	• Restructuring/size and scale • Flatter organization • "Fit in fast" checklist • "Fit for you" card • Delegation of authority • Skills process • Skills focus • Professional careers • Expert professions • Job news • Global processes • Workload study/module
6. Showing concern for quality and productivity	
7. Using and being loyal to the company's products	
8. Communicating/listening effectively	
9. Welcoming the truth	
10. Capitalizing on change	
11. Showing disgust with bureaucracy	
12. Putting never-ending attention to skills improvement	
13. Committing to being a process-managed business	
14. Modeling a work/life balance	
Team	• Diversity council • Diversity training • Flexible work options • Team implementations • Team symposiums • Team-based rewards • 360-degree feedback • Peer recognition • Roles versus job
15. Walking the talk on respect, integrity, teamwork, and excellence	
16. Valuing diversity	
17. Sharing and leveraging knowledge	
18. Acting unburdened by boundaries	
19. Empowering individuals and teams	
20. Energetically building cross-functional/global teamwork	

Win

1. Do you focus on winning—on being the leader in creating the best value for your customers, using technology, integrated solutions, and services?
2a. Are you visibly putting the customer first/company second/unit third in all decisions?
2b. Are you involved with your community?
3a. Do you set aggressive targets?
3b. Are you driven by a common vision of your purpose?
4a. Do you insist on results versus effort?
4b. Do you earn competitive pay and benefits based on personal and company results?
5. Do you hold employees accountable for their commitments?

Execute

6. Do you show concern for quality and productivity?
7a. Do you have a fierce loyalty to the company's products and services?
7b. Do you proudly use what you sell?
8. Do you practice outstanding communications/listening with customers and colleagues?
9a. Do you welcome the truth, even when it's unpleasant?
9b. Is provocative inquiry encouraged?
10a. Do you capitalize on change and quickly adopt new jobs/roles and structure?
10b. Are you open to new ideas?
11a. Do you show disgust with bureaucracy?
11b. Do you know what to do and do it?
12. Do you work continuously to improve your skills?
13. Does your management and measurement system support you becoming a process-managed business?
14a. Are you modeling work/life balance?
14b. Do you work on the right things?
14c. Are you invigorated by your work?
14d. Are you making intelligent choices about balancing your personal life priorities?

Team

15a. Do you model respect, integrity, teamwork, and excellence personally?
15b. Do you expect respect, integrity, teamwork, and excellence from your colleagues?
16. Do you value diverse, dynamic colleagues?
17. Do you share and leverage knowledge broadly?
18a. Do you act unburdened by boundaries of place or thought?
18b. Do you conspicuously share credit for results?
18c. Do you willingly help others in your global company?
19a. Are you empowering individuals and teams?

19b. Do you work by principles, not rules?

20. Are you energetically and visibly displaying cross-functional teamwork?

Ongoing discussions with others in the company are valuable to assess behaviors with the lowest performance and to decide what could be done to improve them.

NORMS AND VALUES

The three commitments of the norm categories are

1. Win
2. Execute
3. Team

The four values are

1. *R*espect
2. *I*ntegrity
3. *T*eamwork
4. *E*xcellence

The resulting acronym helps remember that these are the "RITE" values. Two of them, respect and excellence, may appear to have their origin in the company's basic beliefs, which reinforces the need to engage in dialogue to ensure the current meanings of these values are understood by all.

SYSTEMS, STRUCTURES, AND PROCESSES

Companies require systems, structures, and processes to operate globally. Examples of these include the following:

- *Systems:* Management and measurement systems; Reward and recognition systems
- *Structures:* Hierarchical or team-based structures; Functional or matrix structures
- *Processes:* Customer Relationship Management (CRM); Integrated Product Development (IPD)

These are strong levers to affect behavior since they embody the norms and values of the culture, often implicitly. They are powerful catalysts for change or significant inhibitors to it. When systems, structures, and processes are not aligned with desired new values and behaviors, cultural transformation efforts are ultimately futile.

ASSUMPTIONS

Assumptions are like "givens," and in that respect the following *principles* could be considered as assumptions:

- The *marketplace* is the driving force behind everything a company does.
- At the core, a company depends on *technology to help it with its* overriding commitment to quality.
- The primary measures of success are *customer satisfaction* and *shareholder value.*

- To succeed it has to operate as an *entrepreneurial* organization with a *minimum of bureaucracy* and a never-ending focus on *productivity.*
- Never lose sight of its *strategic vision.*
- Thinks and acts with a sense of *urgency.*
- Outstanding, dedicated *employees* make it all happen, particularly when they work as a *team.*
- It is sensitive to the needs of all *employees* and to the *communities* in which it operates.

Some of the principles overlap with norms and values. Some overlap with behaviors. That is to be expected since they are the foundation of the culture and should be reflected in the other two layers.

Other existing assumptions that we hold and operate by are much more difficult to discover and define. These mind sets are so ingrained that we don't even think about them—it's like fish being the last to discover water. These assumptions include our unconscious, built-in mental models—the lens through which we view the world. They include latent biases and insights, which we view as obvious. We consider these paradigms so given that they are treated as normal since they often reflect assumptions held in our surrounding society. For example, "the bigger my team/unit, the more important/valuable I am" might be an assumption rooted in a hierarchical mind set, whereas "the more I know, share, facilitate, and lead, the more valuable I am" might be an assumption in a knowledge-based team structure. And "the more I know that no body else knows gives me more power over others and will lead to my upward mobility" might be in a politically motivated environment.

If assumptions are supportive of the norms, values, and behaviors of the dynamic culture, there is consistency. If not, there is an uneasy misalignment that requires revisiting, or perhaps discovering for the first time the fundamental assumptions.

Still to be articulated are fundamental assumptions about *human nature, trust, motivation, time frame, and internal competition.* The statements/assumptions in Exhibit 1.8 provide a start to the discussion and offer a few suggestions to spark dialogue and thought. There are many others, and these may not be the right ones yet. The choice of assumptions and meanings behind the terminology has a profound effect on approaches toward teamwork, empowerment, and management processes in a dynamic culture. There is a need to find meaningful ways to contribute to the surfacing of these submerged assumptions. This is difficult, important, and urgent work—and it is just starting.

Before outlining the roles through which IS manager–leaders will accomplish the cultural transformation mission, there is a need to agree on terminology such as "IS security manager–leader."

IS MANAGER, LEADER, OR MANAGER–LEADER

In many companies, the terms *leader* and *manager* are used interchangeably. "Manager" is more likely to appear on a business card. That is, "manager" is used as part of job titles more often than "leader" and implies accountability for both employees and business processes. Managers get business results.

The "leader" label is often applied to famous leaders like Kennedy or Gandhi and to business leaders like Jack Welch of General Electric or Bill Gates of Microsoft. In organizational hierarchies, the employees at the very top are often referred to as "leaders." In team-based organizations, "leaders" and "leadership" can be applied to anyone—most often to "team leaders," "project leaders," "first-line managers," "senior leaders," or "executives." Leaders set direction.

Exhibit 1.8 Moving to a Dynamic Mind-Set

One Set of Assumptions	Dynamic Assumptions
ABOUT HUMAN NATURE	
• Employees basically dislike work, are lazy, need to be coerced and controlled, and prefer to have superiors make their decisions for them.	• Employees basically love being challenged by meaningful work, and are energized when they help make decisions affecting their work environment.
ABOUT TRUST	
• Trust is tied to position power; superiors are not questioned because they must have good reasons for their actions or views.	• Trustworthy employees who display character and competence, and who encourage and open two-way dialogue earn trust.
ABOUT MOTIVATION	
• Extrinsic "carrots and sticks" are what motivate employees.	• Intrinsic satisfaction is what motivates employees—rewards are "hygiene factors."
ABOUT TIME FRAME	
• Short-term survival/success is paramount; we can save our way to profits; daily fluctuations of the stock price affect my mood.	• Long-term survival/success is paramount; we base our actions on the lifetime value of customers and on principles; trends in customer and employee satisfaction affect my mood.
ABOUT INTERNAL COMPETITION	
• Internal competition brings out the best in employees and should be encouraged to stimulate high performance; reward systems should promote trying to do better than peers.	• Internal competition destroys teamwork, inhibits sharing and leveraging knowledge, and demoralizes team members; reward systems should promote collaboration.

Leading or Managing

Terminology in the area of leadership and management can be a semantic minefield. Thousands of articles have been written about managers, leaders, and executives. There has been an explosion of books, videos, and speeches about leadership, especially in the last fifteen years. Unfortunately, most authors are less than crisp in defining their terminology. However, drawing from the essence of what the "experts" say, the following list provides some overall distinctions between leading and managing:

- Leading is *setting the direction;* managing is getting there.
- Leading focuses on the *long-term horizon;* managing focuses on short-term bottom line.
- Leading *employees;* managing processes, systems, and structures.
- Leading is *coaching, empowering, facilitating, serving;* managing is planning, controlling, directing.
- Leading is doing the *right things;* managing is doing things right.
- Leading *change, between paradigms;* managing and operating the status quo, within paradigms.

- Leading *situationally* with *earned power based on competence;* managing from appointed positional power.
- Leading supports the *untidiness of innovation;* managing craves order.
- Leading *inspires faith* in new directions; managing demands proof.
- Leading *relies on trust;* managing relies on control.
- Leading is asking *"What/Why?"*; managing is asking "How?"

Leading, Managing, and Doing

Too easily we start to infer value judgments to these characteristics. We do not need either leading or managing, rather we need both as shown in Exhibit 1.9.

The label "complete leader" for the person that embodies a rich blend of both leading and managing capabilities is preferred. The term *complete manager* would be equally valid. This desired blend of leading and managing is further reinforced by the quote at the end of Joel Barker *Joel Barker's* video *The Power of Vision:*

Vision without action is only a dream;

Action without vision is just passing the time;

Vision with action can change the world.

Resulting from the "complete leader" label in Exhibit 1.9, it is noted that the term *leadership* includes leading, managing, and doing. The working definition of leadership is *"the ability to effectively set/reset direction and model interpersonal behaviors (Leading), align/manage business and HR/Employees processes to accomplish desired business results (Managing), and contribute personally to desired business results (Doing)."*

Exhibit 1.9 Managing and Leading

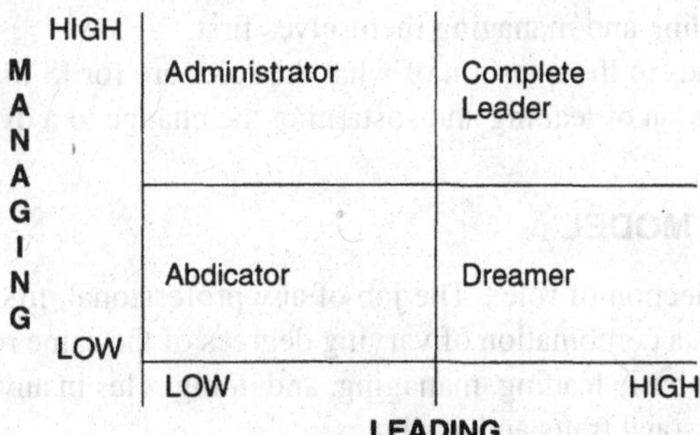

Exhibit 1.10 shows that varying degrees of leading, managing, and doing skills are present in any job. That is, leadership is the umbrella term—leading, managing, and doing are subsets of credible leadership. Exhibit 1.10 also indicates that leadership is expected throughout the organization—it is not just the prerogative of senior managers and executives. Some employees may assume the role of a leader temporarily, in a given situation. Others may be more permanent leaders, such as in senior positions or on some teams. In all cases, the leadership elements that will ensure business success are the same.

The conclusion is that "complete managers" are required to lead and "complete leaders" are required to manage. In terms of the typical organization, "manager–leader" applies

Exhibit 1.10 Elements of Leadership

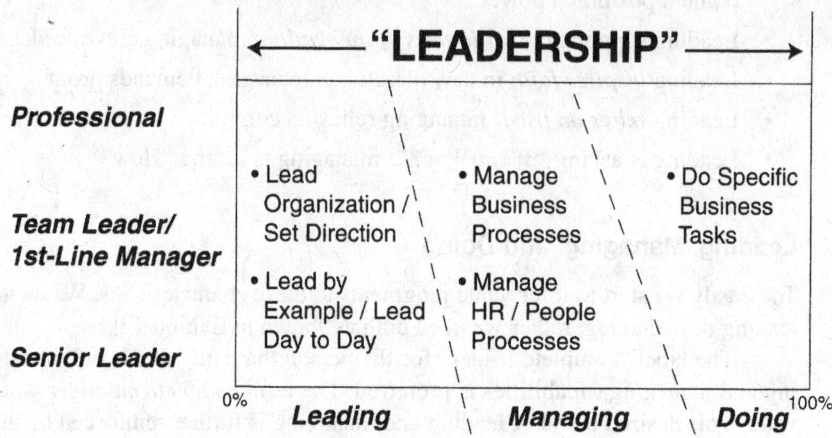

to employees who are often also called "first-line managers," "second-line managers," "senior leaders," or "executives." Some may also be "team leaders."

Self-Managed/Self-Led Employees

Employees are assuming more and more responsibility for their own jobs, careers, skills, self-assessments, and so forth. This is healthy and encourages controlling their own destinies, as opposed to more paternalistic approaches.

The increasing empowerment of employees in all areas allows companies to be more responsive to customers and leads to less dependence on manager–leaders to plan, control, and direct employees and business processes. This is a foundational assumption of this chapter and is consistent with the notion of leaders (which all employees are, at least situationally) leading and managing themselves first.

This leads to the question of what the roles are for IS manager–leaders, as they execute their mission of leading and sustaining the change to a dynamic security culture.

TOTAL JOB MODEL

A job is a collection of roles. The job of any professional, first-line manager, team leader, or executive is a combination of varying degrees of the same roles. The "Total Job Model" shows the five basic leading, managing, and doing roles in any job, with a common underpinning of personal traits and attributes.

As shown in Exhibit 1.11, any job includes five roles, to varying degrees. This may not be clear to everyone today, but manager–leaders can help legitimize these roles for everyone within their organizations. Remember, too, that the "organization" could be a team or a department, as well as larger units. The five roles are as follows:

1. *Leading the organization/Setting direction.* This role is about setting the direction for change and making it happen. It consists of
   - Conceiving and inspiring a shared vision of the organization's future
   - Communicating with an open two-way flow of information
   - Gaining commitment to changes required
   - Networking within and outside the organization

Exhibit 1.11 The Total Job Model

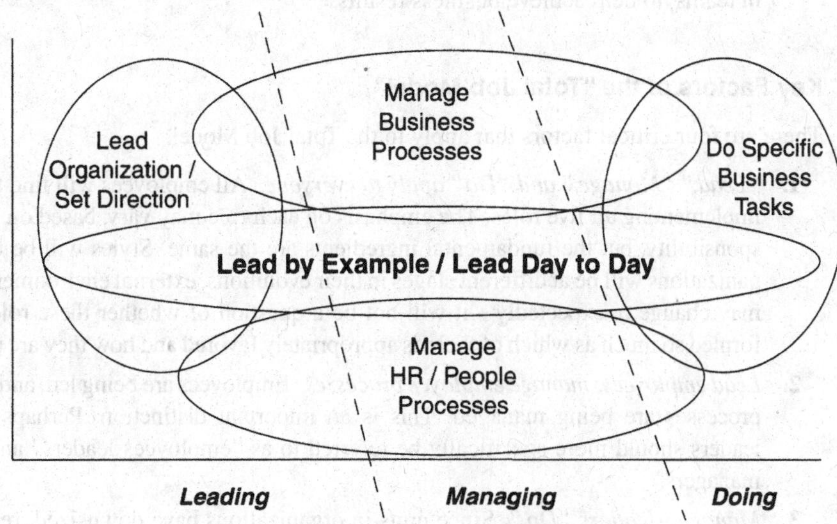

- Aligning the culture with the desired direction and strategies to attain business results for the organization

2. *Leading by example/Leading day to day.* This role consists of displaying interpersonal leadership in hundreds of daily "moments of truth" with individuals and teams.

Note that this touches all other roles and reinforces the interdependencies among the leading, managing, and doing roles. The more senior the leader, the greater the "fishbowl effect"—every action of a CEO is interpreted by the organization as having meaning and intent, whether or not it was intended. This role includes the critical "3 C" descriptors of the manager–leader who is transforming an organization to a dynamic culture:

a. *Coach* (which, in turn, requires Consideration, Courage, Candor, and Character)
b. *Change agent* (which requires Communication, Cheerleading, and personal Commitment)
c. *Collaborator* (which requires Creativity, Competence, and a Common goal)

3. *Managing business processes.* This role consists of

- Managing commitment to the defined ways of doing things
- Challenging business processes that do not support the delivery of profitable solutions to satisfied customers
- Managing financials
- Initiating required improvements to achieve business results

There is an acknowledged paradox that reengineering processes require leading, but once major new processes are operational, they need to be managed, which includes implementing continuous improvements and managing the financial aspects of the business.

4. *Managing HR/Employees processes.* This role ensures that the five HR/Employees management processes, described later, are effectively executed.

5. *Do specific business tasks.* This role consists of performing specific tasks, alone or in teams, to help achieve business results.

Key Factors of the "Total Job Model"

There are four critical factors that apply to the Total Job Model.

1. *"Lead," "Manage," and "Do" apply to everyone.* All employees will find themselves implementing all five roles. The emphasis on each role may vary, based on level of responsibility, but the fundamental ingredients are the same. Styles will be unique, organizations will be at different stages in their evolutions, external environmental factors may change unexpectedly—it will not be a question of whether these roles are performed so much as which of them is appropriately favored and how they are performed.
2. *Lead employees; manage employee processes.* Employees are being led, and Employee processes are being managed. This is an important distinction. Perhaps manager–leaders should more specifically be referred to as "employees leaders" and "process managers."
3. *Manager–leaders "Do."* Since units in organizations have downsized, reduced layers of management, and become more team-based, manager–leaders are finding that they are personally performing more work—in some cases, billable work with external customers. Manager–leaders are increasingly encouraged to maintain technical skills that enable them to perform tasks alone or as team members.
4. *The whole job is greater than the sum of the roles.* Although it is useful to dissect the job of the manager–leader into roles, the job requires a powerful, effective, and unique combination of all roles in each situation. This is graphically acknowledged by showing the "Lead By Example/Leading Day to Day" role touching all the other roles, however, a case could be made for all of the roles overlapping. Just as the essence of a car as a mode of transportation is more than the sum of its engine, wheels, seats, transmission, and so on, so too is a manager–leader more than the sum of the preceding roles or parts. It is the well-rounded and integrated combination of these roles that makes manager–leaders effective.

Each of us has a unique combination of strengths in the various roles, with compensating competencies in some areas offsetting others. In other words, leadership is an art. Our "scientific" analysis of leadership's component roles is simply intended to highlight aspects that contribute to intuitively effective manager–leaders.

Total Job Model Applied to IS Manager–Leaders

The auditor should ask how the IS manager–leaders spent their time and the focus of their day-to-day attention over the last few months. If they were to arrange the five roles from least dominant to most dominant, what would that sequence be? Sequence the following list from 1 to 5, using 1 to indicate the least-dominant role and 5 the most-dominant role.

____ Lead Organization/Set Direction
____ Lead By Example/Lead Day to Day
____ Manage Business Processes
____ Manage HR/Employees Processes
____ Do Specific Business Tasks

List any activities performed by the manager–leaders that do not fit in the above categories. Food for Thought: Would they be more effective in the next six months with a different dominant focus?

The five roles of manager–leaders enable them to accomplish their mission of transforming an organization to a dynamic culture. Exhibit 1.12 shows how the roles contribute to the twenty behaviors of a dynamic culture outlined earlier.

Exhibit 1.12 How the Roles Support Dynamic Culture Behaviors

(H = High Contribution, M = Medium Contribution, L = Low Contribution)

Desired Behaviors	Set Direction	Lead by Example	Manage Business Processes	Manage Human Processes	Do
Win					
1. Focusing on winning/creating best customer value	H	H	H	H	M
2. Putting customer first/company second/unit third	H	H	H	M	M
3. Setting aggressive targets	M	L	H	H	L
4. Insisting on results	M	L	H	H	L
5. Holding employees accountable for their commitments	M	L	H	H	L
Execute					
6. Showing concern for quality and productivity	M	H	H	H	H
7. Using and being loyal to the company's products	M	H	H	M	H
8. Communicating/listening effectively	H	H	M	M	L
9. Welcoming the truth	M	H	L	M	L
10. Capitalizing on change	H	H	M	M	L
11. Showing disgust with bureaucracy	L	H	H	H	M
12. Putting never-ending attention to skills improvement	L	H	M	H	M
13. Committing to being a process-managed business	M	M	H	H	M
14. Modeling a work/life balance	L	H	L	M	M
Team					
15. Walking the talk on respect, integrity, teamwork, and excellence (the "RITE" values)	M	H	H	H	M
16. Valuing diversity	M	H	M	H	M
17. Sharing and leveraging knowledge	M	H	H	M	M
18. Acting unburdened by boundaries	M	H	H	L	M
19. Empowering individuals and teams	M	H	H	H	L
20. Energetically building cross-functional/global teamwork	H	H	H	H	M

HUMAN RESOURCES/EMPLOYEES PROCESSES

The Human Resources (HR)/Employees processes merit more explanation because of their importance. Because they are processes, there are consistent steps that constitute the best way of doing each. Managing the processes, therefore, involves ensuring that the steps are followed properly. (See Exhibit 1.13.)

The quality of execution should live up to the goal of the resulting acronym of which the letters sing the tune, "Nobody does it BEDER" than those who strive to make it Better. The following five people processes are described in more detail:

1. *Balance resources.* This process consists of

- Incorporating planning for the right level of resources directly into the business processes.
- Making sure the appropriate staffing solution/process is used, based on the work that needs to be performed.
- Understanding when to staff internally and when to use external resources and following the appropriate policies and processes when doing so.
- Recruiting and hiring employees using skill-based criteria and reflecting on the diversity in the marketplace.
- Ensuring the optimum balance of employment options, both full and part time, and respecting diverse needs.

Exhibit 1.13 HR/Employees Processes

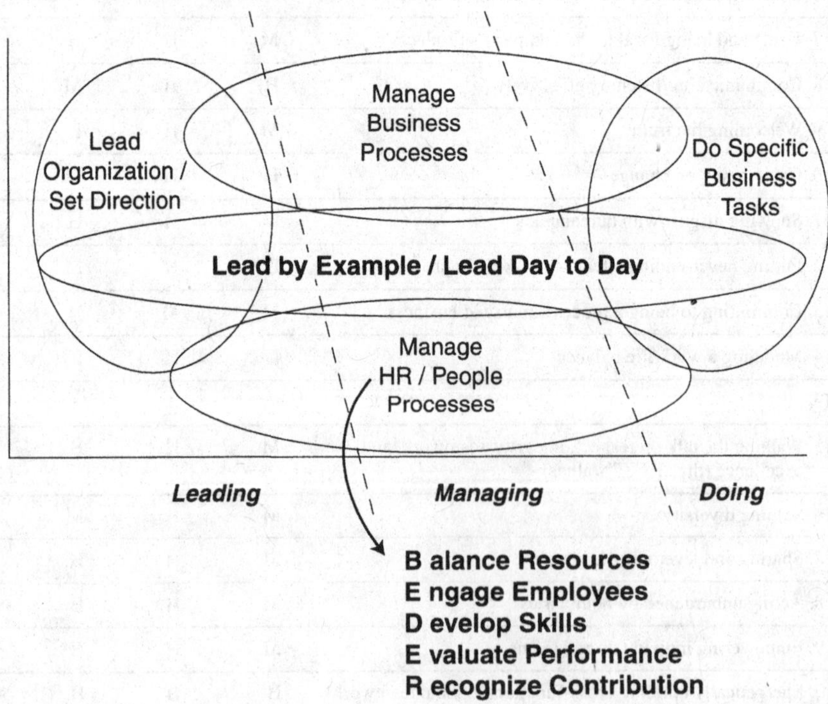

- Using employee development processes the way they are intended.
- Responding to business needs to add to staffing levels and to release employees from the business and doing both with sensitivity and good judgment.

2. *Engage employees.* This process consists of
   - Aligning the vision/mission/values/objectives of employees with the objectives of the organization.
   - Orienting new employees to their new work environment.
   - Creating an environment that accommodates each individual's diverse needs and desires so that they are engaged and energized.
   - Taking the right steps to resolve any engagement or involvement issues with employees (on Conflict Resolution at the end of this chapter).
3. *Develop skills.* This process consists of
   - Assessing what skills are required for the unit as a whole.
   - Ensuring that the unit as a whole has the necessary complement of skills to serve their customers.
   - Supporting and fostering the Individual Skills Plans (ISPs) of unit members.
   - Assigning developmental activities to employees that align with these skills plans.
   - Modeling the way by visibly using the Skills tools and enhancing personal skills.
4. *Evaluate performance.* This process consists of
   - Assessing performance against the planned commitments, with the help of feedback from others.
   - Ensuring performance is rated equitably and fairly within and among related units.
   - Holding the evaluation session.
   - Addressing any commitment issues or opportunities.
5. *Recognize contribution.* This process consists of
   - Compensating employees fairly and equitably by establishing their correct job levels and following the compensation guidelines.
   - Communicating and explaining the total set of compensation programs, in an open and responsive manner.
   - Selecting appropriate rewards and tailoring recognition to the stated preferences of employees.
   - Soliciting input from the unit colleagues on who should be recognized, and how.
   - Taking advantage of the full range of formal awards offered by the organizations.
   - Paying special attention to the simplest, most valued, and most underestimated of all recognitions—a sincere "thank you."

MANAGER–LEADER ACCOUNTABILITY

Normally, a manager–leader is defined as "a person whose job includes accountability for ensuring effective management of employee processes and/or business processes" to achieve business results. This accountability is normally accompanied with a shared responsibility for managing these processes.

Each element of the manager–leader definition is important:

- *"A person whose job includes accountability for ensuring . . ."* because the manager–leader is ultimately accountable for the measurable results from the employees and/or business processes. This *accountability* remains regardless of whether the results are accomplished personally or with others who share responsibility for them, as is common with a team. When the size of a group of employees is large (20 to 100), the manager–leader must share responsibility for many tasks to achieve successful results. However, manager–leaders must still *ensure* that employee and business management tasks are accomplished.
- *"Effective management of employee processes . . ."* because the manager–leader is accountable for the employee or HR processes. Each manager–leader needs to know the employees for whom they are held accountable regarding the employees processes.

  Conversely, every employee needs to be clear who is providing support to them for these processes, especially in a matrix organization. The community of manager–leaders shares the accountability, and employees trust that a process-based approach will ensure consistency among business units.
- *"And/or business processes"* because the manager–leader usually has both employee and business processes accountability. Whereas the employee processes are generic and common throughout an organization, the business processes vary depending on the unit's mandate. Processes such as Customer Relationship Management are consistent throughout sales and services organizations but would not apply to many manufacturing and development units. As with employee processes, the manager–leader can share the responsibility for many of the business process tasks with others but retains accountability for the successful attainment of the business results.

So when the term *manager* is used, it is a shorthand term for a manager–leader whose job includes accountability and shared responsibility for ensuring effective management of employee processes and/or business processes. The manager–leader could be a first-line manager, a general manager, a senior leader, or senior executive. The accountability is common to all of them. This is basic and is certainly not new. What is new is the *fragmentation* of the traditional manager's roles among several employees in many cases.

NEW ROLE OF THE MANAGER

What is new is the *splitting* of the traditional manager roles among several employees. Because of our teaming approach and focus on expertise, what was once done by a single person, "the manager," is now often done by several employees.

A useful phrase to describe this matrix of shared responsibility is *"value net." Organizations* need to build "network-savvy" IS manager–leaders who are totally in touch with how they create value and with how they create the network of relationships that constitute their value net. This network of employees, partners, and suppliers forms a different organizational construct from the one prevalent in many organizations today:

- All "eyes" in the network look to the customer not the manager.
- Control is through process not hierarchy.
- The IS manager optimizes the value-creation process for customers.
- There are new anchor points for the culture: value creation, competence, and teaming.

- IS managers need to be network-savvy practitioners not job holders in the traditional sense.
- Relationships built on trust are vital.

The fragmentation of the traditional management job among several employees is fundamental to the new construct. Examples of specialized managers include the following:

- *Resource coordinator.* This person is often not a manager in the traditional sense but has the responsibility to deploy employees with valued skills on various projects.
- *Project/Proposal leader/Manager.* This person oversees the actual performance of work. Employees move from project to project, so they have a series of such leaders during the course of the year. Some are knowledgeable in the employee's specialty and others are not, depending on the nature of the project. This person's dominant role is the "Manage Business Processes" role in the Total Job Model described earlier.
- *Skills/Competence manager/Mentor.* Because employees are specialists, they want someone who is steeped in their discipline, can guide them on what they should read, know what associations to join, and so on. In services, these are the practice leaders. Elsewhere, it's less formal. This role builds the intellectual capital of the company and concentrates on the "Develop Skills" process in the "Manage HR/Employees Processes" role.
- *Personal development manager.* An individual who oversees the processes involved with employment, transfers, assessment and evaluation, introduction to planning education, handling increases, and so on. They ensure that all five "BEDER" processes are working well in the "Manage HR/Employees Processes" role.
- *Location manager.* Often, if the employee has a "remote" manager, a local manager will handle concerns over personal issues, facilities, and so on. Location managers help ensure a sense of community and belonging for employees with remote management and will usually perform a balanced blend of all five roles in the Total Job Model.

This phenomenon of splitting management roles is happening in many businesses as they move to a virtual, project-based construct. Since it is important to knit these roles together as seamlessly as possible, let's look at how some of them collectively form a value net for the five HR/Employees processes. The example is drawn from a Customer Relationship Management (CRM) environment, although it applies generically to others as well.

SHARED RESPONSIBILITY FOR HR/EMPLOYEES PROCESSES

Some Team Leaders (TLs) and their teams have reached a level of experience and ability in which they share or assume many manager–leader responsibilities. This is especially true when the TL's business and technical expertise allows the TL to lead the team on a day-to-day basis and the manager–leaders span of support is very large. Other TLs may be new and working with a team that is in its early stage of development therefore, the manager–leader may need to be more involved. This spectrum of participation/empowerment can be seen in Exhibit 1.14.

Exhibit 1.15 shows how the fragmented manager roles come together. The "Specific to Team" statement under the TL role in the chart acknowledges the impossibility of defining a one-size-fits-all role for TLs throughout an organization. There is a wonderfully diverse set of team implementations that should be unconstrained by decreed blueprints. The team leader might be the "Skills/Competence Manager/ Mentor"

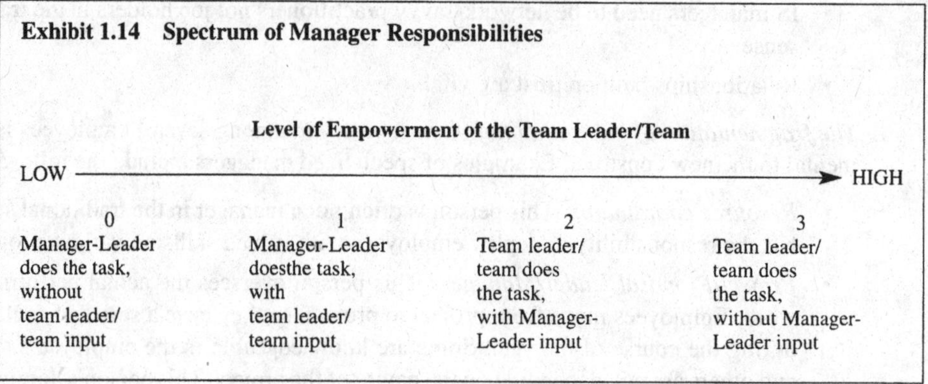

Exhibit 1.14 Spectrum of Manager Responsibilities

described previously or some other "home-based" team which that person returns to between projects.

The role legend at the bottom of Exhibit 1.15 shows that "MGR" refers to the "profile-holding manager." This is the "Personal Development Manager" described previously, who is one of the prime IS manager–leaders described in this chapter.

In cross-functional teams, there may be multiple manager–leaders involved. Also, the leadership of the team will normally be shared among the TLs and the team members.

Are there any powers reserved for manager–leaders related to HR processes that are unlikely to be a shared responsibility with a team leader? Yes. Activities like administering compensation, hiring employees (making the final decision and offer), and managing individual performance issues seem likely to remain as manager–leader responsibilities. Regardless of the level of empowerment, the manager–leader is still accountable for Employees processes working effectively—with more and more shared ownership with others who have been empowered with the responsibility.

As with TLs, the implementation of new roles with processes such as CRM in the Sales and Services (S&S) organization leads to more sharing of the manager's–leader's responsibilities. The manager–leader is still accountable to ensure that new processes are working—there will be multiple employees working with manager–leaders to accomplish the business results, but the process manager–leaders retain accountability for the processes driving those results. *This partnering with others who share the responsibility for the Employees management processes is the essence of the change in the IS manager–leader's roles in the team-based and process-managed matrix of the newer organizations.*

The five roles are built on a foundation of Traits and Attributes that are sought and expected in all manager–leaders including the IS manager–leader.

FOUNDATIONAL TRAITS AND ATTRIBUTES

As shown in Exhibit 1.11, the underpinning of any job is the personal traits/attributes of the employee. Examples of leadership/management traits include integrity, business judgment, courage, achievement orientation, and energy. These are attributes that a dynamic organization looks for in all employees. The following list elaborates these traits:

1. Integrity
   - Demonstrate trustworthiness in your actions.

Exhibit 1.15 The Five HR Processes—Accountability and Responsibility Matrix

	Roles			Process Roles (e.g. CRM)				
	MGR	TL	EE	RC	PTL	PRT		
Balance Resources	A							
• Determine recruitment sources								
• Recruit, select, hire employees		S						
• Transfer/move employees								
• Release employees	↓	P						
		E						
Engage Employees	A	C						
• Position vision/mission/values/objectives								
• Understand job linkages—business/personal		I	R					
• Establish specific objectives		F	R					
- Align and set overall objectives		I	R					
- Assign employees to specific opportunities				R				
- Establish specific project objectives		C			R	R		
- Determine 360-degree input sources, mechanics			R					
• Create environment that enables engagement								
• Provide ongoing feedback, coaching, counseling					R	R		
• Assess level of engagement/involvement		T	R		R	R		
• Agree on "Fit for You" elements		O	R					
• Resolve engagement/involvement issues	↓							
Develop Skills								
• Develop team skills gaps against requirements	A	T						
• Build team skills investment plan		E						
• Assign roles to employees based on skills plan		A						
• Ensure Individual Skills Plans (ISPs) are in place		M						
• Ensure individual/team skills are built			R					
• Measure process effectiveness	↓		R					
Evaluate Performance								
• Gather performance data—360-degree input	A		R					
• Determine overall evaluation			R					
• Conduct evaluation								
• Address commitment issues/opportunities	↓		R					
Recognize Contributions								
• Identify opportunity for acknowledgment	A							
• Determine appropriate acknowledgment					R			
• Deliver acknowledgment—ongoing	↓					R		

Role Legend: MGR = Profile-Holding Manager; EE = Employee; TL = Team Leader; RC = Resource Coordinator; PTL = Proposal Team; PRTL = Project Team Leader; A = Accountable (ensure it is done; has authority to delegate it); R = Responsible (does it)

- Show a constancy of principle and purpose.
- Demonstrate a strong moral fabric.
- Adhere to aforementioned values and principles.

2. Business Judgment ("Smarts")
   - Show the ability to think systematically.
   - Demonstrate creativity and innovation.

- Balance intuition and thoughtfulness.
- Handle complexity and ambiguity well.
- Show oneself to be a "quick study."
- Think ahead and anticipate well.
- Show good common sense and a balanced perspective.

3. Courage
   - Demonstrate the courage of your convictions.
   - Take the risks that should be taken.
   - Stand up and take ownership.
   - Show a willingness to be different.
4. Achievement Orientation
   - Strive to grow and improve.
   - Show a desire to succeed.
   - Set clear and aggressive goals.
   - Take the initiative and lead the way.
   - Show a desire to assume more responsibility.
5. Energy
   - Have high energy.
   - Show energy and inspire others.
   - Balance personal needs.

Traits/Attributes Are Givens

These traits are important in everyone. Consider them as "gating factors"—employees must have them to be IS manager–leaders.

Dynamic companies look for the desired traits when employees are hired, since employees often exhibit them by the time they join organizations—think of them as a starter set of "givens" from some blend of prehiring nature or nurture. The desired traits need to be explicit, refreshed, celebrated, and valued in a reinforcing cultural environment.

Ways to Improve Traits/Attributes

If traits and attributes are important, how can they be developed and improved? To answer this, Exhibit 1.16 compares ways on how both skills and traits/attributes might be improved.

We should hasten to acknowledge that ways to improve both skills and traits/attributes are very similar. *Selection* is important to both. Fundamental to both is some form of *unbiased feedback and interpersonal guidance. Experience* is perhaps the major contributor in both arenas, given high-quality feedback and a climate that motivates one to change and improve. The personal desire to change and continuously improve oneself is essential for lasting learning to occur.

Exhibit 1.16 Improving Skills and Traits/Attributes

Element	Ways to Improve that Element
Skills	Selecting, training, mentoring, coaching, reading, studying, practicing, applying the skill, reflecting, personalized feedback from assessment tools
Traits/Attributes	Selecting employees with the desired traits; receiving 360-degree input; reflecting on experiences and others' reactions; being coached and/or mentored by role models; being rewarded for displaying the traits; receiving honest feedback and coaching when the desired traits are not exhibited; personalized feedback from assessment tools

SPECIFIC SKILLS REQUIRED BY IS MANAGER–LEADERS

What skills do IS manager–leaders need to develop to accomplish their roles? The "Manager-Basic" skills template addresses the skills and behaviors primarily for the four "lead" and "manage" roles. Other skills templates more completely describe the skills needed for the "Do specific business tasks" role, so that role is not the prime focus of the Manager-Basic skills template. The fifty skills in the "Manager-Basic" skills template are listed within the manager–leader roles as indicated in Exhibit 1.17. At a minimum, manager–leaders must assess themselves against at least those skills identified as "key," which are capitalized in **boldface.**

Exhibit 1.17 is called a "Manager-Basic" template to acknowledge that it is a starting level. As stated in the Guidelines for Usage that are built into the online template, different organizations may elect to modify the required proficiency levels to reflect the expectations and requirements of their environments. Level 3 expects more proficiency than in the past and is an acceptable standard for most skills.

PERSONAL LEARNING SPARKS ORGANIZATIONAL LEARNING

It is in the customer's interests, company's interests, and the personal interests of IS manager–leaders to ensure their customer-valued skills are current. This ensures their personal mobility/employability since the ongoing rate of change impacts long-term careers in any one position. In addition, the credibility of IS manager–leaders is greatly enhanced by their professional competence.

Modeling lifelong learning is a corollary of this. IS manager–leaders benefit from self-examination, reflection on their personal purposes, and learning what gives meaning to their lives. On that foundation of inner strength, they build knowledge and skills that enable them to fulfill their personal vision/mission and associated roles, including those that are business related. This "inside-out" approach to leadership can be very powerful.

Finally, IS manager–leaders need to encourage the sharing of knowledge, expertise, and "lessons learned" from successes and failures. Only then will they have progressed from personal mastery and team learning to the organizational learning that raises the level of our combined pool of knowledge and experience, improving our competitive advantage in a dynamic company.

Exhibit 1.17 "Manager-Basic" Skills Template
(Key skills are capitalized in boldface. Proficiency levels are defined in Exhibit 1.18.)

Skills	Proficiency Level
LEAD ORGANIZATION/SET DIRECTION	
• **LEAD AND IMPLEMENT CHANGE**	3
–Facilitate organization change	2
–Build shared commitment	3
• **COMMUNICATION**	3
–Communication—presentation	3
–Communications—written	3
• **FORMAL AND INFORMAL NETWORK**	3
• Leadership (not key because it is covered by the other key skills)	3
• Create client-driven vision	3
–Company vision/mission/strategy	3
• Develop common goal/strategies/plan	3
• Business regulations/standards	1
• Apply business conduct guidelines	3
LEAD BY EXAMPLE/LEAD DAY TO DAY	
• **LEAD BY EXAMPLE**	4
• **USE ADAPTIVE LEADERSHIP STYLE**	3
• **FOSTER TEAM WORK/ENABLE TEAMS**	3
• **EMPOWER AND MOTIVATE**	3
• **PRACTICE DIVERSITY**	3
• Encourage a learning organization	3
• Eliminate barriers/inhibiters	3
• Coaching	3
• Negotiation	3
• Interpersonal communication	3
• Facilitate meetings	3
• Risk awareness/taking	3
MANAGE BUSINESS PROCESSES	
• Understand global operations	2
–Business initiatives	3
–Organization	3
–Management system	3
• Apply basic financial concepts	3
• Organization/business assessment	3

MANAGE HR/EMPLOYEES PROCESSES	
• Implement HR processes	3
1. BALANCE RESOURCES	3
("BALANCE HUMAN RESOURCES")	
• Recruit employees	3
• Release employees from the business	3
2. ENGAGE EMPLOYEES	4
("involve/engage employees")	
• Delegate tasks/responsibilities	3
3. DEVELOP SKILLS	3
("emphasize and foster skills development")	
• Use skills development process	3
• Give career advice	3
4. EVALUATE PERFORMANCE	3
("manage performance of employees")	
5. RECOGNIZE CONTRIBUTIONS	3
("acknowledge employee contributions")	
DO	
• **ARTICULATE COMPANY OFFERINGS/TECH**	2
• **PROBLEM SOLVING/DECISION MAKING**	3
– Analyze problems/situations	3
• Market-driven quality	3
–Client relationships	3
–Quality/problem prevention	3
–Apply project management practices	3
• Internal support tools	3

EXECUTIVE SKILLS VERSUS MANAGER-BASIC SKILLS

The Total Job Model shows executives' jobs with a wider band of "lead" and "manage" skills than for first-line managers. The skill templates for first-line managers and executives use the same foundational skills model. However, the executives' skill template has a higher proportion of "lead" and "manage" skills for the following three reasons:

1. The expected level of proficiency for an executive is higher on some skills.
2. Some skills for executives are more encompassing, even though there are fewer, less granular skills that are explicitly stated.

Exhibit 1.18 Definitions of Proficiency Levels

The proficiency levels are as follows:

Level 0:

Proficiency:	No skill.
Experience:	None.

Level 1:

Proficiency:	Limited skill.
Experience:	None.

Level 2:

Proficiency:	Limited ability to perform. Has general, conceptual knowledge only.
Experience:	Very limited.

Level 3:

Proficiency:	Can perform with assistance. Has applied knowledge.
Experience:	Has performed with assistance on multiple occasions. Has performed in routine situations independently.

Level 4:

Proficiency:	Can perform without assistance. Has in-depth knowledge. Can lead or direct others in performing.
Experience:	Repeated, successful.

Level 5:

Proficiency:	Can give expert advice and lead others to perform. Is sought by others for consultation and leadership. Has comprehensive knowledge with ability to make sound judgments.
Experience:	Extensive, comprehensive.

3. There is a bigger scope implied in the skills for executives than for first-line managers/team leaders because of the larger size of the organizations and business results for which they are accountable.

CONFLICT RESOLUTION

Why would IS manager–leaders be involved in conflict resolution?

Because conflict in any endeavor that requires the interaction of two or more disciplines or, for that matter, minds is inevitable. As the complexity of security increases, the likelihood of differences in opinion and approach increases as a function of the number of variables involved and the amount of time required by the employees in their involvement during or after implementation of projects. Normally, these conflicts arise during implementation because of people's natural resistance to change, scheduling pressures, or initial perceived difficulty of the system to support existing reporting criteria or functionality.

What should the IS manager–leaders look for in conflict resolution strategies? The following answers this important question.

CHARACTERISTICS OF FORMAL CONFLICT RESOLUTION PLANS

Ignoring the inevitable means that manager–leaders will not spend invaluable time and energy dealing with emotions but will keep their focus on finding optimum solutions for the roadblocks. This is so because conflicts in an implementation can be opportunities to hold back, regroup, rethink, reevaluate, and take positive steps including the following:

- Reexamining current business practices (often the latent problems with established practices manifest themselves in conflicts).
- Interfacing in new ways not previously acknowledged because of logistical difficulties and/or complete understanding regarding underlying problems in which the symptoms manifested in conflicts.
- Brainstorming and exploring several perspectives for conflict resolution.
- Allowing those inflicted with real or perceived injuries a forum to express regard for their contribution and for their feedback.

These are important components in ensuring loyal, productive employees during the project and beyond.

CONFLICT AWARENESS

How conflicts are resolved will bear on the relationships among employees and also impact the success of the implementation. Therefore, effective steps need to be taken to manage confrontations and ensure that only positive results are obtained as a result of them. Steps for effective resolution involve establishing approaches specifically geared toward the acknowledgment of differences between project team members and striving for these differences to complement each other by enabling or facilitating the team members to work interdependently instead of independently.

The foundation for building a strong conflict awareness strategy is acknowledgment by the project-managing principals (team leader, coordinator, executive sponsor) that conflicts will arise, but they have to be utilized as positive building blocks instead of letting them be negative energy that will debilitate the spirit and the success of the project.

The second premise is an understanding of the reasons that precipitate conflicts. These can range from the following:

- *Political reasons*—perceived or threatened loss of power or control.
- *Reorganizational reasons*—anticipated coalescence of different units as a function of an integrated system, which disturbs the status quo and creates anxiety about roles within the affected staff.
- *Changes in mandated policy*—these cause the staff to leave the comfort zone of change tolerance.
- *Fear of the unknown*—the most difficult and volatile of conflicts in which reason does not prevail and does not resolve the issues because the adjustment phase was left out.

Paradigm shift—Setting the right attitude for addressing conflicts in an equitable and humane manner will ensure that the benefits received are the benefits required. Recognition and acceptance of the opportunities inherent in conflict resolution will set the tone for the approach to be undertaken and allow for the free exchange of opinions and ideas that are necessary to ensure success in resolution.

A critical step in building conflict resolution strategies is a formal declaration to the team members of the probability of conflict, management's attitude toward it, and the mechanisms being established to cope effectively with the issues as they arise. This step amounts to "flushing out" a potential difficulty before it precipitates and eliminates the possibility of hidden agendas or token acceptance of the team activities or decisions. By declaring that conflict is inevitable and that expectations are set for positive and harmonious resolution, the employees involved in the projects will be less tempted to allow a question or concern to remain buried, which often allows difficulties to ferment and blow out of proportion.

The last and single most important step in building conflict resolution strategies is supplying the "why" in the desire for effective, timely, and complete issue resolution. This personal "why" may be supplied to the team members through:

1. A discussion of the quality-oriented benefits of conflict resolution.
2. An acknowledgment of the contributions the team as a whole can make.
3. An assurance that each member can make individual contributions through issue resolution.
4. An assurance that an organized procedure is designed and will be implemented in order to allow all team members to achieve their personal and cumulative goals.

FORMAT FOR POSITIVE RESOLUTION

First, establish the attitude and approach that both the team leaders and members are required to take. Then, present the structured plan for enactment of conflict resolution and the communication guidelines to be followed during all conflict resolutions to the entire team.

To validate the importance of the resolution tasks, the plan should be presented at the beginning of the project as a formal, written structure. People normally operate comfortably when the ground rules are clearly defined and understood by all players at the outset. By providing written guidelines, the misconception of different standards for different people is eliminated, putting all team members on comfortable communication ground with each other. This is a difficult task and is dependent on the quality and integrity of leadership at play because past experience has always indicated that lip service is usually the case. When people speak up, there can be repercussions, which is the main reason why conflict resolution may appear ideal in theory but improbable in practice and why it fails to secure the desired results.

In the verbal component of the conflict plan, the team leader should pay special attention to the use of "I" statements as a positive tool for clarification of the concept of organized, structured conflict resolution. Conflict is always integrated with emotionality, even if it is couched in totally professional, business-directed terms. By saying, "I believe," "I feel," or "I'm confident that our approach to resolutions will be positive," the leader is recognizing and affirming a personal emotional connection.

In a large team formation (e.g., twelve or more participants), it is more beneficial to use an Issue Coordinator than to have the project team leader assume the duties of logging, monitoring, and documenting each issue that arises. Although the team leader is the appropriate individual to present the issue resolution structure, the issue coordinator should then explain the mechanics and steps being used to ensure complete resolution. The ideal issue coordinator should be a team member with high company visibility and credibility with the other team members.

Using an issue log that adequately defines and categorizes each particular concern is absolutely necessary for organization of conflict resolution. These logs should be provided for all team members so that they have a tool at hand to address their concerns as they arise. The log, stating the description of the problem with the date and name, should be submitted to the issue coordinator who is responsible for the monitoring and follow-up of each particular issue.

The issue coordinator will want to create a summary log that becomes the "tote sheet" for all issues addressed during the implementation. This will become the final tool for the summary and tracking of all concerns that have been successfully satisfied throughout the project period.

When the coordinator has received an issue from a team member, the determination must be made relative to the "ownership" of the particular concern (e.g., if the concern is of a policy nature, the resolution would be referred to decision-making individuals within or outside of the team; if the concern is procedural or system based, then resolution is "owned" by the project team members themselves).

The issue coordinator assigns team members to the task of examining, discussing, and offering viable, mutually agreed-upon suggestions for the resolution. The members selected for the resolution should be composed of representatives from the departments or functions directly impacted by the issue raised. As an example, consider a system-use issue. This would be the responsibility for the creation of product masters. The issue could be, "the input data for the creation of the Master—should it be accounting, purchasing, or engineering?" Only the representatives from each of the applicable departments (i.e., accounting, purchasing, and engineering) would be ideal and therefore should be empowered to examine, discuss, and make a preliminary resolution.

During implementation, conflict also surfaces that involves business practices currently in use, either between or within departments. An example could be a case in which a production manager is concerned about the time it takes purchasing to cut a purchase order after the request has been made. The purchasing manager may be concerned about the increase in costs that results by reducing time. Each party is trying to serve individual department objectives at the expense of the overall company objective for the delivery of the required product in time to meet company requirements of being reliable and competitive in the marketplace.

This is an example of a common issue that, while not necessarily system related, might surface during system implementation and is therefore appropriate to address during the project. In this case, the issue coordinator would assign the two persons most closely affected by the issue to effect the resolution. In cases in which the issues to be addressed do not have the appropriate department representatives, the issue coordinator should solicit the appropriate department management to provide the appropriate human resources to complete an adequate resolution.

After assignment for the discussion of every significant issue has been made, time frames should be developed for discussion and brainstorming, if necessary, and resolution suggestions. The time frame must be pragmatic with reference to the workload of the other team members but should establish a sense of urgency and progress in the timely resolution of all issues.

Once the team members have been assigned to each issue, their preliminary resolution should be brought back to the team for review and acceptance. To explain the mechanics involved in the decision-making process, the team should provide the "what-if" scenarios to assure team members that realistic expectations are being sought. These review periods can be at the start or end of the day, during a reinforcement session, or during regular-scheduled project team meetings. However, the consistency and the seriousness with which they are held are what determines the confidence and respect that they instill within the project. Moreover, the benefits derived from bringing the preliminary resolutions back to the team for their review and acceptance range from the possibility of resolving latent conflicts unenvisaged previously, such as internal departmental problems no one could address previously because of the political nature of the beast; the support and validation to those involved including important feedback to their efforts; and an example of the value of "growing up pains" to the rest of the team. This awareness of "growing up pains" is especially important because it creates a culture of objectivity and reality that issues and conflicts, which are either system or business related, can and will be resolved many times with persistence and patience. A journey of many steps, one forward and three backward, is the prerequisite for accepting small failures in pursuit of continuous improvement strategy, which is the most, if not the only, important strategy for conflict resolution.

If a conflict or issue has not reached a satisfactory, preliminary resolution in the initial discussion between the assigned team members, it is important to reach a tentative compromise while attempts to try to develop a resolution satisfactory to all continue to be synthesized. During this process, the environment should be expanded to include additional input and monitoring by other persons who may provide valuable insight. This may include technical support, management representation, or input from the issue coordinator. However, it is still important to have the original team members lead the discussion, thereby reinforcing the intent and value of the original assignment.

GROUND RULES

When the resolution strategy is initially outlined to all the team members, particular considerations in conflict examination and resolution should be presented, and any adequate explaining should be done at the onset. By providing a set of ground rules to be followed in their meetings, the participating team members will be more apt to stay on task, and the time spent will allow resolution to be reached more quickly and completely.

The rules for effective conflict resolution address behavioral styles in all possible emotional interchanges and provide a self-monitoring check to ensure the open and free exchange of ideas without having the problem of lingering negative repositories.

The rules for effective resolution are as follows:

1. Discuss for resolution, not for the intellectual exercise or just for the meeting. This is an insidious, covert practice that sometimes develops when team members seek attention or attempt to regain control that they may feel is being lost because of the system changes. The issue coordinator should verify the existence and validity of the concern in question through thorough questioning techniques before accepting the assignment. By ensuring that this is the first rule for resolution, petty issues are more likely to disappear.
2. Discussions should concentrate on one specific topic at a time, without floundering and straying into other areas. During the discussion, if other concerns surface or are highlighted that may have a bearing on the original issues, they should be brought to the coordinator's attention, logged, and assigned as a separate issue or concern for resolution. Limiting the scope of each discussion prevents issues from being resolved adequately and in a timely manner. It also causes interference with the specific goals of the meetings.

3. The technique of aggressive silence should be employed. This ensures that each person concentrates on listening to the viewpoint and input of the others involved. No "overtalking" or interrupting should be allowed, so that each participant gets an equal opportunity to state their viewpoint openly. A good rule of thumb is that the number of questions asked by each person should be equal to the number of statements each is making. The questions should help to gain clear understanding of the other person's point of view and to elicit and examine all aspects of the situation surrounding the issue. The objective is to avoid presenting only one side of an issue and not "digging in" for an understanding of the other person's perspective. This increases the chances for positive and complete resolution of the underlying issues.
4. Only positive-response body language should be employed because normally potentially high-quality communication is reserved more by what is seen than by what is heard. Employing positive-response body language means using open, receptive posture and presenting to the other person(s) a face that is free from judgmental expressions. It is also helpful to review the following considerations to keep a conflict discussion focused on the goal of resolution that is in line with the company's operational and managerial framework. The questions to be addressed in effective conflict discussion are as follows:

- What is the relative importance of the issue to each dissenting party? This may bring a discussion to a successful conclusion sooner because the issue being raised is often easily accommodated by the other party. By looking for the relative importance and being aware that this may be the solution at the start, much ado about nothing can be saved.
- Where did the conflict or the issue-causing practice originate (e.g., what person or department has ownership of this particular topic)? It is often better to go back to the beginning of a problem to find the solution than to find an expedient answer.
- How many people would be affected by a change in each relative department? People are more difficult to change than are "things," so primary consideration needs to be given to the number of people involved, which is a determination of the degree of difficulty in effecting the change.
- What would be affected by a change in each relative department? After the number of people involved has been resolved, the degree of difficulty can be measured by the reports, forms, or techniques that would be affected by an alteration in the practice currently being examined.
- What is the view from the top? This should be a "best guess" relative to the concern, if any, that may be presented by management concerning the issue at hand and the potential change mechanisms that are being discussed.
- If, at this point, it is determined that the considerations surrounding the issue make it an "even-up" concern—approximately the same number of people and things will be affected—then the following question should be asked: What is more important, to satisfy my viewpoint and concern or to maintain cooperation with other individual(s) or department(s)?

The exercise of examination and discussion, when focused completely on resolution, may contribute to the company not only by facilitating system integration but also by improving the efficiency of business practices, raising the levels of communication, and increasing the level of company loyalty and employee commitment.

Please bear in mind that this is a review for the auditor. Depending on the nature of the conflict, the resolution process may require far more sophisticated procedures such as diffusion before conflict resolution can be addressed. In such a case, it becomes the auditor's responsibility to communicate the existence of such tension in the workplace. In all cases, evaluating how conflicts are managed and resolved adds value to the client's management function.

SUMMARY

Dynamic companies need IS manager–leaders. They need IS manager–leaders who are *change agents* committed to their transformation to a dynamic culture and who inspire that commitment in others. They need IS manager–leaders who *collaborate* with their global colleagues as they pursue their customers' long-term loyalty and the attainment of their short-term business results. They need IS manager–leaders who understand the big picture, see their roles within it, continuously improve their skills, and *coach* and mentor others' learning. They need dynamic IS manager–leaders who know how and when to lead, manage, and do and are role models for a dynamic company's core values. Dynamic IS manager–leaders enable dynamic organizations! See Exhibit 1.19 for a summary of the IS management process.

Exhibit 1.19 Information Security Management Process

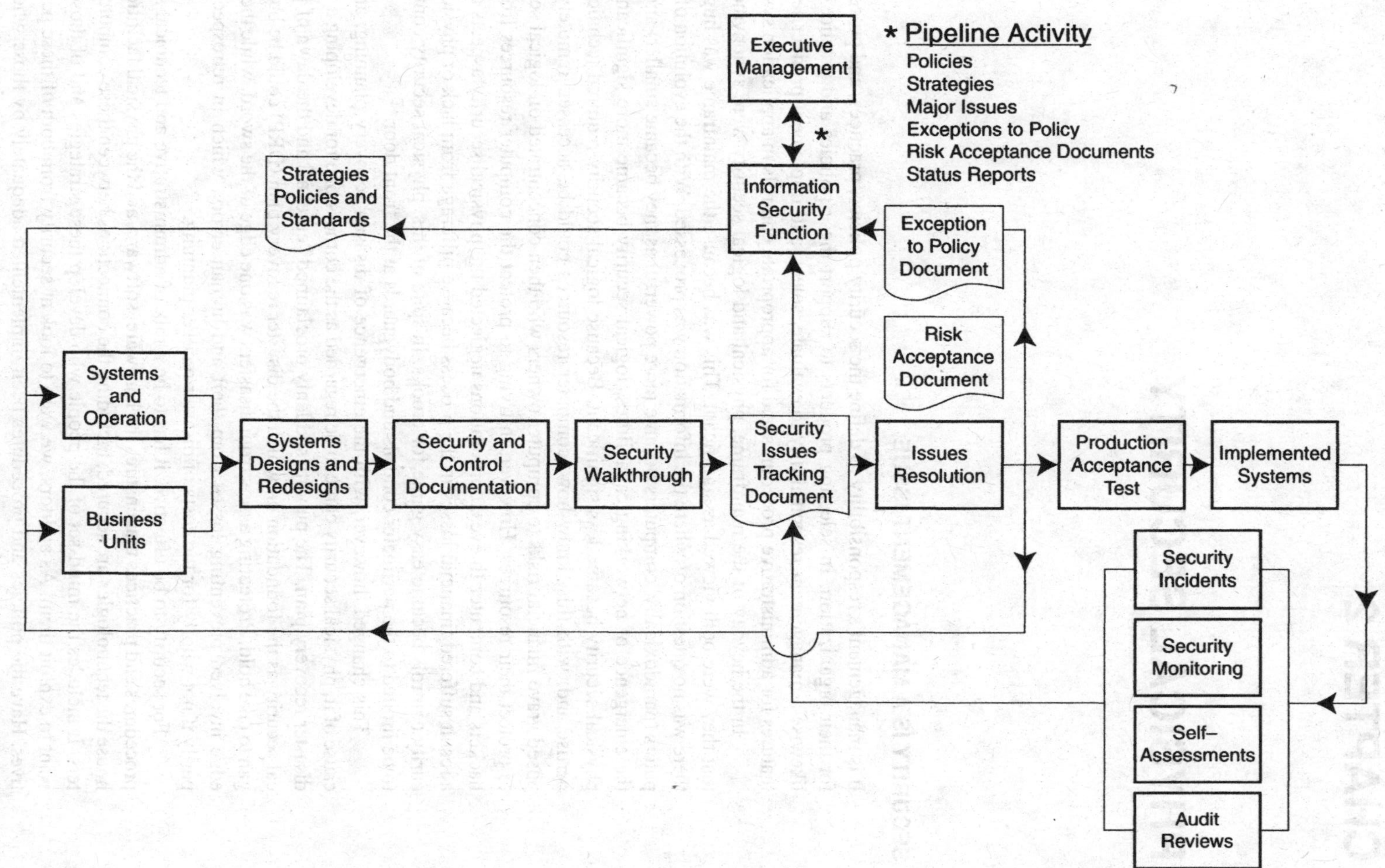

Executive Management
* Pipeline Activity
Policies
Strategies
Major Issues
Exceptions to Policy
Risk Acceptance Documents
Status Reports
Strategies Policies and Standards
Information Security Function
Exception to Policy Document
Risk Acceptance Document
Systems and Operation
Business Units
Systems Designs and Redesigns
Security and Control Documentation
Security Walkthrough
Security Issues Tracking Document
Issues Resolution
Production Acceptance Test
Implemented Systems
Security Incidents
Security Monitoring
Self–Assessments
Audit Reviews

CHAPTER 2

PHYSICAL SECURITY

SECURITY IS A MANAGEMENT ISSUE

It is management's responsibility to define the security policies, practices, and procedures for their organization. In selecting products to support these policies and practices, it is likewise a management responsibility to evaluate, select, and implement product security features for administrative procedures and for appropriate controls in application systems.

In the heyday of the mainframe, physical and logical security were synonymous in that they were both viewed as significant. This was because the mainframe was huge and there was no question of where the information was processed. With the evolution of computers (paradoxically, computers became more powerful as they became smaller) and with the emergence of networking capabilities, logical security became more significant, and physical security became less significant. Because logical security required technical expertise and, with this, know-how, computer resources could be accessed remotely; this posed grave financial risks to computer owners who then concentrated on logical security to protect their resources. However, in trying to protect the computer resources from the hackers and computer thieves, corporations neglected the physical security aspects and as a result suffered financial losses in the process because pilferage from lack of physical security controls became easy game for crooks. In spite of this, physical security continued to be limited to the perimeter controls and bodyguards at the front door.

This changed, however, with the emergence of disaster recovery planning, and because of it, physical security came to be regarded as the cornerstone for developing a viable disaster recovery plan. The pundits suddenly proclaimed "eureka," and the dawn of physical security as the foundation on which the disaster recovery plan (DRP) could be built began to take hold. Protecting assets from disasters was one edge of the sword, while the other edge involved preventing losses from theft and human errors, which in retrospect paid partly if not wholly for the costs of disaster recover planning.

For security to be effective, it has to be a mix of administrative and technical sets of procedures and practices that ensures the hardware, software, and the physical facilities that house the technologies are secured, including the connections between these computer centers. It includes the mind-set of the people who develop these strategies and of those who want to exploit them. As auditors, we want to look at security from both of these perspectives. Have the policies and procedures been implemented adequately by those who have been entrusted with this responsibility? Are the controls adequate to guard against attack from those whom we want to protect against, bearing in mind that these criminals have also put a great deal of thought into their plans?

We can start from the details and work our way to the whole or we can start from the whole and carve out the details. The end result should help us in evaluating the overall security of the organization. From a planning perspective, it is wiser to start from the whole and work our way down by using a divide-and-conquer strategy than to start from pieces and build our way to the whole since it is always easier to break than it is to build.

Therefore, we will start by reviewing physical security and work our way to the technical details of logical security. Following are two reasons why we plan for physical security:

1. Availability
2. Theft of data and/or information

PHYSICAL SECURITY

The first line of defense for most computer systems is physical security. This is especially important due to the decentralized, distributed PC-based computing environments characterized by network infrastructures and critical applications, databases, and complex servers.

Information assets include systems, data, image, text, and voice contained within the internal systems, which support the company's business activities. The computing environments of a company's internal systems can range from large, centralized mainframe computers to distributed networks of personal computers. Across all of these environments, the information security (IS) processes must be implemented to ensure the confidentiality, integrity, and availability of the company's information assets.

The objective of an IS audit is to determine if management processes have been implemented, are effective, and are in compliance with established instructions and standards as formulated in the company security policy. Do they ensure that the company's information resources are protected from unauthorized access or loss?

This requires control of physical access to trusted system components. *Trusted system components* are defined as physical items supporting a computing environment that must have integrity and must be relied on. For example, some trusted system components may include central processing units (CPUs), direct access storage devices (DASDs), control units, or the components of a more distributed computing environment, such as local area network (LAN) and wide area network (WAN) servers and microprocessors.

Some of the dangers that should be eliminated include:

- The ease with which one can gain access to PCs
- The opportunity of using social engineering (e.g., misrepresenting oneself, lying, or tricking someone into giving a person access)
- The opportunity of piggybacking (following someone through a secure door after they swiped their key card)

Additionally, the auditor must determine if the management controls implemented ensure that the computing environments supporting vital business processes are recoverable in the event of a disaster.

The responsibility for the implementation of an effective IS program is assigned according to the company's goals and objectives. Generally, this responsibility is delegated to the information system's organization because of its traditional role as supplier of service for the large centralized virtual machines (VMs) and multiple virtual storage (MVS) computing centers. However, IS is often not the supplier of service for smaller systems like AS/400, UNIX, NT, and LANs that exist at a location. Regardless of the organizational roles and responsibilities, the manager responsible for the IS program within the operating unit, generally the unit corporate information officer (CIO), is responsible for the overall implementation, and line management is accountable for the security of the information resources they own, in all applicable computing environments.

Most business processes (product planning, product development, market forecasting, pricing, billing, accounting, payroll, and so on) depend on effective data processing systems with access to classified information. As more and more classified information is collected into data processing environments, the impact of loss (e.g., theft, fraud, and misuse) becomes significantly greater. State-of-the-art computer centers in corporations are characterized by large pools of shared databases, time-sharing, vast teleprocessing networks, telecommunication connections to noncompany facilities, multiple distributed printers and systems, and thousands of users. Disruption of service or the intentional or inadvertent destruction of data could potentially bring business processes to a halt.

PHYSICAL ACCESS CONTROLS

Theft or damage to information processing resources, unauthorized disclosure or erasure of proprietary information, and interruption of support for proprietary business processes are all risks that managers who own or are responsible for information resources must evaluate. Since physical access to information processing resources exposes the company to all of these risks, management must institute controls to interdict physical access that are commensurate with the risk and potential loss to the company.

Now that the size of the computer is no longer relevant, physical security encompasses all the controls that safeguard system hardware and its contents from damage and from theft not only from those within the premises but also from those without. It protects information resources from corruption due to environmental conditions and assures that unauthorized personnel are denied access to areas containing system equipment and information.

PHYSICALLY SECURING THE COMPANY'S INSTALLATION

Is the plan well formulated and does it address the company's physical security needs as well as its intended future direction? The physical security plan is a living document that is constantly being revised and developed to reflect changing company needs as new information is made available. Ideally, such a plan should be part of the site security policy and should include:

- Description of the computer facilities where the computer resources are located, that is, the boundary that divides your territory from the outside world and all the points in the boundary that give access to the computer resources that your territory houses and protects, that is, gives sanctuary to. These points include entrances, exits, network cable connection, phone outlets, electrical outlets, and any connections that provide connectivity to the outside world.
- Description of the computer resources that are housed in the computer premises (e.g., Human Resources, hardware that includes the central processing unit, system console, terminals, and other peripherals such as printers, disk drives, and tape drives. Software includes the operating system, programs, and data).

- Description of the controlled accessed areas within the premises, what these controlled access areas are, and what they contain.
- Identification of risks (threats) and concern about their likelihood of occurring.
- Controls to guard against these risks and the costs associated if measurable.
- Risks that are being tolerated and accepted and the risk analysis.

The physical security plan with its accompanying documentation is a sensitive document that contains detailed information about the company's risk/control measures. Therefore, it has to be in a neatly compartmentalized form so that you do not have to obtain information from varying sources. However, in practice this may not be the case, and now may be an opportune time to convince the computer management that compiling this information entails good planning. It can also serve many needs (i.e., this same information may be useful in the company's risk analysis when planning for its disaster recovery strategies as well as negotiating any contracts for disaster recovery services and/or insurance).

From firsthand experience concerning the pitfalls that auditors incessantly fall into, the importance of judgment in reviewing the physical security plans cannot be overemphasized. This is because the issues that physical security encompasses—the threats, practices, and protections—are different for practically every site. Physical security is different from organization to organization because the risks and needs of organizations are different. Consequently, always remember to be astute and question your cost-effective principles and your risk assumptions when evaluating the physical security based on any theoretical model. No amount of theoretical knowledge is a substitute for real-world experience that comes from keeping your eyes and ears open and mostly keeping an open mind, albeit skeptically. For the inexperienced, bear in mind that audit is a cumulative process and that waiting for the information to be obtained during the course of your work may lead to a revision of your judgment about risks and materiality before jumping to any conclusions.

PHYSICAL SECURITY PLAN

Are the information assets protected fortuitously or by design? The physical security plan should contain the measures taken to protect the information assets. Companies have established various methods of protecting and restricting access to information processing resources to minimize the risks of loss. The main methods of restricting physical access are by using perimeter controls such as fenced building sites, guards at building entrances, and locked computer rooms. The perimeter of the facilities should have all the access points identified, risks explored, and the method of securing them implemented.

Secured Areas

Once the computer facilities are protected from unauthorized access, subsequent measures are essential to segregate the internal space within the perimeter controls into areas that require different types of protection, thus further restricting access on a need-to-have basis. The type of protection given to these controlled access areas can range from full protection and close surveillance (i.e., tightly secured areas) to limited protection (i.e., loosely secured areas).

Generally, companies have divided internal spaces into two or three zoned areas and have established standards that dictate the kind of protection that is to be afforded to each of these designated controlled areas. For example, the internal space may be divided into three zones: Zone 1, Zone 2, and Zone 3. For the purposes of securing these areas they would normally be referred to as:

- Zone 1 or Tightly Secured Area (i.e., full protection and close surveillance)
- Zone 2 or Loosely Secured Area (i.e., limited protection and surveillance)
- Zone 3 = Internal Space − (Zone 1 + Zone 2)

The security plan defines the requirements for access to Zones 1, 2, and 3 and also the types of computer resources (e.g., computer systems, portable storage media, remote printers, etc.) that are housed within these zones.

Note that Zones 1, 2, and 3 will have to be assigned ownership for accountability considerations, and the owners will be responsible for authorization and maintenance of these areas.

Zone 1 areas are located within Zone 2. Thus, you have to be given access to Zone 2 before you are given permission to enter Zone 1, and this access must include the following additional controls:

- The area owner must be clearly identified.
- The area must be locked, even when attended.
- Access to the area must be restricted to only those authorized by the area owner.
- Access to the area must only be allowed from within Zone 2, and emergency exit doors must have an alarm system.
- Exterior windows are not permitted in ground-floor installations.
- The area must include either slab-to-slab barriers or intrusion detection.
- Access to the area must be controlled electronically, unless specifically exempted by the area owner or equivalent level executive.

The control requirements for Zone 1 areas are:

- Zone 1 class owner(s) should ensure visual inspection of the perimeter walls including the slab-to-slab construction to verify the integrity of their internal space. At a minimum, this inspection should be conducted annually.
- Zone 1 class owner(s) should document the criteria used for determining valid business requirements for access to the Zone 1 area and should authorize access based on these criteria only. Individuals who have routine access to the computing center and who do not meet the documented criteria must have a written justification on file to access these areas.

Zone 2 areas are located within Zone 3 (i.e., computer facilities) and include the following additional controls:

- The area owner must be clearly identified.
- The area is protected from the outside at all times.
- Access to the area must be restricted to only those authorized by the area owner.

Managing Controlled Access Areas

Managers responsible for secured areas are accountable for maintaining effective business controls over the area. Control can be accomplished by a variety of means. Keys, cipher locks, Computer Access Systems (CAS), and guarded entrances are all examples of physical access control. Whichever method is selected must meet all of the following six control requirements:

1. Access is controlled to limit entry to persons authorized to the area. Authorization procedures vary, depending on the level of control and the type of controlled area. In all cases, only persons on the approved access list are considered to be authorized. For Zone 1 and Zone 2 areas, persons allowed temporary access by an authorized person are considered to have one-time authorized access.
2. Persons with authorized access to a controlled access area must have a current business requirement for access. The owner is expected to make the determination of what constitutes a business requirement and to be able to establish that such a determination was made. The Zone 1 area owner(s) will document the criteria used for determining valid business requirements for access to the Zone 1 area and will authorize access based on these criteria. Individuals who have routine access to the Zone 1 area and who do not meet the documented criteria must have a written justification on file.
3. Access authorization must be reviewed as follows:
   - For Zone 1 area the access list is to be verified and signed (hard-copy or electronic) by the class owner at least every six months. Persons with access revoked must be removed from the access list on a timely basis.
   - For Zone 2 area the requirement for periodic review should be at least annually. However, persons who have had their authorization revoked, either by request or implicitly through termination of employment, must be removed from the access list on a timely basis.
   - **Note:** The definition of *timely* is subject to interpretation, but in the absence of a specific standard it will generally be defined as "at the earliest opportunity afforded by management control processes."
4. Emergency exits for Zone 1 area must have working, audible, and monitored alarms. For both safety and security reasons, the alarms must operate on emergency power, and alarm events must initiate investigative action. Periodic verification that emergency exit alarms are functioning should be performed and documented. The Zone 1 area owner must ensure that there is an annual review of all emergency exit alarms.
5. For Zone 1 area an accurate, current log of nonroutine accesses must be kept that reflects the visitor name, time of entry, the escort or authorizer, and the fact of exit. The purpose of the log is to provide a historical record of access and is meant to be a control tool. Therefore, there should be a requirement for management review of this log. If a badge exchange process is used, there must be a local procedure describing how the control over the issuing, retrieval, and inventory of badges is done. The logs of nonroutine access to Zone 1 area must be retained for the current year plus one.
6. Proper operation of the Computer Access System (CAS) and associated devices is the responsibility of the CAS service provider. Any operational defects noted by Zone 1 area owners (e.g., malfunctioning doors, alarms, and so on) should be reported to Security or the CAS service provider immediately.

Installation Responsibility

To ensure that system integrity is effective and to avoid compromising any of the integrity controls provided in the system, the installation must assume responsibility for the information processing resources that are housed within the computer facilities.

These physical access control requirements are applicable to the mainframe environment and midrange environments. The mainframe environment includes CPU, channel attached devices, and physical system/master consoles (i.e., interactive devices providing a command interface to the operating system without having identification and authentication of the operator). The midrange environments include the following:

- IBM AS/400, UNIX
- Microsoft NT
- DEC
- Hewlett-Packard UNIX

Networks (LANs, LAN Connected Systems, and LAN Connected Peripheral Devices) LAN and WAN include the following infrastructure components:

- Segments
  - Jacks
  - Connection media, such as wiring, fiberoptics and wireless connections
  - Repeaters
  - Wiring hubs
- Segment Connection Devices
  - Bridges
  - Gateways
  - Routers
  - Modems
- Segment Management Devices
  - LAN management systems
  - Performance and trace tools
  - Protocol analyzers

LAN Connected Systems include:

- Workstations
- Servers

LAN Connected Peripheral Devices include:

- IBM 4033 LAN Connection for printers and plotters
- Fax servers
- Printers/plotters
- Storage devices

Note: The term *Provider of Service* as used here refers to the organization or management that is providing LAN services on behalf of a LAN Infrastructure Owner and/or LAN Connected System or Peripheral Device Owners.

Classification of System Type

The implementation of physical access controls requires that all systems are classified by their owners as either Type A, Type B, or Type C, as shown in Exhibit 2.1. Normally, systems can be classified based on the scope and value of the service provided. High, medium,

Exhibit 2.1 System Type Classification

Resource/Control	Owner	Type A	Type B	Type C
Mainframe	XYZ	X		
AS/400		X		
HP-Unix		X		
NT-Primary Domain Control		X		
Terminal wiring and network cable		X		
Telephone lines		X		
People	X	X	X	X

or low value is determined based on costs to replace and the ease with which systems can be replaced. This in turn determines where it would be placed in Zone 1, Zone 2, or Zone 3. High-value systems are classified as Type A and require being in Tightly Secured Area, thus in Zone 1. Medium-value systems are classified as Type B and can be placed in Loosely Secured Area, which would be Zone 2. Lastly, low-value systems would be classified as Type C and would require being placed Within Internal Space, which would be Zone 3. The level of physical access controls and for that matter, the logical access controls required are based on the determination of Type A, B, or C systems.

RISK ANALYSIS AND ACCEPTANCE

What at the data processing installation should be protected? The answer is everything. However, 100% security is unrealistic for a number of reasons. For one, it is impossible to anticipate every possible threat or hazard to the information systems environment. For another, total prevention might be too costly to implement. This is where risk analysis, or determining what to protect and to what extent, comes into play.

Judgment is required by the Provider of Service when categorizing a system as having a high, medium, or low value. You do not have to get into complex mathematical equations and probability theories here since these should have been taken care of earlier. You can use a commonsense approach, a commodity that everyone feels heavily indulged with. A general rule of thumb involves the following seven-step process. See Exhibit 2.2, which shows a risk analysis decision matrix.

1. *Determining which assets should be protected:* The information systems environment is made up of a number of elements including physical facilities, personnel, machines (hardware), programs (software), communications equipment, documentation, and information (data). Security can be defined as the "condition of safety of people, facilities, and information from natural and man-made hazards."
2. *Identifying potential threats/hazards:* The list of hazards, headed by errors and omissions, includes such events as fire, water, earthquake, mischief, vandalism, theft, fraud, riot, war, and so forth. The list is virtually endless and by itself is of little value.

Exhibit 2.2 Risk Analysis Decision Matrix

What Equipment to Protect	Threats/ Hazards	Probability of Occurrence	Potential Loss	Cost/Benefit Analysis	Value

One must understand the effects of an undesirable event and the possibility of its occurrence in the evaluation of protective security measures.

3. *Determining the probability of occurrence:* Evidence suggests that accidental events, such as errors and omissions, account for most damage. *Although the consequences of accidental events are limited, they occur with a higher frequency than do intentional events. Intentional acts tend to have more serious consequences per event, but they occur less often.* As a result, all threats and hazards should be addressed so that the likelihood of each happening can be determined.
4. *Calculating the possible loss:* Risk analysis, to be useful, must yield data that describe the cost of loss in terms of cost per unit time, or dollars per year. This is accomplished by estimating the cost associated with an individual event and multiplying by the probability of occurrence for the event to happen. Consideration should be given to the impact of doing business without the affected asset and the cost of reproducing the affected asset in the event of loss.
   - *Costs and Time to Replace:* The actual loss is calculated as Original Cost + Replacement Cost + Incidental Expenses + Legal Fees + Opportunity Cost + Business Loss + Down Time.
   - *Impact on Production:* Production losses, dissatisfied customers, lost credibility, legal suits.
5. *Evaluating the need for protection:* A cost/benefit analysis is required to support the process of deciding whether to implement protective measures. The decision should be based on the cost of implementing and maintaining the protection versus the value of the item being protected. The decision process must be based on the replacement value of the equipment accumulated in one area. When categorizing the systems, the IS manager in conjunction with the security manager may consider additional aspects such as entirely depreciated equipment or equipment for which there is no need for replacement. Also, the state-of-the-art technology involved and the currentness of the version should be considered. If these aspects affect the decision, they must be documented.

   The level of physical access controls selected must be documented and reviewed by the CIO or the manager who owns the service. See Exhibit 2.3.
6. *Documenting the process:* The risk analysis procedure and results should be documented. The results should be understandable and useful to the level of management

Exhibit 2.3 Physical Access Control Requirements

Systems	System Value	Minimum Security Requirements
Type A		
Systems that are *essential* to supporting vital business process	High	Zone Area 1 or in an office room that is locked when unattended
All network communication control units regardless of system service being supported	High	Zone Area 1 or in an office room that is locked when unattended
All network communication control units	High	Zone Area 1 or in an office room that is locked when unattended
Type B	Medium	Zone Area 2
Type C	Low	Zone Area 3

where a decision has to be made on whether to implement protective measures or assume the risk with the associated exposure. In order to demonstrate an effective physical access control process, managers responsible for computing facilities must maintain the following minimum documentation:

- Identification of the area, its use, the level of information supported, the value of the equipment/service, and the level of control required.
- The means of communicating the level of information supported and the security provisions and requirements to users of the facility.

7. *Periodic review and update:* The information systems environment is continually subject to change. Therefore, risk analysis should become an ongoing process that is conducted and reevaluated on a periodic basis to ensure that the cost associated with implementation is achieving the projected benefits to the organization. While the ultimate decision of what risk to accept and what risk to protect against rests with management, risk analysis requires a total team effort. It requires the cooperation of all individuals who can help to evaluate the risk.

AUDIT TESTS

The key control questions within the preceding sections are typical questions that should be addressed when auditing this process. Auditors are encouraged to review the site's process and determine if additions or changes to these questions are required to adequately assess the control posture of the site's process.

The computing environments of internal systems range from large, centralized mainframe computers to distributed networks of personal computers. Across all of these environments, the information security process must be implemented to ensure the confidentiality, integrity, and availability of information assets.

The objective of an information security audit is to determine if management processes have been implemented, are effective, and are in compliance with established instructions and standards to ensure that information assets are protected from unauthorized access or loss. Additionally, the auditor must determine if the management controls implemented ensure that the computing environments supporting vital business processes are recoverable in the event of a disaster.

Secured Area Determination

Objective: Ensure that the provider of service has identified and documented the use, value, and level of security controls required for all information systems and/or equipment.

Approach: Obtain and review the documentation that identifies the area, its use, the value of the information assets or equipment established by the owner, and the level of control required (e.g., system Type A, B, or C and high, medium, or low value). Determine if the owner of the resources has reevaluated the security requirements on a periodic basis or when IS resource value or classification has changed.

Refer to the security policy for details on required information and executive involvement with this document.

Secured Area Access Procedures

Objective: Ensure that there are written procedures that describe the overall control strategy for the protection of trusted system components (e.g., Are there procedures for granting access to the Information System Facility?).

Approach: Review secured access area documented procedures as outlined in the security policy. For networks, access to servers, bridges, and wiring (i.e., the infrastructure) should be restricted from general access, that is, should be in Zone 1. Procedures should outline the effective access control mechanisms for each of the secured areas (Zone 1, Zone 2, and Zone 3) for the following:

- Review of business need as required for routine access
- Access by noncompany visitors, cleanup crews, facility personnel, and so on as required

The procedures should define effective controls to ensure prompt access authorization removal in the case of job changes or separation. Consideration should be made based on the access capabilities defined for an area such as follows:

- Access lists (i.e., group access lists or otherwise)—removal from access list
- Cipher lock—change of lock combination
- Key—change lock or retrieval of keys distributed and regular inventory of keys

Routine Access to Secured Areas

Objective: If a secured internal or restricted space is used for physical access control, ensure that routine access requires appropriate management approval and that access authorizations are revalidated on a regular basis.

Approach: Obtain access lists for secured access areas. Ensure that network infrastructure components are included in your review of information system resources protected by secured space.

Compare secured area access lists, group access list (GAL) or otherwise, to organization chart/information. Note all exceptions (e.g., individual not found) and consider the following cases for inclusion in your sample:

- In I/S but not in operations
- Not in I/S

Check a sample for current access authorization (access authorization may consist of the latest access list verification performed by the space owner or GAL class manager). Ensure that valid business requirement for access can be demonstrated. Ensure that access authorization is reviewed in accordance with standards for secured access areas and restricted space requirements. For non-GAL–controlled areas, verify that the access list is kept current based on level of control required (i.e., zone access 1, 2, or 3).

If the systems are considered Type A (high) or Type B (medium), and nonregular employees are used in the computing center, verify that this has the approval of the Provider of Service senior executive.

Note: If volume is sufficient, Computer Access Audit Tools and Techniques may be used in an ad hoc mode to verify employment status of individuals with access authority.

Secured Area Physical Inspection

Objective: Ensure that procedures and instruction requirements have been adequately implemented to prevent unauthorized access to trusted system components.

Approach: Perform a physical inspection of the secured internal or restricted areas which includes:

- Review nonroutine access log for information required based on requirements defined for specific secured or restricted area (i.e., restricted space or secured access).
- Ensure that all entrances and exits are secured. Verify that alarms have been installed where required and that they work properly.
- Verify that employees are wearing badges and are authorized in the area.

Additionally, for network infrastructure, obtain schematics identifying the components for any networks included in the review and determine the location for all servers, bridges, and gateways. Verify that all components are protected via the appropriate secured access level mechanism.

Management Process/Procedure Review

Objective: Determine if the site's operating procedures adequately address control points specific to the administration of internal computing resources.

Approach: Ensure that users are advised that systems are for company management approved purposes only, especially if confidential data is supported on the system.

Ensure that effective education has been provided to users, including application owners, on their IS security responsibilities as defined in the security policy, and that statements of company "business use" are displayed at system logon.

Objective: Ensure that management awareness of all access to internal systems and data can be demonstrated and that removal of such access is processed when there is no longer a business justification (e.g., at separation or change of assignment).

Approach: Select a random statistical sample of user accesses from the computing environment being audited. For each access selected, verify that

- Management was informed and is aware of the access.
- Access capability is current.

At a minimum, there must be an annual revalidation of access and a quarterly process to assist in the removal of access privileges assigned to employees who have separated or retired. All access privileges must be identifiable to an individual (e.g., a manager may have ownership of nonregular employee access privileges). Refer to the security policy for the frequency with which owning managers should review the nonregular employee access privileges. For persons who have left employment, determine if the access privileges are still active. Three specific tests could be performed to determine if the access privileges are still active:

1. *Continued business need (CBN) for active employees.* For any nonregular access privileges, these should be traceable either to nonregulars (i.e., supplemental employees) on the personnel database, or, in the case of vendors, the access privileges should be traceable to active regular employees. For the latter, determine the site's method for managing vendor access privileges and verify the effectiveness. Provider of Service senior executive approval should be demonstrated for nonregulars who are used in a position where system controls can be bypassed undetected.
2. *Active access privileges assigned to separated employees.* This is a list of all access privileges assigned to employees who have separated but who remain active on the systems. All such access privileges must be explained or accounted for. A subset report that might be reviewed is active access privileges that were used after the date of the employees' separation.
3. *Active access privileges that cannot be "mapped" to personnel (i.e., unknown ownership).* This is a list of all access privileges on the system for which no entry on personnel can be found (this could be due to key entry errors or missing employee serial numbers and so on). All such access privileges must be explained or accounted for. The security policy requires that all access privileges, service machines, and tasks be identifiable to an owner.

For AS/400, a list of users can be obtained using the WRKUSRPRF (Work User Profile) command. For LAN (OS/2) the same tests should be performed. To obtain information about access privileges on the LAN environment, DOMQUERY.CMD and related tools can be used to extract information about each server reviewed. The DOMQUERY.CMD program is a REXX program that uses LAN Server to access information about the LAN environment. It lists all servers, access privileges, groups, and aliases in the domain, along with access control lists (ACLs) for all servers. Alternatively, run '`NET ACCESS d:/TREE`' from an administrator user ID for each server to obtain the ACLs.

STORAGE MEDIA

The controls associated with portable storage media should be implemented in any situation where one group is acting as the custodian of portable storage media for another group. Traditionally, this describes the role of the tape librarian in the main computer center. However, similar controls are applicable to the custodian of portable storage media associated with maintaining the server software on a LAN or any other computing environment. Custodians of portable storage media containing proprietary classified information are responsible for the protection and control of the media.

These controls are not applicable to individuals controlling their own diskettes associated with their microprocessor since the custodial relationship does not exist.

RISK/EXPOSURE

Ineffective controls over portable storage media could result in loss of or unauthorized access to stored data. Potential fraud indicators in this area include:

- Tape inventory and reconciliation performed solely by the librarian
- Inability to explain discrepancies between inventory results and tape library systems
- Procedures that allow tape removal without owner approval

Storage media includes magnetic tape and removable and nonremovable optical or magnetic disks and cartridges. A storage media custodian is an individual who has accepted the responsibility for storage of removable media on behalf of other people. Unlike media used for normal system/data backup purposes, media placed in custodial care is routinely mounted/dismounted for business processing, contains information identified as essential for records retention, or contains information identified as essential for disaster recovery.

Therefore, it must be possible to account for the movement and control of media in a custodian's storage media library.

CONTROL REQUIREMENTS

Portable storage media may not be removed from the control of the custodian without approval from the owner of the data. The designation of data as vital records by the data owner is an indication that the owner has approved its being moved out of the facility on a rotational schedule.

Classification of Storage Media

Classification of information is the data owner's responsibility. Media containing Proprietary Confidential information should be marked accordingly wherever possible. Nonremovable media need not have a classification label on the actual device. Media used for backups, records retention, or disaster recovery may be marked/labeled with a general statement "Property of XYZ Inc. and may contain Proprietary Confidential information and must be protected from unauthorized use or access. Must not be removed from company control without proper authorization and without marking with the Proprietary Confidential information label." This label may also be used on media transported to/from or stored in an authorized retention facility and on locked containers used to transport such media. **Note:** Tape labels have to meet the general label requirement and approval, which has to be obtained from the legal counsel.

Media containing confidential data needs to be labeled with the "Confidential" label when it is removed from the control of a company custodian.

Physical Protection of Storage Media

Media under custodial control and media used for backup, records retention, or disaster recovery must be stored in Secured Zone 1 area or Secured Zone 2 or in an office room in Zone 3 area that is locked when unattended or in a locked cabinet within the Zone 3 area when unattended. Tape drives and media handling devices (e.g., "tape robots," direct access storage "juke boxes") need not be locked when located in a Secured Zone 1 area or Secured Zone 2 area or in an office room that is locked when unattended.

Media used for normal system/data backup purposes is to be kept separate from media placed under custodial control. It must be managed with prudence in order to ensure media availability in case recovery is required but need not be included in the inventory control process applied to media placed under custodial care.

Protecting Backups

Backups are a prerequisite for any computer operation. However, the information stored on backup tapes is extremely vulnerable since there is no operating system's mechanisms of checks and balances and protection to prevent unauthorized people from viewing the data. After the information is written on a backup tape, it can be read by anybody who has physical possession of the tape. For this reason, backups require *as much protection if not more than the computers themselves.*

Control guidelines for backup protection are:

- Backups should not be left unattended in a computer room.
- Entrust backups to only bona fide and bonded messengers.
- Ensure backup tapes are sanitized before being sold or disposed of.
- Backups should be stored at an off-site storage facility in another region if possible.

Backups Should Be Verified.

Backups should be regularly verified to ensure that they contain valid data. It is recommend that a sample of backup tapes be checked at least once a month to ensure this validation.

Backups Should Be Encrypted.

The data stored on the backup tapes should be encrypted to enhance backup security. When you encrypt the backup of a file system you should escrow the encryption key. Otherwise, the information stored on the backup will be useless to you when you lose the encryption key.

Note: If media separation is not possible, then all media must be included in the Custodial Media Inventory Control process described in the following section.

The movement of media to and from an authorized media retention facility must be accounted for by means of transmittal records or equivalent process. Mounting of storage media must be administered in a way that prevents unauthorized access/mounts (e.g., standard label processing, controlled use of bypass label processing [BLP], procedures for the mounting of MVS tapes on VM systems, and so on). Lockable cabinets that are used to store media containing data classified as "Confidential" must have a key control procedure to control access with a key inventory. The key inventory must be reviewed annually.

Custodial Media Inventory Control

Custodians of storage media are responsible for implementing inventory control procedures and performing an accurate inventory reconciliation of the media in the custodial media library at least biannually. The custodial media librarian should participate in the inventory process with at least one person not directly involved in this library operation. Inventory reconciliation must be able to demonstrate the following:

- Beginning inventory (prior ending inventory)

- Plus media in (received from other locations)
- Minus media out (sent to other locations)
- Plus new media added to library
- Minus scrapped media
- Equals current ending inventory (total number of tapes managed by the library)

All discrepancies must be accounted for. All media used in support of the custodial media library, including opened blank or scratch media, as well as media in media handling devices and robot-controlled storage libraries, must be included in the inventory reconciliation.

The manager responsible for the custodial media library must sign the completed inventory documentation. The last inventory reconciliation and supporting documentation (including the previously signed total inventory reconciliation page) must be retained for a predetermined time frame.

Residual Information

Residual information is processable information remaining from prior use (e.g., deleted DASD and tape files, CD-ROMs). Residual confidential data must be made unreadable prior to disposal or noncompany use.

Protecting Local Storage.

Electrical data-processing equipment such as modems and laser printers often contain memory that can download and upload stored information with appropriate control sequences. As a result, when these memories hold sensitive information they pose security risks, especially when the memory is not protected with passwords or encryption devices. Local storage also presents the same security exposure because sensitive information is frequently copied into such local storage without the computer user even being aware of it and consequently not protecting it.

Since computers transmit information faster than printers can print it, printers are equipped with semiconductor memory called "printer spoolers." These receive information faster from the computer but transmit it slowly to the printer. However, they have the ability to copy information in their storage by simply pressing the COPY button on the printer spooler. By pressing this COPY button, everything that has been printed is sent again to the printer for a second time. All that is required to print the sensitive information in the printer's buffer is the opportunity to use the COPY button to make a copy for oneself.

High-speed laser printers contain significant amounts of local storage that can store megabytes if not gigabytes of information. Moreover, they can be programmed to store a copy of any document printed. Unless these buffers are sanitized after the printing is complete, any one with sufficient skill can retrieve all of their contents.

Output of a work group printer is also exposed to theft or copying when the printer is not located in a secured location. Needless to say, printers, plotters, and fax machines should be in secured locations if they are to be used for confidential and sensitive tasks.

Sanitizing Media before Disposal.

Sanitizing is the process that ensures that the data on the tapes have been completely erased. One common sanitizing method involves overwriting the entire tape.

Simply deleting a file on a hard disk does not delete the data associated with the file. Parts of the original data and at times the entire file can be recovered. Hard disks must be sanitized with special software that is formulated for that particular disk drive's model number and revision level.

In cases of highly confidential and security-related materials, the disk or tape should be overwritten several times. Overwriting only once is risky because data can be recovered. Tapes are usually overwritten three times: once with blocks of 0s, then with blocks of 1s, and then with random numbers.

Finally, the tape can be degaussed, that is, running it through a band saw until it is reduced to thousands of tiny pieces of plastic. It is recommended that all media be thoroughly sanitized before disposal.

Function Keys.

Function keys should never be used to store passwords or any other sensitive information such as cryptographic keys.

Smart terminals that are equipped with function keys that can be programmed to send a sequence of keystrokes to the computer just by pressing these keys are often used as a shortcut to store passwords. This exposes the system to security compromises because it gives skillful persons who gain physical access to the terminal also logical access to the computer systems. Moreover, these terminals are also exposed to theft as a result, and when they are stolen, needless to say, the passwords, the cryptographic keys, and any other sensitive information that is stored in them get into the wrong hands.

Unattended Terminals.

Logged-on and unattended terminals allow skillful crooks and disgruntled employees with vandalistic tendencies to access files, sensitive or otherwise, with impunity and with dire consequences. With good planning, these accounts can also be used to launch attacks against the computer system or the entire network with no trace of the perpetrator since the only audit trail will be that of the user of the account. A malicious employee who has a severe grudge against someone could easily send a vicious e-mail to the CEO, creating havoc in the organization.

The bottom line is that all screens should be blanked (use screen savers), and all keyboards should be locked when terminals are unattended even for a short while. If the absence is expected to be long, the user should log off and not expose the company to undue risk. Screen savers that automatically log off the workstation when the keyboard and the mouse have been inactive for ten minutes or so should be used.

Key Switches.

Key switches on the front panel of computers can prevent the system from being rebooted in single-user mode. Some ROM monitors can also prevent the system from being rebooted in single-user mode without a password. Therefore, these key switches and ROM monitor passwords, which enhance security, should be used when available. Nonetheless, computers can be made dysfunctional simply by unplugging them.

Therefore, the most important first line of defense is still the strength of the physical access controls to the computers.

Disposing of Media

Important company material that winds up in the trash can provides information that is useful to hackers or competitors. This material includes plans, designs, preliminary codes, and printouts of software (including incomplete versions)—program printouts collected over time are enough to give experts a complete picture of any software development project especially when the code is well commented. The material can also give important clues about the identity of beta testers, customers, testing strategies, and marketing plans to those who know what they are doing. Information in trash cans provides clues on computers, the types and versions of operating systems in use, serial numbers, patch levels, and so on. Trash has also provided hostnames, Internet Protocol (IP) numbers, account names, and other information critical to a hacker. Listings of complete firewall configurations and filter rules left in wastepaper baskets are a temptation to someone seeking to infiltrate the computers or finding roundabout ways to get into a system.

Materials in trash are always used to figure out important information about a company's personnel and its operations. For example, a company phone book can be used to allow a crook to masquerade as an employee over the telephone and obtain sensitive information including dial-up numbers, account names, and passwords. This is called the art of social engineering. Cursory inside information such as the names, office numbers, and extensions of company officials and their staff facilitates a crook to secure important sensitive inside corporate information as well. The crook just has to convince the operator to obtain the additional information over the phone. Age-old tricks to experienced sleuths. Before disposing of media, the following four important questions need to be asked:

1. Has the value of the information that is discarded been considered carefully?
2. Are there shredders for each location where information of value can be thrown away?
3. Have the users been adequately educated not to dispose of sensitive material in their refuse at work and home but to bring it in to be shredded?
4. Are there provisions to incinerate sensitive wastepaper on-site?

Having the dumpster inside a guarded fence is not enough. It is necessary to know where it goes after it has been picked up and hauled by the trash truck. Is it dumped where it is accessible to anyone who desires to go though the information off of the company's legal boundaries and limits?

AUDIT TESTS

Objective 1

To ensure there are written procedures describing the overall control strategy for portable storage media including inventory control, control of résidual data, assignment of responsibility, and accountability for the media when it is removed from the tape library. Residual data consist of processable information remaining from prior use (e.g., data on scratch tapes, deleted DASD and files, and so on).

Approach.

Review the portable storage media library procedures. Ensure the documented process addresses all portable storage media handling functions such as mounting, labeling, shipping, releasing, returning, storage, and destruction. Coordinate with the auditor's review of logical access controls to ensure that bypass label processing has been adequately protected from unauthorized use. Sample records/documentation associated with portable storage media transactions to ensure that proper approvals were obtained, dates were recorded, and so on. Review the effectiveness of physical controls for portable media, classification and labeling, tape removal procedures, inventory and reconciliation documentation and processes, and procedures for making data classified confidential unreadable prior to disposal or nonproprietary use. Compare inventory entries to the portable media in the library.

Objective 2

To ensure all portable storage media are either assigned a classification or labeled to identify that the contents may contain classified data, that controls ensure accountability for the media when it is removed from the tape library, and that inventory records compare to physical assets. The security policy should stipulate which tapes are permitted to have a generic classification label and which ones must be labeled with the classification.

Approach.
Obtain a copy of the latest inventory of the portable storage media library. Obtain a list of all network media if it is considered to be under custodial care. Determine if data classified confidential is supported on the media. From these inventories, select samples of portable storage media to perform a physical audit. For each inventory entry, verify that the portable storage media can be located, that it is properly labeled, and that the labeling information is consistent with the inventory records. Also, select a sample of portable storage media physically present and verify that it appears correctly on the inventory record/listing.

Objective 3

Ensure that controls have been implemented effectively to prevent unauthorized access to the secured area where the portable storage media is kept (e.g., the tape library). The security policy should identify minimum physical control requirements (e.g., Zone 1 protection) for portable storage media classified confidential.

Approach.
Ensure that all portable media containing classified data is stored and protected in an area commensurate with its classification (reference security policy). Determine who has access to tapes and their associated justification if required.

Objective 4

Ensure that an inventory has been performed and reconciled to the previous inventory at least annually and that inventories and reconciliations have been performed with appropriate separation of duties and reconciliation records maintained (for libraries containing data classified confidential).

Approach.
If a library contains information classified confidential, an inventory of all portable media contained in it must be performed at least annually. Verify that inventory controls exist. Review the last two (current and previous) library inventories and reconciliations to confirm that procedures were followed and exceptions were resolved. Verify that the responsible manager reviewed and signed the completed inventory documentation and that both the physical inventory and the reconciliation were performed with appropriate separation of duties.

PORTABLE STORAGE MEDIA

Are portable storage media protected from unauthorized copying, damage, destruction, or theft? Sensitive or proprietary data are safeguarded by the following:

- Keeping media archived off-site in a locked facility.

- Erasing obsolete data.
- Shredding or securely disposing of console logs or printouts.

Assessment

Completed (Y/N) ________________
WP Reference ________________
Fact Sheet # ________________
Comments

ENVIRONMENTAL CONTROLS

You have now secured the physical access to the computing facilities. The next questions are:

- What are the essential services required for the computers to be operating at optimum levels?
- How will you provide these essential services?
- How will you maintain these essential services?
- How will you monitor these essential services?

Without a doubt, the essential services are

- Power
- Telephone
- Water
- Humidifier

Computers require care and monitoring like all complicated devices and exactly the right balance of physical and environmental conditions to operate at optimum levels. Without this balance, the computer can fail in unexpected and often undesirable ways. Worse still, computers may continue to operate, albeit erratically, painfully producing incorrect results and corrupting valuable data. (For more information about essential service and the associated dangers, see Exhibit 2.4. Also see Exhibit 2.5 for more information about risks and mitigating controls.)

POWER

The power supply can be blown out. What protection do you have?

Even if the power surge doesn't destroy the information on your hard disk, it still may make the information inaccessible until the computer system is repaired. Power surges can come from a variety of sources:

- Electrical noise
- Nature (i.e., lightning, storms)

Exhibit 2.4 Essential Services and Associated Dangers

	R	I	S	K	S
Essential Services	**Fire**	**Smoke**	**Flood**	**Theft**	**Vandals**
Power	X	X			X
Cabling	X	X	X		X
Wiring	X	X			X
Air conditioner			X	X	X
Water			X		X
Humidifier			X		X
Telephone				X	X
People	X	X	X	X	X

- Power surges fatally shorting out the power supply
- Outside and inside saboteurs
- Vandalism

Electrical Noise

Electrical noise is usually generated by heavy equipment, plants, motors, and engines but can also come from fans and even other computers that are in use, which can cause fluctuations in the power supply. For example, an ordinary vacuum cleaner plugged into the same electrical outlet as a workstation can generate a spike capable of destroying the workstation's power supply or even causing a short.

Severe electrical noise can also cause vibration, although vibration can also be caused by other factors. No matter where the vibrations are coming from, they can place an early dent in computer systems. Vibrations, gentle or otherwise, can work printed circuit boards out of their edge connectors and integrated circuits out of their sockets. Hard disk drives can come out of alignment and increase the probability for catastrophic data loss.

The control requirements for electrical noise are:

- There should be no heavy equipment on the electrical circuits that power the computer systems. In fact, the recommended norm is a special electrical circuit with an isolated ground installed for each large computer system.
- There should be a line filter on each of the large computer's power supply.
- There should be static grounding mats installed around the computer area to minimize static.
- There should be a provision to apply antistatic sprays to carpets underneath the computer area to minimize static.

Exhibit 2.5 Risks and Mitigating Controls

Risk/Control	Detective	Preventive	Corrective
Fire	Alarms	Emergency procedures	Fire extinguishers
	Smoke detector	Fire drills	
		Maintenance	CO_2
			Water, dry-pipe
			Halon
			Sprinkler heads
			Disaster recovery plans
			Insurance
Wiring			
Wiring trays, ceilings	Smoke detectors	Rules and regulations	Sprinkler heads
Wiring closets			
Smoke including tobacco	Smoke detectors	Rules and regulations	Cleaning
		Maintenance	
Dust		Maintenance	Vacuum cleaning
Air filters		Maintenance	
		Dust covers	
Humidifiers	Alarms	Maintenance	Vacuum cleaning
Temperature			
Circuit boards or integrated circuits to crack	Temperature alarm	Maintenance	Vacuum cleaning
Water			
Circuit board trace carrying voltage and a trace carrying ground	Water Sensors	Automatic power cutoffs	Disaster recovery plans
	Water Detectors		
			Insurance

- All radio transmitters should be kept at least five feet from the large computers, cables, and peripherals. Radio transmitters such as cellular telephones, walkie-talkies, and other kinds of electronic devices can cause computers to malfunction when they are transmitting. Powerful transmitters can cause permanent damage to systems and can also trigger the explosive charges in some sealed fire extinguisher systems (e.g., Halon).

- There should be signs and instructions posted to prevent portable transmitters from being used in the computer area.

The control requirements for vibration control include ensuring that there is no cause for vibrations around the computers. For example, a simple precaution such as no printer on top of the computer can control vibration.

Lightning

Lightning can generate large power surges that can damage computers. It can also generate an intense magnetic field that can damage magnetic media.

The control requirements for lightning control are:

- During severe lightning storms provisions should be made to turn off and unplug computer systems.
- Backup tapes, if they are kept on magnetic media, should be stored away from the building's structural steel members.
- Surge suppressor outlet strips should be used in severe lightning zones.
- Surge suppressors that include additional protection for sensitive telephone equipment should be used where the law does not require telephone circuits to be equipped with lightning arresters.
- Modems should also be offered additional lightning protection.

Power Supply Control Checklist

Evaluate the adequacy of controls to ensure a constant and nonfluctuating power supply.

1. Obtain and review power supply policy and procedures.
2. Through discussions with the management of the information systems facilities, verify the following:
   a. A UPS/battery/diesel generator has been installed at the site.
   b. The backup systems are regularly tested and monitored.
   c. The power supply is adequate and protected.
   d. A preventative maintenance schedule exists for power supply–related equipment.
3. Obtain and review downtime logs to determine if power fluctuations are affecting operations.
4. Obtain and review maintenance logs to verify that preventative maintenance is taking place.
5. Verify that the security station can monitor the power conditioners for:
   - Operating status
   - Transformer temperature
   - Voltage quality out of range
   - Power fluctuations
6. Are power fluctuations affecting operations?
7. Has a UPS/battery/diesel generator been installed at the site?

8. Does the backup system provide a continuous power supply?
9. Does the backup system merely allow for an orderly shutdown of the computer system?
10. Is emergency battery-operated lighting available when power is off?
11. Is emergency lighting inspected at regular intervals?
12. Can emergency doors be manually operated in the event of power failure?
13. Is the power feed from the distribution transformer to the computer facilities regularly inspected?
14. Are the backup systems tested and monitored?
15. Do the computer facilities have their own separate incoming power supply and cables?
16. Are the incoming power supply lines equipped with surge protectors?
17. Are the circuit control boxes secured from unauthorized personnel?
18. Are the circuit breaker panels properly marked, indicating the equipment being supplied?
19. After each new load is added to the electrical system, is the current drain measured to determine that the circuits are not loaded to capacity and to assure that the total load computed from inventory corresponds to the load as measured?
20. Has the local utility company been informed that a computer is on the line so they can avoid connecting transient prone loads to the same distribution transformer?
21. Are power fluctuations logged to determine if changes to the basic supply are justified?
22. Is there an established action procedure for cycling power back up following failures?
23. In the event that the standby power is not sufficient to power the entire complex, are there procedures in place to turn off nonessential equipment so the electrical load is less than the capacity of the standby generator?
24. Are structural form members grounded to protect against electromagnetic radiation, static discharges, and power line disturbances?
25. Is all equipment connected to a common earth ground?
26. Is there a preventative maintenance schedule for the power supply–related equipment?
27. When was the equipment last inspected?
28. Is it inspected regularly?
29. What is the time interval between inspections?

TELEPHONE SECURITY

In modern times, a computer on its own does not provide the full potential that it harnesses. A modem is one of those devices that enables the computer to communicate with itself or with other computers remotely. The modem is an important part of the computer and its communication capabilities, so its security is equally important.

A modem is an integral part of the computer's communications infrastructure, and it works to let you get information out to others as well as get information to your computer from anywhere as long as you have a telephone line. But in the world of computer security, good communications can be a double-edged sword. While it enables you to get information in and out easily, it can also aid attackers and saboteurs, people you want to guard against. So you need to protect yourself.

Protecting the physical access to the telephone line is as important as securing the computer to which the telephone line and its modem are connected. Some control guidelines include:

1. *Protect physical access to the telephone line.* The telephone line should be physically secure. All junction boxes should be locked. The telephone line itself should be placed in an electrical conduit, pulled through the walls, or at least located in locked Zone 1 areas. Intruders who gain physical access to the telephone line can attach their own modem to the line and intercept telephone calls before they reach the computer. By spoofing, as this is called, the intruder can learn user login names and passwords to further compromise the computer. Intruders can also simply monitor telephone calls, learning all the pertinent information communicated in the process. This way, passwords not only to the system being monitored but also to all the systems to which the users are connected can be compromised.
2. *The telephone line should not allow call forwarding and third-party billing.* If the telephone can be programmed to call forward, an intruder can effectively transfer all incoming telephone calls to another number. If there is a computer at the new number that has been programmed to act like your system, users might be fooled into typing their usernames and passwords. Without third-party billing, people cannot bill their calls to your modem line.
3. *Use leased line where security risk is high.* If all the modem usage is to a single outside location, get a leased line. A leased line is a dedicated circuit between two points provided by the phone company. It acts like a dedicated cable and cannot be used to place or receive calls. As such, it allows you to keep your connection with the remote site but does not allow anyone to dial up your modem and attempt a break-in. Leased lines are more expensive than regular lines in most places, but for security considerations they are cost justified. Leased lines also provide faster communication speeds and, therefore, will transfer data much faster than standard telephone lines and thus are very efficient.

WATER

Water can destroy computers by causing an electrical short. This is what poses the greatest danger. It happens when water provides the contact point between a circuit board trace carrying voltage and a trace carrying ground. Shorts cause an increase in the current load pulled through a trace and as a result heat up the trace and can possibly even melt it. Shorts also destroy electronic components by pulling too much current through them. Water dangers generally arise flooding. Causes of floods are from heavy rains, defective sprinkler systems, and unexpected occurrences such as the toilet overflowing, damages to water pipes and tapes, and even the fire department.

The control requirements for water are:

- Water sensors should be mounted on all floors in the area of the computer system as well as on those adjacent to the area.
- Water detectors should be mounted underneath the raised floors in the computer room and also above it.
- Two alarms, located at different heights, is the preferred norm. The first water sensor should sound an alarm; the second alarm should automatically cut off the power sup-

ply to the computer equipment. Automatic power cutoffs can mitigate the damages and can also save lives when the flood occurs off-hours or when the response time is prolonged due to unmitigated circumstances.

- It is recommended that computers should not be in the basements of buildings in areas that are prone to flooding or if a building has a sprinkler system.

HUMIDIFIERS

Dryness builds up static charge. Humidity prevents this buildup. Computer rooms should not be too dry as this builds up static electricity, the discharge of which destroys information and could also damage the computer itself, which in many cases it does. Conversely, the computer room should not be too humid as this causes condensation on the computer's circuitry, which in turn causes a short in circuitry. A short causes too much current to be pulled through a trace, which heats up the trace and possibly melts it. Shorts damage the electrical circuits and destroy electronic components by pulling too much current through them.

The control requirements for humidity control are:

- For optimal performance, the relative humidity of the computer room should be between 20% and below the dew point, which depends on the ambient room temperature.
- There should be an audible humidity alarm that should ring when the humidity is out of the acceptable range.
- The humidifiers should be well maintained.

The control requirements for air conditioners are:

- Air-conditioning systems are monitored.
- Adequate backup equipment that has been tested for the air-conditioning system.
- Air-conditioning equipment is subject to adequate preventative maintenance.

FIRE

Can your computers survive fires? The control requirements are:

- Functioning fire-extinguishing equipment
- Emergency procedures
- Fire drills
- Insurance

The control requirements for fire-extinguishing equipment are:

- Alarms should be regularly tested.
- Fire equipment should be regularly tested.

Carbon Dioxide (CO_2)

CO_2 asphyxiates fires and causes harm to humans but does not cause environmental degradation.

Automatic Sprinkler Systems

Providing that the computer's power is turned off before the water starts to flow, the risk of damage to computer equipment is low (although disks, tapes, and printouts that are in the open may suffer). However, it is imperative that the computer's power be automatically shut off when the water sprinkler is turned on. Uninterrupted power supplies must be automatically turned off too. Also, the computer must be completely dried out before the power is restored to avoid electrocution of employees. Water with very high mineral content will necessitate the computer's circuit boards being professionally cleaned before turning the power on again.

Computers can now survive exposure to water, and as a result, a water sprinkler system is preferred over a CO_2 system. In addition, a water system lasts longer than a CO_2 system and, therefore, is dependable against major fires. A sprinkler system is also much cheaper and less hazardous to humans.

The "dry-pipe" system is the preferred water-based sprinkler system. It keeps water out of the pipes until an alarm is actually triggered, and it is safer from disasters stemming from leaks and other misfortunes.

The control requirements are:

- Type of fire-extinguishing system used is clearly identified (i.e., CO_2 or dry-pipe system).
- Clear signs and instructions posted in the right places ensure that everyone who enters the computer room sees and understands what to do in case of a fire emergency, especially when the alarm bell rings or sings.
- Imperative to have a functional and regularly tested handheld fire extinguisher by the doorway of the computer room.
- Recharge state of each extinguisher verified and certified every month. Extinguisher gauges also need to be certified as functional.
- Train computer operators in the proper use of the fire-extinguishing equipment as well as emergency and DRP procedures.
- Training schedule that stipulates quarterly drills and regular practice with extinguishers that need to be recharged as per emergency procedures.
- An automatic fire alarm system required that can be "overriden" in cases of false alarms.
- Availability of telephone access for the operators and any person who discovers a fire, a false alarm, or suspicious circumstances that warrant immediate response.

Smoke

The control requirements for smoke damage are:

- Wiring needs to be protected.
- Smoke detectors and sprinkler heads need to be positioned in the right places to protect wires in wiring trays (often above the suspended ceilings) and in wiring closets.

Smoke undoubtedly damages computer equipment. Smoke is a potent abrasive and collects on the heads of magnetic disks, optical disks, and tape drives and on almost all surfaces where it settles. Smoke particles if allowed to accumulate will cause severe disk crashes on most kinds of disk drives that do not have sealed drive compartments.

Smoke is also generated by computers themselves when they become overheated because of constant use or continuously (i.e., 24 hours a day, 7 days a week, for 365 days) being "on." As a result, transformers in video monitors in particular have been known to cause electrical fires. Such fires notoriously produce pungent, acrid smoke that not only causes damage to other equipment but also releases potent carcinogens.

Smoke that comes from tobacco is no exception. Not only is such smoke a health hazard, but it is also a threat to computers and the peripheral equipment. Consequently, this smoke will cause keyboard failures if they are not cleaned more often than normal. In addition, it does create nonsmoker resentment and has led to repercussions that have cost employers dearly in sick days and absenteeism.

While on the subject of smoke, keep in mind the deadly effect of carbon monoxide (CO) and ensure that there is protection from this deadly gas. Carbon monoxide detectors are the first line of defense and usually suffice. They should be installed especially when coal-, oil-, or gas-fired appliances are used. Closed office buildings are very susceptible to buildup of strong concentrations of CO from defective heater venting equipment, from generator exhaust from an uninterruptible power supply (UPS), or from trucks idling outside with their exhaust pointing at the building's air intake.

The control requirements for smoke control are:

- "No Smoking" policy should be enforced.
- Smoke detectors should be installed in every room with or without a computer as long as it has peripheral equipment or terminals. Nowadays most rooms have some computer equipment or the attachments since most office communications involve networks.
- Smoke detectors should be mounted underneath the raised floor as well as on the floors above it.
- Smoke detectors should be mounted above the suspended ceiling tiles as well.

DUST

Does dust destroy data? Just like smoke, dust can collect on the heads of magnetic disks, tape drives, and optical drives. Dust is abrasive and destroys both the recording heads and the media. Dust is also a good conductor of electricity. Large amounts of air and dust get inside the computer with the cooling air required to keep the computers cool. Layers of dust accumulate on the computer's circuit boards and eventually cause the circuits to short and fail.

The control requirements for dust control are:

- Computer rooms should be as dust-free as possible.
- Air filters should be cleaned and replaced on a regular basis.
- Computers and all their peripherals should be vacuumed on a regular basis.
- Dust covers should be used wherever possible.

TEMPERATURE CONTROL

The ambient temperature around the computer needs to be controlled. If it gets too high, the computer's internal cooling system is unable to prevent the internal components from getting damaged. Conversely, if the temperature gets too cold, the system is susceptible to thermal shock when it is turned on, causing circuit boards or integrated circuits to crack. Computers operate optimally from 10° to 32°C or 50° to 90°F. The installation manual should always be referred to for ideal temperature ranges.

The control requirements for temperature control are:

- The computer's manual should be checked to see what the ideal temperature ranges are for the computer.
- Temperature alarms in the computer room must be installed that trigger when the temperature is out of range (i.e., too low or too high). Select alarms that can be connected to phone lines, which can be programmed to dial predefined phone numbers to advise that the computer room temperature is out of range. This may be costly, but some costs are worth the price and pay for themselves many times.
- Computers should be placed where they have from six to twelve inches of open space on each side. This helps the air circulation and the temperature control.
- To detect spurious problems, continuously monitor and record the computer room's temperature and relative humidity. As a general rule of thumb, every 1,000 square feet of office space should have its own recording equipment.
- Log and check recordings on a regular basis.

After completing the above work, the next reasonable step would be to have a discussion with the Information Services personnel to obtain information on environmental monitoring. Evaluate the environmental controls and the functions and procedures that exist to ensure that preventative maintenance is carried out. Steps to take include the following:

1. Obtain and review air-conditioning and humidity control procedures.
2. Through discussions with the management of the Information Services, complete the following environmental control checklist:
   - **a.** The air-conditioning systems are monitored.
   - **b.** There is adequate backup equipment for the air-conditioning system and it has been tested.
   - **c.** The air-conditioning equipment is subject to adequate preventative maintenance.
   - **d.** The computer facilities are protected against water damage from the environmental control systems.
   - **e.** The air-conditioning systems can be shut down automatically or manually in the event of an emergency.
3. Obtain and review downtime logs to determine if air-conditioning failures are affecting operations.
4. Obtain and review maintenance logs to verify that preventative maintenance is taking place.
5. Verify that the security station has an annunciation panel for each air conditioner that displays:
   - Operating status
   - Status of coolant pumps
   - Output pressure at each pump
   - Input pressure
   - Coolant temperature
   - Air temperature to and from room

- Humidity level to and from room
- Flood warning

6. Are air-conditioning failures affecting operations?
7. Are air intakes located to protect against intrusion of smoke, fumes, or harmful particles?
8. Are there permanent temperature recording instruments?
9. Are there permanent airflow recording instruments?
10. Are there permanent humidity recording instruments?
11. Are temperature and humidity controls in critical areas subject to regularly scheduled maintenance?
12. Are there automatic alarm systems for:
    - Temperature control?
    - Humidity control?
    - Chilled water temperature?
    - Air-conditioning compressor overheat?
    - Coolant flow?
    - Motor generator overheat?
13. Is adequate backup equipment for the air-conditioning system available?
14. Have the backup systems been tested?
15. Is the air-conditioning equipment subject to adequate preventative maintenance?
16. When was the equipment last inspected?
17. Is it inspected regularly?
18. What is the time interval between inspections?
19. Do overhead water or steam pipes run through the computer facilities?
20. Are there water detectors underneath the raised floor?
21. Are there adequate drains underneath the raised floor?
22. Are all the drains fitted with valves to prevent reverse flows?
23. Are floors and walls waterproof?
24. Are doors and windows watertight?
25. Are all junction boxes under the raised flooring installed to prevent damage in the event of water seepage?
26. Can water mains be quickly shut off in emergencies?
27. Does the air-conditioning system shut down automatically in the event of a fire alarm?
28. Does the master power off switch also kill all air-conditioning power?

PEOPLE

Are physical access controls implemented to prevent unauthorized access to the computing facilities and to the trusted system components and/or to prevent the loss of information resources as a result of people?

RISK/EXPOSURE

Who causes break-ins?

Who writes computer viruses?

Who steals passwords?

Who causes vandalism?

Who can be notorious threats?

Is it aliens from outer space?

No, the simple answer is men and women. If men and women commit computer security violations ranging from simple errors to complex criminally indictable offenses, then what more needs to be said about this subject to auditors? Auditing computer security exposes weaknesses in controls to restrict access to the trusted components of computing systems. These exposures when exploited subject the company's physical and information assets to loss, theft, or misuse. Weaknesses also expose the facility to interrupted service through intentional or inadvertent actions. The greatest threats are not from the vagaries of the weather or earthquakes but from men and women, as fraud indicators have time and again disclosed. If you take care of men and women, then the rest will take care of itself.

CLASSIFICATION

The level of physical access privileges granted is based on the class levels. Therefore, people need to be grouped into different classes commensurate with their risk profile, which is based on their need to know or on discretionary access control (DAC). The *Department of Defense Trusted Computer System Evaluation Criteria* defines discretionary access control as "a means of restricting access to objects based on the identity of subjects and/or groups to which they belong. The controls are discretionary in the sense that a subject with a certain access permission is capable of passing that permission on to any other subject."

One technique for increasing accountability in security administration is to distribute security-related responsibilities among different users. In Exhibit 2.6, the Information Security Officer is responsible for overall security. The Physical Security Officer is responsible for the physical security and the System Security Officer is responsible for system security. The System Administrator keeps the system running and works with the System Security Officer to plan the system's overall hardware and software needs.

Here the concern is with the physical/organizational controls and not the technical implementation of the logical controls. Conduct control assessment interview(s) with the management responsible for the computing environment and supporting organizations (e.g., user ID administration, database administration); these are necessary to obtain an overview of the management processes and the physical security controls for Zone 1, Zone 2, and Zone 3. See Exhibit 2.7 for mapping classes to Zones.

SECURITY POLICY

Basic Features

The security policy must ensure that management awareness of all physical access to the computing facilities, internal systems, and data can be demonstrated and that removal of

Exhibit 2.6 Security-Related Responsibilities among Different Users

Information Management

Various classes of management positions.

System Security Officer Tasks

- Initiates and monitors auditing policy.
- Determines which users and events are audited.
- Maintains the secure password system.
- Initializes DAC privileges on public files.
- Authorizes new user accounts.
- Checks file systems for sensitive security programs.

System Administrator Tasks

- Implements auditing procedures.
- Inspects and analyzes audit logs.
- Administers group and user accounts.
- Repairs damaged user files and volumes.
- Updates system software.
- Sets system configuration parameters.
- Collects various system statistics.
- Disables and deletes accounts.
- Makes periodic system checks.
- Monitors repeated login attempts.
- Periodically scans file permissions.
- Deals with invalid superuser attempts and invalid network requests.

Operator Tasks

- Installs security-relevant software.
- Performs routine maintenance such as backups.
- Performs online terminal and device tests.
- Responds to user requests for routine system maintenance.

Systems Programmer Tasks

- Installs system upgrades.
- Performs dump analysis.
- Writes programs that conform to security criteria.

Computer User

- Uses the computer resources.

such physical access is processed when there is no longer a business justification (e.g., at separation or change of assignment) in a timely manner.

Physical access capability has to be current. At a minimum, there must be an annual revalidation of physical access privileges and a quarterly process to assist in the removal of physical access privileges assigned to employees who have separated or retired. All physical access privileges must be identifiable to an individual (e.g., a manager may have ownership of nonregular employee physical access privileges). Physical access controls should be used for flagging discrepancies, and the security standards should stipulate the

Exhibit 2.7 People Classes (commensurate with their risk profile) Map to Zones

Class	Zone 1	Zone 2	Zone 3
Information Security Officer			
Physical Security Officer			
System Security Officer			
Information System Management			
System Administrator			
Operator Tasks			
Systems Programmer			
Application Programmer			
Computer Users			
Network Administrators			
Help Desk			
Thieves			

frequency with which owning managers should review the nonregular employee physical access privileges.

The security policy should ensure that effective education has been provided to users when they are given physical access privileges such as CAS, badges, and keys and that they are made aware of their information security responsibilities as defined in the security policy at this time. Provider of Service senior executive approval should be demonstrated for nonregulars who are used in a position where system controls can be bypassed undetected. Documented procedures for completeness, assignment of responsibilities, and compliance should address the following:

- How users are identified (e.g., who authorizes access to a user to the computing environment).
- How resources are identified (e.g., who owns a dataset, minidisk, or subsystem).
- How users are "mapped" to resources (e.g., who authorizes users to or excludes users from which secured areas).
- Any audit trails for access (successful and unsuccessful) that are provided (e.g., who determines what will be audited).
- Any reporting that is provided (e.g., who generates and who reviews).
- How "privileged users" are identified and managed (e.g., who authorizes and what controls have they determined are required).

The site's operating procedures should adequately address control points specific to the administration of physical access to the computing facilities and resources.

Three specific tests should be performed:

1. Continued business need for active employees. Provider of Service senior executive approval should be demonstrated for nonregulars who are used in a position where system controls can be bypassed undetected.
2. Active physical access privileges assigned to separated employees.
3. Active physical access privileges that cannot be "mapped" to personnel (i.e., unknown ownership).

All such physical access privileges must be explained or accounted for. The security policy should require that all physical access privileges, service machines, and tasks be identifiable to an owner.

Audit Approach

Review documentation supporting the level of controls applied to computing facilities (e.g., Zones 1, 2, 3) and verify that appropriate controls have been effectively implemented to prevent unauthorized physical access to trusted system components. Also, review any local procedures describing the overall control strategy for the protection of trusted system components (e.g., procedures for granting access to the computing center, securing unattended microprocessors, and so on).

Now that we have covered the basic requirements for physical security let us evaluate the physical controls for the computer installation. As auditors, always bear in mind that employees will adapt practices that may not fit the ideal model because the employees are the ones who have the real responsibility to get the jobs done and keep the business doors open. Be cognizant of this as well as ensuring that control requirements are cost effective (i.e., they can be financed by management). The main contribution to the audit process should be to ensure that employees have actually adapted a practice that helps the business objectives as well as the control environment objectives and not just the control environment. Risks are different from organization to organization, and this is the basis on which any control environment should be developed. From an audit perspective, objectives should be not to reinvent the wheel but to ensure that physical security has been adequately thought through and designed and also that the physical security plan is a living document that is constantly being developed to reflect changing and new information that is being gathered or obtained.

Audit Checklist

I. Procedures exist to ensure that only authorized personnel have access to the computer facilities, that is, the physical security plan

   Review procedures outlining access to the controlled access areas as documented in the physical security plan (i.e., computer facilities, computer room, communications room, tape library, forms storage area, print distribution room, and so on).

   Through discussions with the management of the computer center, complete the following environmental control checklist:

   1. Are all entry points to the computer facilities secured against unauthorized entry? How are they secured (i.e., electronic access control system)?
   2. Are these entrances monitored by a central system?

3. Is physical access control maintained during power failure?
4. Is access control to the computer room maintained during shifts?
5. Are there provisions to change combinations to safes and locks regularly and especially whenever key personnel leave?
6. Are tape reels secured from unauthorized personnel?
7. Are sensitive forms secured from unauthorized personnel?
8. Is an access log of staff movements within the building maintained by the access control facility?
9. Does the access control facility record violation attempts?
10. Are security violations investigated?
11. Are the electronic access controls equipped with emergency mechanical overrides for emergency personnel?
12. Are all personnel sufficiently security conscious to challenge employees without badges? Unidentified visitors?
13. Are Information Systems personnel required to report all known intentional and inadvertent security violations?
14. Have security arrangements been made for the custodial, electrical, and other in-house maintenance personnel?
15. Have security arrangements been made for vendor personnel?
16. Does entrance to the general office area through the access control system also permit access to the computer room?
17. Are programmers generally prohibited from the computer room?
18. Are users given permission to enter critical areas without an escort?
19. Document and assess the adequacy of:
    a. The security procedures/devices that have been implemented within the computer center.
    b. The efficiency and effectiveness of the access control system.
    c. The security consciousness of the Information Systems personnel.
    d. The security arrangements for the custodial, electrical, and other in-house maintenance personnel.
    e. The security arrangements for vendor support personnel.
    f. The levels of security within the data center.

II. Once the planning and implementation of the physical security measures have been undertaken, the next step is to determine how to access these protected resources. Normally, it is through keys, cipher locks, and electronic controlled access systems (CASs). Again fall back on the review of the physical security plan.

1. Obtain and review administrative procedures for card/key issuance and return.
2. Determine how card/keys are issued and who can authorize card/key issuance.
3. Through discussions with the management of the computer center, document and assess the adequacy of the procedures for:
    a. Issuing card/keys to new and existing staff.

b. Issuing card/keys to outside personnel.

c. Securing "stock" cards from unauthorized use.

d. Returning issued card/keys to "stock."

e. Administering card/key security levels.

4. Obtain a list of all card/key numbers.

a. Identify issued, visitor, and "stock" card/key numbers.

b. Select a sample of fifteen issued cards and test to ensure that they were issued according to procedures.

c. Account for all "stock" card/keys.

d. Verify that card/keys have only been issued to authorized users.

5. Based on (4), identify access privileges for all cards. Select a sample of twenty-five and determine if privileges granted are authorized and appropriate based on the employee's job functions.

6. Based on (4), account for all visitor cards.

a. Are new hires only issued card/keys after they have completed a probation period?

b. Are access restrictions placed upon new hires?

c. Are new hires required to be escorted?

d. Is the access level that is requested verified?

e. Are card/keys that are stored inside the security station protected from theft and unauthorized use?

f. Do "stock" cards have limited access privileges?

g. Are terminated employees required to turn in their card/keys immediately?

h. Are resigning employees required to turn in their card/keys immediately?

i. Are terminated employees escorted?

j. Are returned cards deactivated or destroyed?

k. Is a list maintained detailing all issued, visitor, and "stock" cards and their access levels?

l. Are ID badges required to be worn at all times?

III. Obtain and review administrative procedures for security key issuance and return.

1. Document how security keys are issued and who can authorize them.

2. Through discussions with the management of the computer center, document and assess the adequacy of the procedures for:

a. Issuing security keys to new staff.

b. Issuing security keys to existing staff.

c. Securing security keys from unauthorized use.

d. Returning security keys.

e. Obtaining a list of all security keys.

f. Selecting a sample of fifteen keys and testing to ensure they were issued according to procedures.

g. Accounting for all security keys.

h. Verifying that security keys have only been issued to authorized users.

3. Select a sample of twenty-five persons having security keys and determine if the authorization is appropriate based on their job functions.
4. Select a sample of fifteen employee terminations/resignations/transfers and verify that the security key return procedures were followed.
5. Verify that the security system can place time and day restrictions on specific access cards and is able to logically deactivate access cards.
6. Obtain and review the access log and verify:

a. Staff movements in the building are recorded.

b. Violation attempts are recorded and investigated.

IV. Procedures exist to ensure that visitors' access to the computer center is controlled.

Visitors, maintenance personnel, cleaning crew, consultants, contractors, vendors, and others who have temporary access to the computer facilities and its contents are, in a nutshell, outsiders who pose the same if not greater risk than those in the outside world because they are now inside the guarded territory and with permission. Evaluate the risks of theft from these people with temporary access and determine what detective and preventive controls are available. At the very least, no one from the outside should be allowed unrestricted physical access to the computer and network equipment.

1. Obtain and review visitor sign-in procedures.
2. Through discussions with the management of the physical security, complete document and assess the adequacy of:

a. Visitor sign-in and escort procedures

b. Procedures for maintenance personnel

3. Select a sample of twenty-five visitors over a two-week period and verify that sign-in procedures were followed.

a. Are escorts required to accompany visitors around the computer center?

b. Must visitors wait in an outside lobby for their escort to arrive?

c. Do visitors have to present any ID to pick up their temporary card/keys?

d. Are visitors required to sign in?

e. Are visitors required to sign out?

f. Are VIP visitors treated the same as ordinary visitors with respect to:

- ID authentication?
- Sign in?
- Sign out?
- Escorts?

g. Are visitors restricted from the premises after normal working hours?

h. Are repair or maintenance personnel employed by suppliers permitted entry to critical areas only after proper identification?

i. Are they escorted and supervised at all times?

j. Must repair and delivery personnel formally check out before being allowed to remove any of the installation's property?

TRUSTED INSIDERS

After reviewing the security for the computer facilities and determining that only authorized people can have access to these facilities, the next step is to assess the risk of theft from "trusted insiders." The safeguards include video surveillance, but this is a detective control. Assess the need for preventive controls. One criteria is theft of personal computers, notebooks, memory chips, and small items that can be stolen.

1. Does anyone other than yourself have physical access to your computer?
2. What would happen if that person had a breakdown or an angry outburst and tried to smash your system with a hammer?
3. What would happen if someone in the employ of your biggest competitor were to come into the building unnoticed?
4. In the event of some large disaster in the building, would you lose the use of your computer?
5. If some disaster were to befall your system, how would you face all your angry users?

PREVENTING THEFT

Physically protecting a computer presents many of the same problems that arise when protecting any valuable item. Since an office computer is a valuable commodity and yet it needs to be openly accessed, it is very easy for a thief to steal it or steal from it the data and information that are stored on the computer's disks or, worse still, the system's hardware components such as memory chips, hard disks, modems, and other auxiliaries. It's the value of the loss of the data and information that many times can be devastating more than the hardware itself. To protect against the loss of information, adequate corrective controls such as backup procedures and off-site backup facilities are needed. Backup procedures are also an essential ingredient for the disaster recovery plan. Even with a backup plan, valuable time and resources will still be needed to restore the system. Then there is the added risk that the stolen information or the fact that the information was stolen could result in a tainted reputation or even litigation. Needless to say, computers are among the most expensive possessions owned. Common sense dictates that computers should be in secured areas. However, secured areas should also have the following additional protections.

Raised Floors and Dropped Ceilings

Internal walls that do not extend above the dropped ceilings and beneath the raised floors make it easy for people in adjoining rooms, and sometimes adjoining offices, to gain access to neighboring secured areas.

The control guidelines required with raised floors and dropped ceilings are:

- The building's internal walls should extend above the dropped ceilings so that intruders cannot enter secured areas simply by climbing over the walls.
- Raised floors should have the building's walls extend down to the real floor, thus preventing anyone from sliding below the raised floors.

Entrances through Air Ducts

Air ducts that serve the computer rooms should not be large enough to allow intruders to gain access to secured areas.

The control guidelines for air ducts involve having several small ducts instead of one large enough for a person to pass through when areas that need large amounts of ventilation exist. Although screens can be welded over air vents or even within air ducts to prevent unauthorized entry, this precaution can be rendered useless since screens can be cut.

Glass Walls

Glass walls and large windows frequently add to security risks since they are easy to break—a brick and a bottle of gasoline thrown through a window are enough to cause great damage. Glass walls are also transparent, and as such a potential thief can gain valuable knowledge such as passwords or information about system operations by carefully watching people inside. The control guidelines for glass walls are:

- No glass walls and windows for security-sensitive areas.
- If necessary use translucent glass that does not allow people to see inside.

THREATS

Vandalism

Computer vandalism, if unchecked, can be perpetrated efficiently and effectively and can result in exorbitant expenses.

Ideally, any part of a computer system including the premises that contain the information system resources can be targeted for vandalism. Why? Because vandalism is usually a way out for disgruntled and vengeful employees who are soon to be ex-employees. Therefore, any area that provides easy targets can be vulnerable. Two extremely dangerous areas are described briefly: network cables and network connectors.

Local and wide area networks are vulnerable to vandalism because of the ease with which they can be damaged. All it takes is a vandal to cut a single wire of the Ethernet to disable an entire network of workstations. Fiberoptic cables are even more vulnerable because they are susceptible to damage (fiberoptic cable can be fractured by merely stepping on it, which would be difficult to locate because there would be no break in the coating), they are difficult to repair, and the costs would be enormous.

As mentioned, all it takes is for a vandal to cut a single wire of the Ethernet to disable an entire network of workstations. In addition, a vandal can also electronically disable or damage the entire network simply by removing the terminator at the end of the network cable or by grounding an Ethernet's inside conductor. Ethernet is vulnerable to grounding and network-termination problems. However, all wire-based networks are also vulnerable to attacks of high voltage.

Network cables and network connectors should, therefore, be physically protected and secured in physically secure locations. Ethernet cables should be placed in cable trays or suspended from ceilings with plastic loops. If possible, Ethernet should be run through steel conduit between offices. This would also protect it from network eavesdropping and from fire.

Note: High-security installations use double-walled, shielded conduit with pressurized gas between the layers. Pressure sensors on the conduit break off the traffic and/or trigger a warning bell when the pressure drops, as might occur when the walls of the pipe are penetrated. Placing the wire inside electrical conduits during the initial installation can prevent exorbitant repair and downtime costs.

Protecting Data

There is a strong overlap between physical security and data security (i.e., privacy and integrity). Indeed, the goal of many attacks is not the physical destruction of the computer system but its penetration, access, and theft of sensitive information. This kind of attack can be deadly to any organization. This kind of espionage is referred to as eavesdropping. Eavesdropping is data piracy. All it takes is modest equipment for an eavesdropper to gain knowledge of keystrokes—information on the screen and/or sent to the printer. This mediocre but valuable information reveals passwords and procedures necessary for launching more serious attacks for more complex and sensitive information. In most cases, the victim never learns of the eavesdropper's presence except when the eavesdropper attempts to make use of the stolen information. The following vulnerabilities need special attention with respect to physical access protection.

Wiretapping

Electrical wires radiate electrical currents that cause interference (cross talk) and as such also make them susceptible to wiretapping and eavesdropping. Ensure that wiretapping and eavesdropping are prevented by the following:

- Wires should be protected from eavesdropping by using shielded cable and where possible armored cable for additional protection. Where stringent security is required, cables should be wrapped in steel conduit. The steel conduits can themselves be pressurized with gas since gas pressure monitors can be used to trigger an alarm system in instances of wiretapping. These measures are expensive, and therefore they should be cost justified.
- Routine inspection for physical damage should be done on all wires, especially vulnerable wires such as terminal wires and telephone lines used for modems.
- Unused offices should not have live Ethernet or twisted-pair ports inside them since Ethernet and local area networks are susceptible to eavesdropping.

Departure

Personnel leave, sometimes on their own, and sometimes involuntarily. In either case, a defined set of actions for how to handle the departure is needed. This procedure should include shutting down accounts; forwarding e-mail; changing critical passwords, phone numbers, and combinations; and otherwise removing access to the systems.

In other environments, a departure is quite sudden and dramatic. Someone may show up at work only to find the locks changed and a security guard waiting with a box containing everything that was in the user's desk drawers. The account has already been deleted, all system passwords have been changed, and the user's office phone number is no longer assigned. This form of separation management is quite common in financial service industries and is understood to be part of the job.

CHAPTER 3

IBM AS/400 ARCHITECTURE AND APPLICATIONS

INTRODUCTION

The first AS/400 models based on the 64-bit RISC PowerPC AS processors were announced in June 1995. The ease with which customers migrated to these powerful systems is in testament to the fundamental strength of the AS/400 architecture.

In August 1999, the AS/400 range was again expanded for both hardware and software solutions. A dedicated server for Domino was introduced to allow a choice to deploy Domino solutions on separate servers. The Dedicated Server for Domino is based on the 170 and delivers improved price performance for Domino workload support. Lotus Domino Enterprise Server for AS/400 software was introduced to provide additional options for the office user. An advanced read cache technology was introduced to improve the response times of the input/output (I/O) subsystems. These were just a few of the more exciting announcements.

OS/400 V4R4 and other system software on the AS/400 offer enhanced function in the notable areas of server consolidation, Web serving, network security, network management, Java serving, e-commerce, and database management. With its enduring strength as an integrated system, the AS/400 offers substantial strength for network computing.

Three additional 7XX models were announced in February 1999. Designed to make the AS/400e the most flexible business server available, the AS/400e servers 720, 730, and 740 offer customized performance to match business needs, whether running mostly back-office applications, newer e-business applications, or a mixture of both. Existing AS/400e servers can be upgraded to these new configurations. In the future, upgrade capabilities will enable performance to be fine-tuned to handle changing business environments.

An overview of both the hardware and the software for the current AS/400e includes the 9406 Models 170, 720, 730, 740, and SB1 as well as the 9401 Model 150. V4R3 and V4R4 of the AS/400 operating software support these models. (V4R4 is for the Dedicated Domino Server 170.)

The AS/400e System Handbook is designed to answer the first-level questions that IBM employees, business partners, and customers ask about the AS/400. However, it does not go into considerable detail on the subjects addressed. Therefore, for more information consult the companion manual AS/400 System Builder, SG24-2155, and an IBM sales representative. Also, refer to the IBM online publications and systems such as ViewBlue and PartnerInfo.

AS/400 HARDWARE

- *Model 150:* Provides small businesses with a low-cost, high-performance computing choice. Allows support of about 150 clients, with secure connections to the Internet.
- *Model 170:* Offers departments and small businesses a robust solution that is highly cost effective, is easy to implement, and can upgrade to more than quadruple performance.
- *Model 730/740:* Enterprise-class performance in a manageable, affordable package.
- *Model SB1:* Features eight-way or twelve-way processor configurations specifically tuned for increased processing power and memory.
- *DSD Model:* Three new AS/400 170 servers designed for exceptional price and performance with pure Domino workloads. The first servers in the industry built just for Domino.

CENTRAL CONTROL

Managing a variety of computing environments, including desktop PCs, Windows NT servers, Domino servers, and Java servers, can be a challenging task, to say the least. AS/400 provides a simple solution to this complex task.

AS/400 greatly simplifies PC support by providing native file and print sharing for Windows PCs. No special hardware or software is required for users; AS/400 servers and printers simply show up in their Network Neighborhood. For more complete integration, Client Access Express makes it easier than ever for Windows 95/98/NT PCs to share all AS/400e resources. You can even run Windows NT Server on an Integrated Netfinity Server for AS/400, getting the best of both worlds in a single, easy-to-manage server. And if the network includes more than local PCs, AS/400e gives the graphical tools needed to manage it all—from the Operations Navigator to the Operations Console.

By tightly integrating hardware, software, middleware, and the operating system, AS/400 provides a combination of power, flexibility, and ease of use that can help run the operations smoothly. This design also makes it possible for AS/400 to keep abreast with technology changes. The latest AS/400 hardware enhancements and the newest version of the AS/400 operating system, OS/400 Version 4 Release 4 (V4R4), have been engineered to provide the performance, the tools, and the ease of use needed in critical areas such as e-business, enterprise resource planning, business intelligence, and server consolidation software. With V4R4 the Internet server functions now offer an enhanced graphical user interface (GUI) and expanded digital security. Also, the new WebSphere Application Server transforms the HTTP Server for AS/400 into a Java Web application server.

BRINGING IT ALL TOGETHER

You can create a more manageable information technology infrastructure by consolidating multiple servers onto AS/400e, with its seamless support for Windows NT Server and Windows 95/98 clients. With V4R4, the role of the AS/400 as a consolidated server is enhanced with the delivery of logical partitioning (LPAR).

Logical partitioning lets you run multiple independent partitions—each with its own processors, memory, and disks—within a single symmetric multiprocessing AS/400e. It is ideal for server consolidation, business unit consolidation, mixed production and test environments, and integrated clusters, as well as for supporting multiple national languages and time zones in a single server. Protecting your business from planned and unplanned outages as well as site loss disasters is therefore easier. With the introduction of Cluster Resource Services within the base OS/400 operating system, AS/400 is taking a major step forward. Combined with high-availability applications and expertise provided by IBM Business Partners, V4R4 provides a complete, easy-to-manage clustering solution. With custom server solutions, AS/400e servers are packaged with a choice of applications offered with tailored service, including preloading and support. For in-house development, V4R4 supports the latest generation of object-oriented programming tools and languages including Java, the choice for creating Internet client/server programs. V4R4 also includes the tools you need to update your existing mission-critical solutions.

Business requires that time and resources are used to run the business and not just the computers. The tight integration of AS/400 hardware, operating system, database, input/output devices, middleware, and tools provides significant advantages in performance, ease of use, and reliability, which helps the efficient running of the business. V4R4 provides the updated features and functions needed to run businesses in a networked world without the need for a large IT involvement. And AS/400 can be run from Windows desktop. AS/400 Client Access Express exploits the ease of use of Windows and delivers the power of AS/400 to desktop users. Included as part of Client Access Express is Operations Navigator, which provides a graphical user interface and "wizards" to guide you through system administration tasks. You may install only those functions you need. You can drag-and-drop reports to various printers or the desktop. You can even create desktop "shortcuts" to items in Operations Navigator.

Management Central, a suite of tools integrated into Operations Navigator, makes the management of multiple systems as easy as managing a single system. Real-time performance monitors, asset inventory, software fix management, object packaging, and distribution are just a few of the tools provided to simplify the management of the AS/400 systems.

AS/400 SYSTEM CONCEPTS AND ARCHITECTURE

Why are system concepts and architecture important to understand? Business leaders do not start by choosing a computer system. They start by choosing an application that fits their business needs. Because of that, very often the computer system is considered first. Why should the AS/400 architecture matter? The accelerating rate of change of both hardware and software technologies necessitates that the system selected has been designed with the future in mind. The AS/400 accommodates inevitable, rapid, and dramatic technology changes with minimum relative effort. Is the system future oriented? Paradoxically, the characteristic of the most advanced design and technology is subtle. It accommodates rapidly changing hardware and software technologies in stride—permitting one to fully exploit the latest technologies.

SYSTEM CONCEPTS

The AS/400 is designed and built as a total system, fully integrating all the hardware and software components that a business demands. As a general-purpose business and network system, it is optimized for the required environment with unique benefits.

The AS/400 Advanced Application Architecture is a brilliant, technology-neutral architecture that enables businesses to readily exploit the latest hardware and software technologies without causing disruption to existing application software. The single purpose pervading each aspect of AS/400's architecture is to empower a business with the most advanced technology available, without encumbering it with the complexities that such technologies inevitably contain. In other words, the AS/400 allows you to rapidly deploy advanced business applications and facilitates your business growth. Customers typically decide on required application software first, then select an environment in which to run it. The AS/400 has a plethora of business applications, of which thousands are client/server applications. In addition, the AS/400 provides an excellent platform for Windows NT and Lotus Domino applications. Worldwide support is provided by an impressive network of global partners. A concise and expanded explanation of AS/400's architecture is contained in a renowned book, *Inside the AS/400* (ISBN: 1-882419-66-9), written by the AS/400's chief architect, Dr. Frank G. Soltis. The book is now in its second edition and is published by Duke Communications International.

Technology-Independent Machine Interface (TIMI)

The AS/400 is atypical in that it is defined by software, not by hardware. In other words, when a program presents instructions to the machine interface for execution, it "thinks" that the interface is the AS/400 hardware. But it is not! The instructions presented to that interface have to pass through a layer of microcode before they can be understood by the hardware itself. This design insulates application programs and their users from changing hardware characteristics through this comprehensive layer of microcode. When a different hardware technology is deployed, IBM rewrites sections of the microcode to absorb the fluctuations in hardware characteristics. As a result, the interface presented to the customer remains the same. This interface is known as the Technology-Independent Machine Interface (TIMI). The microcode layer is known as the System Licensed Internal Code (SLIC). The brilliance of this design was dramatically illustrated when the AS/400 changed its processor technology from Complex Instruction Set Computing (CISC) processors to 64-bit Reduced Instruction Set Computing (RISC) processors in 1995. With any other system, the move from CISC to RISC would involve recompiling (and possibly some rewriting) of programs. Even then, the programs would run in 32-bit mode on the newer 64-bit hardware. This is not so with the AS/400 because of TIMI. Customers were able to save programs off their CISC AS/400s, and restore them on their new RISC AS/400s, and the programs would run. Not only did they run, but they were fully 64-bit programs. As soon as they made this transition, customers had 64-bit application programs that ran on a 64-bit operating system containing a 64-bit relational database that fully exploited the 64-bit RISC hardware. TIMI and SLIC have just taken 64-bit RISC processor technology in their stride. These same architectural features will be exploited to fully accommodate post-RISC technologies that may have 96-bit or 128-bit processors.

Many of the frequently executed routines that ordinarily reside in the operating system have been moved to the SLIC. Because the SLIC is closer to the silicon, routines placed there run faster than routines placed "higher" in the machine. There is an important performance gain. Examples of some basic supervisory management functions that are in SLIC are validity and authorization checks.

Operating System OS/400

One of the most dramatic things about AS/400 is that its operating system, OS/400, is a single entity. This section describes the meaning of this concept. Once you buy an AS/400, you do not have to continue shopping for system software components before it is ready to run your business. All of those software components, for relational database, comprehensive security, communications with a broad range of diverse systems, including Internet capabilities, and many more, are already there. They are all fully integrated into OS/400. "Fully integrated" means fully tested, too. All those components, prerequisites for running business applications in the 2000s, work together and are fully tested together so that OS/400 operates as a single entity.

An ordinary machine does not have this approach to its operating system design. An ordinary operating system, which does the basic system housekeeping, needs to have a range of software products added to it before the environment is ready to support modern business applications. Examples include software for the relational database, support for various communications environments, software for security, and support for an interactive environment, multimedia, availability, recoverability, and so on. On an ordinary machine, these software modules are provided by third parties. A customer has to make sure that someone has integrated all these modules and performed the tests necessary to ensure they all function together. When one of the software components has a new release, a customer needs to make sure that component is replaced plus any other software modules that it depends on. The modules need to be at compatible release levels. Also, should a software malfunction occur, how do you establish precisely which modules are causing it? Can you be certain that multiple third-party software vendors will agree with your diagnosis when you blame their software?

There are none of these problems with the OS/400. To achieve the functionality that is standard in OS/400, a customer would integrate typically between ten and twenty-five different modules of software. OS/400 is installed with all these capabilities as standard. When software is updated, a new release of OS/400 is made available. Customers do not have to install individual system software components, nor do they have to check that new releases can coexist.

FULL INTEGRATION INTO THE OPERATING SYSTEM AND THE MACHINE

As noted previously, the AS/400 operating system, OS/400, is conceived as a single entity. This means that facilities such as relational database, communications and networking capabilities, online help, and much more are fully integrated into the operating system and the machine. The user communicates with all components of OS/400 using a single command language or control language (CL).

OS/400 provides tools to handle two different computing environments: systems and servers. The AS/400 continues to provide integrated functions based on the traditional commercial computing environment. The AS/400 client/server dimension combines an open system environment with the AS/400's price and performance and integration of system solutions to extend a complete product package for the server environment.

The computing industry is moving rapidly toward a network-centric world made of global networks. Version 4 of the AS/400 software contains many significant enhancements to the AS/400 capability in this area. The newest release, V4R4, builds on this to make the AS/400 system a key player in this vibrant and vital area. These enhancements to the AS/400 capabilities as a network-centric system are described in this section and the following sections, which contain descriptions of licensed programs.

AS/400e servers include Models 170, 720, 730, 740, 600, 620, 640, 650, S10, S20, S30, S40, and SB1, and the Dedicated Server for Domino is the Version 4. Version 4 of OS/400 runs on all previously announced AS/400 models with PowerPC processors. These are the 9401 Model 150; the 9402 Models 400, 40S, and 436 and packages based on the 400 and 40S; and the 9406 Models 170, 500, 510, 530, 50S, 53S, 600, 620, 640, 650, S10, S20, S30, S40, and SB1 and the Dedicated Server for Domino. Version 4 of OS/400 does not run on earlier models of AS/400 based on Internal Microprogrammed Interface (IMPI) processors. These include the BXX, CXX, DXX, EXX, FXX, 100, 135, 140, 2XX, and 3XX Models.

OS/400 Version 4 is delivered only on CD-ROM to speed loading and to reduce the risk of media errors. Soft-copy manuals are also delivered by CD-ROM.

The AS/400 also has a secondary hierarchical file system developed to support PCs and Office Vision (i.e., AS/400 office productivity products). This file system is totally contained within two object types (*DOC and *FLR). All instances of these objects are stored in the library QDOC. The *DOC object can support the storage of ASCII data (storage is normally in EBCDIC).

Hierarchy of Microprocessors

AS/400 has a range of other processors each dedicated to a particular I/O device type. A single large AS/400 configuration can have well over 200 processors.

The main system processor (which itself can be comprised of twelve separate processors) may encounter a request for data to be read from or written to any I/O device. That request for data is delegated to the particular microprocessor dedicated to that I/O device. Meanwhile, the main system processor continues executing another application program. Nanoseconds (10^{-9} second) is the unit of time used to measure main storage access times. Meanwhile, the main system processor continues with executing another application program. I/O operations are measured in milliseconds (10^{-3} second). This design provides the AS/400 with its outstanding performance in the commercial, transaction-based environment. The AS/400 is designed for business computing, and one of the main characteristics of that environment is that it is I/O intensive rather than compute intensive.

In addition to the benefit of outstanding performance in the business environment, this design gives AS/400 an elegant method of integrating diverse environments into a single, harmonious customer solution. The microprocessors that look after a particular I/O device are accommodated on I/O cards that fit into slots on the AS/400's system bus. One of these cards may be the Integrated Netfinity Server (see #2866 PCI Integrated Netfinity Server for more information). This is a PC on a card, which enables the AS/400 to run Windows NT server, for example. The AS/400's Internet firewall capability also exploits the Integrated Netfinity Server (see IBM Firewall for AS/400 V4R4, 5769-FW1).

Single-Level Storage

Application programs on an AS/400 are unaware of underlying hardware characteristics because of the TIMI. They are also unaware of the characteristics of any storage devices on the AS/400 because of single-level storage.

As with TIMI, the concept of single-level storage means that the knowledge of the underlying characteristics of hardware devices (in this case, the hardware storage devices—main storage and disk storage) resides in the SLIC. All of the storage is automatically managed by the system. Programs work with objects (see the next section on object-based operating), and objects are accessed by name, never by address. No user intervention is ever needed to take full advantage of any storage technologies.

The AS/400's address size is vast. The AS/400 system can address the number of bytes that 64 bits allows it to address. The value 264 is equal to 18,446,744,073,709,551,616. Therefore, the AS/400 system can address 18,446,744,073,709,551,616 bytes, or 18.4 quintillion bytes. To put this into more meaningful terms, it is twice the number of millimeters in a light-year. Light travels approximately 6 trillion miles in one year.

Single-level storage enables another extremely important AS/400 benefit—object persistence. Object persistence means that the object continues to exist in the memory system forever. An ordinary machine requires that information be stored in a separate file system if the information is to be shared or if it is to be retained for a long time. Persistence of objects is extremely important for future support of object-oriented databases. Objects need to continue to exist even after their creator goes away. The AS/400 is uniquely positioned to exploit this characteristic of object persistence. Ordinary systems use a less elegant mechanism that requires them to store their persistent objects in a separate file system with all the attendant performance implications.

AS/400 Logical Partitioning

Logical partitioning is also ideal for companies that want to run mixed interactive and server workloads in a single AS/400 system. Logical partitioning allows the interactive performance of an AS/400 system to be flexibly allocated between partitions. All V4R4 systems have a primary partition with all resources initially allocated to it. Creating and managing secondary partitions is performed from the primary partition. Movement of processors, memory, and interactive performance between partitions can be achieved with only an initial program lead, (IPL), or startup, of the affected partitions. Movement of input output processors (IOP) resources can be achieved without an IPL. Logical partitions operate independently. Communication between partitions is achieved with standard LAN/WAN facilities. OptiConnect software can be installed for high-performance communications between partitions without the need for additional OptiConnect hardware. OS/400 is licensed once for the entire system by its normal processor group, regardless of the number of partitions. License management across partitions is not supported. OS/400 V4R4 must be installed on each partition. Previous releases are not supported on a logical partition.

Logical Partitioning (LPAR)

As the performance of an enterprise class server grows, so does the requirement to divide that performance to run multiple workloads independently. Partitioning enterprise servers has become commonplace in the mainframe market since its introduction in the mid-1980s. Typically, separate partitions are used for test releases of applications or to service multiple business units or companies from a single server.

The AS/400's implementation is an adaptation of the S/390 logical partitions concept with flexible and granular allocation of system resources. The AS/400 logical partition implementation introduces both the flexibility to allocate interactive performance and high-speed internal communications between partitions.

Logical partitioning (LPAR) allows the running of multiple independent OS/400 instances or partitions (each with its own processors, memory, and disks) in an N-way symmetric multiprocessing AS/400e, Model 6XX, SXX, and 7XX. Multiple-system requirements can now be addressed in a single machine to achieve server consolidation, business unit consolidation, mixed production and test environments, and integrated clusters. Each partition's system values can be set independently. Partitions have different system names and may have a different primary or secondary national language or be operated using different time zones.

This flexibility is ideal for banks and other multinational companies that want to centralize operations in a single location yet retain the national characteristics of each system.

OS/400 is licensed once for the entire system by its normal processor group, regardless of the number of partitions. License management across partitions is not supported. OS/400 V4R4 must be installed on each partition. Previous releases are not supported on any logical partition. The following Web site is available for installation support and technical guidance. When planning logical partitions for an AS/400 system, rely on this Web site for information, direction, and management: tips:http://www.as400.ibm.com/lpar/.

It is important to understand that a failure in the primary partition affects all of the logical partitions that are created. For example, if the primary partition is powered down, all of the secondary partitions are also powered down.

OBJECT-BASED OPERATING SYSTEM

An object is a container. Everything the system uses—user and system data structures—is packaged in one of these containers. The objects are encapsulated, which means that you cannot see inside. Inseparable from an object is the list of valid ways in which that object can be used. The AS/400 operating system is object oriented. Everything that is either attached to the AS/400 or takes up storage space is defined as an object. For example, workstations, printers, programs, libraries, users, files, and databases are defined to the operating system as objects. All objects are structured with a common object header and a type-dependent functional portion. Each object on the system is given an object header and description. Object headers and descriptions contain information of audit importance such as the name of the object, the date the object was created or modified, and a listing of other objects that may access the object. By identifying all resources with an object header, the operating system is able to control access to each object by checking the list of authorized users. Each object can be secured.

On the AS/400, instructions can only work on what they are supposed to work on. You cannot have data treated as executable code (so that the processor tries, for example, to execute someone's shoe size) or executable code treated as data (by having something written into the middle of it). Certain instructions apply to all objects, while other instructions work only on specific types of objects. It is not possible to misuse an object, unlike the situation that exists on other systems without an object-based approach. There are two important consequences of an object-based design. The first is that a system built around an object model supports machine independence. This means that technology changes can be made in the environment without affecting application programs. The second consequence is that an object-based design delivers a high level of system integrity.

The AS/400 security structure is dependent on the concept of object ownership to manage programs, files, procedures, and commands, all of which are objects. When an object is created, an owner is assigned. Typically, the owner is the user who created the object. However, another user profile or group profile can be specified as the owner of an object by changing the owner parameter in the creator's user profile. Owners can also be changed with the CHGOBJOWN command.

The assignment of ownership is important because the owner of an object has *ALL authority. With *ALL authority, an owner can grant access, limit access, and modify or delete the object. The owner can also transfer the ownership of the object to another profile. When an owner transfers the ownership right to another profile, the prior owner has the option to either retain or give up *ALL authority to the object. However, an object can have only one owner at a time.

Defining resources, such as data and programs, as objects provides a way of increasing programmer productivity because all information associated with an object is contained in the object's header. *However, the auditor should be aware that an object-oriented architecture can also provide the appearance of controls where they do not actually exist.* Programs and data, which are objects, reside in libraries that are also objects. If security is not set up properly, a programmer or user can be granted different and perhaps conflicting access capabilities to a library and the objects that reside in the library.

CL commands are objects and may have their own security. The default authorization for most CL commands is appropriate for normal system usage. However, in those situations where the default authorization is inappropriate, it may be changed from *USE to *EXCLUDE. Care should be taken when the default authorizations are changed because the command defaults will be reset when a new release of the operating system is installed.

AUTHORITY PARAMETER

The Authority (AUT) parameter can be used to specify the public authority to the object when it is created. The system uses the CRTAUT parameter value from the library in which it was created. The default for this value is *SYSVAL, which means that the value in the QCRTAUT system value is used. The default for the QCRTAUT system value is *CHANGE.

APPLICATION DEVELOPMENT TOOLS (ADTS)

IBM has grouped together application development programs and called the group application development tools (ADTs). These tools help to improve programmer productivity. In addition, these tools can impact the audit and control environment of an AS/400 installation. These tools are:

- Program manager—Programming Development Manager (PDM)
- Full-screen editor—Source Entry Utility (SEU)
- Data file utility—Data File Utility (DFU)
- Screen-design tool—Screen Design Aid (SDA)

Programming Development Manager (PDM)

The Programming Development Manager (PDM) is a utility that allows the user to select a list of objects (e.g., libraries, library members, files, programs) and perform functions (e.g., copy, delete, change, compile, save, rename, restore, run) that are applied to all objects on the list. PDM is integrated with the other application development tools (ADTs) so functions are invoked with the correct parameters based on an object's type and the function selected. For example, if the object selected via PDM is a report program generator (RPG) program, PDM invokes SEU (Source Entry Utility), a full-screen editor with the proper parameters to edit the selected source program.

A control concern with PDM is that object lists can be created based on wild card substring criteria (e.g., all payroll programs, pay****). Therefore, if the organization does not have a standard naming convention, objects may be excluded from the edit/update list generated by PDM. Also, inappropriate use of wild card substring criteria can result in the inappropriate inclusion of objects. Therefore, the use of wild cards in conjunction with PDM should be carefully administered. Naming conventions should be reviewed to determine the impact of wild cards when using PDM.

Source Entry Utility (SEU)

The Source Entry Utility (SEU) is a full-screen editor used to create and maintain source code online. SEU may be used to create and maintain control language procedures, data description specifications (DDSs), and programming language source code, such as RPG, COBOL, and BASIC. SEU includes a syntax checker that checks statement syntax as statements are entered or edited. Following are some of the functions SEU can perform:

- Add, delete, change, move, and copy source code statements.
- Scroll through two different source code members at the same time.
- Locate a specified string of characters.
- Scan and replace a specified string of characters in a source member.

In addition, SEU date stamps each source statement that is added to a source member or modified during an SEU session. The date stamp is recorded in the far right-hand column of each source statement. The date recorded is the current session date maintained by the operating system, which is most likely the date entered when the system was initially program loaded (IPLed). Note that if the system was IPLed with the wrong date, then the SEU session date will also be in error. However, unlike the System/3X products, the system date can be overridden at the initial SEU edit update screen for the current SEU session. *Therefore, controls should be established to ensure that date stamps remain accurate. Because SEU allows a user to modify source code and alter the audit trail, access to SEU should be restricted to authorized personnel.* A detailed discussion of AS/400 security features and control concerns is included in the section on security.

Data File Utility (DFU)

The Data File Utility (DFU) is a utility that allows users to manage the contents of data files by developing simple, online, interactive programs. DFU is linked to a data dictionary that contains the descriptions of databases on the system. By linking DFU to the DDS, a user is able to access both logical and physical files without needing to know the physical characteristics of the data (e.g., field length and type).

DFU allows the user to quickly create programs that will add to, delete from, create, read, move, or modify data files without the need for any other programming procedures. DFU is simple to use and does not require traditional programming experience. *Because DFU is easy to use, applications developed with DFU may not have followed the systems development life cycle, programmed controls may be lacking, and the program may be subject to unknown design flaws.* Use of DFU to modify data files circumvents programmed controls (e.g., editing of data before posting) usually present in traditional application programs. Therefore, the use of DFU should be carefully monitored by management personnel.

Although use is not mandatory, an optional audit control prompt within the DFU permits the creator of a DFU program to specify YES or NO to these inquiries:

- Are additions and deletions of records allowed?
- Are changes to records allowed?
- Do you want to print a log of additions, changes, or deletions?

The DFU program is then executed in accordance with the creator's responses to the preceding questions regardless of who executes the program.

If the audit control logging option of DFU is specified, a detailed record of data file changes made by the DFU program is maintained. Because the audit control prompts within a DFU program can be modified, access to the DFU program must be restricted. The population of DFU changes is difficult to verify because usage of the audit control prompt is optional; therefore, the logs of additions, changes, and deletions have limited audit use. Because DFU allows a user to modify data files without leaving an audit trail, access to DFU should be restricted to authorized personnel. DFU can also be used to perform certain computer-assisted audit techniques (e.g., footing of fields, extracting information).

Users with authority to the DFU command should have "read-only" access to sensitive data files in order to prevent the data in the files from being changed. In order to modify data files with DFU, users must have change authority or greater to the data file.

Screen Design Aid (SDA)

The Screen Design Aid (SDA) is an interactive screen-design tool that allows a programmer to interactively design, create, and maintain application screens and menus. With SDA, a programmer can define input data types (e.g., numeric, alphanumeric) and display attributes (e.g., color, flash, nondisplay) and cursor-sensitive help. These features of SDA may be used to limit application program-dependent data validation. Therefore, during application reviews it may be necessary to examine screen source members.

SYSTEM UTILITIES

Utilities, along with their audit implications, are discussed in the following sections. In addition to the IBM-supplied utilities listed previously, many software vendors have written utilities, productivity aids, training tools, and other system software for the AS/400. Some utilities or packages introduce additional security concerns. Utility programs and operating system functions that are of interest to auditors are as follows:

- Interactive Data Definition Utility (IDDU)
- AS/400 QUERY
- QUERY Manager/400
- Dedicated Service Tools (DSTs)
- User Tools (QUSRTOOL)
- Advanced Printer Function (APF)

Interactive Data Definition Utility (IDDU)

IDDU is an interactive data definition utility that facilitates the creation and maintenance of data dictionaries, file definitions, record format definitions, and field definitions. With IDDU a user can modify or delete record layouts and then link to DFU to modify data stored in the file. *Because IDDU allows a user to modify data definitions and link to DFU without leaving an audit trail, access to IDDU should be restricted to authorized personnel.*

AS/400 QUERY

AS/400 QUERY simplifies database inquiry procedures. QUERY allows users to interactively specify criteria for the extraction, summarization, and presentation of database information. The information can be formatted into a report that can be displayed on a screen or printed. In addition, information can be directed to a file. It is an excellent ad hoc reporting tool.

QUERY uses the data field definitions maintained in a database's data description specifications (DDSs). Therefore, users need only supply the name of the file to be used. Because QUERY applications are created using menus, prompts, and help text, traditional programming experience is not required. QUERY allows limited computations such as totaling fields, averaging fields, and obtaining record counts. In addition, records can be extracted based on specified criteria. QUERY can be a valuable audit tool for accessing database information.

QUERY Manager/400

QUERY Manager/400 is a utility product that is shipped as part of Structured QUERY Language (SQL/400). It is used to perform functions similar to those performed by QUERY and has many of the same audit concerns. It is expected that at some future time, IBM will merge both QUERY functions into one product. *Because neither QUERY product leaves an audit trail, access to them should be restricted to authorized personnel.*

Dedicated Service Tools (DST)

Dedicated service tools (DSTs) are provided to maintain the system and manage disk and printer devices. Examples of these functions include installing the operating system, modifying the licensed internal code of the AS/400, and resetting the password for the QSECOFR (security officer) user profile. DSTs are used when the operating system is not running. They are activated from the system console when the System Key Lock is in the Manual position during an attended IPL.

Based on its purpose, each has been assigned to one of three levels of security available within DST—security, full, and basic. Each level has its own default password that is the same for all AS/400s and is documented in several of the IBM manuals for the AS/400.

DST Level	*Password*	*Use*
Security	QSECOFR	Perform all functions, change the DST passwords, reset the QSECOFR password.
Full	22222222	Perform service functions except the changing of passwords.
Basic	11111111	Perform functions that do not access sensitive data.

All three DST level passwords should be changed by the installation and stored in a sealed envelope in a safe place. With knowledge of the security level password, an unauthorized individual could reset all the other DST level passwords and obtain control of the QSECOFR profile and the ability to change all security options and settings on the system. The QSECOFR is an IBM-supplied user profile that is assigned to the security officer. It is the most powerful user profile on the system and can be used to add, delete, and maintain user profiles, systemwide security options, and access to all data objects.

A user must have access to the system console and the processor to access the DST profile since DST can only be accessed while performing an IPL of the machine. **Note:** DST will never be listed as a profile on the AS/400.

User Tools (QUSRTOOL)

The QUSRTOOL library consists of routines and programs written for AS/400 users and is installed using the normal installation procedure. This library contains the source code for programs that have not been tested as thoroughly as standard OS/400 code. Therefore, IBM does not guarantee their reliability. The only documentation provided for these tools is contained in an online library called QATTINFO. As new versions and modifications of OS/400 are released, some of the tools become part of the operating system. Tools are also added periodically to the library. Between new releases of OS/400, an updated library must be requested from the IBM service engineer.

Some of the tools perform functions that can be used to bypass security such as CHKPWD and DSPPWD, which can be used to display (and capture) new passwords as they are validated. Other tools are useful in performing normal audit functions such as generating random numbers (GENRANNBR), showing the date of last change of a member of a program library (DSPMBRD), locking and unlocking a source code module to assist in controlling program changes (SRCCTL), comparing source code members and displaying summary (CMPSRC2) or detail (CMPSRC) information of any differences, determining the setting of the limited capability parameter for each user (CHKLMTCPB), and displaying the audit log (DSPAUDLOG).

The QUSRTOOL library should be reviewed periodically to scan for programs that may have an impact on security (e.g., CHKPWD). CHKPWD can be used to guess a person's password. CHKPWD only works for the ID signed on at the terminal from which the command is executed. It is also limited to the QMAXSIGN value for attempts.

Advanced Printer Function Utility (APF)

Advanced Printer Function (APF) is a utility that allows the use of different types of fonts, generates bar codes, creates logos, and creates bar graphs. APF has limited audit and control impact.

INITIAL PROGRAMS

Within the user profile, an Initial Program and/or an Initial Menu can be assigned. If an Initial Program is assigned (i.e., the parameter is not specified as *NONE) when the user signs on to the system, the defined program is called automatically. Usually, the Initial Program can display a series of messages at sign-on, a complex password routine, a library assignment, or a control program consisting of a series of programs, possibly ending with a mandatory menu.

This control feature is effective only when the Initial Program provides proper limitations. For example, if the Initial Program allows the user to enter CL commands or has menu options that allow access to powerful data-modifying utilities (e.g., DFU), the effectiveness of this control feature is eliminated. Menus used as Initial Programs should be reviewed by management for options not needed by users and options that allow users to access programs, files, commands, displays, and libraries not related to their job responsibilities.

An example of a potential weakness in the controls provided by a menu is in the IBM-supplied Programmer Menu. This menu allows users to access DFU and SEU. Access to these utilities may be inappropriate for many users. Unless other security measures are in place (e.g., Public Authority is designated as *EXCLUDE on all production programs), use of this menu may allow unauthorized access to sensitive programs and/or data. When the "attention" key on the keyboard is pressed, the operating system interrupts the program that is currently executing and starts executing the program specified in the Attention-key-handling parameter in the user profile or system value. The default setting of this parameter is *NONE, which forces the user back to the Initial Program. This is the desired setting for most users.

The Limited Capability parameter in the user profile defines whether the user can execute certain CL commands or can change the defined Initial Program, Initial Menu, or the Attention-key-handling parameters. The default setting of *NO allows the user to change the aforementioned parameter settings. The desired setting for most users is *YES because it prevents users from changing their initial parameter settings. In addition, LMTCPB (*YES) users are limited to the following CL commands, unless additional commands are added with the ALWLMTUSR command:

- SIGNOFF
- SNDMSG
- DSPMSG
- DSPJOB
- DSPJOBLOG
- STRPCO

The AS/400 operating system has over 200 predefined system menus. Use of these predefined menus should be challenged since the predefined menus may not provide for adequate segregation of duties, particularly in situations where the Initial Menu assigned to a profile allows users to access options conflicting with their job descriptions.

If the Initial Menu user profile parameter is set to *SIGNOFF, then once the Initial Program has finished executing, the user is automatically signed off the system. This is a useful security feature to prevent users from being logged on to the system once they have finished using the system. When designing menus, software vendors should not have functions with different security requirements on the same menu, and menus should not allow access to the command line.

NAMING NOMENCLATURE

The AS/400 operating system uses Library Name/Object Name as the naming convention for objects (e.g., programs, files, procedures). This naming convention includes both the name of the library where the object is stored and the name of the object. Based on this naming convention, the operating system is able to directly locate objects stored on the system by their fully qualified name (library/object). However, the library name is optional and may be omitted. If the library name is omitted, the operating system searches the libraries on the user's library list for the object. An "object not found" message may appear as a result of the library not being on the user's library list. *This is another way to help control access.*

LIBRARIES

Installation management should exercise care in setting up libraries and determining which objects to put into a library. To facilitate security administration, a library should contain objects that are similar by application or use. If this policy is adhered to, appropriate access can be given at the library level instead of at the individual object level. Test and production objects should never be placed in the same library. There are two types of libraries on the AS/400:

1. System libraries
2. User libraries

System libraries contain IBM-supplied programs and utilities, and their names begin with the letter Q. All system libraries should have default Public Access *READ with the exception of the QGPL, QRJE, QTEMP, and QUSRSYS libraries. These may be set to *CHANGE since they are used if libraries are not designated when an object is executed.

User libraries are those created by an installation that contains objects (test, production, and development) created by the installation.

A library list specifies the libraries and the order in which the libraries are searched for objects. The two library lists are QSYSLIBL (the system library list) and QUSRLIBL (the user library list). When an object is referenced without a qualified library name, the user library list is searched sequentially until either the object is found or all libraries on the library list have been searched. The search order can be changed for a user by specifying a current library (*CURLIB), that is, the most used library for that user.

Library search orders can be illustrated by the following example. If Clerk X requests a program named "Program2," each library on Clerk X's library list is searched sequentially starting with the library called LIB_A, LIB_B, and so on, until "Program2" is found in the LIB_X library. However, in a situation where a program by the same name as "Program2" is either accidentally or purposely placed in the LIB_B library ahead of the LIB_X library, then the system executes the program named "Program2" in the LIB_B library. Therefore, the wrong program is executed. *Change control procedures may be defeated by placing unauthorized programs into production in this manner.*

The use of Adopt Authority in conjunction with library lists can also result in security weaknesses. For example, if Clerk Y is allowed to execute the program named "Program3," which adopts the authority of its owner Clerk X, then while Clerk Y is executing "Program3," Clerk Y has the same authority as Clerk X. If "Program3" makes an unqualified call to another program named "Program 3_B," the system searches the library list sequentially for "Program 3_B." Because "Program 3_B" is called by authority of "Program 3," which adopted its owner's (Clerk X's) authority, then "Program 3_B" would also have the adopted authority of "Program 3." Therefore, if Clerk Y were able to add a program named "Program 3_B" to any library ahead of the Sales library on the library list, the program named "Program 3_B" in the library ahead of the Sales library would execute when the unqualified call is made by "Program 3." Because the first occurrence of "Program 3_B" would execute with the adopted authority of Clerk X, it may be possible for Clerk Y to have an inappropriate level of access to objects owned by Clerk X or access rights given to Clerk X. These examples emphasize the importance of using fully qualified object names and preventing users from modifying the contents of the library list.

There are two parameters that control authority to a library.

Authority

The Authority (AUT) parameter can be used to specify the public authority or the authorization list that secures the library. The system uses the CRTAUT value from the QSYS library. This is shipped as *SYSVAL, which means that the value in the QCRTAUT system value is used. The default for the QCRTAUT system value is *CHANGE.

If an authorization list is specified as the parameter for the AUT parameter, the public authority to the library is set to *AUTH. The default value is *LIBCRTAUT.

Create Authority

The Create Authority parameter (CRTAUT) determines the default authority assigned to all new objects created in the library. The authority is set to the value of the QCRTAUT system value. The default value is *SYSVAL.

BACKUP AND RECOVERY

The AS/400 provides a number of options and features to ensure that system and application data are available or can be recovered within a reasonable time period. These include the following:

- Auxiliary Storage Pools
- Journaling
- Commitment Control
- Checksum Protection
- Disk Mirroring
- Redundant Array of Independent Disks (RAID) Protection

AUXILIARY STORAGE POOLS

The auxiliary storage pool allows an installation to determine on which disk drives data are to be stored. With all disk drives allocated to the system storage pool, ASP 1, the AS/400 will store data evenly over all the available disk drives. This presents a risk because should a single disk drive crash, the entire system would have to be restored—not just the single disk. The user has no idea what data were on the failed disk drive. In fact, the auxiliary storage pool (ASP) puts control of the disk into the users' hands; they are now responsible for managing the disk space.

To minimize the risk of data loss, a separate ASP should be established for all save files and journal receivers. This will cause the data files and the save files/journal receivers to be stored on physically separate disk drives, thus reducing the risk of loss. The system storage pool, ASP 1, contains the internal code, operating system, user profiles, and any other data not allocated to another ASP. There can be an additional fifteen user ASPs, labeled 2 to 16.

The audit risk relating to ASPs is that they may fill up, causing the AS/400 to crash. Users must manage ASP storage space. This can be reviewed through the use of WRKDSKSTS (Work with Disk Statistics) and WRKSYSSTS (Work with System Statistics) functions.

JOURNALING

The optional journaling feature is a means of recording changes to data files. It must be started by creating a journal and journal receiver. A journal may be used to reconstruct data files with recorded before and after images of changes, date stamps, and userID of the change. Should the system fail, all entries stored in the journal may be applied to the restored database so that it will be in the same state as it was prior to the system failure. Without this feature, all the transactions performed up until the last backup would have to be recaptured. The journal feature may also be used to create a transaction log and audit trail. Journaling does take disk space and journals need to be monitored and aged accordingly. The command to review the journal receivers on the system is DSPJRNRCV*ALL.

COMMITMENT CONTROL

When a single transaction updates multiple files, there is a risk that data could be corrupted should the system crash before all the files are updated. Commitment control is a feature that uses journaling techniques to record data until the transaction is complete, thereby minimizing the risk of data corruption by ensuring that the transaction is complete before the database is updated permanently.

CHECKSUM PROTECTION

Checksum protection uses an algorithm to store redundant information on one disk about the data residing on several other disks. Should any of the disks fail, checksum is able to use the redundant data to reconstruct the data to the point of failure without having to restore the entire system. This saves a considerable amount of time. This feature does, however, use approximately 15 % of memory to manage. The cost of checksum protection is increased CPU time utilized and additional disk storage space.

DISK MIRRORING

This method of protection stores duplicate data on separate disks. Should one of the disks fail, processing continues using the mirrored disk. The cost of this level of protection is that all write operations are duplicated and available storage is halved. This option is utilized when it is critical for the system to be up and running. Use of this option results in increased performance for read operations since there are two places to read information from.

REDUNDANT ARRAY OF INDEPENDENT DISKS (RAID)

IBM 9337 disk units offer redundant array of independent disks (RAID) technology options. RAID uses data detection and correction techniques in such a manner that if one of the disks in the configuration fails, the system is able to reconstruct the data and continue operating until the disk is repaired or replaced.

This operation is similar to checksum, but the performance impact is improved (over checksum) through hardware features on the disk unit.

SECURITY

Within the AS/400, a level of security can be chosen to meet a customer's needs. These levels range from:

- Minimal security—No passwords are used, and any user can perform any function.
- Password security—Passwords are used, but users can perform any function.

- Resource security—Passwords are required and object usage can be controlled, and users can be restricted to specific functions.
- Resource security and operating system integrity—Passwords are required, and object usage can be controlled. Users can be restricted to specific functions, and using unsupported interfaces is restricted.

The AS/400 security system supports a high degree of granularity (e.g., the ability to grant only the needed level of access) to each individual user defined to the system. Because the security system provides for discrete allocation of access rights, the system is complex. This complexity may result in either inappropriate implementation or accidental security weaknesses. Consequently, security implementation requires careful consideration and implementation. A security journal that logs all security violations is provided. The highest level of security (level 50) enables the AS/400 to operate at the C2 level of trust as defined by the U.S. government.

For departments in which several members have the same duties or requirements, group profiles can be used. There are numerous system values that can be implemented controlling passwords and their expiration dates and what is and is not allowable for a password. Shipped with OS/400 is the publication *Tips and Tools for Securing Your AS/400, SC41-5300,* which provides report generation tools to assist administrators in assessing their implementation of security. Within communications, further security is possible by implementing LU6.2 Session Level Encryption (SLE) for AS/400 applications, which uses LU6.2 communications.

Security features are standard within the OS/400 operating system. These features have been significantly enhanced to accommodate different approaches and strategies to securing objects (e.g., programs, data files). The use of security features is optional, and not all security features need to be used to provide for an effective level of security. Therefore, it is important for the management of the installation to develop a security strategy that utilizes appropriate security features of the AS/400. The risk of inappropriate or erroneous implementation of security features and the accidental or intentional alteration or deletion of data increase without an appropriate strategy for an effective implementation of AS/400 security features.

Major security features, which are discussed more fully later, are listed in the following sections. System Key Lock is the only physical security feature. The others are standard within the operating system and are based on the concept of object ownership and restricting access to objects.

SYSTEM KEY LOCK

The AS/400 is equipped with a four-position System Key Lock (i.e., Manual, Normal, Auto, Secure), as shown in Exhibit 3.1. The System Key Lock is used to limit the functions performed with the system panel. The system panel includes the computer's control panel, the main power switch, and tile manual IPL button. These buttons and switches can be used to physically override or abort logical operations (e.g., switch off the computer and re-IPL the system).

Exhibit 3.1 lists some of the functions that can be performed from the system panel based on the position of the System Key Lock. With the System Key Lock in the Manual position, the AS/400 can be switched on and off by anyone who has access to the main system power switch. In addition, when the System Key Lock is in the Manual position, a user is able to select a different IPL (i.e., boot the operating system) or use dedicated service

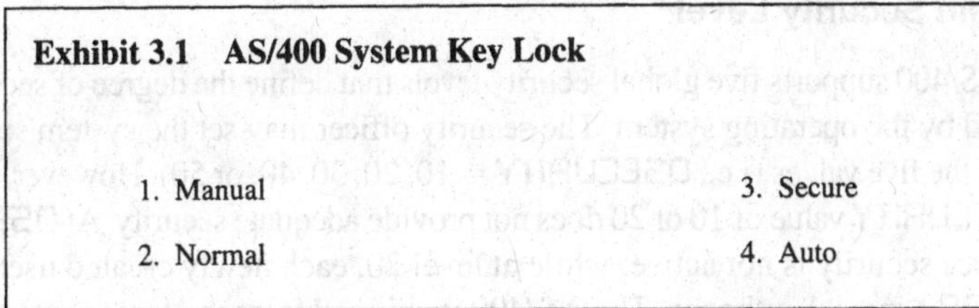

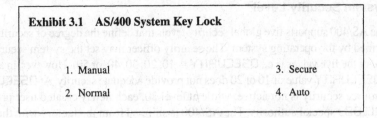

Exhibit 3.1 AS/400 System Key Lock

1. Manual
2. Normal
3. Secure
4. Auto

Exhibit 3.2 Operations by System Key Lock Position

Operations	Manual	Normal	Auto	Secure
Manual IPL	Yes	No	No	No
Auto IPL	Yes	Yes	No	No
Remote IPL	No	Yes	Yes	No
Power Switch (Off)	Yes	No	No	No
Power Switch (On)	Yes	Yes	No	No
PWRDWNSYS	Yes	Yes	Yes	Yes
Run Dedicated Service Tools (DSTs)	Yes	No	No	No

tools that bypass AS/400 security settings, such as *EXCLUDE. With the System Key Lock positioned to either Auto or Secure, users are prevented from manually IPLing the system or using dedicated service tools. Secure is the most protective setting. However, if there are no remote users, Auto provides the same level of security as Secure. See Exhibit 3.2.

Note: Appropriate use of the System Key Lock can significantly reduce the risk of inappropriate use of dedicated service tools or accidental system shutdowns by manual IPLing the system or switching off the power. The key should be removed and placed in a secure location when not in use.

SYSTEMWIDE SECURITY VALUES

The AS/400 has a number of systemwide security parameters that affect the level and type of security implemented. For example, the systemwide options include those needed to define the security level, the password formatting rules, the logging of security violations, and the capabilities of remote users. The systemwide options that affect security are described in the following sections. Each system value includes its name, possible value, default value, and recommended value. Systemwide security values can also be printed for review. Refer to Exhibit 1.3 for the AS/400 sample report.

System Security Level

The AS/400 supports five global security levels that define the degree of security checking performed by the operating system. The security officer may set the system security value to any one of the five values (i.e., QSECURITY = 10, 20, 30, 40, or 50). However, in almost all cases, a QSECURITY value of 10 or 20 does not provide adequate security. At QSECURITY level 10, resource security is not active, while at level 20, each newly created user profile is granted *ALLOBJ special authority. The AS/400 is shipped from the factory with the QSECURITY value set at 10. Any changes to the QSECURITY value are only effective after the next IPL. Changes to the remaining system values are effective immediately.

Control of Confidential Data

The QALWUSRDMN system value contains a list of libraries allowed to contain user domain objects of type *USRSPC, *USPJDX, and *USRQ. These object types are user spaces, user indices, and user queues. If a location wishes to restrict users from passing confidential data, management can restrict the objects of type *USRSPC, *USRIDX, and *USRQ to the QTEMP library, which is a temporary object at level 50, and, therefore, cannot be used to pass confidential data between users.

Password Formatting Options

OS/400 supports a variety of password formatting options. These options can help improve password integrity by making passwords more difficult to guess. Passwords can be controlled on a systemwide basis by using an effective combination of the following options:

- QPWDMINLEN: Controls the minimum length of a password.
- QPWDMAXLEN: Controls the maximum length of a password.
- QPWDRQDDIF: Prevents new passwords from being the same as any of the previous thirty-two passwords used.
- QPWDLMTCHR: Specifies up to ten installation-defined characters that cannot appear in a password.
- QPWDPOSDIF: Forces each character in the new password to be different from the character in the same position in the old password.
- QPWDLMTREP: Prevents characters from being used more than once within a password.
- QPWDLMTAJC: Prevents a user from specifying a password with numbers (0 to 9) next to one another.
- QPWDVLDPGM: Implements a password validation program to perform additional validation.
- QPWDRQDDGT: Ensures that all new passwords have at least one numeric character.

Password Expiration Interval

The system can force all passwords for user profiles to expire by using the system value QPWDEXPITV to set the maximum number of days that a password is valid. When the password expiration interval is reached for a password, the system automatically forces the user to select a new password during the next sign-on procedure. This option does not prevent users from changing their passwords more frequently than the value of this option. The number of days until a password expires is kept in each user profile. The global system value can be overridden in an individual's user profile parameter (PWDEXPITV) for users with needs different from the system value.

Maximum Sign-On Attempts

The system can define the maximum number of unsuccessful sign-on attempts by setting the QMAXSIGN system value of the operating system. With installations running OS/400 Version 2, Release 0 or higher, the security officer can specify the action taken by the system when the number of unsuccessful sign-on attempts is reached by specifying the action taken with the QMAXSGNACN system value. A user with *SECADM special authority and access authority to the user profile object can only reactivate a deactivated user profile. A deactivated user with *ALLOBJ or *SECADM special authority can always sign on at the system console and change the setting of the Revoke parameter to reactivate the profile.

Limiting Security Officer Access

It is possible to prevent users with *ALLOBJ and/or *SERVICE Special Authority from signing on to a workstation, unless they are specifically authorized to use the workstation, by using the QLMTSECOFR system value. This feature enhances security by limiting the number of workstations accessible by users with special authority.

Remote Sign-On Controls

The QRMTSIGN system value determines the action taken by the operating system when a user from a remote system tries to sign on. Remote system users can be required to use normal sign-on procedures or bypass normal sign-on procedures if valid security information is sent with an automatic sign-on.

Limit Number of Device Sessions

The system can prohibit concurrent device sessions for all users with the QLMTDEVSSN value. The global system value can be overridden in the individual user profile parameter LMTDEVSSN. Concurrent device sessions at the same device, however, are not prevented. Concurrent sign-on at multiple physical terminals helps prevent sharing of passwords.

Automatic Configuration of Virtual Devices

The QAUTOVRT system value determines whether pass-through virtual devices (e.g., a user at another AS/400) are automatically configured. This may be a user and physical workstation that are attached to a remote device. The number of sign-on attempts that are allowed at remote devices increases when QAUTOVRT is set to a value greater than zero. The number of attempts allowed through pass-through is QAUTOVRT multiplied by the number of sign-on attempts (QMAXSIGN). If the QMAXSIGN parameter has a value of 5, and the QAUTOVRT a value of 10, a user has fifty attempts at signing on to the system from a remote device.

Automatic Configuration of Local Devices

The QAUTOCFG system value determines whether the system will automatically configure any new local controllers or devices that are added to the system.

Attention Key Program

The QATNPGM system value specifies the program to be called when the user presses the attention key.

Designating a Workstation as the System Console

The system value QCONSOLE states the device address that is assigned the console status. This value can be used to verify which workstation is the system console. All jobs submitted from this console run at priority 10, and it can be used to control jobs and spool files.

System Values that Control Use of Audit Journal

By default most system-generated messages are written to the history journal. The use of a separate audit journal simplifies the review of security-related messages. The audit journal is covered in the section on journals. The system values relating to the audit journal should be set to values that will ensure appropriate actions are logged to meet the organization's security requirements.

Establishing Object Authority Upon Creation

The system value QCRTAUT determines the default public authority to an object upon creation if the following holds true:

The Create Authority library parameter CRTAUT, specifying the public authority to all objects created within the specified library, is set to *SYSVAL (the default for this parameter), and the new object is created with the public authority of *LIBCRTAUT.

Display Sign-On Information

The system value QDSPSGNINF is used to display to the user relevant sign-on information (e.g., date of last sign-on, number of invalid sign-on attempts, number of days until the password expires, if less than seven days) immediately after a successful logon.

Job Time-Out

If a job is inactive for a specified number of minutes as determined by the system value QINACTITV, the system automatically takes action based on the value specified in the system value QINACTMSGQ (e.g., ENDJOB).

System Portion of the Library List

The system value QSYSLIBL specifies the system portion of the library list. This list is intended for IBM-supplied libraries. The objects in the system portion of the library list are searched first, before any libraries in the user portion of the library list. This list can contain as many as fifteen entries. In order to change the QSYSLIBL system value, a user must have both *ALLOBJ and *SECADM special authority.

User Portion of the Library List

The system value QUSRLIBL specifies the user portion of the library list. The libraries in this list are searched after all the libraries in the system portion of the library list have been searched. The list may contain up to twenty-five entries.

SYSTEM AUTHORITY

The AS/400 operating system is object oriented. Everything that is either attached to the AS/400 or uses storage space is defined as an object. For example, workstations, printers, programs, libraries, users, files, and databases are defined to the operating system as objects. Each object on the system is given an object header and description. Object headers and descriptions contain security-related information (e.g., the name of the object, the date the object was created or modified, a listing of other objects that may access the object, and the object type). Two objects of the same name may exist within the same library only if they are of different types. By identifying all resources with an object header, the operating system is able to control logical access to each object.

Normally, logical security is under the control of the operating system. The AS/400 divides logical security into three categories:

1. Special Authority, of which there are seven
2. Specific Authority, of which there are eight
3. *EXCLUDE, which restricts access to objects/resources

Public Authority is the access authority to an object that is granted to a user who does not have Special Authority, Specific Authority, or *EXCLUDE Authority to the requested object.

Special Authority

Special Authority broadly relates to the type of functions and authority required by a class of users to perform their job function. For example, the system operator may require Job Control (*JOBCTL) Special Authority to start and stop jobs and control print queues while a service technician may require Service (*SERVICE) Authority to display and alter system functions. The use of all Special Authorities should be carefully controlled because they grant a privileged level of access to objects.

The seven Special Authorities are:

1. *ALLOBJ (All Object Special Authority). Allows the user access to all system resources even if Specific Authority to the resource has not been given.
2. *SECADM (Security Administrator Special Authority). Allows the user to:
   - Add users to the system.
   - Delete users from the system.
   - Change user passwords.
   - Grant security officer privileges to other users.

3. *AUDIT (Audit Special Authority). Allows the user the ability to:
   - Change auditing characteristics.
   - Use CHGOBJAUD, CHGDLOAUD and CHGUSRAUD commands.
4. *SAVSYS (Save System Special Authority). Allows the user to perform save and restore operations for all resources on the system even if they do not have specific authority.
5. *JOBCTL (Job Control Special Authority). Allows the user to:
   - Change, cancel, hold, and release all files on output queues.
   - Hold, release, and clear job queues and output queues.
   - Hold, release, change, and cancel other users' jobs.
   - Start output devices.
   - Change the running attributes of a job, such as the printer for the job.
   - Stop subsystems.
   - Load the system.
6. *SERVICE (Service Special Authority). Allows the user to perform the display and alter service functions, which permit a user to display and change data.
7. *SPLCTL (Spool Control Special Authority). Allows the user to control spool functions: cancel, delete, display, hold, and release other all spool files on the system.

These seven Special Authorities are assigned to the following five IBM-defined user classes:

1. (*SECOFR) Security Officer
2. (*SECADM) Security Administrator
3. (*PGMR) Programmer
4. (*SYSOPR) System Operator
5. (*USER) System User

When the security officer creates a user profile, the user must be assigned to one of the five predefined user classes listed. If default Special Authorities are desired, the *USRCLS option on the SPCAUT parameter is specified in the user profile.

Based on the active level of security (i.e., 10, 20, 30, 40, and 50), each user class is assigned a default level of authority. Exhibit 1.8 shows the default Special Authorities assigned to each user class under security levels 10 and 20. Exhibit 1.9 shows the default Special Authorities assigned to each user class under security levels 30, 40, and 50.

Note: The default Special Authorities assigned to both the user (*USER) class and the programmer (*PGMR) class may be inappropriate under security levels 10 and 20. Therefore, default Special Authorities assigned to user classes should not be used if the organization is operating at security level 10 or 20. In addition, when changing from levels 30, 40, or 50 to levels 10 or 20, all user profiles are given Special Authorities based on the system defaults in Exhibit 1.8. The user is able to have more or less special authority than the default authorities by overriding the default values. When the operating system is upgraded, the system will reset Special Authorities based on the defaults for the user class assigned.

Specific Authority

There are eight Specific Authorities that are divided into four Object Authorities and four Data Authorities. To work with an object, a user must have the appropriate Object and Data Authorities.

The four Object Authorities are:

1. *OBJOPR (Object Operational Authority). Allows the user to look at the description of an object and to use the object (e.g., READ and UPDATE), as determined by the Data Authorities granted to the user.
2. *OBJMGT (Object Management Authority). Allows the user to move the object, rename the object, and add members to database files.
3. *OBJEXIST (Object Existence Authority). Allows the user to control the object's existence and ownership. This authority is necessary for users who need to delete an object, free storage space of an object, perform save and restore operations for an object, or transfer ownership of an object.

   Note: If a user has *SAVSYS Special Authority, Object Existence Authority is not needed to perform save and restore operations.
4. AUTLMGT (Authorization List Management Authority). Allows the user to add and remove users and their authorities on an authorization list. An authorization list is a list of users authorized to access an object and their authorities related to the object.

The four Data Authorities are:

1. *READ (Read Authority). Allows the user to display the contents of an object or run a program. *READ implies copy.
2. *ADD (Add Authority). Allows a user to add entries to an object.
3. *UPD (Update Authority). Allows the user to change entries in an object.
4. *DLT (Delete Authority). Allows the user to remove entries from an object.

   Note: Unlike some mainframe access control packages, neither the Object nor the Data Authorities are downwardly inclusive (e.g., *UPD does not include the abilities to ADD or READ an object).

IBM has four System-Defined Authorities that are a combination of the four Object authorities and the four Data Authorities. They are used to facilitate assigning authorities. They are:

1. *ALL (All Authority). Provides all Object Authorities and all Data Authorities. The user can control the object's existence, specify the security for the object, change the object, and perform basic operations on the object (e.g., run the program or display the object's contents and description).
2. *CHANGE (Change Authority). Provides Object Operational Authority and all Data Authorities. The user can READ, ADD, CHANGE, and DELETE entries in an object.
3. *USE (Use Authority). Provides Object Operational Authority and READ Authority. The user can run a program or display the object's description or contents. The user is prevented from changing the object, but can copy the object to their own library.
4. *EXCLUDE (EXCLUDE Authority). Prevents the user from accessing the object.

Exhibit 3.3 shows how IBM has combined the Object and the Data Authorities to derive the four System Authorities.

Exhibit 3.3 System Authorities

Authority	System Authorities						
		Object		Data			
	OPR	MGT	EXIST	READ	ADD	UPD	DLT
*ALL	X	X	X	X	X	X	X
*CHANGE	X			X	X	X	X
*USE	X			X			
*EXCLUDE	No system authorities given						

EXCLUDE Authority

*EXCLUDE Authority explicitly prevents a user or a group of users from accessing the named object. If *EXCLUDE is specified, no other authorities can be granted to the object for the excluded profile. Organizations should set the public access parameter for production libraries to *EXCLUDE to assure that only explicitly granted access is permitted. This procedure prevents the accidental granting of access based on public access.

Public Authority

Public Authority is the default level of authority that is granted if access to an object for a specific user or the user's group has not been explicitly granted or denied access. This default Public Authority is determined by the Create Authority library parameter CRTAUT or the Create Authority parameter AUT on the CRTXXX command that was used to create the library or object. The AUT parameter can be modified after creation. The AUT parameter is discussed further later on in this section.

USER PROFILES

The structure used to identify users on the system, control the objects they can access, control what they can do to those objects, and how the system appears to them is their user profile.

A user's ability to access objects on the system is allowed or denied based on the information contained in the user's user profile. A user profile contains the information about a user (or a group of users in the case of a group profile) and the objects the user or group can access. For the purposes of AS/400 security, a "user is anyone using the system, both information systems personnel (e.g., programmers, system operators) and end users (e.g., accounting clerks, terminal operators)."

Consistent with the object orientation of the AS/400 operating system, each user profile is defined as an object. Many of the user's capabilities are defined within a user's profile such as Special Authorities. The user's profile also defines the user's work environment (e.g., initial library, initial program, initial menu, maximum secondary storage, user priority level, attention-key-handling, I/O queues).

A user's profile also contains a list of objects the profile is explicitly authorized to access. The list includes objects owned by the user profile, objects for which the profile has been given ownership due to the transfer of ownership by the previous owner or the security officer, and objects owned by another user profile for which a specific level of access was explicitly granted to this user profile. The list does not include objects that users access via public access, via authorization lists, or via access granted to their group profiles. Certain systemwide values can be overridden in the individual user profile.

A user profile cannot be deleted if it owns any objects. If there is an urgent need to delete a user profile that owns one or more objects, an expedient temporary solution may be to disable the user profile by changing the setting of the STATUS parameter to *DISABLED or the password parameter to *NONE. This prevents anyone from using the profile to sign on to the system. If this solution is used, ownership of the objects should be changed as soon as possible and the user profile deleted.

System-Defined User Profiles

The AS/400 operating system is shipped from the factory with twenty predefined user profiles, all of which begin with the letter "Q." Fourteen are internal profiles with a password of *NONE, which prevents anyone from using them to sign on to the system. The other six user profiles are intended to be used to sign on to the system. Each of these six is initially given the same password as the profile userID, and these profile names and passwords are clearly printed in the AS/400 system documentation. Therefore, installations should change these six IBM-supplied user profile passwords whether or not the user profile is used. Also, the profiles should be disabled until needed.

The six IBM-supplied user profiles and their passwords that can be used to sign on to the system are shown in Exhibit 3.4.

Another IBM-supplied user profile that may be of interest to auditors is QDFTOWN. This profile is given ownership of a restored object when the restored object does not have an originating owner on the system. This may be a result of either the original owner being deleted from the system or never having had an owner because of a transfer from another system. QDFTOWN is needed because all objects on the system must have an owner.

Exhibit 3.4 User Profiles and Passwords

User Profile	Password
1. QSECOFR	QSECOFR
2. QPGMR	QPGMR
3. QUSER	QUSER
4. QSYSOPR	QSYSOPR
5. QSRVBAS	QSRVBAS
6. QSRV	QSRV

Shared User Profiles

The AS/400 operating system does not automatically prevent the concurrent uses of the same user profile and password. Therefore, some installations may share user profiles among groups of individuals. Concurrent use of the same user profile by multiple users reduces user accountability. Thus, sharing of user profiles that reduce user accountability should be discouraged.

GROUP PROFILES

If a number of users on the system require the same access authorities, they can all be made members of one group profile. This method can be used to reduce the management of authorities by controlling multiple users at the group profile level.

A group profile is a user profile that is used to assign the same level of access authority to multiple users. This is accomplished by defining access authority at the group profile level and then assigning each individual user profile to the group profile. One advantage of using group profiles is that the security officer can manage the access rights of individuals at the group level instead of at the individual user profile level. However, it is not required that a user be assigned to a group profile.

Multiple objects, each with a different level of access, can be assigned to a group profile. These same objects can also be assigned to multiple group profiles. However, a user profile can only be assigned to one group profile. For example, if all users in a group need to have the same level of access to an object, the security officer can grant access to the object in a group profile and then assign each individual user profile to the group profile. If one of the users requires a different level of access to the object, that different level of access is defined for that one individual in that user's profile (see the section "Order of Authority Checking"). In addition to possible administrative savings, group profiles also save system storage space and time required in checking security. The use of group profiles is administratively complex without the systemwide use of standard naming conventions for objects and profiles.

Group profiles may be used to sign on to the system. However, doing so makes accountability for their use more difficult. Therefore, it is a good policy to set the passwords of all group profiles to *NONE to prevent them from being used to sign on to the system.

AUTHORIZATION LISTS

An authorization list is a means of specifying the authorities to objects for a list of user profiles. The authorization list feature is used to secure objects. An authorization list identifies user profiles (and their associated authority) that can access the objects secured by the authorization list. Two key features of an authorization list are (1) the security level assigned to each user is independent of other users on the list and (2) the assigned authority applies to all objects secured by the list.

Comparison of Authorization Lists and Group Profiles

The control features of authorization lists are similar to the control features of group profiles in that they both control access to multiple objects. However, differences exist as shown in Exhibit 3.5.

Exhibit 3.5 Authorization Lists and Group Profiles

Authorization List	Group Profile
Users may be assigned different access rights.	All users are assigned the same access rights.
A user is assigned the same access rights for all objects secured by the list.	A user (as part of the group) may have a different access right for each object secured by the group profile.
Users may be listed on multiple authorization lists.	Users can only be assigned to one group profile.
Objects can only be assigned to one authorization list.	Objects can be secured by multiple group profiles.
Objects must be explicitly added to the authorization list.	Objects are authorized automatically to group members when created by a group member if set up to do so.

ADOPT AUTHORITY

This is a security feature that temporarily extends ownership authority to another user profile by allowing the adopting user profile to assume the ownership rights of the object owner.

Adopt Authority is based on the concept of object ownership. Each object (e.g., programs, files, procedures) has an owner, and the owner may be any valid user profile or group profile. However, objects can only have one owner. Object ownership is defined within the user's security profile by either assignment (transfer of ownership from another user who is an owner) or creation (users own the files and programs they create). Owners by default have *ALL authority for the objects they own. For example, owners can grant access to objects, limit access to objects, change objects, or delete objects they own.

The Adopt Authority feature temporarily extends the authority of one user to another user by allowing the adopting user to assume the rights of the other user. The rights extended may be ownership authority at the user profile level. In this case, the adopting user assumes the rights (authorities) contained in the owner's user profile and the owner's rights for all objects secured by the owner's user profile.

Special Authorities can also be adopted. This can provide better security by allowing users who sometimes need to perform a function (such as starting a printer) that requires a Special Authority (*JOBCTL) to do so by adopting authority instead of permanently giving the user the Special Authority. For example, a payroll clerk may not have been given update access rights to the payroll master file. However, the payroll clerk may have been given authority to execute the payroll master file update program, which adopts the authority of its owner, the department manager, who has *ALL authority for the payroll master file. In this case, whenever the payroll clerk executes the payroll master file update program, the clerk adopts the *ALL authority of the department manager and, therefore, is given the same access rights as the department manager. The clerk's adopted *ALL authority for the payroll master file is only valid while the payroll master file update program is in the program stack. Whenever a user executes a program that adopts the owner's authorities, the user assumes the explicit authority of the owner for all objects secured by the owner's user profile. The clerk adopts the authority of the department manager for all resources secured by the department manager's user profile, in particular the *ALL authority for the payroll master file. The adopted authorities remain with the clerk as long as the Payroll Program is executing.

The Adopt Authority feature, if properly used, can greatly enhance security by allowing only predefined programs to modify data. The following command can be used to list programs with Adopt Authority that are owned by a particular user: DSPPGMADP USRPRF (userID).

The Adopt Authority feature applies not only to the program that has been assigned Adopt Authority but also to all other programs that it calls using the CALL command. This extension of Adopt Authority can result in security weaknesses. For example, if an initial menu program that adopts a high level of authority is created, and users are allowed to add programs that are called by the menu, the high level of authority is transferred to the called program.

The use adopted authority parameter (USEADPAUT) of the program that adopts authority determines whether the system uses its adopted authority when issuing the CALL command. When a program is created, the default setting for the USEADPAUT parameter is *YES, which means that the adopted authority is transferred to programs that are called. It is recommended that this parameter be set to *NO to remove the security exposure.

If the TRFCTL command is used, the first program's adopted authority is not passed along. However, if the CALL command is used, the adopted authority of the first program is passed to the next program. The following command can be used to determine if a program ignores Adopt Authority: DSPPGM PGM (library name/program name).

ORDER OF AUTHORITY CHECKING

The AS/400 grants user access based on explicitly defined access rights. The system determines a user's access rights to objects based on the following logic.

The system checks for sufficient authority in the following progression:

1. The Special Authorities assigned in the user's user profile.
2. The Specific Authorities assigned in the user profile.
3. The authorization lists in which the user's profile is defined.
4. The Special Authorities assigned in the user's group profile.
5. The Specific Authorities assigned to the group profile.
6. The authorization lists in which the user's group profile is defined.
7. The default Public Access rights are tested first for specific authority.
8. The authorization lists are checked.
9. The Adopt Authority is checked.

In checking authority to an object, the system first checks authority to the object library. If the authority to the library is adequate, the system will then check authority to the object itself. Access rights are not cumulative, and when an authority is found (even if it is not adequate), authority checking stops. If a user profile, group profile, or default Public Authority indicates *EXCLUDE Authority, the user is denied access to the object because authority checking stops, even if the user is a member of a group or listed on an authorization list that has been granted access to the object. Therefore, the *EXCLUDE Authority should be considered as "Insufficient Authority" rather than "No Authority." The Adopt Authority overrides any specific (and insufficient) authority found.

OTHER SECURITY ISSUES

Job Descriptions

Every job in the system uses a job description during job initiation. This controls the various attributes of a job and prevents the need to specify the same parameters repeatedly for each job. Once a job description has been set up, it can be used by a group of users who require the same initial library list, output queue, and job queue.

A job description also represents a potential security risk. If a job description has a user profile name specified in the USER parameter field, other users on the system with access to the job description will be able to submit jobs using the authority of the user profile specified in the USER parameter of the job description. If the user profile parameter of the job description is set to *RQD, then the job will run under the authority of the user submitting the job.

Another exposure related to job descriptions is the QBATCH description. The QBATCH job description is shipped with USER(QPGMR). Because the job description was created normally (with Public Access *CHANGE), any user on the system who has authority to the SBMJOB command can submit work under the QPGMR user profile. The QBATCH job description should therefore be changed to eliminate this possible exposure. Restricting the SBMJOB command may also minimize the exposure.

Authority Holders

Authority Holders are special security objects that store access authorities for objects. The unique feature of Authority Holders is that they can be created for objects that do not exist on the system. Therefore, a user can create an Authority Holder and allocate access rights to other users for objects that do not exist. Then, when an object by the same name as the Authority Holder is subsequently created or restored, the access rights defined in the Authority Holder are linked to the newly created or restored object. This linking process eliminates the need for the owner of the object or the security officer to grant access rights to the newly created or restored object.

Authority Holders also maintain the access rights defined in the Authority Holder after the object is deleted. Therefore, if the object subsequently is re-created or restored, the object assumes the access rights maintained in the Authority Holder. The Authority Holder feature is useful for applications that create and delete program-described files (e.g., work files) during execution.

The use of Authority Holders most commonly is associated with System/36 applications that have migrated to the AS/400. When migrating from a System/36, an Authority Holder automatically is created for each entry in the resource security file on the System/36 for which a file does not exist at the time of migration. This could result in unneeded Authority Holders that should be deleted from the system. An option in the System/36 Migration Aid software package can be used to prevent Authority Holders from automatically being created.

The use of Authority Holders may result in a security weakness if users are able to create Authority Holders for files that do not exist. For example, a user creates a "dummy" Authority Holder and a file with the same name as the Authority Holder. If the "dummy" Authority Holder is subsequently created, restored, or renamed, the owner of the Authority Holder becomes the owner of the newly created, restored, or renamed file—even if the file was created by another user. In addition, when the file is created, the authorities defined in the Authority Holder override any authorities specified in conjunction with the CREATE command. Therefore, a user may assume a greater level of authority than appropriate.

These weaknesses can be compensated for by controlling access to the CREATE Authority Holder command. When the AS/400 is shipped from the factory, the Public Authority for the CREATE Authority Holder (CRTAUTHLR) command is set to *EXCLUDE. Therefore, only users with all object (*ALLOBJ) Special Authority may use the command. The DSPAUTHLR command may be used to display all Authority Holders on the system.

Authority Holders can be saved by issuing the Save Library command following a Save System or Save Security Data command. Authority Holders can be restored for all user profiles by using the following commands in the sequence shown:

1. RSTUSRPRF USRPRF(*ALL)
2. RSTAUT USRPRF(*ALL)

Journals

The AS/400 equivalent of a history file or console log is the history log that consists of one or more history journal files that are automatically created by the system. As the number of entries increases, a journal eventually fills up, and the system automatically creates another one (in a manner similar to a generation data group on an IBM mainframe) instead of writing over itself or ceasing to record. Depending on the version of the operating system, it is possible to maintain different types of journals. The most common journal types are History, Accounting, and Auditing.

In AS/400 terminology, events are recorded as journal entries. The overall journal is called a file. An object called a journal receiver is attached to a journal and is the entity to which journal entries are actually written. The name of the receivers for each type of journal contain a sequence number. When one receiver fills up, the system automatically creates a new one and uses the next sequence number as the name. To look at events that have been recorded in a journal, the Display Journal (DSPJRN) command can be used to retrieve the specified entries from a receiver, convert them into readable format, and display them on the screen.

Audit Journal

Prior to 0S/400 Version 1, Release 3, all security-related events were written to the History Journal. Beginning with Version 1, Release 3, IBM provided an optional Audit Journal (QAUDJRN in library QSYS) and Journal Receiver, which can be activated using the QAUDLVL system value. Further significant enhancements were added with Version 2, Release 3. Activating the Audit Journal causes the specified categories of security-related events to be written to the Audit Journal in addition to the History Journal. The default is to record security-related events only in the History Journal. *Using the Audit Journal has several advantages from a security point of view.* By segregating security-related events in the Audit Journal, such events are less time consuming to review, and it is easier for the reviewer to spot events that require attention and follow-up action.

Events that occur on the system may be logged at three different levels:

1. Systemwide event logs independent of user or object
2. Events that relate to specific users
3. Events that relate to specific objects

Exhibit 3.6 QAUDLVL System Parameters and Events

Parameter	Event to be Logged
*AUTFAIL	Authority failures are logged.
*CREATE	Object create operations are logged.
*DELETE	Object delete operations are logged.
*JOBDTA	Actions that affect a job are logged.
*OBJMGT	Object move and rename operations are logged.
*OFCSRV	Changes to the system distribution directory and office mail actions are logged.
*PGMADP	Obtaining authority from a program that adopts authority is logged.
*PGMFAIL	System integrity violations are logged.
*PRTDTA	Printing a spooled file and sending output directly to a printer are logged.
*SAVRST	Restore operations are logged.
*SECURITY	Security-related operations are logged.
*SERVICE	Using service tools are logged.
*SPLFDTA	Actions performed on spooled files are logged.
*SYSMGT	Use of system management functions is logged.

Systemwide Event Logs

The events in Exhibit 3.6 may be logged on a systemwide basis by including one or more parameters in the QAUDLVL system value. For this logging to take place, the QAUDCTL system value must include *AUDLVL as one of its parameters. See Exhibit 3.6 for parameters and events.

Individual User Event Logging

The events in Exhibit 3.7 may be logged on an individual user basis by including one or more of the parameters in the AUDLVL user profile parameter. For this logging to take place, the QAUDCTL system value must include *AUDLVL as one of its parameters. See Exhibit 3.7.

Individual Object Access Logging

The QAUDCTL system value, OBJAUD user profile parameter, and OBJAUD value for the object are used for auditing a specific object. The combination of these values determines what specific access will be logged.

If the QAUDCTL system value contains the parameter *OBJAUD, then Exhibit 3.8 applies.

A combination of OBJAUD user profile parameter and the OBJAUD value for the specific object allows the auditing journal to log all users accessing critical objects on the system or specific users accessing critical objects on the system.

Exhibit 3.7 QAUDLVL Individual Parameters and Events

Parameter	Event to be Logged
*CMD	Command strings are logged.
*CREATE	Object create operations are logged.
*DELETE	Object delete operations are logged.
*JOBDTA	Actions that affect a job are logged.
*OBJMGT	Object move and rename operations are logged.
*OFCSAV	Changes to the system distribution directory and office mail actions are logged.
*PGMADP	Obtaining authority from a program that adopts authority is logged.
*SAVRST	Restore operations are logged.
*SECURITY	Security-related operations are logged.
*SERVICE	Using service tools are logged.
*SPLFDTA	Actions performed on spooled files are logged.
*SYSMGT	Use of system management functions are logged.

Exhibit 3.8 OBJAUD Values and Parameters

OBJAUD Value for Specific Object	OBJAUD Parameter Value for User Profile		
	*NONE	*CHANGE	*ALL
*NONE	None	None	None
*USPSPRF	None	Change	Change and Use
*CHANGE	Change	Change	Change
*ALL	Change and Use	Change and Use	Change and Use

Using the commands CHGOBJAUD and CHGUSRAUD can only change the OBJAUD value for the objects and user profiles. These commands are only available to users with *AUDIT special authority. One is able to set the default auditing for objects created at the library level by means of the QCRTOBJAUD system value and the CRTOBJAUD value for libraries. This will affect the auditing value of new objects created. It will not alter the auditing value of objects already existing in the library.

Communications

All AS/400s are sold with at least one communications line (to facilitate IBM remote service diagnosis). This link can provide answers to technical questions, a means of receiving Program Temporary Fixes (PTFs), and a method of reporting problems.

OS/400 provides support for the following protocols:

- IBM Token Ring Network (IEEE 802.5 and IEEE 802.2)
- Ethernet (IEEE 802.3)
- Apple LocalTalk
- Synchronous Data Link Control (SDLC)
- X.21 and X.25
- ISO 9314 (FDDI networks)
- IDLC (ISDN networks)
- Asynchronous
- Binary Synchronous
- TCP/IP

The following communication facilities are available with the AS/400:

- *OSI (Open Systems Interconnect).* Optional AS/400 extensions allow the AS/400 to communicate with other computer environments (both IBM and non-IBM) that are defined by the OSI international standards organization.
- *DDM (Distributed Data Management).* This function of OS/400 allows an AS/400 user access to data on a remote AS/400. It will appear to the user as if the data is located on the local AS/400 since the user will not have to know on which AS/400 the requested data is located.
- *DSPT (Display Station Pass Thru).* This function allows a user to access any other AS/400 in the communications network by signing on to the remote AS/400 directly.
- *APPC (Advanced Program-to-Program Communications).* This communications convention allows a program on one AS/400 system to initiate requests such as starting a program or initiating a database request on a remote system with no assistance from the user.
- *APPN (Advanced Peer-to-Peer Networking).* This manages the logistics for an AS/400 in a communications network by containing details (e.g., location, communications links, available programs, and data) about all the other AS/400 systems in the network. It also selects the most appropriate communications link if more than one exists. It takes into consideration facts such as cost, line speed, and security level.
- *SNADS (Systems Network Architecture Distribution Services).* This is a service that is designed to distribute files and print messages to other systems. It will store items to be distributed until the target system becomes available.
- *ODF (Object Distribution).* This function makes sending programs or information to remote locations much easier. The security considerations that are of major concern are the ones related to the AS/400 as the target system (as opposed to the host system) in any of the three scenarios described previously.

The setting of the QRMTSIGN system value determines the sign-on controls in effect for remote users. The Network Attributes control how an AS/400 communicates with other systems, and they also have a direct impact on the security of the system. The network attributes can be printed by executing the command DSPNETA.

AS/400 PC Support

Personal computers can be attached to an AS/400 and function as an ordinary workstation or download and/or upload data. Controls over the transfer of information are controlled by the object authorizations on the AS/400. An alternate method of controlling this access is via an installation-written exit program, which is executed prior to the execution of each transfer request.

If a PC is disabled because the number of invalid access attempts has exceeded the QMAXSIGN system value, PC Support enables the device, effectively ignoring QMAXSIGN. To prevent this from occurring, the QAUTOVRT value should be set to zero to prevent virtual devices from automatically being configured. A setting of zero, however, may have an impact on other remote users.

PC Support users may be able to bypass menu security even if the LMTCPB (*YES) parameter has been set. Release 2 of AS/400 PC Support allows PC Support users to submit CL commands using the Submit Remote (SBMRMTCMD) command from noninteractive workstations that bypass menu security. Therefore, *PUBLIC access to the SBMRMTCMD command should be set to *EXCLUDE.

The most significant issue relating to the use of PC Support is that once an AS/400 file is transferred to the PC, the file is no longer protected by AS/400 security. Therefore, given the fact that an inappropriate setting of the parameters that relate to PC Support (QAUTOVRT, QMAXSIGN, SBMRMTCMD) can nullify certain aspects of an organization's security system, care should be exercised when installing and using AS/400 PC Support. The ability to read data is equivalent to copy since data can be downloaded easily.

AS/400 Client Access Express for Windows is shipped with OS/400 V4R4 and Operations Navigator. This client can be installed on PCs and works with AS/400 resources. The Express client performs the following functions:

- Runs on PCs installed with Microsoft Windows 95, Windows 98, or Windows NT 4.0 workstation or server operating systems.
- Provides TCP/IP connectivity.
- Uses secured sockets layer (SSL) for client functions to improve TCP/IP network security.
- Uses AS/400 NetServer for PC file serving and network print support.
- Includes Operations Console for both local and remote system console access.
- Contains 32-bit client/server application enablers for the AS/400, such as OLEDB data provider, ODBC driver, Remote Command, and data queues.
- Includes all functions of Operations Navigator for working with AS/400 resources and administering and operating AS/400 systems, plus new graphical interfaces for working with the following AS/400 functions:

    a. SQL performance monitor, SQL scripts, SQL indexes, stored procedures, user-defined functions, and user-defined types (database enhancements)

    b. Virtual private networks (VPN) and application and network security (TCP/IP enhancements)

c. New Management Central system group functions for object packaging and distribution, remote operations, PTF, inventory, and job scheduler

d. Drag-and-drop file system files Server jobs

e. Application administration of third-party plug-ins

f. Java and Visual Basic third-party plug-in enablement

With an AS/400 Client Access Family for Windows license, the preceding functions and PC5250 display, printer emulation, and data transfer are also available.

OUTPUT(*PRINT)

Job Action Network Attribute

The job action network attribute (JOBACN) determines how the system will process incoming job requests. Possible values are:

- *REJECT All input streams are rejected. A message is sent to both the sender and the intended receiver stating that the input stream was rejected.
- *FILE The input stream is filed on the queue of network files for the receiving user. The user is able to display, cancel, or receive the input stream into a database file or submit it to a job queue. A message is then sent to the sender and receiver stating that the input stream was filed.
- *SEARCH The action taken is controlled by the network job table. The default value is *FILE.

PC Support Access Network Attribute

The PC support network attribute (PCSACC) determines how the PC Support program handles requests from personal computers to access objects. The attribute controls whether the personal computer can access objects on the system. Possible values are:

- *REJECT All requests by personal computers to access objects on the AS/400 are rejected. An error message is then sent to the PC application.
- *OBJAUT The request to access an object is verified by the PC Support program. However, access is granted only if sufficient access authority exists.
- Qualified program name The specified installation written program is called if normal authority checking for the object is successful. The program specified is called by PC Support to determine whether the PC request should be rejected. The PC Support program passes information about the user and the requested function to the exit program. The program then returns a code indicating whether the request should be allowed or rejected. A message is sent if the request is rejected or an error occurs. The default value is *OBJAUT.

Distributed Data Management Access Network Attribute

The distributed data management access network attribute determines how the system handles requests from other systems. These requests use the distributed data management (DDM) or the distributed relational database function. Possible values are:

- *REJECT No DDM requests are allowed from remote systems. This does not prevent the system from functioning as the requestor system sending requests to other server systems.

- *OBJAUT The object authority on the system controls remote requests.
- Qualified program name The program specified is called if normal authority checking for the object is successful. The program specified is called only for DDM files and not for distributed relational database functions. The exit program receives a parameter list that identifies the local system user and the request. Once the request has been evaluated, the request is either denied or granted.

Output Queues (Refer to Physical Security).

When output is produced, it is first held in an output queue before it is printed. The output may contain sensitive and confidential information. It is therefore important that such information is protected while waiting in the output queue to prevent it from being displayed, printed, or even copied.

The authority to a spool file is managed by various parameters on the output queue. The owner of a spool file can always access a spool file. It must be noted that the *SPLCTL special authority will allow a user to perform all functions on the spool file, regardless of the security parameters for the spool file. The display data parameter (DSPDTA) of the output queue controls the viewing, copying, and sending of spooled files and the moving of spooled files from one output queue to another. A user cannot view, copy, or send spooled files unless the user has:

- *JOBCTL special authority and the OPRCTL parameter is *YES.
- *CHANGE authority to the output queue if the *AUTCHK parameter is *DTAAUT.
- Ownership of the output queue if the *AUTCHK parameter is *OWNER.

Possible values are:

- *YES A user with *READ authority to the output queue is able to view, copy, or send spool files owned by other users.
- *OWNER Viewing, copying, sending or moving the spooled file is restricted to the owner of the spooled file. If the OPRCTL parameter of the output queue is set to *YES, then any user with *JOBCTL special authority can manage the queue by holding, releasing, or changing the spooled files, but they are restricted from viewing, copying, sending, or moving the spooled file. The default value is *NO.

The authority to check parameter (AUTCHK) of the output queue determines whether users with *CHANGE authority to the output queue allows them to change and delete spooled files owned by other users. Possible values are:

- *OWNER Changing or deleting files is restricted to the user who owns the output queue.
- *DTAAUT Any user with *READ, *ADD, and *DLT authority to the output queue can delete or change the spool files that are owned by other users. The default value is *OWNER.

The operator control parameter (OPRCTL) of the output queue determines the capabilities of a user with *JOBCTL special authority to manage the output queue. If the DSPDTA parameter of the output queue is set to *OWNER, then any user with *JOBCTL special authority can manage the queue by holding, releasing, deleting, and changing the spooled files, but they are restricted from viewing, copying, sending, or moving the spooled file. If the DSPDTA parameter of the output queue is set to *NO, a user with *JOBCTL special authority can perform all functions on the output queue. No authority above the normal user authority is given to a user with *JOBCTL special authority. The default value is *YES.

SYSTEM VALUES

The following twenty-one security system values are listed in alphabetical order. See Exhibit 3.9 for a comparison of functions at different security levels.

QALWUSRDMN

Possible values are:

- *ALL User domain objects of type *USRSPC, *USRIDX, and *USRQ are allowed in any library on the system. Up to fifty library names that may contain user domain objects of type *USRSPC, *USRIDX, and *USRQ.
- Default value: *ALL
- Recommended value: Dependent on the specific requirements.

QATNPGM

Possible values are:

- *NONE No Attention-key-handling program is used by the user.
- *ASSIST IBM Operational Assistant is used. The program specified will be executed when the user presses the Attention-key during an interactive job.
- Default value: *ASSIST
- Recommended value: Dependent on the specific requirements.

QAUDCTL

This system value is used to determine whether auditing is performed on the system. It is effective starting with V2R3 of the operating system. It serves to turn the following attributes either on or off:

- The QAUDLVL system value and AUDLVL user profile parameter.
- The auditing defined for objects by means of the Change Document Library Object Auditing (CHGDLOAUD) command, the Change Object Auditing (CHGOBJAUD) command, and the auditing defined for users by means of the Change User Audit (CHGUSRAUD) command.

Possible values are:

- *NONE No auditing of user actions or objects is performed.
- *OBJAUD Auditing is performed for objects specified by means of the CHGDLOAUD and CHGOBJAUD commands.
- *AIJDLVL Auditing is performed for all functions specified in the QAUDLVL system value, and on the AUDLVL individual user profile parameter, while using the CHGUSRAUD command.

- Default value: *NONE
- Recommended value: Dependent on the specific requirements.

QAUDENDACN

This system value determines the action to be taken by the system if auditing is active but the system is unable to write entries to the audit journal. Possible values are:

- Message CP12283 is sent to the QSYSOPR message queue and QSYSMSG (if it exists) every hour, until the system is able to write entries to the audit journal. The QAUDCTL system value is reset to NONE, and processing continues.
- If an IPL is performed before the auditing function is restarted, the same message is sent to the QSYSOPR and QSYSMSG (if it exists) during the IPL.
- If the system cannot write to the auditing journal, the system will automatically power-down immediately. The system will end abnormally, which may cause a lengthy IPL. When the system is restarted, the following restrictions exist:
  - Sign-on is allowed only at the system console.
  - QAUDCTL is set at *NONE.
  - The user who signs on to the system console must have *ALLOBJ and *AUDIT special authority.
- Default value: *NOTIFY
- Recommended value: Dependent on the specific requirements.

QAUDFRCLVL

This system value determines the frequency with which new audit journal entries are written from memory to disk. This will enable the system administrator to control the amount of audit information that could be lost if the system ended abnormally. Possible values are:

- *SYS The system determines the frequency. This is based on internal system performance. A number between 1 and 100. This figure will determine the number of audit journal entries that can accumulate in memory before being written to auxiliary storage. The larger the number, the less impact there will be on system performance.
- Default value: *SYS
- Recommended value: Dependent on the specific requirements.

QAUDLVL

This system value determines the type of events recorded in the audit journal. Possible values are:

- *NONE No events as specified by the system value QAUDLVL are logged. However, events of individual users based on the user profile parameter AUDLVL will continue to be logged in the journal. These include one or more of the following:
- *AUTFAIL Authority failures are logged.
- *CREATE Object create operations are logged.

- *DELETE Object delete operations are logged.
- *JOBDTA Actions that affect a job are logged.
- *OBJMGT Object move and rename operations are logged.
- *OFCSRV Changes to the system distribution directory and office mail actions are logged.
- *PGMADP Obtaining authority from a program that adopts authority is logged.
- *PGMFAIL System integrity violations are logged.
- *PRTDTA Printing a spooled file and sending output directly to a printer are logged.
- *SAVRST Restore operations are logged.
- *SECURITY Security-related operations are logged.
- *SERVICE Using service tools are logged.
- *SPLFDTA Actions performed on spooled files are logged.
- *SYSMGT Use of system management functions is logged.
- Default value: *NONE
- Recommended value: Dependent on the specific requirements.

QCONSOLE

The system value determines the device name of the console. It is recommended that the console be located in a secure physical environment.

QCRTAUT

Possible values are:

- The public may view but not change the created object.
- The public may change the created object.
- The public may perform any function on the created object.
- The public is specifically excluded from performing any function on the object created.
- Default value: *CHANGE
- Recommended value: *USE

Changing the parameter to a different authority will not change the authority of any existing objects created with the authority as defined by the existing QCRTAUT value.

QCRTOBJAUD

This system value determines the auditing value for a new object if the auditing default for the library is *SYSVAL. The system value is also the default object auditing value for documents without folders. Possible values are:

- *NONE No auditing is performed for the object.
- *USRPRF Auditing is based on the user profile parameter AUDLVL of the user profile accessing the object.

- *CHANGE Every time the object is changed, an audit journal entry is written.
- *ALL When the contents of the object is changed, an audit journal entry is written.
- Default value: *NONE
- Recommended value: Dependent on the specific requirements.

QDSCJOBITV

This system value determines the value in minutes that an interactive job can be disconnected before it is ended. Should users sign on to the system within the time *specified* in this system value, the job will not be disconnected, but users will be brought back to where they were. Possible values are:

- *NONE There is no limit to the time that a job will remain disconnected. A value of 5 to 1,440 minutes.
- Default value: 240 minutes
- Recommended value: Dependent on the specific requirements.

QDSPSGNINF

Possible values are:

- 0 The sign-on information is not displayed.
- 1 The sign-on information is displayed.
- Default value: 0
- Recommended value: 1

QINACTITV

Possible values are:

- *NONE The system does not check the time that a job is inactive. An interval from 5 to 300 minutes.
- Default value: *NONE
- Recommended value: 5 to 30 minutes

QINACTMSGQ

The system value QLNACTMSGQ determines the action to be taken by the system when the period of inactivity specified in the QINACTITV system value is reached. Possible values are:

- *ENDJOB The inactive job, secondary jobs, and/or group job(s) is ended. The inactive job, secondary jobs, and/or group job(s) is disconnected. The QDSCJOBITV system value determines whether the system actually ends the disconnected job. This value does not work for PC Support users.
- Default value: *ENDJOB
- Recommended value: Dependent on the specific requirements.

QLMTDEVSSN

Possible values are:

- 0 Concurrent device sessions are allowed.
- 1 Concurrent device sessions are not allowed.
- Default value: 0
- Recommended value: 1

QLMTSECOFR

Possible values are:

- 0 Users with *ALLOBJ and/or *SERVICE Special Authority are able to sign on to any workstation where they have at least *CHANGE public authority.
- 1 Users with *ALLOBJ and/or *SERVICE Special Authority are only able to sign on to workstations where they are specifically authorized. (*CHG or greater authority is required.)
- Default value: 1
- Recommended value: 1

QMAXSGNACN

This system value determines the action taken by the system when the maximum number of unsuccessful sign-on attempts as specified in the QMAXSIGN system value is reached. Possible values are:

- 1 Only the device is disabled.
- 2 Only the user profile is disabled.
- 3 Both the device and the user profile are disabled.
- Default value: 3
- Recommended value: 3

QMAXSIGN

Possible values are:

- *NOMAX The number of incorrect sign-on attempts is unlimited.
- A value of 1 to 25 This will determine the number of unsuccessful sign-on attempts before the system will take action.
- Default value: 15
- Recommend value: 3 to 5

QPWDEXPITV

Possible values are:

- *NOMAX Users do not have to change their passwords.

- A value of 1 to 365 This represents the number of days before a password expires.
- Default value: *NOMAX
- Recommended value: 30 or higher

QPWDLMTAJC

This system value can be used to prevent a user from specifying a password with numbers (0 to 9) next to one another (e.g., 12345). Possible values are:

- 0 Adjacent numbers are allowed.
- 1 Adjacent numbers are prevented.
- Default value: 0
- Recommended value: Dependent on the specific requirements.

QPWDLMTCHR

Specifies up to ten installation-defined characters that cannot appear in a password (e.g., A, E, I, O, and U). Possible values are:

- *NONE Permits any available character to appear in a password. Up to ten restricted characters, A through Z, 0, 9, #, $, @, and −.
- Default value: *NONE
- Recommended value: Dependent on the specific requirements.

QSECURITY

10, 20, 30, 40, or 50
10
Recommended value: 30 or higher (**Note:** These are IBM set values: 10 equals low security, and 50 equals high security.)

SUMMARY

The AS/400e is brilliant in its architecture. There are many examples of where the AS/400's architecture has delivered on its promise of making the most advanced technology readily and continuously available to its customers. For example, the AS/400 has enabled its customers to give Internet access to existing AS/400 applications.

Through a product known as HTML Gateway that resides within AS/400's operating system, Internet users can access and run AS/400 applications and integrate diverse environments (such as Microsoft Windows NT, firewall, and Lotus Notes/Domino) into AS/400. All customer solutions require a range of hardware and software products from a variety of vendors. The AS/400, through integrating these mixed environments, simplifies the task of managing them. The AS/400 can move from CISC processor technology to RISC processor technology without needing to recompile programs. Programs are saved off the CISC systems, restored on the RISC systems, and run as full 64-bit applications. On ordinary machines recompilation is necessary (sometimes some rewriting), and the resulting programs do not fully exploit the 64-bit hardware. The AS/400's future-oriented architecture has en-

Exhibit 3.9 Comparison of Functions at Various Levels of Security

	QSECURITY =				
Security Function Performed	**10**	**20**	**30**	**40**	**50**
User profile created automatically.	Yes	No	No	No	No
User profile name required.	Yes	Yes	Yes	Yes	Yes
Password required.	No	Yes	Yes	Yes	Yes
Active password security.	No	Yes	Yes	Yes	Yes
Active initial program and menu security LMTCPB(*YES).	No	Yes	Yes	Yes	Yes
Active limit capabilities.	No	Yes	Yes	Yes	Yes
Active resource security.	No	No*	Yes	Yes	Yes
Users have access to all objects.	Yes	Yes	No	No	No
Security auditing available.	Yes	Yes	Yes	Yes	Yes
Programs may not contain restricted instructions.	Yes	Yes	Yes	Yes	Yes
Programs may not use unsupported call interfaces.	No	No	No	Yes	Yes
Enhanced hardware storage protection is available.	No	No	No	Yes	Yes
QTEMP library is a temporary object.	No	No	No	No	Yes
The QALWUSRDMN system value determines the libraries where the objects *USRSPC, *URDX, and USRQ may be created.	Yes	Yes	Yes	Yes	Yes
Pointers in parameters are validated for user domain programs running in system state.	No	No	No	No	Yes
Enforcement of message handling rules between system and user state programs.	No	No	No	No	Yes
A program's associated space cannot be modified directly.	No	No	No	Yes	Yes
Internal control blocks are protected.	No	No	No	Yes	Yes

*At QSECURITY = 20, resource security is active but may not be effective since default *ALLOBJ Special Authority is granted on user profile creation.

abled it to take rapidly changing hardware and software technologies in its stride. This same flexible architecture will continue to serve its users well by enabling its customers to continue to deploy the very latest technologies while causing the minimum possible disruption to their work.

The 64-bit AS/400 architecture has another advantage besides speed: it makes the management of data and applications easier. Why? Because it lets AS/400 assign a unique, permanent address to every piece of data and application inside the system using a technique called single-level storage. Imagine what would happen if you were mayor of a town that had 10,000 buildings and a state law required you to identify them using three-digit addresses and no street names. Obviously, you couldn't give every building its own address.

Imagine how difficult it would be to deliver mail or respond to emergencies in such a town. Believe it or not, many of today's "modern" servers face a similar problem—they cannot assign a unique address to every object in memory or on disk storage. Even though programmers have found clever ways to work around these problems, they all involve extra programming time, added complexity, added costs, and error-prone software. By contrast, single-level storage lets AS/400 mark every object, whether it is in memory or on disk storage, with a unique, permanent address. This reduces the time and staff resources it takes to develop and enhance applications. It also makes the entire system run more efficiently, especially when running multiple tasks. Perhaps most importantly, it makes AS/400 run with fewer software failures. As one customer said, owning an AS/400 means never having to say, "General Protection Fault."

CHAPTER 4

AS/400 AUDIT OBJECTIVES AND PROCEDURES

This section identifies exposures for an AS/400 installation and contains a list of questions the auditor might ask to obtain an overview of the effectiveness of controls in the AS/400 environment. Also identified are the control techniques that might be performed at an AS/400 installation. The control objectives and techniques are not meant to be a comprehensive list, nor is performing all the tests necessary in every situation. What procedures to perform is a matter of auditor judgment, and this can only be determined after all the key risks have been properly assessed and evaluated.

Planning the audit entails obtaining and reviewing the following:

- An organizational chart for the IS function.
- A copy of the program change control policies and procedures.
- A copy of the organization's IS policies.
- A system values report.
- A list of significant user IDs and group IDs.
- A list of significant authorization lists.
- A directory listing for significant production libraries.
- A list of system utilities and compilers.

OPERATIONAL CONTROLS

An effective combination of automated control procedures offered by the computers themselves and manual control procedures designed and developed by management is required to (1) control program development, acquisition, and maintenance of those programs, and (2) control access to data files. This section identifies operational controls that should be considered at all computer installations. These controls are not meant to be a comprehensive list, nor is it necessary for an installation to have all the controls for the internal control structure to be exhaustive. The auditor's overall evaluation of the structure is a matter of judgment determined only after the risks have been assessed at the particular computer installation.

ORGANIZATIONAL STRUCTURE

The organization of an IS department should be designed to provide segregation between operations, systems and applications programming, and data control. Often in midrange computer installations, there are a limited number of IS personnel, and control concerns may result regarding the segregation of duties.

Examples of mitigating controls that may address or monitor a lack of segregation of duties in the IS department are:

- Programmer access to production objects is limited to read-only by using in-built system security features.
- Access to source production programs and compilers is restricted using in-built system security features. Access to these objects is permitted only with management's authorization.
- The audit journal or history log is reviewed by management for unauthorized use of system programs, utilities, and compilers. Unusual activity is logged by user and/or object and is investigated.
- Operations personnel are restricted to an initial program and/or an initial menu thereby restricting processing options.
- Limited capabilities and attention-key-handling are set to prevent MIS and end-user personnel from modifying their initial program and/or an initial menu.
- Object descriptions, which include date of last change, are compared periodically to approved program change forms.
- Physical access to the computer and the system console is limited to authorized personnel.
- Normal sign-on is required for all remote users.
- Modems for the computers are located in secure areas. The modems either are turned off or unplugged when not in use or there are internal security features, such as dial-back or challenge procedures.
- Production source code is maintained off-line.

If no in-house program development is performed, use of purchased software or third-party contract programmers may provide an appropriate segregation of duties in the IS department.

Examples of mitigating controls that may address or monitor a lack of segregation of duties between user and IS departments are:

- Users are assigned an initial program and/or initial menu that restricts options available to each user.
- Limited capabilities and attention-key-handling are set to prevent MIS and end-user personnel from modifying their initial program and/or an initial menu. Management restricts programmers from accessing production data files by using system security features.
- An effective system of reconciling inputs and outputs (e.g., use of batch controls, review of transaction listings) is in place.
- Personnel, independent of authorizing and entering transactions, are responsible for reconciliation and review procedures.

PROGRAM DEVELOPMENT, ACQUISITION, AND MAINTENANCE

An installation should have standards for procedures that control program development, acquisition, and maintenance. An adequate system of establishing standards and reviewing adherence to standards provides controls to ensure that production programs are authorized, tested, and approved before being placed into production. Controls may be achieved by establishing and adhering to the following standards:

- Request forms for program development, acquisition, and maintenance are standardized and approved by information systems and user management.
- All program development, acquisition, and maintenance procedures are adequately tested and reviewed by information systems and user management before being placed into production.
- All programs and changes to programs are properly documented, and documentation is reviewed for propriety.
- The Source Entry Utility (SEU) dates stamp on each source code line is used to determine whether changes made are in accordance with changes authorized.
- Separate production and test libraries are maintained.
- The use of SEU is not allowed in the production environment (i.e., all source code is created and updated in a test environment).
- Source code compare utilities are used to determine change propriety.
- Check-in and checkout procedures are followed for production source code.
- Programmers are restricted from adding new or changed programs to the production library. Only specified operations or information systems management has object existence and management rights (the right to move, rename, grant authority to, revoke authority from, and modify the attributes of an object) for production objects. Public Authority to production source libraries is *EXCLUDE.

Procedures related to the acquisition and subsequent modification of purchased software should also be subject to controls requiring user and information systems approval and appropriate testing before the programs are placed into production. These procedures should be performed whether modifications are done in-house or by outside vendors.

ACCESS TO DATA FILES

An installation should have procedures ensuring that access to data files is restricted to authorized users and programs. The computers provide system security that can be used to restrict access. However, the effectiveness of the security depends on how it is implemented and used.

Examples of installation procedures and controls include:

- Object access rights granted to users are documented and approved by their supervisor.
- Each individual is assigned a unique profile and password.
- Passwords are confidential and difficult to guess.
- Passwords, including the security officer's, are changed periodically.
- Workstations and/or user profiles are deactivated after a reasonable number of password violations. The number of attempts allowed is designated in the system value (QMAXSIGN).

- Access violations are investigated promptly by appropriate management personnel.
- The security officer profile is assigned to only one individual and Special Authority is assigned to a limited number of management personnel who have security responsibilities.
- Security functions may be performed only from a limited number of terminals.
- Public Authority to production data files is *EXCLUDE.
- Users are assigned an Initial Program and/or an Initial Menu limiting access to only those functions necessary to perform their work.
- Limited Capabilities and attention-key-handling are set to prevent MIS and user personnel from modifying their Initial Program and/or an Initial Menu.
- Access to the system is controlled after business hours through the use of automated devices and communication lines commands.
- Access to removable data files (e.g., diskettes, tapes) is restricted to authorized personnel.
- The system is programmed to cancel or deactivate interactive jobs (i.e., terminal session) if there is a specified period of inactivity.
- System Save, Job Control, and Spool Control rights are limited to appropriate authorized personnel.
- Authorization to use restore commands is limited to appropriate personnel.
- Use of data-altering utilities is restricted to authorized personnel and from production environments, and their usage is closely monitored.
- Jobs are executed during scheduled time frames, and deviations from scheduled processing are monitored and reviewed.

BUSINESS CONTINUITY

Organizations are placing more reliance on information processing facilities to support their critical business applications. Therefore, it is important to maintain the availability of this information and the associated processing facilities and to be able to promptly restore critical information processing systems in the event of an interruption of service. Operational controls related to business continuity include:

- Procedures should be in place to regularly measure and assess the impact of interrupted information processing on the business.
- System restoration responsibilities should be assigned and contingency plans prepared by both the IS function and user departments.
- Contingency plans should be documented and tested to ensure timely, controlled recovery of critical information systems.
- On-site and off-site backup for critical information and materials should be instituted.
- Emergency procedures should be developed, and preventive measures should be taken to minimize damage and mitigate the impact on the business from a disaster or disruption of service.

GENERAL CONTROLS

COMPUTER ROOM

Audit Objective

The system environment is adequately secure.

Audit Procedures

Observe the adequacy of the following requirements in the computer room (room requirements depend on size and use of the AS/400(s)):

- Hazard detection tools and equipment
- Air-conditioning equipment
- Protection from risks of water damage
- Support facilities such as a UPS

PHYSICAL ACCESS TO SYSTEM UNIT

Audit Objective

The system unit is physically secure.

Audit Procedures

Observe the physical area surrounding the system unit and evaluate whether it resides in a secure environment (e.g., access by unauthorized individuals is restricted).

- Where is the computer with its peripherals located?
- What physical security measures are used to reduce or prevent access?
- Are visitors (noncomputer room personnel) entering the computer room required to sign in and out and be accompanied?

SYSTEM KEY LOCK

The AS/400 is equipped with a four-position System Key Lock. Each of the positions allows for a different level of system control.

Audit Objective

The System Key Lock is not set to manual or normal, and the key to the System Key Lock is maintained in a secure location.

Audit Procedures

Determine whether the System Key Lock is in the auto or secure position. Determine that the System Key is maintained in a secure location.

- Where is the key to the System Key Lock maintained, and who has access to it?

- What procedures are used/followed when the position of the System Key Lock is changed?
- What is the position of the System Key Lock?

SYSTEM CONSOLE

Audit Objective

The system console is situated in a physically secure location. Certain restricted and sensitive operations can be performed only from the system console. All jobs submitted from this console run at priority 10, and it can be used to control jobs and spool files. The QSECOFR profile can always sign on to the system console, even if the profile is disabled because of invalid password attempts.

Audit Procedures

Review the QCONSOLE parameter on the system values report. Determine that the console device is physically secure. Review the object authority to the device by using the DSPOBJAUT command to determine the device's public authority and the users specifically authorized to use the device. Evaluate whether the object authority is appropriate.

- What is the value of QCONSOLE?
- Is the device specified in the QCONSOLE system value located in a physically secure location? (**Note:** The system console can be physically separated from the system unit.)
- Are all users who are not specifically authorized to use the system console restricted from its use?
- Is the Default Public Authority to the console device set to *EXCLUDE?

DEDICATED SERVICE TOOLS

Audit Objective

Dedicated Service Tools (DSTs) are not used to provide access to sensitive data.

Audit Procedures

During an IPL, with the assistance of the client, observe the client attempt to sign on to DST with the default passwords to ensure that they have been changed. Review the procedures in place to control the use of DST and to ensure that DST passwords are well controlled.

- Have the default passwords for DST been changed?
- Who has access to the DST passwords?
- How often are the DST passwords changed?
- Is the use of DST monitored and logged?

SECURITY LEVEL

Audit Objective

The system security level is set at a sufficient level to provide appropriate security.

Audit Procedures

Review the QSECURITY system value to determine that the system value is set to at least level 30. Level 20 may also be appropriate if Special Authorities have been removed from user profiles since default *ALLOBJ is granted to each user profile at creation under level 20.

- What is the system security level?
- Is the security level ever changed?
- What procedures are used/followed when the security level is changed?
- Who is authorized to change the security level?
- Changes to the system security level are only effective after the next IPL. Therefore it is necessary to verify that the system had an IPL since the QSECURITY value was changed.

ALLOW USER DOMAIN OBJECTS

Audit Objective

Users are not allowed to pass confidential data to other users.

Audit Procedures

Does the client have a need for a high level of security over its processing environment? Is there a need to restrict user domain objects of type *USRSPC, *USRIDX, and *USRQ to specific libraries? Use the System Values report to determine that the QALWUSRDMN parameter has been changed from *ALL to a list of libraries that can contain user domain objects of type *USRSPC, *USRIDX, and *USRQ. Ensure that the libraries indicated in this system value are appropriate.

PASSWORD FORMATTING RULES

Audit Objective

Users are forced to change their own passwords on a regular basis and are prevented from reusing old passwords. Users are prevented from selecting very short, easily guessed passwords because formatting rules are not in effect.

Note: OS/400 has many password formatting options that make it difficult for someone to gain access to the system by randomly attempting to guess passwords.

Audit Procedures

- Is there a security policy that covers passwords?
- What password formatting rules are used (e.g., length, repeat cycles, password life span, repeat characters)?
- What procedures are used to prevent easily guessed passwords?
- What policies and procedures are followed to prevent users from writing down their password?
- Is the need for password confidentiality communicated to users?

- Are all users required to change their password at least once a quarter?
- Are history or audit logs reviewed for possible password violations?
- Does each user have a unique user ID and password?

Use the system values report to determine the following:

- The password expiration (QPWDEXPITV) parameter has been changed from *NOMAX to a reasonable number of days.
- The parameter requiring a new password to be different from the previous 32 passwords is activated (i.e., QPWDRQDDIF is set to 1).
- The minimum password length (QPWDMINLEN) parameter is not lower than 5.
- The maximum password length (QPWDMAXLEN) parameter is greater than 8.

If a password validation program is used, ensure that the additional validation checking performed does not result in users being forced to use passwords that conform to a format that might be easy to guess. The use of a password validation program has a security risk that passwords are copied to a data file by the validation program during input of a new password.

The following parameters have been set to a combination that reasonably prevents easily guessed passwords from being used:

- QPWDLMTAJC
- QPWDLMTCHR
- QPWDLMTREP
- QPWDPOSDIF
- QPWDRQDDGT

MAXIMUM SIGN-ON ATTEMPTS

Audit Objective

The maximum number of unsuccessful sign-on attempts is not set too high. When the maximum number of unsuccessful sign-on attempts is reached, the user ID is revoked and/or the terminal is deactivated.

Audit Procedures

- What is the value of QMAXSIGN and QMAXSGNACN?
- Who is authorized to change the value of QMAXSIGN and QMAXSGNACN?
- Are these values ever changed?

Review the QMAXSIGN value on the system values report and determine if the maximum number of unsuccessful sign-on attempts is set to a reasonable number. The maximum number should not exceed three to five unsuccessful attempts. In addition, determine whether the security officer reviews all unsuccessful sign-on attempts.

With the client's assistance, attempt to sign-on to the system using an invalid password and valid user ID. Attempts should exceed the QMAXSIGN system value to test deactivation of the terminal and/or user ID because of violation attempts. Review the audit log for logging of the unauthorized access attempt. Review the client's follow-up procedures for propriety.

Review the QMAXSGNACN value on the system values report to determine the action taken when the maximum number of unsuccessful sign-on attempts is reached.

LIMIT SECURITY OFFICER ACCESS

Audit Objective

The setting of the QLMTSECOFR parameter has been changed to prevent user profiles with *ALLOBJ and/or *SERVICE to sign on to any workstations that have a public authority of *CHANGE or greater.

Audit Procedures

- What is the value of QLMTSECOFR?
- Is this value ever changed?

Review the QLMTSECOFR value on the system values report to determine that the QLMTSECOFR parameter has been set to 1. Verify that changes to the value are authorized.

REMOTE SIGN-ON CONTROLS

Audit Objective

The setting of the QRMTSIGN parameter has not been changed to a value that will allow unauthorized access to the system via a remote workstation.

Audit Procedures

- What is the value of QRMTSIGN?
- Is there a need for remote users to sign on to the system?

Obtain the value of the QRMTSIGN parameter from the system values report. This should be set to *FRCSIGNON to force display station pass-through users to sign on to the remote AS/400. If there is no need for remote users to access the system, the value should be *REJECT.

LIMIT NUMBER OF DEVICE SESSIONS

Audit Objective

The setting of the QLMTDEVSSN parameter has been changed to prevent users from signing on to more than one workstation at a time.

Audit Procedures

- What is the value of QLMTDEVSSN?
- In what kind of situations do users need to sign on to more than one workstation at a time?
- Which users are allowed to sign on to multiple workstations?

Review the value of the QLMTDEVSSN parameter on the system values report and determine that the QLMTDEVSSN parameter is set to 1. Verify that changes to the value are authorized.

AUTOMATIC CONFIGURATION OF VIRTUAL DEVICES

Audit Objective

The number of attempts allowed through pass-through is QAUTOVRT multiplied by the number of unsuccessful sign-on attempts allowed through QMAXSIGN. The setting of the QAUTOVRT parameter has not been changed to a value greater than 0, thus allowing virtual devices to be configured automatically.

Audit Procedures

- What is the value of QAUTOVRT?
- What is the value of QMAXSIGN?
- In what kind of situations do virtual devices need to be configured automatically?

Review the value of the QAUTOVRT parameter on the system values report and determine that the QAUTOVRT parameter is set to 0. Verify that changes to the value are authorized.

AUTOMATIC CONFIGURATION OF LOCAL DEVICES

Audit Objective

The QAUTOCFG parameter has been set to a value of 0, allowing local devices to be configured automatically.

Audit Procedures

- What is the value of QAUTOCFG?
- In what kind of situations do local devices need to be configured automatically?

Review the QAUTOCFG parameter on the system values report and determine that the QAUTOCFG parameter is set to 0. Verify that changes to the value are authorized.

ATTENTION PROGRAM

Audit Objective

The program that is executed when the attention key is pressed does not grant inappropriate capabilities to users. The ATNPGM parameter in user profiles inappropriately overrides the system value QATNPGM.

Audit Procedures

- What is the value of QATNPGM?
- Does the program grant inappropriate capabilities to users?
- Is the program name qualified by a library name?
- Is there a policy for setting the ATNPGM parameter?

Review the QATNPGM parameter on the system values report and determine whether the program name specified in this parameter grants inappropriate capabilities. If the program is appropriate, verify that the program is qualified by a library name and ensure that the library is part of the appropriate library list.

VIOLATION REPORTING AND FOLLOW-UP

The system will write security-related events to the history journal and also to the audit journal if it has been activated.

Audit Objective

Security-related violations are reviewed and followed up on in a complete and timely manner and the audit journal has been activated. All appropriate activities are being recorded.

Audit Procedures

- Is the audit journal feature activated?
- How often and by whom are history logs/audit journals reviewed?
- What security-related events are being recorded for users of the system?
- What procedures are followed when a security violation is noted?
- Are the history logs/audit journals protected from unauthorized access and modification?
- Who has *AUDIT special authority?
- Who decides what activities to log?
- Is there a requirement for additional logging of specific users' activities on the system in greater detail?
- Is there a need to monitor the use of and changes to specific objects by users?
- Is there a need to monitor the use of and changes to specific objects by specific users only?

Review the settings to the following system values on the system values report and evaluate the appropriateness of the settings:

- QAUDCTL. If audit logging is taking place, the value of this parameter should not be set to *NONE. Verify that the parameter is set to either *OBJAUD, *AUDLVL, or both *OBJAUD and *AUDLVL. It should be set to *OBJAUD if specific object access monitoring is used and *AUDLVL if either specific user and/or all user activity is being monitored.
- QAUDLVL. If the organization is monitoring security-related events for all system users, this parameter should be set to any one or more of the fourteen available values. Ensure that the parameter settings are appropriate to satisfy the needs of the organization and management.
- QCRTOBJAUD. If the organization requires that all objects created on the system have a default auditing value assigned to them, ensure that the parameter is set to one of the available values other than *NONE. Verify that the setting is in line with the organization's security policy or management's requirements.
- QAUDENDACN. Ensure that this value is set to *NOTIFY. If the organization's security policy requires that the system shuts down immediately preventing any further processing should the system not be able to write to the audit journal, the parameter should be set to *PWRDWNSYS. Such a recommendation should only be made after user management fully understands the potential consequences of such a setting.
- QAUDFRCLVL. Setting this parameter to *SYS ensures the best performance. Discuss the current setting with the security administrator and ensure that the setting is appropriate in terms of the organization's needs.

General Procedures

- Evaluate the settings in existence and determine which objects and user activities are logged. Ensure that activity logging meets the organization's security needs and that it is appropriate.
- Examine the documentation supporting the regular review of the history (QHST) log or audit journal. Determine if the review is designed for detection and follow-up of unauthorized access attempts, unauthorized use of system utilities and compilers, and unscheduled processing.
- With management's assistance, attempt to sign on to sensitive objects using unauthorized user profiles. Review the history (QHST) log or audit journal for logging of the attempts.
- Obtain the access authority to the audit and history journals and journal receivers and ensure that access to them is appropriately restricted.
- Determine which system users have been assigned the *AUDIT special authority. Determine that it is appropriate for these users to be given the ability to allocate and remove auditing values for both user profiles and objects and change the system values that relate to audit logging.
- Use the Display User Profile (DSPUSRPRF) command to create an output file containing all user profiles. With the client's assistance, use QUERY, SQL, or a similar utility to print a sample of this file. For the sample of users, review the following user profile parameter settings:
  - Determine that the OBJAUD parameter has been changed from the default setting of *NONE to *CHANGE or *ALL if it is a requirement that an audit record is to be written to the audit journal when the user accesses a specific object. Note that the OBJAUD attribute of objects to be monitored must also be set and that no audit logging will take place if the setting is *NONE, even though the user profile parameter setting is *CHANGE or *ALL.
  - Determine that the AUDLVL parameter has been changed from the default setting of *NONE to any of the twelve available values if additional monitoring of individual user actions is required. Evaluate the appropriateness of the parameter settings and ensure that the parameter settings meet the needs of the organization's security requirements.

For critical objects on the system, use the DSPOBJD command to determine if the setting of the OBJAUD value is appropriate so that access to the object causes an entry in the auditing journal. Note that this setting must be evaluated in conjunction with the OBJAUD user profile parameter if the current setting is *USRPRF. If the setting is *USRPRF, and the user profile parameter is set to *NONE, no audit logging will take place.

To ensure that audit logging of the object takes place regardless of which profile accesses the object, the setting of the objects OBJAUD attribute must be *CHANGE or *ALL. A Query may be developed to help perform the above test.

DEFAULT PUBLIC ACCESS AUTHORITY

Audit Objective

The system value QCRTAUT is set to a value that does not grant inappropriate access to created objects.

Audit Procedures

- What is the value of QCRTAUT?
- Who authorizes changes to QCRTAUT?
- Has the Default Public Access Authority for production programs and files been changed to *EXCLUDE?

Review the QCRTAUT parameter on the system values report and ensure that it has been changed from the default setting of *CHANGE to a setting of *USE or less. Verify that changes to this system value are authorized.

Determine that the production database and production source code files are maintained in a library with appropriately restricted access. Or use the Display Object Authority command and determine whether the Public Authority Access (PUBAUT) parameter for each significant individual production database and production source code file is *EXCLUDE and that the individual accesses allowed are appropriate.

DISPLAY SIGN-ON INFORMATION

Audit Objective

The QDSPSGNINF parameter has been set to 0, preventing the display of sign-on information.

Audit Procedures

- What is the value of QDSPSGNINF?
- Are users instructed to report instances when the sign-on information indicates that unsuccessful sign-on attempts have been made using their user ID, or when the date of last sign-on is incorrect?
- Who authorizes changes to QDSPSGNINF?

Review the QDSPSGNINF parameter on the system values report and ensure that it has been set to 1.

JOB TIME-OUT

Audit Objective

Unattended terminals are being timed out; thus no opportunity is created for an unauthorized user to gain access to the system by way of an active but unattended workstation.

Audit Procedures

- Are inactive jobs canceled/disconnected?
- After how many minutes is an inactive job canceled/disconnected?
- After how many minutes is a disconnected job canceled?
- What is the value of QINACTITV?
- What is the value of QINACTMSGQ?
- What is the value of QDSCJOBITV?

Review the system values report to determine that:

- The QINACTITV parameter has been set at a reasonable number of minutes (e.g., 10 to 30 minutes).
- The QINACTMSGQ parameter has been set to *DSCJOB. This does not work for PC Support users, and it will function like an *ENDJJOB.
- The QDSCJOBITV parameter has been set at a reasonable number of minutes.

SYSTEM PORTION OF LIBRARY LIST

Audit Objective

The system portion of the library list represents a possible security exposure because the libraries on this library list are searched sequentially before those on the user's list. The public authority to the CHGSYSLIBL command has not been changed from *EXCLUDE to a value that grants access to inappropriate users.

Audit Procedures

- Has the object authority to the CHGSYSLIBL command been changed from the default value?
- Who authorizes changes to the system library list?

Using the DSPOBJAUT command, determine whether the access to the CHGSYSLIBL command has been changed from the default value of *EXCLUDE. The libraries on the system list must be reviewed for appropriateness. Verify that all changes to the system library list are authorized.

USER PORTION OF LIBRARY LIST

Audit Objective

The user portion of the library list is searched sequentially after the system portion of the library list for objects that are referenced without a qualified library name. Users can not change their portion of the library list.

Audit Procedures

- Are users allowed to change their library list?
- Are the necessary commands to change the user portion of the library list adequately secured?
- Who authorizes changes to the user library list?

Using the DSPOBJAUT command, determine whether the access to the CHGLIBL, ADDLIBL, RMVLIBL, and EDTLIBL commands has been appropriately restricted. The libraries on the user list must be reviewed for appropriateness. Verify that all changes to the user portion of the library list are authorized.

IBM-SUPPLIED USER PROFILES

Audit Objective

The passwords for the six IBM-supplied user profiles have been changed. The six IBM-supplied user profiles are not used as user or group profiles.

Audit Procedures

- Have the passwords for the IBM-supplied user IDs been changed or set to *NONE?
- Are any of the IBM-supplied user profiles used to gain access to the system as a user profile or group profile?

Determine that the passwords for the six IBM-supplied user profiles have been changed:

Profile	*Default Password*
QSECOFR	QSECOFR
QPGMR	QPGMR
QSYSOPR	QSYSOPR
QUSER	QUSER
QSRV	QSRV
QSRVBAS	QSRVBAS

Display the user profiles using the DSPAUTUSR command and verify that the password for each IBM-supplied user profile is set to *NONE.

SPECIAL USER PROFILES

Audit Objective

User profiles with certain special authorities provide unlimited access to virtually all aspects of the AS/400. Users do not have access to profiles with special authorities that grant levels of access greater than required by their job function.

Audit Procedures

- What users have been assigned Special Authorities?
- Do all users with Special Authority need the assigned Special Authority to perform their job function?

Review all responsibilities of individuals assigned the (QSECOFR) profile and/or any Special Authorities for appropriateness. Use the Display User Profile (DSPUSRPRF) command to create an output file containing all user profiles. With the client's assistance, use QUERY, SQL, or a similar utility to scan this file for each of the Special Authorities (*ALLOBJ, *SECADM, *SAVSYS, *JOBCTL, *SERVICE, *SPLCTL, and *AUDIT). Evaluate the propriety of each user assigned any of these authorities.

By inquiring of information systems personnel, obtain a listing of users who have been given the password to the security officer (QSECOFR) profile. If QSECOFR is being used as a group profile, use the DSPAUTUSR command, sorted by group, to determine security officer group profile members. Evaluate the propriety of each user assigned to this group.

USER PROFILES

Audit Objective

User profiles do not contain parameters that define many of the user's capabilities.

Audit Procedures

- Users are restricted to predefined Initial Programs and Initial Menus.
- Users are not able to break out of their assigned Initial Programs and Initial Menus.
- Users are not able to alter their own user profile parameters.
- Parameters in the user profile cannot override certain system values such as the limiting of device sessions and the forcing of automatic password changes.
- User profile parameters are not set to inappropriate values.
- What policies and procedures are used for the assignment of user IDs?
- Are user capabilities limited to their job function through the use of Initial Programs and Initial Menus?
- Are system values overridden at the user profile level?
- Has the ALWLMTUSR command been used to grant access to additional CL commands?

Review and evaluate the procedures used by the installation to:

- Change the default settings of user profile parameters.
- Determine whether to assign Initial Programs and/or Initial Menus.
- Change installation-standard parameter settings.
- Determine when it is appropriate to override system values in a user profile.

In addition, execute the DSPAUTUSR SEQ(*GRPPRF) OUTPUT(*PRINT) command to print a list of all users and their group profile names in alphabetical order of group name and review a sample of users on the report as follows:

- Review the user profile name to determine that some form of naming convention is used when assigning user profile names (e.g., all groups start with GRP or DPT to indicate group or department, respectively).
- Determine that there are no "generic" profiles (e.g., "ACCOUNTS") or that such profiles are restricted to inquiry only.
- Check to see that the date of the last password change is consistent with the organization's security policy.
- Check that no passwords have been set to *USRPRF.

Use the Display User Profile (DSPUSRPRF) command to create an output file containing all user profiles. With the client's assistance, use QUERY, SQL, or a similar utility to print a sample of this file. For a sample of users, review the following user profile parameter settings:

- Check the date of last sign-on field. If the user profile has not signed on to the system for a reasonably long period of time, check that the profile relates to a current employee.
- If the user profile has a value greater than 3 in the Sign-on Attempts Not Valid field, investigate the user profile and discuss the reason for the invalid sign-on attempts with the security administrator.
- Check that the STATUS field is not set to *DISABLED. If it is, discuss with the security administrator the reason for the setting and whether the profile is still necessary on the system. Some IDs will be disabled but are still valid for processing, such as IDs that own applications.
- Check that the password expiration interval is set to *SYSVAL instead of *NONE or an explicit value.
- Check that the user class parameter and special authorities granted to the user are reasonable given the employee's normal duties.
- If the user is assigned a group profile, capabilities granted by the group profile should be appropriate given the employee's normal duties. Check that the OWNER parameter is set correctly, giving either the user profile or the group profile ownership of objects created by the user profile. Should the OWNER profile be set to *USRPRF, ensure that the group authority parameter is set to give the group appropriate access to the objects created by the user profile.
- If initial programs are used, verify that the employee's Initial Program (INLPGM) is compatible with the employee's normal duties and the initial menu (INLMNU) is set to *SIGNOF~F to ensure that the session is terminated after completion of the initial program. (This helps to avoid unaudited access to the command line.)
- Check that the Limit Capabilities parameter (LMTCPB) is set to *YES to ensure that end users cannot modify their own profiles.
- Check that the attention-key-handling parameter (ATNPGM) is set to *SYSVAL or an appropriate installation-written program to prevent users from using the attention key to escape from their Initial Programs and Initial Menus.
- Check that the maximum storage allowed is set to a reasonable value and is not set at *NOMAX.
- Check that the job description to which the user profile is assigned does not allow the user to submit jobs using the capabilities of a powerful user profile.
- Check that the accounting code parameter is set correctly to accurately monitor usage of system resources by the user if this facility is used by the installation. This should not be set if not used.
- Verify that the output queue and printer device allocated to the user are appropriate, based on the user's job function within the organization.
- Determine that the Limit Device Sessions parameter is set to *SYSVAL and that it has not been overridden at the user profile level.
- Determine that the Display Sign-On Information parameter is set to *SYSVAL and that it has not been overridden at the user profile level.
- Determine that the user's processing priority is set at a level that is appropriate with the organization's policy.

- If audit logging is being used, refer to the section on history logs and audit journals to ascertain what audit procedures need to be carried out on the AUDLVL and OBJAUD parameters.

GROUP PROFILES

The security officer may define a group profile for a group of users with the same capabilities. When a user is assigned to a group, the user is given the system authorities defined in the group profile. Therefore, the authorities assigned to the group should be appropriate for all group members.

Audit Objective

Users have not been granted levels of access by a group profile greater than those required to perform their job function.

Audit Procedures

- What policies and procedures are used for the assignment of individuals to groups?
- Is group membership reviewed on a periodic basis (or when transfers, terminations, or promotions occur)?
- Are the access rights assigned to the group reviewed on a periodic basis?
- Are group profile passwords set to *NONE?

Use the Display Authorized Users (DSPAUTUSR) command and determine which user profiles are group profiles. For a sample of group profiles, obtain a list of all group members and objects authorized by using the Display User Profiles (DSPUSRPRF) command.

Perform the following audit steps on the sample:

- Review reasonableness of the group members assigned to the group profile in relation to the objects authorized to the group profile.
- Check that group profiles do not have passwords and that the password of the *NONE parameter is set to *YES.
- Repeat the audit steps listed under User Profiles on the sample to check that the group profile parameters are appropriate for the group profile.

LIBRARY ACCESS

Audit Objective

Users are not granted levels of access greater than those required to perform their job function.

Audit Procedures

- Which libraries contain sensitive information?
- Is the public authority to these libraries appropriate?
- Who is authorized to access sensitive libraries?

Using the command DSPOBJD OBJ(QSYS/*ALL) OBJTYPE(*LIB) OUTPUT(*PRINT), obtain a list of all libraries on the system. By discussion with client information systems staff, ascertain the significant libraries. These should include live source and object libraries and production data libraries and will be installation specific. The following standard system and utility libraries also should be reviewed to ensure that access authorities to them are appropriate: QSYS, QGPL, QPDA, QPFR, and QSAV, as well as any programming language libraries (e.g., QQRYLIB, QRPG).

Using the DSPOBJAUT OBJ(QSYS/,libname.) OBJTYPE(*LIB) OUTPUT(*) command, display and note the access authorities to each library. For a sample of libraries, determine the following:

- Public Authority is no higher than *USE and preferably *EXCLUDE.
- Users have a maximum authority of *USE to system and utility libraries (except QGPL and QTEMP, which may be *CHANGE), *EXCLUDE to programming language libraries, *USE to production program libraries, *CHANGE to production data, and *EXCLUDE to production source libraries.
- Programmers have a maximum authority of *USE to system and utility libraries, *USE to programming language libraries, *EXCLUDE to production object libraries, *EXCLUDE to production data libraries, and *USE to production source libraries.
- Operators have a maximum authority of *USE to system and utility libraries, *USE to programming language libraries and *CHANGE to production program libraries (if they are part of the change control process), *USE to production data libraries (plus additional emergency authorities if applicable), and *USE to production source libraries.

Note that QSECOFR or an internal profile without a password, such as QSYS, should be the owner of most of the libraries. Also, note that most vendor-written source, object, and data libraries will have an owner that may also be a group profile for end users. This means that users effectively have *ALL authority over vendor-written objects, and therefore access to users must be controlled through package-based controls (e.g., restriction of menu options).

ACCESS TO DATA

When an object is created, the default public access is set to *CHANGE (if the QCRTAUT and CRTAUT parameters have not been changed from the shipped value), which allows users to READ, ADD, UPDATE, and DELETE data.

Audit Objective

Users are not granted levels of access greater than those required to perform their job function.

Audit Procedures

- How are user access rights determined and granted?
- What default level of public access is granted to users?
- How is production data segregated from test data?
- How are programmers prevented from testing programs in productive libraries in a live environment?

Review and evaluate the procedures to issue users access to objects, particularly to data and programs. Review a sample of users' access to objects for reasonableness.

Review and evaluate the procedures used by the client to determine that each user is assigned a unique user profile and password. If a group of users share a profile (i.e., use the same profile to access the system):

- Display the group profile to determine what objects the profile has Specific Authority to use.
- For each object identified previously, use the DSPOBJAUT command to determine that the profile is allowed read-only access.

ACCESS TO PROGRAM LIBRARIES

When an object is created, the default public access is set to *CHANGE (if the QCRTAUT and CRTAUT parameters have not been changed from the shipped value), which allows users and programmers to READ, ADD, UPDATE, and DELETE source code modules and run executable program modules.

Audit Objective

The Default Public Access to objects is set to *EXCLUDE. End users, programmers, and/or operators have not been granted authority access to production program libraries that is incompatible with their assigned job function.

Audit Procedures

- Are separate libraries used for development, test, and production?
- What procedures are followed for the transfer of finished programs into production?
- Who is authorized to add programs to the production libraries?
- How are programmers prevented from accessing production libraries?
- Are production libraries backed up on a regular basis?
- Are production objects assigned to a production ownership ID?

Determine that production program objects are maintained in a separate library(s). Request the DSPOBJAUT report for each production library. Evaluate the propriety of the profiles allowed access and the related level of access (e.g., READ, DELETE, ADD). With the client's assistance, identify the job functions of all individuals whose user or group profile appears in the list and determine whether access levels provide appropriate segregation of duties between programmers, operators, and users (e.g., programmers are allowed read-only access). Verify that the Public Authority (*PUBLIC) access parameter of each production library is *USE or preferably *EXCLUDE. These procedures should be performed at the object level using sampling techniques if access to libraries is not restricted.

AUTHORIZATION LISTS

Audit Objective

Authorization lists do not grant inappropriate access to sensitive objects.

Audit Procedures

- What policies and procedures are used for creating authorization lists?
- How are authorization lists determined?
- Are authorization lists reviewed on a periodic basis?

Obtain a list of authorization lists on the system and determine which lists secure sensitive objects. For these lists, obtain a listing of all user profiles and their access capabilities assigned to these lists and verify the appropriateness of the settings.

JOB DESCRIPTIONS

A job description represents a potential security risk. If a job description has a user profile name specified in the USER parameter field, other users on the system with access to the job description can submit jobs using the authority of the user profile specified in the USER parameter of the job description.

Audit Objective

By using job descriptions, users can not obtain an inappropriate level of access to data files and programs.

Audit Procedures

- Is the security level 30 or lower?
- Are job descriptions used to grant access to sensitive data?
- What procedures are followed to establish job descriptions?
- Are job descriptions reviewed on a regular basis?
- Are there job descriptions on the system with the user profile parameter set to a value other than *RQD?

For system running at security level 30 or lower, use the Display Object Authority (DSPOBJAUT) command and obtain a list of authorities to job descriptions for all job descriptions that have the user profile parameter set to a value other than *RQD.

ADOPT AUTHORITY

The AS/400 operating system allows a program to adopt the system authority of the owner of the program. This feature allows a user who has access to a program to execute the program with the same system authorities as the program's owner. For example, a user with *READ authority could run a program that adopts *ALL authority from the program owner. Therefore, the program adopt feature may allow users unauthorized access to objects.

Audit Objective

Using the Adopt Authority feature, users cannot obtain an inappropriate level of access to data files and programs.

Audit Procedures

- Is Adopt Authority used to grant access to sensitive data?
- What procedures are followed to authorize the use of Adopt Authority?
- Is the use of Adopt Authority reviewed on a regular basis?

Use the Display Programs that Adopt (DSPPGMADP) command to obtain a list of programs that adopt authority of the security officer and all profiles with *ALLOBJ authority. Review the objects authorized to the owner's user profile to determine if access is appropriate for all users using the adopted program.

AUTHORITY HOLDERS

Because access authorities to objects in AS/400 systems are normally removed when the object is deleted, Authority Holders were designed to avoid having to redefine access authorities when objects are deleted and re-created.

Audit Objective

Users cannot create Authority Holders for (temporarily) nonexistent files and use this capability to grant themselves access they should not have.

Audit Procedures

- Who is authorized to create Authority Holders?
- Are unused Authority Holders removed in a timely manner?
- Are access rights for Authority Holders set as low as practical?

Use the Display Authority Holders (DSPAUTHLR) command to list all Authority Holders. If the AS/400 does not currently operate in System/36 mode and Authority Holders are found, determine their purpose.

Review the Public Authority access parameter to the Create Authority Holders (CRTAUTHLR) command to verify that Public Authority access is still *EXCLUDE.

OBJECT OWNERSHIP

User profiles have *ALL Authority to objects they create unless this authority is revoked by the security officer or subsequent owner, if ownership is transferred. In certain situations, authorizations allowed to current or previous owners should be revoked. For example, a programmer creates a program and, therefore, is the owner. When the program is reviewed and transferred into the production library, ownership should be transferred to a production owner, and all accesses except *READ should be revoked for the programmer.

Audit Objective

Programmers do not have *ALL Authority to production programs through ownership.

Audit Procedures

- When programs are transferred into production, is the ownership also transferred to a production profile?

- Are objects owned at the user level or the group level?
- What procedures are followed when ownership is transferred?
- Who assumes ownership of owned objects when an owner/user profile is deleted?

Identify procedures performed by installation personnel to ensure that current or prior ownership of an object does not compromise installation security policies. Evaluate the adequacy of these procedures by reviewing user profiles, including objects owned by programmers and other designated users.

HIGH-RISK UTILITIES

Audit Objective

Access to sensitive utility programs (e.g., DFU, SEU, SDA), which can be used to alter data and/or programs and compilers, is appropriately restricted.

Audit Procedures

- What users have access to sensitive utilities?
- Is the use of sensitive utilities logged and followed up?
- Are all DFU programs required to produce audit trails?

Obtain the Display Object Authority for the Data File Utility (DFU) program and other sensitive utilities on the system. If access is controlled at the library level, obtain the Display Object Authority for the library containing the DFU program or sensitive utility. Determine whether the Public Authority (PUBAUT) access parameter is *EXCLUDE and if individual authorities listed are appropriate. If access to utilities is allowed, verify that users have a maximum of READ only to data files.

Review documentation of review procedures performed by installation personnel who monitor use of these programs and evaluate the propriety of these procedures.

INITIAL PROGRAM

If Initial Programs are not assigned to user profiles or are not properly restrictive, users may have access to sensitive system commands or other objects not otherwise restricted.

Audit Objective

Users do not have access to the operating system command line.

Audit Procedures

- Which users are able to access the command line?
- Which users have limited capability set to *NO or *PARTIAL?
- Are the commands listed on user menus appropriate for their job functions?
- Which commands can limit the capability (*YES) users execute?

With the client's assistance, use the Display User Profile (DSPUSRPRF) command and determine that user profiles have been assigned an Initial Program. Based on installation size, this procedure may be performed on a sample of user profiles.

Evaluate the propriety of the Initial Program assigned based on the individual user's job function. Review the Initial Program assigned, usually a menu, to determine whether options allowing the user to access programs or data files conflict with the installation's segregation of duties conventions.

Review the limited capabilities parameter and verify that it has a setting of *YES. If users have been granted the use of additional commands, verify that the commands grant appropriate capabilities.

PC SUPPORT

PC Support is the utility program that allows users to use a microcomputer instead of a "normal" workstation to access an AS/400. For PC Support to perform functions, such as the transferring of a data file, PC Support ignores menu security.

Audit Objectives

- PC Support users do not store their AS/400 password in a PC file that can easily be compromised.
- The installation has secured production programs and data files using authorization lists or Specific Authorities.
- AS/400 files are secured in the PC environment.
- Users are not able to bypass security by using the submit remote command (SBMRMTCMD).

PC Support users are not able to freely download and upload data files.

Audit Procedures

- Is PC Support used to transfer files?
- Who has access to PC Support?
- Is secured data stored on the PC?
- Is data uploaded to the AS/400?
- What data is downloaded?

Select a sample of microcomputers that are connected to the AS/400 using PC Support and determine that passwords are not stored on the PC.

With the client's assistance, determine the names of the production program libraries and production data files. Use the Display Object Authority (DSPOBJAUT) command to determine whether these resources are appropriately secured from unauthorized use.

Verify that the value of QAUTOVRT and QAUTOCFG is set to 0.

Determine that the Public Authority to the SBMRMTCMD command or the library in which it resides has been set to *EXCLUDE.

Verify that procedures in place to protect sensitive AS/400 data files that have been transferred to the PC are appropriate. Determine the appropriateness of the procedures that are in place to control/limit the uploading of data from the PC to the AS/400.

OUTPUT QUEUES

Audit Objective

Users do not have access to sensitive and confidential data while it is held in output queues.

Audit Procedures

- Is sensitive or confidential information in spooled files on the system?
- Have users been assigned *SPLCTL special authority that gives them access to all information contained in output queues?
- Are the contents of output queues restricted to authorized users?

Ascertain which output queues on the system are used to print sensitive and confidential information. With assistance from the client, review the following output queue parameters:

- Display Data Parameter (DSPDTA)
- Authority to Check Parameter (AUTCHK)
- Operator Control Parameter (OPRCTL)

Ensure that the parameter settings are appropriate to achieve the desired level of security over output queues that hold spooled files containing sensitive and confidential information.

SENSITIVE COMMANDS

Audit Objective

Users do not have access to sensitive system commands.

Audit Procedures

Review the authorities over the following sensitive commands, using the DSPOBJAUT command to ensure that such commands are appropriate:

Command	*Description*
ADDAUTLE	Add Authorization List Entry
ADDDIRE	Add PC-Support User to Distribution Directory
ADDREXBUF	Add REXX Buffer
CHGAUTLE	Change Authorization List Entry
CHGDSTPWD	Change Dedicated Service Tools Password
CHGDTA	Change Database File (using DFU)
CHGNETA	Change Network Attributes
CHGOBJOWN	Change Object Ownership
CHGSYSLIBL	Change System Library List
CHGSYSVAL	Change System Value
CHGUSRPRF	Change User Profile
CLRLFM	Clear Logical File Member
CLRLIB	Clear Library
CLROUTQ	Clear Output Queue
CLRPFM	Clear Physical File Member
CRTAUTHLR	Create Authority Holder
CRTAUTL	Create Authorization List

CRTCBLPGM	Create Cobol Program
CRTCLPGM	Create Control Language Program
CRTLIB	Create Library
CRTOUTQ	Create Output Queue
CRTRPGPGM	Create RPG/400 Program
CRTRPTPGM	Create S/36 Auto Report Program
CRTS36RPG	CRTS36RPGR
CRTSRCPF	Create Source Physical File
DLTAUTHLR	Delete Authority Holder
DLTAUTL	Delete Authorization List
DLTLIB	Delete Library
DLTLICPGM	Delete Licensed Program

BACKUP AND RECOVERY

Audit Objective

Backup procedures for critical/vital information and materials and covering on-site and off-site storage are in place and effectively managed.

Audit Procedures

Are there policies and procedures for backup and off-site storage of program and data files? Perform the following audit procedures:

1. Review backup procedures to check that they are adequate.
2. Determine that all libraries including test libraries are backed up periodically before and after a change.
3. Verify procedures to compare backup tape contents to library listings to ensure that everything is backed up. If saving libraries, verify that all libraries are being saved.
   - Review a sample of libraries to ensure that all objects within each library are saved.
   - Review the report of items not backed up in more than 30 days and items never backed up. **Note:** Performing a SAVSYS does not update the "last saved date" field on the object.
4. As a general rule, the installation should be using the following commands or performing the procedures listed:
   - SAVSYS: Saves the operating system software.
   - SAVLIB: Saves all nonsystem libraries.
   - SAVCHGOBJ: Saves all changed objects from the last SAVLIB date (or date specified).
   - SAVDLO: Saves office documents and PC support (QDOC library).
   - SAVSECDTA: Saves user profiles and access restrictions.
5. Verify that saves are done on a reasonable basis and that the job log is checked to ensure backup is completed successfully. With SAVSECDTA, a SAVSYS now has to

be done only after PTFs are applied since SAVSECDTA saves all the security information done by a SAVSYS. A SAVSYS is normally time consuming, uses substantial resources, and requires a dedicated environment. The following commands should be performed as noted:

- SAVSYS: After changes are made to the operating system.
- SAVLIB: At least weekly, can do 20% of libraries per day. Also has a feature for SAVNONSYS, which saves all nonsystem libraries up to fifty libraries.
- SAVCHGOBJ: Daily.
- SAVDLO: Weekly, depending on volume of AS/400 office users.
- SAVSECDTA: Weekly, to capture all profile and access changes.
- QDOC cannot be saved via SAVLIB or SAVSYS (last saved date will appear empty). Only the SAVDLO command will save the objects within QDOC.

IBM developed a "Save While Active" option that does not force the users out of the application while the save is being performed. The user in the application will be frozen until the save is completed.

Note: The following libraries will not be saved via SAVLIB, so the last saved date field will not be current: QSYS, QSRV, QTEMP, QSPL, QDOC(SAVDLO), QRPLOBJ, QRECOVERY.

6. At least a whole system backup copy should be retained off-site. Review the location's backup scheme.
7. Review backup retention period for adequacy.
8. A listing of the backup tapes should be retained showing what is on each tape and where (e.g., copy of tape index or log or copy of backup schedule). Verify that the content of each tape is easily determined.
9. Verify that journaling (commitment control—program technique) is used for individual applications with high transactions that may be hard to re-create if a loss of data occurred between backups.
10. Verify that off-line backup media are protected from damage and theft. AS/400 security no longer applies to a backup medium to indicate that information can be restored/read on another AS/400.
11. Review the SAVE and RESTORE procedures. Ensure that they have been tested if they have not already been used. Set up test environments to do so.

AUDIT TESTS

System Controls

The Access Control Facility for the AS/400 is integrated into the AS/400 architecture rather than being a product run on top of the operating system (OS/400) like Resource Access Control Facility (RACF).

OBJECTIVE

Verify that only authorized individuals either have or can add, change, or remove user IDs from the system. **Note:** This capability requires the commands CRTUSRPRF (to add users), CHGUSRPRF (to change a user profile), and DLTUSRPRF (to delete users). These commands may be used by the security officer (QSECOFR) or someone with the *SECADM special authority unless access to the commands has been additionally restricted. Authorization to privileged user IDs must be accountable to individuals (i.e., if a Group Profile is permitted, each individual in the Group Profile must be authorized). If a program, especially one running with adopted authority, is used to perform this function, ensure that only authorized individuals can run the program. Programs running with adopted authority always run under the program owner's user profile.

This test should be done concurrently with the Privileged user ID Authorization Test discussed later. The focus of this test is to verify that those individuals actually performing systems administrative tasks have the responsibility to ensure that appropriate management awareness and authorization for the business need exist.

Approach

List all users with the *SECADM privilege. Compare this list with the users authorized to the user profile commands to determine who can add and delete users. The list of privileged users can be obtained using the DSPAUTUSR command. The command authorizations can be obtained using the DSPOBJAUT. If an authorization list is used, the DSPAUTL command will list the individuals on the authorization list. Program ownership and authorization can be displayed using the *DSPPGM command. The specification of the USRPRF(*OWNER) indicates that the program runs with adopted authority.

Audit trails on the AS/400 are limited. The journal can contain information on changes and deletes to user profile. The site may have also implemented additional audit trails for user profile maintenance that should be reviewed. The journal can be reviewed using the DSPJRL command.

How Users Are Identified

For all users of an AS/400, there is a user profile. This profile may contain the following types of information:

- Name (user ID)
- Employee Name or Serial Number
- Password
- User Class controls menu options
- Special Authority includes system resource privileges
- Group Profile whose authority may be used for a job
- Limited Capability (LMTCPB) may limit the user to the functions of the Initial Menu and/or Initial Program
- Initial Program specifies the program to call when the user signs on
- Initial Menu specifies the menu to be shown when the user signs on

For user identification, the areas of concern include how a user ID is added to the system, and how each user ID is then verified (i.e., how does the operating system determine that the user ID is being accessed by the "correct" individual).

USER VERIFICATION

Objective

Ensure that password integrity is effective.

Approach

This is tested two ways:

1. Review the password rules as specified in the system values.
2. Test the rules using a user ID on the system.

Review the system values for the system being tested. If the password syntax rules are not specified in the system values, they may be controlled via the password validation program that is specified in the QPWDVLDPGM value. In this event, all testing must be done using your user ID.

To test for the password interval on privileged user IDs, list the user profiles from the list of privileged user IDs and check the PWDEXPITV parameter.

Using your user ID, try to successfully generate trivial passwords or passwords that do not comply with the requirements of password syntax rules.

Objective

Ensure that there is appropriate control for the use of "shared user IDs." **Note:** There is no software capability, such as found in Resource Control Access Facility (RACF), for managing shared user IDs on an AS/400 system. Shared user IDs should not be allowed without documented procedural controls.

Approach

Obtain the procedures for managing shared user IDs. Procedures should include identification of the user ID and the individuals who have been authorized to the user ID(s). Obtain manual log of user ID assignment (this should include date, time, individual, and, perhaps, purpose). This could be verified against the journal that would show date and time stamp of the changes to a user profile.

Objective

Ensure that all objects on the system have a responsible owner.

Approach

Select a random sample of objects on the system being audited that are not owned by the default owner (QDFTOWN). The object types *FILE, *USRPRF, *PGM, and *LIB are of particular importance. If the system is an office system, the auditor may wish to include document libraries (*DLO) in the sample. Determine if ownership can be attributed to an individual. Review the objects owned by QDFTOWN.

1. Determine if the number of objects owned by QDFTOWN is reasonable.

2. Determine if procedures for finding valid owners for all objects owned by QDFTOWN are adequate.

Note: Object ownership can be viewed using the DSPOBJAUT command.

How Resources Are Identified

All resources on the AS/400 are called objects. The system maintains the following types of information on all objects:

- Owner (a user or group)
- Public Authority (*PUBLIC)
- Specific Authority (individual users or groups)
- Authorization List
- Object Type (file, user profile, program, library, and so on)

This information identifies the object owner; any individuals authorized to access publicly, specifically, or through an authorization list; and the type of object.

Sound security policy requires that all resources be protected from general access unless explicitly required, with formal documentation of the business justification for all exceptions (e.g., system broadcast functions). This implementation relieves not only owners from the requirement to identify the highest classification level of their resources, but also the supplier of service organization from the requirement to "scan" for exposed confidential data.

Objects on an AS/400 cannot exist without an owner. For example, a user profile cannot be deleted until all objects owned by that user are deleted or assigned to another owner. Circumstances may arise in which the system cannot determine an object owner. In that instance, the system assigns ownership to the default owner (QDFTOWN). Objects may be owned by a user or group profile.

Objective

Verify that the access method is effective.

Approach

1. Review the system values, system exits used, and group structure for potential exposures.
2. List the authorizations for a sample of objects.
3. Review the *PUBLIC group, user, and authorization list implementation.

Note: Also ensure that appropriate control mechanisms (e.g., Systems Network Architecture [SNA] Remote Location Configuration List and SNA Distribution Services [SNADS] System Distribution Directory) are used for controlling access from the host systems to the corporate backbone network.

If applicable, obtain from management a registration list of exceptions and determine if the business case seems reasonable. Follow up with control assessment interviews of data owners. Review the object access authorizations for the exceptions and critical system resources.

Note: Object authorizations can be displayed using the DSPOBJAUT command. Authorization lists can be displayed using the DSPAUTL command. System values can be displayed using the WRKSYSVAL command.

How Users Are Mapped to Resources

AS/400 security provides hierarchical methods of controlling access to or exclusion from an object. Access is controlled through *PUBLIC specific or list authorization. Specific authorization is a group or user specified on the objects authorization. List authorization is a group or user on the authorization list specified for an object.

Refer to the organization standard for the minimum requirements for system values, network attributes, and rules for user access to data and resources. Review the exception list to ensure conformance with the standard.

Users can only be in one group. Users may be on multiple authorization lists. Members of groups all have the same authority. Users on an authorization list can have different authorities. Multiple group profiles can have access to an object. An object can have a single authorization list. Groups cannot have other groups as a member.

There are eight basic authorities: *OBJOPR, *OBJMGT, *OBJEXIST, *AUTLMGT, *READ, *ADD, *UPDATE, and *DELETE. Some common combinations of the basic authorities have been given separate names. They are as follows:

- *ALL: Allows unlimited access to the object and its data.
- *CHANGE: Allows unlimited access to the data in the object.
- *USE: Allows data in the object to be read.
- *EXCLUDE: Allows no access to the object or its data.

The authorization search order is as follows:

- User has *ALLOBJ
- User has specific authority for the object (basic authorization)
- User is on the authorization list associated with the object
- The user's group has *ALLOBJ
- The user's group has specific authority for the object (basic authorization)
- The user's group is on the authorization list associated with the object
- *PUBLIC authority for the object
- *PUBLIC authority for the authorization list associated with the object

Note: The first authorization entry found, matching the user and object, is taken. There may be other matches of higher or lower authority, but they are not used.

AUDIT TRAILS

Objective

Ensure that adequate audit trails are generated and audit trail histories are maintained to provide management and/or legal with sufficient documentation for security incident follow-up and resolution. The requirement for a documentation retention period should be documented in the Information Management Plan (IMP).

Approach

Review the latest IMP and ensure that the record retention of history logs and audit journals is in compliance. Corporate standards should dictate minimum audit parameter specifications for QAUDLVL.

What Audit Trails Are Provided

Audit trails are maintained in the history log and journal files. The system value QAUDLVL controls which security-related events are logged to the security-auditing journal. Any user cannot alter a journal entry. *The use of journals is related more to the application design than overall system security.*

Since the use of journals is related more to application design than overall system security, the auditor needs to understand the site's implementation. For example, a program can be written to journal all the activity of the security officer. You can request that the system audit save and restore information, authorization failures, deleted objects, or security-related functions.

PRIVILEGED USERID AUTHORIZATION

Objective

Ensure that a valid business need for privileged users of AS/400s exists and is current. The system security owner should be the authorizer of privileges.

It is important to note the distinction between "security administrative authority," other AS/400 privileges, and those user IDs with access to components of the access control system:

- Security administrative authority is the privilege that is generally used in the performance of adding, deleting, and altering user IDs on a system, (e.g., *QSECADM). Even if the individual owning a user ID or service machine with *QSECADM does not have the job responsibility of "system administration," they are still considered to have this privilege and must comply with the requirements for its authorization.
- Other AS/400 attributes, as described previously, can often be considered as the requirements of system support departments.
- Access to components of the AS/400 access control system is not considered "privileged" in the explicit sense of the term. However, by the potential ability to circumvent the access control system itself, user IDs with access to these components should be considered in performing this test. User IDs in this category would generally belong to the AS/400 system support departments.

Approach

1. Review the management authorization for each privileged user or group and supplement with follow-up control assessment interview(s) with the system security owner as necessary.
2. Review written justifications for long-term (more than two weeks) and short-term (less than two weeks) use. Long-term assignment must be revalidated every twelve months; emergency or short-term assignment must have the approval of the IS manager or a designee.

3. Review the management authorization and business rationale for programs running with adopted authority. Particular attention should be given to programs owned by privileged users.
4. If there is an emergency user ID with privilege(s), review the management authorization process for giving an individual the password.

The list of privileged users can be obtained using the DSPAUTUSR command. If an authorization list is used, the DSPAUTL command will list the individuals on the authorization list. Program ownership and authorization can be displayed using the *DSPPGM command. The specification of USRPRF(*OWNER) indicates the program runs with adopted authority.

How Privileged Users Are Identified and Managed

AS/400 has special authorities and user classes that provide privileges. The six special authorities are not hierarchical. The five user classes are hierarchical. The user class affects what options are shown on the system menus and is a convenient way to assign special authorities to different types of users. These privileges may be assigned directly to the user or to a group.

Special Authorities

- *ALLOBJ: Access to all system resources.
- *SECADM: Create, change, and delete profiles and add directory entries.
- *SERVICE: Access to display and alter service functions.
- *SAVSYS: Access to save/restore operations for system resources.
- *JOBCTL: Control output, job queues, and other users' jobs.
- *SPLCTL: Control spool functions of other users' files.

User Classes (Listed in Hierarchical Order)

- *SECOFR—Security officer
- *SECADM—Security administrator
- *PGMR—Programmer
- *SYSOPR—System operator
- *USER—End user

In addition, any user ID, service machine, or job with explicit access to any of the AS/400 critical resources, whether or not it has security administrator or officer privileges, should also be considered for review in this test.

Programs can be implemented to run with adopted authority. Programs running with adopted authority always run under the authority of the program owner. The adopted authority would include any privileges or authorizations the program owner has. Although attention should be given to programs owned by privileged users, authorized accesses used by these programs may be critical to system resources.

The accelerating pace of technological change is forcing industry to rethink many long-standing rules about organization, strategic partnerships, and relationships with suppliers and customers. The change is exhilarating, but it is also sobering. Only the fittest companies will survive, and even then, only by restructuring the basic building blocks of their business. The laurels will go to those companies with courage, will, and strength to adapt themselves to the changed industry landscape.

SUMMARY

Successful audits of Information Technology (IT) infrastructure are intended to provide an analysis of the physical environment of computing and network hardware components with potential risks and recommendations. If the hardware comprising an IT infrastructure is not secure, neither is the company's data.

The objective of the audits should be to determine whether the infrastructure necessary to successfully manage the AS/400-based computing environment including responsibility for all services related to the physical data center (power, cabling, security, tape mounts, and so on), the operations management, and the network management is at a level that guarantees optimum uptime of the business applications.

If the audit is done well, all components of the environment will be assessed to ensure that they conform to the organization's standards and are stable enough to be included in the infrastructure. The audit will specify standards in the IT environment and establish a computing environment on a predictable stable platform that dramatically reduces the problems and increases the availability of the systems to the users. Those components found to be lacking will be brought into conformance by this exercise, which should implement the target environment with all of its policies, processes, and systems.

These audits may show risks to data security from unauthorized users, poor file security, lapsed passwords, and so on. They may show whether procedures are defined and implemented that ensure that the environment is not changed without appropriate control and whether it is managed and controlled through standardized methods and procedures. Audits also ensure that the integrity of the computing environment is maintained by adequately assessing the impact of any change and testing the proposed change against the full environment. Even a simple, reliable solution carefully implemented will add business value for the organization.

Exhibit 4.1 Sample AS/400 Reports

The following is a list of reports that have audit significance. They can be printed and used to audit the AS/400 platform:

- The System Values Report
- All Libraries On The System
- Library Save And Restore Information
- A Specified Library Description
- All The Objects In A Specified Library
- The Library List For The User Signed On
- The Basic Information From An Object's Description
- The Full Information From An Object's Description
- Service Information From An Object's Description
- Users Authorized To A Specified Object
- All Authorization Lists On The System
- Objects Secured By An Authorization List
- Access Granted By An Authorization List
- Basic Information For A User Profile
- Display All Parameters For All User Profiles
- Authorized Users In User Profile Sequence
- Authorized Users In Group Profile Sequence
- All Job Descriptions On The System
- Contents Of A Job Description
- All Devices On The System
- Program Information
- Programs That Adopt The Owner's Authority
- Authority Holders
- Date Of Last Change For All Programs In A Library
- System Statistics
- Disk Statistics
- Active Job Statistics
- Network Attributes
- Command Information
- Local Hardware
- IBM Software Resources List

APPENDIX 4A AUDIT PROGRAM

4A.1 ENVIRONMENT

This section is related to general environment information. Obtain from IT management the most recently updated strategic planning documentation.

AS/400 INSTALLED

1.1 Note business applications run.

1.2 Are these applications in-house developments or third-party packages?

1.3 Document the structure of the IT department. Is there a clear division of responsibilities between development and operations functions?

1.4 Ascertain who has custody of the QSECOFR password. Arrange for all system enquiries in the work plan to be made with QSECOFR profile.

Note: Enquiries on object authorities will have to be made with QSECOFR profile since any other profile will not have sufficient privilege.

4A.2 SYSTEM VALUES

(ACCESS SECURITY)

System values enable IT to set up the AS/400 to meet specific requirements. However, security can be compromised if inappropriate options are selected or changed. In order to display the setting of a system value, enter the command:

DSPSYSVAL SYSVAL **(SYSTEM VALUE)**

2.1 Determine the installation security level:
QSECURITY
10: No security
20: Password (sign-on) security only

30: Password and resource security
40: Same as level 30 but controls privileged instructions and the machine interface
50: Same as level 40 but with additional integrity checking
Security level 30 must be implemented, and level 40 or level 50 should be considered for clients with high inherent risk.

Note: Although QSECURITY can be dynamically changed, it requires an IPL to become effective.

2.2 Determine the maximum number of sign-on attempts allowed to users:
QMAXSIGN
If the QMAXSIGN value is reached, the workstation device is varied off, and a message is sent to the QSYSMSG message queue if it exists; otherwise, it is sent to QSYSOPR.
NOMAX: The system allows an unlimited number of attempts.
15: IBM default value
The following value is recommended: 3 maximum attempts.
Note: QMAXSIGN is not effective for users accessing the system via Display Station Pass through (DPST). (See subsection 8.5.8).

2.3 Determine the action taken by the system when QMAXSIGN is exceeded as a result of repeated failures to sign on.
QMAXSGNACN
1: Disable device.
2: Disable the user profile.
3: Disable the user profile and the device.
3: Disabling the user profile and the device is recommended.

2.4 Determine the system values governing controls over passwords:

2.4.1 Change frequency:
QPWDEXPITV
*NOMAX: The system allows an unlimited number of days.
1–366: A value from 1 to 366 can be specified.
The following value is recommended: 30.

2.4.2 Minimum and maximum length:
QPWDMINLEN
QPWDMAXLEN
Both values can be from 1 to 10. The following value is recommended: minimum 6 characters

2.4.3 Required number of different previous passwords:
QPWDRQDDIF
0: Password can be the same as previous ones.
1: Password must not be the same as the previous 32 passwords.
2: Password must not be the same as the previous 24 passwords.
3: Password must not be the same as the previous 18 passwords.
4: Password must not be the same as the previous 12 passwords.
5: Password must not be the same as the previous 10 passwords.
6: Password must not be the same as the previous 8 passwords.
7: Password must not be the same as the previous 6 passwords.
8: Password must not be the same as the previous 4 passwords.
The following value is recommended: 1.

2.4.4 List of up to 10 restricted characters:
QPWDLMTCHR
*NONE: There are no restricted characters.
Character string: A list of up to 10 characters that may not be used. Valid characters are A to Z, 0 to 9, and £, $, @, and __.

2.4.5 Limit repeated characters:
QPWDLMTREP
0: Characters can be repeated more than once.
1: Characters cannot be repeated.
2: Characters cannot be used consecutively
The following value is recommended: 2.

2.4.6 Limit adjacent characters:
QPWDLMTAJC
0: Numeric characters are allowed next to each other in passwords.
1: Numeric characters are not allowed next to each other in passwords.
The following value is recommended: 1.

2.4.7 One or more digits required:
QPWDRQDDGT
0: Digits are not required in new passwords.
1: One or more digits are required in new passwords.
Password validated by a special validation program:

2.4.8 QPWDVLDPGM
*NONE: No program is used.
Program-Name: Specify the name of the validation program.
Review any specified program and ensure that it does not allow some users to bypass password security and does not contain "hard-coded" passwords.

2.4.9 Enforcing different characters when passwords are changed:
QPWDPOSDIF
0: The same characters can be used in a position corresponding to the same position in the previous password.
1: The same character cannot be used in a position corresponding to the same position in the previous password.
Recommended if QRWDRQDDIF is found to be onerous.

2.5 Determine current settings for the time-out facility:

2.5.1 QINACTITV
*NONE: No time-out validation.
5–300: Specify the interval for time-out.
QINACTITV specifies how frequently the system will check for inactive jobs and how long a job is permitted to remain inactive when the permitted period has elapsed.
The following values are recommended: 30–60.
The subsystem will send a message to the message queue specified in QINACTMSGQ. A user or program monitoring the queue can then end the job if desired.

2.5.2 QINACTMSGQ

*DSCJOB: The job will be disconnected from any terminal and session processing will stop. The user must sign on and specify the correct password to restart the disconnected job.

Warning: The system cannot disconnect some jobs such as PC organizer and PC text-assist function (PCTA). If the system cannot disconnect an active job, it ends the job instead.

*ENDJOB: Will end any job, secondary job, and/or group job.

MSGQ/LIB: Specify a message queue name and library where the job inactive message can be sent.

Note: *ENDJOB is recommended. Under some circumstances this may not be practical (e.g., if some long-running task is in use, in which case consider *DSCJOB).

2.5.3 Determine the action that the system will take when a job has been disconnected for a given time.

QDSCJOBITV

*NONE: No action is taken.

240: The system ends a disconnected job after 240 minutes.

5–1440: Time interval is minutes after which disconnected jobs will be ended.

Disconnected jobs should be ended after about 15 to 30 minutes, although this will depend to a large extent on the application program environment. Any recommendations should be discussed in detail with management.

2.6 Determine if concurrent device sessions have been limited:

QLMTDEVSSN

0: A user profile can sign on at more than one terminal at once.

1: A user profile cannot sign on at more than one terminal at once.

The following value is recommended: 1.

2.7 Determine if the system value controlling the ability to limit access to workstations for profiles with *ALLOBJ or *SERVICE special authority is being used. Access will be allowed only if the user or QSECOFR profile has been given explicit authority to that workstation.

QLMTSECOFR

0: Users with *ALLOBJ or *SERVICE authority cannot sign on to any display station unless they are specifically authorized to the display station.

1: Users with *ALLOBJ or *SERVICE authority can sign on to any display station that has the public authority specified as *CHANGE.

The following value is recommended: 1.

2.8 Determine the default PUBLIC authority for objects created in a library:

QCRTAUT

*ALL

*CHANGE

*USE

*EXCLUDE

This system value takes effect if:

- The create authority (CRTAUT) for the library is set to *SYSVAL.
- The new object is created with public authority (AUT) if *LIBCRTAUT.

*EXCLUDE or *USE is recommended, but client management should exercise caution when implementing this change because all users usually need *CHANGE to certain objects (e.g., device descriptions, lines, and so on) for normal operation.

2.9 Determine the systemwide attention-key-handling program:
QATNPGM
*ASSIST
*NONE: No attention-key-handling program.
Programme: A user-written program that will handle the attention interrupt.

2.10 Determine the system value QALWOBJRST, which determines whether objects that are security-sensitive may be restored to your system.
QALWOBJRST
*ALL: Any object may be restored to your system by a user with a proper authority.
*NONE: Security-sensitive objects, such as system state programs or programs that may not be restored to the system.
*ALWSYSST: System state objects may be restored to the system.
*ALWPGMADP: Objects that adopt authority may be restored to the system.
*NONE is recommended; however, if the client regularly restores programs and applications then the value should be set to *ALWPGMADP.

4A.3 PROFILES

(ORGANIZATION, ACCESS SECURITY)

User and group profiles should be defined to reflect IT and user department organization, ensuring that appropriate segregation of duties is maintained. Profile attributes and special authorities should reflect users' business functions.

3.1 Display all authorized user and group profiles by entering the command:
DSPAUTUSR SEQ (*GRPPRF)
This will list all group profile names and user profile names within each group of users. It will also list at the bottom any user profile that is not part of a group.

3.2 Evaluate each group profile to ensure that it represents a common group of users with the same or similar business functions.
Where group profiles are used, ensure that the group profiles have a password of *NONE to prevent any unauthorized sign-on.

3.3 Check that the following IBM-supplied profiles have had their original passwords changed:

User Profile	*Original Password*
QSECOFR	QSECOFR
QSYSOPR	QSYSOPR
QPGMR	QPGMR
QUSER	QUSER

Note: With the release of OS/400 V3R1, only QSECOFR is supplied with a password of QSECOFR; all other profiles are now shipped with a value of *NONE.

3.4 Check that the passwords for the following IBM-supplied profiles have been changed, are stored securely, and are only used by authorized IBM engineers:

User Profile	*Original Password*
QSRVBAS	QSRVBAS
QSRV	QSRV

3.5 Check that the passwords for the DST utility have been changed or that the AS/400 key is held by the QSECOFR and that the key lock is in the "Normal" position.

DST Security	*Default*
Level	Password
Security	QSECOFR

(Comment: Performs all DST functions including changing the DST password.)

Full 22222222

(Comment: For service representative to perform all DST functions except password change.)

Basic 11111111

(Comment: For service representative or operator to use functions that do not access sensitive data.)

Note: DST is accessible via the system console during manual IPL and can be used to reset QSECOFR's password to QSECOFR. To use DST, the key lock must be in the "Manual" position.

3.6 Obtain a full listing of user and group profiles:

DSPUSRPRF USRPRF (profile name) TYPE (*BASIC)

For each profile review the following parameters:

3.6.1 GROUP (Group Profile)

Ensure that users are members of appropriate groups related to their business functions.

3.6.2 PWDEXPITV (Password Expiration Interval)

A numeric value means that a specific interval has been set for this user. *SYSVAL means the value is the system default specified in QPWDEXPITV.

3.6.3 SPCAUT (Special Authorities)

*USRCLS

*NONE

*SECADM

*ALLOBJ

*AUDIT

*SAVSYS

*SERVICE

*SPLCTL

*JOBCTL

*IOSYSCFG

See the Technical Guidance notes for guidelines concerning which special authorities should be allocated to which user class.

Generally, production users and developers should not have any special authorities; operators may have *SAVSYS and *JOBCTL. Security officers may have all privileges and IBM engineers *SERVICE. The security administrator should have *ALLOBJ and *SECADM but not *AUDIT.

3.6.4 OWNER Specifies which user profile is the owner of objects created by this user profile.

*USRPRF: The user profile used with the job is made the owner of the object.

*GRPPRF: The group profile is made the owner of newly created objects and is given *ALL authority to the object.

3.6.5 GRPAUT (Group Authority)

*NONE: No authority is given to the group profile when this user creates the object.

*ALL: The user can control the object's existence, specify the security for the object, and change the object.

*CHANGE: The user can add, change, and delete entries in the object or read the contents of an entry in the object.

*USE: The user can run a program or display the contents of a file.

*EXCLUDE: Exclude authority prevents the user from using the object or its contents.

3.6.6 CURLIB (Current Library)

Specifies the name of the user's current library. It should reflect the user's need to perform normal functions. Make a note of this library and check that it is properly secured. (See section 4A.4.)

3.6.7 INLPGM (Initial Program)

Specifies the default initial program for this user when he signs on.

*NONE: No program is called when the user signs on. If a menu name is specified on the initial menu parameter of the user profile then that menu is displayed.

Program-Name: Specify the name of the program that is called when the user signs on.

3.6.8 LMTCPB (Limited Capability)

Specifies whether the user can change the initial program, the initial menu, the current library, and the attention-key-handling program values.

Production users should be locked into application programs or menus at sign-on that do not allow OS/400 command entry. This is done using the limited capability parameter.

Note: If the value is MAIN then the user has menu access to the command line.

*NO: The user can change all the values in the user profile with the CHGPRF command.

*PARTIAL: The initial program and current library values cannot be changed on the sign on display. The initial menu value can be changed and commands can be run from the command line of a menu. A user can change the initial menu value with CHGPRF. The initial program, current library, and the attention-key-handling program values cannot be changed using CHGPRF.

*YES: The initial program, initial menu, and current library values cannot be changed on the sign on display. Some commands can be run from the command line of a menu. The commands allowed are SIGNOFF, SNDMSG,

DSPMSG, DSPJOB, and DSPJOBLOG. The user cannot change the initial program, initial menu, current library, or the attention-key-handling program values using CHGPRF.

Note: Commands can, however, be modified so that they can be executed by a user with LMTCPB (*YES). This is controlled by the ALWLMTUSR parameter, which can be obtained by using the DSPCMD command to display the attributes of a command.

*YES is recommended for production users.

3.6.9 INLMNU (Initial Menu)

The initial menu is shown when the initial program has finished. If INLMNU = *SIGNOFF, the user will be signed off the system when the initial program ends.

*LOGOUT will prevent a user from dropping out to the operating system when a program aborts. Ensure that users have menus and menu options that correspond to their business functions.

3.6.10 LMTDEVSSN (Limit Device Sessions)

*SYSVAL: The system value QLMTDEVSSN is used to determine if the user is limited to one device session.

*NO: The user is not limited to one device session.

*YES: The user is limited to one device session.

The following value is recommended: *YES or *SYSVAL and QLMTDEVSSN = *YES.

Note: *NO is sometimes used to allow multiple sessions on a single terminal.

3.6.11 ATNPGM (attention-Key-Handling Program)

Specifies the attention-key-handling program for this user. If *YES or *PARTIAL is specified on the limited capability parameter, the attention-key-handling program value cannot be changed with CHGPRF.

*NONE: No attention-key-handling program is used by this user.

*SYSVAL: The attention-key-handling program indicated by the system value QATNPGM will be used.

*ASSIST: Program QEZMAIN will be used.

Program-Name: Specify the name of the program that is used by this user.

Review any specified program for adequacy and ensure that it does not give authority to unexpected functions.

3.6.12 STATUS (State of user Profile)

Specifies if the user profile can be used or not.

*ENABLE: User profile can be used.

*DISABLE: User profile cannot be used.

User profiles that are not currently in use should be set to *DISABLE. **Note:** The system profiles QSYS and so on must be set to ENABLE.

4A.4 LIBRARIES

(ACCESS SECURITY, PROGRAM CHANGE)

Appropriate access authority should be defined at the library level to ensure that production data files and programs are protected from unauthorized access and change.

4.1 List all libraries on the system:

DSPOBJD OBJ(QSYS/*ALL) OBJTYPE(*LIB)

Ascertain the use of each library and ensure that production objects (principally files and programs) are in separate libraries from development objects. If there are many production applications, each application should have its own set of libraries.

4.2 Display the contents of a sample of production file and/or program libraries:
DSPLIB (Library Name)
Ensure that only production files or programs are listed.

4.3 Display the object authority for critical production and development libraries:
DSPOBJAUT OBJ(QSYS/library name) OBJTYPE(*LIB)
Ensure that only authorized production users and/or groups have change access and development users have no access. Also check that the owner of the library is an appropriate production user or the security officer.

4.4 The library list specifies the libraries that will be searched when the system attempts to find a program for which a library name has not been explicitly stated. The system search starts at the first entry of the system portion of the library list and then proceeds to the last entry in the user portion. The system loads the first program it finds with the correct name.
Determine the contents of the system portion of the library list:
DSPSYSVAL (QSYSLIBL)
The system library value QSYSLIBL determines the initial settings of the system portion of the library list. This can only be changed with a user with all object (*ALLOBJ) and security administrator (*SECADM) special authorities using the CHGSYSLIBL command.
Determine the libraries specified in the user portion of the library list for a sample of production users.
DSPSYSVAL (QUSRLIBL)
Note: You will need access to the production users to run the command.
You should ensure that only libraries that are specifically controlled are placed on these lists. PUBLIC should not be allowed to add objects to these libraries.

4.5 Review library lists for production users and ensure that only production libraries are listed.

4.6 Evaluate release and change control procedures from the implementation of new or amended production programs or files from development to production libraries.

4A.5 OTHER OBJECTS

(ACCESS SECURITY, PROGRAM CHANGE)

Programs can be compiled to adopt the authority of a production or other privileged users when they are run. Such programs could compromise security by adopting inappropriate authority. Object authorities to data files and programs should be restricted to authorized users. Unrestricted access to these could compromise the integrity of production systems.

PROGRAMS THAT ADOPT AUTHORITY

5.1 Use the DSPPGMADP command to review any programs that adopt the author ity of any production or other privileged user:
DSPPGMADP USRPRF (Profile Name)

5.2 Arrange for DSPPGMADP (QSECOFR) to be run overnight or during a period of low system activity (it may take a long time to run). This will list any programs adopting the security officer's authority. Review reasons for any programs listed.

Ensure that the security officer has a record of such programs and evaluates any new ones before they are made live. Look for programs that allow the user to change object ownership or give access to the command line. Such programs often have obvious names such as QCMD, QCL, CHGOWN, and so on.

AUTHORIZATION LISTS

5.3 To check if any production objects (files, programs, output queues) are protected via authorization lists, run the following to output all authorization lists:

DSPOBJD OBJ (QSYS/*ALL) OBJTYPE (*AUTL)

5.4 Display and review users and production objects to which authorization is obtained via an authorization list:

DSPAUTL (Name of List)

Ensure that only appropriate authorized users have access to production objects.

OBJECT LEVEL SECURITY

5.5 If library level protection is not used, or if the client is of high inherent risk, review the specific object authorities for selected production files and programs using:

DSPOBJAUT OBJ (name of library/name of file) OBJTYPE (*FILE)

and DSPOBJAUT OBJ (name of library/name of program) OBJTYPE (*PGM)

Ensure that only authorized user and group profiles have access to the selected production objects.

Note: Library level security is strongly recommended since it provides a maintainable and relatively easy method of securing most objects.

5.6 With the release of OS/400 V3R1, a new command is available to check for objects that have been altered.

An altered object is usually an indication that someone is attempting to tamper with the system. You may want to run this command after:

- Restoring programs to your system.
- Using DST (Dedicated Service Tools).

Command: CHKOBJITG

Note: CHOKOBJITG requires *AUDIT special authority. Run this command when the system is not busy.

5.7 Review client administration and authorization procedure for granting access to critical system and production objects. Ensure that changes are authorized by object owners.

4A.6 UTILITIES

(ACCESS SECURITY, PROGRAM CHANGE)

The AS/400 is shipped with a number of utilities and commands including:

- SST (System Service Tools)
- DST (Dedicated Service Tools)

- DFU (Data File Utility)
- SEU (Source Entry Utility)
- SDA (Screen Design Aid)
- PDM (Programming Development Manager)
- QUERY

These utilities and commands are available to anyone with access to the command line but are *not* a security risk if resource level security is adequately implemented except SST and DST. Authority to these utilities is controlled via *SERVICE special authority and a password, respectively.

6.1 Determine which users have access to the CHGDSTPWD command using:
DSPOBJAUT OBJ (QSYS/CHGDSTPWD) OBJTYPE (*CMD)
Only the security officer should be allowed to use this command.

6.2 Determine which users have access to the utilities by entering:
DSPOBJAUT OBJ(QSYS/STRDFU) OBJTYPE(*CMD)
DSPOBJAUT OBJ(QSYS/STRSEU) OBJTYPE(*CMD)
DSPOBJAUT OBJ(QSYS/STRSDA) OBJTYPE(*CMD)
DSPOBJAUT OBJ(QSYS/STRPDM) OBJTYPE(*CMD)
Only authorized programmers should have access to these utilities. Public access should be set to *EXCLUDE.

6.3 Determine which users have access to the QUERY facility using:
DSPOBJAUT OBJ(QSYS/STRQRY) OBJTYPE(*CMD)
Only authorized users who have had adequate training should be allowed access to QUERY. Access to the query definitions should be prevented.

COMMANDS

6.4 Review object authority to all security-related commands using:
DSPOBJAUT OBJ (QSYS/command) OBJTYPE (*CMD)

The key commands are:

ADDCFGLE	STRSST
CHGCFGL	WRKOBJ
CRTUSRPRF#2	CRTAUTHLR
CHGUSRPRF#2	DLTAUTHLR#5
DLTUSRPRF#2	SAVSYS#6
CHGDSTPWD#1	CHGSYSLIBL
RSTUSRPRF#3	CHGSYSVAL
RSTAUT#3	PWRDWNSYS#7
STRSST#4	

Ensure that only the security officer and authorized administrators have use of these commands. One or more special authorities are usually required to execute the preceding commands.

These commands can be used by any user and can be used to change the SECURELOC parameter for an APPC device.

#1: Only users with *QSECOFR can use this command.

#2: *SECADM authority required and user must have authority to object.
#3: Only QSECOFR can access unless special authority given. User must also have *SAVSYS special authority.
#4: Require *SERVICE authority.
#5: User must have *ALL authority to the object.
#6: *SAVSYS authority required.
#7: *JOBCTL authority required.

Public authority on these commands should be *EXCLUDE. Any exception should be documented.

You should perform a similar check on the QSYS38 library since the commands are also held there. Enter the command:

DSPOBJAUT OBJ (QSYS38/command) OBJTYPE(*CMD)

6.5 Check all commands from both QSYS and QSYS38 that specify ALWLMTUSR(*YES), that is, are available to users with LIMITED CAPABILITY (*YES). The defaults of SIGNOFF, SNDMSG, DSPMSG, DSPJOB, and DSPJBLOG are acceptable. Note particularly the use of the DFU commands and CHGPFM, which can be used to alter data files.

6.6 Discuss with development staff whether a machine Interface Assembler is available and whether APIs are used in any custom-made applications. Evaluate the security implications of any MI or API level programs.

4A.7 OPERATIONS

(ACCESS SECURITY)

The identity and hence authority of work in the system is determined by job descriptions. Subsystems process work using job descriptions. Printed output is directed to output queues. These features are usually controlled by operations, and inappropriate access to them could result in unauthorized access. (USER ACCESS, GENERAL ACCESS)

JOB DESCRIPTIONS

7.1 Display all job descriptions using the command:
DSPOBJD OBJ (*ALL/*ALL) OBJTYPE (*JOBD)

7.2 Check the object authorities for a sample of production job descriptions:
DSPOBJAUT OBJ (library name/name of job description) OBJTYPE (*JOBD)

7.3 Use the following command to obtain a listing of the job descriptions:
DSPJOBD (Library name/job description)

7.3.1 Ensure that for any JOBD that specifies a user profile (USER = user profile), the PUBLIC authority is set to *EXCLUDE.

Particularly check and ascertain the purpose of any JOBD that has the USER parameter set to:

- QSECOFR
- QSYSOPR
- QSRV
- QSYSOPR
- Production User Profile

Note: The IBM-supplied job description QBATCH in library QGPL specifies QPGMR in the USER parameter and has a PUBLIC access of *CHANGE. This is a security weakness and should be changed.

Note: At security levels 40 and 50 an authority of *USE is also needed to the user profile specified in the job description.

7.3.2 Ensure that for all jobs that specify USER=*RQD, the PUBLIC authority is set to *USE or *CHANGE.

SUBSYSTEMS

7.4 Obtain a list of all subsystems in use on the AS/400 using the command: WRKSBSD (QSYS/*ALL)

7.5 For each subsystem use the menu option to display:
Workstation name entries
Workstation type entries
Communication network entries
Remote location entries

7.6 Check the following subsystem descriptions, which are noninteractive subsystems that have no workstation type entries:

- QBATCH
- QCMN
- QDSNX
- QFNC
- QSNADS
- QSPL

Discuss the reasons for configuring any workstations with management.

7.7 Check the following interactive subsystems that have workstation type entries:

- QBASE
- QCTL
- QINTER
- QPGMR
- QSYSSBSD

7.8 Check that only the following subsystems have workstation entries *CONS:

- QBASE
- QCTL
- QSYSSBSD
- QINTER

7.9 Check that job descriptions for all workstation type or name entries are set to a job description that specifies USER=*RQD.

If a user profile is specified in the job description, then users of the subsystem can logon without entering a user profile or password.

Note: *USERPRF under the job description heading for the workstation entry means that the job description will be taken from the default defined in the user's profile.

7.10 There are no remote location entries in the default system supplied by IBM. If any have been set up, this indicates that this AS/400 is involved either in remote job entry with another system or in distributed data management.

OUTPUT QUEUES

7.11 Obtain a list of all output queues using the command:
DSPOBJD (*ALL/*ALL) (*OUTQ)

7.12 Determine by discussion which output queues contain files that must be protected from change and those that must be protected from display.

7.13 Ensure that only authorized users can change output queue files.
To delete, copy, or re-queue the files on an output queue the user must have at least *USE authority to the library containing the queue and:
(1) *SPLCTL
or
(2) *JOBCTL and the output queue must be *OPRCTL
or
(3) The object authority to the queue must be *CHANGE or *ALL, the authority check parameter for the output queue must be *AUTCHK(*DTAUAT), and DSPDTA must be YES.

7.14 To display the files in the output queue the user must at least have *USE authority to the library containing the OUTQ and:
(1) An object authority to the OUTQ of *CHANGE and AUTCHK (*OWNER) and DSPDTA (YES)
or
(2) An object authority to the OUTQ of *USE and DSPDTA (*YES).
or
(3) An object authority to the OUTQ of *CHANGE and AUTCHK (*DTAAUT)
or
(4) Any of those identified in 7.13.

Note: Use the command WRKOUTQD (library name/output queue) to obtain the AUTCHK, OPRCTL, and DSPDTA parameters and the command DSPOBJAUT (library name/output queue) OBJTYPE (*OUTQ) to obtain the object authorities.

4A.8 NETWORK CONSIDERATIONS
(ACCESS SECURITY)

Users accessing the system from other systems should either be denied or subjected to the same user profile and object authority security controls.

This is a potentially complex area, and care should be taken when making recommendations.

8.1 Use the following command to display the system network attributes currently in use:
DSPNETA

8.2 Review the JOBACN network attribute, which determines how the system processes requests from a remote system. When the system receives an incoming input stream as a target system, it can act as follows:
*REJECT: The input stream is rejected. A message stating the input stream was rejected is sent to both the sender and the intended receiver.

*FILE: The input stream is filed on the queue of network files for the receiving user. The user can display, cancel, or receive the job stream into a database file or submit it to a job queue. A message stating that the input stream was filed is sent to both the sender and receiver.

*SEARCH: The network job table controls the action by using the values in the table. You should enter the command WRKNETJOBE to display the system action on receipt of the input stream. The parameters are:

USER ID: The network ID of the job sender. *ANY means allow any user.

ADDRESS: The network address of the job sender. *ANY means allow any address.

ACTION:

*FILE: The job is placed on the queue of the user to whom it was sent.

*REJECT: The incoming job is discarded.

*SUBMIT: The incoming job is run.

USER: The user profile under whose authority the job will run.

If the action is *SUBMIT, check that only valid users are allowed to submit jobs and confirm that the USER under which they run does not give uncontrolled access to production data or programs. Also ensure that the user profile does not have special authorities such as *ALLOBJ.

There is no risk if ACTION is *FILE or *REJECT, but if it is *SUBMIT and the USER gives authority to production files, then this would increase the risk of unauthorized access particularly if user ID is *ANY or there are unauthorized additions to the list of user IDs.

8.3 Review the PCSACC network attribute, which determines how the system processes requests from attached personal computers.

The significance of the PCSACC parameter is as follows:

*REJECT: Specifies that the system does not allow any PC requests from remote systems.

*OBJAUT: Specifies that all remote requests are allowed, but they are controlled by the object authorizations on this system.

Program-Name: Specifies the name of a user-written exit program that provides additional security to the system object-level security.

8.3.1 If the setting is *OBJAUT, confirm that PC support is actually used. If it is not, PCSACC should be set to *REJECT.

8.3.2 If PC support is in use, then the user's authority to objects is determined by the user profile used by the PC Router and/or the user profile through which the user has signed on. You should be aware that a PC user may be signed on with one user profile and run file transfer requests via the PC Router using a different user profile.

PC users are also not subject to the QMAXSIGN parameter, which prevents repeated but invalid attempts to sign on.

8.3.3 Check the settings for the communications network entry through which PC support access is made.

The IBM default is in subsystem QCMN or QBASE. Using this default a PC user may access the system using the default user profile QUSER. DEFAULT USER should be set to *NONE and the MODE to QPCSUPP to prevent this.

8.3.4 A PC support user can use the "submit remote" command facility without having an interactive workstation display emulation active. Hence, even if a user's profile specifies LMTCPB (*YES), the user can still enter commands. As for DDM (see subsection 8.4.3), access to SBMRMTCMD should be restricted (PUBLIC = *EXCLUDE and only authorized users). It may be necessary to write an exit program (specified in the PCSACC network parameter) to adequately control access in complex environments.

8.3.5 Confirm by discussion with users of PC and DP staff support that user profiles and passwords are not stored in STARTPCS.BAT (or anywhere else on the PC) for automatic sign-on to the AS/400.

8.3.6 If PCSACC = program name, confirm that the program, its library, and source code are adequately secured, documented, and subject to effective change control.

Ensure that they do not allow security to be bypassed.

8.4 Review the DDMACC network attribute, which determines how the system as a remote system processes requests from other systems. Shared folders cannot be controlled by a PC support user-written exit program but can be controlled using a distributed data management (DDM) exit program.

Values controlling access are as follow:

*REJECT: Specifies that the system does not allow any DDM requests from remote systems. However, the system (as a local system) can use DDM to access files on the other systems that allow it.

*OBJAUT: Specifies that all remote requests are allowed, but they are controlled by the object authorizations on this system.

Program-Name: Specifies the name of a user-written exit program that provides additional security to the system object-level security. The program is used to determine whether to allow the request.

8.4.1 If the setting is OBJAUT, confirm that DDM is actually in use. If it is not and PC support is not used, DDMACC should be set to *REJECT.

If DDM is in use, then the local system may be dependent on another remote AS/400 for its security.

The local AS/400 may be the target of a DDM request, or it may be the source of one, or it may be both and the security requirements are dependent on this.

Local system is the source of the DDM request.

8.4.2 Confirm that the library, which is used to store the description of the remotely accessed files, is adequately secured (i.e., PUBLIC = *EXCLUDE and *CHANGE restricted to the security officer or equivalent).

8.4.3 Confirm that SBMRMTCMD (submit remote command), which allows a command to be submitted on the source system and run on the target (or remote system), is adequately restricted (PUBLIC = *EXCLUDE and specific or group user profiles of production users with LMTCPB (*YES)).

Local system is the target of a DDM request.

8.4.4 Use the WRKDEVD (*CMN) command to list all communications device descriptions. For each device of type *APPC, display the description (option 5). This will show the remote location name (RMTLOCNAME), the security parameter (SECURELOC), and the location password (LOCPWD). If the APPC device is APPN capable you will need to use the DSPCFGL QAPPNRMT command to display the SECURELOC parameter for this type of device.

8.4.5 Each subsystem (but usually only QBASE and QCMN) may have one or more communication devices defined to it. To determine which communication device is associated with a subsystem, use the command DSPSBSD and then select option 8 (communication entries). Make a note of the devices and default users that have been defined to each subsystem. If a device of *ALL is defined, then the subsystem will accept requests from any APPC device.

8.4.6 If SECURELOC (*NO) for the device, then the target system allows the source system requests to be handled by the default user specified in the communication network entry for the subsystem. All DDM requests will gain access to objects with the security of the default user profile. If default user is set to *NONE, then DDM requests will fail.

8.4.7 If SECURELOC (*YES), then the source system will send a user profile with the DDM request, and it will be under the authority of this user profile that the request will run. The user profile sent by the source system must be defined on the target system.

Note: If the program name has been specified, then object security still applies, but the program may impose additional restrictions. It may, however, create weaknesses in security if it allows source user profiles to be equated to target user profiles.

8.5 Pass-through Access

Controls over pass-through access depend on the SECURELOC parameter of the device description that defines the source of the request and the setting of the QRMTSIGN system value on the target system.

Pass-through requests are made by using the command STRPASTHR, on which the user can specify the user profile and password to be used on the target system.

8.5.1 Determine the setting of the system value QRMTSIGN using the command: DSPSYSVAL SYSVAL(QRMTSIGN).

8.5.2 The possible values are:

*FRCSIGNON: All pass-through sessions must go through the normal sign-on procedure.

*REJECT: Pass-through sessions are not allowed to start on the remote system.

*SAMEPRF: See below.

*VERIFY: See below.

Program-Name: The program specified will run at the start and end of every pass-through session.

If neither pass-through nor PC support is used by the client, the QRMTSIGN should be set to *REJECT.

8.5.3 A setting of FRCSIGNON does not increase the risk of unauthorized access because the user has to sign on to the target system.

The action taken when *VERIFY or *SAMEPRF is used depends on the SECURLOC parameters as follows:

8.5.4 *SAMEPRF and SECURELOC (*YES)

If the user specifies the same profile on the target system that is being used on the source system, STRPASTHR RMTUSER (*CURRENT), then the target system allows access without need to specify a password. This could be a security risk if, for example, QSECOFR was used.

If the user specifies a different user profile on the target system, regardless of whether the password is valid, the sign-on is rejected.

8.5.5 ***SAMEPRF and SECURELOC (*NO)**

The user may only use the same profile on the target system that is being used on the source system, and a valid password must be included.

8.5.6 ***VERIFY and SECURELOC (*YES)**

If the user specifies the same profile on the target system that is being used on the source system, STRPASTHR RMTUSER (*CURRENT), then the target system allows access without the need to specify a password. Again this represents a potential security weakness unless the target trusts the source system.

If the user specifies a different user profile on the target system, then the request will be allowed provided a correct password is included.

8.5.7 ***VERIFY and SECURELOC (*NO)**

Any attempt to access the target system must include a valid password for the user profile on the target system in the pass-through request.

8.5.8 **Note:** If *VERIFY is specified and the security level is 10, then no passwords are required to sign on.

The number of invalid attempts to access the system (QMAXSIGN) is not necessarily effective for pass-through users.

A pass-through user accesses the system via a virtual device (VRTDEVD), and the user is allocated the first available virtual device that has been configured on the target system.

If a pass-through user exceeds QMAXSIGN, then the virtual device through which he is attempting to access the system is varied off-line. The user may, however, repeat the sign-on request, and the target system will simply assign the next available virtual device up to the maximum number defined on the system. The situation is further complicated if QAUTOVRT is not set to 0 because this allows extra virtual devices to be created automatically beyond those predefined to the system. The maximum number is determined by the value of QAUTOVRT, which can be as great as 9,999.

It is possible to reduce this risk, but the method is complex and not foolproof.

4A.9 SECURITY ADMINISTRATION (ACCESS SECURITY)

Unauthorized attempts to access the system and its resources are recorded in the audit and history logs, in addition to other activities. Therefore, the logs should be reviewed on a regular basis and appropriate action taken when necessary.

AUDIT LOG

9.1 Display the setting of the system values that control audit logging by entering the command:

DSPSYSVAL SYSVAL (system value)

9.2 Determine whether auditing is being carried out:
QAUDCTL
*NONE: No auditing of user actions or access to objects is carried out.
*OBJAUD: Auditing is performed for objects selected using the CHGOBJAUD and CHGDLOAUD commands.
*AUDLVL: Auditing is carried out for all functions selected in the *QAUDLVL system value and the AUDLVL parameter on user profiles.
As a minimum *AUDLVL should be enabled. If auditing of access to particular important objects (libraries, data files, programs, and so on) is required, then *OBJAUD should also be enabled.

9.3 Determine which security-related events are being written to the audit journal:
QAUDLVL
*NONE: No events controlled by the QAUDLVL system value are logged. Events are logged for individual users based on the AUDLVL values of user profiles.
*AUTFAIL: Authority failure events are logged.
*CREATE: Object creates operations are logged.
*DELETE: Object delete operations are logged.
*JOBDTA: Actions that affect a job are logged.
*OBJMGT: Object move and rename operations are logged.
*OFCSRV: Changes to the system distribution directory and office mail actions are logged.
*PGMADP: Obtaining authority from a program that adopts authority is logged.
*PGMFAIL: System integrity violations are logged.
*PRTDTA: Printing a spooled file and sending output directly to a printer are logged.
*SAVRST: Restore operations are logged.
*SECURITY: Security-related functions are logged.
*SERVICE: Using service tools is logged.
*SPLFDTA: Actions performed on spooled files are logged.
*SYSMGT: Use of system management functions is logged.
The following should be enabled: *AUTFAIL, *PGMFAIL, *SECURITY, and *SERVICE. Depending on the client environment it may be appropriate to enable more of the above parameters.
Note: Certain parameters (e.g., *PGMADP, *PRTDTA, *SPLFDTA, and so on) may cause a large number of audit journal entries to be written. This could adversely affect system performance. Discuss any requirement to introduce this level of auditing with management before making any recommendations.

9.4 Determine the auditing value for new objects:
QCRTOBJAUD
*NONE: No auditing is carried out for the object.
*USRPRF: Auditing is carried out based on the settings of parameters in the profile of the user accessing the object.
*CHANGE: An audit record is written whenever the object is changed.
*ALL: An audit record is written for any action that affects the content of the object.
The QCRTOBJAUD system value is used when the auditing default for the library that contains the object is set to *SYSVAL.

A specific recommendation for this system value has not been made. Discuss with management whether default audit logging of access to objects is required.

9.5 For any profiles used for emergency fixes ensure that user profile auditing has been enabled by entering the command:

CHGUSRAUD user profile

Examine the setting of the OBJAUD and the AUDLVL parameters. The OBJAUD parameter should be set to *CHANGE of the user profile. The OBJAUD parameter of the objects accessed by the emergency user should be set to *USRPRF, *CHANGE, or *ALL; otherwise, an audit record will not be written.

The AUDLVL parameter in the user profile should be set to *CMD, *CREATE, *DELETE, *OBJMGT, and *SECURITY.

9.6 For a sample of important production objects (e.g., those containing interest rates or similar information) ensure that object auditing is enabled by entering the command:

DSPOBJD library name/object name object type

The OBJAUD parameter for these objects should be set to *CHANGE or *USRPRF.

Note: Discuss with management any requirements to audit changes to particular objects before making recommendations.

9.7 Confirm that the audit journal is secure. Use the command:

DSPUBJAUT (QSYS/QAUDJRN) OBJTYPE (*JRN)

PUBLIC authority should be *EXCLUDE.

9.8 Discuss with the security officer the procedures for reviewing and reassigning the objects that become owned by QDFTOWN, the default owner user profile.

9.9 Confirm that the authority to QDFTOWN is restricted to the security officer.

DSPOBJAUT (QDFTOWN) OBJ (*USRPRF)

9.10 Confirm that users other than the security officer cannot access objects owned by QDFTOWN.

9.11 Confirm by discussion with the security officer that the procedures for monitoring the use of QSECOFR are adequate.

9.12 Where clients have not used audit journaling a review of the history log can be adequate (see subsections 9.7 and 9.8), although it is not recommended.

Use the DSPLOG command to review security-related messages in the history log.

Select a sample of message types:

- Invalid sign-on attempts (profile and/or password).
- Object authority violations.

Use the command:

DPSLOG LOG (QHST) PERIOD((start-time start-date) (end-time end-date)) MSGID(message-identified) OUTPUT(*PRINT)

9.13 Ensure that the security administrator regularly reviews the history and audit logs for security violations, and takes appropriate follow-up action.

CHAPTER 5

WINDOWS NT SERVER: SECURITY FEATURES

INTRODUCTION

Conducting an audit of the Microsoft Windows NT Server requires a knowledge of the built-in and customized security features of this network. The NT server was designed with some notable objectives in mind. The first of these objectives was extensibility or the ability of the operating system to grow to meet its market demands. The NT server accomplishes extensibility through its modular design, which facilitates the creation of a privileged processor mode known as the kernel mode and a nonprivileged processor mode known as the user mode. It also facilitates the use of objects, the ability to load device drivers, a remote procedure call facility, and the ability for applications to utilize the Windows NT services. All of these features pose their own security issues, which will be addressed later in the chapter.

Another design objective of the NT Server is security. The security within the operating system is a layered security model accomplished through the development of the security subsystems and their associated components such as the LSA, SRM, SAM, and the discretionary access controls. The local security authority (LSA) provides many services to the security subsystem of the Windows NT operating system. It is designed to ensure that the user has permission to access the system by validating the user logon. It manages the local security policy as set by the administrator, generates access tokens, and provides interactive validation services when access is requested for any system object. The LSA also controls the audit policy set by the administrator and writes any messages generated by the security reference monitor (SRM) to the event logs.

SECURITY REFERENCE MONITOR

The SRM is part of the NT executive within the NT kernel as shown in Exhibit 5.1, in which the security functions are highlighted in gray. It is responsible for enforcing all access validation and audit policies defined within the local security authority. In this way, the SRM is designed to protect all system objects from unauthorized access or modification. The SRM is the repository for the system's access validation code, and it is the only copy of that code on any given Windows NT system. This ensures that all protection is provided uniformly to objects on the system. The SRM provides services for validating access to ob-

Exhibit 5.1 Windows NT Server Architecture (Schematic)

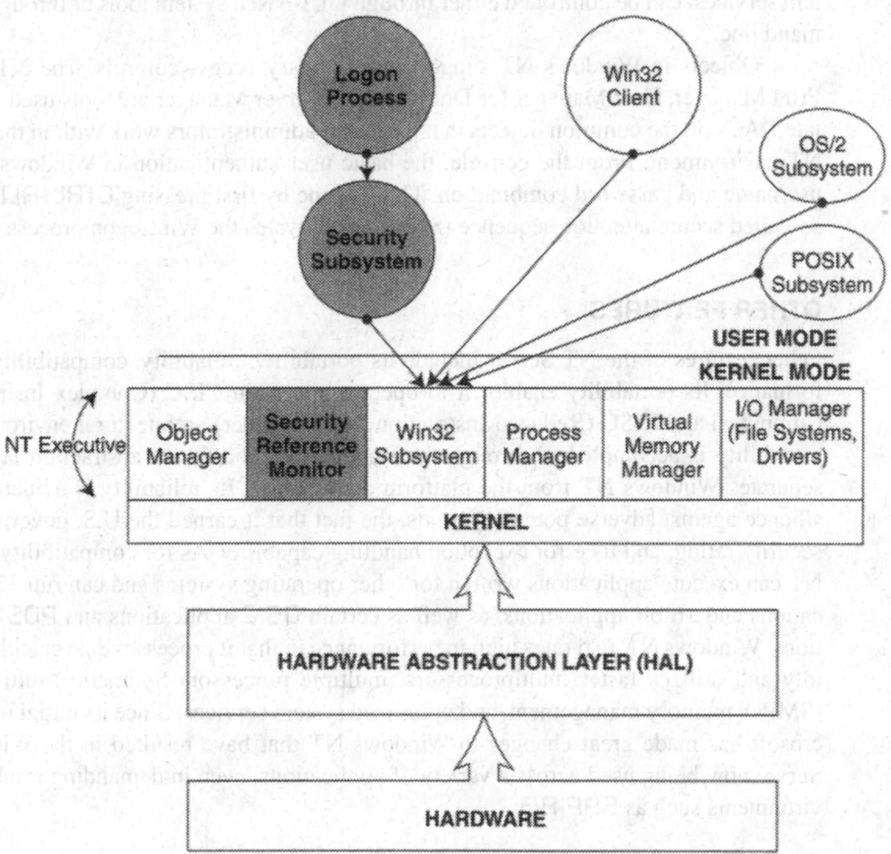

jects, generating audit messages that are subsequently logged by the local security authority, and verifying user accounts for the appropriate privileges.

SECURITY ACCOUNT MANAGER

The security account manager (SAM) controls and maintains the security account database (SAD). The SAD is part of the registry and is not visible to the users during normal processing. The SAD contains account information for all user and group accounts. The SAM provides the user validation service during logon that is used by the local security authority. It compares the cryptographic hash of the password given at logon time with the hashed password stored in the SAD. It then provides the user's security identifier (SID), as well as the SID for any group the user belongs to, to the LSA for the creation of the access token that will be used during that session.

DISCRETIONARY ACCESS CONTROLS

Discretionary access controls (DACs) provide object and resource owners with the means to control who can access resources as well as how much access they may have. Access to system resources, such as files, directories and folders, printers, network shares, and system services, can be controlled either through GUI-based system tools or through the command line.

Objects in Windows NT support discretionary access controls. The NT Explorer, Print Manager, User Manager for Domains, and Server Manager are tools used to manipulate DACs on the common objects that users and administrators work with in the Windows NT environment. From the console, the basic user authentication in Windows NT is the username and password combination. This is done by first pressing CTRL+ALT+DEL, the so-called secure attention sequence (SAS) that activates the WinLogon process.

OTHER FEATURES

Other features of the NT Server include its portability, reliability, compatibility, and performance. Its portability enables it to operate in certain CISC (Complex Instruction Set Computer) and RISC (Reduced Instruction Set Computer) architectural environments. Its portability is accomplished through the Windows NT hardware abstraction layer, which separates Windows NT from the platform architecture. Its reliability is evident in its resilience against adverse potential events, the fact that it earned the U.S. government's C2 security rating, and its error exception handling capability. As for compatibility, Windows NT can execute applications written for other operating systems and can run 32-bit applications and 16-bit applications, as well as certain OS/2 applications and POSIX applications. Windows NT also rates high in performance in that it processes data calculations rapidly and utilizes faster multiprocessors, multiple processors Synthetic Multi Processor (SMPs), memory management, and optimized system services. Since its initial release, Microsoft has made great changes to Windows NT that have resulted in the Windows NT Server now being used across a variety of applications, even in demanding production environments such as SAP R/3.

SECURITY OVERVIEW

Windows NT allows access to resources based on user identity and group membership rather than requiring a password for each resource requested. Windows NT security is based on trusted access that is confirmed by passwords during the logon process. Once the user has logged on, Windows NT compares the user's identity to access permissions stored in objects to determine whether the user has the authority to access the object as requested. The logon process and permissions will be described in more detail later in the chapter, and also how the Windows NT security model provides a safe working environment will be explained. This section discusses the following security features:

- Logon process and user identity
- Objects and security
- Permissions
- Access control lists

LOGON PROCESS AND USER IDENTITY

The method by which a Windows NT domain deals with security is somewhat complex: It starts with the logon process. One has to log on to a domain only once. Subsequently, the computer keeps track of the details of what one can and cannot access; for example, the computer will determine whether a person has access to a particular file or directory. One is not required to justify access privileges with a username and password each time a new server resource or network share is accessed.

This process is something like opening a safe and taking out a set of keys (security identifiers). Once a user has a personal key (account security identifier) for things only the user can access and a key for each of the groups the user belongs to (group security identifiers), the user is in a position to open the resources without requiring another combination. Windows NT automatically creates a "one use only" key ring called a security identifier containing the necessary codes for all the resources a user is allowed access to when logging on. For example, if a user belongs to the finance department, one of the keys the user will receive when logging on is the key to the finance closet. One doesn't have to select the key to use with the security process at all. Windows NT simply tries each of the user's keys and only bothers that person when none of them work.

The CTRL+ALT+DEL logon dialog is the gatekeeper of a Windows NT computer and is presented when the user first logs on to a Windows NT Server. This dialog also appears when the computer is booted and when a user has logged off but left the machine running.

When the Windows NT server is turned on, the Win32 subsystem of the operating system software starts the WinLogon process (a *process* is the micro, utility, or any other program that is within the operating system; in Unix these are referred to as *daemons*), which generates the logon dialog box. When a username and password are entered into the dialog box, the WinLogon process passes that information to a process called the security account manager. When a user logs on to the domain from a network client, the client computer asks for the username and password and (over a network connection) presents them to the SAM. As defined earlier, the SAM is the Windows NT process that is responsible for ensuring that each user (and, by extension, each process started by the user) has only those security privileges established by the system administrator or allocated by default by the operating system.

The security account manager queries the security account database to check the validity of the username. If the name is valid and the password for that user is correct, the SAM generates an access token. The access token contains the user and the user's group memberships in encoded form and passes it back to the WinLogon process or (if connecting via a network client) to the server process maintaining the network client's connection. All processes have access tokens, even those started by the system or by automatic software.

OBJECTS AND SECURITY

The purpose of the Windows NT security system is to control who has access to what. The logon process determines the who; objects in Windows NT are the what. Objects comprise attributes, services, and a permissions list organized into an access control list that users and groups can use to access the services of the object. Most if not all of the resources provided by Windows NT are composed of objects.

An object's attributes are the data contained in the object. Attributes describe such information as the file name, the data contained in a file, and the access control list of permissions. The actions that an object performs are called services. Some examples of object services include Open, Edit, Delete, or Close.

Objects and services grant permissions. For instance, a file contains information to which a user may have access. In other words, the user has Open access, but that user may not have access to the Write service of that object. Windows NT represents its resources as objects, and all objects have access control lists (ACLs) so you can set access permissions for any NT resource based on a user's account or group membership. A typical object could be a type of document. The services that could be performed on this document would include Open, Close, Read, Write, Change, Delete. The attributes of this object would be the File Name, data it contains, and the ACL.

Following are examples of objects that Windows NT contains:

- Directories
- Symbolic links
- Printers
- Processes
- Network shares
- Ports
- Devices
- Windows
- Files
- Threads

Every object has an ACL that Windows NT uses to determine whether users have the authority to access that object.

PERMISSIONS

The logon process defines the user to the operating system, and objects define what the user can access. Permissions define the operations that can be performed on the objects or, more often, the operations the programs can perform on the objects.

Windows NT manages access control by assigning an access token (in the key analogy, an access token is the key ring) when the user logs on. The access token comprises the security identifiers (which are analogous to the keys) for the user account and all the groups to which the user belongs. When the user attempts to access a resource, the security account manager on the computer sharing the resource compares the user's access token to the access control list of the requested object. If one of the security identifiers in the user's security token matches an access control entry in the access control list, the user will be granted access. For example, suppose a user from the engineering group is accessing a file that only members of the engineering domain and administrators are allowed to access. Being a member of the engineering group, the user has a key that will open the resource. Think of the administrator's security ID as the master key that will open anything.

Access Tokens

When logging on, Windows NT assigns the user an access token (i.e., a representation of their account and each group to which the user belongs) that remains valid until the user logs off. Windows NT compares the individual security identifiers (keys) in this token to entries in an object's access control list (locks) to determine whether a user has permission to access the object.

Access tokens are objects. Like any other Windows NT object, they contain attributes and services that describe them to the system and provide their services. Important attributes in the access token include:

- Security ID representing the logged-on user
- Security IDs representing the logged-on user's group memberships
- Permissions allowed for the user

Security ID for Users

Windows NT creates unique security identifiers for each user and group in the user accounts database. Because security IDs are unique, if an account or group is deleted, any new account or group created will not retain the same permissions given to the old account or group. Security IDs can never be repeated, so the system will never mistake one user for another.

Security ID for Groups

Security IDs for groups are like security IDs for users in that they allow certain permissions. Unlike security IDs for users, however, security IDs for groups do not represent an individual user. Rather, these security ID objects contain permissions assigned to groups of users based on some common criteria, such as department or work function. When a user is made a member of a group, the security ID for that group is attached to the user's access token. You will learn more about users and groups and the privileges that can be assigned to them later in the chapter.

When the administrator grants or denies access to an object based on a group, that group's security ID is added to the object's ACL along with the specific permission. Because the access token for a user contains the user's security ID and all the security IDs for groups to which the user belongs, the ACL and the access token will contain a matching ID telling Windows NT which permissions to allow. ACLs and access control entries are covered in detail in the "Access Control Lists" later in this chapter.

More than one ID match may occur if a user is a member of more than one group with permissions to the object. Windows NT combines the access permissions, therefore, if one has **Read** access to an object because they are a member of group A and also **Write** access to the same object because they are a member of group B, one has both **Read** and **Write** access to the object. Permissions are the specific access control entries contained in an object's ACL. An access control entry contains a security ID and the permission to which that security ID is assigned, such as **Read** access, **Write** access, or **Full Control** access.

Attaching Access Tokens to Processes

When a process attempts to access an object, the process's access token is checked against the object's ACL. If the ACL allows the specific access requested, the new process is started and the access token from the calling process is attached to it for the duration of its execution. Because no process can be started without an access token and all processes receive the access token of the process that initiated them, one cannot bypass the security subsystem by starting a process that has a higher security clearance than the process that called it.

ACCESS CONTROL LISTS

Each object has an ACL attribute that describes which user or group accounts have access to the object and what type of access they have. If a user does not have an entry in the ACL allowing access to a service of an object, Windows NT will not allow that user to perform the requested action on that object. For instance, if a user attempts to open a file, the user must have Open and Read access to that file or be a member of a group that has Open and Read access to that file. Otherwise, Windows NT will not allow the user to open the file. ACLs for objects contain access control entries, each of which describes a specific permission for a specific service for a user or a group.

Checking Permissions

When one is requesting access to an object or invoking a service of an object, Windows NT compares the security identifiers in the access token of the calling process to each entry in the ACL. This verifies if the access is explicitly denied to the user or to any group to which the user belongs. It then checks to see if the requested access is specifically permitted. Windows NT repeats these steps until it encounters a deny access or until it has collected all the necessary permissions to grant the requested access. If the ACL does not specifically allow permission for each requested access, access is denied.

Windows NT optimizes access control by performing all security access checking when the object is first opened. All allowable requested accesses are copied into the object's process table when the object is opened. Any subsequent accesses to the object will succeed if the access appears in the process table and will fail if it does not. Owing to this optimization, Windows NT has very little computer overhead for security once an object is started. However, any change to a user's or group's permissions will not take effect for any process currently running until that process is shut down and restarted. It may be necessary to reboot because the user won't be able to shut down and restart many system services. Also, note that only those permissions requested when the object is opened are copied to the object's process table. Consequently, a file opened only for Read, Write access, for example, cannot be deleted until it is closed and then reopened with a Delete request.

Having described the general framework of the security architecture of Windows NT, the next section reviews the components of the security architecture in detail.

DESIGN FEATURES

Windows NT Server utilizes an integrated architecture to authenticate, validate, and record information about security within the operating system.

The overall system architecture is divided into two main areas: the kernel and the user. These are shown in Exhibit 5.1. The segments of the architecture that relate to security are the security reference monitor, security subsystem, and the logon process, which are highlighted on the diagram. Within this architecture, Windows NT is able to apply security to every object and process it controls. This means that every object resident on the Windows NT computer and every process running on that computer are subject to the security controls of the overall architecture.

Logon Process

The Windows NT logon process, which is pictured in Exhibit 5.2, is mandatory for initiating a session with a Windows NT server or workstation. The logon process differs slightly

Exhibit 5.2 Windows NT Logon Process

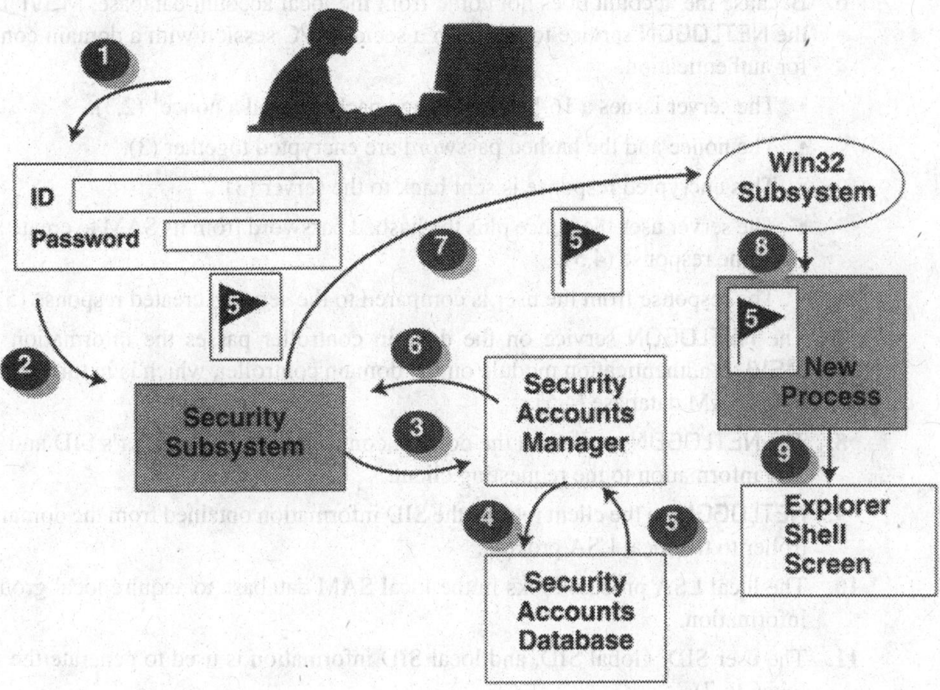

if the user is attempting to log on to a local machine or to a remote server in a network. The logon is a multistep process that follows part A or part B of the following list. The numbers in parentheses correspond with the pictures shown in Exhibit 5.2.

A. Local Machine Logon

1. Press CTRL+ALT+DEL to display a logon dialog box (1).
2. Type the user ID and password (1).
3. Press Enter.
4. The password is hashed and sent to the local LSA (2,3).
5. The LSA makes a call to the MSV1_0 authentication package and compares the hash to the hash stored in the local SAM database (4,5).
6. The LSA creates an access token using the user's account SID and group SIDs returned from the MSV1_0 authentication package (6,7).
7. The NT Explorer Shell opens with the user's access token attached (8,9).

B. Domain Account Logon

1. Press CTRL+ALT+DEL to display a logon dialog box (1).
2. Type the user ID, password, and select the domain (1).
3. Press Enter.
4. The password is hashed and sent to the local LSA (2,3).

5. The LSA makes a call to the MSV1_0 authentication package.
6. Because the account does not come from the local account database, MSV1_0 calls the NETLOGON service to establish a secure RPC session with a domain controller for authentication.
   - The server issues a 16-byte challenge packet called a nonce[1] (2,3).
   - The nonce and the hashed password are encrypted together (3).
   - This encrypted response is sent back to the server (3).
   - The server uses the nonce plus the hashed password from its SAM to create a copy of the response (4,5).
   - The response from the user is compared to the server's created response (5).
7. The NETLOGON service on the domain controller passes the information to the MSV1_0 authentication module on the domain controller, which is in turn compared to the SAM database (4,5).
8. The NETLOGON service on the domain controller returns the user's SID and global SID information to the requesting client.
9. NETLOGON on the client returns the SID information obtained from the domain controller to the local LSA process.
10. The local LSA process looks in the local SAM database to acquire local group SID information.
11. The user SID, global SID, and local SID information is used to generate the access token (6,7).
12. The Explorer Shell opened with the user's access token attached (8,9).

Access Control List

Objects within a Windows NT system have an access control list. ACLs are lists of users and groups that have permissions to access or to operate the specified object. Each object in the Windows NT system contains a security descriptor that is comprised of the security identifier (SID) of the owner of the object, the regular ACL for access permissions, the system ACL (SACL) for auditing, and a group security identifier.

ACLs can contain access control entries (ACEs). There are situations where an ACL will have no ACEs. This is known as a null or empty ACL. Each ACE describes the permissions for each user or group that has access to an object. Access control entries within Windows NT are composed of standard or special permissions categories. Each permission type is valid for both files and directories. Special permissions consist of the six individual permissions, while the standard permissions are combinations derived from the special permissions. These permission levels include NoAccess, which is a level of authority that may supersede all other authorities. Following is an example of the NoAccess permission:

- The local group named Marketing is granted Read access to files in a directory called data.
- The Domain User named joseph, a member of Marketing, is specifically listed as NoAccess to the data directory.

[1] Nonce: a one-time randomly generated number.

- Therefore, joseph is not able to read the files in the data directory while all other members of Marketing may.

The permissions described in the following list and in Exhibit 5.3 may be characterized as new technology file system (NTFS) ACL permissions. The special permissions include:

- **Read (R)** Directory: permitted to view names of files and subdirectories
  Files: permitted to read a file's data
- **Write (W)** Directory: permitted to add files and create subdirectories
  Files: permitted to change file data
- **Execute (X)** Directory: permitted to change to subdirectories
  Files: permitted to run file if it is a program
- **Delete (D)** Directory: permitted to delete directory and subdirectories
  Files: permitted to delete files
- **Change Permissions (P)** Directory: permitted to change directory permissions
  Files: permitted to change file permissions
- **Take Ownership (O)** Directory: permitted to take ownership of directories
  Files: permitted to take ownership of files

The standard permissions are included in Exhibit 5.3.

There are other forms of ACLs in a Windows NT system. These include registry permission ACLs containing two standard permissions and one special permission that contains nine subpermissions for manipulating registry keys. The registry subpermissions are described later. Another type of ACL is the printer ACL for managing printers and documents.

Access Tokens and Security Identifiers

Access tokens are created by the local security authority after SAM validation, as part of a successful logon process. The access token created at this time stays with that particular user's session for as long as they stay logged on. Whenever a user initiates a process during the course of the session, a copy of the token is attached to that process. Once the user logs off, the token is destroyed and will never be used again. Each token contains the following information:

- User's security identifier
- Group security identifiers
- User privileges
- Owner (SID assigned to any objects created during the session)
- Primary group SID
- Default ACL (assigned to any object created by the user)

ACCESS CONTROL: SECURITY MANAGEMENT

Windows NT provides security features in access control. Chief among them is the NT file system. NTFS is one of two file system technologies supported under Windows NT, and it

Exhibit 5.3 Standard Permissions for ACLs

Permission Name	Directory Permission	File Permission	Explanation
NoAccess	None	None	No access to files and directories
List	RX	Not specified	List directory contents Change to subdirectories No access to files unless granted explicitly
Read	RX	RX	List directory contents Change to subdirectories Read data from files Execute programs
Add	WX	Not specified	Create subdirectories Create files No access to existing files unless granted explicitly
Add and Read	RWX	RX	List directory contents Change to subdirectories Create subdirectories Read data from files Execute programs
Change	RWXD	RWXD	List directory contents Change to subdirectories Delete subdirectories Create subdirectories Read data from files Create and modify files Execute programs Delete files
Full Control	All	All	All directory permissions All file permissions Change permissions Take ownership

is the only Windows NT–based file system to provide security functionality at the file and directory level. In addition to providing physical security for a Windows NT Server, which is critical, the NTFS is the only file system that should be utilized if you want to deploy a secure environment.

NTFS is a file system that treats each file and folder as an object. Each object contains attributes that are stored with the object, such as size, name, and security descriptor. The file system itself contains a master file table that keeps track of the information stored on the file system, as well as the information needed to perform a file or directory recovery.

Windows NT provides for granular access control. The basic system design was created with the requirement of discretionary control in mind, as described in the U.S. government's C2 specification. This means the operating system must allow the owner of any object the ability to permit or deny access to that object. Objects include programs, files, directories, processes, printers, and so on. Windows NT accomplishes this level of control through the use of access control lists. When a user executes the logon process, an access token with all the user's rights (name of the authenticated user, any groups the user is assigned to, and so on) is created and follows the user throughout the session. This token is applied to any processes started by the user so the process will have the same rights as the user (inherited token). If the user (or group the user is assigned to) is defined as the owner of an object or part of a group allowed to access an object (as defined in the ACL), access is granted. In all other cases, access is denied. Additionally, in the access control list, a system administrator, or owner of an object, can define what type of access is allowed to the object. These levels of access include Full Control, Change, Read, Write, Execute, Delete, Change Permissions, Take Ownership, and NoAccess.

In addition to the ACL concept, there are additional levels of control. There are twenty-seven specific user rights that can be assigned (or restricted) to users or groups in Windows NT. These levels include the ability to access a computer from the network, to change the system time, to log on to the system locally, the ability to take ownership of objects, and even to shut down the system. Finally, there are specific account restrictions that can be placed on an account to control the user's access to the system. These include password restrictions, logon times, remote access capabilities, group memberships, intruder detection/account lockout, and user-specific profiles.

USER AUTHENTICATION

User authentication, determining a user's identity, is the foundation for Windows NT security. Successful authentication will facilitate access to authorized resources. Unauthorized users that can masquerade as authorized users may gain inappropriate access. *This risk can impact many types of systems and must be addressed through strong procedures, education, and awareness programs.*

Users may be identified by something that they know, something that they have, or something that they are (e.g., a biometric device such as a fingerprint). Single-factor authentication involves just one identification mechanism. This is usually something that users know such as a username and password. When a valid username and password are submitted to the operating system, the user account is looked up in the SAM database. If the account exists, the submitted password is run through a one-way hash function. This one-way hash of the password is compared to the hash in the SAM database. If there is a match, a security token that identifies the user and to what groups the user belongs is built for the session. Changes to a user's rights require that the user log out of the operating system and then log on again for the new rights to take effect.

There are three locations from which users can authenticate themselves to Windows NT:

1. From the console
2. From inside the network
3. From outside the network

From the console, the username and password combination is used. The key combination (CTRL+ALT+DEL) is used because it is a set of keys that has not been used as a "hot key sequence" prior to this usage to avoid conflicts with existing applications. Another reason for this is that the sequence can be implemented at a very low level of the operating system, which helps to protect users from Trojan horse programs. Trojan horse programs are always a potential problem in any operating system that uses a password-based authentication method. One form of a Trojan horse attack substitutes the legitimate logon program for a Trojan program that steals the user's password, somehow records it, and relays it back to the creator.

From another location in the domain, the users can log on remotely. Historically, the remote logon process in many systems involves clear-text transmission of the user's identification and password. This transmission can be monitored and reused to access a user account. This has been a problem for many years with the TCP/IP-based network utilities, such as telnet, that send passwords over networks in clear text. Network administrators (and others) can use debugging and performance monitoring tools to capture the readable identifier and password. The Windows NT "netlogon" process uses encryption to protect the remote logon process.

For non-NT systems, there are other utilities to secure the logon process. The Microsoft User Authentication Module for Macintosh uses the Microsoft Challenge Authentication Protocol (MS-CHAP) installed on the client to encrypt the logon session.

For access from outside the network, Windows NT provides the Remote Access Service (RAS). RAS allows Windows NT's workstations to access NT servers across standard phone lines (plain old telephone service, frame relay, or ATM) or other asynchronous connections, X.25 packet switched networks, or Integrated Services Digital Network lines. RAS uses remote node systems to provide this capability. Remote node systems run the application on the remote user's computer and treat the connection line as an extension of the local area network, sending LAN-style traffic, such as requests for file and print services, over the line, which allows for greater flexibility and security. Because RAS treats the connection line as an extension of the LAN, it is designed to support Windows NT's security model, complete with trust relationships and centralized domain administration. RAS supports a number of authentication protocols for dial-in clients. They include the following:

- The password authentication protocol (PAP) that sends passwords in clear text
- SPAP, which uses two-way encryption for use with the Shiva LAN Rover product
- The U.S. federal government's data encryption standard (DES)
- The Challenge-Handshake Authentication Protocol (CHAP)
- Microsoft's version of this protocol (MS-CHAP)

Windows NT also supports two-factor authentication. Users can optionally use token devices that generate one-time passwords. Windows NT will also support the use of SmartCards. These can take the form of PC cards that plug into a PCMCIA device, or IC Chip cards. Through the use of device drivers and additional hardware (i.e., card readers), the authentication process can be further secured. In addition, SmartCards can store cryptographic key material that can provide digital signatures for authentication, integrity, and nonrepudiation, and encryption that provides confidentiality to network activity. Microsoft is working with a number of hardware vendors to develop implementations based on ISO standards as part of the Personal Computer/SmartCard Workgroup. Applications can use the CryptoAPI to integrate the benefits of SmartCard technology.

The next section describes the logon process and permissions in more detail and explains how the Windows NT security model provides a safe working environment.

USER ENVIRONMENT

Network operating systems such as Windows NT use the concept of user accounts to control security and accountability for the information contained on network servers. Using a process called logging on, which initiates a connection to the network by providing a username and a password, the network is able to identify which user account to use for each person who accesses the network. Logging on enables the network to:

- Present information appropriate for each user.
- Customize the network session for each user.
- Allow the correct access to information for each user.

This section contains explanations of how user accounts are created and maintained, discussions on the topics of security and account policies, and descriptions of ways of grouping users to increase security and administrative control and decrease administrative burden.

USER ACCOUNTS

When first installed, Windows NT Server creates two default accounts: the Administrator account and the Guest account.

Administrator Account

The local Administrator account is established during the installation of any version of Windows NT. This account is powerful and allows full access to the system. When an Administrator account on a PDC is added to the Domain Admin group and the Domain Admin group is then added to the local Administrators group on a workstation, that account can then administer that particular workstation.

The Administrator account cannot be deleted. It cannot be disabled from console login. It can, however, be disabled from network login. In the Windows NT version 4.0 resource kit, a utility program called `passprop.exe` exists. When utilized on a Windows NT system, this program allows the Administrator account to be locked from the network, just as any other regular user account.

In order to secure this account, it must be renamed an obscure value and only be used when necessary. It should be noted that renaming of the Administrator account does not completely obscure it from view. The Administrator account on every Windows NT system has the same SID, therefore making it possible to discover the identity of a renamed Administrator account. If it is necessary to use this account, it should be logged off immediately upon completion of that use. Administrators of Windows NT systems should be assigned their own account, which should be a member of the appropriate administrative group.

Security of the Administrator account may be facilitated by creating an account called Administrator and granting it limited rights and forcing it to be locked out after several invalid access attempts.

Guest Account

The Guest account allows an anonymous logon to the domain. Since the account is a member of the Everyone group, the account has the same access as the Everyone group. By default, the account is disabled and should remain disabled. For additional protection, a strong password should be assigned to the Guest account in case it is accidentally reenabled. The Guest account will only function for anonymous access if it is enabled and has no password.

USER RIGHTS

Access to network resources are defined either by assigning rights to a user to perform specific tasks or by setting permissions directly to objects (files, directories, and devices). As a rule, rights assigned to users override object permissions. The following list details basic rights available on the system and whose default groups should be carefully evaluated:

- *Access this computer from the network.* By default, this right is granted to the Administrators and Everyone groups. Granting this right to the Everyone group allows all users to access the server from the network. As such, the Everyone group should not be assigned this right. A new group should replace the Everyone group in this case, and this group should include users or groups who require the network access.
- *Backup files and directories.* By default, this right is granted to the Administrators, Backup Operators, and Server Operators. Since this right overrides specific permissions placed on objects, users with this right have the ability to copy all files regardless of permissions. As such, carefully scrutinize the users and groups granted this right.
- *Force shutdown from a remote system.* By default, this right is granted to the Administrators, Server Operators, and Power Users in the Windows NT Workstation group. This right allows the specified users or group members to send the Windows NT system a shutdown command from any workstation or server on the network. As such, no group should ever be granted this right.
- *Log on locally.* By default, this right is granted to the Administrators, Backup Operators, Server Operators, Account Operators, Print Operators, and Internet Guest Account groups. Because this right allows the user to log on directly to the console of the server, only the Administrators group should be granted this right.
- *Shut down the system.* This right indicates that the specified users or group members can issue a shutdown command from the system's local console if they are logged on interactively to the console. By default, this right is granted to the Administrators, Backup Operators, Server Operators, Account Operators, and Print Operators. Only members of the Administrators and Server Operators should ever have a need for this right.

In addition to the basic user rights, Windows NT Server offers several advanced user rights. Administration of these rights should be carefully reviewed.

USER ACCOUNTS, GROUPS, AND SECURITY

To provide specific resources to specific users and to secure specific resources against unauthorized disclosure, a network operating system (NOS) has to know the identity of its users. This information is provided to the NOS during the logon authentication. *Logon authenti-*

cation restricts access by ensuring that a valid account name and password are entered into the logon dialog. The logon name identifies each unique user and is distinct for each account in the domain. The password restricts the use of that account to only those individuals who know the password. Normally this account privacy, by virtue of passwords, extends to individuals. When using account groups, two or more people have little reason to share a single account even if their access permissions are the same. For example, suppose Jack and Jill are engineers who need access to the same applications. You could reduce your administrative hassles by having them use the same logon account. This procedure was relatively common on some older mainframe computers and in simpler network operating systems that didn't have a strong concept of grouping. By using the same account, Jack and Jill will have the same security permissions. Unfortunately, Jill won't be able to keep any files private from Jack (she has access to everything he has access to), and if Jack changes his password, Jill won't be able to log on until she finds out what the new password is. Therefore, the better option is to create a group and make Jack and Jill members of that group. In this example you could create at least three groups: engineers, who have access to all engineering-specific files; CAD users, who have access to the computer-aided drafting software; and spreadsheet users, who have access to the spreadsheet software.

Why would you bother creating groups for specific applications though when you could simply secure them with file permissions in such a way that no user could damage the installation? One reason is to control simultaneous access to these applications for licensing purposes. Let's say you have fifty network users but only five CAD licenses. You're using the license manager or a similar tool to track concurrent access to your applications and have discovered that no more than five copies are ever in use at one time—perhaps only five engineers work at your company. But suppose that Snoopy, who is an accountant, launches a copy of the CAD application just to check it out. The license manager tallies up a sixth concurrent user, and your company is out another $5,000 just so Snoopy could draw some lines and boxes. After a user logs on to a domain, the network knows which resources the user is allowed to access and will deny access to resources for which the user does not have specific permission.

User accounts can be grouped together for the assignment of permissions to users. For example, access to financial information can be assigned to the Finance group, and any member of the Finance group inherits permission to access finance information. From an administrative perspective, groups allow administrators to manage permissions at the group level. As such, they can effectively control security without being overwhelmed by the size of the user population in the domain.

User accounts reside on the primary domain controller (PDC). Specifically, in the security accounts manager section of the PDC's registry. Users who are part of the domain are really global users because they can log on to any computer attached to the domain. Local user accounts are set up on individual computers for access only to that specific machine; local user accounts do not provide access to the domain. Domains enable many servers to share accounts. Global user accounts created on the primary domain controller are available to every computer participating in the domain.

Local groups are groups of local user accounts. Global groups are groups of global user accounts that are available to all computers logged on to the network. Local groups can contain global groups and global (domain user) accounts, but the reverse is not true.

Caveat: Do not create a global group with the same name as a local group. These accounts are not the same—members with the privileges of one group will not have the privileges of the other group.

PLANNING

Planning account policies, security structure, naming conventions, and groups provides a foundation from which to create a coherent and secure network environment. Adding users ad hoc, assigning directory permissions when someone has excessive rights, and creating groups only out of necessity produce a disorganized environment that frustrates users and also expose the system to security loopholes. Developing a coherent network environment requires careful planning. Planning should include the following elements:

- Natural groups in the organization, such as Accounting, Finance, Managers, Executives, New Employees, and CAD users. Every conceivable group should be listed.
- A standard naming convention. It is recommended to use the Internet naming convention that prefaces the last name with the first initial. Some organizations prefer to use titles, ranks, or grades as account names, especially if these designations are unique.
- Security permissions for network shares and directories. Determine which network shares you will create and what permissions should be assigned to those shares. Usually on NTFS volumes, you should create a single network share and allow unlimited access to it. Then, you should secure the subdirectories with file-level permissions. With FAT-File Allocation Table volumes, you will have to explicitly share every directory that needs unique permissions.
- Default account policies such as password lengths, account lockout features, and audit policy. Most installations that do not have specific security requirements (e.g., organizations that are not government or defense related) will not need to change account policies from the Windows NT defaults.
- Resource shares that need to be accessed by users of the network. Planning shares up front will keep networked mass storage (i.e., file server) from becoming a morass of disorganized files and directories.

Planning Groups

Well-planned groups will enable administering to users on the network much easier. Experienced administrators seldom assign access permissions to individual accounts. Instead, they create groups and make individual accounts part of those groups. For example, instead of giving individual users access permission to back up systems, the administrator creates a backup group with those permissions and then adds users to those groups. In this way, when the backup process changes (e.g., additions to servers), the administrator only has to make changes to the group account instead of to each individual account. Windows NT Server uses global groups to maintain groups across all computers in a domain. Global groups are different from the local groups that can be created using Windows NT Workstations.

Assigning users to groups allows the administrators to keep track of who needs what resources. For example, word-processing users might need access to the word-processing application, to its data files, and to a shared directory that contains the organization's common documents and templates. All three rights can be given to a group, called Word Processing, and then in one shot the rights can be given to an individual account by adding that individual account to the group. One can assign permissions to everyone in a domain by assigning those access rights to the Domain Users group. Domain Users is the default primary group in a domain. Before creating the network groups for the network, one should determine the network resources on the network the users will need to access. It should be determined what different users have in common, and groups should be created to give users those access permissions. Ideally, one will assign permissions to groups and allow access to users by making them members of the appropriate groups. Groups are normally based on the following criteria:

- Organization functional units (marketing)
- Network programs (word processing)
- Network resources (Canon Laser)
- Location (area 51)
- Individual function (backup operator)

Global groups should be created before creating shares because permissions can be assigned to shares as they are created, as long as the groups already exist.

Naming Conventions

Administering networks requires that consistent and coherent naming conventions be developed. A good naming convention has the following three characteristics:

1. It is easy to use and understand. If users don't understand the naming convention, they won't use it.
2. Anyone familiar with the naming convention should be able to construct an object name in a few moments. For users, the name may include their full name and function in the company. For a printer, the name may include the model number and configuration details, physical location in the building, and the kind of work the printer is intended for.
3. Object names should have obvious and meaningful relationships with objects they correspond to. If objects represent printers, the names should correspond to printers (e.g., the Hewlett-Packard LaserJet III printer on the third floor). If objects are user accounts, users should be able to determine that JASMITH corresponds to John A. Smith.

Constructing naming conventions that produce meaningful names for objects is fairly easy; constructing naming conventions that translate easily in both directions is more difficult.

Security Planning

Security planning involves securing resources from unauthorized access. There are two approaches to security planning:

1. Optimistic, wherein users are allowed maximum permission to access information except in those specific cases in which information should not be available to them.
2. Pessimistic, wherein users are allowed to access only the information they need to perform their jobs.

Both methods are equally valid. The nature of the organization and the work it performs will normally determine what method to choose. For example, governments follow the pessimistic approach because access to their information could pose a security risk to their country. However, most medium to small businesses use the optimistic approach because they may not have information that would be useful to anyone outside their organization.

Pessimistic security policies require more administrative efforts than optimistic policies but they provide greater security and do not rely entirely on the users to safeguard data. Therefore, under a pessimistic policy any time someone needs access to information that is outside the need to know territory, the network administrator has to specifically authorize permission for that person to have access to that information.

Optimistic security policies require very little administrative effort and as such are not as secure. Nearly every user on the network has access to most of the information on it. For that reason, specifically assigning permission to access a resource is usually not necessary.

These two policies are the extremes of the spectrum; most network security policies fall somewhere in the middle. Deciding at the outset where on the spectrum the policy is to fall will provide the guidance for the implementation of the security plan.

PERMISSIONS SUMMARY

The user's access token is created when logging on. It contains the user's identity and the identity of all groups the user belongs to. This access token is compared to each secured resource such as a share, file, or directory that the user attempts to access. These resources contain access control lists that list each security ID permitted to use the resource. If any of the identifiers in the user's access token match identifiers in the resources access control list, the user is allowed access as specified by that access control entry in the access control list.

Share Permissions

Share permissions control how access to a shared resource is managed. Exhibit 5.4 shows the effects of share-level permissions.

File System Permissions

File system permissions complement the basic share-level permissions. Older file systems (e.g., FAT) do not have a rich enough set of file and directory attributes to implement security on a file or directory basis, so file system permissions are not available for these volumes. Share permissions are implemented by the server service to secure access to file systems that do not implement security. File system permissions are available for NTFS volumes only.

Modern file systems like NTFS implement finer security control over the sharing of information with file system permissions, which are assigned to individual files and directories using file system attribute bits that are stored in the directory tables of the file sys-

Exhibit 5.4 Permissions Effect

NoAccess	Prevents access to the shared directory regardless of other allowed permissions.
Read	Allows viewing of contained files and directories, loading of files, and executing software.
Change	Includes all Read permissions plus creating, deleting, and changing contained directories and files.
Full Control	Includes all Change permissions plus changing file system permissions and taking ownership.

Exhibit 5.5 File System Permissions

Permission	Effect
NoAccess	Prevents any access to the directory and its files even if the user has been granted share or file-level full control.
List	Allows viewing and browsing the directory without access to files unless overridden by other file or directory permissions.
Read	Allows the opening of files and executing applications.
Add	Allows the adding of files and subdirectories without Read access.
Change	Includes Add and Read permissions plus Delete.
Full Control	Includes Change permissions plus taking ownership and assigning permissions.

tem. Therefore, file system permissions work even on stand-alone computers. For instance, if a person creates a directory and assigns permissions only for that person, then no one else can access that directory (except administrators) even when other users are logged on to the same machine.

File system permissions can also be used to restrict which files are available to resource shares. Even though a share permission may allow access to a directory, a file system permission can still restrict it. Exhibit 5.5 lists the file system permissions available in NTFS volumes.

Conflicting Permissions

With the myriad of shares, groups, files, and directories that can be created in a network environment, some resource permission conflicts are bound to occur. When a user is a member of many groups, some of those groups may specifically allow access to a resource while other group memberships deny it. Also, cumulative permissions may occur. For example, a user may have Read access to a directory because the user is a domain user but also have Full Control access as a member of the Engineers group. Windows NT determines access privileges in the following manner:

- Administrators always have full access to all resources.
- A specific denial (NoAccess permission) always overrides specific access to a resource.
- When resolving conflicts between share permissions and file permissions, Windows NT chooses the most restrictive. For instance, if the share permission allows full control but the file permission allows read-only, the file is read-only.
- When a user is a member of multiple groups, the user always has the combined permissions of all group memberships.

Combinations of permissions include the NoAccess permission. So if membership in the Engineering group allows access to a directory, but membership in the New_Employee group allows NoAccess, the user will have NoAccess.

Choosing Permissions

Share permissions and file system permissions are two methods for securing files. Use the following criteria to help decide which to use:

- If the user is sharing from the FAT file system, the user cannot use file system security, so the user must share each directory that needs unique permissions.
- If the user needs to secure access to files on a system that users will log on to locally, the user must use file system security. Share security applies only to network connections, not to local users.
- Generally, the user should create the fewest number of shares possible in the networking environment. For instance, rather than sharing each subdirectory on a server, consider sharing just the higher-level directory and then securing the subdirectories with file-level permissions. Some shares should be reserved for sharing hardware devices such as entire hard disks or CD-ROMs.
- File system security allows a richer set of permissions and can be more finely controlled. Use it whenever possible.

POLICY PLANNING

Policies are general operational characteristics of Windows NT. Changing policies basically means changing the default way Windows NT establishes security. Think of policies as the security behavior of Windows NT that affects all users. The four major categories of policies are:

1. Account Policy
2. User Rights
3. Audit Policy
4. System Policy

The user controls the first three, Account Policy, User Rights, and Audit Policy, from the Policy menu of the User Manager for Domains (or the User Manager in Windows NT Workstations) and controls the fourth from the System Policy Editor.

ACCOUNT POLICY

Account Policy allows control over universal security settings for user accounts. The user can set the following user Account Policies:

- Maximum length of time before users are forced to change their password.
- The minimum age if necessary.
- The minimum length of passwords.
- Whether or not passwords must be unique between changes.
- How many passwords a user must rotate among.
- Whether or not account lockouts take place.
- The number of attempts before lockout occurs.
- How long the count remains in effect.
- The length of lockout duration.

- Whether logon hours are strictly enforced.
- Whether users must log on to change their password. In other words, if their logon age expires, can they still change their password or must they contact an administrator?

Defining Security Settings

Windows NT allows modification of the default security settings. The user Account Policy controls the password characteristics for all user accounts across the domain. Exhibit 5.6 details Windows NT Account Policy options and recommendations.

These policies are self-explanatory and usually don't need to be changed unless a specific security policy is in place or a higher level of intrusion attempts is expected (e.g., the server is directly connected to the Internet).

Exhibit 5.6 Windows NT Account Policy Options and Recommendations

NT Policy Feature	Policy Option	Recommendation
Maximum Password Age	Password never expires Expires in *x* days	Password expires in 30 to 60 days*
Minimum Password Age	Allow changes immediately Allow changes in *x* days	Allow changes in seven days
Minimum Password Length	Permit blank password At least *x* characters	Password at least six characters
Password Uniqueness	Do not keep password history Remember *x* passwords	Remember ten passwords
Account Lockout	No account lockout Account lockout	Account lockout selected
Account Lockout	Lockout after *x* bad logon attempts	Lockout after three bad logon attempts
Account Lockout	Reset count after *x* minutes	Reset count after 1,440 minutes (24 hours)
Lockout Duration	Forever (until admin. unlocks) Duration *x* minutes	Select forever
Forcibly disconnect remote users from server when logon hours expire	Selected Not selected	Tied to logon hours specified when user account was created
Users must log on in order to change password	Selected Not selected	Select

*Sixty days would be a permissible password change rate only if strong passwords are implemented. Strong passwords may only be implemented under Windows NT 4.0 at the domain controller. Strong passwords may be implemented using the passfilt.dll program available under service pack 2 of Windows NT 4.0. The strong passwords provided by passfilt.dll are further described in the section on password filtering.

Modifying User Account Policies

Use the following steps when changing Account Policies:

1. Select Start → Programs → Administrative Tools → User Manager for Domains.
2. Select Policies → Account.
3. Select Expires In and enter **30 days** in the Maximum Password Age control.
4. Select At Least and enter **6** in the Minimum Password Length control.
5. Select Account Lockout and enter **5** in the Lockout After control.
6. Select Duration and enter **60** in the Lockout Duration control.
7. Check *Forcibly disconnect remote users from server when logon hours expire.*
8. Click OK.
9. Close the User Manager for Domains.

USER RIGHTS POLICY

User Rights policy allows you to control what activity users can engage in on a specific machine. Rights apply to the system as a whole rather than to specific objects that are controlled by permissions. Exhibit 5.7 shows the rights that are assigned by default to Windows NT.

Unlike permissions, rights affect the overall operation of the computer or domain, not a specific resource. Very few users will have a need to change User Rights unless they don't plan on using the groups that Windows NT provides for certain functions such as server administration or backing up the system. Use the following steps when modifying User Rights:

1. Select Start → Programs → Administrative Tools → User Manager for Domains.
2. Select Policies → User Rights.
3. Select Change the System Time in the right pick box.
4. Click Add.
5. Double-click the Everyone group.
6. Click OK.
7. Close the User Manager for Domains.

AUDIT POLICY

Audit Policy tells Windows NT which security events to track. Auditing creates entries in the Security Event log whenever the event the user wants audited occurs. The user can track events such as failed logons, attempts to change security policies, and other security-critical actions. Specifically, the user can audit the success or failure of the following events:

- Logon and logoff
- File and object access
- Use of User Rights controlled functions
- User and group management activities
- Changes to Security Policy

Exhibit 5.7 Default Rights Assigned by Windows NT

Right	Granted to
Access this computer from network	Administrators, Everyone
Add workstations to domain	No default group
Back up files and directories	Administrators, Backup Operators, Server Operators
Change the system time	Administrators, Server Operators
Force shutdown from a remote system	Administrators, Server Operators
Load and unload device drivers	Administrators
Log on locally	Account Operators, Administrators, Backup Operators, Print Operators, Server Operators
Manage auditing and security log	Administrators
Restore files and directories	Administrators, Backup Operators, Server Operators
Shut down the system	Account Operators, Administrators, Backup Operators, Print Operators, Server Operators
Take ownership of files or other directories	Administrators

- System restarts and shutdowns
- Processes (such as launching applications)

Some security policies require the tracking of failed logon attempts to identify accounts that are subject to frequent failures or to indicate the level of external attack on the network. The user may want to enable auditing if attempts at hacking the system are suspected, even if Security Policy does not specifically prescribe it. Use the following steps when enabling auditing:

1. Select Start → Programs → Administrative Tools → User Manager for Domains.
2. Select Policies → Audit.
3. Select Audit These Events.
4. Check Logon and Logoff Failure.
5. Click OK.
6. Close the User Manager for Domains.

Auditing frequent events like file and object access can seriously degrade the performance of the server. Audit these events only as a last resort when attempting to track down a specific intrusion.

SYSTEM POLICIES

System policies are slightly different from the other policies in that they are managed through the System Policy Editor, which was introduced in Windows NT 4.0. The System Policy Editor provides a convenient way to edit system policies that were previously accessible only through the Registry Editor. The user can modify a number of system settings through the System Policy Editor. Important settings include:

- Programs to run at startup
- Creation of hidden shares
- Print priorities and settings
- RAS security settings
- Availability of logon security features such as banners and shutdown
- File system features
- Local user restrictions
- Disabling Registry editing tools

The System Policy Editor presents a very mixed bag of security settings. The System Policy Editor handles any Registry setting that Microsoft thought someone might like to control. Feel free to browse through the different policy settings in the Registry—but be certain to understand the implications of changing a setting. *System policy changes can lock a computer so securely that even an administrator cannot unlock it.* Use the following steps when modifying System Policy:

1. Select Start → Programs → Administrative Tools → System Policy Editor.
2. Select File → Open Registry.
3. Double-click Local Computer.
4. Expand Windows NT System.
5. Expand Logon.
6. Check Logon Banner.
7. Type **Security Notice** in the Caption input box.
8. Type **UNAUTHORIZED USE OF THIS SYSTEM MAY RESULT IN SERIOUS LEGAL PENALTIES** in the Text input box.
9. Check *Enable shutdown from Authentication* dialog box.
10. Click OK.
11. Close the System Policy Editor.
12. Answer Yes to the Save Changes? prompt.

File system performance (and thereby the performance of the server) can be improved by changing a simple setting in the System Policy Editor.

To use the System Policy Editor, select Registry → Local Computer → Windows NT System → File System and check *Do not update last access time.* This setting disables the NTFS feature that records the last time a file was read (changing a file still updates the time for backup purposes), which eliminates an unnecessary drive seek and directory write each time a read file is dosed. If you still need to audit access to certain files, use file auditing—it does a better job anyway.

With the System Policy Editor you can configure almost any aspect of a Windows NT or Windows 95 user's environment. By editing the Registry directly, the changes you make are made immediately, overriding any policy settings you may have made previously. You can change those settings back either in the User Manager or by using the System Policy Editor. Instead of making changes to the Registry, you can make the changes to a policy file (NTCONFIG.POL for Windows NT and CONFIG.POL for Windows 95) and then save the policy file in the NetLogon directory of the Primary Domain Controller. These policy changes take effect the next time the user logs on to the network. The changes stored in the policy file will be transferred to the registry of the computer logging on to the server, and the changes will overwrite any conflicting settings. Every time the user logs on the changes will be made again, so you cannot simply change the settings back using the User Manager or User Manager for Domains program.

SHARE PLANNING

The following tasks are necessary to manage disk resources:

- Copying and moving files between file systems
- Creating and sharing resources
- Implementing permissions and security
- Establishing file auditing

Creating a coherent shared directory structure is not difficult, but it does require a bit of thinking.

- What resources do users need?
- What natural boundaries or groups might need their own shares?
- What information needs to remain private?

CREATING SHARES

Select a folder, or a mass storage device if sharing the entire device, on the server and share it. Assign permissions for each group to that share as appropriate. For example, consider the directory structure for a server. In our example, let's assign the following directories to the root of one of the drive M: Admin, Apps, Common, Engineering, Finance, Marketing, Research, Software, temp, Users, Winnts4. Each of the directories can have the functions and permissions assigned to them as shown in Exhibit 5.8.

Don't confuse the group created for the Admin department with the built-in Administrators group created for the administration of the domain. Many organizations have an Admin department, so get used to the idea that you will often encounter an Admin group that doesn't have Administrator permissions.

Note that none of the permissions in Exhibit 5.8 contain the Everyone group. Omitting Everyone keeps information private to this domain—users of other domains do not necessarily have access to the shares on this server. Removing Everyone access also keeps guests from accessing information on your server if the Guest account is enabled.

This server is now set up to allow specific users to share specific directories. Marketing users cannot view or use files in the Engineering group. If members of these groups need to exchange files, they can use the common share. The following illustration shows how to create a directory, share it, and assign share-level permissions.

CREATING A NETWORK SHARE

To create a network share:

1. Go to the Desktop and double-click My Computer.
2. Double-click drive C.

Exhibit 5.8 Directory Functions and Permissions

Directory	Function	Permissions
Admin	Files private to members of the Admin department	Admin:Full Control
Apps	Installed applications to be run from the server	Domain Users:Read
Common	Files public to everyone in the domain	Domain Users:Full Control
Engineering	Files private to the Engineering global group	Engineering:Full Control
Finance	Files private to the Finance global group	Finance:Full Control
Marketing	Files private to the Marketing global group	Marketing:Full Control
Research	Files private to the Research global group	Research:Full Control
Software	Applications that can be installed off the network onto local computers	Domain Users:Read
temp	Files used by Windows NT and server resident software	No access is necessary. This directory is not shared.
Users	Container for subdirectories private to each user	Domain Users:Read
Winnts4	The system directory containing Windows NT	No explicit access is necessary. This directory is not shared.

3. Select File → New → Folder.
4. Type **Share** to rename the new folder to share.
5. Right-click the Share folder you just created and select Properties.
6. Click the Sharing tab.
7. Click Shared As.
8. Click Permissions.
9. Click Remove to remove the Everyone permission.
10. Click Add.
11. Select Domain Users in the Groups list box.
12. Click Add.
13. Select Full Control in the Type of Access pick box.
14. Click OK.
15. Click OK. The Share directory is now shared in the domain under share name Share.

SETTING FILE SYSTEM PERMISSIONS

Remember that file system permissions are not available to non-NTFS volumes—the Security tab will not be available. Use the following steps when setting file system permissions on an NTFS volume:

1. Double-click My Computer.
2. Double-click drive C (or an NTFS volume if it is not C).
3. Select File → New → Folder in the window for that drive.
4. Type **Secure** to rename the folder.
5. Right-click the Secure folder you just created and select Properties.
6. Select the Security tab. If the Security tab is not available, you have not selected an NTFS volume.
7. Click Permissions.
8. Select the Everyone → Full Control permission.
9. Select the Finance group you created earlier in the Names list box.
10. Select Full Control from the Type of Access pick box.
11. Click Add.
12. Click OK.
13. Click OK. You have now changed the folder so that only members of the Finance group (and administrators, of course) have access. Try logging on as a nonmember user and accessing this directory.

MANAGING GROUPS

Setting specific permissions for many users of a network can be an error-prone and time-consuming exercise. Most organizations do not have security requirements that change for every user. Setting permissions is more manageable with the security groups concept, in which permissions are assigned to groups rather than to individual users. Users who are members of a group have all the permissions assigned to that group. Group memberships are especially important in large networks.

Groups are useful in many situations. For instance, the finance department in an organization can have permissions set to access all the financial data stored on a computer. You would then create a group called Finance in the User Manager for Domains and make each individual in the finance department a member of this group. Every member of the Finance group will have access to all the financial data.

Groups also make changing permissions easier. Permissions assigned to a group affect every member of the group, so changes can be made across the entire group by changing permissions for the group. For instance, adding a new directory for the finance group requires merely assigning the group permission to the directory to give each member access. This process is much easier than assigning permission to a number of individual accounts.

The two basic types of groups are local groups and global groups. Local groups affect only the Windows NT computer on which they are created. Global groups affect the entire network and are stored on the primary domain controller (PDC). This discussion focuses on global groups.

One individual account can belong to many groups. This arrangement facilitates setting up groups for many purposes. You might define groups corresponding to the functional areas in your organization—administration, marketing, finance, manufacturing, and so on. A group can be created for supervisors, another for network support staff, and another for new employees. For example, a member of the Finance group may have permission to access accounting information and financial statements, but a member of the New Users group may have the No Access permission to accounting information. By assigning membership in both groups, you would be allowing access to financial statements without permitting access to accounting information until the new user becomes a trusted employee and is removed from the New Users group.

All users must be members of at least one group. To enforce this, Windows NT uses primary groups. One cannot remove membership from a user's primary group without assigning the user to a different primary group. By default, in a domain, the primary group is Domain Users. Use the default primary group (Domain Users) rather than the Everyone group to set file system permissions. Members of Domain Users have provided proper logon credentials, but Guests and anonymous network users are members of Everyone.

Windows NT networks also have a special Everyone group that contains all members of the domain and any trusted domains. Resources with Everyone access are available to anyone attached to the domain and trusted domain.

Microsoft Exchange uses the Windows NT group information to define its groups. Therefore, all members of a security group will also become members of message groups when you install Microsoft Exchange.

Global versus Local Groups

Windows NT supports two types of groups: global, or network groups, and local groups that apply only to a single computer. Windows NT servers acting as domain controllers create global groups with the User Manager for Domains. Windows NT workstations can only create groups local to that workstation.

Local groups are not especially important on Windows NT servers because users usually don't log in at the server. All the illustrations in this chapter concern global groups. Local groups can contain global groups, but global groups cannot contain local groups.

Special Groups and Built-in Groups

Windows NT has many built-in groups that cover a wide array of typical functions and have permissions already assigned to support those functions. The Guests local group is included for complete compatibility with Windows NT Workstation and should remain disabled on dedicated servers. A list of the groups built into Windows NT Server is shown in Exhibit 5.9.

Windows NT also includes a special group that does not show up in group lists: Everyone. The Everyone group contains all users attached to the domain in any way, including users on trusted domains and guests, and is used to assign permissions regardless of group membership.

Groups can be created, modified, and deleted with the User Manager for Domains. The following illustration shows how to make a global group. The process for making a local group is similar; simply select the local group menu item.

Creating a Global Group

Use the following steps when creating a global group:

1. Select Start → Programs → Administrative Tools → User Manager for Domains.
2. Select User → New Global Group.

Exhibit 5.9 Windows NT Server Built-In Groups

Group	Type	Function
Account Operators	Local	Members can administer domain user and group accounts.
Administrators	Local	Members can fully administer the server and the domain.
Backup Operators	Local	Members can bypass file security to archive files.
Domain Admins	Global	Members can administer domain accounts and computers in the domain.
Domain Guests	Global	Members have Guest rights to all domain resources.
Domain Users	Global	All domain users are part of this group.
Guests	Local	Members have Guest access to the domain. This group should remain empty.
Print Operators	Local	Members can administer domain printers.
Replicator	Local	A special group for directory replication.
Server Operators	Local	Members can administer domain servers.
Users	Local	Server users.

3. Type **Finance** in the Group Name input box.
4. Type **Members of the Finance and Accounting Departments** in the Description input box.
5. Click OK. To add members to this group from the existing list of users, double-click the Username in the Not a Member of list box. How to add users as they are created will also be shown.)
6. Close the User Manager for Domains.

SPECIAL GROUPS

In addition to the many built-in groups, Windows NT has two groups with special functions: Everyone and Guests. You can use these two groups to create special sets of permissions without creating them yourself.

Everyone

In Windows NT, Everyone is a special group that applies not only to domain users (as does the Domain Users global group) but also to all members of any trusted domains. The Everyone group cannot be deleted or disabled; it is the default permission group granted to any resource when it is shared. Specifically, the Everyone permission must be deleted and permissions assigned to other groups if global access to shared resources is not to be allowed.

Anonymous Users

Anonymous users are accounts attached to the domain that could not provide a valid logon because they do not have an account. Windows NT is not like other network operating systems, such as NetWare or Unix that treat anonymous users as specific accounts. An anonymous user is anyone who failed to log on properly to a Windows NT computer or domain.

Anonymous users are members of the Everyone group. If you allow Everyone access permissions to a share (which is the default), anyone with access to your network will have access to everything on that share.

Besides these two groups, several internal special groups appear in certain instances. Permissions cannot be assigned to these groups, so they are of little consequence, but they do reveal how Windows NT manages groups and connections internally. The internal special groups are:

- Interactive: anyone using the computer locally
- Network: all users connected over the network
- System: the operating system
- Creator/Owner: an alias for the user who created the subdirectory, file, or print job in question

It is not necessary to be concerned with the operation or effect of these groups since they are entirely internal to the function of Windows NT.

MANAGING USER ACCOUNTS

Managing users consists of creating and maintaining user accounts for the people who work on the network. The easiest way to create a user environment is to create the groups first, then create secure shares with permissions assigned by group membership, and finally create users and assign them to groups.

NETWORKED AND LOCAL USERS

As with groups, Windows NT has two types of users—local and global. Local users are users who are allowed to log on to the computer itself. Global users are users who are allowed to log on to the network domain. You create local users with the User Manager included with Windows NT Workstation and Windows NT Servers designated as stand-alone servers. You create global users with the User Manager for Domains included with Windows NT Server on servers designated as primary domain controllers, backup domain controllers, or member servers. Global user accounts are created on the primary domain controller. The primary domain controller replicates its account database to all Windows NT Servers designated as backup domain controllers in the domain. Backup domain controllers will respond to a logon attempt if the primary domain controller fails to log on the client after a short time; that is, the primary domain controller is busy or temporarily unreachable.

SPECIAL BUILT-IN ACCOUNTS

Windows NT creates two user accounts by default: the Administrator account and the Guest account.

Administrator Account

The Administrator account is always present and should be protected with a strong password. This account manages the overall configuration of the computer and can be used to manage security policies, to create or change users and groups, to set shared directories for networking, and to perform other hardware maintenance tasks. This account can be renamed , but it cannot be deleted.

Rename the Administrator account to make guessing its password harder. Hackers know that Windows NT defaults to an Administrator account that cannot be locked out, so they will attempt to hack the password of that account. Changing the Administrator account name defeats this security loophole.

Guest Account

The Guest account enables one-time users or users with low or no security access to use the computer in a limited fashion. The Guest account does not save user preferences or configuration changes, so any changes that a guest user makes are lost when that user logs off. The Guest account is installed with a blank password. If the password is left blank, remote users can connect to the computer using the Guest account. This account can be renamed and disabled, but it cannot be deleted.

Leave the Guest account disabled unless it is needed to allow a specific service to users without passwords. Remember that the special group Everyone includes Guest users and that shares give full control to Everyone by default. If the Guest account is used, be especially careful about share permissions.

CREATING USER ACCOUNTS

User accounts can be added to the NT network in two ways: by creating new user accounts or by making copies of existing user accounts. In either case, changes can be made in these three areas:

- User account information
- Group membership information
- User account profile information

To add a new user account, you will be working with the New User dialog box. When you create users with the User Manager for Domains, you are creating global user accounts.

User Account Properties

The following describes the properties of the user account that are accessible from the New User dialog box:

Field Value

- Username A required text field of up to twenty characters. Uses both uppercase and lowercase letters except ' ',", / \, [ ], ;, :, |, =, +, *, ?, < > but is not case sensitive. This name must be unique among workstation users or among network domain members if attached to a network.
- Full Name An optional text field typically used for the complete name of the user. For instance, a user whose full name is Mae West may have a username of mwest.
- Description An optional text field used to more fully describe users and their positions in the firm, home office, and so on. This field is limited to any 48 characters.

- **Password** A text field up to fourteen characters and case sensitive. This field displays asterisks, rather than the characters typed, to keep the password secure.
- **Confirm Password** A text field used to confirm the password field. This method avoids typing errors that result in unknown passwords. As with the **Password** field, the **Confirm Password** field displays asterisks.
- **User Must Change Password at Next Logon** A checkbox field used to force a password change at next logon. Note that Windows NT will not allow you to apply changes to a user account if this field and **User Cannot Change Password** field are both checked.
- **User Cannot Change Password** A checkbox field that makes it impossible for users to change their own password. This feature is used for shared accounts (such as the **Guest** account) where a user changing the account password would prevent other users of the account from logging on. You would not normally check this account for typical users.
- **Password Never Expires** A checkbox field that prevents a password from expiring according to the password policy. This setting is normally used for automated software services that must be logged on as a user. Note that setting **Password Never Expires** overrides **User Must Change Password at Next Logon.**
- **Account Disabled** A checkbox field that when set prevents users from logging on to the network with this account This field provides an easy way to place an account out of service temporarily.
- **Account Locked Out** This option will be checked if the account is currently locked out due to failed logon attempts. It can be cleared to restore access to the account, but it cannot be set.
- **Groups** button Assigns group membership.
- **Profile** button Activates the user environment profile information.
- **Hours** button Sets the hours during which the user may log on. The default is **Always All Computers.**
- **Logon To** button Specifies which computers the user can log on to the network from. The default is **All Computers.**
- **Account** button Specifies the account expiration date and the account type.
- **Dialin** button Allows users to dial into this computer using Remote Access Service. The **Hours** button can be used to disallow network access for all users when an office is closed, and a policy can be set to forcibly disconnect logged on users when that time occurs. Schedule backups to run in this period to be certain that no files are open during the backup. The NT tape backup utility cannot back up files that are open.

User accounts are administered with the **User Manager for Domains** administrative tool.

Creating a New User Account

The following illustration shows the process of creating new user accounts. (Subsequent illustrations in this chapter assume that you have already opened the **User Manager for Domains.**)

Use the following steps to create a new user account:

1. Log on to the network as an administrator.
2. Click the Start menu and select Programs → Administrative Tools → User Manager for Domains.
3. Select User → New User.
4. Type **mwest** in the Username field.
5. Type **Mae West** in the Full Name field.
6. Type **Movie Star/Pop Culture Icon** in the Description field.
7. Type in any password you want in the Password field. A good password is at least eight characters long and includes at least one punctuation mark. Passwords are case sensitive.
8. Type exactly the same password in the Confirm Password field.
9. Leave the checkboxes as they are for now.
10. Click OK.
11. Do not record this password anywhere. If you forget it, use the Administrator account to assign a new password to this account.

Record the Administrator account password, seal it in an envelope, and put it in a safe or other secure location. Make sure at least one other trusted individual knows where the password is stored.

COPYING USER ACCOUNTS

To create accounts for many users, for instance, in an academic environment where hundreds of students come and go every year, a few basic user account templates can be created and copied as needed. A user account template is a user account that provides all the features new users will need and has its Account Disabled field enabled. To add a user account, the template can be copied. When you copy a user account, Windows NT automatically copies some of the user account field values from the template; you provide the remaining necessary information. Windows NT copies the following values from the template to the new user account:

- Description
- Group Account Memberships
- Profile Settings
- User Cannot Change Password
- Password Never Expires
- User Must Change Password at Next Logon

Windows NT leaves the following fields blank in the New User dialog box:

- Username
- Full Name
- Account Disabled

The Username and Full Name fields are left blank to enter the new user information. The User Must Change Password at Next Logon checkbox is checked by default. As a security precaution, leave this setting if you want to force new users to change from your assigned password when they first log on. Use the following steps to copy a user account:

1. Select the mwest user account in the User Manager for Domains.
2. Select User → Copy or press F8.
3. Enter the following information into the Copy of mwest dialog box. Leave the checkbox fields in their default states.
4. Type **rvalentino** in the Username field.
5. Type **Rudolf Valentino** in the Full Name field.
6. Notice that the Description field is copied from the original New User dialog box. Although it remains correct in this example, it will usually change.
7. Type **ruvaruva!** in the Password field.
8. Type **ruvaruva!** in the Confirm Password field.
9. Explore the User Accounts profile and group settings to note that the assignments for mwest have been automatically assigned to rvalentino. To do this inspection, click the Profile and Group buttons and then click OK to return to the Copy of mwest dialog box.
10. Click OK to complete the creation of the rvalentino account.

Notice that an initial password loosely based on the user's name but mangled according to specific rules was assigned. This method is a relatively secure initial password scheme to keep individuals outside an organization from easily guessing new user passwords. However, the only entirely secure method is to assign randomly generated passwords that are passed to the user through some physical means. Security needs may require more rigorous precautions to keep initial passwords from creating a hole in the security measures.

DISABLING AND DELETING USER ACCOUNTS

When access to the domain is no longer appropriate for a user, the account should be disabled. Leaving unused active accounts in the user accounts database permits potential intruders to continue logon attempts after previously tried accounts have already locked them out. Disabling accounts prevents them from being used, but the account information is retained for future use. This technique is useful for temporarily locking accounts of employees who are absent or for temporarily denying access to accounts that may have been compromised. *Deleting an account* removes all the user account information from the system. If a user account has been deleted and that user requires access again, a new account with all new permissions will have to be set up. Creating a new user account with the same name will not restore previous account information since a unique security identifier and not the user name internally identifies each user account.

Disabling a User Account

Follow the steps below to disable a user account:

1. Double-click user account rvalentino in the User Manager for Domains.
2. Check the Account Disabled field.
3. Click OK to complete the operation.
4. Log off and attempt to log on as rvalentino.

If a user is no longer using the system, delete the user's account instead of disabling it. Deleting an account will destroy all user preferences and permissions, so make sure the user will not require access to the system before deleting the account.

Deleting a User Account

The process for deleting a user account is as follows:

1. Log on to the network as an **Administrator**. Go to the **Start** menu.
2. Select **Programs → Administrative Tools → User Manager for Domains.**
3. Select user account **rvalentino.**
4. Select **User → Delete** (or hit the **Del** key).
5. Click **OK** in the **Warning** dialog.
6. Click **Yes** to confirm the deletion.
7. Log off and attempt to log on as **rvalentino.**

RENAMING USER ACCOUNTS

Any user account with the **User Manager for Domains**, including the **Administrator** and **Guest default** accounts, can be renamed. It may be necessary to change an account user name if an account that is associated with a specific job is assigned to another individual or if an organization changes its network naming policy.

Changing the name does not change any other properties of the account. It may be necessary to change the names of the **Administrator** and **Guest** accounts so an intruder familiar with Windows NT default user account names cannot gain access to your system simply by guessing a password. The steps for renaming a user account are as follows:

1. Log on to the network as **Administrator** and go to the **Start** menu.
2. Select **Programs → Administrative Tools → User Manager for Domains.**
3. Select **mwest** in the **User Accounts** list.
4. Select **User → Rename.**
5. Type **wema** in the **Change To** box.
6. Click **OK** to complete the operation.

EDITING USER ENVIRONMENT PROFILES

User environment profiles allow the change of some default behavior of Windows NT based on the users that are logged on. For instance, the profiles allow you to change the default file location based on the current user or to map a drive letter to a user's home directory on a server if the person is logging on to a network.

User environment profiles also allow you to run a batch file or executable program that changes as each user logs on. This batch file can be used to set paths, environment variables, and drive mappings or for any other purpose that will change from user to user.

Do not use user environment profiles simply to start a program when users log on unless the profile somehow depends on the user's name. The Startup folder provides a much easier method for running programs automatically.

LOGON SCRIPTS

Logon scripts can be used to maintain a consistent set of network connections. In addition, logon scripts provide a way to migrate users from older network operating systems that use logon scripts to Windows NT without changing the user's familiar environment. They are generally not used for individual workstations.

A logon script is usually implemented as a DOS batch file (with a BAT extension), but it can be an executable file under Windows NT 3.5 and later. Certain environment variables enable you to change settings from within a logon script:

- %PROCESSOR% changes to the CPU type of the machine.
- %HOMEDRIVE% changes to the system hard disk drive.
- %HOMEPATH% changes to the user's home path.
- %HOMESHARE% changes to the user's home share name.
- %OS% changes to the operating system being used.
- %USERDOMAIN% changes to the user's home network domain.
- %USERNAME% changes to the user's name.

If you are migrating from Novell NetWare, take advantage of Windows NT Server's ability to process NetWare login scripts without changing them to Windows NT logon scripts. If your network uses Windows clients exclusively and few users run MS-DOS programs, you probably don't need to create logon scripts because your drive mappings will persist from session to session automatically. In addition, environment variables are not as important in this environment as they were in MS-DOS. A lot of hassle can be avoided by using logon scripts only if some functionality is required that cannot be provided any other way. Maintaining logon scripts is an administrative burden that is not necessary for most networks anymore.

HOME DIRECTORIES

Home directories give users a place to store their files. By changing the home directory through the user profile, each user can have a private location in which to store files. Windows NT automatically assigns permissions for that user to access the home directory if it does not already exist. If it does, permissions should be set on home directories so that only the user specified has access to the data in the directory.

Windows NT makes the home directory the default save location for programs that do not specify one in their Save Dialog box. The home directory is also the default directory when launching an MS-DOS prompt. In the user environment profile, these settings can be changed.

CREATING USER DIRECTORIES

Use the following steps to create a user directory:

1. Log on to the network as Administrator.
2. Open the My Computer icon.
3. Open drive C.
4. Click the right mouse button and select New → Folder.

5. Type **users** as the folder Name.
6. Right-click on the folder.
7. Select Sharing.
8. Select Shared As.
9. Click OK.
10. Select Start → Programs → Administrative Tools → User Manager for Domains.
11. Double-click wema in the User Accounts list.
12. Click the Profile button.
13. Select Z in the Connect To pick box.
14. Type **\\{server_name}\users%username%** in the text box. Replace the **{server_share}** text including the brackets with the name of your server.
15. Click OK to close the User Environment Profile dialog box.
16. Click the Profile button again. Windows NT has replaced the environment variable %username% with wema, the name of our user. (Using the %username% variable ensures that the name will be changed when you copy user templates.)
17. Click OK to close the User Environment Profile dialog box.
18. Click OK to close the User dialog box.
19. Click Close in the User Manager for Domains.

When opening the user's folder, you will see that Windows NT has created a directory called wema and that wema has full permissions to the directory—no other users do. Even administrators will not be able to open the directory without first taking ownership of it.

Why create a new share for users when the share path for drive C and the user directory could have been included, thereby eliminating a step and a share? The reason is that unlike most other shares, user directories are likely to be moved between volumes during the lifetime of the server. Having an independent share name is convenient for this purpose. This condition is one of the very rare exceptions to the rule that as few shares as possible should be created and directory permissions should be used to create a secure environment.

Another good idea is to create a volume specifically and only for user files. This technique sets a natural limit to the size user files can take up on your hard disk. This is because Windows NT doesn't support account-based disk quotas like other network operating systems do and as such guarantees your system and boot volumes won't run out of space when those downloaded picture files start taking up too much space.

Windows NT cannot create more than one level of directory structure automatically in the User Environment Profile dialog box. If the path suggested earlier had been entered without having created the user directory first, Windows NT would have set the profile but warned about creating the directory manually. Creating the path for user directories prior to changing the profile information ensures that this step will not be forgotten or the user's name misspelled when creating the directory.

Despite its obvious utility, the Connect Drive Letter to UNC Path function works only on Windows NT clients. It does not function on DOS, Windows, or Macintosh clients. You can still use it to create folders with permissions specific to each user, however.

Although creating home directories is simple, it's a little time consuming. However, you can select multiple users in the user list and use the %username% variable to create many home directories at once.

Profiles

User profiles control Windows NT features such as desktop colors and settings, program groups and start menu settings, and network connections. Because these settings are different for each user, storing them separately allows users to customize and control their Windows NT environment. Bob will always log on to the same environment, even if Susan changes her wallpaper.

Local

Windows NT stores each user's settings in special directories contained in the Profiles directory under your Windows NT System WINNT_ROOT directory. Each user's local profile is stored in a subdirectory named after the user. These directories contain all user-specific settings. A special directory called All Users stores the settings that are global to all users.

Each profile contains many subdirectories. Applications such as Word and Excel store user preferences in the Application Data subdirectory so that shared copies of these applications can maintain different customized features for each user. NetHood contains persistent network connections. Many other directories may exist and contain other settings such as Start menu programs and program groups.

Roaming

Roaming profiles are stored like the local profiles, except that they are stored on a Windows NT Server. Storing one profile on the server, instead of storing a local profile on each of the Windows NT computers that you use, means that changes to your environment will be in effect for all the computers you use rather than just the one on which you made the change.

When specifying a roaming profile in the user settings for your user account, the profile is downloaded from the server every time you log on. Changes you make are then sent back to the server so that they will still be in effect the next time you log on and download the profile. Windows NT profiles affect only Windows NT. Logging on to a Windows 95 computer will not bring down the Windows NT roaming profile.

You may want each user's home directory to contain the user's profile. The %username% environment variable can be used when creating User Directories to automate this process (see the list discussed earlier on the steps to create a user directory).

To create a roaming profile, follow these steps:

1. Select Start → Programs → Administrative Tools → User Manager for Domains.
2. Double-click Administrator.
3. Click Profile.
4. Type **\\name_of_your_server\winnt\profiles** in the User Profile Path input box. (Replace name_of_your_server with the share name of your server and replace winnt with the name of your Windows NT directory share name.) If your Windows NT directory is not shared, use the following path: **\\name_of_your server\c_drive_share\winnt\profiles**.
5. Click OK to close the User Profiles window.
6. Click OK to close the User window.

7. Close the User Manager for Domains.
8. Log on as Administrator on another Windows NT machine in the domain to observe the results.

SUMMARY

Just as providing service to network users is the primary purpose of a network, creating a coherent, secure, and useful user environment is the primary function of network administration. Windows NT Server creates such an environment by using group accounts, security permissions, user rights and policies, and network shares.

Effective groups make administering large numbers of users easy. Rather than assigning permissions to individual users, you can assign rights to groups and simply indicate membership in different groups for each user. Windows NT will manage the combinations of rights for users with multiple group memberships.

Security keeps resources from being exposed to unauthorized access. An optimistic security policy allows maximum access to information and secures only specific information. A pessimistic security policy secures all resources and grants access only where necessary. Both approaches are valid, and the choice will depend on the physical security environment. Windows NT supports two types of secured resources: network shares and file system objects. File system objects provide more control over security than shares do. When resolving conflicting file system and share restrictions, Windows NT chooses the most restrictive permission.

Policies are the general security characteristics of Windows NT. Policy changes affect the entire system, not just individual users or groups. Windows NT implements four types of policies: Account Policies control access to user accounts, User Rights permit or restrict security-related activities, Audit Policy controls the auditing of user activity, and System Policy controls all other security-related system settings.

Setting specific permissions for many users of a network can be an error-prone and time-consuming exercise. Most organizations do not have security requirements that change for every user. Setting permissions is more manageable with the security groups concept, in which permissions are assigned to groups rather than to individual users. Users who are members of a group have all the permissions assigned to that group. Windows NT implements two types of groups: those local to the machine and those global to the domain. Global groups are stored on the primary domain controller and replicated to all backup domain controllers.

User accounts allow you to control security on a per person basis. Every person who accesses a Windows NT domain receives a user account through which identity is established to the network and by which permissions to resources are granted. Windows NT also provides two types of user accounts: accounts local to the machine and accounts global to the domain. As with groups, global accounts are stored on the primary domain controller and backed up to the backup domain controllers. User accounts can have logon scripts, home directories, and roaming user preference profiles to allow users to work comfortably at any computer in the network.

APPENDIX 5A

DOMAINS AND TRUST

A domain is a set of computers with a central security authority, the primary domain controller (PDC), that grants access to a domain. Usually a domain also contains one or more backup domain controllers (BDCs) that provide distributed authentication services to continue authentication services in the event of failure in the PDC as well as load balancing for authentication services. As a rule many types of systems may join a domain, but the PDC and the BDC must be Windows NT systems because of the compartmentalized security they can offer. A domain can be set up to ease viewing and access to resources, to share a common user account database and common security policy, and to allow administrators to enforce a common security stance across physical, divisional, or corporate boundaries. Once users are authenticated to the domain, using either the PDC or a BDC, they can gain access to the resources of the domain, such as printing and file sharing, or access to applications across all of the servers within the domain. This concept of a domainwide user account and password eliminates the need for every machine to provide its own authentication service. Instead, the authentication processes are passed through to the domain controllers for remote authentication against that user account database. This allows machines to be dedicated to servicing individual applications or programs without the overhead of authentication.

The primary function of the PDC is to maintain the security database. A read-only copy of this database is replicated to each BDC on a regular basis to maintain consistency in the environment. Because of the importance of maintaining the security database on the PDC and BDC, strict logical and physical access controls should be implemented.

Trusts are one-way relationships that can be set up between domains to share resources and further ease administration. These relationships allow a user or groups to be created only once within a set of domains yet access resources across multiple domains. There are a number of trust models used to configure domains. The first is the single domain model with only one PDC and, by definition, no trust relationships (see Exhibit 5.10).

The next model is the master domain model for companies who desire centralized security administration. In this configuration, all domains, known as user or resource domains, trust the master domain. The master domain maintains security resources for all of the domains within this structure. This configuration can support up to 15,000 users. There is one trust relationship for every domain that trusts the master domain (see Exhibit 5.11).

The multiple master domain model is designed for larger organizations that desire some centralized security administration. With more than one master domain, administra-

Exhibit 5.10 Single Domain Model

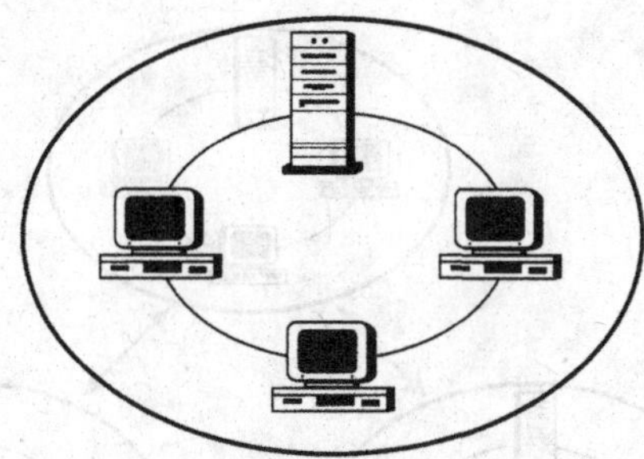

Exhibit 5.11 Master Domain Model

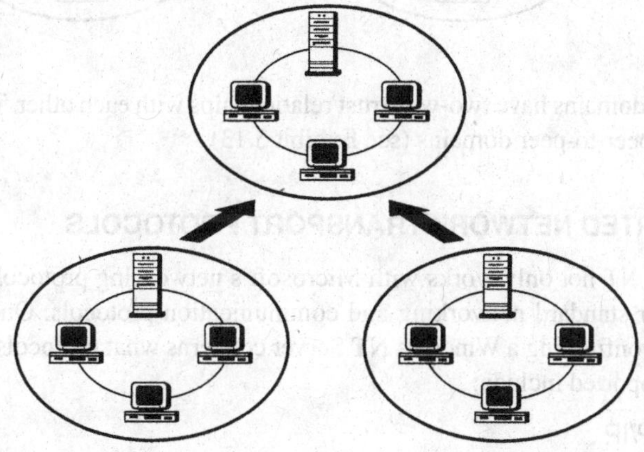

Exhibit 5.12 Multiple Master Domain Model

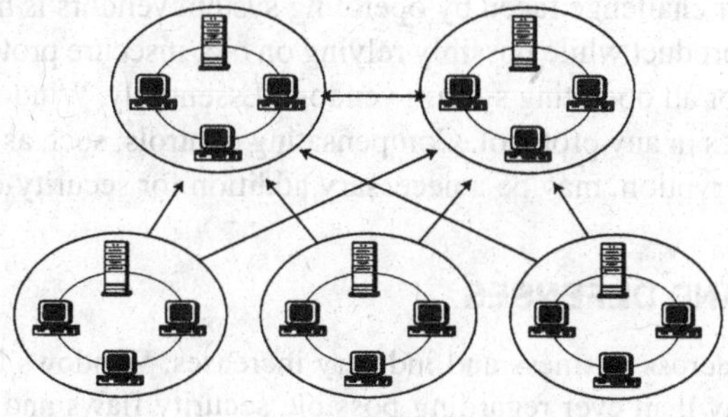

tion needs increase as a result of the need to create all network accounts on each master domain. The two master domains in this case trust each other, while the resource domains have one trust relationship with each of the master domains (see Exhibit 5.12).

Finally, there is the complete trust model. This is designed for larger companies that desire totally decentralized security administration. This configuration presents considerable

Exhibit 5.13 Complete Trust Model

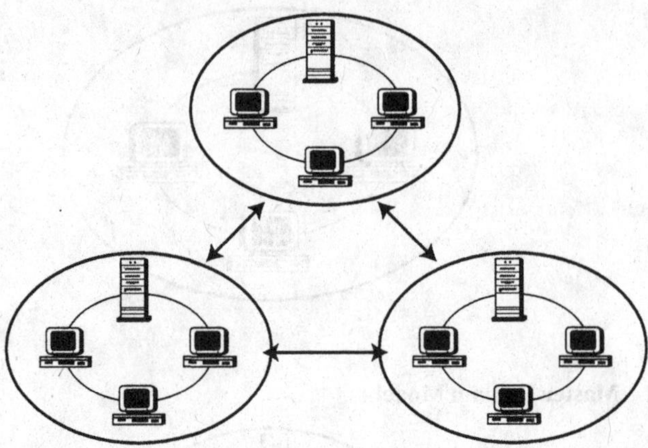

risk as all domains have two-way trust relationships with each other. This concept essentially provides peer-to-peer domains (see Exhibit 5.13).

SUPPORTED NETWORK TRANSPORT PROTOCOLS

Windows NT not only works with Microsoft's networking protocols but also is compliant with other standard networking and communication protocols. One of the top considerations for configuring a Windows NT Server concerns what protocols to install and use. Protocols supported include:

- TCP/IP
- NetBEUI
- NWLink (IPX/SPX)

A major challenge faced by operating system vendors is how to make a secure, standards-based product while possibly relying on old, insecure protocols. This has been an ongoing issue for all operating system vendors. Essentially, Windows NT does not attempt to fix weaknesses in any protocol. Compensating controls, such as the use of link- or application-level encryption, may be a necessary addition for security-conscious organizations.

ATTACKS AND DEFENSES

As its usage across business and industry increases, Windows NT Server has come under closer scrutiny than ever regarding possible security flaws and holes. Exhibit 5.14 examines the various attacks on the Windows NT Server operating system and the defenses put in place in attempts to mitigate them.

Windows NT has been vulnerable to various Denial of Service (DOS) and other attacks that either attempt to retrieve sensitive information or attempt to gain access with permissions greater than those that the attackers own. To provide a secure environment, Microsoft provides fixes in the form of patches and service packs. After being notified of the exposure presented, Microsoft issues fixes. Exhibit 5.14 lists some of the more widespread attacks that have been identified and the associated fix that has been released.

Exhibit 5.14 Windows NT Attacks and Defenses

Attack/Method	Defense
Access Gaining and Information Gathering	
Anonymous User Connections (red button) is used to gain information regarding the administrative account and the network shares that are available.	Insert key into registry that prevents the anonymous user from making a network connection to the server: HKLM\System\CurrentControlSet\Control\LSA\RestrictAnonymous* Type: **REG_DWORD** Value: 1
Remote Registry Access attempts to gain access to the registry, either to retrieve passwords or to change system settings.	Remote registry access is prevented in Windows NT Server version 4.0 by the addition of a Registry key. This key is present by default in a new installation of Windows NT Server 4.0 but is not present by default in Windows NT Workstation 4.0. It may also not be present in a computer that has been upgraded from Windows NT Server 3.51. HKLM\System\CurrentControlSet\Control\SecurePipeServers\winreg
Password Theft and Cracking is an attempt to capture hashed passwords and crack them in order to gain further access to a system.	Increase password encryption in the SAM by applying the features of SP3. Remove anonymous access to the system and tighten registry security.
Weak and Easily Guessed Passwords	Enforce a strong password policy from the domain controller using passfilt.dll. Passfilt.dll is available from Service Pack 2 onward.
Rollback—Rollback.exe is included with Windows NT 4.0. It is a tool that forces the systems configuration back to installation settings.	Rollback may be used as a Trojan horse, and it should be deleted from all systems.
GetAdmin—The GetAdmin program was recently released from a Russian source. GetAdmin allows a regular user to get administrative rights on the local machine.	A security hot fix to patch both GetAdmin and the follow-on issue have been released by Microsoft.
A follow-on to GetAdmin that may bypass the hot fix has just been released.	
Services running under System context could be used to gain access to the registry and other parts of the system as "SYSTEM".	Run Services as accounts other than system wherever possible.
Unsecured Filesystem access using either a DOS- or Linux-based tool gives access to the NTFS file system without any security controls.	Physically secure the server to prevent access to the diskette drive.
Server Message Block (SMB) NetBIOS access. These access ports that are required for file sharing may present an access path, especially when exposed to the Internet or when used in conjunction with a Unix server running the Samba toolset.	Apply Service Pack 3 and disable TCP and UDP ports 137, 138, and 139 on any server connected to an outside network.

Continued

Exhibit 5.14 Windows NT Attacks and Defenses *Continued*

Attack/Method	Defense
Denial of Service	
Telnet to unexpected ports can lead to locked systems or increased CPU usage. Telnet expects connections to be made to port 23 only. By default, Windows NT does not support a telnet daemon.	Apply Service Pack 2 or 3.
The Ping of Death (large ping packet). An attack that has affected many major operating systems has also been found to affect Windows NT. The Ping of Death is caused by issuing ping packets larger than normal size. If someone was to issue the ping command, specifying a large packet size (> 64 bytes), the TCP/IP stack will cease to function correctly. This effectively takes the system off-line until rebooted. Most implementations of ping will not allow a packet size greater than the 64-byte default; however, Windows '95 and NT do allow this exception and can therefore cause or be vulnerable to such a system denial.	This problem was resolved in SP2.
A recent version of this problem has affected Windows NT Server version 4.0 SP3 systems that run IIS and are exposed to the Internet. This was due to a fragmented and improperly formed ICMP packet.	A new hot fix has been released, post-SP3, called the icmp-fix.
'SYN' Flood Attack—A flood of TCP connection requests (SYN) can be sent to an IIS server that contains "spoofed" source IP addresses. Upon receiving the connection request, the IIS server allocates resources to handle and track the new connections. A response is sent to the "spoofed" nonexistent IP address. Using default values, the server will continue to retransmit and eventually deallocate the resources that were set aside earlier for the connection 189 seconds later. This effectively ties up the server, and multiple requests can cause the IIS server to respond with a reset to all further connection requests.	Service Pack 2 provides a fix to this vulnerability.
Out of Band Attacks—Out of Band (OOB) attacks, in which data is sent outside the normal expected scope, have been shown to affect Windows NT. The first OOB attack was identified after Service Pack 2 (SP2), and a patch was released that was also included in SP3. This attack caused unpredictable results and sometimes caused Windows NT to have trouble handling any network operations after one of these attacks. Since the release of SP3, another problem has been identified in the TCPIP.SYS network driver that caused Microsoft networking clients to remain vulnerable to variations of the OOB attack, coming from the Apple Macintosh environment. The OOB attack crashes the TCP/IP protocol stack, forcing a reboot of Windows NT. A subsequent hot fix was released to counter this attack.	Apply Service Pack 3 and the subsequent OOB-fix.

SERVICES THAT ENHANCE OR IMPACT SECURITY

Impact of the Internet

The Internet evolved from the Defense Department's Arpanet, which was first created in the late 1960s. In 1991, commercial traffic was allowed on it for the first time. With commercial use and the subsequent development of the hypertext transport protocol and the World Wide Web that uses it, companies began to connect their corporate WANs to the Internet. The very visible connectivity and accessibility to corporate networks by large numbers of people have created a number of changes in corporate views of data security. The primary impact was one of awareness. In a very short time, nontechnical people started talking about technology. They also started asking about the security of their connections. The hype and misinformation surrounding the Internet's features and risks have created the need for technology solutions and education about technology and security. Anyone can become a content publisher almost overnight. Sharing data with employees, strategic partners, customers, and even competitors has become very easy to do. Naturally, this introduces or enhances the risks to an organization's data.

Internet Information Server

The addition of Internet Information Server (IIS) to the base Windows NT operating system has provided Windows NT Server with new functionality as well as exposing Windows NT to the security risks of the Internet. IIS is integrated with the Windows NT operating system making it an alternative to expand NT Servers to Web servers for intranet and the Internet. IIS also includes standard TCP/IP servers for FTP and Gopher. This Web client-server model provides a method to utilize Windows NT to provide information to people on the internal network as well as on the Internet.

There are many well-known security risks associated with the Internet, and IIS allowed Windows NT to be exposed to them. However, because IIS is coupled with Windows NT Server, it allows for the use of the security features found in the operating system.

In addition, other applications and protocols have been developed in an attempt to limit these security exposures. A few of these applications and protocols have been explored in the following sections as an example of Microsoft's role in Internet technologies. As always, any system exposed to the Internet should be protected using multiple layers of security.

Proxy Server

The Microsoft Proxy Server offers features such as site filtering, access control, request logging, multiple Internet protocol support, caching, and remote administration. This application also integrates with IIS and the Windows NT operating system. The Proxy Server is an optional product, not included with the base operating system.

The Proxy Server assists in preventing network penetration by masking the internal network from other external networks. Client requests can be verified to be sure that they are coming from the internal network. IP packets with destination addresses not defined are prevented from accessing computers on the internal network. This helps to prevent spoofing attacks. Filtering can limit access to specified network addresses, address ranges, subnet masks, or Internet domains. The Proxy Server provides two levels of activity or security logging. User-level authentication is provided between the client and Proxy Server.

Specific protocols can be secured at an individual or group level, or the option to entirely disable access to protocols exists.

Secure Sockets Layer (SSL)

Secure Sockets Layer (SSL) is supported by the Microsoft Proxy Server. This allows a secure session between the server and a client computer. SSL 3.0 is a protocol that provides for mutual authentication and confidentiality between Web browsers and Web Servers. SSL provides a security "handshake" that is used to initiate the TCP/IP network connection. This handshake results in the client and server agreeing on the level of security (i.e., algorithm and key length selection) that they will use and identifies both parties. SSL requires the use of digital certificates and provides both server-side and client-side certificates for the connection. SSL encrypts and decrypts the byte stream of the application protocol being used (for example: HTTP). This means that all the information in both the HTTP request and the HTTP response are fully encrypted, including the Universal Resource Locator (URL) that the client is requesting, any submitted form contents (such as credit card numbers), any HTTP access authorization information (user names and passwords), and all the data returned from the server to the client.

Server-Based Routing

Microsoft has introduced the Routing and Remote Access Service. The new routing features integrate with the Microsoft Proxy Server and provide an added layer of security. Windows NT's routing features support for RIP, OSPF, and DHCP Relay protocols on IP networks and RIP and SAP protocols on IPX networks.

The new service provides the rough equivalent of packet filtering security that can be found on many hardware-based routers. The filtering can be used for packet layer network security and, when used with Microsoft Proxy Server, complements the application layer security. Filters are configured on an exception basis. Users can configure the filter to pass only the packets from the routes listed or pass everything except the packets for the routes specified.

Another security feature provided is Remote Authentication Dial-In User Service (RADIUS). This provides another security and accounting option that can be used with this service. With RADIUS client support, an administrator can elect to use Windows NT Server domain-based database for user authentication or can elect instead to use some other RADIUS server database to perform the authentication.

Point-to-Point Tunneling Protocol

Point-to-Point Tunneling Protocol (PPTP) is a network protocol that facilitates the secure transfer of data from a remote client to a private enterprise server by creating a virtual private network (VPN) across TCP/IP-based data networks. The PPTP protocol encapsulates data for transmission over TCP/IP-based networks. Encapsulation enables plug-and-play software. Any encapsulated software consists of two parts—an interface, which it presents to the outside world, and an implementation, which it keeps private. If a user sends an object one of the messages required by the interface with the appropriate arguments in the agreed-upon format, the object will return to the user a response with the results in the agreed-upon format. PPTP provides a form of secure and encrypted communications over public telephone lines and the Internet. PPTP eliminates the need for expensive, leased-line or private enterprise-dedicated communication servers because PPTP can be used over standard telephone lines.

Authentication of remote PPTP clients is done by using the same authentication methods used for any RAS client dialing directly to a RAS server. Microsoft's implementation of RAS supports the Challenge Handshake Authentication Protocol (CHAP), the Microsoft Challenge Handshake Authentication Protocol (MS-CHAP), and the Password Authentication Protocol (PAP) authentication schemes. After authentication, all access to a private LAN continues to use the Windows NT–based security model. These methods of user authentication are discussed in an earlier section, "User Authentication."

For data encryption, PPTP uses the Remote Access Server (RAS) "shared-secret" encryption process and requires the use of the MS-CHAP authentication process. The data packets are encrypted and then encapsulated into a larger packet for routing over the Internet to the PPTP server.

Network security can also be increased by enabling PPTP filtering on the PPTP server. When PPTP filtering is enabled, the PPTP server on the private network accepts and routes only PPTP packets from authenticated users. This prevents all other packets from entering the PPTP server and private network.

Registry

The registry is a combination of the configuration of hardware and software components with user configuration options. There are five subtrees in the registry. Each of the subtree has a particular purpose. The five subtrees and their purposes are as follows:

- `HKEY_CURRENT_USER` Keeps all the configuration information for the specific users who are logged on.
- `HKEY_USERS` Keeps each user's information who has ever logged on the machine.
- `HKEY_CLASSES_ROOT` Contains information pertaining to the OLE (Object Linking and Embedding)
- `HKEY_CURRENT_CONFIG` Contains information pertaining only to the current settings.
- `HKEY_LOCAL_MACHINE` Contains information pertaining to the hardware settings.

Whenever a user installs software or changes hardware the user is changing the registry. It is therefore sound practice to use front-end tools to change the registry rather than editing it manually through the `REGEDT32` command because the user could accidentally make a parameter change that could stop the machine. Examples of front-end tools are the Control Panel Installation programs and System Policy Editor. The REGEDT32 exe Utility is also used to edit the registry.

Securing the Registry

Securing the registry will help prevent users and others from causing problems for Windows NT by changing registry values, inadvertently or otherwise. All users must have read access to certain portions of the registry in order to function in the Windows NT environment but should not be able to change all registry values or make new registry entries.

The registry supports three types of access permissions:

- **Full Control** Users can edit, create, delete, or take ownership of keys.
- **Read** Users can read any key value but make no changes.
- **Special Access** Users can be granted one or more of ten specific rights to a specific key. These ten specific rights are listed in Exhibit 5.15.

Exhibit 5.15 Registry Subkey Permissions

Permission Level	Description
Query Value	Read the settings of a value entry in a subkey
Set Value	Set the value in a subkey
Create Subkey	Create a new key or subkey within a selected key or subkey
Enumerate Subkeys	Identify all subkeys within a key or subkey
Notify	Receive audit notifications generated by the subkey
Create Link	Create symbolic links to the subkey(s)
Delete	Delete selected keys or subkeys
Write DAC	Modify the discretionary access control list (DAC) for the key
Write Owner	Take ownership of the selected key or subkey
Read Control	Read security information within selected subkey

The following techniques should be used for securing the registry:

- Disable remote registry editing by verifying existence or creating: HKLM\System\CurrentControlSet\Control\SecurePipeServers\winreg
- Disable anonymous access by creating: HKLM\System\CurrentControlSet\Control\LSA\RestrictAnonymous

  Type: **REG_DWORD**
  Value: 1
- Secure the root keys as shown in Exhibit 5.16.
- Secure registry subkeys to limit the access of the Everyone group as shown in Exhibit 5.16 using the following keys and subkeys:
  - HKEY_LOCAL_MACHINE\Software\Microsoft\RPC (and all subkeys).
  - HKEY_LOCAL_MACHINE\Software\Microsoft\Windows NT\Current Version

Exhibit 5.16 Registry Root Key Permissions

Registry Key	Default Setting	Recommended Setting
HKEY_LOCAL_MACHINE	Administrators: Full Control	Administrators: Full Control
	System: Full Control	System: Full Control
	Everyone: Read	Everyone: Read
HKEY_CLASSES_ROOT	Administrators: Full Control	Administrators: Full Control
	Creator/Owner: Full Control	Creator/Owner: Full Control
	System: Full Control	System: Full Control
	Everyone: Read	Everyone: Special Access (defined following)
HKEY_USERS	Administrators: Full Control	No Change
	System: Full Control	
	Everyone: Read	
HKEY_CURRENT_USER	Administrators: Full Control	No Change
	System: Full Control	
	User: Full Control	
HKEY_CURRENT_CONFIG (Windows NT 4.0 only)	Administrators: Full Control	No Change
	System: Full Control	
	User: Full Control	

- Allow special access only to the Everyone group with only four of the ten permissions: Query Value, Enumerate Subkeys, Notify, and Read Control.

WARNING: Using the Registry Editor incorrectly can cause serious, systemwide problems that may require reinstallation of Windows NT. Microsoft cannot guarantee that any problems resulting from the use of the Registry Editor can be solved. Use this tool at your own risk.

FEATURES OF SECURITY

Windows NT is designed to provide an operating system that could be used in many types of implementations, from local application servers and LAN file servers to remote access servers and Internet/intranet Web servers. Windows NT has features for security designed to provide the user with choices of a limited or extensive control implementation, depending on the business needs. Exhibit 5.17 lists the features and their descriptions that either control or implement security.

Exhibit 5.17 Windows NT Security Features

Feature	Description
Local Security Authority (LSA)	The LSA is also referred to as the security subsystem and is the heart of the Windows NT Server subsystem. The LSA provides the following services: • Creates access tokens during the logon process • Enables Windows NT Server to connect with third-party validation packages • Manages the security policy • Controls the audit policy • Logs audit messages to the event log
Security Account Manager (SAM)	The SAM maintains the security account database. SAM provides user validation services that are used by the LSA. SAM provides a security identifier for the user and the security identifier of any groups that the user is a member of. SAM operates as part of the Kernel.
Security Account Database (SAD)	The SAD contains information for all user and group accounts in a central location. It is used by the SAM to validate users. Duplicate copies of the SAD can reside on multiple servers depending on whether a workgroup or domain model is implemented and the type of domain model implemented. Passwords stored in the SAD are stored using a 128-bit cryptographically strong system key.
Security Identifiers (SID)	SIDs are created by the security account manager during the logon process. They are retired when an account is deleted. If an account name was created with the same name as an account that was previously deleted, the SID created will be different from the SID associated with the deleted account.
Security Reference Monitor (SRM)	The SRM is the Windows NT Server component responsible for enforcing the access validation and audit generation policy held by the LSA. It protects resources or objects from unauthorized access or modification. Windows NT Server does not allow direct access to objects. The SRM provides services for validating access to objects (files, directories, and so on), testing subjects (user accounts) for privileges, and generating the necessary audit message. The SRM contains the only copy of the access validation code in the system. This ensures that object protection is provided uniformly throughout Windows NT, regardless of the type of object accessed.
Discretionary Access Controls	Discretionary access controls provide resource owners the ability to specify who can access their resources and to what extent they can be accessed.
Access Tokens	Access tokens are objects that contain information about a particular user. When the user initiates a process, a copy of the access token is permanently attached to the process.
Access Control Lists (ACLs)	ACLs allow flexibility in controlling access to objects and are a form of discretionary access control. They allow users to specify and control the sharing of objects or the denial of access to objects. Each object's ACL contains access control entries that define access permissions to the object.

Exhibit 5.17 (*Continued*)

Logon Process	The interactive logon process is Windows NT Server's first line of defense against unauthorized access. In a successful logon, the process flows from the client system to the server system without exposing the user's password in clear text over the network. The entire logon process is described in an earlier section entitled "Logon Process."
Feature	**Description**
The Registry	The Windows NT Server Registry is an access-controlled database containing configuration data for security, applications, hardware, and device drivers. The registry is the central point for storing these data. The registry contains all user profile information as well as the hashed user password.
Event Logging (Auditing)	Windows NT Server auditing features record events to show which users access which objects, the type of access attempted, and whether or not the attempt was successful. Auditing can be applied to: • System events such as logon and logoff, file and object access, use of user rights, user and group management, security policy changes, restarting and shutting down the system, and process tracking • File and directory events such as read, write, execute, delete, changing permissions, and taking ownership • Registry key access to subkeys • Printer access events such as printing, taking full control, deleting, changing permissions, and taking ownership • Remote Access Service events such as authentication, disconnection, disconnection due to inactivity, connection but failure to authenticate, connection but authentication time-out, disconnection due to transport-level errors during the authentication conversation, and disconnection due to inability to project onto the network • Clipbook page events such as reading the page, deleting the contents of the page, changing permissions, and changing the audit types • Events of significance can be sent to a pager interface to notify security and systems staff
Event Logs	Three logs record system-, security-, and application-related events: 1. The system log records errors, warnings, or information generated by the Windows NT Server system. 2. The security log records valid and invalid logon attempts and events related to the use of resources such as creating, opening, or deleting files or other objects. 3. The application log records, errors, warnings, and information generated by application software, such as an electronic mail or database application.

(*Continued*)

Exhibit 5.17 Windows NT Security Features (*Continued*)

	The size and replacement strategy can be modified for each of the logs. Each logged event's details can be displayed.
Process Isolation	Windows NT was designed to provide process isolation to prevent individual processes from interfering with each other. This is accomplished by providing each process with its own memory space with no access to any other process's memory. This segregation of memory is also designed to prevent data from being captured from the memory space. There is an option to overwrite an individual user's swap or temporary disk space after logout to prevent anyone from reading that user's temporary files and data.
User Account Security	User account security policies are managed through the user manager and consist of account policies and user rights policies. • Account policy controls the way passwords must be used by all user accounts. The major account policy controls include minimum and maximum password age, minimum password length, password uniqueness, forcible disconnection beyond logon hours, and account lockout. • User rights policy allows the granted user to affect resources for the entire system. The basic rights offered by Windows NT Server include access from a network, backing up, changing the system time, remote forcible shutdown, local logon, managing the audit and security log, restoring files, shutting down the system, and taking ownership of objects. Windows NT Server also contains many advanced rights. In total, there are twenty-seven rights that may be assigned to users.
Built-in Accounts	Windows NT Server offers two built-in accounts: the Guest account and the Administrator account. These accounts were created for specific uses and are by default members in a number of default groups. The Guest account is disabled by default.
User Account Properties	The user properties feature allows the administration of user accounts, passwords, password policies, group membership, user profiles, hours of logon, the workstations from which the user can log on, and the account expiration date. In addition, password filtering can be implemented to increase the strength of password security policy.
User Profiles	User profiles enable the Windows NT server to structure and manage the user's desktop operating environment and present the identical environment without regard to the workstation. This file is loaded on logon. The user profile editor allows disabling Run in the file menu and disabling the Save Settings menu item, shows common groups, changes the startup group, locks program groups, restricts access to unlocked program groups, and disables connecting and removing connections in the print manager.
Home Directories	Home directories can be assigned to each user for storage of private files.

Exhibit 5.17 (*Continued*)

Feature	Description
Logon Scripts	Logon scripts are executed on logon by a user. They provide the network administrator with a utility for creating standard logon procedures.
Groups	Groups allow an administrator to treat large numbers of users as one account. Windows NT Server utilizes two types of groups in its tiered administration model: • Local groups are defined on each machine and can contain both user accounts and global groups. Windows NT supplies a number of built-in local group accounts. • Global groups are defined at the domain level and can contain only user accounts from the local domain but not from trusted domains. Windows NT supplies several built-in global group accounts.
Network Models	In a Windows NT network environment it is possible to implement two different network models: the workgroup model or the domain model. • The workgroup model allows peer-to-peer networking for machines that do not participate in a domain. Each Windows NT machine that participates in a workgroup maintains its own security policy and SAD. • The domain model is an effective way to implement security and simplify administration in a network environment. The domain allows the sharing of a common security policy and SAD.
Feature	**Description**
Trust Relationships	The domain model establishes security between multiple domains through trust relationships. A trust relationship is a link between two domains causing one domain to honor the authentication of users from another domain. A trust relationship between two domains enables user accounts and global groups to be used in a domain other than the domain where these accounts are located. Trusts can be uni- or bidirectional and require the participation of an administrator in both domains to establish each directional trust relationship.
Primary and Backup Domain Controllers	Windows NT Server provides domain authentication service through the use of primary and backup domain controllers. If communications to the primary domain controller break, the backup domain controllers will handle all authentication. A backup domain controller may be promoted to a primary domain controller if necessary.
Replication	Windows NT Server uses replication to synchronize the SADs on various servers. This process is automatic. Replication is not restricted to the SAD but can be used to create and maintain identical directory trees and files on multiple servers and workstations. The replication feature contains a security tool to control the import and export of files and directories.

(*Continued*)

Exhibit 5.17 Windows NT Security Features (*Continued*)

Server Administration	The server manager tool enables the following types of administrative activities: • Display the member computers of a domain • Select a specific computer for administration • Manage server properties and services, including start and stop services, and generate alerts • Share directories • Send messages to systems These administrative functions require administrative access.
NTFS	NTFS is the more secure of the two writable file systems supported by Windows NT Server. NTFS is the only file system to utilize the Windows NT file and directory security features. NTFS is a log-based file system that offers recoverability in the event of a disk fault or system failure. The next major release of the operating system will provide an option for file-level encryption.
Legal Notice	The legal notice feature is provided to strengthen the legal liability of individuals who may attempt to access a system without authorization. The feature displays a message to the user after the CTRL+ALT+DEL keystroke combination during the logon process. When the legal notice appears, the user must acknowledge the notice by selecting the OK button in the message box presented.
Fault Tolerance	Windows NT Server has fault tolerance features that can be used alone or in combination to protect data from potential media faults. These features are disk mirroring, disk duplexing, disk striping with parity, and sector hot-sparing.
Tape Backup	The Tape Backup enables backing up and restoration of files and directories. Backups can be full, incremental, differential, custom, or on a daily basis for those files changed on the day of the backup.
Last Known Good Configuration	The last known good configuration feature allows the restoration of the system to the last working system configuration. When used, it discards any changes to the configuration since the last working system configuration. This feature is automatically updated after any system boot.
Emergency Repair Disk	The emergency repair disk allows the restoration of the system to its initial setup state. The emergency repair disk can be used if system files are corrupt and the user is unable to recover the previous startup configuration. Securing the emergency repair disk is of utmost importance since it contains a copy of key pieces of the security accounts database.
Uninterruptible Power Supply Service (UPS)	The UPS feature allows for the connection of a battery-operated power supply to a computer to keep the system running during a power failure. The UPS service for Windows NT Server detects and warns users of power failures and manages a safe system shutdown when the backup power supply is about to fail.

Exhibit 5.17 (*Continued*)

Network Monitor	The Network Monitor allows examination of network traffic to and from a server at the packet level. This traffic can be captured for later analysis, making it easier to troubleshoot network problems.
Task Manager	The Task Manager is a tool for monitoring application tasks, key performance measurements of a Windows NT Server-based system. Task manager gives detailed information on each application and process running on the workstation, as well as memory and CPU user. It allows for the termination of applications and processes.
Performance Monitor	The performance monitor tool enables the monitoring of system capacity and prediction of potential bottlenecks.
Network Alerts	Alert messages can be sent to designated individuals. These messages can report on security-related events, such as too many logon violations or performance issues.
CryptoAPI	This set of encryption APIs allows developers to develop applications that will work securely over nonsecure networks such as the Internet.
Point-to-Point Tunneling Protocol (PPTP)	PPTP provides a way to use public data networks, such as the Internet, to create virtual private network connecting client PCs with servers. PPTP provides protocol encapsulation and encryption for data privacy.
Distributed Component Object Model (DCOM)	Windows NT 4.0 includes DCOM, formerly known as Network OLE, which allows developers and solution providers to use off-the-shelf and custom-created OLE components to build robust distributed applications. Most importantly, it utilizes Windows NT Server's built-in security. It addresses a problem that was frequently associated with OLE applications trying to run as services under Windows NT: Windows NT Server's built-in security did not let OLE services communicate between applications because most applications are launched from a desktop running a different security context from the services. Using DCOM, Windows NT 4.0 now allows communication between different security contexts.
Windows NT Diagnostic Tool	The Windows NT diagnostic tool is used to examine the system, including information on device drivers, network user, and system resources.
Services Administration	The Service Manager enables the access and administration of network and operating system services.
Feature	**Description**
Remote Access Services (RAS)	The RAS administration tools control the remote connection environment.
Administration Tools	The following tools are used in the RAS configuration and administration process: • Network Settings enables the installation and configuration of network software and adapter cards and the ports in which they reside.

(*Continued*)

Exhibit 5.17 Windows NT Security Features (*Continued*)

	• Network Configuration controls the RAS inbound and outbound protocols as well as encryption requirements. Each protocol has subsequent dialog boxes with configuration and control features. • The Remote Access administration tool enables monitoring of specific ports, administration of remote access permissions, and configuration of any callback requirements.
Internet Information Server (IIS)	IIS is an add-on to Windows NT 4.0. Integration of IIS with NT 4.0 allows IIS to have full use of NT 4.0 Server security and directory services. The integration supports logging server traffic to NCSA Common Log File Format as well as any ODBC database. IIS provides Web, FTP, and Gopher services to the Windows NT system.
TCP/IP Support	Windows NT Server supports the TCP/IP protocol and IP address format. The TCP/IP Configuration tool administers TCP/IP as well as SNMP, DHCP, and WINS. The Configuration tool also controls IP routing. Traditional TCP/IP commands such as ARP, NBTSTAT, NETSTAT, PING, TRACERT, and the Unix 'R' commands are supported.
C2 Tool	The C2 tool provides guidance for securing the Windows NT Server to the C2 security standard.

SECURITY CERTIFICATIONS

The U.S. government wrote a series of manuals on computer security over the past few decades, each with a different color of cover. This "Rainbow Series" of manuals includes how to design, build, choose, analyze, and operate a trusted system. The Orange book was released in December 1985 and discussed what criteria to use to evaluate a trusted system. Additional manuals were subsequently produced that expanded the general terms used in the Orange book. They are the Red book, which interprets the Orange book with relation to networked systems, and the Blue book, which interprets the Orange book with relation to subsystems.

The Orange book divides security into four sections, D through A. The D level is minimal protection, while class A is verified protection. In class C there is C1, discretionary security protection, and C2, controlled access protection. Each level states the requirements for the following areas—Security Policy, Accountability, Assurance, and Documentation—and defines what a system must be able to do in each area to meet the requirements of that level.

When a system is evaluated against these criteria, a specific hardware and software configuration is created and used for the evaluation. Once evaluated, government organizations that require the appropriate level of security can purchase the evaluated systems.

The D level has no criteria and is reserved for systems that were evaluated but did not meet the criteria for a higher evaluation class. The C2 level is the minimum acceptable level for certain government uses.

Because of the required rating levels for government usage, the public perception was that if it was good enough for the Department of Defense, it was good enough for commercial use. However, many people today speak of "C2 Security" without understanding the requirements or implications of the certifications. Some of the common misconceptions include:

- If the operating system is certified as C2, it will be C2 in any environment or configuration.
- The C2 standards are appropriate and applicable for all commercial uses.
- The C2 standards include such areas as specific password controls and cryptography usage.

All of the preceding are false. The entire section defining the C2 requirements is just three pages long. It states that users are required to be individually accountable for their actions through logon procedures, the ability to audit security-related events, what the audit records will include, and the requirements of resource isolation.

ITSEC is the United Kingdom's equivalent of the U.S. DOD National Computer Security Center. Conceptually their rating system is the same, except that they divide the ratings into both a functional class (F-C) with F-C2 being equivalent to C2, and an evaluation level (E0 to E6) that defines the level of confidence that a product will meet the functional criteria in as many scenarios as possible. Under this rating scheme, Windows NT has received an F-C2/E3 rating for both the client side and the server side. More detail on these rating levels is available at <www.itsec.gov.uk>.

Microsoft, with intentions of serving the government marketplace and with an understanding of the public's impression of the C2 level of security, designed the architecture of Windows NT to be in compliance with the criteria for Orange book C2 certification, including Red and Blue book compliance. Controls were incorporated that include verification of user actions against the security database, the use of a session token, protection of that security database, the use of a username and password combination to access the system, the ability to audit events on a user-by-user basis for success and failure, access control lists to define access to objects, the NTFS file system to enforce access controls to objects in the system, use of the security reference monitor to control object reuse, memory space protection, and other integrated features. Note that physical control over access to the computer system plays a critical role in C2 compliance and security in general but is not a feature that can be built into the operating system.

As of August 1995, Windows NT 3.5 Service Pack 3 (without networking installed) passed the certification requirements of the NCSC C2 Orange book level. Currently, Windows NT 4.0 with Service Pack 3 is under evaluation. Windows NT 3.51 Workstation and Windows NT 3.51 Server were rated by ITSEC to meet their F-C2/E3 standard levels in October 1996. Windows NT 4.0 has been submitted for ITSEC review. One important point relating to C2 certification is that because of the rigorous level of testing the government does to determine compliance, the testing can take a long period of time. During this period, it is possible for patches, hot fixes, and service packs to be released. If the vendor would like these upgrades included in the evaluation, the process is significantly extended to allow for a review of the patch and the other code that the fix interacts with to make sure that the fix does not introduce a new security vulnerability while fixing a different problem. During an evaluation for either

C2 or E3 certification, the source code of the system is available for review as well as the overall development process. Some of the critical concepts to understand are:

- Out of the box many operating systems (including Windows NT) are considered insecure.
- C2 compliance may or may not meet an organization's security need.
- A C2-level security configuration (this includes no floppy drive and no network connectivity) may be impractical or inappropriate to use in many organizations.
- There are other controls such as physical and monitoring controls that must be addressed for compliance but are not operating system components.
- Availability, which is often critical in many corporate environments, is not one of the criteria for C2 certification.
- An organization must assess the level of risk associated with the data they are attempting to protect, have a policy in place to define what security level is appropriate in their environment, and have monitoring controls in place to determine if the policy is being complied with.
- Using these criteria, a company can appropriately decide if the level of security they have implemented is too much, appropriate, or needs additional controls, such as link level cryptography between a client and a server. In this light, the question is not "is the product C2 certified" but "will this operating system, alone or with additional OEM or third-party tools, meet the security needs of my organization?"

SUGGESTED READINGS

Cowarts, R. *Windows NT 4.0 Server—Workstation Unleashed.* Sams Publishing, 1997.

Daily, S. *Migrating to Windows NT 4.0.* Duke Press, 1997.

Dalton, W., et al. *Windows NT Server 4: Security, Troubleshooting, and Optimization.* New Riders, 1997.

Garms, J., et al. *Windows NT Server 4 Unleashed.* Sams Publishing, 1997.

Grant, G., et al. Troubleshooting with Microsoft: Common Windows NT Problems. *Windows NT Magazine.*

Karanjit, S. *Windows NT Server Professional Reference (4.0).* New Riders, 1997.

Microsoft Corporation. Windows NT Workstation and Server.

Pleas, K. *Windows NT 4.0: Explore the New Features.*

Ramos, F. *Windows NT Security Issues.* Somarsoft Corp.

Sheldon, T. *Windows NT Security Handbook.* McGraw-Hill, 1997.

Sutton, S. A. *Windows NT Security Guide.* Trusted Systems, 1997.

WEB SITES

Microsoft Security (www.microsoft.com/security)

NT Admin FAQ (www.iftech.com/oltc/admin/admin.stm)

NT Bugtraq (ntbugtraq.rc.on.ca)

NT Security (www.ntsecurity.net)

NT Security FAQ (www.it.kth.se/~rom/ntsec.html)

APPENDIX 5B

Windows NT Primary Domain Controller Security Review Program

No.	Category	Control Objectives	Risk	Control Techniques
1	System Configuration	All servers in the domain should be Windows NT 3.51 or higher; no LAN Manager or Windows NT servers previous to version 3.51 should exist within the domain.	Older servers, such as Windows NT 3.5 or LAN Manager, may subject the Windows NT environment to undue security risk.	All Windows NT 3.5 and LAN Manager servers should be eliminated from the domain or upgraded immediately.
1	System Configuration	The latest Microsoft service packs and hot fixes should be installed and properly configured. Service packs and hot fixes should be reapplied after each new software installation.	Current versions of the operating system contain processing and security enhancements. Service packs correct bugs that have been communicated to Microsoft. If the version of the operating system is not current, there is an increased risk that an unauthorized user may be able to exploit weaknesses in the operating system. Certain service packs and hot fixes require system administration intervention such as the running of an application or the manual entry of a registry key into the registry.	Obtain the latest service pack and hot fixes from Microsoft and properly install and configure the service pack and appropriate hot fixes. The latest service pack for Windows NT3.51 is 5, and the latest service pack for Windows NT4.0 is 3.
1	System Configuration	The "system key" options of Service Pack 3 (SP3) should be implemented.	The system key feature of Service Pack 3 provides stronger encryption of the SAM database. Enabling this option decreases the risk that password hashes will be cracked if obtained. A utility has been released that can extract the Windows NT password hashes even with syskey implemented; therefore, this risk is only partially mitigated.	Enable the syskey option

Implementation Techniques	Compliance Assessment Techniques	Compliance Verification Techniques
Upgrade all LAN Manager and Windows NT 3.5 servers to Windows NT version 3.51 or higher.	Verify, through discussion with the company and physical inspection, that each sever is running the Windows NT operating system version 3.51 or higher. This document is only applicable and effective for said versions.	Verify, through discussion with the company and physical inspection, that each sever is running the Windows NT operating system version 3.51 or higher. This document is only applicable and effective for said versions. During specific server reviews, refer to the `<servername>.winmsd.txt` file to verify the version of the operating system.
Browse the Microsoft home page and download the latest service pack. Additionally, view available hot fixes and determine which are necessary to install on target systems. Install the service pack and applicable hot fixes on a test machine to ensure compatibility with existing applications. Ensure that the hot fixes are installed in the correct order by referring to the hot fix documentation and install only after thorough testing.	Determine, by searching the Microsoft home page, the latest available service pack and hot fix versions. Ensure that appropriate patches are installed on each Windows NT server. Confirm that procedures exist to update service packs and hot fixes as new versions are release and new software is installed on the system.	Review the `<servername>.winmsd.txt` and `<servername>.hotfix.txt` files to ensure that appropriate service packs and hot fixes have been applied. Confirm that procedures exist to update service packs and hot fixes as new versions are released and new software is installed on the system. Refer to guidance material and the Microsoft home page to determine the latest service pack version and hot fixes available.
Ensure the system key options are installed by reviewing the setting of the `HKLM\System\Current ControlSet\control\LSA\Secure boot` registry key. Ensure, in a test environment, that this feature is compatible with all installed applications. After testing and installation, update the repair disk. Note that SP3 will no longer be uninstallable.	Determine, through discussion with the network administrator, if this option was considered. If syskey was determined to be viable in this instance, verify that the proper option is set in the registry: `HKLM\System\CurrentControlSet\Control\LSA\Secureboot`. Ensure that sufficient regression testing occurred on a machine outside of the production environment.	Determine, through discussion with the network administrator, if this option was considered. If syskey was determined to be viable in this instance, examine the `<servername>.lsa.txt file` and ensure the value `HKLM\System\CurrentControlSet\Control\LSA\Secureboot` is equal to 1. Verify diskette is protected, if used.
Choose one of the three methods for storing the system key: • obfuscated key on machine • obfuscated key on diskette • password protected key at boot	Verify the choice of the key storage.	Verify knowledge of boot password for the key.

Windows NT Primary Domain Controller Security Review Program

No.	Category	Control Objectives	Risk	Control Techniques
1	System Configuration	The Primary Domain Controller (PDC) should not be utilized for other purposes except those directly related to authentication, such as address assignment or name lookup.	Running applications on a PDC opens the PDC to any vulnerabilities that exist in that application. Additionally, if the PDC is used for other purposes than authentication, there is an increased risk that the server may not possess enough resources to perform both functions adequately.	PDCs should be utilized for authentication and related services only.
1	System Configuration	System services should be running under a secured context.	If services are allowed to interact with the desktop when they are started, there is an increased risk that domain resources may be compromised. In addition, if the service is compromised, the service will be running with too much authority.	No services should have the "Interact with the desktop" check box checked. Services should not run under a global account but rather a local account. Accounts created to run as a service should not be allowed certain rights such as Log On Locally unless required.
2	Networking	Workstation and time restrictions should be enforced when possible.	Restricting users based on workstations and time reduces the risk that unauthorized access will be obtained. These controls should be enforced for users that utilize only one workstation during set hours of the day.	Workstation and time restrictions should be enforced when possible for typical domain users.

Implementation Techniques	Compliance Assessment Techniques	Compliance Verification Techniques
Ensure that all PDC servers are only performing authentication.	Verify that the PDC is only used for authentication by performing the following steps: 1. Open server manager. 2. Select the PDC and choose Services. . . from the computer pulldown menu. 3. Review each running service to determine if it is used for a purpose other than authentication.	Verify that the PDC is only used for authentication by reviewing the <servername>.services file and ensuring that only authentication related services are installed and started. Also, review the <servername>.pulist.txt file to ensure only authentication-related processes are running. Allowable applications include DHCP, WINS, and DNS.
When services are started they should not have the allow service to interact with desktop option selected. Open server manager for each server in question. Open services from the computer pulldown menu. Double-click on each service and verify the settings for Log On As.	Verify that services cannot interact with the desktop by performing the following steps for all servers in scope: 1. Open server manager. 2. Open Services. . . from the computer pulldown menu. 3. Double-click on each service and verify that the Allow services to interact with the desktop option is not selected.	Verify that services cannot interact with the desktop by reviewing the Services Report portion of <servername>.winmsd.txt and noting any services with a Service Account Name of anything other than LocalSystem or any services with a Service Flag of Interactive.
When entering new users or to change existing users perform the following steps: 1. Open User Manager. 2. Open the User Properties by double-clicking on the username. 3. Click the Hours button. 4. Select the appropriate time and click the Allow and Disallow buttons as appropriate. 5. Click OK to confirm changes. 6. Click Logon To button. 7. Verify user access by stations.	Verify the user Logon hours by performing the following steps: 1. Open User Manager. 2. Open User Properties by double-clicking on the username. 3. Click the Hours button. 4. Verify that the hours listed in Blue meet corporate standards. 5. Click the Cancel button to close. 6. Click Logon To button. 7. Verify user access by stations.	Verify the user Logon hours and workstation restrictions by reviewing <servername>.users.txt and determining whether workstation or time restrictions are enforced for any users on the system.

Windows NT Primary Domain Controller Security Review Program

No.	Category	Control Objectives	Risk	Control Techniques
3	Networking	Users should be forcibly disconnected from servers when their login hours expire.	Having users automatically disconnected from the system when their time expires ensures that network resources will not be accessed unless the user is specifically authorized for access during those hours.	Enable the Forced account Disconnect feature in account policies.
3	User Management	All users and groups in the domain should be known and documented by the group responsible for maintaining the Windows NT environment.	If users and groups exist within the domain that are not known or documented, there is an increased risk that the security of the domain may be compromised.	An inventory of users and groups should be performed periodically and checked against an approved listing of users and groups. If "rogue" users or groups are found they should be investigated immediately.
3	User Management	All user and directory management should be performed through Windows NT native tools.	Certain versions of non-Windows NT native administration tools (Windows 95) create user accounts and user home directories in an insecure manner.	Only Windows NT native administration tools should be used to administer users and groups and create directories.
3	User Management	All user accounts should have an applicable, informative full name and description.	Requiring all users to have descriptions and full names minimizes the possibility that an extraneous, unneeded user accounts will be created. Such a user could bypass system administration and be used for unfavorable purposes.	Add an applicable and informative full name and description to each user account.

Implementation Techniques	Compliance Assessment Techniques	Compliance Verification Techniques
Enable the Forced account Disconnect feature in account policies by performing the following steps: 1. Open User Manager. 2. Choose Select Domain from the user pulldown menu. 3. Enter the **Authentication Domain** in the Domain: box. 4. Click OK. 5. Select account from the policies pulldown menu. 6. Select the Forcibly disconnect remote users from server when logon hours expire check box. 7. Click OK. 8. Close User Manager.	Verify that the Forced account Disconnect feature in account policies has been enabled by performing the following steps: 1. Open User Manager. 2. Choose Select Domain. . . from the user pulldown menu. 3. Enter the **Authentication Domain** in the Domain: box. 4. Click OK. 5. Select Account. . . from the policies pulldown menu. 6. Verify that the Forcibly disconnect remote users from server when logon hours expire check box has been checked. 7. Click OK. 8. Close User Manager.	Verify that the Forced account Disconnect feature in account policies has been enabled by reviewing <servername>.policies.txt and ensuring that the "Force logoff when logon hours expire" control is implemented. Verify that logon hours are set for users.
Document all users and groups in the domain. Verify that all users are presently employed with the company by obtaining a list from Human Resources.	Compare user inventory with an actual employee list from Human Resources and verify that all users are current employees. Also determine if there are procedures in place to periodically check the users and groups in the domain against this listing.	Compare user inventory with an actual employee list from Human Resources and verify that all users are current employees. Also determine if there are procedures in place to periodically check the users and groups in the domain against this listing.
Utilize native Windows NT administration tools to administer users and groups and to create directories.	Determine, through discussion with the network administrator and physical review of the system, which tools are used to administer the network. Ensure that all tools are designed specifically for Windows NT.	Determine, through discussion with the network administrator and physical review of the system, which tools are used to administer the network. Ensure that all tools are designed specifically for Windows NT.
When creating users, fill in the full Name and Description fields for the new account in the User Manager.	Verify that all users have full names and descriptions in the appropriate fields by viewing the users in User Manager by performing the following steps: 1. Choose Select Domain. . . from the user pulldown menu. 2. Enter the **Authentication Domain.** 3. Click OK. View all users and verify that they have full names and descriptions.	Review <servername>.users.txt and verify that all users have applicable and full names and descriptions.

Windows NT Primary Domain Controller Security Review Program

No.	Category	Control Objectives	Risk	Control Techniques
3	User Management	Naming conventions should be established and followed for all user accounts. Naming conventions should cover end users, contractors, consultants, and vendors.	Having all users with the same naming convention increases network security, as users can easily be identified and accounts that do not adhere to the naming standard are easily identified. Setting up temporary accounts for contractors, consultants, and vendors with an identifiable naming convention allows these accounts to be easily identified and purged if warranted.	Name all user accounts in accordance with established naming conventions.
3	User Management	User accounts should only be entered in the Authentication Domain's PDC and not on workstations or servers.	Having all user accounts centrally administered by domain increases network security because resource allocation can be controlled. The only accounts that should exist outside of the domain, on local workstations, are the built-in Guest and Administrator accounts.	Remove all user accounts from resource domains, servers, and workstations and move them to their respective authentication domain.

Implementation Techniques	Compliance Assessment Techniques	Compliance Verification Techniques
Name all user accounts in accordance with established naming conventions.	Verify that all users are named in accordance with corporate policy by viewing the users in User Manager by performing the following steps: 4. Choose Select Domain. . . from the user pulldown menu. 5. Enter the **Authentication Domain.** 6. Click OK. 7. View all users and verify that they have been named in accordance with corporate policy.	Obtain a copy of the company's user naming conventions and ensure they are being enforced on all user accounts by reviewing the <servername>.users.txt file. Note whether the naming conventions provide for the ability to identify employees, vendors, and temporary IDs.
Move all user accounts from the resource servers to the authentication domain by performing the following steps: 1. Open User Manager. 2. Choose Select Domain. . . from the user pulldown menu. 3. Enter the **server name.** 4. Click OK. 5. Double-click user account. 6. Write down all visible information. 7. Close user information. 8. With the user account highlighted select Delete from the user pulldown menu. 9. Click OK. 10. Repeat steps 5–9 until all users have been deleted. 11. Choose Select Domain. . . from the user pulldown menu. 12. Enter the **Authentication Domain name.** 13. Click OK. 14. Select New User. . . from the user pulldown menu. 15. Enter all user information. 16. Click Add. 17. Repeat steps 14–16 until all users have been added. 18. Close User Manager.	Note whether the naming conventions provide for the ability to identify employees, vendors, and temporary IDs. Verify that there are no user accounts on each server and workstation by performing the following steps: 1. Open User Manager. 2. Choose Select Domain. . . from the user pulldown menu. 3. Enter the **server or workstation name.** 4. Verify that the only accounts listed are the Default Administrator and Guest accounts. 5. Repeat steps 2–4 until all server and workstations have been verified. 6. Close User Manager.	Review <servername>.users.txt and ensure that end user accounts are only created in the Authentication Domain.

Windows NT Primary Domain Controller Security Review Program

No.	Category	Control Objectives	Risk	Control Techniques
3	User Management	Any account that has not logged into the authentication domain for an extended period of time should be disabled.	Inactive accounts are often used by intruders to break into a network. If a user account has not been utilized for some time, the account should be disabled until it is needed. This minimizes the possibility that an unauthorized user will utilize the account.	Disable all accounts that have not been logged into in accordance with corporate standards. Industry guidelines state that if an account has not been used for 90 days, it is inactive. Enable an account only after being contacted by, and verifying, the user is appropriate.
3	User Management	Accounts of individuals who are no longer employed or do not need their accounts should be deleted.	Having outstanding accounts that are no longer needed increases the risk of unauthorized access.	Delete all unneeded accounts, including vendor accounts, terminated employees, and contractors.

Implementation Techniques	Compliance Assessment Techniques	Compliance Verification Techniques
Disable stale user accounts by performing the following steps: 1. At the command prompt, issue the net user <User Name> command for each user. 2. Note the last login time. If the account has not been logged into in a specified period of time (in accordance with our best practices), this account should be disabled. 3. Disable the account by issuing the net user <User Name./Active:no> **Note:** If a user often authenticates to a BDC rather than the PDC, then this procedure may not provide the true last logon time.	Verify that all inactive user accounts have been disabled by performing the following steps: 1. At the command prompt, issue the net user <User Name> command for each user. 2. Note the last login time. If the account has not been logged into in a specified period of time (in accordance with corporate policy or out best practices), this account should be disabled. 3. Verify through the use of a tool when the last valid logon time was.	Verify that all inactive user accounts have been disabled by reviewing <servername>.users.txt for accounts with a "TrueLastLogon Time" that exceeds the corporate policy.
Remove unneeded user accounts from the authentication domain by performing the following steps: 1. Open User Manager. 2. Highlight the unneeded account and select Delete from the user pulldown menu. 3. Repeat until all unneeded accounts have been removed.	Verify that there are no unneeded user accounts in the authentication domain by performing the following steps: 1. Open the User Manager. 2. Review the list of users. 3. Discuss these users with the network administrator and human resources to determine appropriateness.	Verify that there are no unneeded user accounts in the authentication domain by obtaining a listing of recently departed employees from the HR department and ensuring that the former employee's account have been removed or disabled from the Authentication domain. This information can be found in the appropriate <servername>. users.txt file.

Windows NT Primary Domain Controller Security Review Program

No.	Category	Control Objectives	Risk	Control Techniques
3	User Management	The default Administrator and Guest accounts should be assigned a strong password and renamed immediately after installation.	The Administrator and Guest accounts are known to exist on all Windows NT systems. Consequently, they are one of the first accounts that an intruder will attempt to use. The Administrator account on Windows NT has all system rights and therefore should be the most protected account on the system. If these accounts are not renamed, all an attacker would have to accomplish is brute force guessing a password. Depending on other system settings, this might be easy to achieve in a relatively short period of time without being detected.	Rename the default Administrator and Guest accounts. Assign a strong password to both the accounts. Add an account named "Administrator" and assign it no user rights and no group memberships. Having an account named Administrator with no user rights will aid intruder detection by writing to the audit log.

Implementation Techniques

Rename the default accounts by performing the following steps:

1. Using User Manager highlight the Administrator account.
2. Choose the rename option under the User pulldown menu.
3. Enter a **new account name,** which conforms to corporate standards, in the Change box.
4. Click OK to confirm changes.
5. Double-click on the Administrator account.
6. Enter a **strong password** in accordance with corporate policy in the Password and Confirm Password boxes.
7. Click OK to confirm changes.
8. Choose New User from the User pulldown menu.
9. Enter **Administrator** in the Username box.
10. Enter a **full name** in accordance with corporate policy in the Full Name box.
11. Enter **Administrative Log For Intruder Detection** in the Description box.
12. Enter a **strong password** in the Password and Confirm Password boxes.
13. Ensure that the User Must Change Password at next Logon box is not selected.
14. Select the Password Never Expires check box.
15. Click the Groups box.
16. Select all groups under the Member Of: box.
17. Click the Remove button.
18. Click the OK button to confirm changes.
19. Click the Close button.
20. Perform steps 1–7 for the Guest account and close User Manager.

Compliance Assessment Techniques

Verify, with the network administrator and physical inspection, that the Administrator and Guest accounts have been renamed and assigned strong passwords.

A cracking program can be used to determine if passwords exist and how strong they are.

Some companies may not allow password cracking programs to be run. In that case you may have to accept the word of the system manager regarding password strength.

Compliance Verification Techniques

Review <servername>.users.txt and ensure the default Administrator and Guest accounts are renamed. Also ensure the accounts have been assigned a strong password by executing L0phtcrack against the <servername>.passwd.txt file if permitted.

Windows NT Primary Domain Controller Security Review Program

No.	Category	Control Objectives	Risk	Control Techniques
3	User Management	The default Guest account should be disabled immediately after installation.	The Guest account is known to exist on all Windows NT systems. Consequently, it is one of the first accounts that an intruder will attempt to use. If enabled, an attacker will attempt to login as the Guest and compromise the system. By default, Windows NT 4.0 disables this account; however, a blank password is set.	Disable the default Guest account on all Windows NT systems. The account should remain disabled at all times. If the Guest account is needed for any types of services (i.e., printing), define a new account for that function.
3	User Management	The Replicator account should be adequately secured.	If the directory replicator account and password used by this account are not adequately secured, there is an increased risk that the security of the domain may be compromised.	The Replicator account should have a secure username and password and should not be allowed to override default password policy. The Replicator account should be a member of the Replicators group. (The Replicators group will not have "log on locally" or "access this computer over the network" user rights—only "Log on as service.")

Implementation Techniques

Disable the Guest account by performing the following steps:

1. Using the User Manager open the Guest account.
2. Disable the account by selecting the Account Disabled check box.
3. Click OK to confirm the changes.

Compliance Assessment Techniques

Verify that the Guest account has been disabled by performing the following steps:

1. Open User Manager.
2. Double-click on the Guest account.
3. Verify that the Account Disabled check box is selected.

Compliance Verification Techniques

Review <servername>.users.txt and ensure the Guest account is disabled.

Implementation Techniques

Rename the Replicator account and secure it by performing the following steps:

1. Using User Manager highlight the Replicator account.
2. Choose the rename option under the User pulldown menu.
3. Enter a **new account name,** which conforms to corporate standards, in the Change box.
4. Click OK to confirm changes.
5. Double-click on the Replicator account.
6. Enter a **strong password** in accordance with corporate policy in the Password and Confirm Password boxes.
7. Ensure that the User Must Change Password at next Logon box is not selected.
8. Select the Password Never Expires check box.
9. Click the Groups box.
10. Select all groups under the Member Of: box.
11. Click the Remove button.
12. Add the Replicator account to the Replicators group.
13. Click the OK button to confirm changes.
14. Click the Close button.

Compliance Assessment Techniques

Verify, through discussion with the network administrator and physical inspection, that the Replicator account has been renamed and assigned a strong password. Also ensure that the Replicator account is only a member of the Replicators group. These can be accomplished by performing the following steps:

1. Open User Manager.
2. Verify that an account named Replicator does not exist.
3. Double-click on the renamed Replicator account.
4. Click on the Groups button.
5. Verify that this account is only a member of the Replicators group.

A cracking program can be used to determine how strong the password for this account is.

Some companies may not allow password cracking programs to be run. In that case you may have to accept the word of the system manager regarding password strength.

Compliance Verification Techniques

Review <servername>.users.txt Replicator account security settings and ensure the account has a difficult-to-guess username, belongs only to the Replicators group, and is not overriding default account policies. Also ensure the account has been assigned a strong password by executing L0phtcrack against the <servername>.passwd.txt file, if permitted.

Windows NT Primary Domain Controller Security Review Program

No.	Category	Control Objectives	Risk	Control Techniques
3	User Management	Automatic logon options for servers should not be enabled.	There is an increased risk that an unauthorized user may gain knowledge of a username and password for the domain as the use of this option embeds the password of an account in the registry in clear text.	Ensure the value of the AutoAdminLogon registry key is set to 0.
3	User Management	The default values for automatic logon should not be present.	Even if the automatic logon option is disabled, the default password may still exist in the registry. An unauthorized user may gain access to this key and compromise the system.	Ensure that the DefaultPassword, DefaultUserName, and DefaultDomainName registry keys do not exist.

Implementation Techniques	Compliance Assessment Techniques	Compliance Verification Techniques
Ensure the value of the AutoAdminLogon registry key is set to 0 by performing the following procedures: 1. Open regedt32. 2. Select the hive HKLM\Software\Windows NT\Winlogon. 3. Verify that AutoAdminLogon is set to 0. 4. Close regedt32.	Verify that the value of the AutoAdminLogon registry key is set to 0 by performing the following procedures: 1. Open regedt32. 2. Select the hive: HKLM\Software\Windows NT\Winlogon. 3. Determine if the value of AutoAdminLogon is set to 0. 4. Close regedt32.	Review <servername>.winlogon.txt and ensure the value AutoAdminLogon is set to 0.
Ensure that the DefaultPassword, DefaultUserName, and DefaultDomainName registry keys do not exist by performing the following procedures: 1. Open regedt32. 2. Select the hive HKLM\Software\Windows NT\Winlogon. 3. Delete the keys mentioned above.	Verify that the DefaultPassword, DefaultUserName, and DefaultDomainName registry keys do not exist by performing the following procedures: 1. Open regedt32. 2. Select the hive HKLM\Software\Windows NT\Winlogon. 3. Verify that the keys mentioned above do not exist.	Review <servername>.winlogon.txt and ensure the values DefaultUserName, DefaultPassword, and DefaultDomainName are blank.

Windows NT Primary Domain Controller Security Review Program

No.	Category	Control Objectives	Risk	Control Techniques
3	User Management	Anonymous users that connect with the Null Credentials Logon should be denied access to all systems in the domain. Null session pipes should be disabled.	The Null Credentials Logon gives individuals a method of procuring every share and username that exists on the system. In addition, group memberships can also be discovered. With this information, attackers can start brute force guessing passwords and attempt to compromise the system. **Note:** Some software may not function after these changes. Additionally, the ability to change passwords may be lost. Ensure compatibility by testing. Also, users may be unable to proactively change their password.	Add the registry key `RestrictAnonymous` to the `HKLM\System\CurrentControlSet\Control\LSA\` portion of the registry. The value of this setting should be 1. Review the values on the null session restrictions registry keys in the `HKLM\System\CurrentControlSets\Services\lanmanserver\parameter` portion of the registry.

Implementation Techniques

Add the registry key RestrictAnonymous to the HKLM\System\CurrentControl\Set\Control\LSA portion of the registry by performing the following steps:

1. Open regedt32.
2. Select the key HKLM\System\CurrentControl\Set\Control\LSA.
3. Select Add Value. . . from the Edit pulldown menu.
4. Add RestrictAnonymous to the Value Name: box.
5. Select REG_DWORD for the Data type.
6. Click OK.
7. Enter **1** in the Data: box.
8. Click OK.

In addition, verify that the Null Sessions Access has been restricted by performing the following steps:

1. Open regedt32.
2. Select the hive HKLM SYSTEM\CurrentControlSet\Services\LanmanServer\Parameters.
3. Verify the key RestrictNullSessionAccess is set to 1.
4. Close regedt32.
5. Verify the key RestrictNullPipes is set to the default.
6. Verify the key RestrictNullShares is set to the default.

Compliance Assessment Techniques

Verify that the registry key RestrictAnonymous has been added to the HKLM\System\CurrentControl\Set\Control\LSA portion of the registry by performing the following steps:

1. Open regedt32.
2. Select the key HKLM\System\CurrentControl\Set\Control\LSA.
3. Verify that the registry key RestrictAnonymous:REG_DWORD:0x1 is listed.

In addition, verify that the Null Sessions Access has been restricted by performing the following steps:

1. Open regedt32.
2. Select the hive HKLM\SYSTEM\CurrentControlSet\Services\LanmanServer\Parameters.
3. Verify that the key RestrictNullSessionAccess is set to 1.
4. Close regedt32.

Compliance Verification Techniques

Review <servername>.lsa.txt and ensure the value RestrictAnonymous is set to 1.

Windows NT Primary Domain Controller Security Review Program

No.	Category	Control Objectives	Risk	Control Techniques
4	Password Management	The maximum password age should be set in accordance with corporate security standards and guidelines. Industry guidelines state 60 days.	Without forcing users to change passwords, the risk that a password will have an unlimited useful life after being compromised is increased.	Set the maximum password age in accordance with corporate security standards and guidelines. Industry guidelines state 60 days.
4	Password Management	The minimum password length should be set in accordance with corporate security standards and guidelines. Industry guidelines state 7 characters.	Having an adequate password length increases the difficulty required to guess a password.	Set the minimum password length in accordance with corporate security standards and guidelines. Industry guidelines state 7 characters.
4	Password Management	The minimum password age should be set in accordance with corporate security standards and guidelines. Industry guidelines state 3 days.	Having this feature enabled prevents a user from changing their new password back to the original password, thereby bypassing the password uniqueness control.	Set the minimum password age in accordance with corporate security standards and guidelines. Industry guidelines state 3 days.

Implementation Techniques	Compliance Assessment Techniques	Compliance Verification Techniques
For all servers, set the maximum password age parameter by performing the following steps: 1. Using User Manager, select the Account. . . Option of the Policies menu. 2. Enter the **number of days for the Maximum Password Age.** This should be set in accordance with corporate standards. 3. Click OK to confirm changes. Industry guidelines state 60 days.	For all servers, verify the maximum password age parameter by performing the following steps: 1. Open User Manager. 2. Select the Account. . . Option under the Policies menu. 3. Ensure that the Password Expires In X days radio button is selected. View the number of days for the Maximum Password Age. This should be set in accordance with corporate standards or our best practices. 4. Click OK to exit. Industry guidelines state 60 days.	Review <servername>. policies.txt for compliance with corporate polices relating to maximum password age. If no corporate policy exists, use 60 days as a baseline.
For all servers, set the minimum password length parameter by performing the following steps: 1. Using User Manager, select the Account. . . option of the Policies menu. 2. Enter the **number of characters required for the Minimum Password Length.** This should be set in accordance with corporate standards. 3. Click OK to confirm changes. Industry guidelines state 7 characters.	For all servers, verify the minimum password length parameter by performing the following steps: 1. Open User Manager. 2. Select the Account. . . Option under the Policies menu. 3. Ensure that the At Least X Characters radio button is selected. View the number of characters required for the Minimum Password Length. This should be set in accordance with corporate standards or our best practices. 4. Click OK to exit. Industry guidelines state 7 characters.	Review <servername>. policies.txt for compliance with corporate polices relating to minimum password length. If no corporate policy exists, use 7 characters as a baseline.
For all servers, set the minimum password age parameter by performing the following steps: 1. Using User Manager, select the Account. . . Option of the Policies menu. 2. Enter the **number of days for the Minimum Password Age.** This should be set in accordance with corporate standards. 3. Click OK to close the User Properties. Industry guidelines state 3 days.	For all servers, verify that the minimum password age parameter has been set by performing the following steps: 1. Open User Manager. 2. Select the Account. . . Option under the Policies menu. 3. Ensure that the Allow Changes In X days radio button is selected. View the number of days for the Minimum Password Age. This should be set in accordance with corporate standards or our best practices. 4. Click OK to exit. Industry guidelines state 3 days.	Review <servername>. policies.txt for compliance with corporate polices relating to minimum password age. If no corporate policy exists, use 3 days as a baseline.

Windows NT Primary Domain Controller Security Review Program

No.	Category	Control Objectives	Risk	Control Techniques
4	Password Management	The password uniqueness should be set in accordance with corporate security standards and guidelines. Industry guidelines state 6 passwords.	Requiring unique passwords prevents a user from recycling old passwords that may have been compromised in the past.	Set the password uniqueness in accordance with corporate security standards and guidelines. Industry guidelines state 6 passwords.
4	Password Management	The Service Pack Enhancement, passfilt, should be implemented to enforce strong password controls.	Having a high degree of password strength decreases the likelihood of passwords being guessed by intruders.	Enable passfilt so that not just lowercase letters are required for passwords. Be aware that with Windows 95 companies, passfilt does not enforce case-sensitive passwords. Additionally, the error messages produced by passfilt are often unclear so administrators must stay alert. Finally, know that administrators can create their own dll with their own password rules.

Implementation Techniques	Compliance Assessment Techniques	Compliance Verification Techniques
For all servers, set the password uniqueness parameters by performing the following steps: 1. Using User Manager, select the Account. . . Option of the Policies menu. 2. Enter the **number of passwords for the Password Uniqueness.** This should be set in accordance with corporate standards. 3. Click OK to confirm changes. Industry guidelines state 6 passwords.	For all servers, verify that the password uniqueness parameters have been set by performing the following steps: 1. Open User Manager. 2. Select the Account. . . Option under the Policies menu. 3. Verify that the Remember X Passwords radio button is selected. View the value entered in this field. This should be set in accordance with corporate standards or our best practices. 4. Click OK to exit. Industry guidelines state 6 passwords.	Review <servername>. policies.txt for compliance with corporate polices relating to password uniqueness. If no corporate policy exists, use 6 passwords as a baseline.
For the PDC, enable passfilt by performing the following steps: 1. Open regedt32. 2. Select the Key HKLM\System\CurrentControl\Set\Control\LSA. 3. Edit the Notification Packages value name. 4. Add passfilt to the Value name.	For the PDC, check for passfilt by performing the following steps: 1. Open regedt32. 2. Select the Key HKLM\System\CurrentControl\Set\Control\LSA. 3. View the Notification Packages value name.	Review <servername> lsa.txt to ensure the value Notification Packages contains the passfilt.dll entry. If the Notification Packages value contains an entry of FPNWCLNT.dll, inquire with the company if this is required for connectivity between NT and Novell servers. Also, ensure that the FPNWCLNT.dll exists within the system path and is properly secured. Ensure that the FPNWCLNT.dll is the proper size, date, and version based on the service pack and any hot fixes that are installed.

Windows NT Primary Domain Controller Security Review Program

No.	Category	Control Objectives	Risk	Control Techniques
4	Password Management	The account lockout feature should be enabled, and the related parameters should be set in accordance with corporate security standards and guidelines. Industry guidelines state 3 bad logon attempts and to reset the counter after 1,440 minutes. Accounts should be locked forever or until an administrator manually unlocks them.	Locking out accounts after a specified number of failed login attempts decreases the risk that user accounts will be compromised through brute force attacks.	Enable the account lockout feature and set the appropriate parameters in accordance with corporate security standards and guidelines. Industry guidelines state 3 bad logon attempts and to reset the counter after 1,440 minutes. Accounts should be locked forever or until an administrator manually unlocks them.
4	Password Management	The resource kit utility, passprop, should be utilized to enable lockout on the Administrator account over a network connection.	The Administrator account is susceptible to an infinite number of password guesses over a network connection unless passprop is implemented. Regardless, Administrators should not be able to "access this computer from the network," but this is a good supplemental procedure.	Enable passprop's `adminlockout` function.
4	Password Management	The password for the Administrator account maintained on each server should be changed in accordance with corporate standards and guidelines and be unique across all servers.	The renamed Administrator account on each server is the most privileged account on the system. Therefore, extra care should be taken with its use. Changing the password periodically limits the useful life of any compromised passwords. Requiring unique passwords on different systems limits the exposure to the system if one administrator account is compromised.	Require that the password for the Administrator account on each server is changed periodically and is unique for all servers.

Implementation Techniques	Compliance Assessment Techniques	Compliance Verification Techniques
For all servers, set the account lockout parameters by performing the following steps: 1. Using **User Manager**, select the **Account. . .** Option of the **Policies** menu. 2. Ensure the **Account Lockout** option is enabled. 3. Enter the appropriate settings for **Lockout After Bad Logon Attempts, Reset Count After Minutes,** and **Lockout Duration**. These settings should be set in accordance with corporate standards. 4. Click **OK** to confirm changes.	For all servers, verify the account lockout parameters by performing the following steps: 1. Open **User Manager**. 2. Select the **Account. . .** Option under the **Policies** menu. 3. Ensure the **Account Lockout** radio button is selected. 4. Verify the settings for **Lockout After Bad Logon Attempts, Reset Count After Minutes,** and **Lockout Duration**. These settings should be set in accordance with corporate standards or our best practices. 5. Click **OK** to exit.	Review **<servername>.policies.txt** for compliance with corporate polices relating to account lockout. If no corporate policy exists, use the following as a baseline: • Industry guidelines state 3 bad logon attempts and to reset the counter after 1,440 minutes. • Accounts should be locked forever or until an administrator manually unlocks them. • 1,440 minutes equals 24 hours.
Industry guidelines state 3 bad logon attempts and to reset the counter after 1,440 minutes. Accounts should be locked forever or until an administrator manually unlocks them. From the command prompt, type **passprop/ adminlockout**.	Industry guidelines state 3 bad logon attempts and to reset the counter after 1,440 minutes. Accounts should be locked forever or until an administrator manually unlocks them.	
	Verify that **passprop** has been used to enable lockout of the administrator account over a network connection. From the command prompt, type **passprop** and view the results.	Review **<servername>. passprop.txt** to ensure the Administrator account lockout control is enabled.
Change the passwords on the Administrator-level account by performing the following steps: 1. Using the **User Manager**, open the user account that requires a change of password. 2. Enter the **new password** in both the **Password** and the **Confirm Password** fields. 3. Click **OK** to close the **User Properties**.	Verify, with the network administrator and administrator equivalent users, that Administrator-level account passwords are being changed in accordance with corporate security standards and are unique across all servers. In large multidomain implementations of Windows NT, this may not be a practical policy. An alternative might be a different password within different domains.	Review **<servername>.users.txt** and ensure the Administrator accounts are required to follow default account policies. Also review **<servername>.passwd.txt** and ensure the Administrator account password hashes are unique across servers.

Windows NT Primary Domain Controller Security Review Program

No.	Category	Control Objectives	Risk	Control Techniques
4	Password Management	Default passwords supplied with software packages should be changed upon installation.	Application default passwords are widely known and typically initial targets for attacks. The risk that unauthorized access will be obtained is increased if these passwords are not changed.	Change all default application default passwords upon installation of applications.
4	Password Management	Privileged user passwords should not be widely distributed.	Distribution of privileged account passwords to multiple users weakens the effectiveness of a stringent password policy and reduces user accountability.	Only distribute privileged account passwords to users who require this access for a legitimate business purpose. Each user with a privileged account should have a unique ID and password.
4	Password Management	User-level overrides of password policies should not be enabled for any user accounts except for service accounts.	If user-level overrides of password policies are allowed, there is an increased risk that unauthorized access by users will be obtained.	Remove the User Cannot Change Password and Password Never Expires user overrides of the default password policy.
4	Password Management	All new user accounts should be required to change their password on first logon. There should not be generic or predictable passwords used as a new default. Each new account should be created with a unique and difficult to determine password.	Requiring new users to change their password upon login ensures that the temporary password will not be in use. Additionally, by having users create their own passwords, the chance of their remembering their password is significantly increased.	Require all new user accounts to change their password on first logon.
4	Password Management	Controls should be implemented to ensure the Administrator password is available for emergencies.	System administrators should provide a mechanism to obtain the Administrator password in the event of an emergency to reduce the risk of significant downtime. These passwords should be stored on and off site. They should reside in a physically secure location.	Write down the Administrator password, place it in a sealed envelope, and keep it in secure locations, on and off site, in the event it is needed in an emergency.

Implementation Techniques	Compliance Assessment Techniques	Compliance Verification Techniques
Change the passwords on the appropriate accounts by performing the following steps: 4. Using the User Manager, open the user account that requires a change of password. 5. Enter the **new password** in both the Password and the Confirm Password fields. 6. Click OK to close the User Properties.	Verify, with the network administrator and through physical inspection, that default application passwords have been changed in accordance with corporate security standards.	Review <servername>.users.txt and ensure that any default accounts are required to follow default account policies. Also review <servername>.passwd.txt and ensure that these default accounts' password hashes are unique across servers.
Implement a procedure for distributing privileged account passwords to only users who require this access for a legitimate business purpose.	Review the account password distribution procedure. Verify that privileged account passwords are distributed only to those individuals with a legitimate business need for such access.	Review the account password distribution procedure. Verify that privileged account passwords are distributed only to those individuals with a legitimate business need for such access.
For all servers, disable the user overrides of default password policies by performing the following steps: 1. Using the User Manager, open the user account. 2. Ensure the User Cannot Change Password and the Password Never Expires options are not enabled. If they are enabled, they should be unchecked to disable them. 3. Click OK to confirm changes.	For all users, verify that the user overrides of default password policies have been disabled by performing the following steps: 1. Open User Manager. 2. Double-click on the user account. 3. Verify that the User Cannot Change Password and the Password Never Expires options are not checked. 4. Click OK to exit. 5. Repeat for all users	Review <servername>.users.txt and ensure there are no end user accounts that are allowed to override default account policies.
For all new users added to the PDC, require that they change their password on initial login by performing the following step: 1. When creating a new user with the User Manager Utility, ensure the User Must Change Password at Next Logon box is checked.	Verify, with the network administrator, that the User Must Change Password at Next Logon box is checked when new accounts are created.	Inquire with the company regarding the procedures for creating new user accounts. Determine if the accounts are required to change their password on first logon. Also review the <servername>.users.txt for users who are required to change their password on next logon.
Establish a procedure for keeping the Administrator passwords written down and in a secure location. Establish a second procedure for obtaining the passwords in the event of an emergency.	Verify, through discussion with the network administrator and inspection of written policies, that a procedure exists for the storage and retrieval of the administrator password. Verify that this procedure is followed and that the password is stored in a secured location. Ensure that the retrieval process is known to secondary/emergency administrators.	Verify, through discussion with the network administrator and inspection of written policies, that a procedure exists for the storage and retrieval of the administrator password. Verify that this procedure is followed and that the password is stored in a secured location. Ensure that the retrieval process is known to secondary/emergency administrators.

Windows NT Primary Domain Controller Security Review Program

No.	Category	Control Objectives	Risk	Control Techniques
5	Group Management	The Users local group should only contain the Domain Users global group from the PDC of the Authentication Domain.	Both the Users local group and Domain Users global group are built into the system. All domain users are by default members of the Domain Users global group. There is no need to have additional accounts in the Users local group, and doing so increases the risk that a local system resource will be abused.	Add the Domain Users global group to the Users local group.
5	Group Management	All user accounts, with the exception of the built-in accounts of Guest and Administrator, should be in global groups only. Global groups should be assigned to local groups. The renamed Administrator account should be the only user account in the Administrators local group.	Having all user accounts contained within global groups increases network security by simplifying administration. User accounts should never appear in local groups or have Access Control Lists (ACLs) with any object.	Remove all user accounts from local groups and move them to a respective global group. The renamed Administrator account should be the only user account in the Administrators local group.

Implementation Techniques	Compliance Assessment Techniques	Compliance Verification Techniques
Add the Domain Users global group to the Users local group by performing the following steps: 1. Open User Manager. 2. Choose Select Domain. . . from the user pulldown menu. 3. Enter the **server name** into the Domain box. 4. Click OK. 5. Double-click on the Users Local Group. 6. Domain users should be present. 7. If domain users is not present, click the Add button. 8. Select the Authentication Domain in the List Names From: box. 9. Highlight the Domain Users Global group. 10. Click the Add button. 11. Click OK to confirm the changes. 12. Click OK to close the Local Group Properties box. 13. Close User Manager.	Verify that the Domain Users global group is listed in the Users local group by performing the following steps: 1. Open User Manager. 2. Choose Select Domain. . . from the user pulldown menu. 3. Enter the **server or workstation name** into the Domain box. 4. Click OK. 5. Double-click on the Users Local Group. 6. Verify that Domain users is present as a member of Users. 7. Click Cancel to close. 8. Close User Manager.	Review <servername>.groups.txt and ensure the only end user accounts in the Users local group are those accounts contained within the Domain Users global group from the Authentication Domain.
Remove all user accounts from local groups and move them to a respective global group by performing the following steps: 1. Open User Manager. 2. Double-click on the appropriate Local Group. 3. Domain users should not be present. 4. If domain users is not present, click the Add button. 5. Select the Authentication Domain in the List Names From: box. 6. Highlight the Domain Users Global group. 7. Click the Add button. 8. Click OK to confirm the changes. 9. Click OK to close the Local Group Properties box. 10. Close User Manager.	Ensure that all user accounts are members only of global group by performing the following steps: 1. Open User Manager. 2. Choose Select Domain. . . from the user pulldown menu. 3. Enter the **server or workstation name** into the Domain box. 4. Click OK. 5. Double-click on the Users Local Group. 6. Domain users should be present. 7. Click Cancel to close. 8. Close User Manager.	Review <servername>.groups.txt and ensure that all end users accounts assigned to local groups are done so by the use of global groups.

Windows NT Primary Domain Controller Security Review Program

No.	Category	Control Objectives	Risk	Control Techniques
5	Group Management	User accounts should be logically grouped through the use of global groups in the Authentication Domain.	Global groups simplify network administration by containing logical groups of users. Users should be grouped according to similar job functions, department, or access requirements.	Create global groups in the Authentication Domain and add all applicable user accounts to these groups.
5	Group Management	Naming conventions should be established and followed for all global and local groups. Global groups should have different naming standards than local groups.	Global group names, which can be easily identified, simplify network administration. This increases security because nonstandard groups can easily be identified. Groups should be named in such a fashion that the type of group, group purpose, and/or department could be identified.	Name all local and global groups in accordance with established naming conventions.
5	Group Management	Each group should have a description provided by the application or business manager.	Requiring all groups to have descriptions minimizes the possibility that extraneous, unneeded groups will be created. Such a group could bypass system administration and be used for unauthorized activities.	Add an applicable and informative description for all groups.

Implementation Techniques	Compliance Assessment Techniques	Compliance Verification Techniques
Create global groups according to corporate policy and access needs and add all applicable users accounts to these groups.	Verify, through discussion with the network administrator and review of written policies, that global groups have been created and are utilized in accordance with corporate policy. Ensure compliance with said policies through physical inspection via User Manager.	Inquire with the company regarding procedures for granting users access to resources. Ensure that these procedures require administrators to add end user accounts to global groups (in the Authentication Domain), global groups to local groups, and local groups to resource permissions.
Name all groups in accordance with established naming conventions.	Verify, through discussion with the network administrator and review of written policies, that all groups are named in accordance with corporate policy. Ensure compliance with said policies through physical inspection via User Manager. Note whether the naming conventions distinguish between local and global groups and provide for the ability to identify employee, vendor, and temporary groups.	Obtain a copy of the company's group naming conventions and ensure that they are enforced on all local and global groups by examining the `<servername>.groups.txt` file. Note whether the naming conventions distinguish between local and global groups and provide for the ability to identify employee, vendor, and temporary groups.
For all servers, provide an applicable and informative description for all local groups by performing the following steps: 1. Using **User Manager**, open the appropriate **Local Group Properties** box. 2. Enter an **applicable and informative description** in the **Description** box. 3. Click **OK** to confirm the changes.	Verify that all servers have an applicable and informative description for all local groups by performing the following steps: 1. Open **User Manager**. 2. Double-click on the **Local Group** name. 3. Verify that an applicable and informative description exists in the **Description** box. 4. Click **OK** to exit. 5. Repeat for each local group.	Review `<servername>.groups.txt` and ensure that all groups have an applicable and informative description.

Windows NT Primary Domain Controller Security Review Program

No.	Category	Control Objectives	Risk	Control Techniques
5	Group Management	The Backup Operators, Server Operators, Account Operators, and Print Operators local groups should only contain global groups that are authorized for this purpose.	The Backup Operators, Server Operators, Account Operators, and Print Operators local groups have several privileges associated with them, such as the ability to log on to systems interactively. Therefore, caution should be exercised when adding users to these built-in groups. Having only global groups as members of these groups helps to ensure that the groups will be properly restricted.	Add the authorized global groups to the Backup Operators, Server Operators, Account Operators, and Print Operators local groups on each server in the Authentication and Resource Domain and any workstations in the network environment.
5	Group Management	The special group Everyone should not be used. Using specialized groups will allow the Administrator to have better control over files and directories. **Note:** Certain applications, as well as the Windows NT system directory, will not function without the Everyone group in the ACL. This is more appropriate for data directories.	Using the special group Everyone is very broad and could inadvertently allow an intruder to gain access to system resources. If more broad group naming is required, the Authenticated Users group may be used as a substitute for Everyone.	Replace references to the special group Everyone with Domain Users or Domain application groups. **Note:** Certain applications, as well as the Windows NT system directory, will not function without the Everyone group in the ACL. This is more appropriate for data directories.

Implementation Techniques	Compliance Assessment Techniques	Compliance Verification Techniques
Add the authorized global groups to the Backup Operators, Server Operators, Account Operators, and Print Operators local groups on each server in the Authentication and Resource Domain and any workstations in the network environment by performing the following steps: 1. Open User Manager. 2. Choose Select Domain. . . from the user pulldown menu. 3. Enter the **server name** in the Domain: box. 4. Double-click on the Backup Operator local group. 5. Click the Add button. 6. Select the authorized global groups. 7. Click the Add button. 8. Click the OK button. 9. Repeat steps 4–8 for the Server Operators group. 10. Close User Manager.	Verify that the authorized global groups are members of the Backup Operators, Server Operators, Account Operators, and Print Operators local groups on each server in the Authentication and Resource Domain and any workstations in the network environment by performing the following steps: 1. Open User Manager. 2. Choose Select Domain. . . from the user pulldown menu. 3. Enter the **server name** in the Domain: box. 4. Double-click on the Backup Operator local group. 5. Verify that only authorized global groups are listed. 6. Click the Cancel button. 7. Repeat steps 4–6 for the Server Operators group. 8. Close User Manager.	Review the <servername>.groups.txt and ensure that only authorized users are members of these groups.
Restrict default group access to application and system files and directories by performing the following steps: 1. Open the Windows NT Explorer. 2. Right-click on the file or directory to set the security permissions and select the properties option. 3. Click the Permissions button of the Security tab. 4. Select the Replace Permissions on Subdirectories and the replace Permissions on Existing Files check boxes as appropriate. The Replace Permissions on Subdirectories will place the security permissions that you select on all files and subdirectories under the selected directory, while the Replace Permissions on Existing Files will ensure that all files contained in the directory have the selected security permissions. 5. If a group has access that you want to remove, do so by highlighting the applicable group and clicking	Verify, with the network administrator, that the special group Everyone has been replaced with Domain Users or Domain application groups. If more broad group naming is required, the Authenticated Users group may be used as a substitute for Everyone.	Review <servername>.perms <drive letter>.txt and ensure the special group Everyone is not allowed access to any files on the system.

Windows NT Primary Domain Controller Security Review Program

No.	Category	Control Objectives	Risk	Control Techniques
5	Group Management	Other than the built-in global groups, no global groups should exist outside of the authentication domains.	Global groups simplify network administration by containing logical groups of users. There is no need to create global groups on resource domains. Doing so only decreases the ability of the network manager to effectively manage the network.	Delete all global groups (other then the default global groups) contained in resource domains and re-create them in the Authentication Domain.

Implementation Techniques	Compliance Assessment Techniques	Compliance Verification Techniques
the **Remove** button. The special group everyone's permissions should be removed from all files and directories on the system. If all users require this access, it should be granted to the **Users Local Group**. 6. Click the **Add** button to include the applicable groups to be granted permissions. When you have selected all the applicable groups, click the **OK** button to confirm these additions. 7. Grant the **Type of Access** for each group by highlighting the applicable group and selecting **Access** from the **Type of Access** box. These **Permissions** should be set in accordance with corporate system standards. 8. Click the **OK** button to confirm these changes. 9. After the security permissions have been changed, click the **OK** button to close the file and directories properties window. **Note:** Certain applications, as well as the Windows NT system directory, will not function without the Everyone group in the ACL. This is more appropriate for data directories.		
Delete all global groups (other then the default global groups) contained in resource domains and re-create them in the Authentication Domain.	Verify, through discussion with the network administrator and physical inspection, that no global groups exist in the resource domains.	Review the <servername>.groups.txt and ensure no global groups exist in nonauthentication domains.

Windows NT Primary Domain Controller Security Review Program

No.	Category	Control Objectives	Risk	Control Techniques
5	Group Management	Access Control Lists (ACLs) for files and directories should only specify local groups as having access. ACLs should not specify individual user accounts or global groups as being granted or revoked access.	In Windows NT, only local groups should be granted rights to resources. All users should be placed in global groups, and global groups should be placed in local groups. This ensures that the environment has a structured method of administration and decreases the possibility that users will be granted excessive rights.	Utilize local groups to grant permissions to files and directories.
6	File System Access and Management	The Windows NT File System (NTFS) should be used on all partitions. Additionally, there should be no unformatted space on the drive.	NTFS associates permissions with each file and directory. Using these permissions, different levels of access can be granted or denied to different groups of users. Under NT, file access is based solely on file permissions.	All File Allocation Table (FAT) or High Performance File System (HPFS) partitions should be converted to the Windows NT file system (NTFS). HPFS is not supported under Windows NT 4.0. Any file systems in that format would have to be converted during the 3.51 to 4.0 upgrade.
6	File System Access and Management	Application and system directories should not allow Write, Delete, Change Permissions, or Take Ownership to users. The built-in special group should have no permissions.	Granting excessive permissions to applications could lead to their abuse or deletion.	Set the default permissions for users to be as restrictive as possible on application directories. Remove all permissions for the built-in special group of Everyone. If these types of permissions are needed, create new groups that contain the appropriate users and have the required permissions.
6	File System Access and Management	Data files should be stored in segregated directories external to the application and system directories, possibly in the data owners' home directories, or the application-specified data directory.	Data files should be placed in separate directories to help prevent the changing of directory permission levels that may accidentally flow down to executable program files. It is also good practice to separate data from application files in order to grant the appropriate level of security for each type of file.	Separate application files from data files.

Implementation Techniques	Compliance Assessment Techniques	Compliance Verification Techniques
Implement a procedure to utilize local groups for granting permissions to files and directories.	Verify that a procedure exists to ensure that permissions for files and directories are only granted to local groups. Make certain, through discussion with the system administrator, that this procedure is followed.	Review <servername>.perms <drive letter>.txt and ensure that only local groups are granted access to files and directories.
Open Disk Administrator to view the partition information and file system for all drives. Issue the following command to convert the FAT partitions to NTFS: At the command prompt enter the following command: **convert X: /fs ntfs /v, Where X is the drive to be converted.**	Verify that the NTFS file system is being used and that there is no unformatted or nonpartitioned space by performing the following steps: 1. Open Disk Administrator. 2. View the partition information and file system for all drives.	Review the <servername>.perms <drive letter>.txt and ensure that all drives reviewed use the NTFS file system and that there is no unformatted or nonpartitioned space.
Implement a procedure to set default permissions for users to be as restrictive as possible on application directories and to remove all permissions for the built-in special group Everyone. If these types of permissions are needed, create new groups that contain the appropriate users and have required permissions.	Determine, with the network administrator, the appropriate (most restrictive) level of permissions for application and system directories. Verify that this level of access is granted. Ensure that the special group Everyone has no file system permissions. Under certain circumstances, ensure that new groups are created to manage relaxed permissions.	Determine, with the network administrator, the appropriate (most restrictive) level of permissions for application and system directories. Verify that this level of access is granted by reviewing <servername>. perms<drive letter>.txt and ensuring that end users are not allowed excessive permissions to application files and directories. Under certain circumstances, ensure that new groups are created to manage relaxed permissions.
Implement a procedure to place data files in separate directories from the application and system directories.	Verify that a procedure exists to ensure that application and data files are segregated. Ensure, through physical inspection, that application files and data files are located in separate directories or on separate drives.	Verify that a procedure exists to ensure that application and data files are segregated. Ensure, through physical inspection, that application files and data files are located in separate directories or on separate drives.

Windows NT Primary Domain Controller Security Review Program

No.	Category	Control Objectives	Risk	Control Techniques
6	File System Access and Management	Certain directories that contain sensitive Windows NT system files should be secured (these directories are listed in the implementation checklist).	If unauthorized users gain access to sensitive system files, they could execute a Trojan horse or create a denial of service on the PDC.	Restrict access to sensitive Windows NT directories (listed in the implementation checklist).

Implementation Techniques

Restrict access to the following directories by performing the following steps:

1. Open the Windows NT Explorer.
2. Right-click on the file or directory to set the security permissions and select the Properties option.

The following directories should be secured:

C:\
C:\winnt\
C:\winnt\system32
C:\winnt;\system32\drivers

The following permissions should be set:

Administrators	Full Control
Server Operators	Change
Everyone	Read
Creator/Owner	Full Control
System	Full Control

3. Click the Permissions button of the Security tab.
4. Select the Replace Permissions on Subdirectories, and the Replace Permissions on Existing Files check boxes as appropriate. The Replace Permissions on Subdirectories will place the security permissions that you select on all files and subdirectories under the selected directory, while the Replace Permissions on Existing Files will ensure that all files contained in the directory have the selected security permissions.
5. Click the OK button to confirm these changes.
6. After the security permissions have been changed, click the OK button to close the file and directories properties window.

Compliance Assessment Techniques

Verify that permissions on the following directories comply with the recommendations by performing the following steps:

1. Right-click on the directory in Explorer.
2. Choose Properties.
3. Select the Security tab.
4. Click the Permissions button.
5. Compare the current permissions to the recommendations.
6. Repeat for all listed directories.

Directories:
C:\
C:\winnt\
C:\winnt\system32
C:\winnt\system32\drivers

Recommended Permissions:

Administrators	Full Control
Server Operators	Change
Everyone	Read
Creator/Owner	Full Control
System	Full Control

Compliance Verification Techniques

Review the <servername>.perms<system drive letter>.txt and ensure the following permissions are in place for the:

Directories:
C:\
C:\winnt\
C:\winnt\system32
C:\winnt\system32\drivers

Recommended Permissions:

Administrators	Full Control
Server Operators	Change
Everyone	Read
Creator/Owner	Full Control
System	Full Control

Windows NT Primary Domain Controller Security Review Program

No.	Category	Control Objectives	Risk	Control Techniques
6	File System Access and Management	The `c:\winnt\system32\config` directory contains the SAM, audit files, and other registry files. These should be secured from unauthorized use.	If unauthorized users gain access to this directory, they could view the audit files or attempt to get access to the SAM if they crash the server.	Restrict access to the `c:\winnt\system32\config` directory to prevent unauthorized access.

Implementation Techniques

Restrict access to c:\winnt\system32\config by performing the following steps:

1. Open the Windows NT Explorer.
2. Right-click on the file or directory to set the security permissions and select the Properties option.

The following permissions should be set:

Administrators	Full Control
Everyone	List
Creator/Owner	Full Control
System	Full Control

3. Click the Permissions button of the Security tab.
4. Select the Replace Permissions on Subdirectories and the Replace Permissions on Existing Files check boxes as appropriate. The Replace Permissions on Subdirectories will place the security permissions that you select on all files and subdirectories under the selected directory, while the Replace Permissions on Existing Files will ensure that all files contained in the directory have the selected security permissions.
5. Click the OK button to confirm these changes.
6. After the security permissions have been changed, click the OK button to close the file and directories properties window.

Compliance Assessment Techniques

Verify that permissions on the following directory comply with the recommendations by performing the following steps:

1. Right-click on the directory in Explorer.
2. Choose Properties.
3. Select the Security tab.
4. Click the Permissions button.
5. Compare the current permissions to the recommendations.
6. Repeat for all listed directories.

Directory:
C:\winnt\system32\config

Recommended Permissions:

Administrators	Full Control
Everyone	List
Creator/Owner	Full Control
System	Full Control

Compliance Verification Techniques

Review the <servername><perms<system drive letter>.txt and ensure the following permissions are in place for:

Directory:
C:\winnt\system32\config

Recommended Permissions:

Administrators	Full Control
Everyone	List
Creator/Owner	Full Control
System	Full Control

Windows NT Primary Domain Controller Security Review Program

No.	Category	Control Objectives	Risk	Control Techniques
6	File System Access and Management	The c:\winnt\system32\spool directory contains the printer drivers and files. These should be secured from unauthorized use.	If unauthorized users gain access to this directory, they could gain access to printer settings and drivers.	Restrict access to the c:\winnt\system32\spool directory to prevent unauthorized access.
6	File System Access and Management	The replication directories contain login scripts, policies, and other user-sensitive data that is replicated among servers. These should be secured from unauthorized use.	If unauthorized users gain access to these directories, they could gain access to user data, policies, and login scripts. That type of information could contain password information or be replaced with Trojan horses.	Restrict access to the replication directories so that only authorized users have access.

Implementation Techniques

Restrict access to c:\winnt;\system32\spool by performing the following steps:

1. Open the Windows NT Explorer.
2. Right-click on the file or directory to set the security permissions and select the **Properties** option.

The following permissions should be set:

Administrators	Full Control
Print Operators	Full Control
Everyone	Read
Creator/Owner	Full Control
System	Full Control

3. Click the **Permissions** button of the **Security** tab.
4. Select the **Replace Permissions on Subdirectories** and the **Replace Permissions on Existing Files** check boxes as appropriate. The **Replace Permissions on Subdirectories** will place the security permissions that you select on all files and subdirectories under the selected directory, while the **Replace Permissions on Existing Files** will ensure that all files contained in the directory have the selected security permissions.
5. Click the **OK** button to confirm these changes.
6. After the security permissions have been changed, click the **OK** button to close the file and directories properties window.

Compliance Assessment Techniques

Verify that permissions on the following directory comply with the recommendation by performing the following steps:

1. Right-click on the directory in Explorer.
2. Choose **Properties.**
3. Select the **Security** tab
4. Click the **Permissions** button.
5. Compare the current permissions to the recommendations.
6. Repeat for all listed directories.

Directory:
C:\winnt\system32\spool

Recommended Permissions:

Administrators	Full Control
Print Operators	Full Control
Everyone	Read
Creator/Owner	Full Control
System	Full Control

Compliance Verification Techniques

Review the <servername>. perms<system drive letter>.txt and ensure the following permissions are in place for:

Directory:
C:\winnt\system32\spool

Recommended Permissions:

Administrators	Full Control
Print Operators	Full Control
Everyone	Read
Creator/Owner	Full Control
System	Full Control

Restrict access to replication directories by performing the following steps:

1. Open the Windows NT Explorer.
2. Right-click on the file or directory to set the security Permissions and select the **Properties** option.

Verify that permissions on the following directories comply with the recommendations by performing the following steps:

1. Right-click on the directory in Explorer.
2. Choose **Properties.**
3. Select the **Security** tab.

Review the <servername>. perms<system drive letter>.txt and ensure the following permissions are in place for the following directories:

Directory:
C:\winnt\system32\repl

Windows NT Primary Domain Controller Security Review Program

No.	Category	Control Objectives	Risk	Control Techniques

Implementation Techniques	Compliance Assessment Techniques	Compliance Verification Techniques
The following directory permissions should be set: C:\winnt\system32\repl Administrators Full Control Server Operators Full Control Everyone Read Creator/Owner Full Control System Full Control C:\winnt\system32\repl\import Administrators Full Control Server Operators Change Everyone Read Creator/Owner Full Control Replicator Change Network No Access System Full Control C:\winnt\system32\repl\export Administrators Full Control Server Operators Change Creator/Owner Full Control Replicator Read System Full Control 3. Click the **Permissions** button of the **Security** tab. 4. Select the **Replace Permissions on Subdirectories** and the **Replace Permissions on Existing Files** check boxes as appropriate. The **Replace Permissions on Subdirectories** will place the security permissions that you select on all files and subdirectories under the selected directory, while the **Replace Permissions on Existing Files** will ensure that all files contained in the directory have the selected security permissions. 5. Click the **OK** button to confirm these changes. 6. After the security permissions have been changed, click the **OK** button to close the file and directories properties window.	4. Click the **Permissions** button. 5. Compare the current permissions to the recommendations 6. Repeat for all listed directories. *Directory:* C:\winnt\system32\repl *Recommended Permissions:* Administrators Full Control Server Operators Full Control Everyone Read Creator/Owner Full Control System Full Control *Directory:* C:\winnt\system32\repl\import *Recommended Permissions:* Administrators Full Control Server Operators Change Everyone Read Creator/Owner Full Control Replicator Change Network No Access System Full Control *Directory:* C:\winnt\system32\repl\export *Recommended Permissions:* Administrators Full Control Server Operators Change Creator/Owner Full Control Replicator Read System Full Control	*Recommended Permissions:* Administrators Full Control Server Operators Full Control Everyone Read Creator/Owner Full Control System Full Control *Directory:* C:\winnt\system32\repl\import *Recommended Permissions:* Administrators Full Control Server Operators Change Everyone Read Creator/Owner Full Control Replicator Change Network No Access System Full Control *Directory:* C:\winnt\system32\repl\export *Recommended Permissions:* Administrators Full Control Server Operators Change Creator/Owner Full Control Replicator Read System Full Control

Windows NT Primary Domain Controller Security Review Program

No.	Category	Control Objectives	Risk	Control Techniques
6	File System Access and Management	The c:\winnt\repair directory contains a backup copy of the SAM and needs to be protected against unauthorized access.	If unauthorized users gain access to a backup copy of the SAM, they can run a password cracker and possibly guess user passwords.	Restrict access to the c:\winnt\repair directory so that only authorized users have access.
6	File System Access and Management	The default system shares for file systems should be disabled and re-created under standard share security. The default admin level shares are: C$, D$. . . and Admin$.	Windows NT creates special administrative-level shares by default that have preset security levels. These shares provide access to the root level of each NT drive and the NT system root directory.	Document the default shares and their directories. Disable them permanently if they are not required. Re-create new shares to those directories if needed with appropriate permissions.

Implementation Techniques	Compliance Assessment Techniques	Compliance Verification Techniques
Restrict access to c:\winnt\repair by performing the following steps: 1. Open the Windows NT Explorer. 2. Right-click on the file or directory to set the security Permissions and select the Properties option. The following permissions should be set: Administrators Change 3. Click the Permissions button of the Security tab. 4. Select the Replace Permissions on Subdirectories and the Replace Permissions on Existing Files check boxes as appropriate. The Replace Permissions on Subdirectories will place the security permissions that you select on all files and subdirectories under the selected directory, while the Replace Permissions on Existing Files will ensure that all files contained in the directory have the selected security permissions. 5. Click the OK button to confirm these changes. 6. After the security permissions have been changed, click the OK button to close the file and directories properties window.	Verify that permissions on the following directory comply with the recommendations by performing the following steps: 1. Right-click on the directory in Explorer. 2. Choose Properties. 3. Select the Security tab. 4. Click the Permissions button. 5. Compare the current permissions to the recommendations. 6. Repeat for all listed directories. *Directory:* C:\winnt\repair *Recommended Permissions:* Administrators Change	Review the <servername>.perms<system drive letter>.txt and ensure the following permissions are in place for: *Directory:* C:\winnt\repair *Recommended Permissions:* Administrators Change
Disable the shares in the registry by performing the following: 1. Open regedt32. 2. Select the Key HKLM\System\CurrentControlSet\Services\Lanman Server\Parameters 3. Value:AutoShareServer 4. REG_Binary is the Data type. 5. Change value to 0. 6. Click OK. Create new shares to these points if necessary.	Verify the existence of the default shares by checking the Share button under the Server Manager. If none exist, verify the registry key by checking the value of the HKLM\System\CurrentControlSet\Services\Lanman Server\Parameters key. The value should be 0.	Review <servername>.shares.txt to ensure only authorized users are allowed access to the shares.

Windows NT Primary Domain Controller Security Review Program

No.	Category	Control Objectives	Risk	Control Techniques
7	Sensitive System Privileges and Utilities	Permissions on shares must not allow Write, Delete, Change Permissions, or Take Ownership to the special group Everyone. Permissions on shares should be equivalent to the permissions on files within the share.	Shares allow users to access resources remotely on the network. Consequently, care should be taken when granting share rights. In particular the default system groups should not be granted permissions that would allow members of these groups to abuse the system.	Set the default permissions for the default group Users in accordance with permissions set on the files within the share. The built-in special group Everyone's access should be removed on all share permissions.

Implementation Techniques

Restrict share permissions by performing the following steps:

1. Using the Server Manager, highlight the applicable server and select the shared directories option under the Computer menu.
2. Highlight the share and view its properties by selecting the Properties button.
3. Click on the Permissions button to view the Users who have access to this share via the network.
4. Click the Add button to include the applicable groups to be granted access to this share and select the groups you wish to grant access to. When you have selected all the applicable groups, click the OK button to confirm these additions.
5. Grant the Type of Access for each group by highlighting the applicable group and selecting the access from the Type of Access box. These Permissions should be set in accordance with corporate system standards.
6. If the special group Everyone has access to the share, this access should be removed by highlighting the member and clicking the Remove button.
7. Click the OK button and then the Yes button to confirm these changes.

Compliance Assessment Techniques

Verify that share permissions are properly restricted by performing the following steps:

1. Open Server Manager.
2. Highlight the applicable server and select the shared directories option under the Computer menu.
3. Highlight the share and view its properties by clicking the Properties button.
4. Click on the Permissions button to view the Users who have access to this share via the network.
5. Verify that only appropriate groups have been granted access to this share. Verify that the special group Everyone does not have access.
6. Click the Cancel button to close.
7. Repeat for all shares.
8. Close Server Manager.

Compliance Verification Techniques

Review <servername>.shares.txt to ensure only authorized users are allowed access to the shares. Permissions should only be granted to groups. The special group Everyone should not be allowed access to the share.

Windows NT Primary Domain Controller Security Review Program

No.	Category	Control Objectives	Risk	Control Techniques
7	Sensitive System Privileges and Utilities	Access to sensitive system utilities should be removed from all users who do not require this access for a legitimate business use.	If user accounts are granted access to potentially sensitive utilities, there is an increased risk that the user may gain information that could be used to compromise the security of the domain or perform actions that may affect the security and productivity of the domain.	Remove user access to system utilities that do not require this access for a legitimate business use.
8	Maintenance and Operations	If standard user profiles are used they should be maintained on the PDC.	If standard profiles are utilized they should reside on the PDC, where their access can be controlled and changes can be monitored. Having standard user profiles on local systems can easily, lead to their modification, and/or abuse.	Move all standard user profiles, if implemented, to the PDC in the Authentication Domain.

Implementation Techniques	Compliance Assessment Techniques	Compliance Verification Techniques
For all servers, disable the ability for normal users to access sensitive system utilities by performing the following steps: 1. Open the Windows NT Explorer. 2. Right-click on the utility to be restricted and select the Properties option. 3. Click the Permissions button of the Security tab. 4. Click the Add button to include the applicable groups to be granted security permissions. 5. Select the groups you wish to add to the security permissions. When you have selected all the applicable groups, click the OK button to confirm these additions. 6. Grant the Type of Access for each group by highlighting the applicable group and selecting the Access from the Type of Access box. These permissions should be set in accordance with corporate system standards. 7. If the special group Everyone or the group Users have permissions to the utility, they should be removed by using the Remove button. 8. Click the OK button to confirm these changes. 9. After the security permissions have been changed, click the OK button to close the file properties windows.	Verify, through discussion with the network administrator and physical inspection, that sensitive system utilities are properly restricted. Sensitive utilities include: Regedt32.exe Poledit.exe User Manager for Domains Server Manager Resource kit utilities Auditing tools	Review the <servername>.perms<system drive letter>.txt and ensure the sensitive system utilities are properly protected.
Move all standard user profiles, if implemented, to the PDC in the authentication domain.	If standard profiles are used, verify, through discussion with the network administrator and physical inspection, that all such profiles reside in the Authentication Domain and obtain the applicable policies and procedures.	If standard profiles are used, verify, through discussion with the network administrator and physical inspection, that all such profiles reside in the Authentication Domain and obtain the applicable policies and procedures.

Windows NT Primary Domain Controller Security Review Program

No.	Category	Control Objectives	Risk	Control Techniques
8	Maintenance and Operations	Windows NT's screen saver should be enabled with the password protection feature turned on. When not being used, accounts should be logged off from the system console.	Enabling the Windows NT screen saver with the password protection minimizes the chances that an unattended servers and workstations will be broken into.	Enable the Windows NT screen saver with the password protection feature active.
9	Fault Tolerance Backup and Recovery	A disaster recovery plan should be set in accordance with corporate security standards and guidelines.	Without a properly configured and tested disaster recovery plan, the system is open to extended downtime.	Establish a proper backup rotation plan in accordance with company policy. The registry must be backed up using a third-party backup tool or the regback utility from the resource kit. Backups should be cycled through an off-site storage location along with the copies of the emergency repair disks.
9	Fault Tolerance Backup and Recovery	An uninterrupted power supply must be used with all Windows NT PDCs. This will provide power for the system to be shut down in the event of power loss or degradation.	Not using a UPS will make the system more open to corruption and will increase the risk of losing user data in the event of a power loss.	An uninterrupted power supply that is fully compatible with Windows NT should be used. Using Windows NT–compatible UPS will allow for a graceful shutdown of the Windows NT system, minimizing the amount of system file corruption and data loss.
10	Physical Access	Two copies of the Emergency Repair Disk should be made with each placed in a physically secure location.	The Emergency Repair Disk contains critical information referencing users and file system details. This information could be detrimental if an unauthorized user obtained it. Two copies of the disk should be made: one for on-site storage and one for off-site storage. Both copies should be located in physically secure areas.	Create two copies of all critical Windows NT systems' Emergency Repair Disk. Store one copy on site and another at a secure remote location.

Implementation Techniques	Compliance Assessment Techniques	Compliance Verification Techniques
Enable the native Windows NT screen saver by performing the following steps: 1. Right-click on any blank area of the desktop. 2. Select the **Properties** option. 3. Select the **Screen Save** tab of the **Display Properties** box. 4. Select a screen saver from the pulldown box. 5. Click on the **Password Protected** check box and set an appropriate time to enable the security feature of the screen saver. 6. Click **OK** to close the **Display Properties** box.	Verify that policies exist to mandate that password protect screen savers are enabled on all machines. Attempt to disable the screen saver on a randomly selected machine and the PDC by moving the mouse or pressing a key on the keyboard. Verify that you are prompted for a password.	Review <servername>.desktop.txt and ensure the values ScreenSaverActive and ScreenSaverIsSecure are equal to 1.
Note: Be sure to run RDISK/S before backups are created so that the Repair directory is up to date.	Inquire with the company regarding policies and procedures for updating of the Emergency Repair Disk on periodic basis. Check the file dates in the repair directory to assure they are not out of date.	Inquire with the company regarding policies and procedures for updating of the Emergency Repair Disk on periodic basis. Review the <servername>.dir<system drive>.txt and ensure the dates on the files in the <system drive>:\winnt\repair are current.
N/A	Inquire with the company regarding the controls in place to mitigate a loss of power. If the server is protected by an individual UPS, inquire whether the UPS is integrated with Windows NT operating system. Then, ensure that the PDC is connected to a functioning UPS system.	Inquire with the company regarding the controls in place to mitigate a loss of power. If the server is protected by an individual UPS, inquire whether the UPS is integrated with Windows NT operating system. Then, ensure that the PDC is connected to a functioning UPS system.
Run RDISK and click "Create Repair Disk." Reminder: RDISK only creates the default information on the disk when the /S switch is not used.	Ensure that a procedure is in place to create, update, physically secure, retrieve, and utilize the Emergency Repair Disk. Verify that the Emergency Repair Disk exists, is not out of date, and is physically secured. Ensure that proper individuals are aware of the recovery process.	Ensure that a procedure is in place to create, update, physically secure, retrieve, and utilize the Emergency Repair Disk. Verify that the Emergency Repair Disk exists, is not out of date, and is physically secured. Ensure that proper individuals are aware of the recovery process.

Windows NT Primary Domain Controller Security Review Program

No.	Category	Control Objectives	Risk	Control Techniques
11	Auditing, Logging, and Monitoring	If network managers are being used, SNMP should be installed in a secure fashion.	It is important to note that SNMP should not be run with the default community known as "public." This would be a potential security breach. The SNMP database of errors and alerts must be protected if used in the Windows NT environment because it can contain information on host or router operating systems, network interfaces, address translation, and protocol software. This information could be used to compromise an environment by "spoofing" or "denial-of-service."	If the Windows NT system is equipped with SNMP, ensure that the access to this service information is limited to daily monitoring and alert warnings to management.
11	Auditing, Logging, and Monitoring	Auditing should be enabled for Logon and Logoff.	A hacker might be trying to guess a user's password and gain access to the system. Without auditing, this might go undetected.	Enable auditing for logon and logoff, for both success and failure.
11	Auditing, Logging, and Monitoring	Auditing should be enabled for File and Object Access.	Without auditing on files and objects, hackers might have enough time to figure out a way around compensating controls. For example, hackers might try to access files they do not have read access to. In addition, it is possible to detect a virus outbreak if write access auditing for program files, such as files with `.exe` and `.dll` extensions, is enabled.	Enable auditing for file and object access for success and failure.

Implementation Techniques	Compliance Assessment Techniques	Compliance Verification Techniques
Remove the default community "public" and input the correct name by performing the following steps: 1. Open Control Panel's Network applet. 2. Choose the Services Tab. 3. Double-click the SNMP service. 4. Disable the "public" community and enter the appropriate name. 5. Click OK.	Verify that the default community "public" is not being used by performing the following steps: 1. Open Control Panel. 2. Double-click the Network applet. 3. Choose the Services Tab. 4. Double-click the SNMP service. 5. View the community settings. 6. Click OK.	Inquire with the company whether SNMP is being used to monitor the server. If SNMP is being utilized, inquire whether the community name has been changed from "public" to a difficult-to-guess name.
Enable the Auditing for system logons and logoff by performing the following steps: 1. Using the User Manager, select the Audit option from the Policies menu. 2. Ensure the Audit These Events button is selected. 3. Enable both the Success and Failure check boxes for Logon and Logoff auditing option. 4. Click the OK button to confirm these changes.	Verify that Auditing has been enabled for system logons and logoff by performing the following steps: 1. Open User Manager. 2. Select the Audit option from the Policies menu. 3. Ensure the Audit These Events radio button is selected. 4. Verify that both the Success and Failure check boxes for Logon and Logoff auditing option have been selected. 5. Click the OK button to exit.	Review <servername>.policies.txt to ensure auditing is enabled for successes and failures for logons and logoffs.
Enable the Auditing for file and object access by performing the following steps: 1. Using the User Manager, select the Audit option from the Policies menu. 2. Ensure the Audit These Events button is selected. 3. Enable both the Success and Failure check boxes for File and Object Access auditing option. 4. Click the OK button to confirm these changes.	Verify that Auditing has been enabled for system file and object access by performing the following steps: 1. Open User Manager. 2. Select the Audit option from the Policies menu. 3. Ensure the Audit These Events radio button is selected. 4. Verify that both the Success and Failure check boxes for File and Object Access auditing option have been selected. 5. Click the OK button to exit.	Review <servername>.policies.txt to ensure auditing is enabled for successes and failures for file and object access.

Windows NT Primary Domain Controller Security Review Program

No.	Category	Control Objectives	Risk	Control Techniques
11	Auditing, Logging, and Monitoring	Auditing failures should be enabled for Use of User Rights.	A user might try taking ownership of files they do not have access to in order to edit them. Or, a user who somehow got physical access to a PDC might try logging in locally. Without auditing, these events might not be detected.	Enable auditing for Use of User Rights failure only.
11	Auditing, Logging, and Monitoring	Auditing should be enabled for User and Group Management.	If a user is granted access above what they deserve, it would be important to know who made those changes. Without auditing User and Group Management, it would be impossible to know within Windows NT.	Enable auditing for User and Group Management success and failure.
11	Auditing, Logging, and Monitoring	Auditing should be enabled for Security Policy Changes.	If changes are made to the Security Policy, where users are granted access to resources they should not have been, it is important for an administrator to be able to determine who made those changes.	Enable auditing for Security Policy Changes success and failure.

Implementation Techniques	Compliance Assessment Techniques	Compliance Verification Techniques
Enable the Auditing for Use of User Rights by performing the following steps: 1. Using the User Manager, select the Audit option from the Policies menu. 2. Ensure the Audit These Events button is selected. 3. Enable the Failure check box for Use of User Rights auditing option. 4. Click the OK button to confirm these changes.	Verify that Auditing has been enabled for Use of User Rights by performing the following steps: 1. Open User Manager. 2. Select the Audit option from the Policies menu. 3. Ensure the Audit These Events button is selected. 4. Verify that the Failure check box Use of User Rights auditing option has been selected. 5. Click the OK button to exit.	Review <servername>.policies.txt to ensure auditing is enabled for failures for Use of User Rights.
Enable the User and Group Management by performing the following steps: 1. Using the User Manager, select the Audit option from the Policies menu. 2. Ensure Audit These Events button is selected. 3. Enable both the Success and Failure check boxes for User and Group Management auditing option. 4. Click the OK button to confirm these changes.	Verify that Auditing has been enabled for User and Group Management by performing the following steps: 1. Open User Manager. 2. Select the Audit option from the Policies menu. 3. Ensure the Audit These Events radio button is selected. 4. Verify that both the Success and Failure check boxes for User and Group Management auditing option have been selected. 5. Click the OK button to exit.	Review <servername>.policies.txt to ensure auditing is enabled for successes and failures for User and Group Management.
Enable the Auditing for Security Policy Changes by performing the following steps: 1. Using the User Manager, select the Audit option from the Policies menu. 2. Ensure the Audit These Events button is selected. 3. Enable both the Success and Failure check boxes for Security Policy Changes auditing option. 4. Click the OK button to confirm these changes.	Verify that Auditing has been enabled for Security Policy Changes by performing the following steps: 1. Open User Manager. 2. Select the Audit option from the Policies menu. 3. Ensure the Audit These Events radio button is selected. 4. Verify that both the Success and Failure check boxes for Security Policy Changes auditing option have been selected. 5. Click the OK button to exit.	Review <servername>.policies.txt to ensure auditing is enabled for successes and failures for Security Policy Changes.

Windows NT Primary Domain Controller Security Review Program

No.	Category	Control Objectives	Risk	Control Techniques
11	Auditing, Logging, and Monitoring	Auditing should be enabled for Restart, Shutdown, and System.	Only authorized users should have the capability to change the state of a system. This activity should be especially scrutinized on all servers.	Enable auditing for Restart, Shutdown, and System for success and failure.
11	Auditing, Logging, and Monitoring	Auditing should be disabled for Process Tracking.	Process Tracking will not help much in determining any security breaches. It is more useful for debugging a program that doesn't function correctly. If used, Process Tracking will generate thousands of audit entries in a few seconds, thereby flooding the log.	Do not select success or failure for Process Tracking.

Implementation Techniques	Compliance Assessment Techniques	Compliance Verification Techniques
Enable the Auditing for Restart, Shutdown, and System by performing the following steps: 1. Using the User Manager, select the Audit option from the Policies menu. 2. Ensure the Audit These Events button is selected. 3. Enable the both the Success and Failure check boxes for Restart, Shutdown, and System auditing option. 4. Click the OK button to confirm these changes.	Verify that Auditing has been enabled for Restart, Shutdown, and System by performing the following steps: 1. Open User Manager. 2. Select the Audit option from the Policies menu. 3. Ensure the Audit These Events radio button is selected. 4. Verify that both the Success and Failure check boxes for Restart, Shutdown, and System auditing option have been selected. 5. Click the OK button to exit.	Review <servername>.policies.txt to ensure auditing is enabled for successes and failures for Restart, Shutdown, and System.
Disable auditing for Process Tracking by performing the following steps: 1. Using the User Manager, select the Audit option from the Policies menu. 2. Ensure the Audit These Events button is selected. 3. Deselect both the Success and Failure check boxes for the Process Tracking auditing option. 4. Click the OK button to confirm these changes.	Verify that Auditing has been enabled for Restart, Shutdown, and System by performing the following steps: 1. Open User Manager. 2. Select the Audit option from the Policies menu. 3. Ensure the Audit These Events radio button is selected. 4. Verify that both the Success and Failure check boxes for the Process Tracking auditing option have been deselected. 5. Click the OK button to exit.	Review <servername>.policies.txt to ensure auditing is not enabled for successes and failures for Process Tracking.

Windows NT Primary Domain Controller Security Review Program

No.	Category	Control Objectives	Risk	Control Techniques
11	Auditing, Logging, and Monitoring	Logs containing auditing information should be secured.	Audit logs may contain sensitive information about the system and can be used to compromise the system. In addition, if logs are unsecured it would be possible to delete them in order to eliminate an audit trail.	Logs should be secured to prevent them from being viewed or deleted by unauthorized individuals.
11	Auditing, Logging, and Monitoring	All audit files should be archived and purged in accordance with corporate standards.	Having all reviewed audit files archived and purged ensures that if they are needed they will be available and at the same time guarantees that unauthorized users cannot pursue the audit files to identify system patterns.	After audit files have been adequately reviewed in accordance with corporate standards and guidelines, all audit files should be archived and purged.

Implementation Techniques	Compliance Assessment Techniques	Compliance Verification Techniques
The Auditors and System groups should have Full Control of the following files and no other permissions should be specified: c:\winnt\System32\config\APPEVENT.EVT c:\winnt\System32\config\SECEVENT.EVT c:\winnt\System32\config\SYSEVENT.EVT **Note:** The System group is a built-in special group, and the Auditors group will need to be created by an administrator.	Verify that permissions on the following files comply with the recommendations by performing the following steps: 1. Right-click on the file in Explorer. 2. Choose Properties. 3. Select the Security tab. 4. Click the Permissions button. 5. Compare the current permissions to the recommendations. 6. Repeat for all listed files. *Files:* c:\winnt\System32\config\APPEVENT.EVT c:\winnt\System32\config\SECEVENT.EVT c:\winnt\System32\config\SYSEVENT.EVT *Recommended Permissions:* Auditors Read System groups Change	Review the <servername>.perms <system drive letter>.txt and ensure the following: *Files:* c:\winnt\System32\config\APPEVENT.EVT c:\winnt\System32\config\SECEVENT.EVT c:\winnt\System32\config\SYSEVENT.EVT *Recommended Permissions:* Auditors Read System groups Change
Review the audit files in accordance with corporate standards and guidelines. Properly back up the audit logs and then purge them from the system.	Ensure that policies exist to archive and purge audit files. Verify, through discussion with the network administrator, that these procedures are followed.	Ensure that policies exist to archive and purge audit files. Verify, through discussion with the network administrator, that these procedures are followed.

Windows NT Primary Domain Controller Security Review Program

No.	Category	Control Objectives	Risk	Control Techniques
11	Auditing, Logging, and Monitoring	Auditing of sensitive system and application files and directories should be enabled.	Auditing access to sensitive system and application files and directories increases the chances that unauthorized access to the system will be detected and terminated in a timely manner.	Enable Windows NT native auditing feature on all sensitive system and application files and directories.

Implementation Techniques

Enable Windows NT native auditing feature on all sensitive system and application files and directories. Identify these directories per the corporate standards. In addition, the following Windows NT system directories and files within should be audited:

C:\winnt\
C:\winnt\repair
C:\winnt\system32
C:\winnt\system32\config

The following items should be audited:

Write: Select Success & Failure
Delete: Select Success & Failure
Change Permissions: Select Success & Failure
Take Ownership: Select Success & Failure

Compliance Assessment Techniques

Verify that the Windows NT native auditing feature has been enabled for all sensitive system and application files and directories by performing the following steps:

1. Right-click on the directory in Explorer.
2. Choose Properties.
3. Select the Security tab.
4. Click the Auditing button.
5. Compare the current audit settings to the recommendations.
6. Repeat for all listed directories.

Directories:
Those stated in the best practices, plus

C:\winnt\
C:\winnt\repair
C:\winnt\system32
C:\winnt\system32\config

Recommended Settings:
Write: Select Success & Failure
Delete: Select Success & Failure
Change Permissions: Select Success & Failure
Take Ownership: Select Success & Failure

Compliance Verification Techniques

Review the <servername>.perms <system drive letter>.txt and ensure the sensitive system files are being audited for the following actions:

Directories:
Those stated in the best practices, plus

C:\winnt\
C:\winnt\repair
C:\winnt\system32
C:\winnt\system32\config

Recommended Settings:
Write: Select Success & Failure
Delete: Select Success & Failure
Change Permissions: Select Success & Failure
Take Ownership: Select Success & Failure

Windows NT Primary Domain Controller Security Review Program

No.	Category	Control Objectives	Risk	Control Techniques
12	Auditing, Logging, and Monitoring	Auditing of sensitive system registry keys should be enabled.	Auditing access to sensitive system registry keys increases the chances that unauthorized access to the system will be detected and terminated in a timely manner.	Enable Windows NT native auditing feature on all sensitive system registry keys.

Implementation Techniques

Enable Windows NT native auditing feature on all sensitive system registry keys. Identify these keys per the corporate standards. In addition, the following keys should be audited:

HKLM\SYSTEM
HKLM\SOFTWARE
HKCR

The following items should be audited:

Set Value: Select Success & Failure
Create Subkey: Select Success & Failure
Create Link: Select Success & Failure
Delete: Select Success & Failure
Write DAC: Select Success & Failure

Compliance Assessment Techniques

Verify that the Windows NT native auditing feature has been enabled for all sensitive system registry keys by performing the following steps:

1. Open regedt32.
2. Click on the appropriate key.
3. Choose Auditing. . . from the Security pulldown menu.
4. Compare the current audit settings to the recommendations.
5. Repeat for all listed keys.

Keys:
Those stated in the best practices, plus

HKLM\SYSTEM
HKLM\SOFTWARE
HKCR

Recommended Settings:
Set Value: Select Success & Failure
Create Subkey: Select Success & Failure
Create Link: Select Success & Failure
Delete: Select Success & Failure
Write DAC: Select Success & Failure

Compliance Verification Techniques

Review the <servername>.HKLM.txt and ensure the HKLM\SYSTEM, HKLM\SOFTWARE, HKCR portions of the registry are being audited for the following actions:

Keys:
Those stated in the best practices, plus

HKLM\SYSTEM
HKLM\SOFTWARE
HKCR

Recommended Settings:
Set Value: Select Success & Failure
Create Subkey: Select Success & Failure
Create Link: Select Success & Failure
Delete: Select Success & Failure
Write DAC: Select Success & Failure

Windows NT Primary Domain Controller Security Review Program

No.	Category	Control Objectives	Risk	Control Techniques
11	Auditing, Logging, and Monitoring	The event viewer should be allocated sufficient space for audit logs.	If events are overwritten before they can be reviewed, there is an increased risk that continuous unauthorized activity may go undetected.	The event viewer should be allocated adequate disk space to store all audit logs. The disk space needed should be based on size of the domain and review intervals of the audit logs.
12	Security Administration Activities	Unauthorized individuals should not be allowed to remotely edit the registry.	There is an increased risk that an unauthorized user may gain knowledge about the PDC and domain and even attack the system with denial of services or Trojan horses, if they can access the registry.	Set the `winreg` registry key permissions to comply with corporate standards. Industry guidelines state that only Administrators have full control.

Implementation Techniques	Compliance Assessment Techniques	Compliance Verification Techniques
Set the amount of space that is being allocated by performing the following steps. 1. Open Event Viewer. 2. Select Log Settings. . . from the Log pulldown menu. Set the log settings according to corporate standards. The following are industry guidelines: Security: 5–10 MB (Overwrite after 14 days) System: 1–2 MB (Overwrite after 14 days) Application: 1–2 MB (Overwrite as needed) 3. Click Close. **Note:** If a log is set in the above manner, for example, Security Log 5MB, 14 days, the log can be filled the first day, and no events would be logged for the next 13 days. Log sizes should be based on the size of the system including the number of users if logon and logoff is going to be tracked.	Verify that sufficient space is allocated for log files by performing the following steps: 1. Open Event Viewer. 2. Select Log Settings. . . from the Log pulldown menu. 3. Select appropriate log file in the Change Settings for Log List box. 4. Compare current settings to the recommended settings. 5. Click Cancel. 6. Close Event Viewer. *Log:* Security *Settings:* 5–10 MB (Overwrite after 14 days) *Log:* System *Settings:* 1–2 MB (Overwrite after 14 days) *Log:* Application *Settings:* 1–2 MB (Overwrite as needed) **Note:** If a log is set in the above manner, for example, Security Log 5MB, 14 days, the log can be filled the first day, and no events would be logged for the next 13 days.	Review the <servername>. eventlog.txt for the value of MaxSize and ensure adequate disk space is allocated *Log:* Security *Settings:* 5–10 MB (Overwrite after 14 days) *Log:* System *Settings:* 1–2 MB (Overwrite after 14 days) *Log:* Application *Settings:* 1–2 MB (Overwrite as needed) **Note:** If a log is set in the above manner, for example, Security Log 5MB, 14 days, the log can be filled the first day, and no events would be logged for the next 13 days. Log sizes should be based on the system including the number of users if logon and logoff is going to be tracked.
Secure the winreg registry key by performing the following steps: 1. Open regedt32. 2. Select the key HKLM\System\ CurrentControlSet\Control\ SecurePipeServers\ WinReg. 3. Choose Security | Permissions from the pull-down menu bar. 4. The permissions should be in accordance with corporate standards. Industry guidelines state: Administrators: Full Control 5. Close regedt32.	Verify an appropriate security setting on the winreg registry key by performing the following steps: 1. Open regedt32. 2. Select the key HKLM\System\ CurrentControlSet\Control\ SecurePipeServers\ WinReg. 3. Choose Permissions. . . from the Security pulldown menu. 4. Compare the permissions to the recommended settings. 5. Close regedt32. *Recommended Setting:* Administrators: Full Control	Review <servername>.hklm.txt and ensure the permissions on the value HKLM\System\ CurrentControlSet\Control\ SecurePipeServers\WinReg are restricted to only authorized users. *Recommended Setting:* Administrators: Full Control

Windows NT Primary Domain Controller Security Review Program

No.	Category	Control Objectives	Risk	Control Techniques
12	Security Administration Activities	Parts of the registry run programs at startup should be configured to not allow unauthorized users to edit the list of programs.	With its default permission levels, any locally logged on user can change the value of the Run key to point to a Trojan horse program. This Trojan horse can be anything from malicious code to a program that, when run as administrator equivalent, dumps the password hash.	Set the Run and RunOnce registry keys permissions to comply with corporate standards or industry guidelines.

Implementation Techniques

Secure the Run and RunOnce registry keys by performing the following steps:

1. Open regedt32.
2. Select the following keys independently:

HKLM\SOFTWARE\Microsoft\Windows\CurrentVersion\Run

HKLM\SOFTWARE\Microsoft\Windows\CurrentVersion\RunOnce

3. Choose Security | Permissions from the pull-down menu bar.
4. The permissions should be in accordance with corporate standards.

Industry guidelines state:

Creator Owner: Full Control
Administrator: Full Control
System: Full Control
Everyone: Read

5. Close regedt32.

Compliance Assessment Techniques

Verify an appropriate security setting on the Run and RunOnce registry keys by performing the following steps:

1. Open regedt32.
2. Select the appropriate key.
3. Choose Permissions. . . from the Security pulldown menu.
4. Compare the permissions to the recommended settings.
5. Close regedt32.

Keys:
HKLM\SOFTWARE\Microsoft\Windows\CurrentVersion\Run

HKLM\SOFTWARE\Microsoft\Windows\CurrentVersion\RunOnce

Recommended Settings:
Creator Owner: Full Control
Administrator: Full Control
System: Full Control
Everyone: Read

Compliance Verification Techniques

Review <servername>.run.txt and ensure the following:

Keys:
HKLM\SOFTWARE\Microsoft\Windows\CurrentVersion\Run

HKLM\SOFTWARE\Microsoft\Windows\CurrentVersion\RunOnce

Recommended Settings:
Creator Owner: Full Control
Administrator: Full Control
System: Full Control
Everyone: Read

Windows NT Primary Domain Controller Security Review Program

No.	Category	Control Objectives	Risk	Control Techniques
12	Security Administration Activities	Parts of the registry contain sensitive system information like performance data, the logon process, and security information. These registry keys should be configured to not allow unauthorized users to edit the list of programs.	If an unauthorized user could read these registry keys, they might gain access to sensitive system resources or be able to learn information about the PDC.	Set the registry keys' (listed in the implementation checklist) permissions to comply with corporate standards or industry guidelines.
12	Security Administration Activities	Certain registry keys should be secured to prevent unauthorized access to the PDC's configuration.	If an unauthorized user could read these registry keys, they might be able to launch a denial of service attack or upload a Trojan horse.	Set the registry keys' (listed in the implementation checklist) permissions to comply with corporate standards or industry guidelines.

Implementation Techniques	Compliance Assessment Techniques	Compliance Verification Techniques
Secure the following registry keys by performing these steps: 1. Open regedt32. 2. Select the following keys independently: HKLM\SOFTWARE\MICROSOFT\WindowsNT\CurrentVersion\PerfLib HKLM\Software\Micorsoft\WindowsNT\CurrentVersion\Winlogon HKLM\SYSTEM\CurrentControlSet\Control\LSA HKLM\System\CurrentControlSet\Services\LanManServer\Shares 3. Choose Security | Permissions from the pull-down menu bar. 4. The permissions should be in accordance with corporate standards. *Industry guidelines state:* Creator Owner: Full Control Administrator: Full Control System: Full Control Everyone: Read 5. Close regedt32.	Verify that appropriate security settings exist on the following registry keys by performing these steps: 1. Open regedt32. 2. Select the appropriate key. 3. Choose Permissions. . . from the Security pulldown menu. 4. Compare the permissions to the recommended settings. 5. Close regedt32. *Keys:* HKLM\SOFTWARE\MICROSOFT\WindowsNT\CurrentVersion\PerfLib HKLM\Software\Micorsoft\WindowsNT\CurrentVersion\Winlogon HKLM\SYSTEM\CurrentControlSet\Control\LSA HKLM\System\CurrentControlSet\Services\LanManServer\Shares *Recommended Settings:* Creator Owner: Full Control Administrator: Full Control System: Full Control Everyone: Read	Review <servername>.hklm.txt and ensure the following: *Keys:* HKLM\SOFTWARE\MICROSOFT\WindowsNT\CurrentVersion\PerfLib HKLM\Software\Micorsoft\WindowsNT\CurrentVersion\Winlogon HKLM\SYSTEM\CurrentControlSet\Control\LSA HKLM\System\CurrentControlSet\Services\LanManServer\Shares *Recommended Settings:* Creator Owner: Full Control Administrator: Full Control System: Full Control Everyone: Read
Secure the following registry keys by performing these steps: 1. Open regedt32. 2. Select the following keys independently: HKCR (all subkeys) HKLM\SOFTWARE HKLM\SOFTWARE\MICROSOFT\RPC (and all subkeys) HKLM\SOFTWARE\MICROSOFT\WindowsNT\CurrentVersion\	Verify that appropriate security settings exist on the following registry keys by performing these steps: 1. Open regedt32. 2. Select the appropriate key. 3. Choose Permissions. . . from the Security pulldown menu. 4. Compare the permissions to the recommended settings. 5. Close regedt32. *Keys:* HKCR (all subkeys) HKLM\SOFTWARE	Review <servername>.hklm.txt and ensure the permissions on the values HKCR (all subkeys) HKLM\SOFTWARE HKLM\SOFTWARE\MICROSOFT\RPC (and all subkeys) HKLM\SOFTWARE\MICROSOFT\WindowsNT\CurrentVersion\ HKLM\SOFTWARE\MICROSOFT\WindowsNT\CurrentVersion\AeDebug

Windows NT Primary Domain Controller Security Review Program

No.	Category	Control Objectives	Risk	Control Techniques

Implementation Techniques

HKLM\SOFTWARE\MICROSOFT\ WindowsNT\CurrentVersion\ReDebug

HKLM\SOFTWARE\MICROSOFT\ WindowsNT\CurrentVersion\ Compatibility

HKLM\SOFTWARE\MICROSOFT\ WindowsNT\CurrentVersion\Drivers

HKLM\SOFTWARE\MICROSOFT\ WindowsNT\CurrentVersion\ Embedding

HKLM\SOFTWARE\MICROSOFT\ WindowsNT\CurrentVersion\Fonts

HKLM\SOFTWARE\MICROSOFT\ WindowsNT\CurrentVersion\Font Substitutes

HKLM\SOFTWARE\MICROSOFT\ WindowsNT\CurrentVersion\Font Drivers

HKLM\SOFTWARE\MICROSOFT\ WindowsNT\CurrentVersion\FontMapper

HKLM\SOFTWARE\MICROSOFT\ WindowsNT\CurrentVersion\FontCache

HKLM\SOFTWARE\MICROSOFT\ WindowsNT\CurrentVersion\ GRE_Initialize

HKLM\SOFTWARE\MICROSOFT\ WindowsNT\CurrentVersion\MCI

HKLM\SOFTWARE\MICROSOFT\ WindowsNT\CurrentVersion\ MCIExtensions

HKLM\SOFTWARE\MICROSOFT\ WindowsNT\CurrentVersion\Port (all subkeys)

HKLM\SOFTWARE\MICROSOFT\ WindowsNT\CurrentVersion\ TypeInstaller

HKLM\SOFTWARE\MICROSOFT\ WindowsNT\CurrentVersion\ProfileList

HKLM\SOFTWARE\MICROSOFT\ WindowsNT\CurrentVersion\Windows 3.1MigrationStatus(all subkeys)

HKLM\SOFTWARE\MICROSOFT\ WindowsNT\CurrentVersin\WOW (all subkeys)

HKLM\Sytem\CurrentControlSet\ Services\UPS

HKEY_USERS;default

1. Choose Security | Permissions from the pull menu bar.
2. The permissions should be in accordance with corporate standards.

Compliance Assessment Techniques

Industry guidelines state:

Creator Owner: Full Control
Administrator: Full Control
System: Full Control
Everyone: Read

5.Close regedt32.

HKLM\SOFTWARE\MICROSOFT\RPC\ (and all subkeys)

HKLM\SOFTWARE\MICROSOFT\Windows NT\CurrentVersion\

HKLM\SOFTWARE\MICROSOFT\Windows NT\CurrentVersion\ReDebug

HKLM\SOFTWARE\MICROSOFT\Windows NT\CurrentVersion\Compatibility

HKLM\SOFTWARE\MICROSOFT\Windows NT\CurrentVersion\Drivers

HKLM\SOFTWARE\MICROSOFT\Windows NT\CurrentVersion\Embedding

HKLM\SOFTWARE\MICROSOFT\Window sNT\CurrentVersion\Fonts

HKLM\SOFTWARE\MICROSOFT\Windows NT\CurrentVersion\FontSubstitutes

HKLM\SOFTWARE\MICROSOFT\Windows NT\CurrentVersion\FontDrivers

HKLM\SOFTWARE\MICROSOFT\Windows NT\CurrentVersion\FontMapper

HKLM\SOFTWARE\MICROSOFT\Windows NT\CurrentVersion\FontCache

HKLM\SOFTWARE\MICROSOFT\Windows NT\CurrentVersion\GRE_Initialize

HKLM\SOFTWARE\MICROSOFT\Windows NT\CurrentVersion\MCI

HKLM\SOFTWARE\MICROSOFT\Windows NT\CurrentVersion\MCIExtensions

HKLM\SOFTWARE\MICROSOFT\Windows NT\CurrentVersion\Port (all subkeys)

HKLM\SOFTWARE\MICROSOFT\Windows NT\CurrentVersion\TypeInstaller

HKLM\SOFTWARE\MICROSOFT\Windows NT\CurrentVersion\ProfileList

HKLM\SOFTWARE\MICROSOFT\Windows NT\CurrentVersion\Windows3.1Migration Status (all subkeys)

HKLM\SOFTWARE\MICROSOFT\Windows NT\CurrentVersion\WOW (all subkeys)

HKLM\System\CurrentControlSet\ Services\UPS

HKEY_USERS\.default

Compliance Verification Techniques

Recommended Settings:
Creator Owner: Full Control
Administrator: Full Control
System: Full Control
Everyone: Read

HKLM\SOFTWARE\MICROSOFT\Windows NT\CurrentVersion\Compatibility

HKLM\SOFTWARE\MICROSOFT\Windows NT\CurrentVersion\Drivers

HKLM\SOFTWARE\MICROSOFT\Windows NT\CurrentVersion\Embedding

HKLM\SOFTWARE\MICROSOFT\Window sNT\CurrentVersion\Fonts

HKLM\SOFTWARE\MICROSOFT\Windows NT\CurrentVersion\FontSubstitutes

HKLM\SOFTWARE\MICROSOFT\Windows NT\CurrentVersion\FontDrivers

HKLM\SOFTWARE\MICROSOFT\Windows NT\CurrentVersion\FontMapper

HKLM\SOFTWARE\MICROSOFT\Windows NT\CurrentVersion\FontCache

HKLM\SOFTWARE\MICROSOFT\Windows NT\CurrentVersion\GRE_Initialize

HKLM\SOFTWARE\MICROSOFT\Windows NT\CurrentVersion\MCI

HKLM\SOFTWARE\MICROSOFT\Windows NT\CurrentVersion\MCIExtensions

HKLM\SOFTWARE\MICROSOFT\Windows NT\CurrentVersion\Port (all subkeys)

HKLM\SOFTWARE\MICROSOFT\Windows NT\CurrentVersion\TypeInstaller

HKLM\SOFTWARE\MICROSOFT\Windows NT\CurrentVersion\ProfileList

HKLM\SOFTWARE\MICROSOFT\Windows NT\CurrentVersion\Windows3.1Migration Status(all subkeys)

HKLM\SOFTWARE\MICROSOFT\Windows NT\CurrentVersion\WOW (all subkeys)

HKLM\System\CurrentControlSet\ Services\UPS

HKEY_USERS\.default
are restricted to only authorized users.

Recommended Settings:
Creator Owner: Full Control
Administrator: Full Control
System: Full Control
Everyone: Read

Windows NT Primary Domain Controller Security Review Program

No.	Category	Control Objectives	Risk	Control Techniques
12	Security Administration Activities	The last username and default username should not be displayed at login.	There is an increased risk that an unauthorized user may gain knowledge of the company domain naming standards and a name to use in gaining access to the domain if the last username is displayed at logon.	Set the DontDisplayLastUserName registry entry with a value of 1 and delete any username contained within the registry key DefaultUserName.
12	Security Administration Activities	It should not be possible to shut down the PDC without logging on.	If users could shut down the PDC without logging on, no audit trail would be created, and unauthorized users might be able to shut the PDC down.	Set the ShutdownWithoutLogon registry entry with a value of 0.
12	Security Administration Activities	The system should not be shut down if the audit log becomes full.	In some cases, it might be necessary to shut down the server when the audit log becomes full, ensuring that an audit trail is always in existence. However, it is not normally necessary to enable this on a PDC.	Set the CrashOnAuditFail registry entry with a value of 0. A value of 1 should be set under certain circumstances to shut down the machine but is normally unnecessary.
12	Security Administration Activities	The auditing of all user rights should be disabled.	Auditing all user rights will generate a very large number of audit entries because all user rights, including Bypass traverse checking, are enabled.	Set the FullPrivilegeAuditing registry entry with a value of 0. A value of 1 should be set under certain circumstances to audit all user rights but is normally unnecessary.

Implementation Techniques	Compliance Assessment Techniques	Compliance Verification Techniques
Set the DontDisplayLastUser Name registry entry with a value of 1 and delete any username contained within the registry key DefaultUserName by performing the following steps: 1. Open regedt32. 2. Select the hive HKLM\SOFTWARE\Microsoft\WindowsNT\CurrentVersion\Winlogon. 3. The key DontDisplayLast Username should be set to 1. 4. Close regedt32.	Verify that the DontDisplayLast UserName registry entry is set to a value of 1 and that there is no username contained within the registry key DefaultUserName by performing the following steps: 1. Open regedt32. 2. Select the hive HKLM\SOFTWARE\Microsoft\Windows NT\CurrentVersion\Winlogon. 3. Verify that the key DontDisplayLastUsername is set to 1. 4. Verify that the key DefaultUserName has no value. 5. Close regedt32.	Review <servername>.winlogon.txt and ensure the value DontDisplayLastUserName is set to 1.
Set the ShutdownWithout Logon registry entry with a value of by performing the following steps: 1. Open regedt32. 2. Select the hive HKLM\SOFTWARE\Microsoft\WindowsNT\CurrentVersion\Winlogon. 3. The key ShutdownWithoutLogon should be set to 0. 4. Close regedt32.	Verify that the ShutdownWithout Logon registry entry is set to a value of 0 by performing the following steps: 1. Open regedt32. 2. Select the hive HKLM\SOFTWARE\Microsoft\WindowsNT\CurrentVersion\Winlogon. 3. Verify that the key ShutdownWithoutLogon is set to 0. 4. Close regedt32.	Review <servername>.winlogon.txt and ensure the value ShutdownWithoutLogon is set to 0.
Set the CrashOnAuditFail registry entry with a value of 0 by performing the following steps: 1. Open regedt32. 2. Select the hive HKLM\SYSTEM\CurrentControlSet\Control\Lsa. 3. The key CrashOnAuditFail should be set to 0. 4. Close regedt32.	Verify that the CrashOnAuditFail registry entry is set to a value of 0 by performing the following steps: 1. Open regedt32. 2. Select the hive HKLM\SYSTEM\CurrentControlSet\Control\Lsa. 3. Verify that the key CrashOnAuditFail is set to 0. 4. Close regedt32.	Review the <servername>.lsa.txt and ensure the value CrashOnAuditFail is set to 0. Review <servername>.lsa.txt and review the value FullPrivlegeAuditing. If it is a highly secure server, the setting should be 1; otherwise, it should be 0.
Set the FullPrivilegeAuditing registry entry with a value of 0 or 1 by performing the following steps: 1. Open regedt32. 2. Select the hive HKLM\SYSTEM\CurrentControlSet\Control\LSA. 3. The key FullPrivilegeAuditing should be set to 0 or 1. 4. Close regedt32.	Verify that the FullPrivilegeAuditing registry entry is set to a value of 0 or 1 by performing the following steps: 1. Open regedt32. 2. Select the hive HKLM\SYSTEM\CurrentControlSet\Control\LSA. 3. Verify that the key FullPrivilegeAuditing is set to 0 or 1. 4. Close regedt32.	**Note:** Setting this value to 1 greatly increases the number of events logged in the Event Viewer.

Windows NT Primary Domain Controller Security Review Program

No.	Category	Control Objectives	Risk	Control Techniques
12	Security Administration Activities	If all companies run Windows NT, then only Windows NT Challenge Response authentication should be accepted.	Windows NT supports LanManager Challenge Response and Windows NT Challenge Response authentication. Because the LanManager uses a weaker form of encryption, a hacker may potentially be able to crack the password hash if they sniff it as it traverses the network.	Set the LMCompatibility Level registry entry with a value of 2 if all companies run Windows NT. Otherwise, set it to a value of 1, which only sends the LM hash if it is required. **Note:** This requires the LM hot fix or Service Pack 4.
12	Security Administration Activities	Only administrators should be scheduling jobs.	The schedule service could potentially allow an unauthorized user to execute malicious code as an administrator.	Set the SubmitControl registry entry with a value of 0.
12	Security Administration Activities	Individuals should only be members of the Administrators group if absolutely necessary. Individuals managing files and shares should be Server Operators. Individuals managing accounts should be Account Operators. Individuals managing printers should be Print Operators, and individuals performing backups should be Backup Operators. These accounts should not be allowed to log on locally except for Administrators and Backup Operators if backups of the PDC are not done remotely.	Assigning individuals to the Administrators group may grant them excess user rights. These excess rights may allow them to perform unwarranted administrative functions.	Grant individuals the minimum necessary rights to perform their job function by placing them in appropriate user groups.

Implementation Techniques	Compliance Assessment Techniques	Compliance Verification Techniques
Set the LMCompatibilityLevel registry entry with a value of 1 or 2 (Set to 2 if all companys are Windows NT) by performing the following steps: 1. Open regedt32. 2. Select the hive HKLM\System\CurrentControlSet\Control\LSA. 3. The key LMCompatibilityLevel should be set to 1. 4. Close regedt32. **Note:** This requires the LM hot fix or Service Pack 4.	Verify that the LMCompatibilityLevel registry entry is set to a value of 1or 2 by performing the following steps: 1. Open regedt32. 2. Select the hive HKLM\System\CurrentControlSet\Control\LSA. 3. Verify that the key LMCompatibilityLevel is set to 1 or 2. 4. Close regedt32.	Review <servername>.lsa.txt and review the value LMCompatibilityLevel. If the environment being reviewed is strictly Windows NT, the value should be equal to 2. If the environment is mixed, the value should be equal to 1.
Set the SubmitControl registry entry with a value of 0 by performing the following steps: 1. Open regedt32. 2. Select the hive HKLM\SYSTEM\CurrentControlSet\Control\LSA. 3. The key SubmitControl should be set to 0. 4. Close regedt32.	Verify that the SubmitControl registry entry is set to a value of 0 by performing the following steps: 1. Open regedt32. 2. Select the hive HKLM\SYSTEM\CurrentControlSet\Control\LSA. 3. Verify that the key SubmitControl is set to 0. 4. Close regedt32.	Review <servername>.lsa.txt and ensure the value SubmitControl is set to 0.
Open User Manager for Domains and implement the following: Individuals managing files and shares should be Server Operators. Individuals managing accounts should be Account Operators. Individuals managing printers should be Print Operators, and individuals performing backups should be Backup Operators. These accounts should not be allowed to log on locally except for administrators and backup operators if backups of the PDC are not done remotely.	After discussion of users and user roles with the network administrator, open User Manager for Domains and ensure the following: Individuals managing files and shares are Server Operators. Individuals managing accounts are Account Operators. Individuals managing printers are Print Operators, and individuals performing backups are Backup Operators. These accounts should not be allowed to log on locally except for administrators and backup operators if backups of the PDC are not done remotely.	Review the <servername>.rights.txt and ensure only authorized users are granted User Rights. Verify the following: Individuals managing files and shares are Server Operators. Individuals managing accounts are Account Operators. Individuals managing printers are Print Operators, and individuals performing backups are Backup Operators. These accounts should not be allowed to log on locally except for administrators and backup operators if backups of the PDC are not done remotely.

Windows NT Primary Domain Controller Security Review Program

No.	Category	Control Objectives	Risk	Control Techniques
12	Security Administration Activities	The Guest account should not be able to view the System Event Log and the Application Event Log.	The System and Application Event Log could contain sensitive information about the PDC that guests could use to attack the system.	Set the RestrictGuestAccess registry entry with a value of 1.
12	Security Administration Activities	The "Access this Computer from the Network" standard user right should be restricted to ensure the PDC is secure from outside threats and that if Administrators accounts are compromised, the entire domain won't be.	If an Administrator account is compromised, it would not be able to compromise the PDC from the network. In addition, nonauthorized users will not be able to access the PDC from the network.	Restrict who can access the PDC from the network.

Implementation Techniques	Compliance Assessment Techniques	Compliance Verification Techniques
Set the RestrictGuestAccess registry entry to a value of 1 by performing the following steps: 1. Open regedt32. 2. Select the following hives independently: HKLM\System\CurrentControl Set\Services\EventLog\System HKLM\System\CurrentControl Set\Services\EventLog\ Application 3. Set the key RestrictGuest Access to 1. 4. Close regedt32.	Verify that the RestrictGuest Access registry entry is set to a value of 1 by performing the following steps: 1. Open regedt32. 2. Select the following hives independently: HKLM\System\CurrentControlSet\ Services\EventLog\system HKLM\System\CurrentControlSet\ Services\EventLog\application 3. Verify that the key RestrictGuestAccess is set to 1. 4. Close regedt32.	Review <servername>. eventlog.txt and ensure the values RestrictGuestAccess is set to 1 for the system, application, and security entries.
Restrict user rights by performing the following steps: 1. Open User Manager. 2. Choose Policies from the pulldown menu and choose User Rights. . . 3. Scroll through the Rights and find "Access this Computer from the Network." 4. Edit the Grant To list to be commensurate with corporate standards. Industry guidelines state: • Users • Server Operators • Account Operators • Print Operators • Backup Operators 5. Click OK on the new window to confirm changes. 6. Close User Manager.	Verify who has the "Access this Computer from the Network" user right by performing the following steps: 1. Open User Manager. 2. Choose Policies from the pulldown menu and choose User Rights. . . 3. Scroll through the Rights and find Access this computer from the network. 4. Verify that the list of users is commensurate with corporate standards and best practices. 5. Click Cancel. 6. Close User Manager. Industry guidelines state: • Users • Server Operators • Account Operators • Print Operators • Backup Operators	Review the <servername>. rights.txt and ensure only authorized users are granted the "Access this Computer from the Network" user right. The following guidelines can be used: • Users • Server Operators • Account Operators • Print Operators • Backup Operators

Windows NT Primary Domain Controller Security Review Program

No.	Category	Control Objectives	Risk	Control Techniques
12	Security Administration Activities	The "Add Workstation to the Domain" standard user right should be restricted to ensure that unauthorized users cannot add miscellaneous machines to the domain.	Users should not be adding machines to the domain unless they are authorized. They might be able to add a domain controller and compromise the SAM.	Restrict who can add computers to the domain.
12	Security Administration Activities	The "Backup Files and Directories" standard user right should be restricted because anyone with this user right can bypass resource ACLs and read all files.	There should be a segregation of duties between Administrators, users, and individuals who can back up files. Individuals with this user right can bypass the ACL of a file and read any file they want.	Restrict who can add backup files.

Implementation Techniques	Compliance Assessment Techniques	Compliance Verification Techniques
Restrict user rights by performing the following steps: 1. Open User Manager. 2. Choose Policies from the pulldown menu and choose User Rights. . . 3. Scroll through the Rights and find "Add Workstation to the Domain." 4. Edit the Grant To list to be commensurate with corporate standards. Industry guidelines state: • Administrators • Server Operators 5. Click OK on the new window to confirm changes. 6. Close User Manager.	Verify who has the "Add Workstation to the Domain" user right by performing the following steps: 1. Open User Manager. 2. Choose Policies from the pulldown menu and choose User Rights. . . 3. Scroll through the Rights and find "Add Workstation to the Domain." 4. Verify that the list of users is commensurate with corporate standards and best practices. 5. Click Cancel. 6. Close User Manager. Industry guidelines state: • Administrators • Server Operators	Review the <servername>.rights.txt and ensure only authorized users are granted the "Add Workstation to the Domain" user right. The following guidelines can be used: • Administrators • Server Operators
Restrict user rights by performing the following steps: 1. Open User Manager. 2. Choose Policies from the pulldown menu and choose User Rights. . . 3. Scroll through the Rights and find "Backup Files and Directories." 4. Edit the Grant To list to be commensurate with corporate standards. Industry guidelines state: • Backup Operators 5. Click OK on the new window to confirm changes. 6. Close User Manager. Compliance Assessment	Verify who has the "Backup Files and Directories" user right by performing the following steps: 1. Open User Manager. 2. Choose Policies from the pulldown menu and choose User Rights. . . 3. Scroll through the Rights and find "Backup Files and Directories." 4. Verify that the list of users is commensurate with corporate standards and best practices. 5. Click Cancel. 6. Close User Manager. Industry guidelines state: • Backup Operators	Review the <servername>.rights.txt and ensure only authorized users are granted the "Backup Files and Directories" user right. The following guidelines can be used: • Backup Operators

Windows NT Primary Domain Controller Security Review Program

No.	Category	Control Objectives	Risk	Control Techniques
12	Security Administration Activities	The "Change the System Time" standard user right should be restricted because anyone with this user right can change the system time, which in turn could misconfigure the time on all member servers.	Accuracy of the system time is a prerequisite for an audit trail because knowing who was accessing resources at a specified time could implicate a user. The entire audit, event monitoring, and logging system is based on time and therefore requires that time not be tampered with. Security policies, such as those for account lockout and expiration, are based on the system time	Restrict who can change the system time.
12	Security Administration Activities	The "Log on Locally" standard user right should be restricted so that normal users cannot interact with the PDC.	Individuals that interact with the PDC can usually get access to very sensitive system resources or create denials of service.	Restrict who can interact with the PDC.

Implementation Techniques	Compliance Assessment Techniques	Compliance Verification Techniques
Restrict user rights by performing the following steps: 1. Open User Manager. 2. Choose Policies from the pulldown menu and choose User Rights. . . 3. Scroll through the Rights and find "Change the System Time." 4. Edit the Grant To list to be commensurate with corporate standards. Industry guidelines state: • Administrators • Server Operators 5. Click OK on the new window to confirm changes. 6. Close User Manager.	Verify who has the "Change the System Time" user right by performing the following steps: 1. Open User Manager. 2. Choose Policies from the pulldown menu and choose User Rights. . . 3. Scroll through the Rights and find "Change the System Time." 4. Verify that the list of users is commensurate with corporate standards and best practices. 5. Click Cancel. 6. Close User Manager. Industry guidelines state: • Administrators • Server Operators	Review the <servername>.rights.txt and ensure only authorized users are granted the "Change the System Time" user right. The following guidelines can be used: • Administrators • Server Operators
Restrict user rights by performing the following steps: 1. Open User Manager. 2. Choose Policies from the pulldown menu and choose User Rights. . . 3. Scroll through the Rights and find "Log on Locally." 4. Edit the Grant To list to be commensurate with corporate standards. Industry guidelines state: • Administrators • Backup Operators (only if the backups are performed locally) • Server Operators 5. Click OK on the new window to confirm changes. 6. Close User Manager.	Verify who has the "Log on Locally" user right by performing the following steps: 1. Open User Manager. 2. Choose Policies from the pulldown menu and choose User Rights. . . 3. Scroll through the Rights and find "Log on Locally." 4. Verify that the list of users is commensurate with corporate standards and best practices. 5. Click Cancel. 6. Close User Manager. Industry guidelines state: • Administrators • Backup Operators (only if the backups are performed locally) • Server Operators	Review the <servername>.rights.txt and ensure only authorized users are granted the "Log on Locally" user right. The following guidelines can be used: • Administrators • Backup Operators (only if the backups are performed locally) • Server Operators

Windows NT Primary Domain Controller Security Review Program

No.	Category	Control Objectives	Risk	Control Techniques
12	Security Administration Activities	The "Manage Auditing and Security Log" standard user right should be restricted so that only designated auditors can view and delete the PDC's logs.	There should be a segregation of duties between Administrators, users, and individuals who can audit the PDC's logs. Since individuals with this right can clear a security log, they have the ability to attempt an attack on the system and then delete the log, although a security control inherent in Windows NT is that the first entry in the new log states that the old log was cleared and by whom. Only authorized individuals, such as the Security Officer or the Internal Auditor, should be given this right. Those types of individuals should be members of an Auditors group.	Restrict who can audit the PDC.
12	Security Administration Activities	The "Restore File and Directories" standard user right should be restricted because anyone with this user right can bypass resource ACLs and read and write to all files.	There should be a segregation of duties between Administrators, users, and individuals who can restore files. Individuals with this user right can bypass the ACL of a file and read or write to any file on the PDC.	Restrict who can add restore files from backups.

Implementation Techniques

Restrict user rights by performing the following steps:

1. Open User Manager.
2. Choose Policies from the pulldown menu and choose User Rights. . .
3. Scroll through the Rights and find "Manage Auditing and Security log."
4. Edit the Grant To list to be commensurate with corporate standards.

Industry guidelines state:

- Auditors (must be created)

5. Click OK on the new window to confirm changes.
6. Close User Manager.

Compliance Assessment Techniques

Verify who has the "Manage Auditing and Security log" user right by performing the following steps:

1. Open User Manager.
2. Choose Policies from the pulldown menu and choose User Rights. . .
3. Scroll through the Rights and find "Manage Auditing and Security Log."
4. Verify that the list of users is commensurate with corporate standards and best practices.
5. Click Cancel.
6. Close User Manager.

Industry guidelines state:

- Auditors (must be created)

Compliance Verification Techniques

Review the <servername>.rights.txt and ensure only authorized users are granted the "Manage Auditing and Security Log" user right. The following guidelines can be used:

- Auditors (must be created)

Review the <servername>.rights.txt and ensure only authorized users are granted the "Restore File and Directories" user right. The following guidelines can be used:

- Backup Operators

Restrict user rights by performing the following steps:

1. Open User Manager.
2. Choose Policies from the pulldown menu and choose User Rights. . .
3. Scroll through the Rights and find "Restore File and Directories."
4. Edit the Grant To list to be commensurate with corporate standards.

Industry guidelines state:

- Backup Operators

5. Click OK on the new window to confirm changes.
6. Close User Manager.

Verify who has the "Restore File and Directories" user right by performing the following steps:

1. Open User Manager.
2. Choose Policies from the pulldown menu and choose User Rights. . .
3. Scroll through the Rights and find "Restore File and Directories."
4. Verify that the list of users is commensurate with corporate standards and best practices.
5. Click Cancel.
6. Close User Manager.

Industry guidelines state:

- Backup Operators

Windows NT Primary Domain Controller Security Review Program

No.	Category	Control Objectives	Risk	Control Techniques
12	Security Administration Activities	The "Shut Down the System" standard user right should be restricted to prevent unauthorized individuals from shutting down the PDC and causing a denial of service.	Individuals who can shut down the PDC could cause a denial of service or degrade the performance of the network depending on the BDC configurations.	Restrict who can shut down the PDC
12	Security Administration Activities	The "Take ownership of Files or Other Objects" standard user right should be restricted so that no one can manipulate a file they do not already own.	This is a very powerful user right because individuals can ignore the ACL of an object, take ownership of the object, and change the ACL to what they want.	Restrict who can take ownership of files or other objects.

Implementation Techniques	Compliance Assessment Techniques	Compliance Verification Techniques
Restrict user rights by performing the following steps: 1. Open User Manager. 2. Choose Policies from the pulldown menu and choose User Rights. . . 3. Scroll through the Rights and find "Shut Down the System." 4. Edit the Grant To list to be commensurate with corporate standards. Industry guidelines state: • Administrators • Server Operators 5. Click OK on the new window to confirm changes. 6. Close User Manager.	Verify who has the "Shut Down the System" user right by performing the following steps: 1. Open User Manager. 2. Choose Policies from the pulldown menu and choose User Rights. . . 3. Scroll through the Rights and find "Shut Down the System." 4. Verify that the list of users is commensurate with corporate standards and best practices. 5. Click Cancel. 6. Close User Manager. Industry guidelines state: • Administrators • Server Operators	Review the <servername>. rights.txt and ensure only authorized users are granted the "Shut Down the System" user right. The following guidelines can be used: • Administrators • Server Operators
Restrict user rights by performing the following steps: 1. Open User Manager. 2. Choose Policies from the pulldown menu and choose User Rights. . . 3. Scroll through the Rights and find "Take Ownership of Files or Other Objects." 4. Edit the Grant To list to be commensurate with corporate standards. Industry guidelines state: • No one 5. Click OK on the new window to confirm changes. 6. Close User Manager.	Verify who has the "Take Ownership of Files or Other Objects" user right by performing the following steps: 1. Open User Manager. 2. Choose Policies from the pull-down menu and choose User Rights. . . 3. Scroll through the Rights and find "Take Ownership of Files or Other Objects." 4. Verify that the list of users is commensurate with corporate standards and best practices. 5. Click Cancel. 6. Close User Manager. Industry guidelines state: • No one	Review the <servername>. rights.txt and ensure only authorized users are granted the "Take Ownership of Files or Other Objects" user right. The following guidelines can be used: • No one

Windows NT Primary Domain Controller Security Review Program

No.	Category	Control Objectives	Risk	Control Techniques
12	Security Administration Activities	The "Act as Part of the Operating System" advanced user right should be restricted so that no one can act like the "system." This right is required by some applications such as BindView.	The "Act as Part of the Operating System" right is one of the most powerful rights within Windows NT. It allows the designated accounts to act as a trusted part of the operating system and can therefore do anything regardless of other rights.	Restrict who can act as the "system."
12	Security Administration Activities	The "Bypass Traverse Checking" advanced user right should be available to Everyone. **Note:** This is a divergence from the book, which specifies that the Administrator, Server Operator, and Backup Operator groups are the only ones to have bypass traverse checking on the PDC.	If Everyone is removed from this user right, POSIX-compliant applications could cause a denial of access when they try to traverse subdirectories.	Ensure that Everyone has the right to bypass traverse checking. **Note:** The "Bypass Traverse Checking" right allows Windows NT to be configured in a POSIX-compliant manner. It allows users to traverse subdirectories regardless of parent permissions.

Implementation Techniques	Compliance Assessment Techniques	Compliance Verification Techniques
Restrict user rights by performing the following steps: 1. Open User Manager. 2. Choose Policies from the pulldown menu and choose User Rights. . . 3. Select the "Show Advanced User Rights" check box. 4. Scroll through the Rights and find "Act as Part of the Operating System." 5. Edit the Grant To list to be commensurate with corporate standards. Industry guidelines state: • No one 6. Click OK on the new window to confirm changes. 7. Close User Manager.	Verify who has the "Act as Part of the Operating System" user right by performing the following steps: 1. Open User Manager. 2. Choose Policies from the pulldown menu and choose User Rights. . . 3. Select the "Show Advanced User Rights" check box. 4. Scroll through the Rights and find "Act as Part of the Operating System." 5. Verify that the list of users is commensurate with corporate standards and best practices. 6. Click Cancel. 7. Close User Manager. Industry guidelines state: • No one	Review the <servername>.rights.txt and ensure only authorized users are granted the "Act as Part of the Operating System" user right. The following guidelines can be used: • No one
Ensure user rights by performing the following steps: 1. Open User Manager. 2. Choose Policies from the pulldown menu and choose User Rights. . . 3. Select the "Show Advanced User Rights" check box. 4. Scroll through the Rights and find "Bypass Traverse Checking." 5. Ensure that the special group Everyone is granted this right. 6. Click OK on the new window to confirm changes. Industry guidelines state: • Everyone 7. Close User Manager.	Verify who has the "Bypass Traverse Checking" user right by performing the following steps: 1. Open User Manager. 2. Choose Policies from the pulldown menu and choose User Rights. . . 3. Select the "Show Advanced User Rights" check box. 4. Scroll through the Rights and find "Bypass Traverse Checking." 5. Verify that the list of users is commensurate with corporate standards and best practices. 6. Click Cancel. 7. Close User Manager. Industry guidelines state: • Everyone	Review the <servername>.rights.txt and ensure only authorized users are granted the "Bypass Traverse Checking" user right. The following guidelines can be used: • Everyone

Windows NT Primary Domain Controller Security Review Program

No.	Category	Control Objectives	Risk	Control Techniques
12	Security Administration Activities	The "Log on as a Service" advanced user right should be restricted so that no one can act as a service.	The "Log on as a Service" right allows a user to log on as a service, similar to those required by virus scanners and faxing software. These services run in the background without any interaction from any additional users. Some services have Full Control over the system and could be very powerful if configured in that manner.	Restrict who can log on as a service.
12	Security Administration Activities	The "Modify Firmware Environment Variables" advanced user right should be restricted so that users can't modify the system environment variables that affect certain programs.	The "Modify Firmware Environment Variables" right allows users to modify the system environment variables that affect certain programs. If a variable is modified, it could be set to point to a batch program that launches a Trojan horse or denial of service.	Restrict who can modify firmware environment variables.

Implementation Techniques	Compliance Assessment Techniques	Compliance Verification Techniques
Restrict user rights by performing the following steps: 1. Open User Manager. 2. Choose Policies from the pulldown menu and choose User Rights. . . 3. Select the "Show Advanced User Rights" check box. 4. Scroll through the Rights and find "Log on as a Service." 5. Edit the Grant To list to be commensurate with corporate standards. Industry guidelines state: • Replicators 6. Click OK on the new window to confirm changes. 7. Close User Manager.	Verify who has the "Log on as a Service" user right by performing the following steps: 1. Open User Manager. 2. Choose Policies from the pulldown menu and choose User Rights. . . 3. Select the "Show Advanced User Rights" check box. 4. Scroll through the Rights and find "Log on as a Service." 5. Verify that the list of users is commensurate with corporate standards and best practices. 6. Click Cancel. 7. Close User Manager. Industry guidelines state: • Replicators	Review the <servername>. rights.txt and ensure only authorized users are granted the "Log on as a Service" user right. The following guidelines can be used: • Replicators
Restrict user rights by performing the following steps: 1. Open User Manager. 2. Choose Policies from the pulldown menu and choose User Rights. . . 3. Select the "Show Advanced User Rights" check box. 4. Scroll through the Rights and find "Modify Firmware Environment Variables." 5. Edit the Grant To list to be commensurate with corporate standards. Industry guidelines state: • Administrators 6. Click OK on the new window to confirm changes. 7. Close User Manager.	Verify who has the "Modify Firmware Environment Variables" user right by performing the following steps: 1. Open User Manager. 2. Choose Policies from the pulldown menu and choose User Rights. . . 3. Select the "Show Advanced User Rights" check box. 4. Scroll through the Rights and find "Modify Firmware Environment Variables." 5. Verify that the list of users is commensurate with corporate standards and best practices. 6. Click Cancel. 7. Close User Manager. Industry guidelines state: • Administrators	Review the <servername>. rights.txt and ensure only authorized users are granted the "Modify Firmware Environment Variables" user right. The following guidelines can be used: • Administrators

Windows NT Primary Domain Controller Security Review Program

No.	Category	Control Objectives	Risk	Control Techniques
12	Security Administration Activities	Certain advanced user rights should either be granted to no one or to Administrators only. These rights are listed in the implementation checklist.	These advanced user rights could be used to compromise the PDC if they are granted to the wrong individuals other than Administrators. They are very powerful and do not need to be granted to normal users.	Restrict who is granted these advanced user rights (as listed in implementation checklist).

Implementation Techniques

Restrict user rights by performing the following steps:

1. Open User Manager.
2. Choose Policies from the pulldown menu and choose User Rights. . .
3. Select the "Show Advanced User Rights" check box.
4. Scroll through the Rights and find the following:

Should be granted to Administrators:

- Create a pagefile
- Debug programs
- Increase quotas
- Increase scheduling priority
- Load and unload device drivers
- Profile single process
- Profile system performance

Should be granted to no one:

- Create a token object
- Create permanent shared objects
- Generate security audits
- Lock pages in memory
- Modify firmware environment variables
- Replace a process-level token

5. Edit the Grant To list to be commensurate with corporate standards or the above industry guidelines.
6. Click OK on the new window to confirm changes.
7. Close User Manager.

Note: The standard user right "Force shutdown from a remote machine" and the advanced right "Log on as a batch job" are not listed anywhere in ESAS because they are not implemented in Windows NT 4.0 and have no consequences.

Compliance Assessment Techniques

Verify who has certain user rights by performing the following steps:

1. Open User Manager.
2. Choose Policies from the pulldown menu and choose User Rights. . .
3. Select the "Show Advanced User Rights" check box.
4. Scroll through the Rights and find the following:

Group A:

- Create a pagefile
- Debug programs
- Increase quotas
- Increase scheduling priority
- Load and unload device drivers
- Profile single process
- Profile system performance

Group B:

- Create a token object
- Create permanent shared objects
- Generate security audits
- Lock pages in memory
- Modify firmware environment variables
- Replace a process-level token

5. Verify that the list of users is commensurate with corporate standards and best practices.
6. Click Cancel.
7. Close User Manager.

Industry guidelines state:

- Group A (Administrators)
- Group B (No one)

Note: The standard user right "Force Shutdown from a Remote Machine" and the advanced user right "Log on as a Batch Job" are not listed anywhere in ESAS because they are not implemented in Windows NT 4.0 and have no consequences.

Compliance Verification Techniques

Review the <servername>.rights.txt and ensure only authorized users are granted the following user rights. The following guidelines can be used:

Should be granted to Administrators:

- Create a pagefile
- Debug programs
- Increase quotas
- Increase scheduling priority
- Load and unload device drivers
- Profile single process
- Profile system performance

Should be granted to no one:

- Create a token object
- Create permanent shared objects
- Generate security audits
- Lock pages in memory
- Modify firmware environment variables
- Replace a process-level token

Windows NT Primary Domain Controller Security Review Program

No.	Category	Control Objectives	Risk	Control Techniques
12	Security Administration Activities	The company's legal department should be consulted, and consideration should be given to implementing a legal warning message to be displayed during login.	Displaying a legal warning ensures that users are aware of the consequences of unauthorized access and assists in conveying the protection of corporate assets.	Set the registry value LegalNoticeCaption and LegalNoticeText to "Authorized Use Only" and "The Use of this System is Restricted to Authorized Persons Only. All Others will be Prosecuted to the Full Extent of the Law," respectively.
12	Security Administration Activities	Services that compromise the security of the domain should not be started.	If the company has services running that compromise the security of the domain, there is an increased risk that domain resources will be compromised.	Disable any unnecessary or insecure services running.
12	Security Administration Activities	Services that provide enticement information should be disabled.	Certain services (Messenger and Alerter) allow users to get enticement information about the domain and its resources.	The Messenger and Alerter services and any other services that provide users enticement information should be disabled when possible.

Implementation Techniques	Compliance Assessment Techniques	Compliance Verification Techniques
For all servers, enable the display of legal text by performing the following steps: 1. Open the Registry Editor (regedt32.exe). 2. Select the Software\Microsoft\WindowsNT\CurrentVersion\Winlogon subkey of the HKLM hive. 3. Enter the appropriate text in the LegalNoticeCaption and LegalNoticeText values. 4. Close the Registry Editor.	Verify that an appropriate Legal Notice has been created and cleared with the Legal Department. Ensure that the Legal Notice is implemented on all machines by attempting to log on to selected machines and verifying the existence of a legal notice.	Review <servername>.winlogon.txt and ensure the LegalNoticeCaption and LegalNoticeText values contain adequate legal text.
N/A	Verify that there are no services running on the PDC that could lead to unnecessary risk and exposure by performing the following steps: 1. Open Server Manager. 2. Select the PDC and choose Services. . . from the computer pulldown menu. 3. Review each running service to determine if it may compromise the security of the PDC.	Verify that there are no services running on the PDC that could lead to unnecessary risk and exposure, by reviewing <servername>.services.txt and ensuring that unnecessary or insecure services are not running.
N/A	Discuss with the network administrator the use of Messenger and Alerter. If these services are not used, be sure that they are stopped.	Review <servername>.services.txt and determine if the Messenger and Alerter services are running. If the services are running, inquire with the company if they are necessary to support applications or services running on the server (e.g., backup software).

CHAPTER 6

UNIX

INTRODUCTION

This chapter on Unix provides instructions on performing specific security-related tasks and explains the underlying concepts of security concerns. It also contains procedures and guidelines essential to administering the Unix computer as a trusted system. According to the industry-standard Department of Defense Trusted Computer System Evaluation Criteria, a trusted system is one that "employs sufficient hardware and software integrity measures to allow its use for processing simultaneously a range of sensitive or classified information."

PLANNING FOR SECURITY

The focus of this section concerns the need for a comprehensive security policy. To ensure that the policy is implemented and maintained, tasks must be distributed to various personnel.

The U.S. Computer Security Act of 1987 cast new urgency on computer security in all business segments. The act stipulates that if financial loss occurs as a result of computer fraud or abuse, the company, not the perpetrator, is liable for damages. Thus, the ultimate responsibility for safeguarding information lies with individual businesses themselves.

Systems processing sensitive or proprietary data are inherently targets for mischief or damage. Damage can be accidental, physical, or intentional, as in the malicious use of software. Since Unix was developed for an environment of cooperating users, not all security flaws have been corrected programmatically. Unauthorized persons gaining access to sensitive material might wreak considerable havoc to the system.

SECURITY POLICY

To protect system and data integrity, a business entity should establish a comprehensive security policy governing computer use. A computer security policy is a statement of rules that govern the behavior of users to ensure system and data integrity. The following basic principles govern good security:

- Commit management to security.
- Control physical equipment.
- Educate employees to know what is expected of them.

- Design administrative procedures to increase security.
- Segregate and compartmentalize data.
- Disconnect unused terminals and mass storage devices.
- Never perform any task as super user that can be performed with a lesser privilege.
- Do not trust what others can alter.
- Require users to be on the system purposefully, on a "need-to-know" basis.
- Have users report any unusual or irresponsible activities to authorities. These activities might include unaccounted-for programs or unexpected software behavior.

Besides software features, administrative support is essential for achieving a workable security policy. When drafting a security policy, be sure to address the following questions:

- What facilities require protection?
- Which data warrant protection?
- Who is allowed access to the system and under what circumstances?
- What permissions and protections are required to maintain security?
- How can the system security policy be enforced by physical, procedural, and system mechanisms?

Physical Security Policy

Physical security safeguards system hardware from damage. It protects software from corruption as a result of environmental conditions and assures that unauthorized personnel are denied access to areas containing system equipment. Hardware includes the central processing unit (CPU), system console, terminals, and other peripherals such as printers, disk drives, and tape drives. Software includes the operating system, programs, and data. Restrict physical access to areas containing system equipment by:

- Using perimeter controls, such as locked computer rooms, fenced building sites, and guards at building entrances.
- Using antitheft protection designed for desktop computers.
- Issuing keys and ID badges.
- Physically securing access to terminal wiring and network cables.
- Safeguarding sensitive or proprietary data by keeping media archived off-site in a locked facility.
- Erasing obsolete data.
- Shredding or securely disposing of console logs or printouts.

Procedural Security Policy

Although practices may differ depending on the type of computer involved, the procedural security policy should govern the following:

- Use of equipment and systems operation.
- Management of software and data, including the following:
  - How computer-processed information can be accessed, manipulated, and monitored to maintain system safeguards.

- Information handling throughout the system's life cycle.
- Use of system security features, including frequency of audit review and analysis
- Physical storage of data.

Common security practices include the following:

- Restrict login access to software to those with a legitimate need.
- Have users log off or use the `lock` command when not using their terminals.
- Decentralize computer duties by rotating operators.
- Store backup tapes at bonded, off-site depositories.

System Security Policy

System security tasks such as auditing should be performed by authorized security personnel only. However, users might use security features such as action control lists (ACLs) that are applicable to user files. Maintaining system security involves:

- Identification of users. All users must have a unique login identity, or ID, that identifies them as legitimate system users. An ID consists of an account name and password, and without it, a user cannot log in to the system.
- Authentication of users. When a user logs in, the system authenticates the user's password by checking for its existence in `/etc/passwd` or `/.secure/etc/passwd`.
- Authorization of users. At a system level, Unix provides two kinds of authorized computer use: regular and super user. Individual users also may be granted or restricted access to system files through traditional file permissions and access control lists.
- Auditing of users. Unix enables the auditing of computer usage by user, system call, and event.
- Educating users. All users are responsible for security. A security policy is effective only if the users are informed of its contents and trained in its use.

The guidelines to follow for a system security policy are:

- Centralize security responsibilities with a clearly defined security officer, and make sure that all users know who to call if a security breach is suspected.
- Prepare a list of security guidelines and distribute it to all computer users.
- Have the security guidelines reviewed by management to establish compliance at all levels.
- Review and update the guidelines periodically as technology and needs change.
- Disseminate information about the policy changes promptly.
- Consider installing a file of security guidelines in every new user's account.
- Consider factors of human nature in working to gain acceptance of a security policy.
- Emphasize the benefits derived by a sound security policy.
- Keep the security policy consistent with the "corporate culture" of the organization.
- Do not make the system any more restrictive than necessary. Poorly chosen or excessively rigid security measures often force users to develop loopholes to maintain productivity.

KEY SECURITY PERSONNEL

One technique for increasing accountability in system administration is to distribute security-related responsibilities among different users. In the following model, recommended by the National Computer Security Center, the system Security Officer is responsible for overall system security, while the system administrator keeps the system running and works with the system Security Officer to plan the system's overall hardware and software needs.

System Security Officer's Tasks

The system Security Officer's tasks are:

- Initiates and monitors auditing policy.
- Determines which users and events are audited.
- Maintains the secure password system.
- Initializes DAC privileges on public files.
- Authorizes new user accounts.
- Checks file systems for `setuid/setgid` (set user ID/set group ID) programs.

System Administrator's Tasks

The system administrator's tasks are:

- Implements auditing procedures.
- Inspects and analyzes audit logs.
- Administers group and user accounts.
- Repairs damaged user files and volumes.
- Updates system software.
- Sets system configuration parameters.
- Collects various system statistics.
- Disables and deletes accounts.
- Makes periodic system checks.
- Monitors repeated login attempts.
- Periodically scans file permissions.
- Deals with invalid `su` (substitute user, or super user) attempts and invalid network requests.

System Operator's Tasks

The system operator's tasks are:

- Installs security-relevant software.
- Performs routine maintenance such as backups.
- Performs online terminal and device tests.
- Responds to user requests for routine system maintenance.

System Programmer's Tasks

The system programmer's tasks are:

- Installs system upgrades.
- Performs dump analysis.
- Writes programs that conform to security criteria.

SECURE SYSTEM SETUP

This section provides a strategic road map for setting up a secure system. Key topics covered include setting up the system, enabling auditing, and maintaining the system after implementing the security features.

SYSTEM ADMINISTRATION MANAGER REVIEW

System Administration Manager (SAM) is used to perform security-related system administration tasks. SAM, a window environment reserved for users with super user capabilities, queries the user through each step, focuses choices, and protects the user from corrupting critical files. It avoids introducing mistakes or compromises that might breach security. The following security-related system administration tasks can be performed with SAM:

- Turning auditing on and off.
- Setting the audit monitor and log parameters.
- Viewing audit logs.
- Viewing and modifying audit options for users, events, and system calls.
- Converting to a trusted system.
- Managing user accounts.

INVOKING SAM

Invoke SAM by typing: **/usr/bin/sam.** Select the following area you wish to work in:

- In the X Window System interface, double-click on the area title.
- In the text terminal interface, move the highlight through the SAM list items using the arrow (▼, ▲) keys and press <Return>.

For details on the differences between the X Window System interface and the text terminal interface, consult your system administrator. Specific tasks provide detailed information on SAM usage.

SETTING UP A SECURE SYSTEM

The procedures presented here cover all of the tasks required to implement a secure (trusted) system. Determine whether the following steps were followed:

- Plan prior to conversion.
- Install the system from tape.

- Convert to a secure (trusted) system.
- Enable auditing to set up the secure system.

Prior to Conversion Plan

Prior to the conversion plan, the following steps must be taken:

1. Assess the auditing needs.
   - How was the size of your audit log files determined?
   - How were the events and users to audit decided?
   - How was the frequency to evaluate your audit logs determined?
2. Establish an overall security policy.
   - How were the security requirements of the work site identified?
   - At both the administrative and user levels, how were the written guidelines reflecting the realistic needs of the work site established?
   - How were all personnel-administrators and individual users informed of their security responsibilities?
   - What procedures were in place to keep security guidelines updated and all users informed as requirements changed?
3. Were all existing files on the system inspected for security risks? This is mandatory the first time a secure (trusted) system is installed. Thereafter, files should be examined regularly, or when a security breach is suspected. How was it determined that no security breaches existed before proceeding to the next section?

Installing the System

The system should not be updated but should be installed from tape because the effectiveness of security features may be compromised if the system files were altered. The steps that should be taken are:

1. The file system should be backed up for later recovery of user files.
2. The Unix operating system should be installed from tape.
3. The user files should be recovered from the backup media.
4. `Product Description Files (pdfs)` for each product fileset installed on the system should be created. These should be used as a reference when checking for security breaches in the future.
5. No other operations should occur before conversion. After step 4, proceed directly to the conversion task that is described as follows.

Conversion to a Secure (Trusted) System

When Unix is converted to a secure (trusted) system, the conversion program:

- Creates a new, secure password file called `/.secure/etc/passvd`.
- Copies the `/etc/passvd` file into `/etc/passwd.old.sav`, a file with restrictive permissions.

- Moves encrypted passwords from the **/etc/passwd** file to the **/.secure/etc/passwd** file and replaces the password field in **/etc/passwd** with an *.
- Forces all users to use passwords.
- Creates an audit ID number for each user.
- Sets the audit flag on for all existing users.
- Converts the **at**, **batch**, and **crontab** files to use the submitter's audit ID.

Prerequisites

Before running the conversion program:

1. Be sure that the directory **/etc/filesets** contains the **AUDIT** fileset. To check for this fileset enter: **ls /etc/filesets / grep AUDIT.** If the system returns the message **AUDIT**, the fileset is there and the user can proceed. If nothing is returned, it probably means that during installation all filesets were not chosen. Add the **AUDIT** fileset.
2. Verify that the **/etc/newconfig/auditrc** file has been copied to **/etc/auditrc** by typing **ls /etc/auditrc.** If the system returns the message **/etc/auditrc not found**, use the following command string to copy the file: **cp /etc/newconfig/auditrc /etc/auditrc**.
3. Verify that the **/etc/rc** file calls the **/etc/auditrc** file by typing: **more /etc/rc.** Locate the text **Here is the heart of the rc script**: in the **/etc/rc** file and verify that the following lines appear before it:

   ```
   audit-start ()

   {#Start up the auditing subsystem # if [ -x /etc/auditrc] & /etc/auditrc
   then
   echo "Audit subsystem started"
   fi}
   ```

   Insert these lines if they are not there and insert the subroutine called **audit-start** at the end of the list of calls in the **standalone** section and in the **localroot** section of this file.

To convert to a secure (trusted) system:

1. Invoke **SAM** by typing: **/usr/bin/sam.**
2. Highlight **Auditing and Security** and activate **open**.
3. Press Y to begin the conversion process. As the system is converted, the user will receive messages concerning the progress of the conversion.

The auditing subsystem is now ready to be enabled.

Enable Auditing

The system supplies default auditing parameters at installation. Some of these defaults are activated automatically, some have to be enabled. Before turning auditing on, go through the steps that follow.

From the "Auditing and Security" window, the auditing status of users, events, or system calls can be changed. To make changes, enter the appropriate functional area by highlighting either **Users**, **Events**, or **System Calls**.

1. By default, the audit status for all users is set to y. Verify that if this screen is modified, adequate justification is documented.
2. The event types admin,].logon, and moddac are selected as defaults by the system. Both Audit Success and Audit Failure are set to y. This is the minimum event type selection recommended for running a secure system. To activate these default event types, enter the "Events" functional area, highlight these events, and choose Audit both success and failure from the "Actions" menu. Verify that this has been done.
3. To enter the "Set Audit Monitor and Log Parameters" window, choose Log/Monitor Params from the "Actions" menu in any of the "Auditing and Security" functional areas (Users, Events, or System Calls). Exhibit 6.1 describes the parameters set here and shows the default values supplied automatically at installation. The audit file interaction is discussed later in more detail.
4. Assess the size of your file systems using the bdf command. Use the Shell escape from SAM by pressing the Shell key and executing the bdf command at the shell prompt by typing: **bdf.** This provides the following information about the file systems:
   - Size in kbytes.
   - Amount of space used in kbytes.
   - Amount of space available in kbytes.
   - Capacity by percentage.
   - Mounted on.

Exhibit 6.1 Audit Monitor and Log Parameters

SAM Screen Entry	Default	What Is Being Set Here
Primary log file path name	/.secure/etc/auditlog-1	The full pathname of the file set to collect auditing data initially.
Primary log file switch size (AFS)	5,000 kbytes	The Audit File Switch size for the primary audit log file.
Auxiliary log file path name	/. secure/etc/auditlog-2	The full pathname of the backup file for collecting auditing data.
Auxiliary log file switch size (AFS)	1,000 kbytes	The Audit File Switch size for the backup audit log file.
Monitor wake-up interval	1 minute	How frequently you want audomon to check the state of the auditing system when it is approaching either AFS or FSS.
Allowable free space minimum (FSS)	20%	The FSS value is the File System Switch point, the minimum amount of file space allowed on the file system before a switch to a backup file is attempted.
Percentage of log size limit to trigger warnings	90%	When either the AFS or FSS point is nearing this percentage, audomon will send out its initial warning message.

Following is an example of the possible output of the bdf command:

Filesystem	*kbytes*	*Used*	*Available*	*Capacity*	*Mounted on*
/dev/dsk/c2000d0s0	23,191	19,388	1,483	93%	/
/dev/dsk/c2000d0s5	207,267	184,224	2,316	99%	/mnt
/dev/dsk/c3d0s2	120,942	13,374	95,473	12%.	/mnt/oth
/dev/dsk/c2d0sl0	121,771	48,273	61,320	44%	/usr/tool

5. Choose a file system with adequate space for the audit log files. For example, using the system supplied default for the primary audit log file would mean that:
   - **a.** The /. secure/etc file system must have more than 5,000 kbytes available for the primary audit log file.
   - **b.** It must have more than 20% of its file space available.

   The following errors can occur if file system space is inadequate:
   - **a.** If the primary audit log file resides in a file system with less than 20 percent file space available, the system immediately switches to the auxiliary audit log file when auditing is invoked.
   - **b.** If the file system chosen has insufficient space to handle the indicated audit file switch size (i.e., 5,000 kbytes), the system issues the following warning: May not have completed task . . . current audit file /.secure/etc/auditlog-1 insufficient space available on audit file system, specify a different audit file or select a smaller AFS auditing system unchanged.
6. Provide a new pathname for the auxiliary audit log file. The primary and auxiliary audit log files should reside on separate file systems. Since each installation of Unix is different, it is not known which file systems are available at the user's installation. Hence, the default situation has both the primary and auxiliary log files residing on the same file system, / .secure/etc.
7. These parameters can now be enabled and auditing turned on. Leave the default answer of y at the question "Turn auditing ON?" and leave the default of (y) at the query Make changes permanent (live beyond reboot)? if you wish these parameters to become the new default parameters. Press the Perform Task key.

The system is now ready for normal operation as a secure system.

SECURE SYSTEM MAINTENANCE

Once the system is up and running, one should periodically verify file system security and also check for security breaches on a regular basis.

CREATING PRODUCT DESCRIPTION FILES

One should create Product Description Files (pdfs) for each of the product filesets installed on the system to be used as a basis for later comparison. The pdf files created will contain a single-line entry for each file having the following information:

Field	*Comments*
pathname	Absolute.
owner	Either symbolic or numeric ID.
group	Either symbolic or numeric ID.
mode	Symbolic representation as displayed by the ls-l command.
size	Size of the file in bytes. Major and minor numbers are listed for device special files.
links	Number of hard links to pathname.
version	Numeric value, reported by what(l).
checksum	File contents computed by a checksum algorithm. This field reflects the slightest change to a file, even a single character.
linked-to	Indicates whether the file has symbolic or hard links.

Fields are separated by colons (:) and comment lines begin with percent signs (%).

An example of a pdf entry is:

```
% Product Description File
% UX-CORE fileset
/bin/ls:bin:bin:-r-xr-xr-x:94208:6:64.1:3245:
/bin/ll : bin: bin: -r-xr-xr-x:94208:6:64.1:3245:/bin/ls
% total size is 154,712 bytes.
% total size is 153 blocks.
```

Producing pdf files is a simple task involving the use of the mkpdf(1M) command. Mkpdf(1M) finds each file, gathers statistics on it, and tabulates those statistics in the format shown previously. The following example shows how to produce pdfs for all filesets currently installed using the sh(l) or ksh(l) login shell. One must be a super user to execute these commands.

```
Release='uname -a'
date='date'
is /etc/filesets /
while read fileset
do
  comment="Fileset $fileset, Release $release, $date"
  echo processing $comment
  mkpdf -c "$comment" /etc/filesets/$fileset /system/$fileset/pdf
done
```

The resulting pdfs will reside in files named /system/$fileset/pdf, for example, /system/UX-CORE/pdf.

VERIFYING FILE SYSTEM CONSISTENCY

To verify that system files have not been altered, one would use the pdfck(1M) command to compare current file statistics against the Unix release file system statistics collected and stored in /system/$fileset/pdf. To verify:

1. Run the pdfck(1M) command. Pdfck does not produce output unless it finds discrepancies.
2. Examine the results, paying particular attention to changes in:
   - Mode permission bits.
   - Owner ID and group ID.
   - Checksum— discrepancies.

USING PDF FOR CUSTOMIZED FILESETS

Use the same procedures as before to verify file consistency for customized systems.

1. Create a prototype file list and run the mkpdf(1M) command on that list to produce a pdf.
2. Archive that pdf somewhere safe.
3. To verify the consistency of the listed files, run the pdfck command using the archived pdf file as a baseline. Pdfck will read each entry in the file, gather the current statistics, compare it to the baseline, and report any discrepancies.

PLANNING USER ACCESS TO SYSTEM AND FILES

This section covers basic information on password security, system and user file permissions, and file access control using ACLs.

PASSWORD SECURITY

The password is the most important individual user identification symbol. With it, the system authenticates a user to allow access to the system. Since they are vulnerable to compromise when used, stored, or even known, passwords must be kept secret at all times.

The System Security Officer and every user on the system must share responsibility for password security. The security policy should be based on the following assumptions:

- A password is assigned when a user is added to the system.
- A user's password should be changed periodically.
- The system must maintain a password database.
- Users must remember their passwords and keep them secret.
- Users must enter their passwords at authentication time.

Password Responsibilities

The System Security Officer performs the following security tasks:

- Assigns the initial system passwords.
- Maintains proper permissions on the /etc/passwd and /.secure/etc/passwd files.
- Assigns the initial passwords to all new users.
- Establishes password aging.
- Deletes or nullifies expired passwords, user IDs, and passwords of users no longer eligible to access the system.

Every user must observe the following rules:

- Keep password secret at all times.
- Change the initial password immediately.
- Remember the password (never write it down).
- Report any changes in status and any suspected security violations.
- Change password periodically.
- Make sure no one is watching when entering the password.
- Choose a different password for each machine on which there is an account.

Criteria of a Good Password

Observe the following guidelines when choosing a password:

- A password should have at least six characters. It must contain at least two alphabetic and one numeric or special character. Special characters can include control characters and symbols such as asterisks and slashes.
- Do not choose a word found in a dictionary, even if you spell it backwards. Software programs exist that can find and match it.
- Do not choose a password easily associated with you, such as a family or pet name, or a hobby.
- Do not use simple keyboard sequences, such as `asdfghjkl`, or repetitions of your login (e.g., login is `ann`; password is `annann`).
- Misspelled words or combined syllables from two unrelated words make suitable passwords.
- Consider using a password generator that combines syllables to make pronounceable gibberish.

Note: Keep your password private. It is a security violation for users to share passwords.

Password Encryption

All passwords are encrypted immediately after entry and stored in the `/.secure/etc/passwd` file. Only the encrypted password is used in comparisons.

Two Password Files

A trusted system maintains two password files: `/etc/passwd and /. secure/etc/passwd`. Every system user has entries in both files, and `login` looks at both entries to authenticate login requests.

The `/etc/passwd` file is used to authenticate a user at login time. The file contains descriptions of every account on the Unix system. Each entry consists of seven fields separated by colons. When a system is converted to a trusted system, the encrypted password, normally held in the second field of `/etc/passwd`, is moved to the `/ . secure/etc/passwd` file and an asterisk holds its place in the `/etc/passwd` file. A typical entry of `/etc/passwd` in a trusted system looks like this:

```
robin: *: 102:99: RobinTewes : /mnt/robin: /bin/csh
```

The fields contain the following information (listed in order):

1. User (login) name consisting of up to eight characters.
2. Encrypted password field held by an asterisk instead of an actual password.
3. User ID (uid), an integer less than 60,000.
4. Group ID (gid), taken from the /etc/group file. The gid must be an integer less than 60,000.
5. Comment field used for identifying information such as the user's full name.
6. Home directory, the user's initial login directory.
7. Login program pathname, executed when the user logs in.

The user can change the encrypted password field (second field) by invoking the passwd(1) command, the comment field (fifth field) with the chfn(1) command, and the login program pathname (seventh field) with the chsh(1) command (see the *Unix Reference Manual*). The system administrator sets the remaining fields including the user and group IDs (uid and gid) and audit ID (aid). The aid must be unique; the uid should be unique.

Key security elements are held in the / . secure/etc/passwd file, accessible only to super users. Each entry of / . secure/etc/passwd consists of four fields separated by colons. A typical entry looks like this:

```
robin: a9x0EmtQsK6qc: 101: 1
```

The four fields of the / . secure/etc/passwd file contain the following information (listed in order):

1. User (login) name consisting of up to eight characters
2. Encrypted password
3. Audit ID
4. Audit flag: l=on, 0=off

General users cannot alter any fields in /.secure/etc/passwd.

Eliminating Pseudoaccounts

By tradition, the /etc/passwd file contains numerous "pseudoaccounts." These entries are not associated with individual users and they do not have true interactive login shells. Sometimes these entries have a star in their password field; sometimes they have a password.

Some of these entries, such as date, who, sync, and tty, have evolved strictly for user convenience. To tighten security, these entries should be eliminated from the /etc/passwd so that these programs can be performed only by a user who is logged in. This also prevents a hacker who knows the password of a pseudoaccount from establishing a remote file access connection to the system without a legitimate login.

Other such entries remain in /etc/passwd because they are owners of files. Among them are bin, daemon, adm, uucp, lp, and hpdb.

Manipulating Password Files

The following library routines can be used to access information in the password files:

getpwent	Get password entries from /etc/passwd and / . secure/etc/passwd
getspwent	Get password entries from /. secure/etc/passwd
putpwent	Write password file entries to /etc/passwd
putspwent	Write password file entries to /.secure/etc/passwd

Refer to the *Unix Reference Manual* for detailed specifications.

FILE PERMISSIONS

Unix controls all privileges through user accounts. To the system there are only two kinds of accounts: root and all others. The security system administrator must consider many factors, such as program use and how the programs function, to set appropriate file permissions that help ensure system security without losing functionality.

Consider the principle of "least privilege" and whether a user legitimately needs file access when setting permissions.

Root

Root, or the super user, is a user whose effective user ID is zero. Super users can access and modify any file. In a trusted system, the super user is also the user with the most responsibility for maintaining the security and integrity of the system.

Many commands and system calls can be executed successfully only by a super user. Super users can perform tasks such as the following:

- Invoke any executable command in the system.
- Override any protection placed on user files.
- Add and remove system users.
- Perform other system functions.

Root Use Guidelines

Commands and system calls used only by the system administrator are reserved for the super user. To protect the system, observe the following:

- Restrict knowledge of the root password to a minimum number of people—one, if possible. The root password should be held in strictest secrecy and changed periodically.
- All root accounts should have PATH set (in .profile or . login) to some default that does not contain the current directory ("dot"). The following PATH is recommended:

  bin: /usr/bin: /etc
- Most system administration tasks should be performed by invoking SAM, because its menus restrict choices and thus reduce damage potential.
- If the root user forgets the root password, reboot the system in single-user state and reassign the password.

- Super users should construct at and cron jobs carefully. When at and cron are executed, the system searches the path set by root.
- Set your file creation mask with a umask of 077 before creating a file. This restricts read and write permissions to the file owner by default.
- Do not leave executables where they were developed. Restrict access to executables under development.

System Files and Directories

Permissions on essential Unix programs should be set as restrictively as possible without losing functionality. Most should be set to prevent users from writing to them. These include:

- directories and commands contained in /, bin, /dev, /etc, /usr, /usr/bin, /usr/lib, and /usr/spool
- /ux
- /etc/rc
- /etc/inittab

Only root should be able to write to /etc/passwd. Only root should be able to read from and write to /etc/ . secure/passwd.

PROTECTING KEY SUBSYSTEMS

Programs with owners such as bin, uucp, adm, lp, and daemon encompass entire subsystems and represent a special case. Since they grant access to files they protect or use, these programs must be allowed to function as pseudoaccounts with entries listed in /etc/passwd.

```
root:* :0:3/: /bin/sh
daemon: *: 1:5/ :/bin/sh
bin:*:2:2/bin:/bin/sh
adm: *: 4: 4/usr/adm: /bin/sh
uucp : * :5: 3/usr/spool /uucppublic: /usr/ lib/uucp/uucico
lp: *: 9: 7/usr/spool/lp: /bin/sh
```

A key factor to the privileged status of these subsystems is their ability to grant access to programs under their jurisdiction without granting a user ID of zero. Instead, the setuid bit is set and the uid bit is set equal to the specified subsystem (for example, uid is set to lp).

Once set, security mediation of that subsystem enforces the security of all programs encompassed by the subsystem, not the entire TCB. However, the subsystem's vulnerability to breach of security is also limited to the subsystem files only. Breaches cannot affect the programs under different subsystems (for example, programs under lp do not affect those under daemon).

CRITERIA FOR MODES

The permission bits of Unix programs are set according to the principle of least privilege, which allows access to any object based on "need to know/use" only. The number of setuid-to-root files has been reduced to minimize the risk of Trojan horses or other security breaches. Wherever possible, all setuid programs have been changed to setgid. By default, both owner and group are designated bin. Some setuid programs require a different owner. For example, passwd must be owned by root, but it belongs to group bin.

Directories that do not change often (static directories) should not have any **write** permission whatsoever. Their modes are set to 555, for example:

/bin	555	dr-xr-xr-x	bin	Bin
/dev	555	dr-xr-xr-x	bin	Bin
/lib	555	dr-xr-xr-x	bin	Bin

Directories to which files are added or deleted often (dynamic directories) need **write** permission, for example:

/usr/spool	755	drwxr-xr-x	bin	Bin

Only **execute** and **read** bits of standard binaries (both **setuid** and **setgid**) should be set:

/bin/sh	555	r-xr-xr-x	bin	Bin
/bin/su	4555	r-sr-xr-x	root	Bin
/bin/ps	2555	r-xr-sr-x	bin	Sys

The same guidelines for static and dynamic directories are applicable to executables, scripts, and databases (e.g., **/etc/utmp**, **/etc/wtmp**).

SECURITY CONSIDERATIONS FOR DEVICE FILES

Access to all devices in a system is controlled by device special files that enable programs to be device independent. These files have been shipped with permission settings that enable proper use and maximum security. If installing any other special files, please refer to the **insf** command manual entry or the **/etc/newconfig/mkdev** file for the correct permission settings.

Since device special files can be as vulnerable to tampering as any other file, observe the following precautions:

- Use only Unix-supplied device drivers in your kernel. If you write your own device driver, you invalidate the **Trusted Computing Base**.
- Protect the memory and swap files—**mem**, **kmem**, and **swap**—from casual access, since these files contain user information that has a potential for sabotage. For example, a program that watches memory for an invocation of the **login** program might copy the password from **login**'s buffers when a user types it in.
- All device files should be kept in **/dev**.
- Write-protect all disk special files from general users to prevent inadvertent data corruption.
- Read-protect disk special files to prevent disclosure.
- Terminal ports on Unix systems may be writable by anyone if you are allowing users to communicate by using the **write** or **talk** programs. Only the owner, however, should have **read** permission.
- Individual users should never own a device file other than a terminal device or personal printer.

PROTECTING DISK PARTITIONS

Although disks can be divided into partitions, the concepts described here are applicable to all disks by considering the entire disk as a partition.

- Disk partitions should be readable only by root.
- Since ownership and permissions are stored in the inode, anyone with write permission to a mounted partition can set the user ID for any file in that partition, regardless of the owner, bypassing the chmod() system call and other security checks.
- If a program, such as a database, requires direct access to the partition, that partition should be reserved exclusively for the program and never mounted. Program users should be informed that the file's security is enforced by its permission settings, rather than by the Unix file system.

SYSTEM ACCESS BY MODEM

System access by modem poses security problems similar to those of device special files. To protect against system penetration, observe the following precautions:

- Require the use of a hardware dial-back system for all interactive modems, rather than allowing users to dial in directly, so that the system can authenticate authorization. This will help prevent break-ins by trial and error.
- Require an additional password from modem users by adding an entry for the modem device in the /etc/dialups and possibly /etc/d_passwd files.
- Have users renew their dial-in accounts frequently to ensure that access lists are kept current.
- Cancel modem access promptly when a user is no longer in a company's employ.
- Establish a regular audit schedule (such as four times per year) to review remote usage.
- Maintain adequate protections on the modem access to the system. Connect the modems and dial-back equipment to a single Unix CPU, and allow the use of network services to reach the destination CPU from that point.
- Exceptions to dial-back must be made for UUCP access. Additional restrictions are possible through proper UUCP configuration. Another potential exception is file transfer via kermit.
- If a security breach with unknown factors occurs, shut down the network and telephone access to the computer and inform the network administrator. Open the computer to external access only after identifying and remedying the breach.
- To maximize security when configuring a dial-back modem system, dedicate the dial-out mechanism to the dial-out function only. It should not be configured to accept dial-in. Use another modem on another telephone line for the dial-in service.

MANAGING USER ACCOUNTS

Every user account can potentially enforce or break system security. The organization of user accounts can advance or detract from security goals.

Ideally, users should have easy access to the files, directories, and programs needed for their work and should not be able to use resources they do not need. Through selective privileges, the user can acquire access to resources as needed. In keeping with the concept of least privilege, users should receive the lowest privilege level needed to perform a given task and only for the time needed.

Note: For basic instructions on managing user accounts, refer to the *System Administration Tasks Reference Manual.*

The guidelines to follow for managing user accounts are:

- Use SAM to administer user accounts.
- Group users according to task, security level, and needs. Create specific groups for people working on the projects whose work is confidential.
- The /etc/profile file should deny write permission to general users. Use /etc/profile for mandatory system settings, such as ulimit, instead of placing them in the individual user's .profile file. Further protect /etc/profile by using trap to intercept signals sent to the shell from the same user at another terminal. See the pages on sh(1) or ksh(1) in the *Unix Reference Manual* for information on using the special commands ulimit and trap.
- Maintain a list of what systems the users have accounts on, for accountability and assistance in thoroughly removing a user once the person leaves the organization.

GUIDELINES FOR ADDING A USER ACCOUNT

The guidelines for adding a user account are:

- Use SAM to add a user account.
- Include the user's full name and a work-related identifier (such as phone number) in the fifth field of /etc/passwd. Do not include confidential information, since anyone can read this file.
- Develop a . profile (or . cshrc for C-shell users) file with suitable security settings, including well-defined PATH variables and restrictive umask. Unix default PATH variables are satisfactory. For basic security, set the umask at 022, to create default file permissions of -rw-r- -r- -, which allow only the file owner to write a file.
- Place system directories (written as absolute pathnames) in the user's search path before the home directory.
- Do not include in a user's path variable any open or temporary directories such as /usr/tmp. This will make it less likely that the user will be trapped by an intruder's bogus program whose name matches a standard program.
- Use a separate login name and user ID number for each user to promote accountability.
- Do not assign login names beginning with a number. Chown interprets such strings as user IDs.
- Do not create generic guest accounts. They increase the risk of system penetration because typically they are not well maintained. Even temporary accounts should have sole ownership.
- Place a security policy file in the home directory of a new user's account to call attention to security policy.
- If appropriate, set password aging.

PASSWORD AGING ON USER ACCOUNTS

When creating a new user account with the SAM interface, password aging can be initiated by placing the necessary information in the password field. For example, one can add a new user, force that user to enter a password at initial login and establish password aging by entering the following in SAM's highlighted field "Enter Password":

,81..

This series of characters, the comma followed by digits and two dots, causes the user to receive the message Your password has expired at initial login, and requires the user to enter a password. Once the password is established, the user is required to change the password every ten weeks and no sooner than three weeks.

See passwd(4) in the *Unix Reference Manual* for full details on establishing password aging.

GUIDELINES FOR DEACTIVATING A USER ACCOUNT

Sometimes it is necessary to deactivate an account temporarily, or pending removal. Deactivate the account as soon as it is established that the user no longer needs access. The administrative task involves the following procedure:

- Before deactivating the account, invoke who to see whether the user is logged in. If so, communicate via write or other means to ask the user to log out.
- Verify that the user has no active processes by typing **"Ps -fu <user>,"** then kill any current processes before deactivating the account.
- Inform other users in the same group of the intention to remove the account. They may then copy needed files or adjust absolute pathnames and environment variables.
- Invoke SAM to deactivate the account.

GUIDELINES FOR REACTIVATING A USER ACCOUNT

The following guidelines can be used to reactivate a user account:

- Use SAM to reactivate a user account.
- To allow the user to set the password, respond to the SAM query for a password with ,.. and on logging in the user is prompted to set a new password.

GUIDELINES FOR REMOVING AN ACCOUNT

To reduce the chance of system penetration, remove an account as soon as a user leaves an organization or no longer requires computer access. To remove an account follow these steps:

- Make a backup copy of the user's directory tree so that the account can be reconstructed if necessary.
- Remove all the files and other objects in the user's hierarchy by using the recursive form of the rm command rm -rf <home_directory>.
- Locate any files owned by the user but residing in other users' hierarchies by using find / -user <user> -print. Consider who should own them. Remove any trivial files. Transfer ownership of necessary files to the logical owner by using the chown(1) command.

- Search the system for files owned by the user after removing the home directory structure. Look for a file in /usr/spool/cron/crontabs. Remove reference to the user in cron. allow and cron. deny.

  rm /usr/spool/cron/crontabs/<user>
- Look for the user's at jobs, which by default are found in /usr/spool/cron/atjobs. To remove them, type the following commands:

  at -l

  at -r <job_number>

  Remove reference to the user in at . allow and at . deny.
- Remove the user's mailbox from /usr/mail.
- Use the find(1) command to locate all files in which the user is explicitly included in an ACL entry, as follows:

  find <user> -hidden -acl '<user>.%' -print

  If appropriate, notify the file owner and remove the ACL entry.
- Remove reference to the user in /usr/lib/aliases or redirect the user's mail, if appropriate.
- A user might have accounts on other systems that one does not administer. Inform other system administrators to remove the user.
- Use SAM to remove the account.

GUIDELINES FOR MOVING A USER ACCOUNT

Moving a user account from one system to another is trickier than it seems.

- Use SAM to add the user to the new system.
- Make sure the user's uid and gid do not already exist on the new system. If either does, the user must be reassigned a new one for the new system, and the uid and/or gid of all of the user's files must be changed. Do so from the user's home directory, referred to as an absolute pathname:

  find <directory> -user <old_uid> -exec chown <new_uid> {} \;

  or

  find <directory> -group <old_gid> -exec chgrp <new_gid> {} \;
- Copy the user's files from the old to the new system.
- Remove or deactivate the user from the old system.
- Move the user's /usr/mail/<user> file.
- If acquiring a user from a system one does not administer, or the user is moving from a less to more secure environment, check the user's files carefully for setuid/setgid programs. Remove any setuid/setgid programs that might compromise security.

GUIDELINES FOR ADDING A GROUP

Because teams of employees typically require access to common files and directories, define groups of users in the /etc/group and link it to /etc/logingroup. All members of a group acquire the group ID (gid) when logging in. Users can belong to more than one group; access to resources can be governed by group membership. The administrator should have sole access to /etc/group and /etc/logingroup, which are manipulated using the newgrp and chgrp commands (for /etc/group) or through the login command or initgroups library routine (for the /etc/logingroup file). (Refer to the system administration reference manual for details on the use of specific systems.)

Groups may be used to deny access by individuals to objects such as shared memory segments and message queues. To deny access using groups, one can create a group that contains all users except the individual denied access. For files, use ACLs to set selective access.

When adding a group:

- Use SAM to add a group.
- Place users with similar needs or in the same project in the same group. This enables users to make links to each other's data, or conveniently access it rather than having to copy files or directories unnecessarily.
- Add a group any time a new project joins the user base.
- Do not assign group names beginning with numbers because the chgrp command treats such names as a gid.
- Group and user IDs in /etc/group and /etc/passwd should be consistent, although no tool exists to verify the consistency. Make sure that both contain the same group ID whenever a change is made.
- Create a new group for a user who needs privacy for development or other highly confidential work.

GUIDELINES FOR REMOVING A GROUP

Following are the guidelines for removing a group:

- Groups without members should be removed, but first find any files or directories with the group's ID. Conduct the search from a directory where you would expect to find the gid and refer to the directory as an absolute pathname. Invoke the following command: find <directory> -group <group_name> -print.
- Either assign new group IDs to these files or remove them.
- Use SAM to remove a group.

GUIDELINE FOR MODIFYING A GROUP

The following is the guideline for modifying a group:

- Use SAM to modify a group.

CONTROLLING FILE ACCESS SELECTIVELY

Unix already enables nonprivileged users or processes to set access to files and other objects through the user and/or group identity (see passwd(4) and group(4) in the *Unix Reference Manual*). This level of control is accomplished by setting or changing a file's permission bits to grant or restrict access by owner, group, or others (also see chmod(2) in the *Unix Reference Manual*).

ACCESS CONTROL ENTRIES

Access control lists are a key enforcement mechanism of discretionary access control (DAC), for specifying access to objects by users and groups more selectively than traditional Unix mechanisms allow, based on the user's legitimate need for access.

ACLs offer a greater degree of selectivity than permission bits by allowing the file owner or super user to set (permit or deny) access to individual users or groups.

An ACL consists of sets of entries associated with a file to specify permissions. Each entry specifies for one user-ID/group-ID combination a set of read, write, and execute/search access permissions, and is represented in the syntax (user. group, mode). ACLs are supported for files only.

Comparing ACLs and File Permissions

To understand the relationship between access control lists and traditional file permissions, consider the following file and its permissions:

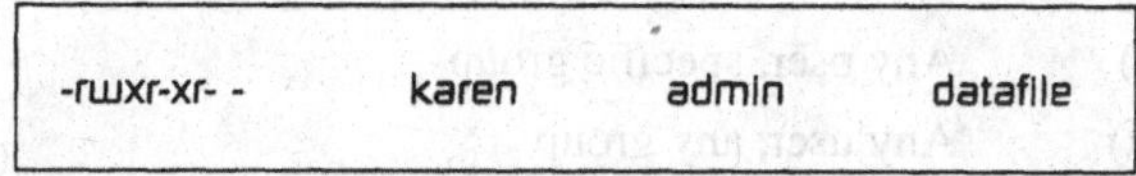

The file owner is user karen.

The file owner's group is admin.

The name of the file is datafile.

The file owner's permissions are rwx.

The file group's permissions are r-x.

The file other permissions are r- -.

In an ACL, user and group IDs can be represented by names or numbers found in /etc/passwd. The following special symbols can also be used:

% No specific user or group

@ Current file owner or group

Base ACL Entries Equal File Mode Permissions

When a file is created, three base access control list entries are mapped from the file's access permission bits to match a file's owner and group and its traditional permission bits. Base ACL entries can be changed by the chmod() and setacl() system calls.

(uid.%, mode)	Base ACL entry for the file's owner
(%.gid, mode)	Base ACL entry for the file's group
(%.%,mode)	Base entry for other users

(Except where noted, examples are represented in short form notation. See the section on ACL notation.)

Granting Selective Access with Optional ACLs

Optional access control list entries contain additional access control information that the user can set with the setacl () system call to further allow or deny file access. Up to thirteen additional user-group combinations can be specified. For example, the following optional access control list entries can be associated with the file:

(mary. admin, rwx)	Grant read, write, and execute access to user mary in group admin.
(george.%,- - -)	Deny any access to user george in any group.

Access Check Algorithm

ACL entries can be categorized by four levels of specificity based on their user and group IDs. In access checking, ACL entries are compared by effective user and group IDs in the following order:

(u.g, rwx)	Specific user, specific group
(u.%, rwx)	Specific user, any group
(%.g, rwx)	Any user, specific group
(%.%, rwx)	Any user, any group

Once an ACL entry is matched, only other entries at the same level of specificity are checked. More specific entries that match take precedence over any less specific matches.

In the Berkeley model, a process might have more than one group ID, in which case more than one (u.g, mode) or (%.g, mode) entry might apply for that process. (See setgroups(2) in the *Unix Reference Manual.*) Under these circumstances, the access modes in all matching entries (of the same level of specificity, u.g or %.g) are mode together. Access is granted if the resulting mode bits permit. Since entries are unique, their order in each entry type is insignificant.

Because traditional Unix permission bits are mapped into ACLs as base ACL entries, they are included in access checks. If a request is made for more than one type of access, such as opening a file for both reading and writing, access is granted only if the process is allowed all requested types of access. Note that access can be granted if the process has two groups in its groups list, one of which is only allowed read access and the other is only allowed write access. Even if the requested access is not granted by any one entry, it may be granted by a combination of entries as a result of the process belonging to several groups.

ACL Uniqueness

All ACL entries must be unique. For every pair of u and g values, there can be only one (u.g, mode) entry; one (u.%, mode) entry for a given value of u; one (%.g, mode) entry for a given value of g; and one (%.%,mode) entry for each file. Thus, an ACL can have a (23.14, mode) entry and a (23.%, mode) entry, but not two (23.14, mode) entries or two (23.%,. mode) entries.

How to Use ACL Notation

Supported library calls and commands that manage ACLs recognize three different symbolic representations:

operator form	Used to input entire ACLs and modify existing ACLs in a syntax similar to that used by the chmod(1) command.
short form	Easier to read, intended primarily for output. The chacl(1) command accepts this form as input to interpret output from the lsacl(1) command.
long form	A multiline format easiest to read, but supported only for output.

The base ACL entries of our example file are represented in the three notations as follows:

Operator form karen.%.= rwx, %.admin = rx, %.% = r

Short form (karen.%,rwx) (%.admin , r-x) (%.%, r- -)

Long form rwx karen.%

r-x %.admin

r- -%.%

Some library calls and commands use a variant format known as ACL Patterns (described later in this section).

Operator Form of ACLs (Input Only)

Each entry consists of a user identifier and group identifier, followed by one or more operators and mode characters, as in the mode syntax accepted by the chmod(1) command. Multiple entries are separated by commas.

```
user . group operator mode [ operator mode] . . . , . . .
```

The entire ACL must be a single argument, and thus should be quoted to the shell if it contains spaces or special characters. Spaces are ignored except within names. A null ACL is legitimate and means either "no access" or "no changes" depending on context. Each user or group ID may be represented by:

name Valid user or group name.

number Valid numeric ID value.

% Any user or group, as appropriate.

@ Current file owner or group, as appropriate; useful for referring to a file's u.% and %.g base ACL entries.

An operator is required in each entry. Operators are:

= Set all bits in the entry to the given mode value.

+ Set the indicated mode bits in the entry.

- Clear the indicated mode bits in the entry.

The mode is an octal value of zero through seven or any combination of r, w, and x. A null mode denies access if the operator is =, or represents "no change" if the operator is + or -.

Multiple entries and multiple operator-mode parts in an entry are applied in the order specified. If more than one entry or operator for a user and group are specified, the last specified entry or operator takes effect. Entries need not appear in any particular order.

Note that the chmod(1) command allows only u, g, o, or a to refer symbolically to the file owner, group, other, or all users, respectively. Since ACLs work with arbitrary user and group identifiers, @ is provided as a convenience. The exact syntax is:

```
acl     ::= [entry[,entry]. . .]
entry   ::= id . id op mode [op mode]. . .
id      ::= name I number I % I @
op      ::= = I + I -
mode    ::= 0..7 I [char[char]. . .]
char    :: = r I w I x
```

Using chacl to Set ACL Entries (Operator Form)

Note: For basic instructions on setting access control list entries, see the information on the chacl(1) command in the *Unix Reference Manual.*

The following example sets the %.% entry to restrict other users to only reading myfile.

```
chacl '%.% = r' myfile
```

The following allows user bill in any group to write the file, assuming that no restrictive entry is more specific than the bill .%. entry (for example, a bill. adm entry that denies writing). (For information on the order in which ACLs evaluate access, see the section "Access Check Algorithm.")

```
chacl 'bill.%. +w' myfile
```

The following ACL contains two entries. The first one deletes write- and adds read-capability to the entry for user 12, group 4. The second entry denies access for any unspecified user in any unspecified group. The two entries are separated by a comma and a required space.

```
chacl '12.4-w+r, %.%. =' myfile
```

The following pair of entries sets the current user entry for the file's owner to allow both read and execute and results in adding write and execute capabilities for other users (the % .% entry). Note that a mode character (x) is repeated for illustration.

```
chacl '@.% = 5, %.% + xwx' myfile
```

Short Form of ACLs (Input and Output)

Short form differs from operator form in several ways:

- Entries are separated by parentheses rather than commas.
- Each entry specifies the mode, including all mode bits. It is not possible to change the mode value with + and - operators. However, the comma functions like the = operator in operator form.
- For clarity, hyphens represent unset permission bits in the output of the mode field and are allowed in input. This resembles the mode output style used by the ls -l command.

Multiple entries are concatenated. For consistency with operator form, a dot (.) is used to separate user and group identifiers.

On output, no spaces are printed except in names (if any). Identifier numbers are printed if no matching names are known. Either identifier can be printed as % for "any user or group." The mode is always represented by three characters: (r, w, and x) and padded with hyphens for unset mode bits. If the ACL is read from the system, entries are ordered by specificity then by numeric values of identifier parts. On input, the entire ACL must be delimited by quotation marks to retain its quality as a single argument, since it might contain spaces or special characters such as parentheses. Spaces are ignored except within names. A null ACL is legitimate and means either "no access" or "no changes" depending on context. User and group identifiers are represented as in operator form. The mode is represented by an octal value of zero through seven or any combination of r, w, x. A null mode denies access.

Redundancy does not result in error; the last entry for any user.group combination takes effect. Entries need not appear in any particular order. The exact syntax is:

```
acl   ::= [entry[entry]. . .]
entry ::= (id . id,mode)
id    ::= name | number | % | @
mode ::= 0..7 | [char[char]. . .]
char  :: = r | w | x
```

Examples of ACL Entries in Short Form

The following is a sample ACL as it might be printed. It allows user jpc to read or execute the file while in group adm, it denies user ajs access to the file while in group trux, it allows user jpc in any group (except adm) to only read the file, any other user in group bin may read or execute the file, and any other user may only read the file.

```
(jpc.adm,r-x) (ajs.trux,- - -) (jpc.%,r- -) (%.bin,r-x) (%.%,r- -)
```

On input, the following example allows other users to only read myfile:

```
chacl '(%.%,r)' myfile
```

The following sets write-only access for user bill in any group:

```
chacl '(bill.%, -w-)' myfile
```

The following sets the entry for user 12 in group 4 to allow read and write:

```
chacl '(12.4,wr)' myfile
```

The following sets the base ACL entry for the file's owner to allow both read and execute, and sets write and execute capabilities for other (%,%) users:

```
chacl '(@.%, 5) (%.%, xwx)' myfile
```

Long Form of ACLs (Output Only)

Each entry occupies a single line of output. The mode appears first in a fixed-width field, using hyphens (unset mode bits) for easy vertical scanning. Each user and group identifier is shown as a name, if known, a number, if unknown, or % for "any user or group." Entries are ordered from most to least specific then by numeric values of the identifiers. Note that every ACL printed has at least three entries, the base ACL entries (i.e., uid.%,%.gid, and %.%).

The exact syntax is:

```
acl   = entry [<newline>entry]
entry = mode<space>id.id
mode  = <r ξ - > <w ξ -> < x ξ ->
id    = name ξ number ξ %
```

Here is the same ACL as in an earlier example, printed in long form.

```
r-x    jpc.adm
- - -  ajs.trux
r- -   jpc.%
r-x    %.bin
r- -   %.%
```

ACL Patterns

Some library calls and commands recognize and use ACL patterns instead of exact ACLs. This allows operations on all entries that match the patterns. ACL syntax is extended in the following ways:

Wildcard user and group IDs	A user or group name of * (asterisk) matches the user or group ID in any entry including % (any user or group).
Mode bits on, off, or ignored	For operator-form input, the operators =, +, and - are applied as follows: = Entry mode value matches this mode value exactly + These bits turned on in entry mode value - These bits turned off in entry mode value When only + and - operators are used, commands ignore the values of unspecified mode bits. Short form patterns treat the mode identically to the = operator in operator form.
Wildcard mode values	A mode of * (asterisk) in operator or short form input (e.g., ajs.%* or ajs.%,*) matches any mode value, provided no other is given in an operator-form entry. Also, the mode part of an entry can be omitted for the same effect.
Entries not combined	Entries with matching user and group ID values are not combined. Each entry specified is applied separately by commands that accept patterns.

The following command locates files whose ACLs contain an entry that allows **read** access and denies **write** access to any **user .group** combination.

```
find / -acl '*.*+r-w' -print
```

The following matches entries for any user in **group bin** and for user **tammy** in any group, regardless of the entries' mode values. Matching optional ACL entries are deleted and mode values in matching base ACL entries are set to zero:

```
chacl -d '%.bin, tammy.*=*' myfile
```

The following matches all entries, deleting optional entries and setting mode values of base ACL entries to zero:

```
chacl -d '(*.*,*)' myfile
```

WORKING WITH ACL FUNCTIONALITY

New ACL Commands and Programs

This section describes the new programs available to manipulate a file's access control list information. For the detailed specifications, refer to the *Unix Reference Manual.*

Commands

chacl(1)	Change (add, modify, delete, copy) access control lists of files, restrict access to files, convert specified ACL information into base permission bits.
getaccess(1)	List access rights to files.
lsacl(1)	List access control lists of files.

System Calls

getaccess(2)	Get a user's effective access rights to a file.
getacl, fgetacl (2)	Get access control list information.
setacl, fsetacl (2)	Set access control list information.

Library Routines

acltostr (3c)	Convert ACL structure to string form.
chownacl (3c)	Change owner and/or group represented in a file's access control list.
cpacl, fcpacl (3c)	Copy the access control list and mode bits from one file to another.
setaclentry, fsetaclentry (3c)	Add, modify, or delete an entry in a file's access control list.
strtoacl (3c)	Parse and convert ACL structure to string form.
strtoaclpatt (3c)	Parse and convert ACL pattern strings to arrays.

Existing Unix Core Programs and ACLs

Optional ACL entries are affected by numerous Unix commands, system calls, and subroutine libraries; sometimes in unexpected ways. This section identifies issues critical to using familiar Unix programs on a system in which access control lists are implemented. For the detailed specifications, refer to the *Unix Reference Manual* for the specific entry.

The general purpose commands and system calls are:

chmod(1)	Use the -A option to retain ACLs.
chmod(2)	All optional ACL entries are deleted when chmod() is executed. Use getacl() and setacl() to save and restore the permission bits of ACL entries.
cpset(1)	Cpset does not set a file's optional ACL entries.
find(1)	New functionality enables find to identify files whose ACL entries match or include specific ACL patterns.
ls(1)	In long form, ls indicates the existence of ACLs by displaying a + after the file's permission bits.
mailx(1)	Mailx does not support optional ACL entries on /usr/mail/* files.
compact(1)	These programs copy optional ACL entries to the new files they create.
compress(1)	
cp(1) ed(1)	
makecdf(1)	
pack(1)	
unpack(1)	

The file archive commands are:

frecover(1M), fbackup (1M)	Use only these programs to selectively recover and backup files. However, use the -A option when backing up and recovering files for use on systems that do not implement ACLs.
ar(1), cpio(1)	These programs do not retain ACLs when archiving and restoring. They use the st_mode value returned by stat ().
ftio(1)	
shar(1)	
tar(1)	
dump(1m)	
restore(1M)	

The configuration control commands are:

SCCS, RCS	The commands in these packages do not support ACLs. As a general practice, do not place optional ACL entries on system software. They are not preserved across updates.

Access control lists use additional, "continuation inodes" when creating new file systems. Consider them when using the following programs. The file system commands are:

fsck(1M)	Fsck returns the number of files with optional ACL entries as a value for icont. Use the -p option to clear unreferenced continuation inodes.
diskusg(1m), ncheck(1m)	These commands ignore continuation inodes.
mkfs(1M)	Allow for continuation modes on new disks.

ACLs in a Network Environment

ACLs are not visible on remote files by Remote File Access (RFA) or Network File Systems (NFS), although their control over access permissions remains effective. Individual manual entries specify the behavior of various system calls, library calls, and commands under these circumstances. Use caution when transferring a file with optional entries over a network, or when manipulating a remote file, because optional entries may be deleted with no indication.

CONTROLLING USER ACCESS TO DIRECTORIES AND FILES

This section explains the following concepts:

- How to list and change directory and file permissions.
- How to restrict access to directories and files using access control lists (ACLs).
- How to protect directories from file tampering.

ASSIGNING FILE PERMISSIONS TO SPECIFIC USERS AND GROUPS

In a traditional Unix system, the ls -l command can be used to see a full listing of a file's permissions and ls -ld to list a directory's permissions. The chmod(1) command enables the user to change the mode permissions of directories and files.

On a secure system, to assign permissions to specific users and groups, use the lsacl(1) command to see what permissions are associated with a given file and the chacl(1) command to change the access control lists of the file.

Listing File Permissions

To see exactly who can access certain files and directories and what permissions are set on them, use the lsacl command. The general form of the lsacl command is as follows:

```
$ lsacl file_ name
```

The system will respond with a listing in this general form:

```
(user.group, mode)... file_name
```

where (**user.group, mode**) is an ACL entry (there will always be at least three ACL entries), and **file_name** is the name of the file or directory for which a listing is needed. The following exhibit describes what each element of an ACL entry means:

This element . . .	*Means . . .*
User	The user's login name; a percent sign (%) in this position means all users.
Group	The user's group; a percent sign (%) in this position means all groups.
mode	The permissions allowed: **read (r), write (w), execute/search (x)**. A dash (-) means a permission is denied (for example, **rw-** means that **read** and **write** permissions are allowed, but **execute/search** permission is denied).

Suppose you run the **lsacl** command on **myfile**:

```
$ lsacl myfile
(sally.adm,rw-) (leslie.%,r- - -) (%.mtg,r- -) (%.%.,- - -) myfile
```

Interpret the preceding listing as follows:

(sally. adm,rw-)	The user **sally** while in the group **adm** has **read** and **write** permissions (**rw-**) on **myfile**.
(leslie.%,r- -)	The user **leslie** while in any group (%) has **read** permission (**r- -**) on **myfile**.
(%.mtg,r- -)	Any user (%) in the group **mtg** has **read** permission (**r- -**) on **myfile**.
(%.%,- - -)	No other user (%) from any other group (%) has **read, write**, or **execute** permissions (- - -) on **myfile**.

The following section explains how to change file and directory permissions using ACLs.

Changing Permissions

Like the **chmod(l)** command, which enables one to change general permissions on files and directories, the **chacl(l)** command allows one to grant or restrict file access to or from specific users or specific groups of users. For example, you may want a particular file or directory to be accessible to only one other person. To do so, use the **chacl (change acl)** command to grant or restrict file access to or from specific users or groups of users.

How the chmod and chacl Commands Interact

Since both the **chmod** and the **chacl** commands can be used to change access permissions, an awareness of how the two commands interact is necessary.

- The **chcl** command is a superset of the **chmod** command. Any specific permissions assigned to the **chcl** command are added to the more general permissions assigned with the **chmod** command. For example, suppose you use the **chmod** command to allow only yourself **write** permission to **myfile**. You can use the **chcl** command to make an exception and allow your manager **write** permission to **myfile** also. Users other than yourself and your manager will still be denied **write** permission as previously specified by the **chmod** command.

- Use **chmod** with the **-A** option when working with files that have additional permissions assigned with the **chcl** command. The additional permissions will be deleted if the **-A** option with **chmod** is not used. For example, to keep ACL permissions on the file **myfile**, enter **$ chmod -A number myfile.**

Using the chacl Command

The general form for the **chacl** command is as follows:

$ chcl ' user.group operator mode' file_name

user Indicates the user's login name; a percent sign (%) in this position means all users.

group Indicates the user's group; a percent sign (%) in this position means all groups.

operator Indicates whether you are adding or denying permissions to existing ACL entries or whether you are adding new ACL entries. A plus sign (+) adds permissions, a minus sign (-) denies permissions, and an equals sign (=) means "this permission exactly," and is usually used when adding new ACL entries.

mode Indicates the permissions allowed. Possible modes are **read (r)**, **write (w)**, and **execute/search (x)**. An operator (explained previously) immediately precedes the mode (e.g., **+rw** adds **read** and **write** permissions; **-rw** denies **read** and **write** permissions).

File_name Indicates the name of the file for which you want to specify access.

Suppose your user name is **Ali**, and you are in the group **users**. If you need to limit access to **myfile** so anyone in your group can read the file, but *only* you and your manager (**Yusuf**) can both **read** from and **write** to the file, follow these steps:

- First, use the **chmod** command to protect **myfile** so your group can read it, but only you can both **read** from and **write** to the file. (*Note:* If you have any previously set ACL entries, **chmod** deletes them unless the **-A** option is used):

  $ chmod 640 myfile

- To view the permissions just set, run the **ll** command on **myfile**:

  $ ll myfile

  -rw-r- - - - - 1 Ali users 236 Dec 8 14:04 myfile

  The **ll** command shows that **owner (Ali)** has **read** and **write** permission on **myfile**; **group (users)** has only **read** permission; and **other** has no access to the file.

- Now use the **lsacl** command to compare the preceding long listing with the ACL entries:

  $ lsacl myfile

  (Ali.%,rw-) (%.users,r- -)(%.%,- - -) myfile

  The **lsacl** command shows that **Ali** in any group (%) has **read** and **write** permission to **myfile**; anyone (%) in the group **users** has **read** permission to **myfile**; and everyone else has no access to **myfile**.

Exhibit 6.2 Using chacl Command

If you want to . . .	Use this command . . .
Create a new ACL entry allowing the user cyc in any group (%) read and write (=rw) access to myfile.	$ chacl 'cyc.%=rw' myfile
Modify an existing ACL entry allowing all users (%) in all groups (%) read (+r) access to foofile.	$ chad '%.%+r' foofile
Modify an existing ACL entry denying all users (%) in the adm group write (-w) access to afile.	$ chacl '%.adm-w' afile
Create a new ACL entry denying user jon in the mkt group read, write, or execute/search access to olddir.	$ chacl 'jon.mkt=' olddir

- To specify that your manager, who is in a different group (mtg), should have read and write access to myfile, use the chacl command to create a new ACL entry for myfile:

  $ chacl ' yusuf.mtg=rw' myfile
- Now run the ll command on myfile:

  $ ll myfile

  -rw-r- - - - - + 1 Ali users 236 Dec 8 14:04 myfile

  The plus sign (+) at the end of the permissions string means that additional permissions (in the form of optional ACL entries) exist for myfile.
- Run the lsacl command to view these optional ACL entries:

  $ lsacl myfile

  (yusuf.mtg,rw-)(Ali.%,rw-) (%.users,r- -)(%.%.,- - -) myfile

  The lsacl command now shows that, in addition to the previous ACL entries, yusuf of the group mtg has read and write permission to myfile.

Because directories are also files, the same technique of using lsacl and chacl can be used to set selective access to directories.

Exhibit 6.2 further illustrates ways to use the chacl command.

PROTECTING DIRECTORIES FROM FILE TAMPERING

If a directory is writable, anyone can remove its files, regardless of the permissions on the files themselves. The only way to ensure that no files can be removed from a directory is to remove write permission from that directory. For maximum protection this technique can be applied to the directory of a user account.

1. Create a confidential directory. To hide the directory's name from routine view, use a dot (.) as the first character of its name.

   $ mkdir .secret
2. Move sensitive files into the directory.

   $ mv report1 report2 .secret

3. Use ll -d to view the permissions set on the directory.

   $ ll -d .secret

   drwxrwxr-x 1 leslie users 236 Dec 8 14:04 .secret

4. Use the chmod(1) command to change the permission modes of the directory to restrict access to the owner only.

   $ chmod g=,o= .secret

   The symbolic notation denies read, write, and execute access to members of the group (g) and all other (o) users.

5. List the permissions on the directory.

   $ ll -d .secret

   drwx- - - - - 1 leslie users 236 Dec 8 14:04 .secret

6. To allow another person to access that directory also, use the chacl(1) and lsacl(1) commands.

   $ chacl 'yusuf.%=rwx' .secret

   $ ll -d .secret

   drwx- - - - - + 1 ali users 236 Dec 8 14:04 .secret

   The plus sign (+) after the permission modes indicates that ACLs are set on the directory.

7. Use the lsacl command to list the ACLs.

   $ lsacl .secret

   (ali.%,rwx) (%.users,- - -) (%.%,- - -) (yusuf.%.,rwx) .secret

   In this example, only the users Ali and Yusuf can access the directory secret.

The default umask setting in a secure (trusted) system is should be set to 022. This means that all directories created will have a default permission mode of 755, granting access of drwxr-xr-x. All files created will have the default permission mode of 644, granting access of rw-r- - r- -.

OPERATING SYSTEM AND FILE PROTECTION

Let us discuss how the operating system and files should be protected. This section provides tools that one can use to:

- Assess system files for potential security risks and then converting it to a secure (trusted) system.
- Review system files for routine security maintenance.
- Locate suspicious files in case of security breach.

Before you install Unix, you must inspect your system for files that pose a potential risk to security. Thereafter, on a regularly scheduled and ongoing basis, and whenever you suspect any breach of security, examine your system to locate problem files.

LOOKING FOR SETUID AND SETGID PROGRAMS

Since setuid and setgid programs pose the greatest security liability to a system,

- Note which programs are setuid and setgid.
- Stay vigilant of any changes to them.

- Investigate further any programs that appear to be needlessly setuid.
- Change the permission of any unnecessary setuid program to setgid.

The long form of the ls command (ll or ls -l) shows setuid programs by listing s instead of - or x for the owner-execute permission. It shows setgid programs by listing s instead of - or x for the group-execute permission. The audit techniques are:

- To locate setuid or setgid programs in the hierarchy, list the files returned by the find command:

```
$ find $HOME \( -perm -4000 -o -perm -2000 \) \
-exec ls -ld {} \;
```

- Periodically, find and list all setuid programs:

```
find / -hidden -perm -4000 -exec ls -ld {} \;
```

Or, list setuid and setgid programs in system directories:

```
find [directories] \( -perm -4000 -o -perm -2000 \) \
-exec ls -ld {} \;
```

- Review the output for the following unexpected results:
  - Expect to find system files, but they should display the same permissions as shown in the pdf files provided unless they have been customized.
  - Setuid-to-root programs are the most significant.
  - Setuid to other users are less significant, but might warrant concern.
  - Users normally should not have setuid programs, especially setuid to users other than themselves. Do not run a user's personal setuid program, since you may not know what that program may be doing.
- Examine the code of all programs imported from external sources for destructive programs known as "Trojan horses."
- Never restore a setuid program for which there is no source to examine. If suspecting trouble, delete the file.
- Most locally written programs reside in /usr/local/bin and may be restored if you know exactly what they do.

VERIFYING PASSWORD FILE SECURITY

Before conversion, passwords are located in /etc/passwd. In a trusted system, passwords are located in / .secure/etc/passwd.

No empty password fields in either password file should be permitted. The conversion tools replace any empty password fields in /etc/passwd with ,.. to force the user to select a password on first login. Nonetheless, even this leaves a potential for security breach by allowing any user to set the password for that account. The audit concerns are:

- Before converting to a trusted system, look for empty password fields or fields that force the user to set a password by typing awk -F: '$2 == " " $2 == ",..." ' </etc/passwd.
- Once the system has been converted to a trusted system, periodically look for password fields or fields that force the user to set a password by typing awk -F: '$2 == " " $2 == ",..."' </.secuxe/etc/passwd.

- On a trusted system, the password fields of the /etc/passwd file should contain an asterisk. To find deviations, type awk -F: '$2 ! = "*" ' /etc/passwd.
- Every user should have a unique user ID (uid), and should have the same uid on each computer system for which one has an account. To locate duplicate user IDs, type sort -t: +2n /etc/passwd ξ \awk -F: '{if (duplicate == $3) print; duplicate = $3}. Only root and users with root privileges (user ID of 0) should be found. Inspect those accounts to make sure that the users warrant root privilege. Assign new user IDs to any ordinary users with duplicate IDs.

PROTECTING USER ACCOUNTS

Home directories should not be writable because they allow any user to add and remove files from them. To find home directories that are writable by others, run:

```
find 'awk -F: '{print $6}' /etc/passwd` \
-prune -perm -02 -exec ls -ld '{}' \;
```

Here is an example of output:

```
drwxrwxrwx      6    cwagner    topaz    2048    Feb 16  07:18
/mnt/topaz/cwagner
drwxrwxrwx      2    ekr        topaz    1024    Aug 10  19:88
/mnt/topaz/ekr
drwxrwxrwx      10   achoy      topaz    2048    Jun 8   12:49
/mnt/topaz/achoy
drwxrwxrwx      2    gnuss      topaz    1024    May 5   15:12
/mnt/topaz/gnuss
drwxrwxrwx      15   jacques    topaz    3072    Jum 13  17:35
/mnt/topaz/jacques
```

Set directory permissions to drwxrwxr-x, to grant write permission only to group members:

```
chmod 775 [directory]
```

If confidentiality requires that even group members be denied write access to a directory, set the permissions to drwxr—xr—x:

```
chmod 755 [directory]
```

Users' .profile, .cshrc, and .login files should not be writable by anyone other than the account owner. To find those that are writable by group members or others, run:

```
find 'awk -F: '{printf "%.s/.profile\n", $6}' /etc/passwd' \
-prune -perm -022 -exec ls -l '{}' \;
find 'awk -F: '{printf "%s/.cshrc\n', $6}' /etc/passwd' \
-prune -perm -022 -exec ls -l '{}' \;
find 'awk -F: '{printf "%s/.login\n", $6}' /etc/passwd' \
-prune -perm -022 -exec ls -l '{}' \;
```

The message "find: cannot stat. . ." means that the user does not have the file listed. This is a warning only and can be ignored.

A user's .rhosts file should not be readable or writable by anybody other than the owner. This precaution prevents users from guessing what other accounts you have, as well as preventing anyone from editing the .rhosts file to gain access to those systems. To find readable or writable .rhosts files, run:

```
find 'awk -F: '{printf "%s/.rhosts\n", $6}' /etc/passwd' \
-prune -perm -066 -exec ls -l '{}' \;
```

In this command, awk prints the sixth field (the home directory) of every entry in /etc/passwd, followed by the string .rhosts and a carriage return (\n). This output is then evaluated by the option of find, which searches for and displays a long listing (ls -l) of any entries that grant read or write permissions to group or other (-066).

The message "find: cannot stat . . . " is returned if the user does not have a .rhosts file. This is a warning only and can be ignored.

Use of a ..netrc file is discouraged, since it bypasses .login authentication for remote login and even contains the user's unencrypted password. If used at all, .netrc must not be readable or writable by anyone other than its owner. To find readable or writable .netrc files, run:

```
find 'awk -F: '{printf "%s/.netrc\n", $6}' /etc/passwd' \
-prune -perm -066 -exec ls -l '{}' \;
```

Some systems maintain an /etc/securetty file, which should not be writable. If it exists on the system, use ls -l /etc/securetty to verify that its modes are correct.

MAINTAINING DEVICE FILE SECURITY

To ensure the integrity of devices, check the device special files for potential security hazards. Character and block special devices should reside only in /dev. To find and list files of a particular type (such as b for block special files, c for character special files, or d for directories), type

```
find / -hidden -name /dev -prune -o -type b -exec ls -l {} \;
```

Devices found anywhere other than /dev should be removed unless they have been added for a specific reason. No individual user should own a device file.

Before mounting disks or other mountable devices of unknown origin, first check its files for special files and setuid programs:

```
ncheck -s /dev/dsk/ [device name]
```

This program, which takes several moments to run, provides only a first impression of the unmounted device. It returns inode and file names relative to slash (/). It cannot give a long listing of the unmounted files' permissions.

If deciding that any of the listed setuid files might pose a risk, mount the device special file with its setuid bit inhibited as follows:

```
/etc/mount -o nosuid /dev/dsk/[device name] [mount point]
```

Consider this only a temporary measure, and be sure to investigate the problem promptly. Delete the file if it threatens system security.

RISKS TO THE UNIX OPERATING SYSTEM

This section addresses both preventive and emergency risk management by discussing the risks associated with **setuid** and **setgid** programs and describing how Unix safeguards the operating system environment.

OVERALL RISK MANAGEMENT GUIDELINES

Follow these steps for converting to a trusted system:

1. Familiarize yourself with the elements of the system comprising the Trusted Computing Base (TCB). The Trusted Computing Base (TCB) contains all the elements of the computer system (hardware, firmware, and software) necessary to create a protected environment and allow for its use in processing a range of sensitive or classified information. The TCB consists of the kernel and all key operating system components, including **login**, **getty**, **backup**, **restore**, **sam**, and other utilities essential to run and support the system. The TCB enforces security policy by controlling access to code and data on which the protection is based and by providing auditing capability.
2. Leave system file permissions set restrictively to maintain secure usage.
3. Safeguard system programs by limiting the impact of **setuid** programs whenever possible.
4. Use ACLs to restrict or permit access to data selectively.
5. Both system software and user files pose security risks. Before converting to a trusted system, be sure that all existing user files are free of security hazards. Also, review the sction on **setuid** programs.

If satisfied that the system is free of security hazards, install the new system software and convert to a trusted system.

Let us review the following before discussing the **setuid** and **setgid**:

Discretionary Access Control

The Department of Defense Trusted Computer System Evaluation Criteria defines discretionary access control (DAC) as "a means of restricting access to objects based on the identity of subjects and/or groups to which they belong. The controls are discretionary in the sense that a subject with a certain access permission is capable of passing that permission on to any other subject."

The traditional Unix system provides sets of permissions for user, group, and others. Access control lists extend this mechanism by allowing users to add sets of permissions or restriction for specific users and groups.

Subjects

Subjects are active entities: persons, processes, or devices that cause information to flow among objects or that change the system state. All subjects are a potential target of auditing on a trusted system.

Objects

Objects are passive entities: files, directory trees, programs, bits, bytes, fields, processors, stack registers, video displays, keyboards, clocks, printers, network nodes, and anything that contains or receives information on a system. Because access to an object implies access to the information the object contains, objects require protection. Certain controlled objects require special attention:

- Root directory.
- Sensitive files such as `.rhosts` and password files.
- Configuration files such as `inetd. sec`.
- Public directories.
- Log files.

To ensure security, set `umask` as restrictively as possible and assign ACLs as needed to all files whose access a user intends to limit. For further directions, refer to ACLs and `umask(l)` in the *Unix Reference Manual.*

Least Privilege

The principle of least privilege requires each subject in a system to be granted only as much privilege as is needed to perform authorized tasks. Users should be able to access information based only on a valid "need to know." These criteria help to limit damage resulting from accident, error, or unauthorized use.

Accountability

To ensure that individual users are held accountable for their activities online, the conversion program to a trusted system creates an audit ID (`aid`) that identifies every user uniquely and associates that user with every process invoked. The `aid` and Unix auditing functionality enable authorized personnel to evaluate auditable events, which are actions potentially capable of allowing access to, generating, or releasing sensitive information. See the section on auditing including audit IDs.

SET USER ID (SETUID) AND SET GROUP ID (SETGID) PROGRAMS

The `setuid` and `setgid` programs have the following characteristics. These comments also apply to `setuid` and `setgid` shell scripts. Most programs that run `setuid` can be run `setgid` just as successfully.

- A `setuid` program is one whose `setuid` bit is on.
- A `setgid` program is one whose `setgid` bit is on.
- The `setuid` and `setgid` bits are indicated by the `s` (or `S`) in the `owner-execute` (for `setuid`) or `group-execute` (for `setgid`) position of the file permission modes.

  For example, in `/bin/passwd` the `setuid bit` is set to its owner, `root`:

```
ll /bin/passwd
-r-sr-xr-x     1 root     bin      110592 Jul 21 12:55 /bin/passwd
```

In /bin/ps, the setgid bit is set to its group, sys:

```
ll /bin/ps
-r-xr-sr-x    1 bin    sys    116736 Jul 21 12:55 /bin/ps
```

How IDs Are Set

The steps for setting IDs are:

- The ruid and rgid are inherited from the login process, which sets the uid and gid. The uid and gid are located in /etc/passwd.
- The aid is also set at login time and is located in / .secure/etc/passwd. The aid does not change when running setuid and setgid programs.
- The login command also changes the ruid and euid (real and effective user ID) and rgid and egid (real and effective group ID).
- The su command changes the euid and ruid.
- The newgrp command can change the gid.
- Setuid and setgid bits are set by using the chmod() system call or command. Use chmod 4000 for the setuid bit, chmod 2000 for the setgid bit.

Why setuid Programs Can Be Risky

Whenever any program is executed, it creates a process with four numbers: real and effective user ID (ruid and euid) and real and effective group ID (rgid and egid). Typically, these ID pairs are identical. However, running a setuid or setgid program changes the euid or egid of the process from that associated with the owner to that of the object. The processes spawned acquire their attributes from the object, giving the user the same access rights as the program's owner and/or group.

- If the setuid bit is turned on, the privileges of the process are set to that of the owner of the file.
- If the setgid bit is turned on, the privileges of the process are set to that of the group of the file.
- If neither the setuid nor setgid bit is turned on, the privileges of the process are unchanged.
- If a program is setuid-to-root, the user gains all privileges available to root. This is dangerous, because the program can be used in a way to violate the TCB.

Kinds of Attacks

Most common "attacks" to the system are due to operator error! However, a system attacker can exploit setuid and setgid programs, most often in one of two ways:

1. By having a setuid or setgid program execute commands defined by the attacker, either interactively or by script.
2. By substituting bogus data for the data created by a program.

A discussion of computer attacks is beyond the scope of this section. Interested readers can refer to industry periodicals for articles on this subject. However, maintaining appropriately restrictive file permissions on system programs strengthens computer assurance.

Guidelines for Limiting setuid Power

A privileged program is more powerful than other programs because it gives the user the capability of doing something the user is not otherwise allowed to do. If misused, such privilege can threaten system integrity. The user must not add setuid-to-root programs to an existing trusted system. Adding a setuid-to-root program changes the system configuration and might compromise security.

Enforce restrictive use of privileged programs through the following suggestions:

- Use setuid only when absolutely necessary.
- Make sure that no setuid program is writable by others. Write permission allows attack by Trojan horses.
- Whenever possible, use setgid instead of setuid to reduce the scope of damage that might result from coding flaws or breaches of security.
- Periodically search the file systems for new or modified setuid and setgid programs. If tampering is suspected, remove the setuid bit. Before reinstating the setuid bit, examine the program thoroughly or rebuild it from trusted sources.
- Know exactly what the setuid and setgid programs do, and verify that they do only what is intended. Failing this, remove the program or its setuid attribute.
- If a setuid program must be copied, make sure that the modes are correct on the destination file.
- Write setuid programs so that they can be tested on noncritical data without setuid or setgid attributes. Apply these attributes only after the code has been reviewed and all affected users are satisfied that the new programs maintain security.

Guidelines for Writing setuid Programs

The following guidelines minimize risk when writing setuid and setgid programs:

- Do not write setuid-to-root programs. If possible, write the programs setuid-to-user (user other than root) or setgid.
- Make sure that a setuid program does not create files writable by anyone other than its intended user.
- Reset the euid before making an exec system call. Be aware that exec may be called within other library routines, and be wary of using routines (including popen, system, execlp, and execvp) that fork a shell to execute a program.
- When writing setuid programs, use setresuid(2) around the pieces of code that require privileges to reduce the window of vulnerability.
- Close all unnecessary file descriptors before calling exec ().
- Ensure that all variables (PATH, IFS, and umask) in the program's environment are sufficiently restrictive.
- Do not use the creat() system call to make a lock file. Use lockf () or fcntl () instead.

SECURE SYSTEM INITIALIZATION

Unix sets up a safe operating environment at the start of most `setuid-to-root` programs by calling a special library function to establish the following conditions:

- Environment variables are set to only those values necessary for the proper operation of `setuid` programs. Since Trojan horses typically attack improperly set `PATH` and `IFS` variables, these are set to predetermined values: `PATH` is set to `/bin: /usr/bin` and `IFS` is set to `space, tab`, and `newline`. All other environment variables are deleted.
- All file descriptors other than standard input, standard output, and standard error are closed.
- All alarms are turned off. All interval timers are set to zero.

These safeguards increase the assurance that known programs are executed in a known environment.

EXEMPTED SYSTEM PROGRAMS

The library function cannot be applied to some programs because to do so would inhibit their specified behavior. Instead, the following programs have been carefully examined for flaws:

`at(1), crontab(1)`	Specified shell environment variables are retained when the commands are executed.
`hpterm(1), xterm(1)`	Some file descriptors other than standard input, standard output, and standard error remain open.
`newgrp(1)`	All exported variables retain their value.
`su(1)`	The environment is passed along unchanged.

OTHER TYPICAL SOFTWARE THREATS

Since Unix is a relatively open system, once having logged in the user has access to virtually all available functionality. Although Unix has numerous built-in software restrictions (including passwords, account and group management, and access control), it is vulnerable to penetration, which leads to destruction or compromise of material or data. Be aware of the following penetration techniques.

Spoofing

Spoofing is a technique used to masquerade a hostile program as a system program. A classic example prompts the user to log in, thereby capturing the person's login and password. Instruct users to report any unexpected system query for their password once logged in.

Time Bombs

A time bomb is a program that remains inactive until triggered by a program such as an `at(l)` job, which is scheduled to run at a set time. A time bomb might be as harmless as a program that displays blinking Christmas trees on everyone's terminal screen on Christmas Eve, or as harmful as a program set to reformat the root disk at 11:59 P.M. October 12.

Trap Door

A trap door is a hidden software or hardware mechanism that circumvents system protections by acting differently from documented behavior. A trap door is often activated subtly, such as by "random" key sequence at a terminal, or it might be built in to a program by the software developer.

Trojan Horse

A Trojan horse is a seemingly useful computer program containing additional (hidden) functionality that exploits the program's capabilities to the detriment of security. For example, a program might copy a sensitive file for the creator of the Trojan horse.

Trojan horses are frequently located in a directory searched before the system directories in a user's `PATH`. Trojan horses also might arrive online as a "gift" with some "undocumented features."

- Never begin `PATH` with the user's current (.) directory.
- Be vigilant against Trojan horses when unpacking archives of software. The `shar` format is especially dangerous. Never unpack archives as `root`.
- Never blindly compile and execute the source code without first examining it for software threats.
- Be wary of using programs that require privilege to operate, especially if you have the binaries without the source. If the programs must be used, back up the system completely before loading the code, and watch for changes to the password file and other sensitive areas.

Viruses

Viruses are covert code segments programmed to reproduce rapidly, debilitate hosts, and spread through a variety of carriers.

Worms

Worms are independent programs that, like viruses, migrate through a system for harmful purposes. The 1988 Internet Worm invaded 6,000 Unix systems, including 308 government-affiliated sites.

TRUSTED NETWORKING

From the perspective of security, networked systems are more vulnerable than stand-alone systems. Networking not only increases system accessibility, but also a greater risk of security violations. An open system such as Unix allows extensive public access over networks to information in unencrypted form. While you cannot control security over the network, you can control security of each node on the network to limit penetration risk without reducing the usefulness of the system or user productivity.

Following the principle of least privilege, all network management programs should be owned by a protected, network-specific account such as `uucp` or `daemon`, rather than `root`. This section provides information on:

- Controlling administrative domain.
- Understanding network services.

- Protecting passwords when using RFA.
- Using `inetd.sec` to restrict outside access.
- Denying access with /etc/ftpusers.
- Mounting files in an NFS environment.
- Safeguarding link-level access.

CONTROLLING ADMINISTRATIVE DOMAIN

An administrative domain is a group of systems connected by network services that allow users to access one another without password verification. An administrative domain assumes their host machine has already verified system users. In other words, network services assume security is established at the system level. See Exhibit 6.3 for examples of administrative domains:

- A user on system `sales` need not enter a password to read an NFS-mounted file on system `mfg`, because `sales` verified the password when the user logged in. Systems `mfg` and `sales` are in the same administrative domain.
- A user on system `legal` executes `rlogin` to establish a remote session on system `sales`. System `legal` is not listed in /etc/hosts .equiv on `sales`, so `sales` requires the user to provide a password. Systems `legal` and `sales` are not in the same administrative domain.
- Systems `design` and `sales` are not in the same administrative domain. However, because `design` and `mfg` are in the same domain and `mfg` and `sales` are in the same domain by association with `mfg`, `design` and `sales` are indeed in the same administrative domain.

Exhibit 6.3 Examples of Administrative Domain

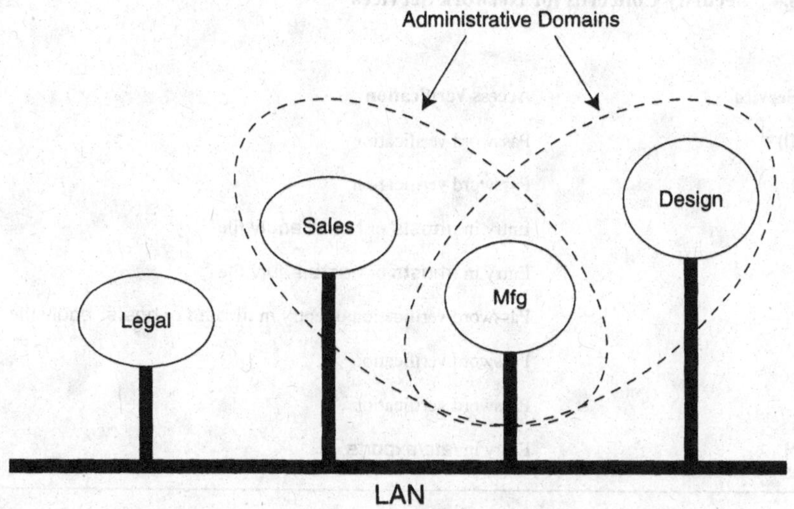

UNDERSTANDING NETWORK SERVICES

Unix provides various networking services, each providing a means of authentication either through password verification or authorization set up in a file on the remote system. For information on using the services, refer to the system reference manual specific to each service. Exhibit 6.4 identifies some of the major security concerns related to these network services.

PROTECTING PASSWORDS WHEN USING REMOTE FILE ACCESS

Potentially, any super user can make a network special file anywhere in the file system and use it to gain access to any other system on the network.

To prevent this, remote file access (RFA) requires one to respecify their password to the netunam(1) command. However, this command also allows one to specify their password on the command line. This poses a serious security risk. If one uses netunam in a script, they should not enter their password in the command line, as they will be doing so in an unencrypted state. It will also be exposed to anyone who runs ps, and thus gets broadcast messages.

USING INETD.SEC TO RESTRICT OUTSIDE ACCESS

Except for remote file access (RFA) and network file transfer (NFT), access control to individual network services can be set in /usr/adm/inetd. sec, an optional security file for the Internet daemon. To explicitly allow or deny use of most networking services requires that they be listed on a per-machine or per-subnet basis.

The syntax of entries in /usr/adm/inetd.sec is:

<service name> <allow/deny> <host/net addresses, host/net names>

Service name is the official name (not alias) of a valid service in the file /etc/services. The service name for RPC-based services (NFS) is the official name (not alias) of a valid service in the file /etc/rpc. The wildcard character * and the range character - are permitted in addresses.

Exhibit 6.4 Security Concerns for Network Services

Network Service	Access Verification
netunam(1)	Password verification
dscopy(1)	Password verification
rcp(1)	Entry in .rhosts or hosts.equiv file
remsh(1)	Entry in .rhosts or hosts.equiv file
rlogin(1)	Password verification or entry in .rhosts or hosts. equiv file
telnet(1)	Password verification
fip(1)	Password verification
mount(1M)	Entry in /etc/exports

Refer to the *Unix Reference Manual* entry **inetd.sec(4)** for complete details on the syntax and use of this file.

DENYING ACCESS WITH /ETC/FTPUSERS

Ftpd(1M), the file transfer protocol server, is run by the Internet **daemon** (see **inetd(1M)**) when a service request is received at the port indicated in the **/etc/services**.

Ftpd rejects remote logins to local user accounts named in **/etc/ftpusers**. Each restricted account name must appear alone on a line in the file. The line cannot contain any spaces or tabs. User accounts with restricted login shells in **/etc/passwd** should be listed in **/etc/ftpusers** because **ftpd** accesses local accounts without using their login shells. **Uucp** accounts also should be listed in **/etc/ftpusers**. If **/etc/ftpusers** does not exist, **ftpd** skips the security check.

FILES MOUNTED IN NETWORK FILE SYSTEM ENVIRONMENT

A Network File System (NFS) is used to:

- Save file space.
- Maintain consistent file usage.
- Provide a lean, cooperative user environment.

NFS streamlines file-sharing between server and client systems by controlling access via the **/etc/exports** file. Entries in **/etc/exports** provide permission to mount a file system existing on the server onto any client machine. Once a file system is put into **/etc/exports**, the information is available to anyone who can do an NFS mount.

Thus, the NFS client user can access a server file system without having logged in to the server system. RFA and diskless clusters also provide access to files hooked up to a remote CPU, but do not bypass password authentication.

Server Vulnerability

Server security is maintained by setting restrictive permissions on the **file /etc/exports**. Root privileges are not maintained across Network File System (NFS). Thus, having root privileges on a client system does not provide you with special access to the server.

The server performs the same permission checking remotely for the client as it does locally for its own users. The server side controls access to server files by the client by comparing the user ID and group ID of the client, which it receives via the network with the user ID and group ID of the server file. Checking occurs within the kernel.

A user with privilege on an NFS client can exploit that privilege to obtain unlimited access to an NFS server. Never export any file system to a node on which privilege is granted more leniently than from your own node's policy.

Client Vulnerability

In earlier releases of Network File System for workstations, the **/dev inode** had to reside on the client disk. Network File System now allows for the **/dev inode** containing the major and minor numbers of a client-mounted device to exist on the server side. This opens the possibility for someone to create a Trojan horse that overrides permissions set on the client's mounted device by accessing the device via the file and inode number found on the server side.

Although lacking permission to make a device file on the client side, a cracker wanting to sabotage the client can create an undermining device file, such as /dev/kmem, using root permissions on the server side. The new /dev file is created with the same major and minor number as that of the target device on the client side, but with the following permissions:

```
crw-rw-rw-
```

The cracker can then go to the client, log in as an ordinary user, and using Network File System can open up the newly created server-side device file and use it for devious means (e.g., to wipe out kernel memory on the server, read the contents of everyone's processes, or other mischief).

SAFEGUARDING NETWORK FILE SYSTEM–MOUNTED FILES

The following steps are used to safeguard the NFS files:

1. If possible, make sure that the same person administers both client and server systems. Alternatively, require that administrators of both client and server systems coordinate their efforts.
2. Maintain uniformity of user ID and group ID for server and client systems.
3. Stay vigilant of /dev files in file systems exported from server.
4. Restrict write access to the /etc/passwd and / .secure/etc/passwd client files.
5. For strictest control, audit every host that is accessible through the network.

LINK-LEVEL ACCESS

Link-level access is a very powerful facility that permits a programmer to access the link driver on the host directly. In the wrong hands, this capability can enable an ordinary user to fabricate any network packet including network control packets.

Everything transmitted on the system is enclosed in a packet with a header and body. The header contains all administrative information including control, routing, timing, and billing data. Sometimes this is the critical part of the transmission, rather than file content itself. Since Unix protocols each have their own administrative layers, information becomes more and more encapsulated the more protocols a packet travels through. To protect link-level access, make sure that the files /dev/ether*, /dev/ieee*, and /dev/lan* are owned and writable only by root.

SAFEGUARDING NETWORK SECURITY

This section provides techniques for checking the security of network control files.

IDENTIFYING ADMINISTRATIVE DOMAIN

Following are the steps to identify and control an administrative domain. The example used in these steps assumes that the computers you can reach on your network are named for corporate departments, such as **finance**, **sales**, and **mktg**, and that you are working on a machine named **hq**.

1. List the nodes to which you export file systems.

```
cat /etc/exports
```

The **/etc/exports** file lists entries that consist of the pathname of a file system followed by a series of names of computers and names of groups of computers. Any entry consisting of only a pathname without being followed by a computer name is a file system available to every computer on the network. All pathnames should be associated with specific computers.

The **/etc/exports** entries might contain names of groups of computers. You can find out what individual machines are included in a group by checking **/etc/netgroup**. If the output of the command **cat /etc/exports** is:

```
/u1 mfg mktg
/u2 personnel
/u3 mfg design quality
```

you can conclude that **hq, mfg, mktg, design, personnel**, and **quality** are part of one administrative domain.

2. List the nodes that have equivalent password databases.

```
cat /etc/hosts . equiv
```

The **/etc/hosts . equiv** file lists the names of computers with equivalent password files. If the output of this command is:

```
legal
mfg
mktg
quality
```

you can conclude that **hq, mfg, mktg, design, personnel, quality**, and **legal** are part of one administrative domain.

3. Verify that each node in the administrative domain does not extend privileges to any unincluded nodes. Repeat steps 1, 2, and 3 on each of these machines: **mfg, mktg, design, personnel, quality** and **legal**.

For example, suppose that most of these machines extend privileges only to computers within the administrative domain, but **mktg** also exports file systems to **sales**. Repeat steps 1, 2, and 3 for the machine called **sales**.

4. Control root and local security on every node in the administrative domain. A user with super user privileges on any machine in the domain can acquire those privileges on every machine in the domain. Follow the system security procedures described elsewhere in this manual to protect root privilege on each machine.

5. Maintain consistency of user name, **uid**, and **gid** among password files in the administrative domain. To verify consistency of systems in the domain, compare their password files.

For example, if you are working on system **hq** and wish to check consistency with **mfg**, whose / file system is remotely mounted to **hq** as **/nfs/mfg/**, type the following sequence of commands:

```
% awk -F: '{printf "%s %s %s\n", $1, $3, $4}' \
/etc/passwd . /tmp/hq-pwd
```

```
% awk -F: '{printf "%s %s %s\n", $1, $3, $4}' \
/nfs/xyz/etc/passwd . /tmp/mfg-pwd
% diff /tmp/hq-pwd /tmp/mfg-pwd
```

The awk commands print the values of the first, third, and fourth fields of /etc/passwd (user name, uid, and gid, respectively) to temporary files. Then, any output produced by running the diff command on the temporary files indicates inconsistency between the two /etc/passwd files. Edit one or both /etc/passwd files to make them consistent.
The /etc/passwd files of a local (hq) and remote (mfg) system can be compared by using rcp(1) instead of NFS. You might choose to use these commands if you do not have NFS and mfg is listed in the /etc/hosts . equiv file of hq, making it a member of hq's administrative domain:

```
% rcp mfg:/etc/passwd /tmp/mfg-passwd
% awk -F: '{printf "%s %s %s\n", $1, $3, $4}' \
/etc/passwd > /tmp/hq-pwd
% awk -F: '{printf ' "%s %s %s\n", $1, $3, $4}' \
/tmp/mfg-passwd > /tmp/mfg-pwd
% diff /tmp/hq-pwd /tmp/mfg-pwd
```

6. Maintain consistency among any group files on all nodes in the administrative domain. If you are working on system hq and you wish to check consistency with system mfg, and mfg's / file system is remotely mounted to hq as /nfs/mfg/,

```
% diff /etc/group /nfs/mfg/etc/group
```

If you see any output, the two /etc/group files are inconsistent. The manual entry on diff(1) will explain how to interpret the output. Edit one or both of the files, making them the same. For a non-NFS method:

```
% rcp mfg:/etc/group /tmp/mfg-group
% diff /etc/group /tmp/mfg-group
```

In both cases, if you see no output the two /etc/group files are consistent and you are done.

VERIFYING PERMISSION SETTINGS ON NETWORK CONTROL FILES

Modes, owners, and groups on all system files are set carefully. Their correct values are recorded in product description file (pdf) databases. All deviations from these values should be noted and corrected.

Particular attention should be paid to network control files that reside in /etc and are notable targets because they provide access to the network itself. Network control files should never be writable by the public. Among these are:

- networks — Network names and their addresses
- hosts — Network hosts and their addresses
- hosts.equiv — Remote hosts allowed access equivalent to the local host
- services — Services name database
- exports — List of file systems being exported to NFS clients
- protocols — Protocol name database

- `inetd.conf` Internet configuration file
- `netgroup` List of networkwide groups

CONTROLLING FILE SYSTEM EXPORT

The `/etc/exports` file defines which file systems can be exported to other systems. Each one-line entry should have at least two fields: the first is the name of the file system being exported, the second and subsequent name the systems to which the file system can be exported. If fewer than two fields are present, the file system can be shipped anywhere in the world.

Verify that no file system can be universally exported:

```
sed -e'/^\#/d' -e '/^[space, tab]*$/d' /etc/exports | awk 'NF < 2'
```

This command examines `/etc/exports`, removes all comment lines, removes all null lines (lines containing only spaces or tabs), and then searches the file for lines with fewer than two fields.

GUIDELINES FOR HANDLING NETWORK SECURITY BREACHES

If a network security breach occurs because of an unknown cause:

- Shut down the network and telephone access to the computer.
- Inform the network administrator immediately.
- Allow external access to the computer only after identifying and eliminating the problem.

A security breach can present itself in many different ways:

- Someone might report unexpected or destructive behavior by a common program.
- The user might notice a sudden increase in the system's load average, causing the computer not to respond well.
- `Read/write` permissions or ownership might be changed from what is expected.
- The byte count of any system files changes unexpectedly.

Anything that seems to deviate from normal system behavior might suggest tampering. If one suspects a security breach, such as a virus or worm, one should handle it by limiting its immediate impact.

1. Shut down the system. If users can be given a warning, use the more courteous shutdown command:

   ```
   /etc/shutdown [-r | -h] [grace_period]
   ```

   or

   ```
   /etc/shutdown [-r | -h] [-d device] [-f lif_file] [grace_period]
   ```

2. Bring the system to a sudden halt by using `/etc/reboot -q` if an infiltrating program is actively corrupting the system. Allowing for a grace period by using shutdown might allow more time for further corruption. Also, the system might not respond to system load.

   Note: Once rebooted, some systems would ask to autoboot from the primary boot path enabled. Others would return without asking. Press any key within 10 seconds to override this option. See the system administrator's manual and follow procedures for rebooting the system in single-user state.

3. One should bring the system up in a single-user state, its barest minimum. This limits the impact that is subject to symptoms. From a single-user state, analyze the problem and clean it up. This brings up the system without any local file systems being mounted. By killing all processes, one has effectively stopped a virus or worm from causing more damage.
4. Mount all file systems using `/etc/mount -a`. Until their integrity has been verified, set restrictive directory permissions (`drwx------`) to prevent users from accessing the questionable files. This is a short-term solution only. Think in terms of what went wrong? Examine the audit trail, password file, and login files for clues.
5. Run the `pdf` programs, `ncheck` and `find` commands, as described in step 10 to compare file size from the previously backed-up system to the current one. Examine the date that files were last written, byte count, inodes, and ownership. Suspect any files whose sizes differ unexpectedly. Remember, however, that some system files, especially network files, might have been customized and therefore differ from the default system software.
6. Copy contaminated files to tape to save as evidence.
7. Under some circumstances, one might not be able to reboot, or one might not trust the reboot program (`/etc/init`) itself. If so, one must reinstall the entire system.
8. If one is uncertain of the scope of damage, it is recommended that Unix be reinstalled from the system tapes. Even if it is believed that the offending file has been found and the architecture of the problem understood, the possibility still exists that the worm, virus, or Trojan horse might have propagated itself. Therefore, it is advisable to reinstall the system completely.
9. After reinstalling, it must be decided if any user files, or other files not reinstalled from tape have been corrupted.
10. Mount users' home directories and run the `find` and `ncheck` commands described earlier to uncover any additional compromised files.
11. If the breach was an unauthorized access of the machine, under most circumstances the point of entry will be apparent. Disable those accounts, replacing the password entries with an asterisk. The root user then has to change the password at the console by hand.
12. Inform all system users of a security breach and ask them to check their accounts for anything unusual. Instruct users to run `ls -lt` to look for unexpected changes to files, such as time of last modification for file creation or mode change, which might suggest tampering.
13. Analyze evidence to determine how the breach occurred and what can be done to prevent recurrences.

TECHNICAL AUDIT CONCERNS

Computer risks on the Internet have a lot to do with the Unix operating system, which is very powerful and includes many more features and utility functions than any other operating system. Unfortunately, incorporating all of these powerful features made it a security risk. Many of the attacks on Internet computers exploit weaknesses in the Unix operating system. An example would be to somehow get administrator status and then delete everyone's accounts. Therefore, one of the methods of protecting information is to restrict access to it by using the operating system of the computer privileges. Another method is to encrypt the information.

Utilities

Unix utilities are used as building blocks for bigger programs. Many Unix utility programs are used in this way. Therefore, make sure the sensitive utilities are protected.

Popular Unix data filtering utilities are:

Utility	*Purpose*
cat	Copy input to output
grep	Search for strings in the input
Sort	Sort lines in the input
Cut	Extract columns from input
Sed	Perform editing operations on input
tr	Translate characters in the input to other characters

TCP/IP Concepts

The key concepts are:

- Hardware addresses.
- Software addresses.
- Host names and IP addresses.
- Routers, Bridges, and Gateways overview (A gateway is a host that contains interfaces between two or more networks that pass or forward datagrams between the networks. Gateways store information about the topology of the network in the form of a routing table with entries keyed on destination IP addresses. Each entry in the table consists of a destination address, gateway address, and a pointer to the directly connected network the gateway resides on.
- Translating IP addresses to hardware addresses.
- Protocols and Ports.
- The TCP/IP Protocol Stack.
- Network.Host Numbers -> Netmask -> Network Address.
- Networks and Routers.
- The /etc/hosts file.
- Review planning documents with respect to Domain Name Space topology, that is and Subnet topology.
- Review how the TCP/IP configuration was made.
- Was the TCP/IP configuration tested? (Note: use.ifconfig).
- ifconfig—command can be used to configure a networking interface as well as to change its configuration on the fly, including temporarily taking the interface out of service.

- **Run:** You can run the command line **ifconfig -a** at any time to see a list of interfaces currently configured and their parameters.
- **ttl - time to live;** The sending host specifies how long (**ttl**) in seconds live. Once ttl reaches zero the packet is discarded.
- Options: The options that are infrequently used in IP datagrams follow:
  1. **Source Route**: A list of internet addresses through which the datagram must pass.
  2. **Record Route**: The nodes which the datagram passes through are instructed to return their Internet address. Thus, we may determine the route taken by a datagram.
  3. **Time Stamp**: The time it takes for the datagram to pass through the nodes is returned to the host. This allows measurement and comparisons of network performance.
  4. **Checking Remote Hosts**: A host can send the **ICMP Echo Message** to see if a remote system's Internet Protocol is up and operational. The Unix **PING** command uses this message.

TCP/IP Commands

The TCP/IP commands are:

rlogin	Provides a login to a remote system.
telnet	Provides a remote login to a remote system and a suite of commands to perform special functions such as copying files over the network.
rcp	Does remote copying of files over the network.
rcmd	Executes commands on a remote system over the network.
ftp	A file transfer program that provides a suite of file transfer utilities.
netstat	Provides statistics that measure the load and efficiency of the network's hardware and data transfer environments.
Ping	Examines network connectivity and efficiency of the network in transferring packets.

Some other commonly used TCP/IP applications that provide services to the user's interactive processes are:

Domain Name Services (DNS)	Maps IP addresses to the names assigned to the network devices.
Network File System (NFS)	Allows file systems and directories to be shared by various hosts on the network.
Routing Information Protocol (RIP)	Provides forwarding of datagrams through the network through designated devices assigned by Internet address.

Name Services

Name Services designates a unique network name (i.e., domainname) and address (i.e., IP number) for each host, and specifies the path or communication channels (i.e., the routes) through which a remote host must reach that host. A name indicates what we seek, an address tells where it is, and a route specifies the path that we take to get there.

To communicate, a host on a network must have the following five features:

1. A unique address (i.e., an IP address in either NIS or the /etc/host table).
2. A broadcast address allowing it to receive a message sent to all similarly addressed hosts (i.e., the ifconfig command executed at boot-up time: ifconfig -a, vi/etc/tcp, /ifconfig /* searches for ifconfig)

   TCP/IP /* Network Configuration manager -> change IP address -> ping IP address e.g., ping 157.178.173.4 /* to see if the network is operational and online.

   Or ping net 'n' to

   Telnet

   Vi /etc/hosts

   or grep ifconfig/etc/tcp to verify that the tcp startup script has a proper ifconfig command with the correct natmask and broadcast address for each interface on the system.

3. It must be able to determine which hosts and users it may communicate with (i.e., have entries in the /etc/host table and /etc/passwd file).
4. It must know through which paths (i.e., routes) it may send data to reach known and unknown destinations (i.e., a route table).
5. It must have the capability to select the packets on the network that are addressed to it, and be able to discard or forward packets that are not addressed.

The three network name services that provide the preceding capabilities and provide the capability to manage the Network are:

1. the /etc/host/table services /* review this file */
2. Network Information Services (NIS)
3. Domain Name Services (DNS)

MANAGING THE NETWORK WITH /ETC/HOSTS TABLE

The /etc/hosts file, also called the host table, contains the network addresses and names of hosts on a network. Note: The host table may be superseded by either the Domain Name Service (DNS) or (NIS). However, even though these network services may be in use, the host table may still be needed to:

- Provide information about important hosts (including itself) when DNS or NIS is not running.
- Supplement DNS or NIS with additional information.

The Internet Protocol Network Address

If a network is to be connected to the Internet Network, one must have a range of IP numbers assigned to the machines through the Internet Central Network Authority. Each root network must be assigned a unique 32-bit IP address and an Internet Network Name, and each host is assigned a unique IP address and hostname. The IP address and hostname are distributed to network servers on the local network, and may be distributed to servers on the extended network.

Common Network Configuration and Management Tables Files

Ethers File

Control Objective: Use of /etc/ethers reduces the overhead on the local host and speeds network access. The Ethers File found in /etc/ethers contains information regarding the 48-bit ethernet addresses of hosts and gateway hosts on the Internet. This information may be enclosed in a frame so that there is no need to utilize arp (Address Resolution Protocol) to resolve or map IP numbers to ethernet interface numbers.

For each host on an ethernet network, there should be a single line in the ethers file containing the following information:

Ethernet-Address	*Official-host-name*
8:0:20:0:fc:6f	laidbak

Network File

Control Objective: /etc/networks list networks on the Internet. Review to determine none of the listed files are security threats.

Protocol File

Control Objective: Review the protocol file to ensure that authorized protocols are being used and there are no security exposures. The file is in /etc/protocols.

Services File

Control Objective: Review the services file to ensure that authorized services are being used and there are no security exposures. The file is in /etc/services.

Host.equiv *File*

Control Objective: Review the hosts.equiv file to ensure that the list of trusted hosts and users are authorized and that there is no danger of breaches of system security or damage.

The file /etc/hosts.equiv contains a list of trusted hosts. Cross-reference the name of the hosts to /etc/passwd file of the system. This file controls which hosts can remotely log on or execute a number of commands called RCP commands without specifying a password. This file is controlled by root or super user accounts.

Home/.rhosts *File*

Control Objective: The file /Home/.rhosts contains a list of trusted users. Ensure that rhosts file does not grant permissions for "trusted" remote hosts and users without specific authorization. Rhosts file can grant permission for "trusted" remote hosts and users to use local usernames without specifying the corresponding user passwords. This file is normally controlled and configured to grant remote access to local accounts.

The RPC (Remote Procedure Commands) are a suite of commands of Berkley Remote utilities (such as rlogin,rcmd, rcp, (or rsh), rwho, and ruptime) that are initiated by a local host but executed on a remote host across the network but are transparent to the user and appear as locally executed commands. They are a potential breach of the Unix system security and require an added form of security protection.

/* You can make a user's login shell restricted by putting rksh or ksh -r in the user's /etc/passwd entry. Also review the user's .profile and environment files after they are run.

Subnetwork Addresses

Determine if there is a planned subnet topology based on constraints and performance needs. Obtain defined netmasks, network numbers, broadcast, and IP addresses for any interfaces on the network. What physical layer media cable types is in use? That is, thick ethernet, thin ethernet, 10baseT, 100baseT, Token Ring, and FDDI. Each has a limit to the number of hosts that can be attached to a single segment of cable. As an organization adds more nodes to the network, one may reach the limit of the cable type. Determine the number of subnetworks. How many subnets have been configured?

The advantages are:

- It provides for increased security controls.
- It reduces traffic on a large network as more services are more widely dispersed.
- It provides for more efficient management and distribution of network administrative tasks and databases to selected parts of the network.
- It provides more effective administrative and security to a subgroup of an organization.

Look at the /etc/hosts database.

ROUTING

Routing issues are:

- Configuring a router.
- Route configuration.
- Getting and interpreting routing information.

  The /etc/gateways file:

  ```
  # cat /etc/gateways
  # netstat -r
  # netstat -rn
  ```
- Configuring other LAN and WAN interfaces.
- Configuring the Point-to-Point Protocol (PPP).
- Tuning Serial Line kernel parameters.
- Internet address and domain name registration.

PPP File Usage

1. Outgoing PPP request detected.
2. pppd contacted to make connection.

3. pppd looks in ppphosts; gets remote system UUCP name /etc/ppphosts.
4. UUCP subsystem invoked, looks in system file, gets phone number (/usr/lib/uucp/Systems).
5. UUCP looks in Devices file to select tty line and invoke dialer (/usr/lib/uucp/Devices).

Kernel Configuration for TCP/IP Networking

Most Unix systems do not come especially configured for networking. For these systems, network modules must be downloaded from the software media and configured into the kernel so that TCP/IP services are incorporated into the operating system. Review the process and determine how this configuration was done and by whom:

- How often is the configuration reviewed to determine adequacy?
- A unix system that has been network configured will start a number of daemons to enable network services at multiuser boot times. Which daemons are started depend on the particular configuration of the system and the network services that are required.
- Determine which daemons have been selected to be started. (Generally, the network daemons started at multiuser boot times are activated by the boot files in the /etc/rc directory.)

Other daemons are not started at boot time but may be invoked on demand (as needed) by a super-server daemon inetd ('i-net-d'), sometimes called the Internet daemon. The Internet super daemon (inetd) listens for connection requests with the network services daemons listed in the /etc/inetd.conf and starts those daemons on demand, thus saving memory and process table resources. When an inetd started process completes its execution, inetd terminates the process. Utilizing the inetd daemon to invoke processes only when needed reduces system overhead.

Therefore, determine what daemons can be invoked on demand by the inetd and by whom and when. The following daemons are started to add functionality for multiuser mode:

pppd	The point-to-point protocol only starts if configuring an /etc/ppphosts file.
snmpd	The Simple Network Management Protocol (SNMP) daemon will only be started if configuring the /etc/snmpd.conf file. If these files are configured, set up the system as a SNMP agent.
named(ADMN)	The named daemon will only be started if an /etc/named.boot file has been configured.
routed or gated	One must configure the file /etc/gated.conf for gated to start. Otherwise, routed will start by default. The behaviour of routed may be modified by the existence of /etc/gateways.
xntpd	This daemon is used to synchronize the kernel's clock using time servers on the Internet. The Internet daemon will only start if an /etc/ntp.conf. file has been created.
lpd	This line printer will only start if any of the printers have been configured as either print servers or clients and thus have an /etc/printcap file on the system.

Network Daemons *Not Started*

Several daemons are not started by the /etc/tcp script because their start-up code is commented out. To start any of these deamons, edit the /etc/tcp file and uncomment their start-up code.

Irdd	This daemon is an alternative to either routed or gated.
timed rwhod	This daemon is an older and less reliable alternative to the xntpd broadcast.
rarpd	Replies to reverse ARP.

Starting TCP/IP

The sd command is required to start TCP/IP if the system is configured for the two highest levels of security. sd resides in the /usr/sbin directory. The command line would be: sd/etc/tcp/ start. Ensure that the sd command is restricted.

The Inetd *Super Daemon (*/etc/inetd.conf*) File:*

- The inetd.conf file lists all the server daemons that should be started by inetd (e.g., rlogind and telnetd).
- Has several entries commented out, preventing inetd from starting them.
- Has several entries commented out that provide alternative ways for inetd to run daemons with entries that may or may not be commented out.
- Can be modified using a standard text editor.

The inetd daemon listens for connection requests to daemons providing Internet services (e.g., rlogind, telnetd), and then spawns the requested server process. The daemons that inetd listens for are listed in the /etc/inetd.conf file by default, though this can be changed from the command line that starts inetd.

/etc/services *File*

Cross-reference entries in this file to /etc/inetd.conf file.

Booting from the Network

There are two ways that devices booting from the network can get their boot information by using:

1. BOOTP (the boot protocol). The bootpd (boot protocol daemon) resides in the /etc/bootptab file. Another file to watch for is bootpgw.
2. RARP (reverse address resolution protocol). RARP only allows devices to discover their IP address. BOOTP allows devices to discover other things including the IP address, netmask, name of file that holds the kernel, name of server that holds the kernel and more.

Downloading the Device's Kernel

Once a device that boots from the network knows its IP address (and possibly other information if it uses BOOTP), it can download its kernel. There are two methods commonly used to download kernels: TFTP and NFS.

1. One way a file can get its kernel is to transfer it via the trivial file transfer protocol (TFTP). No user authentication is required. As a result it presents a huge potential

security risk because no password is required to retrieve the file. Review the /etc/inetd.conf file to see whether the tftpd file is enabled. (-s indicates it is enabled).

2. Make sure that the firewall takes the proper attention to BOOTP, RARP, and FTP protocols such as:
   - Never have a gateway broadcast or rebroadcast (with bootpgw) any of these packets to networks outside the enterprize network (i.e., on to the Internet).
   - Never allow TFTP packets from outside your enterprise network into your network.
   - Restrict TFTP directory access by ensuring that tftpd is started with the arguments -s dir, where dir is the name of the directory that contains only downloaded files. This prevents malicious people from downloading any publicly readable, yet network-sensitive file (e.g., /etc/passwd).
3. Review the ftpaccess file to ensure that it is not installed by default and review the file for the following entries:
   - passwd-check
   - chmod
   - delete
   - overwrite
   - log commands
   - log transfers
   - banner
4. Determine the kinds of restrictions placed on FTP use such as control of what kind of usernames can be used to access the FTP server. Prevent users from accessing the FTP server as root and other sensitive accounts. Also account names presented must:
   - Exist on the system or be anonymous or ftp if anonymous ftp is configured.
   - Not have a null password.
   - Not exist in the /etc/ftpusers file unless it is anonymous.
   - Have a login shell that exists in the /etc/shells file.
   - Ensure that ftpd sessions are logged in the syslog file.

Configuring Trusted Access

Trusted Access allows users to utilize the enterprise network in a way that is more convenient and more secure via the rlogin command. If trusted access is not configured for the rlogin command, it will prompt users for a password. This password is transmitted across the network and may even be on the Internet. Packets containing these passwords are relatively easy to intercept and identify and thus can compromise the security of the enterprise network. Keep in mind the following:

- If trusted access is set up, no password is necessary for rlogin.
- If trusted access is not set up, the rcmd and rcp commands do not even work.

Trusted Access can be set up at the host or user level or both.

Configuring Trusted Host Access

Trusted host access allows you to indicate that one host trusts all the users on another host that have identical login names to use the rlogin, rcp, and rcmd without specifying a password.

One must be root to configure trusted access at the host level. This configuration consists of editing the /etc/hosts.equiv file. Each entry in the /etc/hosts.equiv specifies the remote system that is trusted. The root account can never be equivalenced by an entry in the /etc/hosts.equiv file. If the network is connected to the Internet, always use fully qualified host names in this file for security reasons.

Configuring Trusted User Access

Trusted user access allows users on one system to indicate which users from another system they trust to use their account via the rlogin, rcp, and rcmd commands without providing a password. Unlike trusted host access, trusted user access can be created for users on different machines with different login names.

One can configure trusted user access for users or they can do it for themselves by creating or modifying a file called .rhosts in the user's home directory. The format is the same as in the /etc/hosts.equiv file.

TCP/IP Performance Tuning

Troublemaking performance problems associated with TCP/IP are typically the result of too much traffic. The cause of the traffic can involve several factors:

- Physical layer performance.
- Networking card performance.
- Machine performance.
- Network loads.
- Data corruption.
- Distribution of resources to appropriate nodes and networks.

If the network appears to be performing poorly, any combination of the preceding factors may be the cause.

Data Corruption

Data can be corrupted in several ways:

- Via echoes.
- Improperly terminated cable.
- Detecting echoes with a cable scanner.
- When packets are transmitted to a host faster than its networking card can buffer the packets.
- Increased traffic.

Network performance problems may also be due to overloading physical layer capabilities. The tools for diagnosing performance problems include Ping-f.

The commands to use are:

netstat ls - 1 Lists the files that show the owner.
Netstat-i Displays stats about each network interface.
netstat-s Displays packet stats.

Network File System

NFS allows you to make entire file systems or directories on one host available to many other hosts, which treat the disk space as though it were their own.

How are file systems on disks mounted? Manually they are mounted using the **mount(ADM)** command and automatically at system start-up through entries in the **/etc/dfault/filesys** file. This is equivalent to the **/etc/fstab** file found on Berkley and System V systems.

Who has access to the **mount(ADM)** and **/etc/dfault/filesys** commands? Review the **/etc/dfault/filesys** for the following entries:

```
passwd=string /* an optional password prompted at mount request time. */
fsck=yes,no, dirty, prompt
rcmount=yes,no, prompt
fstyp=type
nfsopts=opts
```

The mount command may also be used to mount a file system or directory of a remote computer on to a mount point on the local host. Two conditions must be met to accomplish this:

- Network communication must be established between the two.
- The remote host must assign the local host the permission to mount its file system.

fsck *Checks the File Integrity*

When a file system is mounted over a mount point directory, it replaces the mount point directory with its own root directory.

Server Configuration

Server configuration is a matter of listing which directories the server should export and to which clients they are to be exported. Review the **/etc/exports** file to see how anonymous **UIDs** are treated and to review the list of file systems the NFS server is willing to share with other systems and in what way it is willing to share them. Note: The script that starts the **NFS daemons** is **/etc/nfs**. This script will only start the **daemons** necessary if the **/etc/export** file exists. Normally an empty **/etc/export** file is created so that in the future when an **NFS** server is required, the **daemons** will already be running. However an empty **/etc/export** file creates security exposures.

Network File System Performance

The **nfsstat** file displays **NFS** statistics (reset these stats by typing **nfsstat -z**. The use of **NFS** opens the system to additional security risks, all of which are manageable but must be handled. **NFS** security issues include the following:

- **Setuid** and **setgid** bits on files on NFS servers. Files marked with the **setuid** and **setgid** bits pose a risk to remote systems mounting the files via **NFS** like they do the local system on which they physically reside. Further, an NFS file server may have a setuid file that one does not want to be setuid on NFS clients. Therefore, ensure that the nosuid option to the mount command is specified. Specifying this flag means that NFS will not honor the setuid permission on files accessed through NFS.

- Root privileges. All NFS operations pass the UID and GID of the process requesting I/O operations from the client to the server. However, this may be dangerous if the UID is 0 (i.e., the process on the client is running as root). Therefore, NFS normally passes the UID -2 to the NFS server if the UID on the client is root. You can force NFS to pass the UID 0 to the server by specifying: root=host[:host...] where host is a fully qualified host name in the /etc/exports file. Review the use of forced UID 0 to determine the appropriateness.

Network Information Services

Network Information Services (NIS) provides one with an easy way to maintain user equivalence throughout the enterprise network, including full integration with account administration tools. The NIS user should be able to answer the following questions:

- What is NIS?
- How is it configured?
- How is it administered?
- What is the client-server architecture of NIS, including the various kinds of NIS servers?
- What are the NIS maps and list what maps are configurable by default?
- What are the NIS management tools?
- The daemons used to implement NIS perform what function?

The importance of user equivalence cannot be underestimated. As the size of the network increases, the administrator's ability to maintain user equivalence with manual methods becomes impossible. NIS was created to solve the problem of distributing a user's account information throughout the enterprise domain in an efficient way.

By default, NIS distributes the following files:

/etc/passwd/etc/group
/etc/hosts
/etc/ethers
/etc/netgroup/etc/protocols
/etc/services

In addition, NIS information can be included in many other network-related files including:

/etc/exports
/etc/hosts.equiv
.rhosts
/etc/auto.master

NIS *Security Issues*

NIS opens several potentially large security holes in the network. With care, these holes can be plugged.

One should only distribute administrative accounts if the password for administrative accounts including root should be the same on all machines running NIS. This means that if someone were able to crack root's password on one machine on the network, they would have it for all of the machines on the network. If any machine is allowed to set the binding of a host, then a devious person could send the hosts a ypset command that causes them to bind to this devious person's NIS server. This person would have account names all ready to go that had UID 0 (i.e., root privileges). This person can now control the hosts.

TCP/IP Administration

TCP/IP functionality is configured by the following:

- The role of the /etc/tcp file in initializing the TCP/IP environment.
- The function of the inetd daemon.

BOOTY AND RARP
/etc/shells/ files
Anonymous FTP
Trusted user access

TCP/IP should be tuned for better performance and functionality.

AUDITING

Auditing allows one to record user access to objects. The resulting record can show such things as repeated attempts by a user to assume a level of privilege that exceeds the user's approved level (i.e., super user). By checking the audit record one can monitor system activities. Once you follow the procedures outlined in this section concerning the installation of the new operating system and conversion to a secure (trusted) system, you are ready to begin auditing. The auditing subsystem allows one to audit selected users performing selected types of activities on the system.

Users are audited through their association with their audit ID numbers, assigned automatically by the system. The audit ID (a number ranging from 0 to 60,000) is kept in the / .secure/etc/passwd file, which can only be read by super users. When an audited user logs in, any action (also selected for auditing) performed by that user is traceable to the user through the audit ID.

Select actions you wish to monitor such as file deletions. Choose to audit any action you select such as:

- When the action is attempted and either succeeds or fails.
- Only when the action is attempted and fails.
- Only when the action is attempted and succeeds.

The types of activities that need to be monitored are:

- Use of identification and authentication mechanisms such as login.
- File manipulations such as opens, closes, deletions, and creations.
- Security-related actions such as turning the auditing system on and off and changing the password file.
- Printing.

SELECT EVENT TYPES FOR AUDITING

To simplify the selection of actions to be audited, system activities with similar behavior are grouped together in categories called *event types.* Selecting one of these event types to be audited automatically turns auditing on for all processes in that category. However, system calls for auditing can be selected without selecting the event type that they belong to. Also, system calls selected for auditing because of their association with a particular event type can be removed.

Exhibit 6.5 shows the event types (and the processes associated with them) that can be selected for auditing.

Exhibit 6.5 Event Types

Event Type	Description of Action	Associated Processes
Create	Log all creations of objects (files, directories, other file objects)	creat(2), mknod(2), mkdir(2), semget(2), msgget(2), shmget(2), shmat(2), pipe(2)
Delete	Log all deletions of objects (files, directories, other file objects)	rmdir(2), semctl(2), msgctl(2)
Moddac	Log all modifications of objects' Discretionary Access Controls	chmod(2), chown(2), umask(2), fchown(2), fchmod(2), setacl(2), fsetacl(2)
Modaccess	Log all access modifications other than Discretionary Access Controls	link(2), unlink(2), chdir(2), setuid(2), setgid(2), chroot(2), setgroups(2), setresuid(2), setresgid(2), rename(2), shmctl(2), shmdt(2), newgrp(1)
Open	Log all openings of objects (file open, other objects open)	open(2), execv(2), ptrace(2), execve(2), truncate(2), ftruncate(2), lpsched(1M)
Close	Log all closings of objects (file close, other objects close)	close(2)
Process	Log all operations on processes	exit(2), fork(2), vfork(2), kill(2)
Removable	Log all removable media events (mounting and unmounting events)	smount(2), umount(2), vfsmount(2), rfa_netunam(2)
Login	Log all logins and logouts	login(1), init(1M)
Admin	Log all administrative and privileged events	stime(2), cluster(2), swapon(2), settimeofday(2), sethostid(2), privgrp(2), setevent(2), setaudproc(2), audswitch(2), setaudid(2), setdomainname(2), reboot(2), sam(1M), audisp(1M), audevent(1M), audsys(1M), audusr(1M), chfn(1), chsh(1), passwd(1), pwck(1M), init(1M)
Ipccreate	Log all ipccreate events	socket(2), bind(2), ipccreate(2), ipcdest(2)
Ipcopen	Log all ipcopen events	connect(2), accept(2), ipclookup(2), ipcconnect(2), ipcrecvcn(2)
Ipcclose	Log all ipcclose events	shutdown(2), ipcshutdown(2)
Ipcdgram	Log ipc datagram transactions	udp(7) user datagram
uevent 1, uevent2	Log user-defined events	See the following section "Streamlining Audit Log Data."

STREAMLINING AUDIT LOG DATA

Some processes invoke a series of auditable actions. To reduce the amount of audit log data collected and to provide for more meaningful notations in the audit log files, some of these processes are programmed to suspend auditing of the actions they invoke and produce one audit log entry describing the process that occurred. Processes programmed in this way are called *self-auditing programs.*

For example, when the login program is invoked it opens, reads, and closes several files to gather the necessary information for logging a user into the system. Each of these opens, reads, and closes may be an auditable action. However, since login is a self-auditing program, the auditing subsystem does not record these subsequent actions. Instead, it makes one entry in the audit log file to record that UserX has logged in to the system (see Exhibit 6.6).

The following processes have self-auditing capabilities:

chfn(1)	Change finger entry.
chsh(1)	Change login shell.
login(1)	The login utility.
newgrp(1)	Change effective group.
passwd(1)	Change password.
audevent(1M)	Select events to be audited.
audisp(1M)	Display the audit data.
audsys(1M)	Start or halt the auditing system.
audusr(1M)	Select users to be audited.
init(1M)	Change run levels and users logging off.
lpsched(1M)	Schedule line printer requests.
pwck(1M)	Password/group file checker.
sam(1M)	The System Administration Manager performs self-auditing for certain security-related tasks.

Self-auditing programs are useful for streamlining the audit data collected on the system. Therefore, two event types, UEVENT1 and UEVENT2, are reserved for self-auditing programs you may want to write. See the following section for guidelines on how to write self-auditing programs.

Exhibit 6.6 Self-Auditing Process

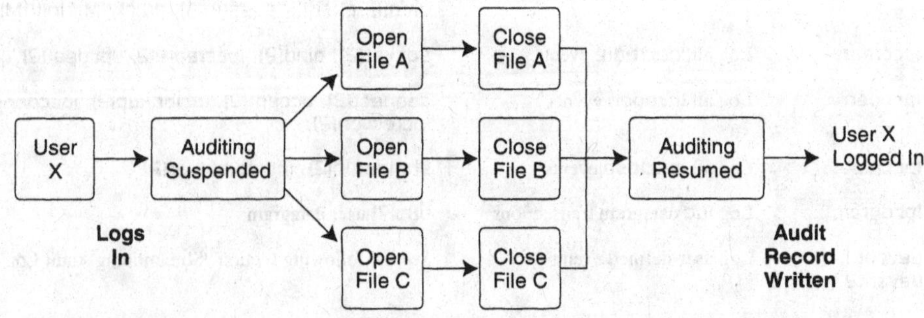

WRITING PROGRAMS

Users with super user permission may wish to write their own programs to streamline auditing data. Use the **audswitch** and **audwrite** system calls to suspend process-by-process auditing of a program and to generate a summary audit record. One can suspend auditing (**audswitch(AUD_SUSPEND)**), choose key points in the program to generate an auditing record (**audwrite**), and then resume regular auditing (**audswitch(AUD_RESUME)**).

Self-Auditing Program

Following is an example of a self-auditing program:

```
#include <stdio.h>

#include <sys/audit.h>
void writerec();
struct self_audit_rec audrec;
main() {
   char *errmesg, *wr_string;
   int fd;
/* suspend auditing for this self auditing process */
if (audswitch(AUD_SUSPEND)) {
   fprintf(stderr,"You do not have privilege
   to access this command\n");
   exit(1);
};

/* do the work that isn't to be audited */
/* open the test file */
if((fd=creat("test_file", 0666))== -1) {
   errmesg="could not create test file\n";
   fprintf (stderr, errmesg);
   writerec(errmesg,3);
}
/* write "that's all folks" to the test file */
wr_string="that's all folks\n";
if(write(fd,wr_string,strlen(wr_string))== -1) {
   errmesg"could not write to test file\n";
   fprint (stderr,errmesg);
   writerec(errmesg,3);
}

/* tell the user what we did */
```

```
errmesg="successfully created *that's all folks* file\n";
printf (errmesg);

/* write *successfully* audit record */
writerec(errmesg,0);

}

/* routine to write an audit record and exit */
static void
writerec(mesg,err)
   char *mesg;
   int err;
{
   extern struct self_audit_rec audrec;

   /* copy output message int audit record body - aud_body.text */
   strncpy (audrec.aud_body.text, mesg, MAX_AUD_TEXT);

   /* initialize the audit record header */
   /* 1. set ah_error to return value */
   /* 2. set ah_event to specify the type of event */
   /* 3. set ah_len to specify the length of the aud_body.text*/
   audrec.aud_head.ah_error = err;
   audrec.aud_head.ah_event = EN_UEVENT1;
   audrec.aud_head.ah_len = strlen(mesg);

   /* resume auditing */
   audswitch(AUD_RESUME);

   /* write the audit record */
   audwrite(&audrec);

   exit (err);
}
```

Note: If the auditing system is turned off at the time the program is run, audwrite returns successfully, but no auditing record is written.

Refer to the *Unix Reference Manual* for more information on how to write self-auditing programs.

AUDIT RECORD

For each event audited, the following information is recorded in the audit log file:

- Date and time of event.
- Audit ID of the user generating the event.
- Subject (user/process).
- Type of event.
- Success and/or failure of event.
- Origin of request (tty) for identification/authentication events.
- Name of an object introduced to or deleted from a user's address space.
- Description of modifications made by the system administrator to the user/system security databases.
- Other information relevant to the event.

AUDIT LOG FILES

All auditing data is written to an audit log file. One can specify two files to collect auditing data, the primary log file and the (optional) auxiliary log file. These files should reside on two different file systems. The growth of these files (and the file systems on which they reside) is closely monitored by the audit overflow monitor daemon, audomon, to ensure that no audit data is lost.

The primary log file is where audit records begin to be collected. When this file approaches a predefined capacity (its Audit File Switch (AFS) size), or when the file system on which it resides approaches a predefined capacity (its File Space Switch (FSS) size), the auditing subsystem issues a warning. When either the AFS or the FSS of the primary log file is reached, the auditing subsystem attempts to switch to the auxiliary log file for recording audit data. If no auxiliary log file is specified, the primary log file continues to grow. Exhibits 6.7 and 6.8 show what happens as this file grows.

The example assumes that:

- Only the primary audit log file has been specified.
- It resides on a file system with no other user files competing for space.

The primary audit log has reached 90 percent of its AFS size. Audomon, which is monitoring the state of the auditing system, issues the warning message shown to the system console.

The primary audit log has passed the first warning point and reached the AFS size. The system attempts to switch to an auxiliary audit log file, but finding none, issues the indicated message periodically to the system console.

In Exhibit 6.9, the primary audit log has grown past its AFS size and reached 90 percent of the space allocated to it on the file system. The message sent indicates that the audit file system is approaching capacity.

In Exhibit 6.10, the primary log file has reached FSS. The message shown is sent periodically to the system console. If other activities consume space on the file system, or the file system chosen has insufficient space for the AFS size chosen, the File System Switch point could be reached before the Audit File Switch point.

Exhibit 6.7 The Primary Audit Log Approaches AFS

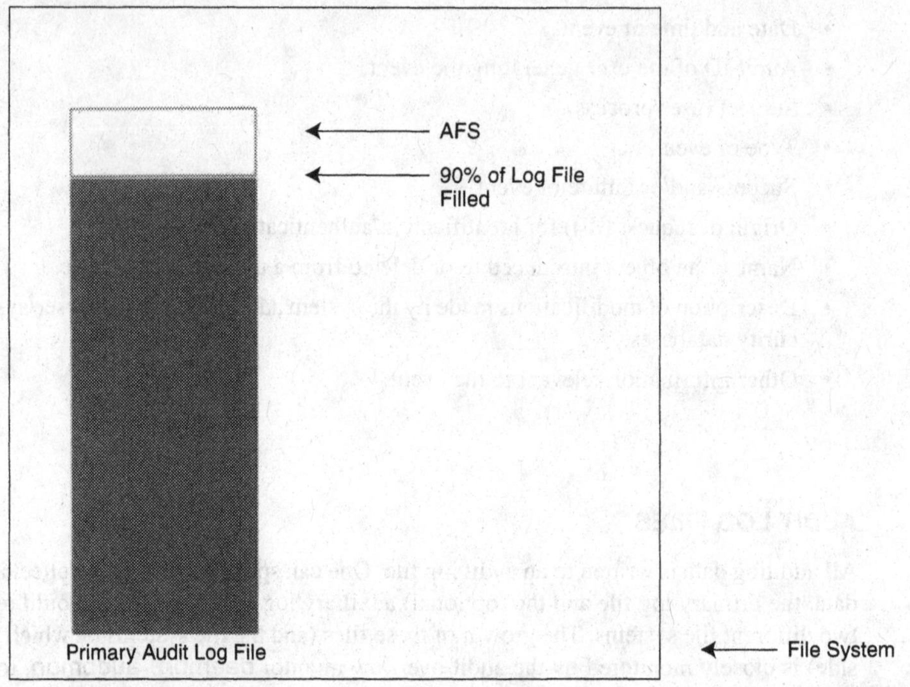

AuditConcern

If the primary audit log continues to grow past the FSS point, a system defined parameter, min_free, could be reached. *All auditable actions are suspended for regular users at this point.* Restore the system to operation by archiving the audit data or specifying a new audit log file on a file system with space.

If, as shown in Exhibit 6.11, an auxiliary log file is specified on a different file system from the primary log file, when the primary log file reaches either AFS or FSS the system switches to the auxiliary log file. From this point the auxiliary log file becomes the new primary log file and the growth stages proceed as in the first example. Note: Specify both a primary and an auxiliary log file that reside on different file systems for best results.

DEFINING AUDITING SYSTEM PARAMETERS

To define parameters:

1. Assess the auditing needs.
   a. How was the size of the audit log files determined?

Exhibit 6.8 Primary Audit Log Reaches AFS

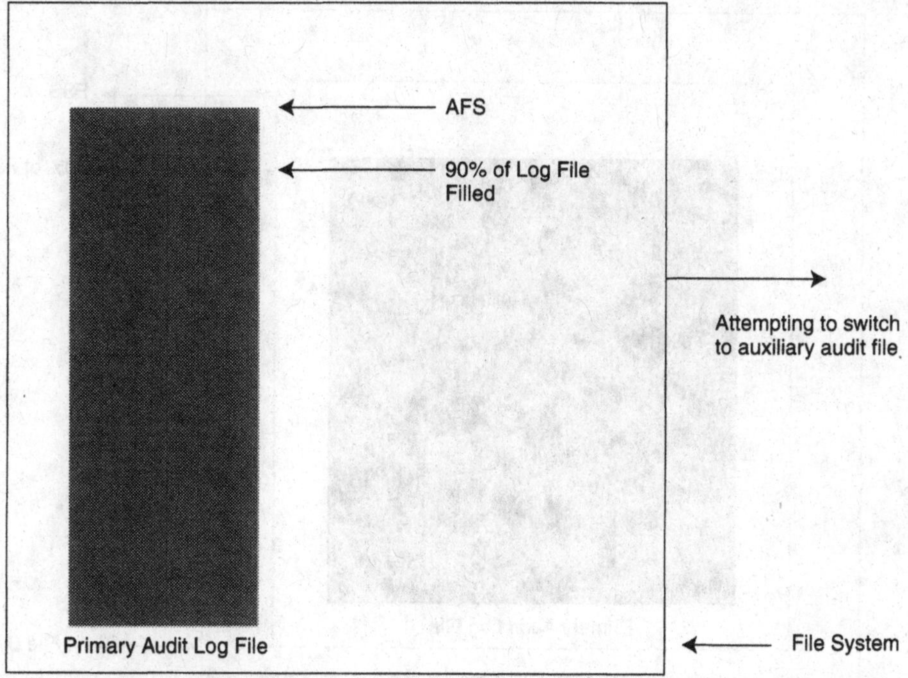

Message: "Current audit file size is _____ kilobytes. An attempt to switch to the backup file failed."

b. How were the events and users to audit decided?

c. How was the frequency to evaluate the audit logs determined?

2. Establishment of an overall security policy.

a. How were the security requirements of the work site identified?

b. How were the written guidelines at both administrative and user levels that reflect the realistic needs of the work site established?

c. How were all personnel-administrators and individual users informed of their security responsibilities?

d. What procedures were in place to keep security guidelines updated and all users informed as requirements changed?

3. Were all existing files on the system inspected for security risks. This is mandatory the first time a secure (trusted) system is installed. Thereafter, files should be examined regularly or when a security breach is suspected.

Exhibit 6.9 Primary Audit Log Approaches FSS

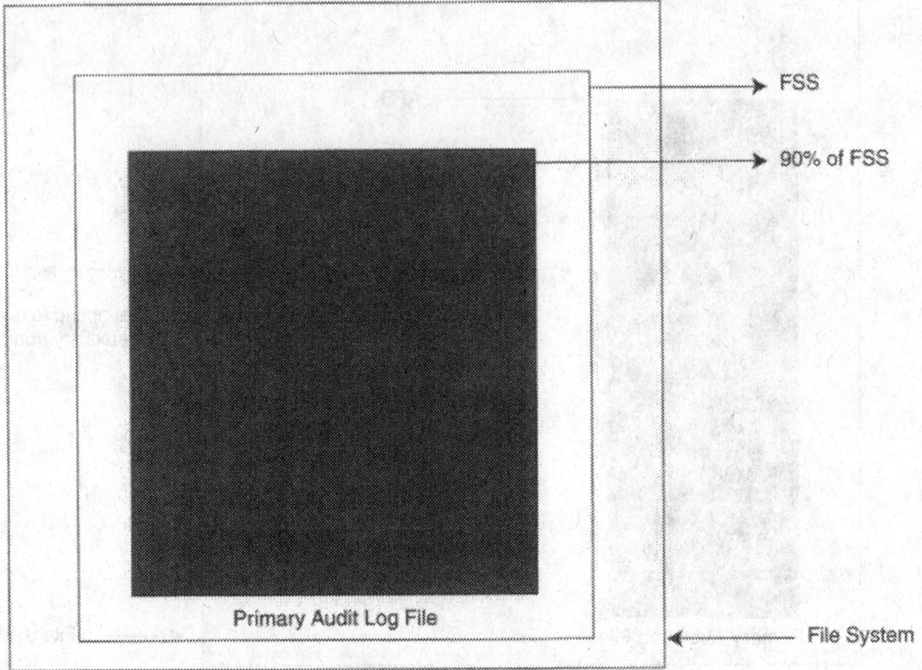

Message: "Audit system approaching file space switch point. Free space left on file system _____%"

AUDITING TASKS

Auditing tasks include information regarding the default auditing system parameters supplied at installation and procedures for:

- Setting audit monitor and audit log parameters.
- Turning auditing on or off.
- Selecting users to be audited.
- Selecting events to be audited.
- Selecting system calls to be audited.
- Viewing audit log files.

Exhibit 6.10 Primary Audit Log Reaches FSS

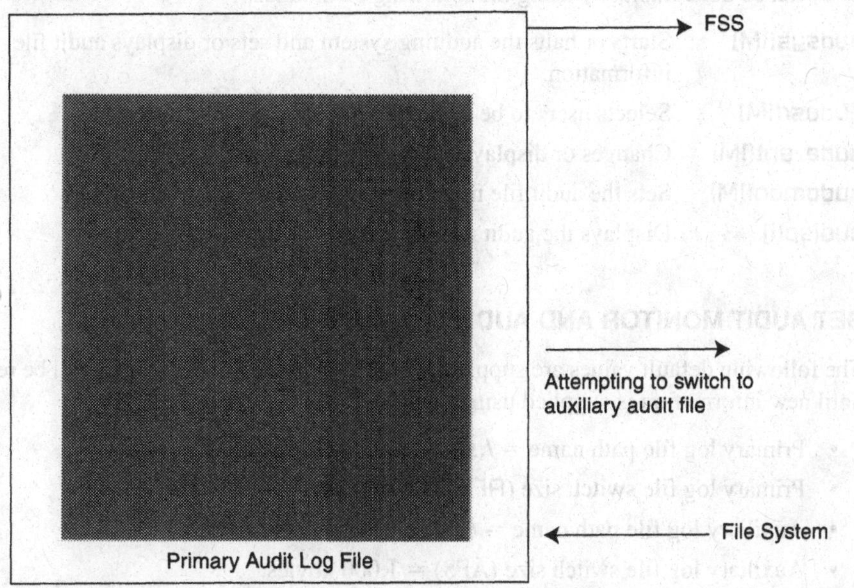

Exhibit 6.11 Primary and Auxiliary Audit Log Files

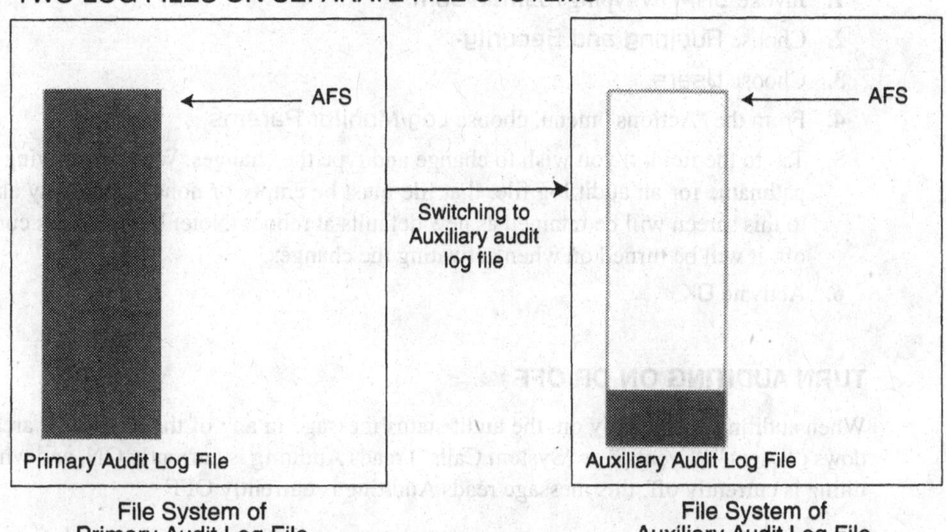

Using SAM to perform all auditing tasks is recommended since it focuses choices and helps to avoid mistakes that might cause a breach in security. However, all auditing tasks can be done manually using the following commands:

audsys(1M) Starts or halts the auditing system and sets or displays audit file information.

audusr(1M) Selects users to be audited.

audevent(1M) Changes or displays event or system call status.

audomon(1M) Sets the audit file monitoring and size parameters.

audisp(1) Displays the audit record.

SET AUDIT MONITOR AND AUDIT LOG PARAMETERS

The following default values are supplied by the system automatically and will be retained until new information is supplied using SAM:

- Primary log file path name = /.secure/etc/auditlog-1.
- Primary log file switch size (AFS) = 5,000 kbytes.
- Auxiliary log file path name = /. secure/etc/auditlog-2.
- Auxiliary log file switch size (AFS) = 1,000 kbytes.
- Monitor wake-up interval = 1 minute.
- Allowable free space minimum (FSS) = 20%.
- Start sending warning messages when log reaches = 90%.

Procedure

When securing the system, to alter any of the preceding parameters:

1. Invoke SAM by typing /usr/bin/sam.
2. Choose Auditing and Security->.
3. Choose Users.
4. From the "Actions" menu, choose Log/Monitor Params...
5. Tab to the field(s) you wish to change and type the changes. When specifying a new pathname for an audit log file, that file must be empty or nonexistent. Any changes to this screen will be retained as new defaults at reboot. Note: If auditing is currently off, it will be turned on when activating the changes.
6. Activate OK.

TURN AUDITING ON OR OFF

When auditing is currently on, the audit status message in any of the functional area windows ("Users," "Events," or "System Calls") reads Auditing is currently ON, and when auditing is currently off, this message reads Auditing is currently OFF.

Procedure

Secure the system and perform the following steps:

1. Invoke SAM by typing /usr/bin/sam.
2. Choose Auditing and Security Π.
3. Choose Users.
4. Take one of the following actions:
   a. To turn auditing *on,* from the "Actions" menu, choose Turn Auditing ON.
   b. To turn auditing *off,* from the "Actions" menu, choose Turn Auditing OFF.
5. You are informed by a message box of the change you have requested. Activate OK to continue.
6. The "User Audit Status" window now indicates the change requested.

Note: Use this menu item to turn auditing on and off when audit log file and monitor parameters stay the same. When changing audit log file and monitor parameters, choose the Log/Monitor Params. . . menu item to make the changes and turn auditing on or off.

SELECT USERS TO BE AUDITED

An audit flag is set to on for all existing users at initial conversion to a trusted system. To change the selection of audited users on the system do the following procedure.

Procedure

Secure the system and follow these steps:

1. Invoke SAM by typing /usr/bin/sam.
2. Choose Auditing and Security Π.
3. Choose Users.
4. Highlight the users whose auditing status is to be changed.
5. To change the auditing status of the highlighted users, choose one of the following from the "Actions" menu:
   a. Audit Users
   b. Don't Audit Users
6. A confirmation message will be received from the system. Activate OK to continue.

Note: The y or n next to the name of each highlighted user will be changed to reflect the choice. New users added to the system are automatically audited. You must enter this screen to turn auditing off for any new user that you do not wish to have audited.
Note: Changes to this option take effect at next login. For example, if user 1 is added to the list of users being audited, and user 1 is currently logged on, user 1's actions are not audited until user 1 has logged off and back on.

SELECT EVENTS TO BE AUDITED

The following event types are recommended as a minimal set of auditable events. They are supplied by the system as default event types and become activated when the Perform Task key is pressed.

- Login
- Moddac
- Admin

All system calls associated with a specific event type are audited automatically when that event type is selected for auditing. See the *Unix Reference Manual* for a list of event types and their associated system calls and commands.

Procedure

Secure the system and follow these steps:

1. Invoke SAM by typing /usr/bin/sam.
2. Choose Auditing and Security Π.
3. Choose Events.
4. Highlight the events whose auditing status is to be changed.
5. To change the auditing status of the highlighted events, choose one of the following items from the "Actions" menu:
   a. Audit for success only
   b. Audit for failure only
   c. Audit for both success and failure
   d. Audit for neither success nor failure
6. A confirmation message will be received from the system. Activate OK to continue.

Note: The y or n in the appropriate column next to the name of each highlighted event will be changed to reflect the choice.

SELECT SYSTEM CALLS TO BE AUDITED

All system calls associated with selected event types are audited automatically. The following is a list of the system calls and commands associated with the system-supplied default event types.

login	login(1), init(1M)
moddac	chmod(2), chown(2), umask(2), fchown(2), fchmod(2), setacl(2), fsetacl(2)
admin	stime(2), cluster(2), swapon(2), settimeofday(2), set hostid(2), privgrp(2), setevent(2), setaudproc(2), audswitch(2), setaudid(2), setdomainname(2), reboot(2)

To select additional system calls to be audited, or to remove system calls that have been selected because of their association with a selected event type, do the following procedure.

Procedure

Secure the system and follow these steps:

1. Invoke SAM by typing /usr/bin/sam.
2. Choose Auditing and SecurityΠ.
3. Choose System Calls.
4. Highlight the system calls whose auditing status is to be changed.
5. To change the auditing status of the highlighted system calls, choose one of the following items from the "Action" menu:
   a. Audit for success only
   b. Audit for failure only
   c. Audit for both success and failure
   d. Audit for neither success nor failure
6. A confirmation message will be received from the system. Activate OK to continue.

Note: The y or n in the appropriate column next to the name of each highlighted system call will be changed to reflect the choice.

View Audit Logs

Auditing accumulates a lot of data. SAM gives you the opportunity to select the data you want to view.

Procedure

Follow these steps:

1. Invoke SAM by typing /usr/bin/sam.
2. Choose Auditing and Security Π.
3. Choose Users.
4. From the "Actions" menu, choose View Audit Log. . .
5. Tab to the field(s) you wish to change and type the changes. You may change the following items:
   a. Whether the log output is directed to the screen or to a file.
   b. The name of the file to which log output is to be directed.
   c. Whether to view the records of successful events, failed events, both, or neither.
   d. Which log file to read.
   e. Which user login to view.
   f. Which tty to view.
   g. Which events or system calls to select for viewing. When specifying a new pathname for an audit log file, that file must be empty or nonexistent.

6. Use the default settings on this screen or alter them to suit particular needs.
7. Activate OK.

Note: It may take a few minutes to prepare the record for viewing when working with large audit logs.

Examples

The following sample record from an audit log file shows a failed attempt to open the secure password file:

```
Users and aids:
hesh
69
Selected the following events:
5
All ttys are selected.
Selecting successful & failed events.
TIME             PID  E  EVENT  PPID  AID  RUID  RGID  EUID  EGID  TTY
890620 14:31:30  570  F  5      567   69   69    11    69    11    ttysr
[ Event=open; User=hesh; Real Grp=topaz; Eff. Grp=topaz; Origin=hpkang; ]

    RETURN_VALUE 1 = -1;
    PARAM #1 (file path) = 1 (cnode);
                           0x000e0000 (dev);
                           6418 (inode);
          (path) = /.secure/etc/passwd
    PARAM #2 (int) = 0
    PARAM #3 (int) = 438
```

The initial lines identify information for which the audit log file was searched. Following in tabular form the record shows:

- The year, month, and day (in this case 1989, June, 20th).
- Time of day (in this case 1400 hours, 31 minutes, 30 seconds).
- Process ID (in this case 570).
- Whether the action failed or succeeded (in this case F for failed).
- Event number identified with the event type (in this case 5).
- Parent Process ID (in this case 567).
- Audit ID of the user (in this case 69).
- Real User ID (in this case 69).
- Real Group ID (in this case 11)
- Effective User ID (in this case 69).

- Effective Group ID (in this case 11).
- The tty of the audited event (in this case ttysx) int open (path, of lag [, mode]).

  Self-auditing commands conform to the same tabular format. For example,

  890621 14:12:38 1063 S 9218 1062 76 0 11 0 11 ttyuo

  [Event=login; User=nlb; Real Grp=topaz; Eff.Grrtopaz; Origin=hpkang;]

  SELF-AUDITING TEXT: User= nlb uid=2419 audid=76 Successful login

INTERPRETING AUDIT LOG DATA

Since auditing produces large amounts of data, be discriminating in the selection of event types and users to audit. Selection of all events and all users for auditing could result in an overwhelming amount of data as well as a very rapid filling of disk space. The use of self-auditing programs when appropriate for the operation can help significantly.

When viewing the audit data be aware of the following anomalies:

- Audit data may be inaccurate when programs that call auditable system calls supply incorrect parameters. For example, calling the kill(2) system call with no parameters (i.e., kill()) produces unpredictable values in the parameter section of the audit record.
- System calls that take filename arguments may not have device and inode information properly recorded. The values will be zero if the call does not complete successfully.
- Auditing of the super user while using the SAM interface to change event or system call parameters will result in a long audit record. For example, when you add an event type to be audited in SAM a record will be produced for each event type and system call being audited, for both success and failure if both are turned on, not just for the new event type being added.

MANAGING AUDIT LOG RESOURCES

Because auditing produces large amounts of data, auditing resources need to be managed carefully. The following guidelines should prove helpful:

- Be selective when choosing events and users for auditing.
- Once an audit file is full, immediately respecify the destination file for audit log entries.
- Archive the full audit file onto tape to free up disk space.

An online audit file should be retained for at least 24 hours and all audit records stored off-line should be retained for a minimum of 30 days.

ADMINISTERING THE AUDITING SYSTEM

It is recommended to use the following guidelines when administering the system:

1. Check the audit logs once a day at a minimum.

2. Review the audit log for unusual activities such as:
   - Late hours login.
   - Login failures.
   - Failed access to system files.
   - Failed attempts to perform security-related tasks.
3. Quickly remove users who no longer have access to the system.
4. Prevent overflow of the audit file by archiving daily.
5. Revise current selectable events periodically.
6. Revise audited users periodically.
7. Do not follow any pattern or schedule for event or user selection.
8. Set site guidelines. Involve users and management in determining these guidelines.

Performance Considerations

Auditing increases the system overhead. When performance is a concern (such as in a real-time environment), the system administrator has to weigh security versus performance. Being selective about what events and users are audited can help reduce the impact of auditing to an acceptable level.

USING AUDITING IN A DISKLESS ENVIRONMENT

Audit log files are context dependent files (cdfs). On a diskless duster with server and clients, each cluster node (cnode) records its own audit data. All cnode records are merged into a single audit file viewable using SAM. This merged audit record is shown when using the "View Audit Files" window in SAM. To view a specific subelement, specify the cdf wanted. For example, type / /.secure/etc/auditlog_1+/cnode_name.

BACKUP AND RECOVERY IN A SECURE ENVIRONMENT

Since implementing Unix security features requires that one completely install (not update) Unix Operating System, one needs to back up and recover the entire file system. This section provides security guidance to supplement other information sources and provides security guidelines for file system management tasks such as:

- Backup and recovery.
- Mounting and unmounting a file system.
- System shutdown.

BACKUP SECURITY PRACTICES

For basic instructions on backing up system files, refer to the *System Administration Tasks* manual and fbackup(1M) in the *Unix Reference Guide.*

Orderly backup of files safeguards data against loss by archiving information that can be retrieved in case of system failure or user error. Ensure that a thorough set of procedures has been established and adhered to at all times.

- Use only fbackup(1M) and frecover(1M) to back up and recover files selectively. Before attempting these tasks, reference should be made to the specific pages in the *Unix Reference Guide* for full information.
- Only fbackup(1M) and frecover(1M) retain access control lists (ACLs). However, use the -A option of these commands when backing up and recovering files for use on systems that do not implement ACLs.
- If one plans to recover the files to another system, it should be ensured that the user's username and group name on both systems (the system to which files are being backed up from and recovered to) are consistent.
- Remember that the backup media is sensitive material. Allow access to the media only on the basis of proven need.
- Label backup tapes and store them securely. Off-site storage provides maximum security. Keep archives for six months then recycle the media.
- Since backup takes time and uses considerable media, a schedule should be set up according to how much data one can afford to lose. Criteria include system use, available media, and storage space. Daily incremental and full weekly backups are recommended.
- Be mindful of the security risks posed by automated backup. Be sure that the tape holds the intended contents of the incremental backup. Safeguard the tape against tampering. Do not leave the tape unattended; retrieve it promptly when backup has been completed.
- Be sure that the tape is mounted on the correct output device.
- If backing up to reel tape, be sure that the write ring is in place.
- If backing up to cartridge tape, be sure that the tape is write-enabled.
- Once system backup is complete, remove the write ring on the reel tape or write-disable the cartridge.
- If all files must be backed up on schedule, request that all users log off before performing the backup. However, fbackup(1M) does the best it can by backing up active file systems without interrupting regular work. The backup(1M) command warns if a file is changing while the backup is being performed.
- Examine the log file of the latest backups to identify problems occurring during backup. The backup log file should have restrictive permissions set.

RECOVERY SECURITY PRACTICES

The ability to recover data after user error or system failure endears the user to coworkers and management alike. More importantly, recovery of current data is critical to protecting computerized information. Observe the following precautions:

- Use only the frecover(1M) command to recover files and retain access control list information. However, use the -A option with frecover(1M) when recovering files for use on systems that do not implement ACLs.

- frecover(1M)— allows one to overwrite a file. However, the file retains the permissions and ACLs set when the file was backed up.
- When recovering files from another machine, one might have to execute the chown(1) command to set the user ID and group ID for the system on which they now reside if the user and group do not exist on the new system. If files are recovered to a new system that does not have the specified group, the files will take on the group ownership of the person running frecover(1M). If owner and group names have different meanings on different systems, recovery results might be unexpected.
- Keep the recovery system tape locked up or otherwise physically secured. Allow access to the archive only on the basis of proven need.
- Power failure should not cause file loss. However, if someone reports a lost file after a power failure, look for it in /lost+found before restoring it from a backup tape.
- To verify contents of the tape being recovered, use the -I option of frecover(1M) to preview the index of files on the tape. Note, however, that existing permissions of a file system are kept intact by the backup; frecover(1M) prevents one from reading the file if the permissions on the file forbid it.
- Examine the file listing for overly liberal permissions, setuid, setgid, or sticky bits. Change attributes if warranted, using the chmod(1) command with the -A option, since ACLs might be present. See the *Unix Reference Guide* for detailed specifications.
- Never recover in place any critical files such as /etc/passwd or those in /.secure. Instead, restore the file to a /tmp directory, and give this directory permission drwx------, preventing anyone else from using it, even if others will be able to use the files after verifying their identities and moving them to their final destinations. Compare the restored files with those to be replaced, to ensure that all current data is preserved. Make any necessary changes then move the files into place.

  If this precaution is not followed, a user added to the system after the system has been backed up and possibly after the /etc/passwd file has been changed would be unable to log in unless the current and archival files had been reconciled.
- Never recover /dev files in place. If one does and then tries to reboot, the system is likely to hang and will be unable to reboot.

  Device files can be recovered in /tmp. One must then manually create any missing files based on what is on the tape and recovered to /tmp.
- In another /dev recovery scenario, suppose the disk had crashed and one had no way to recover from their own system. A coworker might have a running system. One could then roll their disk over to their coworker's system and mount their disk in /mysys, owned by root and with permissions set to drwx------. Then one could cd/mysys and recover the /dev files in place. Retrieve their disk and boot up.
- Auditing is not enabled automatically when one has recovered the system. One has to ensure to turn auditing on.

MOUNTING AND UNMOUNTING A FILE SYSTEM

Mounting a file system can create security problems

- If not done carefully.
- If the media being mounted contain compromising files.

- In an NFS-configured computer environment.

This section is intended to provide a security perspective on these tasks. The /etc/mount command enables one to attach to an existing filetree by using removable file systems and disks or disk partitions.

The mount command uses a file called /etc/mnttab that contains a list of available file systems and their permissions. The /etc/mnttab file should be writable only by root, but readable by others. Observe the following precautions when mounting a file system or disk:

- Create a mount point directory (such as /mnt) on which to mount a new file system. Never mount a file system in the directory tree already containing files because those files will become inaccessible.

  The mount point of a mounted file system acquires the permissions and ownership of the file system's root directory.
- Use base mode permissions and access control list entries on disk pathnames to control access to disks.
- Use the -r option of the mount command to maintain the write protection of tape drives and disks.
- When mounting a new or foreign file system, assume that the medium is insecure.
  - Create a directory restricted to root by setting its permissions at 700 drwx- - - -. Mount the foreign file system read-only at that location, for example, by loading the disk and typing mount /dev/diskl /securefile -r.
  - Check all directories for special objects and privileged programs, and verify the identity of every program.
  - Run ncheck -s to scan for setuid and setgid programs and device files and investigate any suspicious findings. Remove any unnecessary setuid and setgid permissions from files. These precautions are especially important if a user requests that you mount a personal file system.
  - Run the fsck program to verify that the file system is not technically corrupted.

  Only after performing these tests should you unmount the file system and remount it in its desired location.
- Be sure to unmount all mounted file systems of a user whose account you are disabling or removing.

SHUTTING DOWN A SYSTEM SECURELY

Shutdown is used to halt the system in an orderly fashion for maintenance, installation, or powering down, without adversely affecting the file system. After a grace period, shutdown

- Kills all unnecessary processes.
- Forces the contents of the file system's I/O buffers to be written to the disk (with the sync command).
- Places the system in single-user state (also known as system-administration mode, or run-level s).

Shutdown can also abruptly halt or reboot the system. Since it is run only from the system console by a user logged in with `root` privileges, shutdown must be performed conscientiously to maintain system security.

Observe the following security precautions when bringing down the system:

- Instruct users to log out before starting final shutdown procedures.
- When invoking the shutdown command, set a grace period to allow stragglers to log out and processes to complete.
- Always use reboot or shutdown to halt the CPU. If you simply pull the plug or push the reset button, all the processes halt and `syncer` cannot write the memory buffers on to the disk.
- Never leave the system in the system-administration (`s`) run level any longer than necessary. Shutdown does not self-audit, and it turns auditing off.
- Do not physically `write`-protect a mounted file system, since this prevents `syncer` from updating the hard disk.
- Complete the shutdown before taking off-line any disk drives or other peripherals. Do not take a disk off-line without syncing and unmounting the file system on the disk.
- If the computer is halted and the last command involving output to the file system was not a reboot or shutdown, a superblock might be corrupted. The `fsck` program can be used to detect superblock inconsistency.

APPENDIX 6A

GLOSSARY OF UNIX TERMS

Administrative domain	A group of systems connected by network services that allow users to access one another without password verification.
Audit File Switch point (AFS)	The point of saturation of the audit log file when auditing attempts to switch the recording of log data to a backup file.
Audit ID	A number assigned by the system and unique to each user, used to identify users for auditing purposes.
audomon	The auditing system monitor daemon.
Auxiliary log file	A backup file used for collecting auditing data.
Discretionary access control (DAC)	A means of restricting access to objects based on file permission modes that can be set by the owner.
Event type	System activities with like behavior that have been grouped together for use by auditing.
File System Switch point (FSS)	The point of saturation of the file system where the audit log file resides when auditing attempts to switch the recording of log data to a backup file.
Least privilege	Users receive the lowest level of privilege necessary to perform their tasks.
Min-free	A system-defined saturation point for file systems.
Password	A private character string used to authenticate an identity.
Primary log file	The current file used by auditing for collecting data.
SAM	The System Administration Manager. A menu-driven package that simplifies some of the most commonly performed system administration tasks.
Self-auditing programs	Programs that can suspend low-level auditing of certain processes.

`setgid` program	A program whose group ID is set to grant a user privileges equivalent to that of the program group.
`setuid` program	A program whose user ID is set to grant a user privileges equivalent to that of the program owner.
Trap door	A hidden software or hardware mechanism that circumvents system security.
Trojan horse	A computer program containing additional functionality that exploits the program's capabilities for destructive ends.
Trusted computing base (TCB)	All protection mechanisms within a computer system (including hardware, firmware, and software) responsible for enforcing the security policy. Security effectiveness is based on both the TCB mechanisms and its correct implementation by system administrative personnel.
Trusted system	A system that employs sufficient hardware and software security measures to allow its use for processing sensitive material.
Virus	Code segments that replicate themselves through a system destructively.
Worm	A program that migrates through a system for harmful purposes.

APPENDIX 6B

UNIX ENVIRONMENT CONTROL FEATURES

NIS Unix Environment Control Features

No.	Audit Test	Control Objective	Risk
1	Check for the existence of NIS with /usr/bin/ypwhich.	NIS is a distributed database system that lets many computer systems share password files, group files, and other files over the network.	
2	Review the output of command: domainname.	Domainnames and NIS Server names are easy to guess.	Domainname should be hard to guess. It can be used with NIS to grab password files.
3	Review NIS password file with command: ypcat passwd.	All user identification codes defined in the NIS password file have a password.	This increases the risk that unauthorized users log in to these unprotected accounts. Once this access is achieved, the unauthorized user has access to a user's configuration files and any system processes owned by that user. In addition, the user may then attempt to gain further access to the system by exploiting other weaknesses.
4	Review the NIS password file with the preceding command looking for any user account that has a UID of 0.	Root level identification codes are defined on local servers and are not provided domainwide access through the NIS password file.	This increases the risk that administrative users have privileged access to systems that are not required for their job functions. Users that have access to these systems as root have the ability to modify or delete system configuration files, system processes, and modify or delete sensitive user data files.
5		Duplicate UIDs are not permitted and should not exist in the NIS password file.	Duplicate UIDs increase the risk that unauthorized users will modify or delete files created by another user, and accountability is in jeopardy.
6	Review the script output of the ypcat passwd command. Note the number of users listed as compared with the entire user population. Review the list with the system administrator and verify that the level of access is appropriate for the listed users.	Only users who require domainwide access are included in the NIS password file.	Users with domainwide access may have privileges that go beyond their job responsibilities. They may perform unauthorized functions or access sensitive files.

Finding	Control Techniques
	Avoid using obvious domainname.
	The system administrator should immediately assign passwords to these accounts, then notify each user of their assigned password and ask that they log in and change their password. If no user is associated with the user ID, the user ID should be removed from the NIS password file.
	The system administrator should remove any privileged identification codes from the NIS password file.
	The system administrator should delete any duplicate UIDs and create new unique identification codes for each user. The ownership of any files owned by the duplicate users should be changed to match the newly created UIDs.
	The system administrator should restrict users access where appropriate by removing users from the NIS password file.

NIS Unix Environment Control Features

No.	Audit Test	Control Objective	Risk
7	Review the script output of the ypcat passwd command. Identify users that have access to the shell (i.e., access to /bin/sh, /bin/csh, or /bin/ksh located in the last field of the NIS password file. Review the list with the system administrator and verify that users with shell access require that access for their job functions.	End users are not provided command line access to the Unix operating system.	Access to the command line via a shell (the command line interpreter) increases the risk that users access unauthorized commands, data, and configuration files.
8	Review the script output of the ypcat passwd command and identify generic user identification codes. Review the list of generic users with the system administrator to define their use and purpose.	The use of generic user identification codes is not permitted and not evident within the system.	Generic user identification codes limit accountability on user action performed while logged in as a generic user. Even if the system is logging all events of the generic user. In addition, default, generic users, such as the "guest" identification code are normally targeted by intruders attempting to gain access to a system.
9	Review NIS+ password file for issues with the command: niscat passwd.org_dir.		
10	Review output of command: ypcat group.	Verify that there are no duplicate GIDs.	This increases the risk that unauthorized users will modify or delete files created by another user.
11	Review output of: ypcat passwd ypcat group.	Verify that only authorized and approved user codes are members of privileged groups.	Identification codes listed in privileged groups such as GID=0 have access to group writable files created and owned by the root user. This increases the risk that sensitive system configuration files will be changed or deleted.

Finding	Control Techniques
	In order of effectiveness: 1. Replace the shell located in the last field of the NIS password file with a menu program. 2. Give users a restricted shell with no access to `cd`, `rm`, `cat`, and other sensitive commands.
	The system administrator should deactivate the generic users and remove them from the NIS password file. It should be investigated whether or not all users who currently access the system via the generic ID can be moved to individual IDs with a similar environment.
	The system administrator should delete any duplicate GIDs and create new unique group identification codes for each group. The group ownership of any files owned by the duplicate groups should be changed to match the newly created GIDs.
	The system administrator should remove any user codes that do not need access to the GID=0 group.

NIS Unix Environment Control Features

No.	Audit Test	Control Objective	Risk
12	Review the NIS services output with the command: ypcat services.	The FTP service defined by NIS is configured on the "well-known port" of 21. The Telnet service defined by NIS is configured on the "well-known port" of 23. The mail or smtp service defined by NIS is configured on the "well-known port" of 25.	Many router-based access control lists (ACL) filter TCP/IP packets based on the port being accessed. Configuring these services on any port other than the "well-known port" increases the risk that unauthorized users will bypass the controls of the router ACLs. Many publicly available programs called "port scanners" will identify open ports and the service to which they are assigned on the host.
13	Review the output of ypcat services and netstat -na.	Only properly configured and approved services are being provided in the nonprivileged port range. (Ports greater than 1,023.)	Many third-party software packages require the ability to communicate to other hosts on the network within the nonprivileged port range. Open ports increase the risk that unauthorized users will gain access to the system.
14	Review the NIS hosts file with the command: ypcat hosts.	Only valid, authorized, and known hosts are listed in the NIS hosts file. Review the list with the administrator and verify that all hosts are valid and approved to be in the NIS domain.	Unneeded or unauthorized hosts in the NIS hosts file increases the risk that unauthorized users gain access to hosts within the NIS domain.
15	Review the NIS hosts file.	Review output and review the list with the system administrator. Verify that all hosts are within the NIS domain.	Hosts in the NIS hosts file from outside the domain increase the risk that unauthorized users gain access to hosts within the NIS domain.
16	Review the output of: ypcat services, /etc/inetd.conf file and netstat –a.	Review output for the running of the NIS rstat daemon.	The rstat daemon gives an intruder information about the host, including when the machine was last booted, how much CPU it is using, how many disks it has, and how many packets have reached it, load average, network traffic, etc.
17	Review output of the preceding.	Review the output for the running of the NIS rusers daemon.	Rusers provides information on users on the host. It provides information on how busy the machine is and on login accounts an intruder can use in an attack. Obtained account information can be used by a scanner or attacker in a brute force attack.
18	General NIS issues.	NIS Yellow Pages (YP) service or YPBind is running.	NIS (Network Information Service) contains data such as host files, password files, and e-mail aliases for entire networks. It allows a remote user to obtain copies of the NIS password map information. An intruder who possesses the NIS domainname (often set up as a derivative of the public domainname) can steal information helpful in guessing passwords and gaining unauthorized access.

Finding	Control Techniques
	If the FTP, Telnet, and SMTP services are configured on ports 20 and 21, 23 and 25 respectively, no recommendation is required. However, if the service is configured on any other port, the system administrator should reconfigure the service on to the standard ports.
	If the open ports are required, no recommendation is required. However, the system administrator should remove unnecessary ports from the list.
	If all hosts are required, no recommendation is required. However, the system administrator should remove any unnecessary hosts from the list.
	If all hosts are required, no recommendation is required. However, the system administrator should remove any unnecessary hosts from the list.
	Disable service by commenting out the rstat entry in the /etc/inetd.conf file. Restart the inetd process.
	Disable service by commenting out the rusers entry in the /etc/inetd.conf file.
	If possible a different approach should be taken to the distribution of this type of information to servers. There are several commercial packages as well as many homegrown systems that accomplish these tasks in a more secure way.

Local Users and Groups: Unix Environment Control Features

No.	Audit Test	Control Objective	Risk
19	Review the output of: cat /etc/passwd. Note if the second field in the file contains "x,*,!" or an encrypted password string.	The password file should be shadowed and does not include encrypted passwords.	Unshadowed password files increase the risk that unauthorized users will attempt to gain access to the system by cracking user passwords.
20	Review output of: cat /etc/passwd.	Verify that all user identification codes defined within the local password file have a password.	This increases the risk that unauthorized users log in to these unprotected accounts. Once this access is achieved the unauthorized user has access to a user's configuration files, and any system processes owned by that user. In addition, the user may then attempt to gain further access to the system by exploiting other weaknesses.
21	Review output of: cat /etc/passwd for UID=0.	Verify that there is only one root level identification code defined on the local server. User identification codes with the UID = 0 are root equivalent accounts.	Multiple UID=0 identification codes increase the risk that users have system access privileges that are not required for their job functions. In addition, unauthorized users who target privileged identification codes have multiple opportunities to gain root access.
22	Review output of: cat /etc/passwd for duplicate UIDs.	Verify that duplicate UIDs are not permitted and do not exist in the local password file.	Duplicate UIDs increase the risk that unauthorized users will modify or delete files created by another user, and accountability is in jeopardy.
23	Review the script output of the cat passwd command. Identify users that have access to the shell (i.e., access to /bin/sh, /bin/csh, or /bin/ksh located in the last field of the password file. Review the list with the system administrator and verify that users with shell access require that access for their job functions.	End users are not provided command line access to the Unix operating system.	Access to the command line via a shell (the command line interpreter) increases the risk that users access unauthorized commands, data, and configuration files.

Finding	Control Techniques
	The system administrator should shadow the password file.
	The system administrator should immediately assign passwords to these accounts, then notify each user of their assigned password and ask that they log in and change their password. If no user is associated with the user ID, the user ID should be removed from the local password file.
	The system administrator should remove all UID=0 identification codes, except root. Users should be required to log in to their own unprivileged identification codes and "su" to root.
	The system administrator should delete any duplicate UIDs and create new unique identification codes for each user. The ownership of any files owned by the duplicate users should be changed to match the newly created UIDs.
	In order of effectiveness: 1. Replace the shell located in the last field of the password file with a menu program. 2. Give users a restricted shell with no access to cd, rm, cat, and other sensitive commands.

Local Users and Groups: Unix Environment Control Features

No.	Audit Test	Control Objective	Risk
24	Review the script output of the `cat passwd` command and identify generic user identification codes. Review the list of generic user with the system administrator to define their use and purpose.	The use of generic user identification codes is not permitted and not evident within the system.	Generic user identification codes limit accountability on user action performed while logged in as a generic user. Even if the system is logging all events of the generic user. In addition, default, generic users, such as the "`guest`" identification code are normally targeted by intruders attempting to gain access to a system.
25		Duplicate GIDs are not permitted and should not exist in the group file.	Duplicate GIDs increase the risk that unauthorized users will modify or delete files created by another user, and accountability is in jeopardy.
26	Review output of: `cat /etc/passwd` `cat /etc/group`.	Verify that only authorized and approved user codes are members of privileged groups. Such as GID=0.	Identification codes listed in privileged groups, such as GID=0 have access to group writable files created and owned by the `root` user. This increases the risk that sensitive system configuration files will be changed or deleted.

Finding	Control Techniques
	The system administrator should deactivate the generic users and remove them from the password file. It should be investigated whether or not all users who currently access the system via the generic ID can be moved to individual IDs with a similar environment.
	The system administrator should delete any duplicate GIDs and create new unique identification codes for each group. The ownership of any files owned by the duplicate groups should be changed to match the newly created GIDs.
	The system administrator should remove any user codes that do not need access to the GID=0 group.

NFS: Unix Environment Control Features

No.	Audit Test	Control Objective	Risk
27	Review the output of: cat /etc/exports command. Verify that the root or "/" partition is not being exported.	The root partition of a Unix host is not exported for use by any other system.	Root access to exported file systems may allow a privileged user on a remote system unrestricted access to the exported files. This user could then modify or delete any files on the exported file system.
28	Review the output of command: showmount -e hostname for the NFS exports that the machine is telling.	Only authorized file systems are exported by use for other systems.	Unauthorized exported file systems being exported may allow users on remote systems unrestricted access to the exported files. These users can then modify or delete any files on the exported system.
29	Review the output of: cat /etc/exports. Verify the permissions granted on the exported file systems.	File system partitions, such as /usr should be exported read-only.	Exporting file system partitions with read-write access increases the risk that unauthorized users will make changes to system configuration files. These changes may lead to additional unauthorized access or a denial of the services being provided by the system.
30		Application or user file systems should be exported with the nosuid option.	Exporting file systems without the nosuid option increases the risk that nonprivileged users on the system will obtain privileges by executing an SUID command file. By obtaining privileges on the system the user would be able to modify or delete files.
31		All NFS exports are fully qualified domainnames.	Exporting to hosts without fully qualified names increases the risk that a compromised DNS server will allow access to the exported file systems.
32	General NFS		

Finding	Control Techniques
	If a requirement exists to export the root partition the system administrator should export the file system with read-only permissions. However, if the file system is not required to be exported the system administrator should remove the file from the /etc/exports file. If these file systems are required, if possible, explicitly specify each node that can NFS mount the directories.
	All exported file systems should be listed in /etc/exports preferably with Read Only access. If the file systems have not been approved, they should be removed from /etc/exports.
	If the file system is required to be exported the system administrator should configure the export to be read-only within the /etc/exports file.
	The system administrator should export application or user file systems with the "nosuid" parameter.
	Ensure that only fully qualified hostnames are used in defining hosts in the /etc/exports file.
	Ensure that export lists do not exceed 256 characters.

Trusted Hosts (Hosts within the network that are trusted allow users access without password authentication.) Unix Environment Control Features

No.	Audit Test	Control Objective	Risk
33	Review the output of the command: cat /etc/hosts.equiv. Verify that there are no entries within this file. In addition, verify that there is no "+" entry in this file, which would allow any user on any hosts unauthenticated access to the system.	Ensure that there are no trusted hosts within the network.	Any entries in this file increase the risk that an unauthorized user will gain access to the system from a remote system without entering a password. After gaining access this user could modify or delete files and may have access to sensitive processes running on the system.
34	Review the output of the command: cat /etc/.rhosts /etc/rhosts. Verify that there was no file found in the root directory. Additionally, review the policies and procedures surrounding these files with the system administrator.	A root level rhosts file should not exist on the system.	The existence of this file increases the risk that unauthorized users will gain access to the root identification code. **Note:** .rhosts files are easily exploited for unintended purposes. For example, hackers who break into computer systems frequently add their usernames to unsuspecting users' .rhosts files so they can more easily break into the systems in the future.
35	Review the output of the command: find / -name .rhosts –print. Verify that there were no files found on the system.	The use and creation of .rhosts files should not be permitted within the environment.	The existence of these files increase the risk that unauthorized users will gain access to user accounts on the system.
36	Review the files output of the individual rhosts files from the prior step.		The existence of these files increase the risk that unauthorized users will gain access to user accounts on the system.

Finding	Control Techniques
	The system administrator should either remove the hosts.equiv file or remove all entries from within it.
	The system administrator should remove the /.rhosts or /rhosts file.
	The system administrator should remove all .rhosts files located on the system. In addition, the system administrator should create a cron job which searches for and removes these files on a regular basis (i.e., weekly).
	Ensure that any .rhosts files that are required on the system contain only hostnames that are directly controlled within the same network. The systems Administrator should remove any hosts that do not fit this criteria.

General System: Unix Environment Control Features

No.	Audit Test	Control Objective	Risk
37	Verify the operating system level and hostname with the command: uname –a.	Discuss with the administrator the application and schedule of security patches upgrades.	Older versions or unpatched versions of operatings systems often have security vulnerabilities that are exploitable either remotely or locally on the server.
38	Review the services output with the command: cat /etc/services netstat –a. And verify if the services, are running or not, especially if they are on the nonstandard ports.	The FTP service defined is configured on the "well-known port" of 21. The telnet service defined is configured on the "well-known port" of 23. The mail or smtp service defined is configured on the "well-known port" of 25.	Many router-based access control lists (ACLs) filter TCP/IP packets based on the port being accessed. Configuring these services on any port other than the "well-known port" increases the risk that unauthorized users will bypass the controls of the router ACLs. Many publicly available programs called "port scanners" will identify open ports and the service to which they are assigned on the host.
39	Review the output of cat /etc/services and netstat -na.	Only properly configured and approved services are being provided in the nonprivileged port range. (Ports greater than 1,023.)	Many third-party software packages require the ability to communicate to other hosts on the network within the nonprivileged port range. Open ports increase the risk that unauthorized users will gain access to the system.
40	Review the output of the command: cat /etc/inetd.conf.	Ensure that only necessary services are running on the host out of the inetd daemon.	The standard Unix "out of the box" configuration leaves many unnecessary services running which could open the server up to denial of service failures as well as additional entry or information gathering points to an intruder.
41		Ensure that the finger service is not running.	The finger daemon increases the risk that unauthorized users obtain sensitive information about users on the network that could enable them to gain unauthorized access to user accounts.

Finding	Control Techniques
	It is recommended that the operating system be upgraded or that all security patches be applied.
	If the FTP, Telnet and SMTP services are configured on ports 20 and 21, 23 and 25 respectively, no recommendation is required. However, if the service is configured on any other port, the system administrator should reconfigure the service on to the standard ports.
	If the open ports are required, no recommendation is required. However, the system administrator should remove unnecessary ports from the list, and add definitions for needed ones to /etc/services.
	Limit the number of services that are running on the server to those that are needed. Many services have more secure replacements.
	The system administrator should remove the finger daemon from the system start-up files or /etc/inetd.conf.

General System: Unix Environment Control Features

No.	Audit Test	Control Objective	Risk
42		Ensure that the TFTP (trivial file transfer protocol) has been disabled or is running with the secure option. AIX flags: -i Logs the IP address of the calling machine with error messages. -n Allows the remote user to create files on your machine. -r Attempts to convert the IP address to the appropriate host name before it logs messages. This flag must be used with the -l flag or the -v flag. -s Turns on socket-level debugging. -v Logs information messages when any file is successfully transferred by the tftpd daemon. This logging keeps track of who is remotely transferring files to and from the system with the tftpd daemon.	Use of TFTP increases the risk that unauthorized files are transferred across the network. For example, if the /etc/passwd file is transferred across the net, a user could run a cracker program on the password file and obtain unauthorized passwords.
43	Review output of command: cat /etc/tftpaccess.ctl to look at the access control associated with TFTP.	This is potentially an AIX specific file. TFTP reads through this file for lines that start with allow: or deny:. Other lines are ignored. If there is no file, access is allowed. The allowed directories and files minus the denied directories and files can be accessed. For example, the /usr directory might be allowed and the /usr/ucb directory might be denied. This means that any directory or file in the /usr directory, except the /usr/ucb directory, can be accessed. The entries in the file must be absolute pathnames.	

Finding	Control Techniques
	If there is no need to utilize TFTP then the system administrator should remove it from the /etc/inetd.conf file. Otherwise restrict it by invoking the -s option, which restricts its use to a specific directory.
	The file should be write-only by the root user and readable by all groups and others (that is, owned by root with permissions of 644). The user nobody must be able to read the file. Otherwise, the tftpd daemon is not able to recognize the existence of the file and allows access to the entire system. The search algorithm assumes that the local pathname used in the tftp command is an absolute pathname. It searches the /etc/tftpaccess.ctl file looking for allow:/. It repeatedly searches for allowed pathnames with each partial pathname constructed by adding the next component from the file pathname. The longest pathname matched is the one allowed. It then does the same with denied names, starting with the longest allowed pathname matched. For example, if the file pathname were /a/b/c and the /etc/tftpaccess.ctl file contained allow:/a/b and deny:/a, one allowed match would be (/a/b) and no denied match starting with /a/b would be made, and access would be allowed. If the file contained allow:/a and deny:/a/b, one allowed match would be made (/a) and one denied match starting with /a (/a/b) would be made, and access would be denied. If the file contained allow:/a/b and also contained deny:/a/b, access would be denied because allowed names are searched first.

General System: Unix Environment Control Features

No.	Audit Test	Control Objective	Risk
	FTP Access		
44	Review the output of the command: cat /etc/ftpusers to review the ftp access restrictions.	The use of the FTP (file transfer protocol) should be restricted.	Without the existence of the /etc/ftpusers file any user listed in the /etc/passwd file can transfer files across the network. This increases the risk that unauthorized files are transferred across the network.
45	Review the above output. Note the system users included within it. Review the list with the system administrator to determine which system users do not need FTP functionality.	System identification codes should be restricted from using FTP.	System users who are not listed in the /etc/ftpusers file can transfer files across the network. This increases the risk that unauthorized files are transferred across the fnetwork.
46	Review the above output. Users who do not specifically require use of FTP should be identified and restricted from using it. Review the list with the system administrator to determine which users don't need FTP access.		End users not listed in the /etc/ftpusers file can transfer files across the network. This increases the risk that unauthorized files are transferred across the network.
	System Files		
47	Review the output of the command: ls –als /etc by looking at system configuration files such as passwd, hosts, services, and inetd.conf that control the security of the system but are not writable by any user other than root.	System configuration files should be writable only by root.	System configuration files writable by other users increase the risk that unauthorized users delete or modify these files.
48	Review the output of the command: ls –als /bin ls –als /usr /bin ls -als /sbin.	System files such as su, login, and passwd should be writable only by root.	System configuration files writable by other users increase the risk that unauthorized users delete or modify these files.
49	Review the output of the command: ls –als /.	System files such as vmunix, .login, .profile, and .cshrc should not be writable only by root.	This increases the risk that unauthorized users delete or modify these files, including files created by other users.

Finding	Control Techniques
	The system administrator should create the /etc/ftpusers file and at a minimum the following identification codes should be included: This includes the root account, any guest accounts, uucp accounts, accounts with restricted shell, and any other account which should not be copying files across the network.
	The system administrator should include the following system users in the /etc/ftpusers file: root, bin, uucp, nuucp, sync, hpdb, and sys as well as other system ids.
	The system administrator should include the following users in the /etc/ftpusers file: any guest accounts, accounts with restricted shells, and any other account which should not be copying files across the network.
	The system administrator should reduce the permission settings on these files to be writable only by root.
	The system administrator should reduce the permission settings on these files to be writable only by root.
	The system administrator should reduce the permission settings on these files to be writeable only by root.

General System: Unix Environment Control Features

No.	Audit Test	Control Objective	Risk
50	Review the output of the commands: xhost and cat /etc/X0.hosts to review X11-based settings.	X11-based software has been configured in a secure manner by explicitly allowing access to only those addresses on the network that require access.	Unsecured X Windows access allows an unauthorized individual to capture user keystrokes to obtain login IDs and passwords. In addition, an unauthorized user could issue keystrokes as if the user on the vulnerable computers had typed the command (e.g., rm -R *), or export the entire X screen to a remote computer on the network.
51	Review the output of the command: find / -type f -a -perm -4000 -print.	SUID files are authorized, inventoried.	Files that are SUID increase the risk that the user executing the file will escape to a shell. Once at the shell prompt, the user would retain the same access as the actual owner of the file.
52	Review the output of the command: find / -perm -2 ! -type l –print. Review the list with the system administrator to identify any files that are proprietary, sensitive, or confidential.	Application and user files should not writable by any user other than owner.	This increases the risk that unauthorized users modify or delete these files.
53	Review the output of the command: find / -name .netrc –print. Review the files output by this command.	The use of scripts or reference files containing unencrypted passwords should not be permitted within the environment.	The existence of reference files or scripts with unencrypted passwords increases the risk that unauthorized users will gain access to user identification codes on the system.
	Profiles and logins		
54	Review the output of the commands: cat /etc/profile and the files output by: find / -name .profile –print find / -name .login –print find / -name .cshrc –print find / -name .bashrc –print	User file creation default settings are configured to restrict write access to files by other users.	Improperly setting the umask variable in the user's .profile, .login or .chsrc file increases the risk that unauthorized users will modify or delete files created by other users.

Finding	Control Techniques
	The system administrator should execute the command: xhost -. Other security steps include: 1. Specifying individual computers that are permitted to access the X-Windows server. 2. Protecting the command xhost by making the owner root and giving it the permissions of 700, this will allow read, write, and execute access by root only. 3. Ensuring that the xserver is started in a secure manner. Do not execute the -noauth command when starting the X windows. 4. If running the MIT X server use MAGIC-COOKIE by entering the following command: xinit-,xserver,-auth $HOME/.Xauthority.
	The system administrator should verify that these files are proper and needed for the functioning of the system, reducing permissions where possible. Additionally, the system administrator should create a static inventory list of the remaining files and create a cron job that searches for and reports any newly created SUID files on a regular basis (i.e. weekly).
	The system administrator should reduce the permission settings on these files where possible.
	The system administrator should remove all .netrc files located on the system. In addition, the system administrator should create a cron job that searches for and removes these files on a regular basis (i.e., weekly).
	The system administrator should correct any problems noted by changing the umask command in the .login, .cshrc, or .profile script file for these users to 027. This results in the following access to any files created by the user: Owner: read, write, execute; Group: read, execute; World: no access.

General System: Unix Environment Control Features

No.	Audit Test	Control Objective	Risk
55	Review the output of the preceding commands.	Users are restricted from exiting start-up scripts prior to their completion.	Improperly set traps allow users to break out of login shells or scripts and access the command line. Once command line access is achieved users can read sensitive configuration files and attempt to gain further system privileges.
56	Review the output of the preceding commands.	The user PATH variable is configured in a secure manner.	Insecure PATH variables increase the risk that users will be "spoofed" by common system commands such as "ls" (list files), which is executed instead of the system ls. For example, an unauthorized user could write a program that performs certain functions and call the program ls. When an authorized user invokes the ls command the bogus ls program could be executed.
57	Review the output of the commands: SUNOS: cat /etc/ttytab SOLARIS: cat /etc/default/login HPUX: cat /etc/securetty.	Users are required to log in as unprivileged users from every terminal except the console.	Allowing users to log in to the system directly as root from any host on the network, including PCs increases the risk that an unauthorized user will gain privileged access to the system.
58	Review the output of the command: rpcinfo –p. Verify that all RPC programs are appropriate.	Only known RPC programs should be running on TCP and UDP ports.	Unknown or unauthorized RPC programs being provided by either TCP or UDP increase the risk that unauthorized users will gain access to the system.

Finding	Control Techniques
	The system administrator should correct any problems by setting the traps at the beginning of the profile (i.e., .login, .cshrc, or .profile).
	The system administrator should construct the PATH variable so that directories are searched in the following order: (A) System directories, (B) Application directories, (C) User directories (if needed), (D) "." or the current directory (if needed). At no time should a world writable directory be included in any user PATH statement.
	Proper setup should include: Depending on the operating system the method to secure this function will vary. For those systems not specified the control must be placed in the individual user's profile. SUNOS: Review the script output of the cat /etc/ttytab file, only the console entry should be defined as "secure." Solaris: Review the script output of the cat /etc/default/login file and verify that the command CONSOLE=/dev/console has been uncommented. HPUX: Review the script output of the cat /etc/securetty file and verify that the entry "console" is the only entry in the file.
	The system administrator should disable any unknown or unauthorized RPC programs running on the system.

General System: Unix Environment Control Features

No.	Audit Test	Control Objective	Risk
59	Review the output of the commands: ifconfig -a ifconfig -a lan0 ifconfig -a lan1 ifconfig -a lan2 ifconfig -a le0 ifconfig -a le1 ifconfig -a le2 ifconfig -a hme0 ifconfig -a hme1 ifconfig -a hme2 Verify that all network address configurations are appropriate.	All network interfaces are configured appropriately (i.e., promiscuous mode is not enabled).	This increases the risk that a network sniffer is active or could be activated by an unauthorized user.
60	Review the output of the command: netstat –rn netstat –a. Verify that all routes are appropriate.	Ensure network traffic is properly routed through the corporate network.	Improperly routed network traffic may allow unauthorized users to view the network traffic.
61	Review the output of the command: arp –a. Verify that all hosts are appropriate.	Only authorized hosts should be available to communicate on the network.	Unknown hosts on the network increases the risk that unauthorized users will gain access to the system.
62	Review the output of the command: tail -50 /var/adm/sulog with the Administrator to ensure that only authorized users are accessing root.	Ensure that users who access root have that access logged and that the log is reviewed on a regular basis.	Users accessing root have the ability to modify or delete any file on the system.
63	Review the output of the command: dmesg and the policy of system restarts, note any discrepancies.	The system is restarted only when authorized.	Unauthorized system restarts may indicate an unauthorized user attempting to gain privileged access or that a serious configuration or application problem exists.
64	Review the output of the command: cat /etc/syslog.conf.	Ensure that there is adequate logging of system activities.	Insufficient logging will result in a lack of an audit trail in the event of an unauthorized access. With good logging and monitoring Administrators are often given early warnings for hardware and software errors or problems.
65	Review the output of the command: cat /etc/resolv.conf.	Ensure that the correct nameservers and domainname are being used on the machine.	The wrong information could substantially slow down many network requests if reverse lookups are used.

Finding	Control Techniques
	The system administrator should reconfigure any network interface that has been misconfigured.
	The system administrator should work with the network group (or administrator) to configure the network routing appropriately.
	The system administrator should investigate and remove any unknown and unauthorized hosts on the network.
	The system administrator should change the root password and ensure that only authorized users receive it.
	The system administrator should review the system messages on a regular basis and investigate any unplanned system restarts.
	The administrator should review the system log messages on an active basis with alerts being sent off if there are problems.
	Ensure that the DNS lookup information in /etc/resolv.conf is correct.

CHAPTER 7

NETWORKS

Exhibit 7.1 Network Architecture

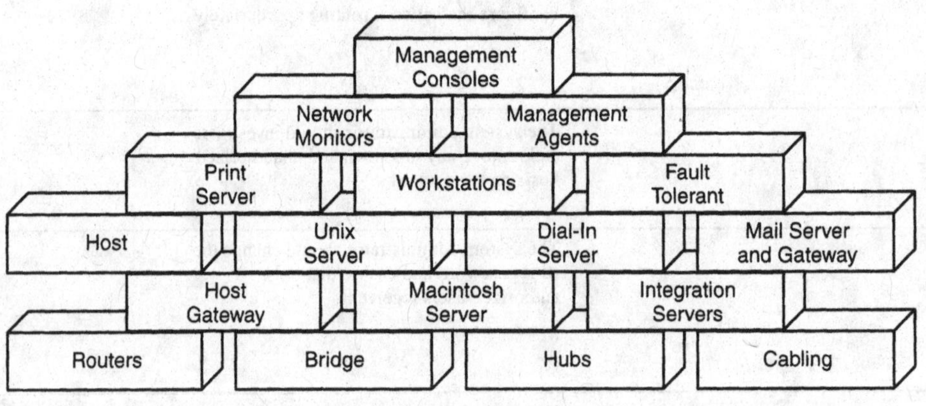

INTERNETWORKING

OVERVIEW

What is an internetwork? An internetwork is a collection of individual networks connected by intermediate networking devices that functions as a single large network. Internetworking refers to the industry, products, and procedures that meet the challenge of creating and administering internetworks.

DEVICES

The three classes of internetworking devices are the hubs (Ethernet hubs) that operate at Layer 1, data link switches that operate at Layer 2, and the network touters that operate at Layer 3.

Communication Devices

The first building block of data internetworking involves getting more than one computer to talk to each other. Devices for this first building block function by transporting information between connected systems. Methods of transport include physical media, data packaging, route determination, and data forwarding. Examples of these are:

- RS-232 (Serial Interface)
- Ethernet used in LAN

Exhibit 7.2 Internetworking Devices

Cable Connectors

1 Bayonet, BNC or 'Stab' ^ 'Twist'
2 RJ-45 (expanded phone connector)
3 D connectors, 9 pin
4 B connectors

Network Cards Based on:

1 Network type
2 Bus type
3 Media type

Network Types

1 Ethernet
2 Token Ring
3 Arc Net
4 Appletalk

Bus Types

1 ISA (8 or 16 bit) bus
2 PCI bus (for IRO Performance, 32 bit)
3 PCMCIA (PC Card-Notebook type of connections)
4 MCA (Microchannel architecture bus-based on the original IBM's P52)
5 NuBus (architecture for the Macintosh)

Media Types

Close Network Interface Cards Based on Type of Media Used:

1 Coax
2 Twisted pair
3 Fiberoptic
4 Microwave
5 Infrared
6 Radio

Settings on the Network Cards

1 IRQ settings
IRQ = default 1-15
Set the same IRQ setting on each one on the system
2 I/O port address
—Main keys should be unique
—Are they the same on each card on the network
3 RAM address
—Where BIOS or address of the BIOS will reside
—If this is incorrectly set, then the system will lock up

Exhibit 7.3 Media Types Media Concerns

#		Cost	Ease of Installations
1	Coax	Moderate, cable inexpensive	Relatively easy
2	Twisted pair		
(i)	Unshielded twisted pair (UTP)	Low	Easy if inside walls, outside walls, around corners
(ii)	Shielded twisted pair	Moderately higher than UTP	Fairly easy
	Legend Bandwidth capacity: amount of information that can be transmitted at the same time		
	Node capacity: number of connections (i.e., point to point or multiple)		
3	Fiberoptic	High	Difficult transmission if wire is broke–no transmission
	Wireless Transmission		
4	Terrestrial (point to point)	Moderate to high	Difficult
	(ii) Satellite	High	Difficult
5	Infrared—laser		
	(i) Point to point	Very high	Difficult
	(ii) Broadcast	Depends on equipment—very high	Easy
6	Radio		
	(i) Low power, single frequency	Moderate	Simple
	(ii) High power, single frequency	High	Difficult
	(iii) Spread spectrum	Moderate	Difficult

Bandwidth Capacity	Node Capacity	Attenuation	Electromagnetic Interference (Sniffer) EMI
10 Mbps	30 nodes per segment of cable	Low, therefore long-distance transmission	Moderate vulnerability
Up to 10 Mbps; can go to 155 Mbps	2 nodes per segment (i.e., 2 connections, one at each end of cable, point to point)	High, therefore short-distance transmission	High vulnerability
1 Mbps up to 155 Mbps	2 nodes per segment, (point to point or to hub)	High, therefore short-distance transmission	Moderate vulnerability
			Resistance to traffic on the network. High attenuation means low distances, low attenuation means long distances
		EMI (interference): noise gets in or information sniffed out	
Up to 2 Gbps (typically 100 Mbps	Point to point (2 nodes per segment)	Low, therefore logon distance uph 2 km	Not vulnerable to sniffing, good for manufacturing industries
1-10 Mbps (e.g., between two large buildings)	2 nodes	Depends on atmospheric conditions (e.g., thunderstorms)	High vulnerability
1-10 Mbps, larger distances	2 nodes	Depends on atmospheric conditions	High vulnerability
100 Kbps–16 Mbps	Application dependent	Depends on light quality	Vulnerability = 0, only affected by intense light vulnerable to interception.
Less than 1 Mbps	Application dependent	Depends on light quality and purity	Vulnerability = 0, only affected by intense light vulnerable to interception.
1–10 Mbps		High	High
1–10 Mbps		Low	High
2–6 Mbps		High	Fair vulnerability: more secure than (i) or (ii) above

- Token ring used in LAN
- IP (Internet Protocol)
- IPX (Novel Networks)
- SNA (IBM's Preferred Network Solution)

Interoperability

The second building block of data internetworking is interoperability. Interoperability encompasses the ability to effectively exchange information between similar and dissimilar systems. The most well-known similar system interoperability solution is the Internet (ASCII, IP). The most well-known dissimilar system interoperability solution is EBCDIC (SNA) <> ASCII (IP), where EBCDIC and ASCII are character representation.

CONTROL REQUIREMENTS

Determine how much thought was put into the design of the network. What topologies were selected and how?

DIFFERENT TYPES OF NETWORKS

The first networks were time-sharing networks that used mainframes and attached terminals. Such environments were implemented by both IBM's System Network Architecture (SNA) and Digital's network architecture.

Local area networks (LANs) evolved around the PC revolution. LANs enabled multiple users in a relatively small geographical area to exchange files and messages and to access shared resources such as file servers.

LOCAL ACCESS NETWORK

A LAN is an interconnected group of systems that covers a single geographic location or site. LANs are typically used for data services and voice. Examples of LAN solutions include:

- Ethernet (10, 100, 1,000 Mbps, 1 Gbps)
- Token ring
- FDDI (Fiber Distributed Data Interface)

Wide area networks (WANs) interconnected LANs across normal telephone lines (and other media), thereby interconnecting geographically dispersed users.

WIDE ACCESS NETWORK

A WAN is a communication system that interconnects multiple geographic sites (i.e., around the world). WANs are typically used for voice, data, and video. Some WAN solutions include:

- Frame Relay
- ISDN

- ATM
- T1, T3

Today, high-speed LANs and switched internetworks are becoming widely used, largely because they operate at very high speeds and support such high-bandwidth applications as voice and videoconferencing.

Internetworking evolved as a solution to three key problems:

1. Isolated LANs
2. Duplication of resources
3. Lack of network management

Isolated LANs made electronic communication between different offices or departments impossible. Duplication of resources meant that the same hardware and software had to be supplied to each office or department, as did a separate support staff. This lack of network management meant that no centralized method of managing and troubleshooting networks existed.

INTERNETWORKING CHALLENGES

Implementing a functional internetwork is no simple task. Many challenges must be faced especially in the areas of connectivity, reliability, network management, and flexibility. Each area is key in establishing an efficient and effective internetwork.

Reliable communication is the first consideration. The challenge when connecting various systems is to support communication between disparate technologies. Different sites, for example, may use different types of media, or they might operate at varying speeds.

Another essential consideration, reliable service, must be maintained in any internetwork. Individual users and entire organizations depend on consistent, reliable access to network resources.

Manageability is the ability to manage and control the network and the visibility to see the conditions as they work. Furthermore, network management must provide centralized support and troubleshooting capabilities in an internetwork. Configuration, security, performance, and other issues must be adequately addressed for the internetwork to function smoothly.

Flexibility, the final concern, is necessary for network expansion and new applications and services among other factors.

ISO HIERARCHY OF NETWORKS

Large networks typically are organized as hierarchies. A hierarchical organization provides such advantages as ease of management, flexibility, and a reduction in unnecessary traffic. Thus, the International Organization for Standardization (ISO) has adopted a number of terminology conventions for addressing network entities. Key terms that are defined in this section include end system (ES), intermediate system (IS), area, and autonomous system (AS).

An ES is a network device that does not perform routing or other traffic-forwarding functions. The typical ES includes such devices as terminals, personal computers, and printers.

An IS is a network device that performs routing or other traffic-forwarding functions. The typical IS includes such devices as routers, switches, and bridges. Two types of IS networks exist: intradomain IS and interdomain IS.

- An intradomain IS communicates within a single autonomous system.
- An interdomain IS communicates within and between autonomous systems.

An area is a logical group of network segments and their attached devices. Areas are subdivisions of autonomous systems.

An AS is a collection of networks under a common administration that share a common routing strategy. Autonomous systems are subdivided into areas, and an AS is sometimes called a domain.

Networking is a complex endeavor, and breaking it into digestible pieces is why a layered network model was developed. The OSI model enables the network to be broken down into logical layers (i.e., the seven layers), which ideally specifies and groups the functions that need to be performed at each layer. These functions within each layer are further broken down into tasks.

The layered network task model facilitates specialization by the age-old concept of division of labor, and this in turn enhances simplicity and increases standardization, which further helps competition and drives costs down. More importantly, this layered approach facilitates intervendor product interoperability. Now one can determine what products are in use and how much interoperability is taking place.

OSI MODEL

OSI (Open Systems Interconnection) is a standard description or reference model for how messages should be transmitted between any two points in a telecommunications network. Its purpose is to guide product implementors so that their products will consistently work with other products. The reference model defines seven layers of functions that take place at each end of a communication. Although OSI is not always strictly adhered to in terms of keeping related functions together in a well-defined layer, many, if not most, products involved in telecommunication make an attempt to describe themselves in relation to the OSI model. It is also valuable as a single reference view of communication that furnishes everyone a common ground for education and discussion.

Developed by representatives of major computer and telecommunications companies in 1983, OSI was originally intended to be a detailed specification of interfaces. Instead, the committee decided to establish a common reference model for which others could develop detailed interfaces that in turn could become standards. OSI was officially adopted as an international standard by the ISO. Currently, it is Recommendation X.200 of the ITU-TS.

The ITU-T (for Telecommunication Standardization Sector of the International Telecommunications Union) is the primary international body for fostering cooperative standards for telecommunications equipment and systems. It was formerly known as the CCITT. It is located in Geneva, Switzerland.

The V Series Recommendations from the ITU-TS are summarized below. They include the most commonly used modem standards and other telephone network standards. Prior to the ITU-T standards, the American Telephone and Telegraph Company and the Bell System offered its own standards (Bell 103 and Bell 212A) at very low transfer rates. Another set of standards, the Microcom Networking Protocol, or MNP Class 1 through Class 10 (there is no Class 8), has gained some currency, but the development of an international set of standards means these will most likely prevail and continue to be extended.

The V Series Recommendations from the ITU-TS

Standard	Meaning
V.22	Provides 1200 bits per second at 600 baud (state changes per second)
V.22bis	The first true world standard, it allows 2400 bits per second at 600 baud
V.32	Provides 4800 and 9600 bits per second at 2400 baud
V.32bis	Provides 14,400 bits per second or fallback to 12,000, 9600, 7200, and 4800 bits per second
V.32terbo	Provides 19,200 bits per second or fallback to 12,000, 9600, 7200, and 4800 bits per second; can operate at higher data rates with compression; was not a CCITT/ITU standard
V.34	Provides 28,800 bits per second or fallback to 24,000 and 19,200 bits per second and backward compatibility with V.32 and V.32bis
V.34bis	Provides up to 33,600 bits per second or fallback to 31,200 or V.34 transfer rates
V.35	The trunk interface between a network access device and a packet network at data rates greater than 19.2 Kbps. V.35 may use the bandwidths of several telephone circuits as a group. There are V.35 Gender Changers and Adapters.
V.42	Same transfer rate as V.32, V.32bis, and other standards but with better error correction and therefore more reliable
V.90	Provides up to 56,000 bits per second downstream (but in practice somewhat less). Derived from the x2 technology of 3Com (US Robotics) and Rockwell's K56flex technology.

An industry standard, Integrated Services Digital Network (ISDN) uses digitally encoded methods on phone lines to provide transfer rates up to 128,000 bits per second. Another technology, Digital Subscriber Line, provides even faster transfer rates.

The main idea in OSI is that the process of communication between two end points in a telecommunications network can be divided into layers, with each layer adding its own set of specially related functions. Each communicating user or program is at a computer equipped with these seven layers of function. So, in a given message between users, there will be a flow of data through each layer at one end down through the layers in that computer and, at the other end, when the message arrives, another flow of data up through the layers in the receiving computer and ultimately to the end user or program. The actual programming and hardware that furnishes these seven layers of function is usually a combination of the computer operating system, applications (such as the Web browser), TCP/IP or alternative transport and network protocols, and the software and hardware that enable a signal to be put on one of the lines attached to the computer.

OSI divides a telecommunications network into seven layers. The layers are in two groups. The upper four layers are used whenever a message passes from or to a user. The lower three layers (up to the network layer) are used when any message passes through the host computer. Messages intended for this computer pass to the upper layers. Messages destined for some other host are not passed up to the upper layers but are forwarded to another host.

Exhibit 7.4 Seven-Layer OSI Model

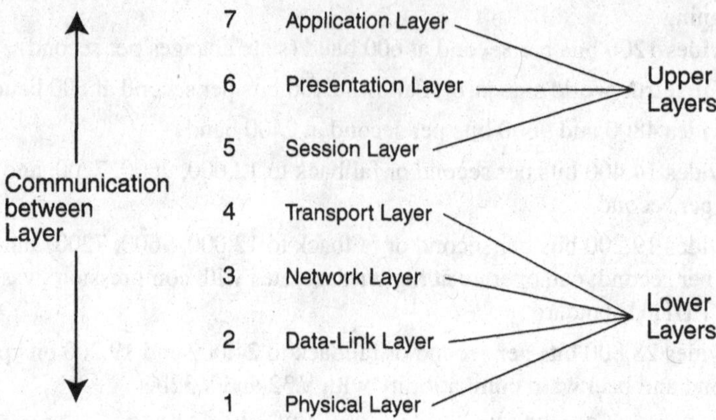

COMMUNICATING DATA THROUGH ENCAPSULATION

The entire packet from a layer is inserted in the data field of the layer below it. This continues until Layer 1 is reached. Large packets may be split up into multiple smaller sections for insertion (see Exhibit 7.4). The packet traverses the network, and the destination peer layer "unwraps" the data portion of the packet and processes what it finds. This may include passing it to a higher layer. Remember that data communication goes from the Application Layer down → Presentation → Session → Transport → Network → Data Link → Physical.

It is at the Physical Layer that it traverses to its destination where it is unwrapped layer by layer from Physical → Data Link → Network → Transport → Session → Presentation → Application. The Application Layer of the destination is where the packet is processed. Following is a discussion of the seven layers.

OSI LAYER 1: PHYSICAL LAYER

The first layer in the OSI model is the Physical Layer, which consists of the hardware. This layer conveys the bitstream through the network at the electrical and mechanical level. It provides the hardware means of sending and receiving data on a carrier.

This layer defines the following:

- Electrical levels and signals that are used for clocking and synchronization
- Transmission distances
- Physical connectors
- Bringing link up and down (voltage)

Examples of hardware are:

- EIA/TIA—232 (RS-232)
- v.35
- HSSI—Serial Interface
- BRI (ISDN)

V.35 The trunk interface between a network access device and a packet network at data rates greater than 19.2 Kbps. V.35 may use the bandwidths of several telephone circuits as a group. There are V.35 Gender Changers and Adapters.

Basic Rate Interface in ISDN BRI (ISDN)

In the Integrated Services Digital Network (ISDN), there are two levels of service: the Basic Rate Interface (BRI), intended for the home and small enterprise, and the Primary Rate Interface (PRI in ISDN), for larger users. Both rates include a number of B channel and a D channel. The B channels carry data, voice, and other services. The D channel carries control and signaling information.

The BRI consists of two 64-Kbps B channels and one 16-Kbps D channel. Thus, a Basic Rate user can have up to 128-Kbps service. The PRI consists of 23 B channels and one 64-Kbps D channel in the United States or 30 B channels and 1 D channel in Europe.

The typical cost for Basic Rate usage in a city like Kingston, New York, is about $125 for phone company installation, $300 for the ISDN adapter, and an extra $20 a month for a line that supports ISDN.

HSSI—High-Speed Serial Interface

The High-Speed Serial Interface (HSSI) is a DTE/DCE interface developed by Cisco Systems and T3plus Networking to address the need for high-speed communication over WAN links. The HSSI specification is available to any organization wanting to implement HSSI.

HSSI is now in the American National Standards Institute (ANSI) Electronic Industries Association (EIA)/TIA TR30.2 committee for formal standardization. It has recently moved into the ITU-T (formerly the Consultative Committee for International Telegraph and Telephone [CCITT]) and the ISO and is expected to be standardized by these bodies.

HSSI defines both the electrical and the physical DTE/DCE interfaces. It therefore corresponds to the Physical Layer of the OSI reference model. HSSI technical characteristics are summarized below.

HSSI Technical Characteristics.

Characteristic	Value
Maximum signaling rate	52 Mbps
Maximum cable length	50 feet
Number of connector pins	50
Interface	DTE-DCE
Electrical technology	Differential ECL
Typical power consumption	610 mW
Topology	Point to point
Cable type	Shielded twisted pair wire

EIA/TIA—

Cabling standards are set by the American National Standards Institute (ANSI), the Electronic Industry Associations (EIA), and the Telecommunications Industry Associations (TIA).

OSI LAYER 2: DATA LINK LAYER (THE VIRTUAL WORLD)

The second layer in the OSI model is the Data Link Layer. This layer provides synchronization for the physical level and does bit-stuffing for strings of 1s in excess of 5. It furnishes transmission protocol knowledge and management.

It consists of hardware and software (built in to firmware). This layer defines:

- Bitstream formatting into "frames"
- Physical addressing
- Network topology (bus, star)
- Error modification (end stations)
- Flow control

The Data Link Layer contains two sublayers: LLC (Logical Link Control) and MAC (Media Access Control).

Some LAN technologies combine Layer 1 and Layer 2 in today's real-world networking environments. LAN/MAN (Metropolitan Area Network) examples are:

- Layers 1 and 2 combined
- Common IEEE 802.X standards
    - 802.2 Defines LLC protocol that all 802.X standards can use
    - 802.3 Ethernet (CSMA/CD)
    - 802.4 Fast Ethernet, 100 BaseT
    - 802.5 Token ring
    - 802.6 Dual fiberoptic bus (MAN)
    - 802.11 Windows LAN using CSMA/CA
    - 802.12 100 VG -Any LAN (Hewlett-Packard)

OSI LAYER 3: NETWORK LAYER

This layer handles the routing of the data (sending it in the right direction to the right destination on outgoing transmissions and receiving incoming transmissions at the packet level). The Network Layer does routing and forwarding. It has two significant components: Routed Protocol (IP) and Routing Protocol.

Routed Protocol has a transport mechanism that one can put data into to move it through the network, and it runs at Layer 3. A routing protocol is actually a program that runs in a router that keeps track of where all the network addresses are and the network segments and what the network looks like so that the routing protocol can make its way through the network (see Exhibit 7.5).

Network Layer (WAN)

x.25 (the original Layer 3-Packet-Switched Network)

Exhibit 7.5 Frame Relay Cloud

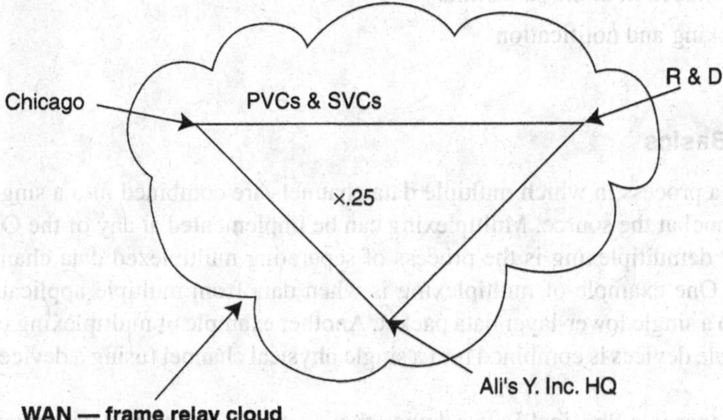

VC — virtual circuit
PVC — permanent virtual (always available)
SVC — switched — created when needed

De facto = standard is accepted as a standard due to its widespread use

Network Layer Addressing

The logical or software address is put into the networking software at Layer 3. It contains a network portion (user defined) and a node portion (created from a MAC address). The node portion is often the MAC address (Layer 2 burnt address from the manufacturer).

Routed protocol has the information necessary at the packet level to make hierarchical addressing and path decision making possible. The hierarchical address structure makes scaling large networks possible.

Roundtrip Protocol maintains the routing-forwarding tables that are used to decide the best way to get from here to there (the concept is metrics—the preferred path). It maintains the constant communication between the network routers needed for up-to-date information about network conditions. It makes the tremendously complex network underneath seem transparent to the end station.

OSI LAYER 4: TRANSPORT LAYER

The fourth layer in the OSI model is the Transport Layer. This layer manages the end-to-end control (e.g., determining whether all packets have arrived) and error checking. It ensures complete data transfer and quality of service. This layer also ensures a transparent, reliable, consistent way to use the network (no long pauses, etc.).

Layer 4 tasks include:

- Flow control—controls information
- Multiplexing ability for more than one program in the network computer to use the network connection at the same time
- Error checking and notification

Multiplexing Basics

Multiplexing is a process in which multiple data channels are combined into a single data or physical channel at the source. Multiplexing can be implemented at any of the OSI layers. Conversely, demultiplexing is the process of separating multiplexed data channels at the destination. One example of multiplexing is when data from multiple applications is multiplexed into a single lower-layer data packet. Another example of multiplexing is when data from multiple devices is combined into a single physical channel (using a device called a multiplexer).

A multiplexer is a Physical Layer device that combines multiple data streams into one or more output channels at the source. Multiplexers demultiplex the channels into multiple data streams at the remote end and thus maximize the use of the bandwidth of the physical medium by enabling it to be shared by multiple traffic sources. Some methods used for multiplexing data are time-division multiplexing (TDM), asynchronous time-division multiplexing (ATDM), frequency-division multiplexing (FDM), and statistical multiplexing.

In TDM, information from each data channel is allocated bandwidth based on preassigned time slots, regardless of whether there is data to transmit. In ATDM, information from data channels is allocated bandwidth as needed, by using dynamically assigned time slots. In FDM, information from each data channel is allocated bandwidth based on the signal frequency of the traffic. In statistical multiplexing, bandwidth is dynamically allocated to any data channels that have information to transmit.

Error-Checking Basics

Error-checking schemes determine whether transmitted data have become corrupt or otherwise damaged while traveling from the source to the destination. Error checking is implemented at a number of the OSI layers.

One common error-checking scheme is the cyclic redundancy check (CRC), which detects and discards corrupted data. Error-correction functions (such as data retransmission) are left to higher-layer protocols. A CRC value is generated by a calculation that is performed at the source device. The destination device compares this value to its own calculation to determine whether errors occurred during transmission. First, the source device performs a predetermined set of calculations over the contents of the packet to be sent. Then, the source places the calculated value in the packet and sends the packet to the destination. The destination performs the same predetermined set of calculations over the contents of the packet and then compares its computed value with that contained in the packet. If the values are equal, the packet is considered valid. If the values are unequal, the packet contains errors and is discarded.

CONNECTION-ORIENTED AND CONNECTIONLESS NETWORK SERVICES

In general, networking protocols and the data traffic that they support can be characterized as being either connection oriented or connectionless. In brief, connection-oriented data handling involves using a specific path that is established for the duration of a connection. Connectionless data handling involves passing data through a permanently established connection.

Connection-oriented service involves three phases: connection establishment, data transfer, and connection termination.

During the connection-establishment phase, a single path between the source and destination systems is determined. Network resources typically are reserved at this time to ensure a consistent grade of service, such as a guaranteed throughput rate.

In the data-transfer phase, data are transmitted sequentially over the path that has been established. Data always arrive at the destination system in the order in which the data were sent.

During the connection-termination phase, an established connection that is no longer needed is terminated. Further communication between the source and destination systems requires that a new connection be established.

Connection-oriented network service carries two significant disadvantages over connectionless: static-path selection and the static reservation of network resources. Static-path selection can create difficulty because all traffic must travel along the same static path. A failure anywhere along that path causes the connection to fail. Static reservation of network resources causes difficulty because it requires a guaranteed rate of throughput and, thus, a commitment of resources that other network users cannot share. Unless the connection uses full, uninterrupted throughput, bandwidth is not used efficiently. Connection-oriented services, however, are useful for transmitting data from applications that do not tolerate delays and packet resequencing. Voice and video applications are typically based on connection-oriented services.

Connectionless network service does not predetermine the path from the source to the destination system, nor are packet sequencing, data throughput, and other network resources guaranteed. Each packet must be completely addressed because different paths through the network may be selected for different packets, based on a variety of influences. Each packet is transmitted independently by the source system and is handled independently by intermediate network devices. Connectionless service, however, offers two important advantages over connection-oriented service: dynamic-path selection and dynamic-bandwidth allocation. Dynamic-path selection enables traffic to be routed around network failures because paths are selected on a packet-by-packet basis. With dynamic-bandwidth allocation, bandwidth is used more efficiently because network resources are not allocated a bandwidth that they will not use.

Connectionless services are useful for transmitting data from applications that can tolerate some delay and resequencing. Data-based applications typically are based on connectionless service.

In summary, connection-oriented service ensures the pathway is open for transfer between one joint and another and also ensures reliability of the pathway. Connection-oriented services have a mechanism within them to correct errors that occur along the way and to handle retransmission so that the program does not have to have any of these resources. The program that is using this transport service is Transport Control Protocol (TCP/IP). This is a connection-oriented reliable service that uses acknowledgments to ensure delivery along with automatic retransmission of bad/lock packets. It can adjust transmission rate dynamically according to network conditions through the "sliding window" dynamic buffer resizing method.

Connectionless service offers the best-effort delivery; however, the network does not guarantee that the information gets there. The program using this service is User Datagram Protocol (UDP/IP). This is a connectionless service with no acknowledgments, and error checking needs to be handled by the next layer up.

The preceding are lower-layer protocols, that is, Physical → Data Link → Network → Transport. The upper-layer protocols are Session → Presentation → Application.

OSI LAYER 5: SESSION LAYER

This layer sets up, coordinates, and terminates conversations, exchanges, and dialogs between the applications at each end. It deals with session and connection coordination. It also handles tasks associated with establishing, managing, and terminating connections between Presentation Layer (Layer 6) entities. An example would be AppleTalk's ZIP (Zone Information Protocol), which coordinates the AppleTalk name-binding process.

OSI LAYER 6: PRESENTATION LAYER

This is a layer, usually part of an operating system, that converts incoming and outgoing data from one presentation format to another (e.g., from a text stream into a pop-up window with the newly arrived text). Sometimes called the Syntax Layer, the Presentation Layer handles tasks associated with data coding, conversion, and representation. Detail task items include:

- Common data representation formats for dissimilar systems (ASCII CIP<>EBCDIC (IBM/SNA)
- Data compression/decompression
- Data encryption and deencryption communication (secure system)

OSI LAYER 7: APPLICATION LAYER

This is the layer at which communication partners are identified, quality of service is identified, user authentication and privacy are considered, and any constraints on data syntax are identified. (This layer is not the application itself, although some applications may perform Application Layer functions.)

The Application Layer is the highest layer. This layer interacts directly with the application using the network resources available through the lower layers. Typical Layer 7 tasks include:

- Identifying communication partners
- Determining resources available
- Synchronizing communication between systems

Examples include:

- FTP (TCP/IP) File Transfer Protocol
- SMTP (TCP/IP) Simple Mail Transfer Protocol for e-mail

Exhibit 7.6 Ethernet—Four Common Implementations

Name	Transmission Rate	Topology	Media/Cabling
10 Base T	10 Mbs	Star	UTP
10 Base F	10 Mbs	Star	Fiberoptic
10 Base 2	10 Mbs	Bus	50-ohm thin coax
10 Base 5	10 Mbs	Bus	50-hm thin coax

10 Base T—Ethernet Network

10 Base F—Fiberoptic

LAN NETWORKING TOPOLOGIES

Common LAN networking topologies are DIX (Digital, Intel, and Xerox). See Exhibit 7.6 for common implementations.

IMPLEMENTING ETHERNET

Carrier Sense Multiple Access with Collision Detect

Different devices on a network may try to communicate at any one time, so access methods need to be established. Using the Carrier Sense Multiple Access with Collision Detect (CSMA/CD) method, a device first checks that the cable is free from other carriers and then transmits while continuing to monitor the presence of another carrier. If a collision is detected, the device stops transmitting and tries later. In a CSMA network with collision detection, all stations have the ability to sense traffic on the network.

Data is framed into a stream of bits—ones and zeros—for physical transmission. The information at the Data Link Layer or the Frame Layer of the Ethernet is similar to that in Exhibit 7.7, and the information at this layer is called a frame. CSMA/CD is an example of a protocol that works at this level. Purpose equals name. It checks the cable to see if there is already another PC transmitting (Carrier Sense), allows all computers to share the same bandwidth (Multiple Access), and detects and retransmits collisions. Essentially, it is the highway patrol of the Network Access Layer.

Exhibit 7.7 Ethernet Frame

Preamble	SOF	Destination address	Source address	Length field	Data	FCS

SOF—Start of Frame

FCS—Frame Check Sequence

TOKEN RING

A token ring network is a local area network (LAN) in which all computers are connected in a ring or star topology and a binary digit- or token-passing scheme is used in order to prevent the collision of data between two computers that want to send messages at the same time.

The token ring protocol is the second most widely used protocol on local area networks after Ethernet. The IBM Token Ring protocol led to a standard version, specified as IEEE 802.5. Both protocols are used and are very similar.

The IEEE 802.5 token ring technology provides for data transfer rates of either 4 or 16 megabits per second. Very briefly, here is how it works:

Empty information frames are continuously circulated on the ring. When a computer has a message to send, it inserts a token in an empty frame (this may consist of simply changing a 0 to a 1 in the token bit part of the frame) and inserts a message and a destination identifier in the frame.

The frame is then examined by each successive workstation. If the workstation sees that it is the destination for the message, it copies the message from the frame and changes the token back to 0. When the frame gets back to the originator, it sees that the token has been changed to 0 and that the message has been copied and received. It removes the message from the frame.

The frame continues to circulate as an "empty" frame, ready to be taken by a workstation when it has a message to send. The token scheme can also be used with bus topology LANs.

The standard for the token ring protocol is Institute of Electrical and Electronics Engineers (IEEE) 802.5.

The Fiber Distributed-Data Interface (FDDI) also uses a token ring protocol.

The Token Ring adapter is available in IEEE 802.5 and IBM versions. Token Ring is more reliable because it uses Token. Stations are linked together by MSAUs (Multiple Station Access Units), also known as MAUs.

ANSI FIBER DISTRIBUTED DATA INTERFACE

Fiber Distributed Data Interfaces (FDDIs) also have tokens, commonly referred to as fast token ring. These tokens have a primary ring and a secondary ring, an extra level of fault tolerance, and the use of fiberoptics.

WAN NETWORKING TOPOLOGIES

Wide area network technologies consist of two types: point to point and frame relay.

NETWORK INTERFACES

PHYSICAL LAYER INTERFACE

Physical Layer Interface One

Technology one is EIA/TIA (RS-232). Layer 1 specifications include:

- Connectors associated with it are: -DB-9 9pin and -DB-25 25 pin
- From 19.2 to 115 kbps max cable transmission speed rating
- DCE/DTE Interfaces
  - DCE: Data Communication Equipment provided by the carrier is from MCI or AT&T

  - DTE: Data Terminal Equipment (i.e., router or other device)
- Send and receive pins
- Control pins on the interface
- Asynchronous—no timing clock, therefore has to synchronize itself (i.e., end nodes cannot synchronize themselves).

Physical Layer Interface Two

Layer 2 specifications include:

- ITU-T Standard (International Telecommunications Union Telecommunication Standard)
- Defines v.35 connector physical characteristics
- Also can be used on packet-network speeds up to 48 Kbps
- Capable of 4 Mbps in other applications
- DCE/DTE interfaces
- Send and receive control pins
- Synchronous (timing clock used to synchronize bit streams)

Physical Layer Interface Three (High Speed Serial Interface)

Layer 3 specifications include:

- Created by CISCO, under review by ISO and ITU-T for standardization
- Defines High Speed Serial Interface (HSSI) connector physical characteristics
- Capable of 52 Mbps
- DCE/DTE interfaces
- Send and receive control pins
- Synchronous (timing clock used to synchronize bit stream)

Physical Layer Interface Four (ISDN Basic Rate Interface)

Layer 4 specifications include:

- Defines two 64-Kb B channels for data, one 16-Kb D channel for signaling, framing control, and general overhead.
- Defines the "Terminal Adapter." A modem-like device to connect DTE devices to the ISDN circuit.

DATA LINK LAYER INTERFACE

Point-to-point (WAN) Implementations

The point-to-point implementations are:

- SLIP—Serial Line Interface Protocol (early Unix implementation mainly used with RS-232)
- PPP—Point-to-Point Protocol

- Next generation of SLIP
- Works over most WAN serial links, DSO, T1, T3, ISDN
- Includes encryption, multiple protocol support, error control, security, dynamic IP addressing, automatic connection negotiations
- Three frame types are Link Control Protocol frame (LCP), Network Control Protocol frame (NCP), and data frame

Data Link Layer Interface (WAN)—Frame Relay

Frame relay is an upgrade from X.25. It is the fastest of the WAN protocols listed because of its simplified framing, which has no error correction. It must use the high-quality digital facilities of the phone company and therefore is not available everywhere (see Exhibit 7.5). For the WAN frame types see Exhibits 7.9 and 7.10.

The Integrated Services Digital Network (ISDN) is shown in Exhibit 7.11.

Data Link Layer Interface (WAN)—Asynchronous Transfer Mode

The Asynchronous Transfer Mode (ATM) specifications include:

- Fixed length, 53-byte cell switching protocol. The two types are:
  - UNI: User to Network Interface
  - NNI: Network to Network Interface
- Uses PVCs and SVCs like frame relay
- Introduced QOS (Quality of Service) features
- Physical layer speeds for T1 (1.54 Mbps to 2.4 Mbps)

See Exhibit 7.12 for the ATM cells.

Exhibit 7.8 Frame Relay

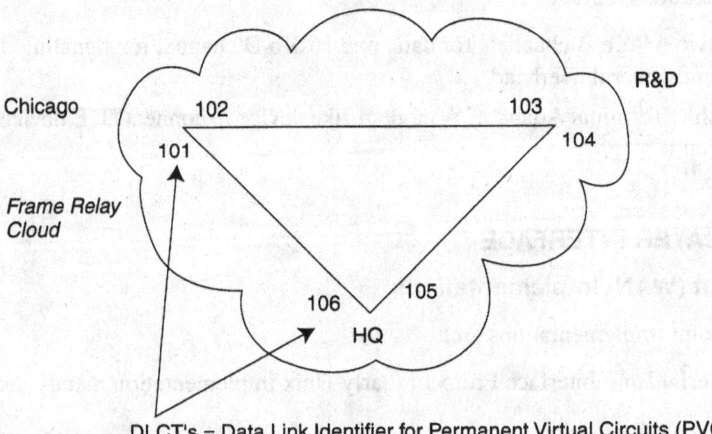

Exhibit 7.9 PPP Frame

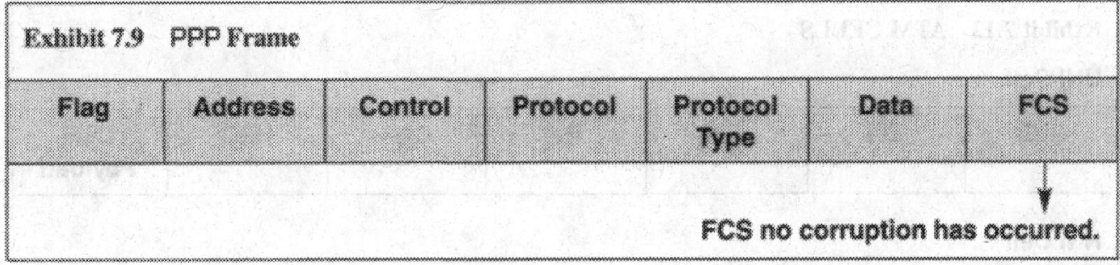

Exhibit 7.10 Frame Relay Frame

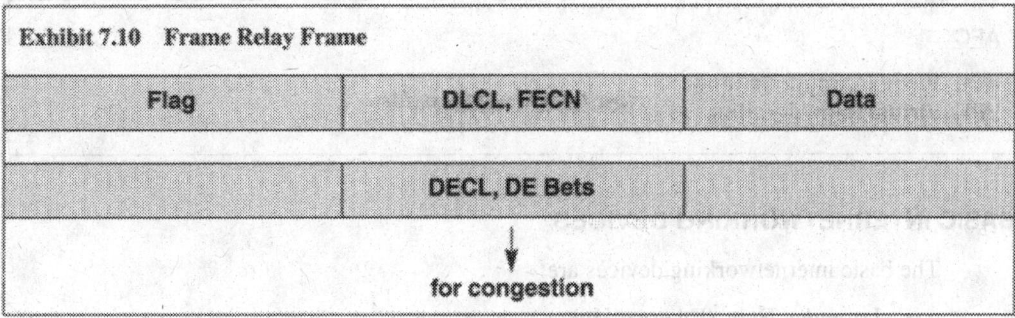

Exhibit 7.11 ISDN (Integrated Services Digital Network)

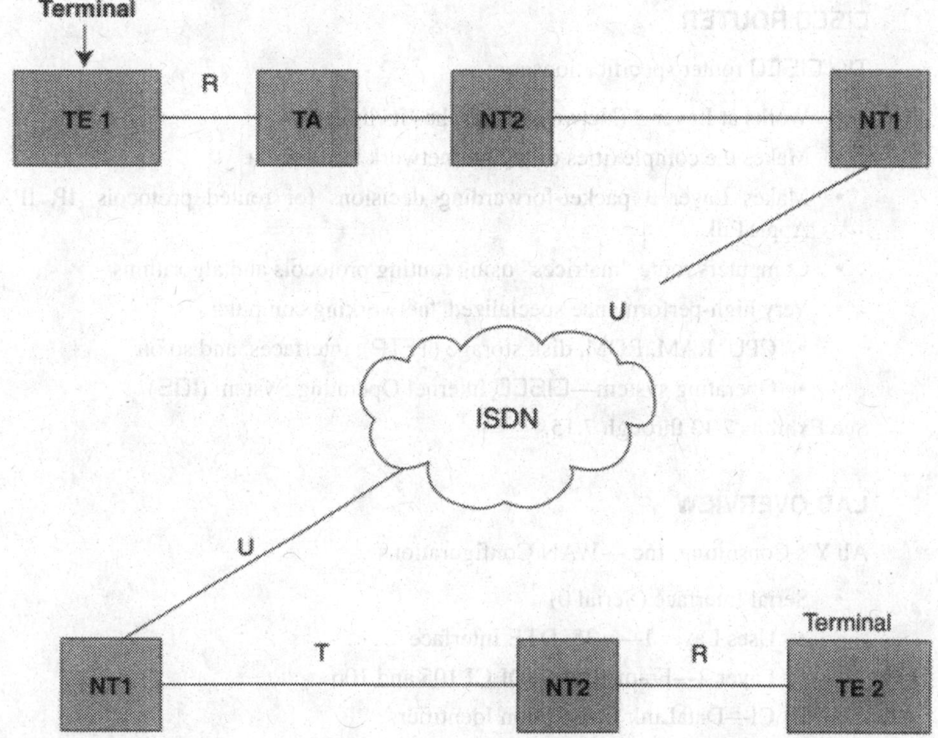

Exhibit 7.12 ATM CELLS

UNI Cell

GFC	VPI	VCI	PT	CLP	HEC	Data Payload

NNI Cell

YPI	YCI	PT	CLP	HEC	Data Payload

AFC

VCI—Virtual Circuit Identifier
VPI—Virtual Path Identifier ***How to and who it is for***

BASIC INTERNETWORKING DEVICES

The basic internetworking devices are:

- Layer 1—Hubs (Ethernet Hubs)
- Layer 2—Data Link Switches
- Layer 3—Network Routers

CISCO ROUTER

The CISCO router specifications are:

- Works at Layer 3 (Network Layer, has its limits)
- Makes the complexities of an internetwork transparent
- Makes Layer 3 packet-forwarding decisions for routed protocols, IP, IPX, and AppleTalk
- Computers route "matrices" using routing protocols and algorithms
- Very high-performance specialized "networking computers"
  - CPU, RAM, ROM, disk storage (TFTP), interfaces, and so on
  - Operating system—CISCO Internet Operating System (IOS)

See Exhibits 7.13 through 7.15.

LAB OVERVIEW

Ali Y's Consulting, Inc.—WAN Configurations

- Serial Interface (Serial 0)
  - Uses Layer 1—v.35, DTE Interface
  - Layer 2—Frame Relay, DLCI 105 and 106
- DLCI—DataLink Connection Identifiers
- Ethernet Interface (Ethernet 0)

Exhibit 7.13 Routing and Routed Protocols

- Layer 1—10 Base T (UTP)
- Layer 2—Ethernet, 10 Mbps, IEEE 802.3 Ethernet frames
- Token Ring Interface (Token ring 0)
  - Layer 1—UTP
  - Layer 2—Token ring frames, 16 Mbps, IEEE 802.5 frame format

Router

- Main Console Port
- Auxiliary Port—Modem attachment
- Transreceiver—*Token ring attached to May

R&D Site Router

- Serial Interface (Serial 0)
  - Layer 1—v.35, DTE
  - Layer 2—Frame Relay, DLCE 103 and 104

Exhibit 7.14 Routing Table

IP Address	Port	Metric
210.157.64.1	1	10
210.157.64.2	2	10
210.157.64.3	3	10

Exhibit 7.15 Ali Y's Consulting, Inc.

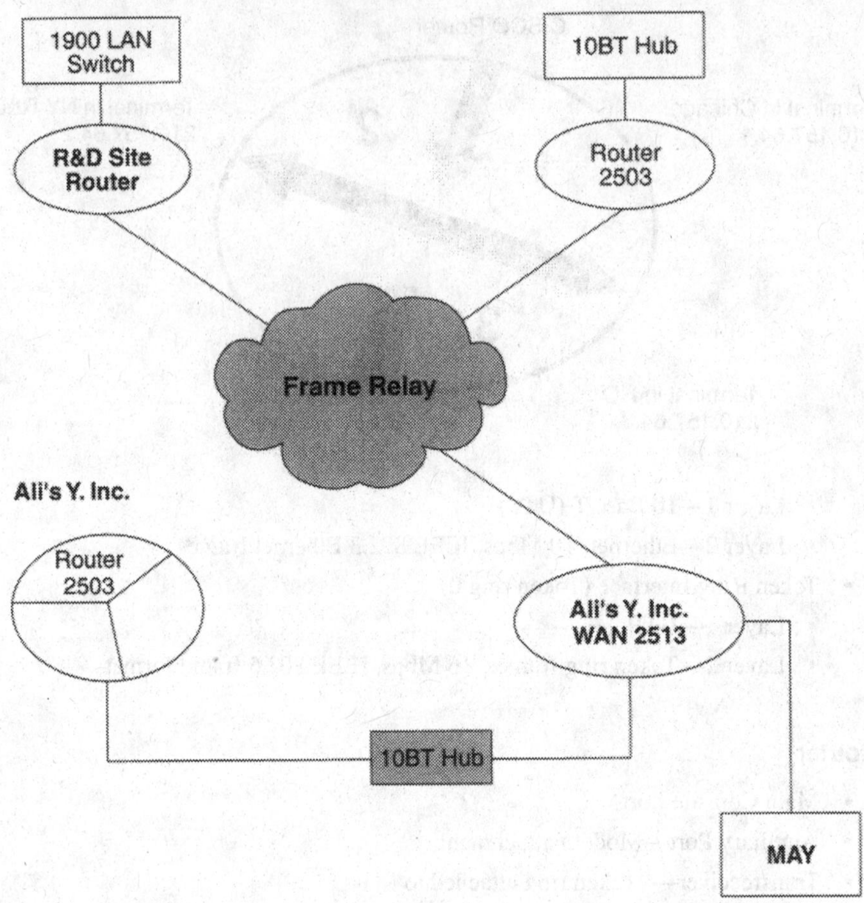

- Ethernet Interface (Fast Ethernet 0)
  - Layer 1—100 Base T (UTP)
  - Layer 2—ISL-100 Mbps (VLAN trunk, VLANS 1 and 3)

POWER UP AND BASIC ROUTER ACCESS USING FTTP SERVER

NVRAM—Nonvolatile RAM
Power up the router
System bootrap message
Load proceed
Interfaces that are attached, network and node numbers
Access to router
*User mode ">"—this shows user mode
*Privilege mode; ENTER enable → ENTER password→
#indicates privilege mode

Internet Operating System (IOS) EFC Modes:

- User Mode ">"
  - Lowest level of access
  - Basic nondisruptive tasks permitted only
  - Cannot view router configuration
- Privileged Mode "#"
  - Highest level of access
  - Complete access to all commands and configuration
  - Configuration information and configuration modes

A LOOK INSIDE

Wealth of Show Commands:

- Show running-config—Displays router configuration in RAM.
- Show startup-config—Displays configuration stored in NVRAM (power up).
- Show flash—Shows formatting and contents of flash memory.
- Show buffers—Displays statistics for router buffer pools.
- Show memory—Shows router memory statistics.
- Show process CPU—Shows active processes (programs) in router.

Other Commands:

- Show protocols—Shows information on all the protocols the router is configured to support, includes network addresses.
- Show slacks—Memory slack utilization and interrupts.
- Show version—System hardware, IOS version, sources of config files and boot images.
- Show <protocol> interface <interface id>—Shows all selected interface information.

*Configuration register value: This should be the *value: 0X2102* ← most important 3:32
Configuration register is 0X2102
Virtual configuration register:

- 16-bit register in special area of NVRAM
- Visible in results of "show version" in privileged mode
- Hexadecimal value 0x2102—Default
- First 4 bits (0 × 2) control boot actions, "boot field"

0 × 0—Router starts in ROM monitor mode
0 × 1—Router starts from ROM IOS image
0 × 2—Normal startup from flash.
See documentation for other start-up uses.

INTERNET OPERATING SYSTEM

IOS image—stored locally in the flash memory:
Global Configuration Mode 9/25/99

```
# config terminal
# Boot system flash
# exit
# manage configured from "Terminal"
# Copy running - config startup-config
[ OK ]
```

IOS Start-up

IOS load and start-up sequence commands (from global config mode):

- Boot system flash—normal, flash-based IOS load
- Boot system tftp <tftp (put server address here)
- Boot system ROM—router boots from ROM version of IOS

Router Configuration Modes

IOS configuration modes:

- Global: Router (config) #
- Interface: Router (config.if)#
- Subinterface: Router (config.subif)#
- Line: Router (config.line)#
- Router: Router (config.router)#
- IPX Router: Router (configIPX.rotuer)#

Managing Config and IOS files:

- IOS image—binary executable image (router)
- Config file—text file (in NYRAM)
- Copy to external location (i.e., tftp server)

IOS File Handling:

- Copy tftp flash—copies IOS image from tftp server to flash memory
  - Watch that spelling
  - Flash is erased first
- Copy flash tftp—copies IOS from router's flash memory to tftp server
- Routers can be tftp servers
  - tftp server <file name>

Configuration File Loading:

- Configuration file contains router's running instructions
- CLI configuration commands enter the running config immediately

X.7 (f) CLI = Command Line Interface

Configuration File Management Commands:

- **Copy running-config startup-config**—copies **config** file in RAM to NVRAM for start-up.
- **Copy tftp running.congfig**—copies configuration information to NVRAM.
- **Copy running.config tftp**—copies RAM-based running **config** to **tftp** server.
- **Copy startup.config tftp**—copies NVRAM configuration file to the **tftp** server.

Commands:
#Copy tftp flash verifying checksum OK verification process upgrading CPSCO router.
Another Common Task → backup copy
#copy running.config tftp
need IP address ← <Remote Host>
(i.e., 157.100.128.20)
Broadcast address means that it will look at all the interfaces attached to the router.

ROUTERS IN CISCO SERVICES

1. **CISCO** 12000 ASR(Argabit Switch Router)
   - Targeted at ISP (Internet Service Provider)
   - WAN interface speeds from T3(52 Mbps) to OC-48(2.4 Abps)
2. **CISCO** 7500 Series
   - CISCO's premier multiprotocol router
   - WAN interface speeds from T1(1.54 Mbps) to OC-12(622 Mbps)
   - Run CISCO IOS
3. **CISCO** 7200 Series
   - Run CISCO IOS
   - WAN interface for T1(1.54 Mbps) to GC=3(1.50 Mbps)
4. **CISCO** 4000 Series
   - Run CISCO IOS
5. **CISCO** 3600 Series
   - High-performance CPU
6. **CISCO** 2500 Series
   - Runs **CISCO** IOS—**<some commands in all areas>**
   - WAN interface speeds up to T1(1.54 Mbps)

   T1 (1.54 Mbps)

   OC-12 (622 Mbps) *WAN interface specials*

LAN interface speeds from 4 Mbps to 100 Mbps

CISCO LAN SWITCHES

- Typically work at Layer 2 (Data Link)
  - New generation of switches have Layers 3 and 4 sensitivity

- Makes Layer 2 frame-forwarding decisions based on MAC port
- Very high performance specialized "data link" computers
  - CPU, RAM, ROM, disk storage, (UTP), interfaces, and so on
  - Operating System CISCO IOS Switching

CISCO 1900/2000 series:

- LAN Interface Speeds from 10 Mbps to 100 Mbps
- Used for high-performance "backbone" applications

CISCO LAN HUBS

- Works as Layer 1 (i.e., Physical Layer)
- Acts as an electrical-signal "repeater" and fans out devices
- Available in 10-Mbps and 100-Mbps versions

FIREWALL

WHAT IS A FIREWALL?

Let us start by defining our terms. Just what is a firewall? The standard definition of a firewall is a device that prevents the hazards of the internet or intranet from extending to a local network. Or, more specifically, it is a system that enforces a boundary between two (or more) networks.

The most realistic definition of a firewall is simply "the implementation of the internet security policy. If one does not have a security policy, one does not have a firewall. Instead, one has a thing that is sort of doing something, but one does not know what it is trying to do because no one has said what it should do."

While the installation and configuration of a firewall is often a complex art, the most difficult aspect of proper firewall implementation is determining the specific and appropriate type of firewall architecture to implement, especially when there are over thirty different types of firewalls. Making the proper and intelligent choice is not so simple.

Selecting a firewall architecture for the environment is only possible when one defines their criteria and specific needs for a firewall. Trying to buy the "Best Firewall" without qualifying one's firewall needs will only result in a false sense of security. In fact, it might turn out to be just the opposite. An improper firewall can give an organization a false sense of security, which in turn makes their security vulnerabilities much greater.

In summary, a firewall is only as good as:

- The security policy rule base that one enables.
- The devices connected to the firewall.
- The operating system and its configuration.
- The person or persons that installed and configured the firewall.

It is important to realize that a firewall is not a security panacea. There are some things a firewall simply cannot do or prevent. Some of them are:

- Stop internal attacks.
- Fill in the deficiencies of a security policy.
- Be a magic security blanket.

- Protect against hostile applets or malicious ActiveX or Java code (although some firewall vendors offer this as a software add-on).
- Stop connections that do not go through it (dial-up analog lines).
- Protect against viruses (while virus protection is possible via software add-ons, the native firewall architecture is not concerned with viruses and their eradication).
- Protect against new threats.

SECURITY POLICY

Before getting into the details of the various firewall architectures, let us take a look for a moment at the need for an effective network security policy. The security policy is the document that details an enterprise's network security considerations. The problem of setting up a firewall without a policy is similar to having a policeman who does not know what the laws are. Only when a security policy is in place can a company genuinely start their search and implementation for the best firewall for their environment.

For a security policy to be effective, it has to be a document that is created according to the needs of the company it is written to serve. It must identify the potential threats to networks, computers, services, and information within the organization, in addition to the procedures and polices that are to be implemented by staff to access those risks.

An example of a policy that relates directly to a firewall is the question of what to do with an unknown packet. There are two possibilities: allow the packet into the network or reject the packet. What occurs depends on how the firewall is set up. There are two possible states in which the firewall can be set up, they are:

- Approach #1: Deny any service (or packet) not expressly permitted.
- Approach #2: Permit any service (or packet) not expressly denied.

Most firewalls follow the secure principle of Approach #1.

As for policies, the best procedure to follow involves the four Ps of network security:

- Paranoid
- Prudent
- Permissive
- Promiscuous

The best approach is usually a combination of all four.

COMMON INTERNET THREATS

There are scores of threats on the internet. Following are a few of the more insidious problems that a firewall will attempt to fix:

- SMTP (e-mail). SMTP is the internet e-mail protocol transport service. There are many problems with SMTP. One of the primary problems is that when one gets a message, there is no way to verify that the person whose name appears in the "From" section is actually the sender of the message.
- Sendmail. Sendmail has often been the hacker's choice of entry (via its security holes) into a network. Sendmail is the application that handles all of a systems e-mail. Sendmail has a history of technical problems and is known to be remarkably

difficult to configure. While there may be more than 250,000 CNEs (Certified NetWare Engineers) in the United States, there are only a limited number of people who really understand Sendmail.

- DNS. DNS (Domain Name Service) is a database that maps usernames and hostnames. A security issue with DNS is that it provides a place to search for the IP address of trusted machines.

FIREWALL ARCHITECTURES

Now that the preliminaries have been covered, let us discuss the nitty-gritty about firewall architectures. The firewall architecture is where the core capabilities and functionality of the firewall is determined.

The three leading types of firewalls in use are:

1. Application gateway/proxy
2. Circuit-level gateway
3. Packet filter

Application Level Gateway/Proxy Firewalls

This is the type of firewall that looks for valid application-level data before allowing a connection to initiate. An application-level gateway firewall inspects the application-level data in all packets. The firewall has a specialized version of the application running on it. A Telnet application on the firewall would appear as a Telnet client to a user and as a Telnet client to the server.

Application-level gateway firewalls use a proxy. The proxy is a firewall mechanism that replaces the IP address of a host on the internal (secure) network with its own address for all traffic passing through.

Most applications and circuit-level gateways include a built-in proxy for added security. This is because hiding the address of an internal host makes it much more difficult for outside attackers to target specific devices inside of the firewall.

Many hackers and penetrators will attempt to try a variety of ways to get into a network by exploiting applications. The internet worm of 1988 in which the penetrator exploited holes in the Sendmail program is an example of this. The function of an application-based firewall is to prevent such penetrations from occurring. This is because the application level is generally the prime zone of attack favored by hackers.

Circuit-Level Gateway Firewalls

This is the type of firewall that will validate the TCP and UDP sessions before opening a connection or circuit through the firewall. The firewall will examine the session setup to verify that valid TCP or UDP handshaking exists and will not forward the packet until the handshaking process is complete. Once the session is established, the firewall maintains a table of authorized connections and lets data pass through when the session information matches an entry in the table. When the session is completed, the entry is removed from the table and the circuit is terminated until another process starts anew.

A circuit-level firewall can only validate a connection at the Session Layer (Layer 4), therefore, it is less secure than an application gateway once a session is initiated since any application can run over that connection.

Packet Filter

Packet filtering allows one to control a connection based on the source and destination address and the protocols being used in that session. A packet-filter firewall (which is one of the most basic types of firewalls) is one that inspects each packet at the Network Layer (Layer 3). Packet filtering uses permission rules to grant or deny access from one source address (the host) and port (service) to a second destination address and port. A packet filter is generally considered to be the least secure type of firewall, but it makes up for that in its speed (which is quick) and its transparency (users do not have to do anything special, nor does code need to be recompiled). Once a TCP port is defined as accepting traffic, the firewall might let any packet with the same port number pass through. This also means that any other application or session with the same port number could pass through the firewall. Low-level packet filter capabilities are available on a router.

The concern with a packet filter is that it only has a myopic view of the network. Since it operates at the Network Layer, it can only see (and protect) the three lowest layers of the network. In addition, its limited security means that it cannot provide protection against IP spoofing attacks, nor is it a packet filter firewall that has adequate logging facilities.

The packet filter works on the six main headers in an IP packet. Those headers are:

1. IP source address
2. IP destination address
3. Protocol (TCP, UDP, or ICMP)
4. TCP or UDP source port
5. TCP or UDP destination port
6. ICMP message type

STATEFUL INSPECTION

Stateful inspection was invented by Check Point Software Technologies (Redwood, CA: www.checkpoint.com), makers of the FireWall-1 product. Check Point was awarded a U.S. patent (patent 5,606,668) in February 1997 for its stateful inspection technology. Stateful inspection is packet filtering with a brain. It intercepts the packet at the Network Layer (Layer 3) and then analyzes the data in the packets. Stateful inspection maintains the "state" and "context" of the user's request so that when the data are returned via the firewall, it is able to verify whether or not the data was specifically requested. Stateful inspection attempts to track open, valid connection without the need to process a rule for each packet.

PACKET FILTERS

Packet Filter Advantages:

- Speed
- Sufficient for nonbusiness critical environments
- Generally less expensive
- Flexible
- Transparent
- Can be implemented on existing routers

- Application independent
- Good scalability

Packet Filter Disadvantages

- Management features generally lacking
- Easier to spoof
- Logging features are generally lacking
- Does not support user authentication
- Cannot automatically hide network and system addresses from public view
- Cannot provide protection against an application-level attack (e-mail, Web, Java, and so on)
- Susceptible to sophisticated IP fragmentation and source routing attacks
- Cannot screen above Network Layer
- Some protocols do not operate fully in a filters environment (such as NFS, NIS/YP, Berkeley "r" commands)
- Cannot provide time of day access control

CIRCUIT-LEVEL GATEWAY

Circuit-Level Gateway Firewall Advantage:

- Prevents direct connection between internal and external machines

Circuit-Level Gateway Firewall Disadvantages:

- Client software on the internal network must be modified
- Operates only at the Session Layer (Layer 4)

APPLICATION-LEVEL GATEWAY

Application-Level Gateway Firewall Advantages:

- Generally offers higher level of security
- Allows for a great deal of customization for disabling or modifying specific commands, protocols, or services
- Proxies prevent direct connection between internal host and external, untrusted hosts
- Supports strong end user authentication (SecurID, S/Key, Safeword, and so on)
- Excellent logging
- Can automatically hide network and system addresses from public view
- Able to provide time of day access control

Application-Level Gateway Firewall Disadvantages:

- Generally more complex
- Slower than stateful inspection and packet filtering

- Must support every application that one wants to use through the firewall
- In some environments, adequate WAN bandwidth can be a limitation
- Poor scalability
- Requires more horsepower on the firewall device
- More difficult to set up and configure
- Lack of application proxy means the application cannot be run
- Some services, such as chat and talk, are very difficult to develop a proxy for
- Not transparent to the end user

STATEFUL INSPECTION ADVANTAGES AND DISADVANTAGES

Stateful Inspection Advantages:

- Intelligence
- More secure than a standard packet filter
- Better protection against spoofing
- Flexible in their ability to add new applications, services, and protocols
- Faster than proxy-based firewalls
- Good scalability

Stateful Inspection Disadvantages:

- Cannot provide protection against an application level attack
- CPU intensive
- Cannot automatically hide network and system addresses from public view

CAVEAT

How does a company make the correct decision about buying a firewall? First, if the firewall vendor makes a claim such as "The best firewall available, no hacker has ever cracked it," drop that company from your short list. No reputable firewall vendor would make such a preposterous claim. The fact that a vendor has a public hacker challenge does not prove anything. These challenges are generally random tests that do not have a baseline testing method. The fact that no problems were found does not mean that no problems exist. And if you were a hacker with devious intent, you would not want to publicize the security vulnerability that you found; instead, you would want the vendor to ship a defective product and then attack the companies using the product.

Also, do not get caught up by the number of awards that the firewall vendor has. Even if the firewall was awarded the Interop "Best-of-Show" award, that does not necessarily mean that the product is right for an organization.

CHOOSING A FIREWALL

SECURITY AUDIT

A good place to make a decision about the appropriate firewall is with a security audit. A security audit is an organization's internal security staff, or an external staff, performing a thorough investigation of the security architecture. Everything from policies and procedures to network operating system configuration is evaluated. The results of the audit can provide a potent indication of what the appropriate firewall architecture should be.

Another benefit of an audit is that it allows a company to better understand their real requirements as opposed to their perceived requirements. A common mistake that a lot of companies make is that they focus too much on a firewall's capabilities and feature set while ignoring their own requirements. The right firewall architecture choice cannot be made until a requirements analysis has been performed.

When choosing a firewall, the bottom line is to avoid fads in firewalls and simply purchase the best firewall that minimizes an organization's risks and vulnerabilities while maximizing its levels of protection.

By far, the majority of security threats to corporate information and computing resources come from inside the company. Mission-critical intellectual property, trade secrets, customer lists, and strategic plans are all vulnerable when accessed from inside the firewall.

The latest industry studies show that 75 to 84 percent of breaches originate internally. According to a Broadview and Associates report, the competitive landscape for security software vendors in 1998 included a "recognized need for internal security solutions." This spurs the search for a cost-effective solution for simplifying and hardening security from inside the company, behind the firewall.

Organizations are increasingly relying on mission-critical client-server programs and systems to remain competitive. Distributed computing environments are known for their openness, flexibility, and scalability. On the other hand, these same computing environments create barriers to resource access control and consistent security policies. The design and wide use of distributed systems have created the following security challenges:

- Distributed access from multiple locations makes it difficult to manage and secure networks and systems.
- Distributed data storage spanning multiple servers multiplies the number of files and programs that need to be secured.
- Numerous diversified platforms make it difficult to implement consistent security policies, leading to management difficulties and a reduction in system security.
- Limited operating system (OS) security. The Unix operating system was designed with inadequate security because the primary intent was to provide users with easy access to shared resources. Although the NT operating system attempts to address security, several of the security issues that are common to Unix environments still exist with NT.

Key solutions involve the following:

- Applying a single integrated security solution for system, network, file, and program access control that operates between the OS and all applications.
- Eliminate the superuser security threat that comes from compromising the "root" account in Unix and the "NT Administrator" account in NT.
- Make the security system simple to deploy with "Default Security Policies" where only the "exceptions" need to be managed in the form of user groups.
- Provide a uniform and comprehensive framework for security policy administration, auditing, and real-time monitoring that enables accountability and helps improve security policies.

SOLVING THE SUPERUSER PROBLEM

The superuser concept was created in the early stages of Unix development. At that time, most systems were stand-alone and required a simple way to facilitate system administration in a multiuser environment. An easy solution was to create an account called `root` that had the privileges to do everything on the system. As both the number of applications and the need to connect machines with networks grew, the superuser power extended far beyond what it was originally meant to be.

Another way to win access to superuser privileges is by running a program with the `setuid` permission. The `setuid` mechanism was created to allow certain system programs run by regular users to obtain `root` account privileges in order to access protected files or resources.

The presence of interactive superuser (or `root`) access in Unix results in the following security problems:

1. The superuser power overrides all system protections. As a superuser with `root` access, one can view files owned by anyone, modify system configurations, disrupt network connections, copy hard disk or database files, and circumvent system security by introducing viruses or Trojan horses into the operating system.

2. There is no way to establish accountability for important system administration functions. On most Unix systems, a generic username is used for the superuser ID called the `root` account. This user account is used by all system Administrators to perform administrative tasks. There is no way to identify who has logged in as the superuser.

The presence of programmatic superuser (or `setuid`) access in Unix results in the following security problems:

1. Enables the creation of a "backdoor," which is a popular way to break into a Unix system. This involves stealing the superuser's password, creating a `setuid` program, and waving this `setuid` program on the system for future tampering. Afterwards, the creator of the backdoor logs in to the system as a regular user, runs the `setuid` program, and acquires superuser privileges. As a superuser, the hacker can then anonymously move throughout the network stealing or destroying information without fear of identification or retaliation.

2. System Administrators often write their own `setuid` programs to provide added system administration capabilities. Backdoors that are created by these programs can cause security breaches that are generally not detected until a significant loss occurs.

Many methods have been tried to resolve these problems. Unfortunately, most of them are either incomplete or too complicated to implement and manage.

There is a new methodology that allows one to work from a secure level by eliminating the superuser threat and then explicitly allowing access to administrative privileges and computing resources. This approach funnels all administration tasks that require interactive `root` access to one tool that delegates and monitors administrative tasks. Access is secured by assigning Security Administrator roles to administrative users of the security solution. In addition, all custom programs requiring `setuid` privileges are funneled through one tool.

These software and hardware barriers stand between the private internal network and its connection to the outside world such as the internet. The firewall provides an extra layer of protection and regulates and controls communication.

GENERAL BACKGROUND INFORMATION

What kind of planning has been carried out in the design of the firewall and the overall security?

1. What should be protected? For example, information, computing facilities, data storage facilities, or communication facilities (i.e., voice hacking, free long-distance phone calls).
2. What should be protected against? For example, intrusion, denial of service, or information theft. Firewalls help prevent intrusions (i.e, properly configured firewalls reduce the number of accounts accessible from the outside that are vulnerable to guesswork).
3. What is expected from the firewall?
4. Can the firewall log internet activity efficiently?
5. Does it collect information about the system and network use and misuse efficiently?
6. Is the company aware that the firewall cannot protect it against malicious insiders and that the firewall can also not protect the company against connections that do not go through it?
7. A firewall can only protect against known threats.
8. A firewall cannot protect against viruses.
9. Has the company documented and performed risk assessment over all the services that can be provided or used over the internet? For example, electronic mail or Simple Mail Transport Protocol (SMTP), File Transfer (FTP), Remote Terminal Access (Telnet), Usenet news (NNTP), HTTP, DNS, Finger, Whois.
10. Is the company aware of its weakest link and weakest point. Are all aspects of security evenly attended to so as to minimize the exposure of weakest links and weakest points?
11. What is the company's stance with respect to security? Is it restrictive or permissive?
12. Is it the Default Deny Stance or is it Default Permit Stance?
13. Have the services the users want been adequately examined?
14. Have the security implications of these services (i.e., risk assessments) been adequately conducted?
15. Have the strategies to provide these services safely been carefully considered?
16. Are users allowed to set up unauthorized servers?
17. Are any authentication tools (TIS Internet Firewall Toolkit [FWTK], Kerberos) used?
18. Are any analysis tools (COPS, Tiger, Tripwire, Satan, ISS) used?
19. What packet-filtering tools (Screened, ipfwadm, Drawbridge, Karlbridge) are used?
20. What steps are taken to keep the firewall current and sophisticated?
21. A firewall is a computer usually running the Unix operating system and firewall software. Was it downloaded from the URL or was it purchased as a separate product?
22. How has the effectiveness of the firewall been determined?
23. Data circuits (links can be bottlenecks). Who is doing the planning?

NETWORKING

The trend in networking is to simplify administration and control costs by adding additional functionality to existing hardware. But with security and virtual private networks (VPNs), some managers are taking an alternate route: adding stand-alone specialized hardware to their networks to better manage security and encryption.

Dedicated hardware for network security is winning converts for three main reasons.

1. First, it improves network performance because encryption-based security processes can bog down a network. The DES (Data Encryption Standard), for example, can require as much as twenty-five times more processing power than a regular IP packet.

2. Second, because the technology is so complex and at the same time increasingly strategic, administrators are not willing to risk problems that can arise when integrating new software into existing products.

3. Third, some network managers believe it is simply safer to keep encryption information separate from the rest of the network.

What are the must-have network operating system skills?

1. Installation, configuration, and troubleshooting. When it comes to troubleshooting problems, one needs to be able to tell whether it is hardware or software related—if one is not well rounded in that, it can be a downfall.

2. A fundamental knowledge of the operating system's operation and administrative tasks is necessary, and not just the what and how, but the why and when also. It is not enough to know how to add a user and how to configure a network protocol or how to install a server. One must understand how all three interact and the effect they all have on each other.

3. Applications developers need to know the network infrastructure services like domain name services, directory services like Lightweight Directory Access Protocol, security services, proxy services, and firewall services. And they need to know network applications like the Novell file service or Network File System in Unix.

All operating systems today have known weaknesses that provide opportunity for attack. While it is the operating system manufacturer's responsibility to provide patches to plug security holes, it is the user's responsibility to learn the operating system, implement the security available, and ensure that those patches are applied. One should disable all protocols and services that are not needed, remove unused profiles, and ensure that passwords are not obvious.

Many attacks begin with physical access to the PC to install "sniffer" programs, copy password files for later decryption, or add a new account, any of which can be done in as little as fifteen seconds.

1. In an office environment, never leave the PC without signing off.
2. Ensure server access is restricted.
3. Do not leave disks or backup tapes lying around.
4. Lock up that little piece of paper with one's password on it.
5. Finally, whenever anyone leaves the company, disable their account immediately.

How do users who have an internet connection ensure that traffic between their network and the outside world is secure and controlled? If one can tolerate the restrictions imposed with this type of connection, use it to reduce the effort required to secure the environment.

MODEM

Numerous options are available for connecting a personal modem on an existing network. These options include analog, ISDN, cable, and various flavors of digital subscriber lines—all generally equivalent from a security standpoint.

But does the ISP maintain a robust firewall? Cable modems, for example, use a fixed, real IP address, usually from an ISP-allocated address range known to hackers. If the ISP does not protect you, you must learn more about network security. Otherwise, many shared resources, such as personal files, are available for public consumption.

BROWSER

What about the browser? Hackers spend disproportionate efforts hacking Microsoft products like Internet Explorer (IE). There are a number of IE security holes that allow hackers and malicious Web sites to crash the browser or worse. This does not mean that Netscape Navigator is safe either.

Avoid many problems by steering clear of Web sites you do not trust and by disabling Java, JavaScript, and ActiveX unless absolutely required. When planning to do business on the internet, get the browser version that supports strong encryption and use Secure Sockets Layer (SSL) or Secure HTTP (S-HTTP) whenever personal information is sent.

CONDUCTING BUSINESS ACROSS THE INTERNET

Leased line networks and remote access equipment have been replaced in favor of virtual private networks (VPNs) offering substantial infrastructure and supporting cost savings. To enable secure private communications, implement the following:

- Tunneling
- Authentication
- Encryption
- Key management technologies

Because these technologies are not "battle-hardened," VPNs are vulnerable to attacks. They will remain so until the emerging protocols, standards, and products mature.

Three critical VPN components are:

1. Security (access control, authentication, and encryption)
2. Traffic management (making sure that critical applications are delivered reliably and with the highest possible performance)
3. Policy-based network management (the ability to manage the entire network from one central console to one easy-to-install turnkey solution).

How does one stay familiar with the latest viruses and fixes as well as other security issues on Web sites such as www.cert.org or www.NTSecurity.net? The enemy is likely more experienced, but a little prevention can go a long way. Often the technology, like firewalls that guard against internet hackers, is improperly configured. How does one take a proactive role to find vulnerabilities when troubleshooting a problem? Even when the firewall is configured well, how does the Security Administrator decide what to give users access to and what to lock them out of? It is best to begin by giving users no access and build from there.

PERFORMANCE

High availability is a significant internet customer requirement. What percentage of internet services are highly available today in a cluster environment? Can the service be automatically or manually moved off one TruCluster node to another, providing guaranteed availability?

Performance is another key requirement for internet applications. The following questions pertain to the performance level of internet systems:

1. How does one tune the internet systems for optimal performance?
2. Does the installation interface allow system managers to adjust kernel-tuning parameters? What parameter values have been specifically designed to improve the performance of Web servers, proxy servers, FTP servers, mail servers and relays, gateway systems, and firewall systems?
3. Do you have what is needed to get started right away on the internet—set up Web browsers, build a security scheme, and get internet mail? Do you have the utilities to create and automatically install a home page. If so, what are they?
4. How does one reduce the cost and complexity of managing networks, systems, databases, and applications?
5. Virus scanning takes so many resources out of the firewall. How does one manage scanning on the firewall?
6. Antivirus and intrusion detection systems are all very CPU intensive, and one cannot afford to have the firewall down for even a minute. What do you do?

CONFIGURATION

The firewall can be configured in such a way as to restrict individuals from sending e-mail out of the company and barring them from having access to the internet. External access may also be limited because few companies would allow access to files and information by the general public or competitors.

Firewall technologies are available. For example, simple packet filters will deny access to any piece of information in which the source and destination address have not been authorized by the system. To set up the filters, define a set of rules for the filtering code. This will allow the system to decide whether the packet should be allowed to pass or not.

NETWORK ADDRESS TRANSLATION

NAT (Network Address Translation) is the translation of an internet Protocol (IP) address used within one network to a different IP address known within another network. One network is designated the inside network and the other is the outside. Typically, a company maps its local inside network addresses to one or more global outside IP addresses and unmaps the global IP addresses on incoming packets back into local IP addresses. This helps ensure security since each outgoing or incoming request must go through a translation process that also offers the opportunity to qualify or authenticate the request or match it to a previous request. NAT also conserves on the number of global IP addresses that a company needs and lets the company use a single IP address in its communication with the world.

NAT is included as part of a router and is often part of a corporate firewall. Network administrators create a NAT table that does the global-to-local and local-to-global IP address mapping. NAT can also be used in conjunction with policy routing. NAT can be statically defined, or it can be set up to dynamically translate from and to a pool of IP addresses.

NAT allows internal internet addresses or internet protocols to be hidden. Packets sent from a host behind the firewall will appear to have been sent from the firewall's external address. This makes the sender invisible to the internet, which makes it difficult for hackers to track down the network information and addresses required. Has NAT been set up? How?

Stateful inspection is the most sophisticated technology available. Firewalls modeled around this technology interrogate the packets based on source, destination, protocol, and communications port. Is stateful inspection technology available (i.e., that interrogates the packets based on source, destination, protocol, and communications port)?

Does the design provide both router and bridge configurations? The router setup is most common for commercial firewalls that receive a packet, compare it to the rules defined, and either permit or deny access to another network. This scenario often requires several network changes including managing static routing tables, and it can make it an easy target for hackers. To address these issues, the firewall was built on top of a secure operating system.

MONITORING

Another significant requirement is monitoring. Having the right monitoring or detection tools is incredibly important to reacting to a breach. Monitoring can be broken down into three crucial questions:

1. What is being detected?
2. How quickly can it be detected?
3. How often is the detection tool updated?

Even with detection, few companies have any idea what to do if they find a breach. It has become common knowledge that most do very little, except perhaps improve their security system. Few companies legally pursue hackers according to industry observers. Thus, there have to be procedures available to react to a breach even if it will not be pursued legally.

SECURITY

The critical security tasks include network protocol analysis and security and network management solutions.

These tasks should be followed during all stages of network development and security—from planning and design to implementation and ongoing management. They include:

- Operational tasks
- Software distributions
- Event alerts
- System monitors of Total Virus Defense from within the IT environment

Specific integration points include the following:

- Remote deployment and updating of Total Virus Defense products.
- Distribution of virus signature updates to all supported Total Virus Defense clients and servers across the network.
- Automated polling of virus signature files across the network to monitor file aging and identify systems that require updating.
- Central monitoring of virus event logs across the network.
- Centralized display of Total Virus Defense event alerts to identify unprotected systems, noncompliant or outdated virus protection, and specific virus activity.

The Total Virus Defense suite should provide complete virus security at all possible points of entry across the network including the desktop, file server, e-mail server, and internet gateway.

Security is a concern with any internet application. Part of the total function involves using 128-bit encryption, plus a firewall, plus user passwords. These security levels have become accepted as industry standards. Remote management security procedures are:

- Generate a public/private key pair with Netscape Enterprise Server.
- Generate a certificate request.
- Look up the company's Dun and Bradstreet (DUNS) number.
- Submit the certificate request with the DUNS number to VeriSign.
- Retrieve the Digital ID using the PIN number sent by VeriSign. (This procedure is too involved for most users to follow.)

NETWORK INFORMATION SERVICES

Network Information Services (NIS) provides you with an easy way to maintain user equivalence throughout the enterprise network including full integration with account administration tools.

1. What is NIS?
2. How is it configured?
3. How is it administered?
4. What are the client-server architectures of NIS including the various kinds of NIS servers?
5. What are the NIS maps? List what maps are configurable by default.
6. What are the NIS management tools?
7. Obtain a list of `daemons` used to implement NIS including their functionality.

A final point to consider is whether security issues are addressed by incorporating strong encryption, authentication, and secure firewall traversal features.

DOCUMENTATION CHECKLIST

The documentation checklist includes:

- Organizational charts and job descriptions for personnel of the IS.
- Documentation pertaining to the overall solid design and functionality of the firewall.

- Wide area network (WAN) topologies indicating the names of all LANs and the network locations including WAN transmission methods used (X.25, Frame-relay, T1, dial-up, and so on). This should be cross-referenced to the documentation on the network systems such as Novel, Banyan, and so on.
- Data circuits (links can be bottlenecks). Who is doing the planning?
  28.8 kb/s v.34 over POTS
  56, 64, or 128 kb/s over ISDN BRI
  256, 384 kb/s using fractional T1
  1.5 Mb/s using T1
  45 Mb/s using T3 or Sonet
  30 Mb/c over cable TV
- Detailed network topologies for all local area networks within and without the organization should include all significant points of reference for:
  - Routers (types, make, model); access to routing tables and Domain Name System (DNS), which decide how to route data.
  - Firewalls (Is the firewall performing the router functions, or is there a separate router and where is it placed?) It should normally be placed outside the firewall (on the internet side). Is the firewall purchased as a product, or was it downloaded from the URL?
  - Gateways
  - File servers (How many? What are they? List of all file servers)
  - Host processing systems (Unix, mainframe, and so on)
  - Network and node IP addresses
  - Link transmission methods (Ethernet, token ring, and so on)
- Names of significant applications in use and where they reside on the system with a security matrix detailing access privileges of the owners of the applications and users, including their profiles.
- Description of `TCP/IP` services (`Telnet`, `ftp`, `nfs`, `tftp`, and so on) necessary to support these applications.
- Access to the network control files for significant systems in audit scope (`/etc/inetd.conf`, `/etc/hosts.equiv`, `/etc/exports`, and so on).
- Printout of router configuration files for routers that connect to external networks or routers that are used to segment server networks from the user networks.
- Printout of firewall configuration files and log files.
- Network Operations and Security Policies and Procedures (add security profiles of all users of the system classified by the following functions: Administrators, Security Officers, developers, system engineers, and programmers).
- Determine if any risk assessment has been performed and if so what the overall security assessment of the system is (i.e., if the security is adequate before going on to reviewing the firewall).
- Determine if packet-filtering blocks dangerous services such as RCP and other "r" services such as (`rlogin`, `rsh`, `rcp`).
- Determine if packet-filtering tools are used.

FIREWALL CHECKLIST

The firewall checklist includes the following questions:

- How was the specific and appropriate type of firewall architecture determined?
- What was defined as the criteria and specific needs for a firewall?
- Have the firewalls been linked with stand-alone intrusion detection and antivirus software running on separate servers?
- Is the firewall tightly integrated with antivirus scanning and network monitoring features that can respond to a wider range of network security attacks?
- Was an inward-looking role for firewalls formed (i.e., to position multiple firewalls between offices to protect against internal misuse of departmental servers)? These are referred to as intranet firewalls. Perhaps most notably, the firewall will turn its attention inward to fend off internal attacks as well, which are generally viewed as more common than assaults from the outside.
- Does the firewall scan all relevant internet traffic, including HTTP, FTP, and SMTP, for viruses in real time? The software automatically cleans, deletes, and even quarantines viruses for future analysis and origin tracing.
- Do the firewall capabilities enable a protective perimeter around the user's PC? Access to and from the PC can be limited by application, network port, IP address, or even to a particular time period. With the increasing importance of security for internet, intranet, and extranet resources, are individual PC users looking for more control over who accesses their PC?
- Are the rules well designed and make it easy to define source and destination addresses and ports?

Security issues are addressed by incorporating strong encryption, authentication, and secure firewall traversal features.

FILTERS

Spam Filter

The spam filter is designed to prevent junk e-mail from clogging the corporate network. It is implemented by using internet gateway traffic scanning software.

Content Filtering

Content filtering involves:

- Providing products that block unwanted viruses or malicious code, including a process that guards against unwanted content.
- Scanning internet or e-mail traffic for viruses and scanning e-mail content for particular keywords, domains, and e-mail addresses. Spam and viruses are two of the most unwelcome visitors on private and public networks.
- Addressing the growing spam problem inflicting the approximately 75 million business e-mail users in the United States.

- Blocking distribution of viruses, spam, and other inappropriate message content.

E-mail can now be used to distribute confidential or inappropriate information, which can raise a number of serious legal issues. Can different filters be applied to different groups of people at different times of the day? How is the corporate policy implemented and centrally controlled by the company's IT experts, ensuring that the filter is effective and hassle-free for corporate end users?

FIREWALL TESTS

Possible Tests:

- Install SMS and digital "sledgehammers."
- Attempt to bypass it with basic TCP scans, fragmented packet scans, and SYN and FIN scans.
- Attempt to overwhelm it with SYN and ICMP floods.

Rules are well designed and make it easy to define source and destination addresses and ports. Permitting dynamic port selection applications such as RealAudio and NetMeeting through the firewall is often difficult, but solutions include dependency masks. Dependency masks let you define the next sequence of protocols to allow after the initial ones have been established. For example, with RealAudio you can define TCP for the control connection and User Datagram Protocol for the following data connection.

TECHNICAL AUDIT PROGRAM

INTERNET AND FIREWALL CONFIGURATION SECURITY

Purpose: Determine that the connection to an external network, such as the internet, is secured with an application gateway firewall and that the firewall is properly configured to secure internet traffic.

A. Obtain a detailed network diagram of the firewall network configuration (router, DNS server, firewall host system, Web server, and so on) with hostnames and IP addresses.
   - Determine that all of the physical and logical components of the firewall network are managed by the same group and that the control procedures and policies are well documented and updated regularly.
   - Review the firewall network operations and control procedures to ensure that procedures are documented and in place to back up security and configuration files and to properly restore these files after system failures and software or operating system upgrades.
   - Using the network diagram as a guide, observe the physical connections between the various components noting proper labeling of all physical connections and that all physical connections are consistent with the diagram. Investigate any connections that link portions of the firewall network to networks or links not documented in the network diagram.
   - Determine that the firewall has only two network interfaces: the link to the external network and the link to the internal network.

- Determine that the router that connects to the internet has only two interfaces: one that connects to the internet service provider and a second that connects directly to the firewall or one that connects to the sacrificial network outside of the firewall.
- For all systems (Web server, DNS server, router, firewall) on the sacrificial network, determine that each component has no links to any other parts of the network or to other networks.

B. Review the router configuration file for the router that connects to the internet service provider. Determine that adequate filters are in place to detect and drop incoming services that are not authorized to be used on any of the components located on the sacrificial network (possibly Telnet, snmp, bootp, and so on).

C. Ensure that the application gateway firewall's host operating system has been properly modified to disable services that could be used to subvert the security of the firewall software program:

- Review the /etc/inetd.conf file and the /etc/rc start-up files to ensure that all standard network services have been disabled (by commenting out # their entries).
- Execute the command netstat at the firewall operating system prompt and review the output (it should show no routes available) to ensure that IP datagram routing has been disabled in the operating system kernel.
- Review the contents of /etc/hosts.equiv, $HOME/.rhosts, and $HOME/.netrc to ensure that these files are empty or do not exist on the system.
- Review the /etc/passwd file to ensure that only the root account and one firewall administration account are active (not including login-disabled system accounts—bin, wheel, and so on). Assess controls over access to these accounts—passwords, logging, and review.
- Review the directory structure to ensure that no other application programs, language compilers, interpreters, or other utilities are loaded on the system.

D. Review the configuration of the firewall software. Often, a configuration file can be printed out and reviewed.

- Identify all supported and active network application proxies along with the indication as to where connections may be initiated from (this may be noted as "trusted network" for connections initiated from the internal network and "untrusted network" for connections initiated from the external network—internet) and compare this to the internet policy description of authorized services. Investigate any deviations from policy.
- For all proxies that allow network connections to be initiated from the internet (Telnet, ftp, and so on), ensure that strong authentication controls are implemented within the password (challenge-response, encryption) or that **** what about tftp***** third-party security schemes have been implemented (SecureID, S/key).
- For all proxies that allow network connections to be initiated from the Internet, there should normally be restrictions (based on IP addresses or hostnames) on the source of such connections and the systems on the internal network that an internet user may access. Assess the need for these restrictions and review the configuration of such access controls.

- Review ID and password controls—authorizations for IDs, password format, and aging controls.
- Review and assess the use of groups to assign services and access capabilities to users.
- \For generic proxy programs that may be in use, review the port number and IP source and destination restrictions to ensure that they are correctly designed to restrict this traffic. Assess the need and implementation of compensating controls such as router filters.
- For each proxy, determine that adequate logging mechanisms have been activated and that logs are reviewed on a timely basis.
- Determine that audit alerts have been adequately designed to alert management on a real-time basis of security events that require prompt attention (alerts such as snmp traps, e-mail messages, pagers, and so on).
- Identify and assess the appropriateness of Administrators with access to view and modify the firewall configuration. Review the configuration change log (many firewall products support this) and investigate several changes with the Administrator to ensure they are authorized changes.

For more detailed information on a technical network audit, refer to the section "Safeguarding Network Security" in Chapter 6. Specifically note the subsections "Technical Audit Program" and "Managing Network with /etc/hosts Table."

CHAPTER 8

DISASTER RECOVERY PLANNING

INTRODUCTION

Online, real-time applications have become commonplace in all business environments. In fact, because computer systems and business goals are often interdependent, computer applications are essential to business success. The proliferation of business-critical, real-time transaction processing makes the availability of information processing a key issue. However, the very nature of user-interactive, online systems significantly complicates a recovery strategy.

EMERGING TECHNOLOGIES

Recent technological advances not only provide great utility to the organization but also increase the reliance on technology. Even short-term downtime of critical applications can jeopardize the business as it halts production and services. However, despite hardware redundancies and fault-tolerant operating systems, fires, floods, and numerous other disasters pose a risk that a comprehensive recovery plan should address. Look at the emerging technologies such as end-user computing, networks, electronic data interchange, and electronic commerce.

END-USER COMPUTING

End-user computing is a derivative of the microcomputer revolution. Processing power no longer resides solely in the computer room but can be on any user's desk. As microcomputer-processing power increases, more powerful and user-friendly software languages and tools are being furnished to end users. Instead of waiting for the data processing department to develop and enhance an application, end users may develop it themselves. Many mission-critical applications currently reside on minicomputers or microcomputers that are completely under the control of end users. Thus, the ability to process end-user applications in the event of a disaster may be crucial to an organization.

NETWORKS

Local area networks (LANs) and wide area networks (WANs) allow users to share common data files. Hundreds of users can be connected via a common file server(s). A LAN is generally confined to a small geographic area, such as a department, while a WAN covers a larger area. LANs and WANs are designed to allow end users to share information quickly and easily. In many cases, end users maintain critical applications contained on their local area network(s).

ELECTRONIC DATA INTERCHANGE

There has been steady growth in the acceptance and use of electronic data interchange (EDI) in business functions. The number of EDI users has increased significantly in the past five years. Major corporations are requiring there trading partners to replace paper transactions with electronic transactions. A business that relies on EDI to perform routine business functions may be unable to process transactions or receive deposits if the EDI system is not operating.

E-COMMERCE

The growth of end-user computing (EUC), local and wide area networks, and microcomputers further underscores the need for disaster recovery plans (DRPs). In most organizations, even a comprehensive and tested DRP may not address all the necessary computing resources. The design, development, implementation, and recovery of systems is no longer the domain of the IT professional. The ultimate responsibility for recovery of key business assets rests clearly with senior management. The role of audit is to help management fulfill this responsibility by providing complete, timely, and accurate reviews of the organization's DRP.

Comprehensive and functional DRPs are necessary because today's automated information services critically affect the very life of IT. Within moments of a disruption in system availability, IT may experience inefficiencies and inconveniences. As a direct result of the pervasive nature of critical real-time systems, computer disasters are now viewed as potential corporate disasters.

KEY COMPONENTS OF A SUCCESSFUL DISASTER RECOVERY PLAN

Successful DRPs are complete, current, and well documented. Specifically, the plan should describe the role of senior management, the recovery team's responsibilities, the distribution of completed plans, cost-effectiveness and operational feasibility, plan testing, recovery alternatives, critical operational procedures, and other emergency information that may be used in a long-term recovery environment. Specific statements regarding each of these areas will help to ensure that the DRP is comprehensive and complete enough to minimize the need for critical decision making in a crisis situation.

In order to establish a comprehensive and effective recovery plan, the direct support and involvement of senior management is essential. Responsibility for disaster recovery ultimately rests with senior management. As part of their overall responsibility for the assets in the organization, senior management must ensure that adequate resources are available for planning, testing, and maintaining a comprehensive plan. For recovery planning to be truly effective, management should issue a formal statement outlining its commitment to DRPs throughout the organization.

MANAGEMENT COMMITMENT AND FUNDING

Disaster recovery requires additional resources and broader distribution of DRP responsibilities across the firm. The technology group is no longer the sole provider and sponsor for the firm's DRP since the technology itself is no longer isolated in the controlled environment of major data centers.

As with any business program, the DRPs should be cost-effective and operationally feasible. Senior management should identify the proper scope of the DRPs based on the objectives of the plan, potential causes of business interruptions, possible economic consequences of disaster, potential legal liabilities, and organizational and nonorganizational resources affected. It is possible to reduce costs by developing a plan that deals with only the worst-case scenarios. This comprehensive plan with the worst-case scenarios will be easy to modify for use following a less serious disaster.

Senior management should also determine the operational feasibility of the DRPs. This step involves critically assessing the ability and desire of the organizational staff to implement approved recovery procedures, and the likelihood that key personnel will remain in a disaster situation to actually implement the plan should be addressed. Determining how recovery team members and other employees will react to a disaster situation directly affects the structure and content of the DRPs.

Since audit is familiar with many of an organization's business units, they can act as catalysts to empower senior management into sufficient funding allocation and heightened DRP awareness within the firm according to the audit findings. Recommendations for DRP education, ownership, and expenses may need to be allocated among the various business groups. Some organizations have taken such recommendations to heart and have even begun to include disaster recovery responsibilities in their business manager's job description and evaluation process.

If a company is in the early stages of disaster recovery planning, there will be a significant level of program development effort required, which will level out as the DRP program moves into maintenance and testing mode. In the early stages of planning, disaster recovery planners should solicit audit support in obtaining senior management's commitment to resources and assignment of DRP responsibilities throughout the firm. Audit can work with management to communicate the following messages:

- Disaster recovery planning is a vital exercise.
- Management is committed to implementing an effective DRP program.
- Management will employ and deploy the required resources.
- These are the DRP team assignments.
- Team participation and cooperation is key to our success.
- This is what is expected of you.

Audit support in gaining management's commitment will ensure that support continues through all stages of the DRP.

Audit should play an equally important role in the disaster recovery planning process in a number of ways in which it can add value to the development and ongoing testing, maintenance, and support of the disaster recovery plans and strategies. However, the appropriate level of audit participation should be aligned with the organization's overall audit plan, availability of appropriate audit resources, and the existence and maturity level of the organization's disaster recovery program.

Audit is in the unique position of having access to related initiatives across the organization. They also have unique access to senior management and the board of directors. These attributes should be explored and tapped as a benefit to any DRP program. Therefore, leveraging the audit process in the disaster recovery program makes sense.

However, audit should abstain from highlighting only the negative aspects of organizational processes or controls. Disaster recovery planners as a result are vulnerable to this audit scrutiny, which frequently results in reports to senior management that only highlight weaknesses in the existing DRP program.

Audit should avoid recommendations to management for a strengthened DRP process when in doing so does not add value to the DRP strategies. This is especially true of audit findings that are typical of cursory review such as:

- A specific business area does not have a disaster recovery plan.
- A specific business area has a disaster recovery plan. However, the findings, comments, and concerns relate to the weaknesses in the documentation and not to the plans and strategies themselves, which in itself suggests that audit has not expended significant effort in reading and comprehending the plans. This may be because they are not in a position to do so because of lack of expertise and, as a result, their recommendations are not meaningful and practical.

It is not surprising then that those disaster recovery planners may be reluctant to freely share ideas, thoughts, and concerns with audit and as a result sever their alliance with audit. This becomes a sad state of affairs. To overcome this, audit's traditional "critique and report" role should be reevaluated and possibly enhanced.

Audit should be capable of providing more value during the process than an "after the fact" exceptions report, which to most in the organization appears to be an attempt to "shoot holes" in the DRP process instead of being a part of it. Audit's approach to participating in the disaster recovery planning process should be a fully integrated one since this is a business, technology, and operational issue. Audit participation may cover the entire program or may be limited to one or more of the specific categories described later in the chapter. Audit's overall objective should be to ensure that the organization has an effective disaster recovery program in place and that it is kept current and tested on a regular basis. Reports to senior management should communicate a clear and independent message on the status of the program, highlighting any identified issues and areas for improvement. Measures of disaster recovery success and mechanisms for ongoing management reporting should also be established. Lastly, audit can and should monitor the business groups' participation in the DRP program and provide management with ongoing progress reports.

Presented following are several specific areas where audit can add value and become an important part of the disaster recovery process.

RECOVERY TEAM

Disaster recovery teams should include senior managers, information systems department personnel, and end users that are qualified to help the organization recover from business interruption. Specific recovery teams may be organized to handle damage assessment, off-site facility administration, communications, hardware, software, and general logistics.

The DRPs should also include a notification section that contains the names, home addresses, and telephone numbers of key personnel who need to be contacted in the event that a decision is made by senior management to declare a disaster at a critical processing site. This notification section should also contain procedures and organizational charts identifying the appropriate sequence for contacting recovery team members following a disaster declaration.

DISASTER PREPAREDNESS

In today's highly competitive corporate environment, which increasingly depends on information technology for continued survival, the definition of a disaster becomes more significant. How should management define a disaster?

First, begin by assessing the organization's dependency on information technology. *A disaster could then be defined as any unplanned or spontaneous event or condition that renders the organization unable to use its information technology and causes significant loss of essential services.*

Not every event is a disaster, even though it might be perceived as such. Thus, there are classifications of exposure:

- Interruption—Any disruption of operations that causes only limited corporate consequences. An operational failure may fall into this category.
- Emergency—A disaster or a significant interruption, depending on its duration and the impact to the continued survival of the organization.

Criteria to consider when defining a disaster include the degree of dependency placed on information technology and the quality of the organization's DRP.

A DRP cannot depend on the participation of any particular individual or group of individuals. The plan should describe key activities and critical decisions in sufficient detail so that any available staff member can perform required recovery tasks.

A DRP should be as comprehensive as possible and should document preestablished criteria for making critical decisions in a crisis atmosphere. The plan should also provide details of required recovery actions and document retention policies. This information will become an important resource for the recovery process.

A DRP should include and emphasize the actions intended to protect the organization, management, and staff members from being victimized by those who would take advantage of the organization's situation. *The requirement for preparing, organizing, and reviewing disaster recovery documentation has the added benefit of building a defense against lawsuits and unjustified charges.*

Although a DRP should be based on a worst-case scenario (e.g., the entire information technology facility becomes unavailable for an extended period of time), emphasis should be placed on defining recovery procedures for basic interruptions that, if not addressed efficiently, might result in a full-scale disaster. Some potential causes of business interruptions include:

- Fire
- Vandalism
- Sabotage (external/internal)
- Fraud
- Power failures
- Riot/civil disorder
- Human error
- Terrorist actions
- Plane crash
- Computer hackers
- Earthquake
- Hurricane or tornado
- Theft
- Flood

The first step in determining the potential impact of a disaster is to identify the essential assets that need protection. One way to do this is to perform an impact study. Some essential assets (e.g., facilities, hardware, and software) might be tangible and easily identified and their value easily calculated. However, the value of data is more difficult to assess because it depends on its relative value to management. The following categories should be considered when developing an inventory of essential assets requiring protection:

- Facilities
- Data
- Software
- Personnel
- Data processing hardware
- Communications circuits
- Communications hardware

These assets are susceptible to any of the threats listed as probable causes of business interruptions. Management is responsible for recognizing the probable causes of business interruptions and, to the extent possible, taking steps necessary to protect critical information technology operations. Auditors should assess the risk of exposure and the adequacy of precautionary steps to prevent or minimize the effects of disaster. It can be expensive to develop and maintain a DRP. Designing a DRP is a labor-intensive task and can take a year or more to complete.

BUILDING A CASE FOR DISASTER RECOVERY

Audit has an opportunity to communicate the need for a DRP program to senior management. Audit must emphasize the risks of not being ready and able to recover and continue the firm's critical business functions, not complying with regulatory requirements, not meeting contractual obligations and service level agreements, and not providing an adequate level of awareness within the organization.

Audit may also be well positioned to compile information throughout the organization on risks and potential threats to facilities and business processes because of their close examination of these areas during other scheduled audits. Furthermore, audit can often compile and share DRP benchmarking data and leading-practices information across business units and locations. Audit could also obtain information on DRP plans, strategies, and practices from similar organizations or other firms within an industry grouping, which can assist in a company's DRP efforts.

BUSINESS IMPACT ANALYSIS

The business impact analysis (BIA) is the foundation of effective disaster recovery planning. It must originate from the individual business areas and should highlight business strategy as well as inherent risks and critical threats to achieving business goals. As such, it will represent the business area's risk assessment of its financial, operational, competitive, and systems environments. The more defined the BIA is, the easier it will be to justify the expense of the disaster recovery program to senior management.

Audit should help make this process less subjective and more quantifiable through the use of appropriate measurement tools and risk assessment techniques. Remember, this is what audit does regularly. This is an area of expertise.

Audit's most significant contribution to the BIA process is one of validation. At a minimum, they should review and validate the following components:

- Business process inventories
- Business process owners
- Resource listings, including systems inventories
- Business impact information (financial and nonfinancial)
- Critical time periods
- Interdependencies
- Recovery time frame objectives
- Recovery resource requirements

Obtaining audit's evaluation and validation of the preceding items will enhance the DRP's framework and serve to strengthen its effectiveness not only for the eyes of management but also in the event of a disruption.

STRATEGY SELECTION

Disaster recovery strategies range from providing fully functional alternate sites to "quick ship" programs, which may be internally or externally provided. Based on the BIA, a suitable strategy should be selected to provide the organization with the necessary recovery resources within its predetermined recovery time objectives (RTOs).

Audit should review the strategy to ensure that it is in line with the overall business process and fits the organization's bigger picture. Audit can also perform independent reviews of vendor contracts and agreements as well as liaise with procurement and legal departments during this process. The key is to ensure that the selected recovery strategies and all assumptions surrounding those strategies have been adequately and independently reviewed.

These assumptions may include:

- Assuming that the alternate facility will be available at crisis time.
- Assuming that the alternate facility is a certain distance away and unlikely to be affected.
- Assuming that key personnel will be available to facilitate recovery.
- Assuming that identified vendors and alternates will be available to provide products and services.

Audit should work with the disaster recovery planner to ensure that there are no "surprise" audit findings after the DRP program is implemented. It is far more efficient and effective to build audit requirements into the DRP process during development than to retrofit a DRP program with audit-required controls.

PLAN PREPARATION

Since individual business managers are ultimately responsible for the successful execution of the plan in the event of disruption, they should assume ownership of the plan. They should provide the time and resources to clearly document the detailed recovery procedures necessary to resume and continue critical business activities.

Audit should share concerns and expectations up front during the development of the disaster recovery plans, as it will streamline the process to implement the auditor's suggestions during the development of the plan. The auditor should conduct independent reviews of both the initial draft and final plans.

It is important that the audit group be satisfied with the level of detail in the documented recovery procedures. As audit cannot be expected to be expert in every business process across the organization, it should monitor the review and approval of DRP plan sections or modules by appropriate key managers including department/functional managers, technology managers, facilities' managers, DRP team leaders, and executive team leaders and managers.

Another area in plan preparation where audit can help involves DRP software tools. Audit can often provide assistance with software selection activities and act as a liaison with the procurement department to ensure the right vendors are involved and the right package is ultimately selected. Audit should also get involved with vendor support and program change management issues since each part of the final DRP will depend on every other part.

PASS THE TEST

Exercising the plan means validating it. It is also a method for training those responsible for recovery activities and a test to ensure the completeness and accuracy of plan documentation. This process is more than a one-day event. Tests can range from a structured walk-through conducted via table discussion to full-business resumption simulation conducted at an alternate site with full-user participation.

Audit should independently assess the effectiveness of the testing process. This includes participation in all phases of the testing cycle including the initial preparation prior to test date, the test exercise itself, and the posttest activities.

In the pretest or preparation phase, assessment should commence with audit monitoring the initial planning meetings. This will confirm that the right people are represented and working together to formulate an adequate test scope, discussing expectations and prior test results, assigning responsibilities, and properly preparing for the upcoming test exercise.

This is a perfect time for audit with their respective business expertise to review the current plans and determine that they accurately articulate the business area's critical path and have included all interdependencies. It is a critical step to perform this "sanity check," for if the plan is incomplete and does not sufficiently cover the critical business functions, then one might ask, "How worthwhile is the test?" or "Why are we incurring the expense of this test?"

Next, audit plays a key role during the test exercise itself. Audit should not only act as independent observers but also perform many adjunct functions that day. These include:

- Performing a facility review of the alternate site and surrounding area
- Independent testing of security and technology configurations
- Observation testing to ensure that test scripts are successfully completed within the RTOs
- Confirming that adequate support personnel are available
- Verifying that there is adequate ongoing communications during the exercise (including kickoff and wrap-up meetings with all the participants, shift turnover, and problem-solving meetings with the tech staff, etc.)
- Observing that problems are logged, properly handled, and resolved
- Performing an inventory check on equipment by reconciling both vendor contacts and the business plan requirements

- Ensuring that disengagement procedures are properly executed
- Observing the final sign-out process for test participants

The final phase of audit's participation would include:

- Attendance in the postmortem meetings
- Performing postanalysis audit runs, where appropriate
- Continuous follow-up on open issues
- Consolidated reporting on progress across the firm

By including audit and making it an integral part of all phases and aspects of the testing stage of the DRP, contingency planners and senior management can make sure that in the event of a real emergency the plan is effective and fully assembled.

TESTING THE DISASTER RECOVERY PLAN

For an increasing number of organizations the loss of their computer systems will have a devastating effect. In spite of this, surveys indicate that only a small number of organizations have invested in a DRP, and regrettably only a very small number of these plans are more than a token gesture toward the audit function. Even where companies have created a reasonable disaster recovery strategy and have documented a plan, in many cases these plans have never really been tested. An out-of-date, untested plan is perhaps more dangerous than not having a plan at all because it lulls everybody in the organization into a false sense of security. A plan exists but will it suffice in the event of a real emergency?

Why is it that organizations do not test their disaster recovery plans? There are two main reasons that can be considered the great myths of disaster recovery testing. These are:

1. "I don't need to test because my technical staff is committed to their role and will resolve all the problems when a disaster occurs."

Most staffs are committed and will perform beyond their normal expectancies in times of crisis. But if the plan has not been tested, there is a better-than-average chance that some of the procedures will not work (i.e., the backups not saving the data necessary to recover the system) and the whole plan will fail with dire consequences throughout the organization.

2. "I cannot test the plan because there is no suitable system available to use in the test and the vendor will not make such a system available to me."

The exercise is perceived as too costly and too difficult to perform. This is a common excuse with organizations that have subscribed to an external service such as a cold site with a supplier agreement for replacement equipment or a hot site solution.

As we will see, the current operational system is often quite satisfactory for testing low-level tasks such as backup and restore procedures, and with suitable planning a great deal of disaster recovery testing can be accomplished with very little expenditure.

TYPES OF TESTS

The methodology described following will provide one with a good basis for creating tests to prove the accuracy and validity of the disaster recovery plan. Testing is essential if a plan is to keep pace with changes in technology and company objectives.

A series of test programs needs to be developed and conducted before the disaster recovery plan is complete and accurate. Following are four classes of tests:

1. Hypothetical (dry run of plan processes)
2. Component (can have multiple component tests)
3. Module (can also be combined with other modules)
4. Full (requires stand-alone machine time)

Depending on the size and complexity of the computer facility, it may not be appropriate to conduct all testing phases. One may wish to omit the module tests and go directly to a full test, or it may not be possible to conduct a full test, in which case perform as many module tests as practicable. Timings should always be recorded during each test, other than the hypothetical test, to verify the time frame required to fully restore the system. If the timing falls outside the time frame stipulated in the plan, the plan and/or the recovery method should be reviewed.

Hypothetical Test

The hypothetical test is an exercise to verify the existence of all necessary procedures and actions specified within the recovery plan and to prove the theory of those procedures. It is a theoretical check and should be conducted every six months. The exercise is generally a brief one, taking approximately two hours to conduct, and is designed to look at the worst-case scenario for equipment, ensuring that the entire plan process is reviewed.

Component Test

A component is the smallest set of instructions within the recovery plan that enables specific processes to be performed. For example, the process System Load/IPL, involves a series of commands to load the system. However, in a recovery situation this may differ from normal operational requirements. Certain functions may need to be enabled or disabled to suit the new environment. If this is not fully tested, incompatibility problems with other components are high. Component testing is designed to verify the detail and accuracy of individual procedures within the recovery plan and can be used when no additional system can be made available for extended periods.

Examples of component tests are:

- Backup procedure
- Off-site tape storage
- Assembly location
- Restore procedure
- Recovery site inspection
- Security package start-up

Module Test

A module is a combination of components. The ideal method of testing is for each component to be individually tested and proven before being included in a module. (Some of these components may be performed and verified during normal daily operational activities.) The aim of module testing is to verify the validity and functionality of the recovery procedures when multiple components are combined. If you are able to test all modules, even if you are unable to perform a full test, then you can be confident that the business will survive a major computer center disaster. It is when a series of components are combined without individual tests that difficulties occur.

Examples of module tests are:

- Alternate site activation
- Network recovery
- Database recovery
- System recovery
- Application recovery
- Run production processing

Full Test

The full test verifies that each component within every module is workable and satisfies the strategy and time frame requirements detailed in the recovery plan. The test also verifies the interdependencies of various modules to ensure that progression from one module to another can be effected without problems or loss of data.

There are two main objectives associated with a full test:

1. To confirm the total *elapsed time* to establish that the production environment meets the plan objective.
2. To prove the *efficiency* of the recovery plan to ensure a smooth flow from module to module.

To achieve the first objective, a computer system of the similar capacity and speed must be available for the estimated time frame as stipulated in the plan. This is not critical to achieving the second objective.

SETTING OBJECTIVES

Each test is designed around a worst-case scenario for equipment since this will ensure that the entire plan is examined while catering to all possible disastrous situations. Base tests around best-case scenario for staffing to ensure that all participants are involved and that all available expertise is on hand to understand and resolve each issue in the process of building a complete plan.

Appropriate personnel should note any weaknesses or opportunities to improve the plan for action. Once confident that the recovery plan is effective, other scenarios for staffing can be tested (i.e., worst case) to verify that the procedures are complete and can be performed by less technical personnel. Only when every requirement associated with each component has been documented and verified can the recovery plan be said to be complete and functional. It is very important that all aspects of the test are properly examined before a commitment is made to invoke the test.

Because it is a test, some considerations will be necessary that perhaps would not be so in a real disaster. For example, a test may require agreement with business units to prevent any impact to production, or require that all change control be frozen for a period, or require discussions with the building superintendent to ensure that no electricity or air conditioning maintenance is planned. This may result in the test being rescheduled or conducted over a weekend. The last thing management or participants of the test want is for the test to be canceled because a simple item has been overlooked. This would be a waste of time, commitment, and money.

Sample test objectives include:

- Recover systems at the standby site and establish an environment to enable full accommodation of the nominated applications.
- Present a fully documented set of procedures to successfully obtain and utilize off-site tapes to restore the system and critical applications to the agreed-upon recovery point as set out in the recovery plan.
- Successfully recover system/application/database data from the off-site backup or tapes.
- Present detailed documentation on how to restore the production data as stipulated in the recovery plan to the agreed-upon recovery point (e.g., start of day).
- Present fully documented procedures for establishing communication lines/equipment to enable full availability and usage by appropriate areas (e.g., business units, data entry, users, and so on).
- Establish communication lines/equipment as set out in the plan.
- Examine the designated alternative site and confirm that all components are as noted in the site handbook.

DEFINING THE BOUNDARIES

Test boundaries are needed to satisfy the disaster recovery strategy, methodology, and processes. The management team must also consider future test criteria to ensure a realistic and obtainable progression to meet the end objectives. Opportunities to test actual recovery procedures should be taken whenever possible (e.g., a purchase of new or additional equipment, vendor agreements, use of hot site, or a loan of system at site, or cold site). Management must also include observers for audit and data security services.

Scenario

The scenario is the description of the theoretical disaster, and it explains the various criteria associated with such a disaster. For example, the scenario should outline what caused the disaster and the level of damage sustained to the equipment and facilities and whether or not anything can be salvaged from the wreckage. The purpose is not to get bogged down in great detail but to explain to all participants what is or is not available, what tools can or cannot be used, what the objective of the exercise is at the time the disaster occurred, and the planned recovery point.

Note: The objective of testing is to have a fully validated recovery plan. However, testing should not be made difficult during the initial phases. Complicated testing programs, which have not previously been verified, will only delay this objective and waste resources.

Test Criteria

Not all tests will require all personnel to attend. The test criteria advises all participants, including observers when appropriate, where they are to be located and the time and day the exercise will take place. The role of the observer is to give an unbiased view and to comment on areas of success or concern to assist in future testing.

Assumptions

There will need to be some assumptions made. This allows a test to achieve the results without being bound by other elements of the recovery plan that may not have been verified yet. Assumptions allow prerequisites of a particular component/module to be established outside the test boundaries.

Examples are:

- All technical information documented in the plan, including appendices, is complete and accurate.
- All purchases (equipment/furniture, etc.) can be made in the time frame required.
- Tapes and other equipment recalled from off-site are valid and usable.

TEST PREREQUISITES

Before any test is attempted, it must be verified that the recovery plan is fully documented in all sections, including all appendices and attachments referenced to each process. Each of the participating teams in a test must be aware of how their role relates to other teams, when and how they are expected to perform their tasks, and what tools are permissible. It is the responsibility of each team leader to keep a log of the proceedings for further improvement and to prepare better for future tests.

Briefing Session

No matter whether it is a hypothetical, component, module, or full test, a briefing session for the teams is necessary. The boundaries of the test are explained, and the opportunity to discuss any technical uncertainties, provided.

Depending on the complexity of the test, additional briefing sessions may be required, one to outline the general boundaries, another to discuss any technical queries, and perhaps one to brief senior management on the test's objectives. The size of the exercise and number of staff involved will determine the time between the briefing session(s) and the test. However, this time period must provide sufficient opportunity for personnel to prepare adequately, particularly the technical staff. It is recommended that the final briefing be held no more than two days prior to a test date to ensure that all activities are fresh in the minds of the participants and the test is not impacted through misunderstandings or tardiness.

An agenda would be:

- Team objectives
- Scenario of the disaster
- Time of the test
- Location of each team
- Restrictions on specific teams
- Assumptions of the test
- Prerequisites for each team

Checklists

Checklists are used to provide the minimum preparation for all of the test types. Checklists are directly related to specific modules of the recovery plan, and all sections relevant to a particular test must be verified as complete before a test date is set.

Because these checklists follow the various modules associated with the recovery plan, only those parts applicable to the forthcoming test are compulsory prerequisites for that test. However, it is recommended that all sections of the checklist be completed as soon as possible. The following sample checklists show the detail required.

Documentation Checks

Maintaining currency of the documentation contained within the recovery plan is essential to not only the success of the tests but also, more importantly, to the recovery of critical business activities in the event of a real disaster. There are a number of important documents that need to be monitored, maintained, and issued for both testing and emergency situations. They generally fall into two main groups.

General.
Following is a list of general preparations:

- Prepare and maintain a twelve-month test schedule
- Regularly advise all teams of the test schedule
- Maintain business impact information if applicable
- Maintain documented test procedures
- Prepare a floor plan of each team's location during tests
- Maintain a supply of special forms (e.g., security, authorizations, checklists, etc.)

Plan.
Review the recovery plan to ensure the following are maintained and current:

- Team objectives and responsibilities
- Team procedures
- Team actions
- All low-level procedures (components) including:
  - Operations procedures
  - Operations schedule
  - Application runbooks
  - Disaster recovery fallback runbooks
  - Network configuration diagrams
  - Escalation procedures
  - Contact list
  - Security logs/registers
  - Alternative site manual
  - System configuration
  - Storage requirements

- Change control activities
- Sequence of application recovery
- Critical applications
- Simultaneous updates of master and team recovery plans
- Test high-level flowchart (road map) master

SYSTEM MODULE CHECKS

The first module required to establish a system after a disaster is the system module. It covers the items necessary for staff to proceed once the hardware is installed, and progresses to the point where application and/or database recovery can commence. (Network/communications is covered as a separate module.)

The first section, off-site tapes, forms a critical component of system recovery. (An additional checklist under this heading is also located in the applications/database module.)

Off-Site Tapes

Questions to ask regarding off-site tapes include:

- Is there a regular review of backup procedures?
- Are critical files/records (e.g., backups) stored off-site on a daily basis?
- Are these tapes sent off-site immediately after creation?
- Do you have a list of tapes required for each recovery step? Off-site?
- Can the tapes be retrieved from the off-site location in the required time frame?
- Are there any authorizations or passwords required to collect these tapes? Can the designated person collect them?
- Is the process of getting tapes documented in the plan?
- Has the process of obtaining tapes from the off-site location been tested? How often? Without warning?

System

Questions to ask about the system include:

- Do you have a listing of tapes to be used in the recovery of the system and all subsystems?
- Is this documented and is a copy off-site and in the plan?
- Do you know and understand the sequence of restoring the system?
- Is this documented in the plan?
- Have these procedures been tested/proven?
- Have you performed this process before by yourself? Assisting others?
- Are your backup copies current (e.g., PTFs, fixes/patches, upgrade level, etc.)?
- Do you know the time frame to restore the system to recovery point as stated in the plan?
- Can you restore the operating system and is this documented in the plan?

- Can you restore each subsystem and are they documented in the plan?
- Do you know what time and day you have to recover to? Start of current day (SOD)? End of previous day? Midday? Is this in the plan?
- Do your recovery procedures reflect the correct backup tapes to be used? (For example, if recovering to SOD, the backup tapes will probably have the previous day's date.)
- Do you know the recovery point (e.g., SOD or end of day [EOD] checkpoint recovery?) Is this documented in the plan?
- Can you recover the databases to the SOD?

The Plan

Questions to ask about the plan include:

- Can you forward-recover the databases to the point of failure? Is this documented in the plan?
- Do you know how to verify the integrity and currency of the databases?
- Who is to perform this task and is it documented in the plan?
- Does this person need to formally authorize this fact?
- Can you IPL the system and is it fully documented in the plan?
- Are these procedures accurate; that is, can your manager use them to load the system?
- Are there any processes that are not included in the recovery plan? If not, why not?
- Has your vendor/supplier/maintainer checked and verified all procedures?
- Do you have documented and verified procedures to:
  - Initialize disk drives
  - Restore system (reload)
  - Reboot from stand-alone backup
  - Perform restarts
  - Restore other libraries
  - Initialize catalogues
  - System start-up
  - Application restore
  - Database restore
  - Set unit addresses
  - Perform restarts

Cold Site Checks

Questions to ask about the cold site include:

- Does everyone know the location of the recovery site?
- Have all those who will be located there visited the site?
- Have you checked the access to and from the location?

- Is the equipment stated/contracted to be on-site actually there?
- Have you tested the equipment to verify it as fully functional?
- Do you know your procedures to invoke a DRP at this site?
- Does the site have a security system and do you know how to program/use it?
- Are all the cables, phones, power, telex, and modems of the agreed-upon type and quantity to meet recovery needs?
- Have you verified as functional, the air conditioners, lights, phones, and power?
- Is their sufficient floor and office space to meet your needs?
- Have you checked the access for entry and exit of equipment and staff?
- Do you have a diagram showing the network/system configuration and floor plan?
- Do you know the emergency evacuation procedures of the site?
- Does the fire fighting equipment meet the required standards, and has it been recently checked?
- Is all this documented in a site manual?
- Do you have a copy of the site manual in your possession?
- Does the site satisfy all your recovery communications/network equipment needs?
- Is anyone else situated at this location?
- If so, are they totally isolated from your equipment/communications (e.g., cable moves, security risk, physical risk)?
- Is a method in place to check regularly the readiness of the facility?
- Are all critical consumable (special forms) located in controlled conditions and at multiple locations?

Third-Party Hot Site Checks

Questions to ask about third-party hot site checks include:

- What peripheral equipment do you require to meet your disaster needs as stated in the recovery plan?
- What system size/capacity do you require to run in disaster mode?
- Is the hot site equipment (e.g., system, peripherals, communications) compatible to your existing production site?
- What is the maximum time frame acceptable before you must commence the recovery process?
- Does the site have tape library facilities?
- Do you regularly review the site to check all these items?
- What will the status of the system be on occupation of the hot site (e.g., powered up/down, operating system, configured)?
- If powered up, what levels of release, patches, and so on?
- What procedures are in place to ensure the hot site system remains current?
- Have you performed any tests on this system at this site?
- Is there any special software licensing requirements when running at a second location under recovery mode?

Warm/Hot Site Checks

Questions to ask about warm/hot site checks include:

- Do you have a DRP machine at this location?
- Is the system a development or second production machine?
- Is the system large enough to allow the DRP system and all its requirements to be loaded (e.g., CPU/disk capacity, tape/cart drives, speed to meet user satisfaction)?
- Do you know which files/libraries you need to remove from the DRP system to provide sufficient space?
- Do you wish to keep the data on the DRP machine and restore it after a test or actual disaster?
- If not, do you have a plan to clear or prepare this system for both testing purposes and the actual disaster?
- Do you have procedures to perform this clearing function (backup and delete)?
- Do you have cleanup procedures for the DRP machine at the completion of the test to enable return to normal processing?

ANALYZING THE TEST

While testing is in itself beneficial, an effective recovery plan can only be achieved by constructive analysis of each test and the test's results through a postmortem. This also maintains the momentum gained from the test, which is critical to the process of building a workable plan.

Many staffs see disaster recovery as an additional workload; however, with time and constructive and regular involvement, staffs develop a greater commitment.

Debriefing Session

If the company has a dedicated DRP team or coordinator assigned permanently, then this team or coordinator would have the responsibility of conducting the briefing and debriefing sessions. If not, the responsibility lies with the command team leader.

The format is to discuss the results and findings of the test with a view to improving the recovery plan for future exercises. From these discussions, a set of objectives is developed for later inclusion in the report. An agenda could be:

- Overall performance
- Team performance
- Observations
- Areas of concern
- Next test (type and time)

Test Report

Each team leader has the responsibility of maintaining a log of events during each test. The information gathered from these logs, in addition to the postmortem report by the test manager, is used to produce a test report. Any areas of improvement are noted for action, assigned to an appropriate team member, and given a realistic completion date. A sample format could be:

- Executive summary
- Objective results
- Performance
  - Overall
  - Teams
- List of actions

Always bear in mind that "No test is considered a failure, as any information gained through an exercise such as this can only be of benefit, even if the objectives are not met."

Maintenance Matters

Maintaining the DRP must be proactive and must be an ongoing effort. Certain significant changes in the business like reorganizations, the roll-out of a new system or application, or new expanded business products should trigger an immediate update to the DRP. Business managers need to understand that they are responsible for DRP updates since these updates are a part of the business process.

Audit should contribute knowledge and awareness of these trigger items, since they are typically members of the normal production environment, while examining aspects of the production business regularly. They know the big picture and should be able to discern when one department's changes will affect another department's daily operations. Any change should be examined closely by audit, which will be able to determine its effect on the DRP.

Audit should ensure that adequate DRP-related controls are in place. Audit should periodically verify that production change control procedures include a checkoff item for including disaster recovery updates and that disaster recovery requirements are addressed in a system's development life cycle before they go into production. Additional relevant areas that audit should review include system backup and recovery procedures, records retention programs, off-site storage procedures, security (physical and logical), and general facilities controls.

Critical Operation Procedures

A successful DRP is comprehensive and detailed. In addition to describing procedures relating to data processing, the plan should outline procedures to maintain general business operations. Specific statements in the plan should describe assignments for organizing the temporary work site while progressing with the cleanup, salvage, and restoration procedures at the disaster site. Other general business concerns include providing employees with transportation, food, medical care, and dependent care. Insurance coverage should also be reviewed periodically to ensure that each and every employee is adequately covered. Also, a safety stock of preprinted forms should be available to help maintain uninterrupted business processing. Finally, the recovery team should ensure that power, telecommunications, and postal service will be available at the alternate site and restored at the disaster site as soon as possible.

Evaluate and Assess

As mentioned before, audit should be an ally in the disaster recovery process. If this is not the case, a reevaluation and redefinition of roles might be in order. Audit should be the independent group to monitor and report the progress and effectiveness of the disaster recovery program. They should also confirm that senior management is receiving the right message and not a false sense of security when it comes to disaster recovery readiness. The following statements should be considered "warning signs" that may indicate a false sense of security among an organization's management:

- "We have a disaster recovery plan for technology."
- "We conduct annual plan tests at our vendor facility."
- "We have a DRP software package."
- "If I am affected by disaster, so are my competitors."

Statements such as these indicate that the company's DRP program may not be comprehensive. Audit should recognize these symptoms and recommend solutions for bringing the DRP program to the appropriate level. Audit should work with disaster recovery planners and business managers to identify synergies with other enterprise-wide activities, such as corporate standards, self-assessment compliance programs, awareness programs, DRP expense reporting, plan development, and the development and use of monitoring tools.

Audit may often feel like "referees" in a large corporate effort. They are regularly asked to "enforce the rules" of a well-controlled and operated environment. Disaster recovery planning is clearly one area in which audit can shed the "striped shirts," don their company's "team colors," and participate and add value to the critically important DRP process.

Distribution of Completed Plans

Members of disaster recovery teams and senior managers should receive a copy of the completed DRPs. It is also advisable to consider providing copies of the plan to external groups such as police and fire departments that may help with disaster prevention and recovery. However, the DRPs should be considered a proprietary document, and they should not be distributed indiscriminately, either internally or externally.

As described in the previous section, the DRPs should not be dependent on the participation of any individual or team. A disaster could result in the unavailability, injury, or death of key recovery team members. It is also possible that essential members of the recovery team may find the recovery process overwhelming and resign from their positions. Therefore, to help prevent chaos following a disaster, the DRPs should contain enough detail to allow available staff to begin implementing the recovery process as quickly as possible following a disaster. A complete, up-to-date set of plans should also be maintained in an accessible off-site location to ensure accessibility when needed.

AUDITING THE DISASTER RECOVERY PLAN

GENERAL QUESTIONS

Overview

1. Does the DRP include at least the following sections:
   - Senior Management Responsibilities Overview
   - Short-Term Disaster Recovery Strategies

- Long-Term Disaster Recovery Strategies
- Recovery Team Responsibilities and Procedures
- Notification of Staff Members
- Backup Sites and External Support Agreements
- Data Center Operations and Critical Procedures
- Data Center Specifications and Inventories
- Emergency Procedures and Information

The plan should contain specific information and procedures for evacuation of buildings, staffing responsibilities, assessing damage, and prioritizing critical jobs.

Plan Organization and Assignments

2. Is the DRP clear, concise, complete, and current? The plan should cover all key business areas and related data. Specific assignments of the recovery team and appropriate notification procedures should also be clearly defined in the plan.

Hardware and Software Requirements

3. Does the DRP provide for adequate hardware and software to resume the necessary level of operation following a disaster? Hardware considerations should include requirements related to operations, data retention, supply storage, PCs, and telecommunications. Also, the plan should include an inventory of all software needed to fully resume processing operations.

Legal Requirements and Liabilities

4. Does the DRP protect key business records and contracts? Procedures should exist for backup and off-site storage and control of documents such as major contracts, employee information statutory files, confidential materials, and other documentation.

Off-Site Storage

5. Does the DRP insulate the corporation from financial loss as a result of loss of data? This should be the primary consideration of the DRP. The DRP should include pickup and delivery services at the off-site storage facility, the potential for electronic vaulting of key data and programs, and available emergency delivery service in the event of disaster. The DRP should also include appropriate costs of storage, convenience and adequacy of the facility location, and specific restrictions imposed by the storage facility.

Third-Party Facility

6. Two critical areas related to third-party facilities are adequacy and scrutiny. Accordingly, does the DRP ensure that all third-party facilities are able to meet the corporation's technical needs? Audit should conduct physical inspections of storage vaults, facility access restriction procedures, and other security controls to ensure that they are maintained at a standard that is acceptable to the organization. Formal agreements should address the right to use the backup site, notification of changes and alterations at the backup site, notification required before occupying the site, length of stay permitted, testing procedures, assistance available from the backup site, and adequacy of office space.

Backup Sites

7. Does the DRP adequately describe operations and procedures presently in use at the data center, plus any unique procedures developed for use at the internal backup site? This information allows staff members (other than those most familiar with the tasks) to quickly resume critical processing. The DRP should define critical data, documentation, and supplies that are to be stored at the internal backup site. It should also include notification procedures of when and how to move personnel, equipment, and supplies to the alternate site. The DRP should address the adequacy of the computer room layouts, building specifications, and security provisions.

Testing

8. Do the periodic tests of the DRP fulfill audit objectives by:

- Determining the adequacy of the off-site storage facilities and existing recovery procedures? Information will be obtained concerning availability of off-site files and the documentation necessary for efficient recovery.
- Identifying deficiencies in recovery capabilities and related internal controls? Plan testing will also help assess management's command of the situation and its ability to adapt to unusual situations.
- Identifying and evaluating the cost and effectiveness of continuing operations at an alternate site?

Audit should compare the criticality of the controls being tested with the strength of the test results. If they are equal (i.e., if there is high criticality and a high level of compliance), then the disaster recovery procedures should be considered adequate. Differences between compliance and criticality may suggest that resources associated with the control are being overused or underused

Critical Application Selection

9. Does the DRP adequately identify critical files necessary for operation and efficient recovery? It is important to verify that adequate procedures exist for backup, documentation, and storage of critical files.

End-User Computing

10. Is the DRP designed to protect and recover data at all levels within the organization? In addition to addressing mainframe-based data, DRPs should also provide policies and procedures for protecting and recovering programs and data developed by end users for use on personal computers.

Insurance

11. Does the organization maintain adequate insurance coverage to ensure restoration following a disaster? The organization's insurance should also protect against business losses resulting from the inadequate performance of a third-party vendor.

DOCUMENTATION QUESTIONS

1. Has a comprehensive DRP been developed?
2. Where is the plan stored?
3. Does the plan contain:
   a. Configuration document?
   b. Locations of backups?
   c. Staffing and responsibilities?
   d. Training in DRP skills?
   e. Testing?
   f. Identification of critical data?
   g. Recovery time frames?
   h. Alternate processing facility?
4. When was the plan last tested?
5. Was a thorough review of test results performed and a conclusion drawn?
6. Was the plan updated based on the results of the test?
7. Are critical backups stored off-site?
8. How often is data taken off-site? How is the data taken off-site?
9. Has a disaster recovery plan been developed for each type of significant disaster?
10. Is the formal disaster recovery plan regularly updated as processing conditions and personnel change?
11. Is insurance coverage for computer disasters regularly reviewed for adequacy?

Disaster recovery plans should be reviewed (typically on an annual basis), tested, and reevaluated at least once every six months to ensure that the procedures are complete, practical, feasible, and timely. Testing should include at least one detailed walk-through of the plan's procedures. Periodically the organization should conduct announced and/or unannounced simulated disaster drills of the information system function both locally and at remote sites. Testing can consist of a modular approach if the entire plan cannot be tested feasibly at one time.

PLAN ORGANIZATION AND ASSIGNMENTS: FORTY-NINE-POINT CHECKLIST

1. Does the DRP contain a statement of objectives and assumptions?
2. Does the DRP identify different levels of disruption such as disaster, loss of individual system configuration components, and temporary loss of resources?
3. Does the DRP describe scenarios for each potential disaster identified by information systems management? Examples of potential disasters include:
   - Interruption of communications
   - Destruction of programs
   - Destruction of databases
   - Excessive transaction volume
4. Does the DRP define what a disaster is, who may declare one, and how to implement recovery procedures?

5. Does the DRP define procedures for each recovery area identified as a result of the risk analysis process? For example:
   - Application system recovery
   - Telecommunications system recovery
   - Systems software recovery
6. Does the DRP describe alternate operating and processing procedures of electronic data interchange (EDI)?
7. Does the DRP also describe maintaining communications with the value-added network?
8. Is there an authorized list for updating the DRP and destroying old copies?
9. How frequently is it reviewed or revised? Does the DRP contain required management approval signatures?
10. Does the DRP describe who is responsible for updating the plan to reflect changes in operation, hardware, personnel, software, and telecommunications?
11. Does the DRP consider cost/benefits of a hot versus a cold site processing facility?
12. Does the DRP require storage of at least one complete, current copy of the plan at a secure and accessible off-site location?
13. Does the DRP identify the test team and the procedures the team should follow in documenting the physical testing of the plan?
14. Does the DRP specify procedures for conducting regularly scheduled tests of the entire plan and documenting those results?
15. Does the recovery team include key representatives from the following business entities:
    a. Data processing management
    b. Data administration
    c. User departments
    d. Telecommunications (voice and data)
    e. Facilities management
    f. Computer operations
    g. Systems and applications programming
    h. Personnel, security, audit, and vendor representatives
16. Are senior managers officially assigned the responsibility for initiating disaster recovery procedures?
17. Does the DRP provide for assigned alternates for each permanent team member? Do the alternate team members know of this assignment? Do they know their job responsibilities?
18. Does the DRP list the addresses and telephone numbers of the team members, users, vendors, and alternate site?
19. Does the DRP provide a clear procedure for notifying vendors and alternate-site contacts of a disaster?
20. Does the DRP provide for training recovery team members to fulfill their assigned roles?
21. Does the DRP address the definition of team members functions at the task level?

These definitions should include functions such as:

- **a.** Coordination of the DRP between departments
- **b.** Damage assessment
- **c.** Application system immigration
- **d.** Equipment
- **e.** Communications and system software
- **f.** Relocation of data center operations
- **g.** Personnel transportation
- **h.** Data preparation
- **i.** Arrangement for supplies
- **j.** Administration of DRP
- **k.** Security and salvage
- **l.** New facilities preparation

22. Has an inventory of data processing and end-user essentials (i.e., pens, paper, preprinted forms, lists, etc.) required for recovery been prepared?

23. Does the DRP contain current job descriptions of key personnel? (**Note:** Current job descriptions allow nonincumbents to fill key roles, if necessary, following a disaster.)

24. Does the DRP contain the current home telephone numbers and addresses of key staff personnel for disaster notification? How often is the list reviewed?

25. Are the recovery responsibilities of data processing and end-user personnel part of the DRP? These duties and responsibilities would include:

- **a.** Transfer of application and job control statement program libraries
- **b.** Restoration of telecommunications software and systems documentation
- **c.** Acquisition of supplies and documentation from off-site storage location
- **d.** Migration of application systems
- **e.** Salvage operations
- **f.** Assisting in rebuilding the data center
- **g.** Staff training procedures

26. Does the organization have plans for controlled public press releases following a disaster?

27. Do all staff members know who to call in times of emergency or where the emergency telephone list is located?

28. Have attempts been made to create and sustain employee interest in the prevention of fire, theft, and other causes of disaster?

29. Have alternates been assigned to all disaster recovery jobs in case the primary handler is absent?

30. Has a disaster recovery planning team or equivalent been established?

31. Has an emergency organizational chart been developed?

32. Has an employee call-in list been prepared for use during a disaster?

33. Are there general community procedures designed to notify the entire workforce, by radio or TV, in the event of a serious disaster?

34. Are management personnel able to run the computer center in the event that non-management personnel are unavailable?
35. Has a personal skills inventory been conducted to identify special employee skills that could be used during an emergency?
36. Is access to the data library restricted to designated librarians, even during disaster periods?
37. Has a recovery team been assigned so that they can begin work immediately in the event of a disaster?
38. Is user management heavily involved in computer disaster recovery planning?
39. Are computer personnel in key positions of authority bonded?
40. Has the staff been trained in fire alarm, bomb threat, and other emergency procedures?
41. Has the staff been adequately instructed in what to do when an emergency alarm sounds?
42. Have computer center personnel been trained to protect confidential data during periods of disaster recovery?
43. Do all security procedures remain in effect during a disaster recovery period?
44. Are disaster recovery responsibilities included in the appropriate job descriptions?
45. Are new or transferred employees immediately trained in disaster recovery procedures and assigned appropriate responsibilities?
46. Is there a complete listing of all supplies and copies of all forms available at a second site?
47. Has the DRP been reviewed by senior management and approved by all responsible managers?
48. If extra copies of the disaster recovery plan are maintained, are they regularly updated?
49. In the event of a disaster, have sufficient funds been allocated for transportation, operating expenses, emergency supplies, and so on?

VITAL BUSINESS PROCESS OWNER

The following questions must be answered by members of management who own a vital business process:

1. Have you ensured that the vital business process can fulfill its mission in the event of a disaster?

   (C) All processes evaluated
   (A) Target date
   (AE) Target date

2. Have you prepared disaster recovery plans that include vital business process recovery requirements as well as service commitment requirements from suppliers of service?

   (C) Disaster recovery plans prepared
   (A) Target date
   (AE) Target date

3. Have you planned and conducted a review of the disaster recovery plan in the past year, updating and resolving any deficiencies discovered during the review?

(C) Reviewed within the past year
(A) Target date
(AE) Target date

4. Has a disaster recovery test been conducted within the last two years, resolving any problems or exposures discovered during the test?

(C) Tested within the past two years
(A) Target date
(AE) Target date

5. If you manage your own computing facility (i.e., local area networks, RISC machines, and so on) supporting the vital business process, have you answered the Supplier of Service section?

(C) Supplier of service section applicable/not applicable
(A) Target date
(AE) Target date

C—Compliance, A—Action plan in progress, AE—Action plan ending date, R—Risk Acceptance target date

SUPPLIERS OF SERVICE

The following questions must be answered by members of management who are suppliers of services essential to the recovery of the vital business process (i.e., information systems services, site services, site security) and who must negotiate service level agreements with owners of vital business processes defining services committed in the period following a disaster until normal operations are restored.

1. Have you negotiated service level agreements with owners of vital business processes who are on your service/system?

(C)
(A) Target date
(AE) Target date
(R) RISK number
(RD) Target date

Prepare disaster recovery plans covering their service commitments and protect it off-site.

2. Do you have a disaster recovery plan for your service/system that will recover the vital business processes as committed in the service level agreement?

(C)
(A) Target date
(AE) Target date
(R) RISK number
(RD) Target date

3. Is your disaster recovery plan for your service/system current? (Current means being updated within the last twelve months.)

(C)
(A) Target date
(AE) Target date
(R) RISK number
(RD) Target date

Suppliers of information systems services, in addition to the requirements for all suppliers of service, must assist the vital business process owner in the following:

- The design of tests to demonstrate recovery capability at alternate facilities using disaster recovery information protected off-site.
- The frequency of testing, test schedules, and where the tests will be conducted and the participants.

4. Have you tested your disaster recovery plan for your service/system recently? (Recently means being within the last twelve to twenty-four months.)

(C)
(A) Target date
(AE) Target date
(R) RISK number
(RD) Target date

Negotiate written service level agreements with managers of alternate internal computing facilities for the recovery of the vital business processes.

In addition to the effort in support of vital business processes, suppliers of information systems services must develop timetables for restoring computing services capabilities at the affected site using local estimates of availability of hardware products, telecommunications lines, raised floor, chilled water, and so on. User management should be informed of the proposed schedule and advised to make alternate arrangements if the schedule is felt to be unacceptable.

5. Have you included in your service level agreement alternate site agreements and developed and communicated recovery schedules to user management recently? (Recently being within the last twelve to twenty-four months.)

(C)
(A) Target date
(AE) Target date
(R) RISK number
(RD) Target date

6. Have you evaluated all locations for which you are responsible (i.e., local and remote) for compliance with the disaster recovery of vital business processes instruction? Requirements?

(C) All locations evaluated
(A) Target date
(AE) Target date

7. Have you evaluated the VBP owner test schedules to verify that each VBP has been tested within the last twenty-four months?

(C) All VBPs

(A) Target date

(AE) Target date

8. Do you report to VBP management and the CIO when testing is not in compliance with testing schedules?

(C) VBP management informed date

(A) Target date

(AE) Target date

See Exhibit 8.1 for a sample disaster recovery plan.

Exhibit 8.1 Ali Y's Consulting, Inc.

Disaster Recovery Plan

Location: Central Maintenance

Date Completed: 1/10/00 **Prepared By: Ali Yusuf**____________________

Last Date Revised: 1/10/00________________ **Revised by: N/A**____________________

Type of Loss	**Short-Term Action Plan**		**Long-Term Action Plan**		**Date of Last Backup**
Vendors	*Ongoing*	**Priority**	*Ongoing*	**Priority**	
We currently have alternative suppliers for virtually all needed production equipment.	If we were to lose a key vendor, we would shift to another. We could possibly pay a premium for the short term.		Continue negotiating pricing and delivery with alternative vendors.		
Utilities	*Up to 5 Days*		*Up to 6 Months*		
Power outage in the shop	If it is local to the shop, Mr. XX would be capable of performing his tasks from a network site at Plant Eng. If it is the entire city, then he would revert to manual POs. All necessary shop work would either be transferred or performed at one of the plants with utilities.		If the outage was for a significant period of time, Mr. XX could reinstall his software on another system. Most of the other shop tasks would continue to be transferred to other areas. Maintenance personnel would be redirected to the plants.		
Natural Disasters	*Indefinitely*		*Up to 7 months*		
Complete destruction of facility	Part procurement would revert to manual POs. Other maintenance operations would be transferred or performed in one of the remaining plants.		Rebuild facility.		

Computers	*Up to Days/Hour*		*Up to Days/Hour*		
Spare parts	Is networked and can be performed within Plant Eng. If complete system is down, we revert to manual POs and update system when back online. Information is backed up weekly and is stored off-site.		Same as short term.		
Key Equipment	*Up to Days/Hour*		*Up to Days/Hour*		
Any	If any piece of equipment is lost, machining operations are sent to Northside Machining in Huntingburg for processing.		Any piece of equipment in the shop can be replaced within 8 weeks.		

Continued

Exhibit 8.1 Ali Y's Consulting, Inc. (continued)

Disaster Recovery Plan

Location: Corporate Office

Date Completed: 1/00/00 **Prepared By: Ali Yusuf**

Last Date Revised: ____________ **Revised by:** ____________

Type of Loss	**Short-Term Action Plan**		**Long-Term Action Plan**		**Date of Last Backup**
Vendors	*Up to Days/Hour*	**Priority**	*Up to Days/Hour*	**Priority**	
Contractors	We have alternative contractors for all areas.		Same		
Suppliers	Several alternative suppliers are available on short notice.		Same		
Utilities	*Up to 1 Day*		*Up to Days/Hour*		
Electrical power outage	City will repair most outages within one day. Transformers are in stock.		Necessary office personnel will relocate to Plant number 22 office.		
Water supply disruption	Provide a 24-hour fire watch for fire protection.		Same		
	Provide a tanker for sanitary water supply.		Same		
Gas supply disruption	Provide LP tank within 24 hours.		Provide larger tank and switch to LP.		
Telephones:					
If we lose the switch	Can be replaced within 2 days (some parts in stock. Can use HOT phones and fax machines).		Same		
If we lose GTE central office in Jasper	Move operations to Plant 22 (for up to 50 people, can be set up within a day).		Move to Plant 22 (have all that is necessary within . 2 weeks)		

Natural Disasters	*Up to Days/Hour*		*Up to Days/Hour*		
Complete destruction of facility	Those that require hookup to the LAN or WAN will move to Plant 22 where temporary offices would be set up. Others would operate at another plant or out of their homes.		Same as short term. Set up temporary offices on site.		
Computers	*Up to Days/Hour*		*Up to Days/Hour*		
Mainframe	Uninterupted power supply (for 30 minutes).				
Key Equipment	*Up to Days/Hour*		*Up to Days/Hour*		
ADT disruption	Appoint security guard.				
HVAC breakdown	Repaired by contractors within one day.		Replace units within one week (will bring in temporary heat or AC).		

Continued

Exhibit 8.1 Ali Y's Consulting, Inc. (continued)

Disaster Recovery Plan

Location: **Customer Service**

Date Completed: xx-xx-xx | **Prepared By:** Ali Yusuf

Last Date Revised: ____________ | **Revised by:** ____________

Type of Loss	**Short-Term Action Plan**		**Long-Term Action Plan**		**Date of Last Backup**
Vendors	*Up to Days/Hour*	**Priority**	*Up to Days/Hour*	**Priority**	
N/A					
Utilities	*Up to Days/Hour*		*Up to Days/Hour*		
N/A					
Natural Disasters	*Up to Days/Hour*		*Up to Days/Hour*		
N/A					
Computers	*Up to Days/Hour*		*Up to Days/Hour*		
N/A					
Key Equipment	*Up to Days/Hour*		*Up to Days/Hour*		
N/A					

INDEX